OLYMPIC CITIES

The first edition of *Olympic Cities*, edited by John and Margaret Gold, provided the first full overview of the changing relationship between cities and the Olympic events since 1896. This substantially revised and enlarged edition builds on the success of its predecessor. Three years on, its coverage takes account of important new scholarship as well as adding reflections on the experience of staging Beijing 2008 and Vancouver 2010, the state of preparations for London 2012, and the plans for the Games scheduled for Sochi in 2014 and Rio de Janeiro 2016.

The first of the book's three parts provides overviews of the urban legacy of the four component Olympic festivals: the Summer Games; Winter Games; Cultural Olympiads; and the Paralympics. The second part comprises systematic surveys of five key aspects of activity involved in staging the Olympics: finance; place promotion; security; urban regeneration; and tourism. The final part consists of ten chronologically arranged portraits of host cities, from 1936 to 2016, with particular emphasis on the first four Summer Olympic Games of the twenty-first century. An Afterword stresses the role and strengthening of the Olympic brand.

As controversy over the growing size and expense of the Olympics continues unabated, this book's incisive and timely assessment of the Games' development and the complex agendas that host cities attach to the event will be essential reading not only for urban and sports historians, urban geographers, planners and all concerned with understanding the relationship between cities and culture, but for anyone with an interest in the staging of mega-events.

John R. Gold is Professor of Urban Historical Geography at Oxford Brookes University. Margaret M. Gold is Senior Lecturer in Arts and Heritage Management and an Associate of the Cities Institute at London Metropolitan University.

Planning, History and Environment Series

Editor:

Emeritus Professor Dennis Hardy, High Peak, UK

Editorial Board:

Professor Arturo Almandoz, Universidad Simón Bolivar, Caracas, Venezuela and Pontificia
Universidad Católica de Chile, Santiago, Chile

Professor Gregory Andrusz, London, UK

Professor Nezar AlSayyad, University of California, Berkeley, USA

Professor Robert Bruegmann, University of Illinois at Chicago, USA

Professor Meredith Clausen, University of Washington, Seattle, USA

Professor Robert Freestone, University of New South Wales, Sydney, Australia

Professor John R. Gold, Oxford Brookes University, Oxford, UK

Professor Sir Peter Hall, University College London, UK

Emeritus Professor Anthony Sutcliffe, Nottingham, UK

Technical Editor

Ann Rudkin, Alexandrine Press, Marcham, Oxfordshire, UK

OLYMPIC CITIES

City Agendas, Planning and the
World's Games, 1896–2016

Second Edition

edited by

John R. Gold

and

Margaret M. Gold

Routledge
Taylor & Francis Group

LONDON AND NEW YORK

First edition published 2008
by Routledge

This edition published 2011
by Routledge
2 Park Square, Milton Park, Abingdon, Oxon, OX14 4RN

Simultaneously published in the USA and Canada
by Routledge
270 Madison Avenue, New York, NY 10016

Routledge is an imprint of the Taylor & Francis Group, an informa business

Typeset in Aldine and Swiss by PNR Design, Didcot
Printed and bound in Great Britain by TJ International Ltd, Padstow, Cornwall

This book was commissioned and edited by Alexandrine Press, Marcham, Oxfordshire

British Library Cataloguing in Publication Data
A catalogue record of this book is available from the British Library

Library of Congress Cataloging in Publication Data
Olympic cities: city agendas, planning, and the world's games,
1896-2016 / edited by John R. Gold and Margaret M. Gold. — 2nd ed.
    p. cm. — (Planning, history and environment series)
   Includes bibliographical references and index.
   ISBN 978–0–415–48657–6 (hbk : alk. paper) — ISBN 978–0–415–48658–3
(pbk : alk. paper) — ISBN 978–0–203–84074–0 (ebk) 1. City
planning—History. 2. Municipal government—History. 3. Municipal
services—History. 4. Olympics—History. 5. Olympics—Planning. 6. Olympics—
Management—History. I. Gold, John Robert. II. Gold, Margaret M.
   HT166.O4 2011
   307.1'21609—dc22
                              2010016608

ISBN13: 978–0–415–48658–3(pbk)
ISBN13: 978–0–415–48657–6(hbk)
ISBN13: 978–0–203–84074–0(ebk)

For David Pepper

Contents

Preface ix

Acknowledgements xiii

The Contributors xv

List of Acronyms xix

1   Introduction 1
    John R. Gold and *Margaret M. Gold*

Part I   The Olympic Festivals

2   From A to B: The Summer Olympics, 1896–2008 17
    John R. Gold and *Margaret M. Gold*

3   The Winter Olympics: Driving Urban Change, 1924–2014 56
    Stephen J. Essex

4   The Cultural Olympiads: Reviving the Panegyris 80
    Margaret M. Gold and *George Revill*

5   The Paralympic Games 108
    John R. Gold and *Margaret M. Gold*

Part II   Planning and Management

6   Financing the Games 131
    Paul Kitchin

7   Promoting the Olympic City 148
    Stephen V. Ward

8   Olympic Security 167
    Jon Coaffee and *Peter Fussey*

9   Urban Regeneration and Renewal 180
    Jon Coaffee

10 Olympic Tourism 194
    Mike Weed

Part III   City Portraits

11 Berlin 1936 215
    Monika Meyer

12 Mexico City 1968 233
    Michael Barke

13 Montreal 1976   247
    Daniel Latouche

14 Barcelona 1992   268
    Francisco-Javier Monclús

15 Sydney 2000   287
    Beatriz García

16 Athens 2004   315
    Margaret M. Gold

17 Beijing 2008   340
    Ian G. Cook and *Steven Miles*

18 London 2012   359
    Graeme Evans

19 Rio de Janeiro 2016   390
    John R. Gold

20 Afterword   403
    John R. Gold and *Margaret M. Gold*

References   407

Index   437

Preface

Anyone looking at the second edition of a book published only a few years previously has every reason to ask why the revisions were necessary. In our case, an essential part of the rationale lies in the need for updating. Three years on from when the manuscript of the first edition was delivered (March 2007), we are now able to reflect on the experience of staging the Summer Games in Beijing 2008 and the 2010 Winter Games in Vancouver. Moreover, the relentless onward movement of the calendar of Olympic and Paralympic festivals means that there are now further developments that need attention. At the time of writing, the major structures for the next Summer games in London 2012 are recognizably taking shape and plans are pressing ahead on two Games that had not yet been allocated to host cities when the previous edition went to press, namely, the Winter Games scheduled for Sochi in 2014 and the Summer Games in Rio de Janeiro in 2016. The slight change in the book's title – now extending to 2016 rather than 2012 – reflects this changing situation.

Yet the business of dealing adequately with the multifaceted festivals that comprise the modern Olympic and Paralympic Games involves far more than adding new events to the list covered. The Olympics have a remarkable tendency to become the focus of new debates. In this respect, concerns about environmental sustainability, security and, in particular, legacy have impacted upon thinking about the Games and have prompted the staging of innumerable symposia to discuss emerging problems and shared challenges. Often involving a mixture of academics and practitioners, these events have stimulated and sometimes underwritten a further wave of new publications about the Olympics that, at their best, have helped to move scholarship decisively forward. In addition, there has been a notable outpouring of new studies about the history of the Olympics and on topics such as bidding processes, tourism, spectacle, and branding. Understandably, therefore, an essential part of the purpose of this new edition has been to take stock of this new literature and give adequate recognition to its findings.

Having emphasized the need for change, however, it should also be stressed that the core aim of this book remains precisely the same. In broad outline, it seeks to draw on the expertise of an international group of authors to examine comparatively the experience of cities that have hosted the Olympics in the years from the creation of the modern Games in 1896 through to the present day and beyond to 2016. As such, it remains a book framed around historical analysis, seeking not just to account for past Games but also to chronicle recent and future Olympics in light of established and emerging narratives. For a festival as immersed in precedent and invented tradition as the Olympics, we believe that this comprises an eminently appropriate approach to set alongside much of the instant punditry now on offer.

In terms of structure, we have retained the same multilayered approach to our subject matter as in the previous edition, with the chapters arranged into three main parts. The book opens with chronologically-arranged surveys of the broad trends in staging the Games; followed by chapters that scrutinize significant themes arising from cities acting as host; and then by a representative selection of city portraits – understandably concentrating on the period from the 1960s onwards when host cities became more interested in using the Olympics as a catalyst for development. Adopting a tripartite structure that seeks both thematic insight and chronological coverage inevitably means revisiting the same festivals at several points in the text from different angles and perspectives. In addition, the correct balance between allowing authors scope for initial context and removing unnecessary repetition by employing cross-references is difficult to achieve, but we hope that the results are acceptable. Certainly, we would like to express our sincere gratitude to our contributors for their patience with the editorial process and for their willingness to redraft material to benefit the book as a whole.

Certain elements of standardization and conventions deserve some clarification. Statements of expenditure frequently occur in local currencies and exchange rates at points in the past are not always easy to obtain, especially when sources are unclear about precise dates. Where possible, we have attempted to use pound sterling or US dollar equivalents, and all sums where dollars are shown without qualification relate to the US currency. In addition, anyone familiar with using Olympic documentation, especially Official Reports, will realize that there are often different language versions available. We have retained the linguistic version used by our contributors in cited references, even though this means that different language versions of the same publication might be listed separately in the consolidated bibliography. Finally, Olympic sport is a realm in which institutional acronyms abound. Our policy is to present acronyms in their most common form regardless of the language from which they are derived. Thus, for example, the abbreviation COJO (standing for Comité d'Organisation des Jeux Olympiques) is used in relation to Games held in Francophone nations, whereas the body concerned is normally referred to as an OCOG (Organising Committee for the Olympic Games) elsewhere. To avoid confusion, a full listing of all such acronyms occurs at the start of this text, with our practice being to provide names of bodies in full wherever they first occur in a chapter.

As ever, we have incurred a variety of debts in the process of preparing this book. Dennis Hardy and Ann Rudkin supplied the stimulus to develop the initial idea and Graeme Evans supplied valuable contacts. The International Planning History Society supplied an invaluable opportunity to gather an initial group of contributors together at its Biennial Meeting in Barcelona in 2004. The School of Social Sciences and Law at Oxford Brookes University and the London Metropolitan Business School at London Metropolitan University have provided finance and other assistance to facilitate our work. We would particularly like to acknowledge the assistance of the British Olympic Association for allowing us access to source materials and Martin McElhatton, Chief Executive of Wheel Power, for sparing generous amounts of time to show us round the Stoke Mandeville Stadium. We would like to record our thanks to Brian Chalkley, Jo Foord, Willy Guneriussen, Elsa-Minni Heimgard, Lorraine Johnston, James Kennell, Peter Larkham, Chuck Little, Sarah Loy, Kat Martindale, Jill Pearlman and Matthew Taylor for various and sundry kindnesses. Iain, Josie, Thomas and Jenny tolerated the things that did not happen in order to allow us time and space to complete this text. Finally, we have great pleasure in dedicating this book to David Pepper, a man for whom sport occupies its proper place in life.

John and Margaret Gold
West Ealing
July 2010

Acknowledgements

We are grateful to the following for permission to reproduce the illustrations as recorded below:

Barcelona City Council 14.6

CCCB-Salvat 14.2, 14.3, 14.4, 14.5

Jon Coaffee: 9.1, 9.2, 9.3

Colegio de Arquitectos de Catalunya: 14.1

Ian Cook 17.1

Graeme Evans 17.1

Fluid: 18.8

Beatriz García: 15.1, 15.2, 15.3, 15.4. 15.5

Gerkan, Marg and Partner 11.5

IOC/Olympic Museum Collections 3.2. 3.4

Monika Meyer-Künzel: 11.3

Andy Miah: 17.2, 17.3

The following illustrations are either from historic postcards or from now defunct publishing houses for which no successor can be found: 2.2, 2.3, 2.4, 2.5, 2.6, 2.7, 4.1, 11.1, 11.2, 11.4.

All remaining photographs were taken by the editors. Other artwork and maps were compiled by the contributors.

The Contributors

Michael Barke is Reader in Human Geography at Northumbria University, Newcastle upon Tyne. His research interests include the study of socio-economic change in southern Spain, the historical geography of North East England and place promotion in the United Kingdom. His publications include *Tourism in Spain: Critical Issues* (CAB International, 1996).

Jon Coaffee is Professor of Spatial Planning at the University of Birmingham and a member of the Centre for Urban and Regional Studies in the University's Business School. His research interests revolve around the interplay of planning, regeneration, urban management and security policy. He is the author of *The Everyday Resilience of the City* (Palgrave, 2008) and *Terrorism, Risk and the Global City* (Ashgate, 2003, 2009).

Ian G. Cook is Professor of Human Geography at Liverpool John Moores University and formerly Head of the Centre for Pacific Rim Studies. He is the joint editor or author of eight books of which the most recent are *The Greening of China* (China Intercontinental Press, Beijing, 2004), *New Perspectives on Aging in China* (Nova Science Publishers, New York, 2007) and *Aging in Asia* (Nova Science Publishers, New York, 2009).

Stephen J. Essex is a Reader in Human Geography at the School of Geography, Earth and Environmental Science, University of Plymouth. His teaching and research focuses on urban and rural planning, especially the infrastructural implications of the Olympic Games and post-war reconstruction planning. He has co-authored a number of journal articles and book chapters on the urban impacts and planning of both the Summer and Winter Olympic Games with Professor Brian Chalkley (also at the University of Plymouth).

Graeme Evans is Professor of Urban Cultures and Regeneration and Director of the Cities Institute at London Metropolitan University where he leads research projects under the EPSRC's Sustainable Urban Environments programme. His book *Cultural Planning: An Urban Renaissance?* (Routledge, 2001) was the first to consider culture and city planning from both historic and contemporary perspectives.

Peter Fussey is a Senior Lecturer in Criminology and Terrorism Studies at the University of East London. His main research interests concern the dissemination and application of technological surveillance to tackle crime and terrorism. He is also researching the form and impact of London's 2012 security operation and conducting ethnographic research into organized criminality in East London's Olympic market place. Recent work includes *Securing and Sustaining the Olympic City* (Ashgate, 2010 co-authored with Jon Coaffee, Gary Armstrong and Dick Hobbs) and *Terrorism and the Olympics* (Routledge, 2010 co-edited with Andrew Silke and Anthony Richards).

Beatriz García is the Director of 'Impacts 08 – The Liverpool Model', a longitudinal research programme into the impact of Liverpool's becoming European Capital of Culture (ECoC), jointly undertaken by the University of Liverpool and Liverpool John Moores University. She acted as academic collaborator to the Palmer/Rae team evaluating the impact of 1995–2004 European Capitals of Culture for the European Commission, has been academic advisor to the London 2012 Culture and Education team since the bid stage, and is a member of the IOC Postgraduate Research Grant Selection Committee. In 2009, she was appointed as a member of the DCMS Science and Research Advisory Committee. Her monograph *The Olympic Games and Cultural Policy* (2010) is published by Routledge.

John R. Gold, Professor of Urban Historical Geography in the School of Social Sciences and Law at Oxford Brookes University, is the author or editor of fourteen previous books on urban and cultural subjects. He is currently working on the third of his trilogy on architectural modernism in Great Britain, entitled *The Legacy of Modernism: Modern Architects, the City and the Collapse of Orthodoxy, 1973–1990*. In addition, he and Margaret Gold are working on *Festival Cities: Culture, Planning and Urban Life since 1945* (for publication in Routledge's Planning, History and Environment series, 2011); and on a four-volume set, *The Making of Olympic Cities,* for Routledge's Major Works series (2011).

Margaret M. Gold is Senior Lecturer in Arts and Heritage Management at London Metropolitan University and an Associate of the University's Cities Institute. She is the joint author of *Imagining Scotland* (Scolar Press, 1995) and *Cities of Culture* (Ashgate, 2005). She is currently working with John Gold on *Festival Cities: Culture, Planning and Urban Life since 1945* (for publication in Routledge's Planning, History and Environment series, 2011); and on a four-volume set, *The Making of Olympic Cities,* for Routledge's Major Works series (2011).

Paul Kitchin is Lecturer in Sport Management at the University of Ulster where he teaches strategic finance, marketing and sports policy. Paul is currently Deputy Editor of the *International Journal of Sports Marketing and Sponsorship* and an editorial board member of the *International Journal of Sport Management and Marketing*. Paul has seven years experience working with United Kingdom third-sector sporting organizations in the provision of research, planning and consultancy services.

Daniel Latouche is Research Professor of Political Science in the Centre for Urban and Cultural Studies of the National Institute of Scientific Research (Montreal). He is the author of numerous books on issues of ethno-cultural relations, constitutional design, forecasting and urban economic development. His recent interests deal with territorial planning in West Africa, the contribution of urbanism to ethnic accommodation, the impact of artistic and cultural clusters, and 'cultural adjustment' as a contributor to modernity.

Monika Meyer is head of the research area 'Urban and Regional Development in Europe' at the Leibniz-Institute of Ecological and Regional Development, Dresden, and a member of the Deutsche Akademie für Städtebau und Landesplanung. Her main fields of work are urban development and mega-events.

Steven Miles is Professor of Urban Culture at the University of Brighton. He is interested in the impact of consumption upon city life and in particular the role of consumer culture in the context of social change in China. His publications include *Consuming Cities*, Palgrave Macmillan, 2004 (with Malcolm Miles) and *Spaces for Consumption* (2010).

Francisco-Javier Monclús is Professor of Urbanism at the University of Zaragoza, Spain. He was Convenor of the 11th International Planning History Society Conference in 2004 and since 2005 has worked as Planner for the Consortium Zaragoza Expo 2008. He is co-editor of the journal *Perspectivas Urbanas* and his books include the *Atlas Histórico de Ciudades Europeas* (CCCB, 1994–1996), *Culture, Urbanism and Planning* (Ashgate, 2006) and *El Urbanismo de las Exposiciones Internacionales* (Ediciones UPC, 2006). An English version of the last book was published recently as *International Exhibitions and Urbanism: The Expo 2008 Project* (Ashgate, 2009).

George Revill is Senior Lecturer in Geography at the Open University. His research interests include cultural histories of travel and transport and the study of music, landscape and national identity. Publications include *Representing the Environment* (Routledge, 2004, with John R. Gold) and *Railway* (Reaktion, 2010).

Stephen V. Ward is Professor of Planning History at Oxford Brookes University. He was President of the International Planning History Society (2000–2006) and was formerly Editor of the journal *Planning Perspectives*. His books include *Selling Places* (Routledge, 1998), *Planning the Twentieth-Century City* (Wiley, 2002) and *Planning and Urban Change*, second edition (Sage, 2004).

Mike Weed is Professor of Sport in Society and Director of the Centre for Sport, Physical Education and Activity Research (SPEAR) in the Faculty of Social and Applied Sciences at Canterbury Christ Church University. He is author of *Olympic Tourism* (Elsevier, 2008) and *Sports Tourism: Participants, Policy and Providers* (Elsevier, 2009), as well as editor of *Sport and Tourism: A Reader* (Routledge, 2008). He is Editor of the *Journal of Sport and Tourism* (Taylor & Francis), has acted as Guest Editor for issues of *European Sport Management Quarterly*, *European Journal of Sport Science* and *Psychology of Sport and Exercise*.

List of Acronyms

The list below contains an alphabetical listing of acronyms used substantively in the text rather than simply for bibliographic purposes:

ACOG	Atlanta Committee for the Olympic Games
AOBC	Athens 2004 Olympic Bid Committee
ATHOC	Athens Organising Committee for the Olympic Games
BBC	British Broadcasting Corporation
BOCOG	Beijing Organising Committee for the Games of the XXIX Olympiad
COJO	Comité d'Organisation des Jeux Olympiques
CONI	Comitato Olimpico Nazionale Italiano
COOB	Barcelona Olympic Organising Committee
DCMS	Department of Culture, Media and Sport (UK)
FIFA	Fédération Internationale de Football Association
IBC	International Broadcast Centre
ICC	International Coordinating Committee of the World Sports Organisations
IF	International Federation
IOC	International Olympic Committee
ISMGF	International Stoke Mandeville Games Foundation
IPC	International Paralympic Committee
LDA	London Development Agency
LOCOG	London Organising Committee of the Olympic and Paralympic Games
NBC	National Broadcasting Corporation (USA)
NOC	National Olympic Committee
OCOG	Organising Committee for the Olympic Games
ODA	Olympic Delivery Authority
ROCOG	Rio de Janeiro Organising Committee for the Olympic Games
SOCOG	Sydney Organising Committee for the Olympic Games
TOP	The Olympic Programme
TOROC	Organising Committee of the XX Turin 2006 Olympic Winter Games
WWF	World Wildlife Fund

Chapter 1

Introduction

John R. Gold and Margaret M. Gold

On 11 November 2008, Tessa Jowell, then the British Secretary of State for Culture, Media and Sport, addressed a group of chief executive officers from the leisure industry at a private dinner.[1] As part of her assessment of the progress being made towards preparing the sites for London to become the 'Olympic City' for 2012, she turned to the broader, troubled macroeconomic context of the time, especially the threat posed by impending global recession. 'Had we known what we know now', she mused, 'would we have bid for the Olympics? Almost certainly not' (Osborne and Kirkup, 2008, p. 1).

Her thoughts were not intended for public circulation but, predictably, were leaked to the press. Before Jowell could repair the damage – stating that she had been taken out of context, that the Games would be a boon rather than a handicap during any economic slowdown, and that 'she was expressing what she thought would have been the commonly held view rather than one she shared herself' (Blitz, 2008, p. 4) – her words had attracted considerable interest. The Olympics are the foremost of the genre commonly described as 'mega-events' – cultural and sporting festivals that achieve sufficient size and scope to affect whole economies and to receive sustained global media attention (Getz, 1997; Roche, 2000; Horne and Manzenreiter, 2006). More than any other sporting festival they focus the eyes of the world on the host city before, during and after the event and here, as so often before, the media were quick to respond.

For the domestic press, the gift of a quickly-regretted pronouncement provided a lens by which British journalists could bring two prevailing newsworthy themes into focus for their readers, namely: longstanding misgivings over what the real costs of the Games might be; and more recent preoccupations with the implications of the so-called 'credit crunch'. Familiar questions about whether or not the Olympics were a responsible way to spend money given their opportunity cost could again resurface (e.g. Anon, 2008; Lyons, 2008). Internationally, media reactions varied but mostly tended towards amusement and hostility. Newspapers and broadcasting networks in countries that had been recent Olympic hosts gave prominence to the story, with varying degrees of understanding for a successor's apparent misgivings. The media in countries with cities that were unsuccessful in the bidding competition for 2012 generally adopted a more jaundiced view. The London correspondent of the French daily newspaper *Le Figaro*, for example, felt little need to mask his wry amusement at the Minister's discomfort. This, after all, was the event for which the British had so enthusiastically competed just 3 years before, successfully defeating what the French media still regarded as a superior bid from Paris. Now, under the headline 'The Olympic Games already too expensive for London', he opined that, while the Games would not be cancelled, the British government's search for retrenchment might seriously impair their impact (Vanlerberghe, 2008; see also Samuel, 2008).

Agencies actively involved in bringing London 2012 to fruition immediately reacted to limit the damage. The government's press officers worked overtime to assure the public that the project remained on time and within budget. The press and broadcasting media were quickly invited to watch clearance work at the Olympic Park, including ample photo opportunities with the Minister, clad in safety helmet and goggles, watching the demolition of the first of fifty-two pylons which had supported the power-lines that previously crisscrossed the site (Pierce, 2008). It was a subtle reminder that the future Olympic Park was no longer a blank canvas and that the proposals had already started to become reality, constraining the scope for change. For his part Boris Johnson, the Mayor of London, stressed that the developments underway for London 2012 'will prove a vital shot in the arm for the city when it needs it most'. Moreover, the benefits would not just be short-term. In a short statement that encapsulated most of the elements associated with the notion of the 'legacy' that the Olympics would bequeath, he observed:

> I believe London is extremely fortunate to be hosting the Games in 2012… They will bring the world to London, raise the city's profile, provide a focus for a broad range of policies and hopefully encourage young people in the capital to aspire to great sporting achievement… Huge public funds have been allocated but large amounts of private money have also been locked in. This unprecedented level of investment will deliver iconic buildings, major improvements in transport infrastructure, crucial housing and beautiful parks – all of this in a part of the city neglected for decades. (Hart, 2008)

The Ascendance of Legacy

In the event, the furore quickly dissipated. Within a few days, the storm that had been brewing for some weeks around the 'credit crunch' finally broke in its full ferocity, effectively pushing all other matters off the front pages. The huge levels of indebtedness achieved by banks throughout the world made it seem that the £9.325 billion promised for London 2012 was really rather good value since, unlike the astronomic sums needed to cover the bankers' losses, the taxpayers would receive something tangible in return. Yet, even without the intervention of external circumstances, Boris Johnson's evocation of the concept of 'legacy' would have been regarded as providing a perfectly robust defence of the Olympic project in the face of criticisms of the expense incurred in staging the Games. 'Legacy', however conceived, has rapidly become the touchstone by which host cities judge the worth of staging the Olympics. In times of need, it can be pressed into service in support of contentions about the value of the Games since the truth or otherwise of assertions involving legacy are based on faith and accurate judgment about the merits, or otherwise, of the matter may well lie many years in the future.

It had not always been thus, although any discussion of this point has to differentiate between explicit usages of the term 'legacy' and the interest that host cities have shown in the substance of that term. The former is itself a relatively recent occurrence in Olympic discourse; limited perhaps to the last 16 years. By contrast the latter, in the sense of cities pursuing lasting beneficial outcomes has a much longer history.

To elaborate: the vision propagated by the founders of the modern Games that underpinned their revival deliberately sought to take the Olympics to the four corners of the earth through making it an ambulatory festival awarded to designated cities. The Olympic movement, as represented by the International Olympic Committee (IOC), sought to encourage longer-term sporting outcomes in host nations by staging the Games in this manner. By contrast, the value of the event for the host city came from the honour of holding the Games, for which it would provide suitable premises and facilities. Naturally, the organizers of earlier Games were aware of the economic potential the Games might have, particularly in the area of tourism but, given the attachment to amateurism and antipathy to profit on the part of the IOC, it was considered inappropriate to glory in what the Games would do for the city rather than for sport and the pleasure of its citizens (McIntosh, 2003, pp. 450, 452).

In the fulness of time, the Games' organizers saw that much more could be achieved as a by-product of being nominated to stage the Olympics. Berlin 1936, for example, saw the Summer Games used as a medium for the Third Reich's spectacular representations of the New Germany, albeit with a surprisingly small impact upon the host city apart from the completion of an enormous sports complex on the city's outskirts. Rome 1960, the first Games held after the end of the period of Austerity that followed the Second World War, saw the first thoroughgoing attempt by a host city to attach a general exercise in urban development to the festival. Over time, a tacit bargain effectively developed between the IOC and the host city, particularly as mediated by its Organizing Committee for the Olympic Games (OCOG). In broad terms, this allowed the Games to be used to address the needs of the home city in return for the extraordinary investment of time and effort needed to stage the modern Games. By the time of Barcelona 1992, the balance had altered so dramatically that only 17 per cent of total expenditure actually went on the sports element of the Games compared with 83 per cent on urban improvement.

In the 1990s, the issue of sustainability entered the frame. In 1994, the IOC adopted the principle that the candidate cities for Summer and Winter Games should also be evaluated on the environmental consequences of their plans.

This was matched by the decision to make 'environment' into the 'third pillar' of the Olympic movement's core philosophy of Olympism, alongside 'sport' and 'culture'. In 1996, the Olympic Charter was itself amended to assert that one of the IOC's roles is 'to encourage and support a responsible concern for environmental issues, to promote sustainable development in sport and require that the Olympic Games are held accordingly' (quoted in Pitts and Liao, 2009, p. 67). In October 1999, the Olympic Movement published its own Agenda 21 document as a response to the recommendations of the 1992 Rio Earth Summit to serve as a 'useful reference tool for the sports community at all levels in the protection of the environment and enhancement of sustainable development' (IOC, 2006c, p. 10). To a large extent, the idealistic tenor of environmentalism conveyed by these measures struck a resonant note with the Olympic movement – itself not adverse to idealism. Yet it may also be argued that the sustainability agenda gave the IOC the chance to respond to accusations of 'gigantism', in which it was charged with requiring host cities to expend vast amounts of resources in constructing and staging a one-off mega-event. Direct advocacy of environmental responsibility helped to show that the movement was addressing these issues by seeking to reduce the impact of the Games and to ensure that future generations of the city's residents gained lasting benefits from the expenditure.[2]

The new and explicit concern for legacy emerged at much the same time that the sustainability agenda was being consolidated. The word 'legacy' itself had previously had a patchy and non-specific usage in Olympic parlance, largely lacking the conceptual impedimenta now attached to it. The first significant mention of the word *per se* occurred in the city of Melbourne's bid document for the 1956 Games (McIntosh, 2003, p. 450), but that was an isolated occurrence – particularly as there was no further use of the term in the Official Reports prepared for the Olympic Games after Melbourne 1956. This did not mean, of course, that the organizers were indifferent to achieving a beneficial outcome for the host city. At Melbourne, for example, the OCOG's Official Report talked of putting resources to good use and creating 'a continuing asset' (Organizing Committee, 1958). For Rome 1960, the Official Report comments on 'meeting ever-increasing needs' (Organizing Committee, 1958) and the Montreal Summer Games in 1976 were intended to leave an 'inheritance of benefit' (Organizing Committee, 1976).

Legacy, in the contemporary sense, started to be used in a concerted manner in the Official Reports for Los Angeles with eleven mentions (LAOOC, 1985) and the Winter Games in Calgary 1988 with forty-two mentions (COWGOC, 1988). As measured by the Official Reports, the notion of legacy then became increasingly entrenched in thinking, with Atlanta 1996 recording seventy-one mentions, forty-three for Sydney 2000, fifty-five for Salt Lake City 2002 and twenty-three for Athens 2004 (see respectively ACOG, 1990; SOCOG, 2000b; SLOC, 2002; and ATHOC, 2005). The informal and *ad hoc* usages of the term, however, were in many ways racing ahead of substantive definition. It could clearly consist of a broad package of sporting, urban regenerative and environmental elements.

Equally, the term could encompass a disparate range of intangible ingredients that includes skills, sports and cultural participation, volunteering, national pride and city status.

In attempting to come to terms with the growing diversity, therefore, a symposium met under IOC auspices in 2002 to consider the relevant theory and practice. After extensive deliberations, it concluded (IOC, 2003*b*, p. 2) that:

> the effects of the legacy have many aspects and dimensions, ranging from the more commonly recognized aspects – architecture, urban planning, city marketing, sports infrastructures, economic and tourist development – to others ... that are less well recognised ... the so called intangible legacies, such as production of ideas and cultural values, intercultural and non-exclusionary experiences (based on gender, ethnicity or physical abilities), popular memory, education, archives, collective effort and voluntarism, new sport practitioners, notoriety on a global scale, experience and know-how...

This all-encompassing definition delimits a broad category, within which further differentiation has been made by establishing dichotomies. The one recognized by the symposium was tangible (measurable) versus intangible legacy (non-measurable), but other dichotomies, often sharing common ground, have subsequently been added. They include direct (arising from investment in the Olympics) versus indirect (associated) legacy; short term versus long term; and hard (physical structures and infrastructure) versus soft (other tangible and intangible outcomes). In addition, other terms like 'pregacy' have become a jocular way of identifying impacts occurring before the event.

Considerations of the hydra-headed beast now known as legacy arise at many points in this text, but at the outset, it is worth making four points that help to contextualize the subject. The first is that despite now ostensibly being central to the *raison d'être* of the Games, no city to date has yet undergone a full and rigorous longitudinal evaluation of the legacy from an Olympic Games. In attempting to gain better data, for example, the IOC established the Olympic Games Global Impact (OGGI) project in 2005 by which candidate and then host cities are committed to look at the economic, environmental and social impact of the Games over a period of 12 years, namely when the city applies (baseline report); in the preparation phase; a report on staging the Games completed a year after the Games have ended; and a closing report supplied 3 years after the end. Although Athens 2004, Turin 2006 and Beijing 2008 cooperated in limited ways with this project, Vancouver 2010 and London 2012 will be the first hosts to go through the full cycle and their final reports are not due until 2013 and 2015, respectively. What is available in the meantime, therefore, is an assortment of different reports from past Olympics, official and unofficial, completed on the basis of a wide variety of methodologies and modes of analysis. In each case, the objectives of policy only emerged as each succeeding OCOG has refined and operationalized its initial goals. As Girginov and Hills (2008, p. 2092) rightly note, such legacies are 'constructed and not given'.

The second point concerns the tendency to accent the positive. Even though some commentators do talk about 'neutral' or 'negative' legacy, the case that city managers make for legacy predominantly involves its intergenerational benefits, in that future citizens will be repaid handsomely for costs borne by current citizens. This positive slant may prove to be rhetoric, given the numerous instances when inadequate or overambitious planning, poor stadia design, the withdrawal of sponsors, and heavy cost overruns have bequeathed legacies of debt and environmental damage (e.g. see Tomlinson, 1999; Payne, 2006; and Mangan, 2008).

It is not part of the function of this book to debunk the Games or argue on the basis of that experience that their impact on host cities is necessarily adverse. What is apparent from the standpoint of Olympic cities, however, is that staging the Games is now divorced from the economic rationale that surrounds almost all other festivals. The Olympics are commonly hailed as mega-events that will bring a highly desirable package of benefits to the host city including, *inter alia*, boosting a city's economy, improving its international standing, repositioning it in the global tourist market, promoting urban regeneration, revamping transport and service infrastructures, creating vibrant cultural quarters, establishing a network of high-grade facilities that could serve as the basis for future bids, and gaining a competitive advantage over rivals. Nevertheless, looked at another way, the Olympic festivals are also prime candidates for classification as 'megaprojects'. Defined as prestige schemes involving large-scale and high-risk investment over a lengthy period, megaprojects notoriously suffer heavy cost overruns, often failing to deliver the supposed benefits and regularly provoking financial crises (Flyvbjerg *et al.*, 2003; see also Hall, 1980). Indeed, the Olympics may suffer more in this respect than other megaprojects by virtue of having an immutable deadline for completion. When works run behind timetable, this can add further cost pressures by forcing organizers to instigate high-cost emergency building programmes, with round-the-clock working and additional contractors, in order to get laggard projects back on schedule.

Acknowledgment of these unwelcome characteristics, however, is rarely countenanced before winning the bid and almost never once the Games have been awarded – the prime reason why Tessa Jowell's utterances caused such consternation. The right to host the Olympics represents the ultimate accolade that a city can earn on the world stage. To surrender that right would invite universal ridicule and inflict a mortal blow on the standing of the host city in the international urban pecking order. Expenditures might be disputed and lower priority events, such as the Cultural Olympiad or associated youth programmes, might have their budgets slashed, but the prestige element of the expenditure will go ahead. Ways will be found to finance the Games regardless of the logic of the balance sheet, probably with the nation as a whole rather than the Olympic city picking up the bulk of the bill. Without cost as an effective constraint, debate inevitably centres on the seductive promise of legacy to sustain popular enthusiasm and drive the project ahead. Boris Johnson's instincts, therefore, were certainly in line with current expectations about the role of Games' organizers and city managers.

The third point concerns the balance of sports to non-sports legacy. It goes without saying that sports-related elements are a key dimension in the equation, particularly for the IOC which is not altogether happy about the over-identification of notions of legacy with the interests of the host city and the approach that this appears to embody. Certainly bid documents by candidate cities pay close attention to sports legacy, which routinely incorporates four interrelated and overlapping themes. The first is sports infrastructure. With the Summer Games requiring new, renovated or temporary facilities for around thirty sports, there is always likely to be a stock of new facilities available for elite or local use. The second, sports development, comprises encouraging sports participation for its own sake or for instrumental reasons (for example, promotion of public health or for tackling unequal access to sports opportunities). The third, sports performance, relates to raising standards and promoting excellence. The final element, sports tourism, involves travel to participate in or watch sporting events. Taken collectively, however, these various aspects of sports legacy are often easier to propose conceptually than to achieve, especially in terms of sports participation and inculcation of public health.

The final point involves inclusion and exclusion. Anything that involves long-term legacy from an Olympic Games, and the passing of resources from one generation to the next, immediately invokes questions of equity – about who gains and who bears the costs. Issues connected with intergenerational equity were mentioned above, but various other forms of equity also arise. Although detailed discussion of these matters lies beyond the scope of this chapter,[3] it is possible to recognize, in outline, at least four dimensions of equity connected with Olympic legacy. The first, social equity, refers to situations in which people within the society have equal rights and opportunities with respect to the gains to be realized from legacy, regardless of their class or status. The second, economic equity, recognizes that wealth created as part of the legacy of the Games is distributed fairly throughout the community. The third, environmental equity, offers a safe, healthy, productive, and sustainable environment for all.[4] The fourth, spatial equity, deals with fairness of distribution of legacy outcomes regardless of location. These four loosely-defined dimensions, of course, represent ideal states that are difficult to implement and pursuit of one may create tensions with others. Nevertheless, there is little doubt that these problems of definition and tensions need to be resolved if host cities are to make full sense of the indeterminate notion of legacy.

Flexibility and Durability

These points about legacy, which are reinforced at many points in this book, are testimony to the flexibility of the Olympics – itself an important factor in the durability of these festivals. The Olympics have frequently embraced many agendas, absorbed new ideas and priorities, and adapted to changing times. Certainly, there is nothing new in recasting the Olympics as a device capable of delivering goals other than those directly arising from sport, since the Games have been continually invented and reinvented since their reintroduction in the 1890s.

An important example stems from the cultural dimension of the Olympics. The ancient Games at Olympia, as chapters 2 and 4 show, were not just sporting festivals, but represented gatherings of all the people (*panegyris*) and featured art, oratory, music and poetry as well as athletics. When revived in 1896, the founders of the modern Olympics sought to revive a semblance of that style of assembly by adopting a pan-cultural approach that regarded sports, the arts, technology and culture as mutually enriching and interrelated aspects of human life. From the outset, therefore, cultural programmes that might serve as lasting enhancements to the lives of the societies that staged the modern Games were attached to the Olympic festivals, even if host cities have sometimes chosen to downplay this dimension.

This breadth of interpretation was merely a foretaste of what was to come. On the sporting front, the Games soon came to embrace events that either had a primarily regional appeal or had no ancient equivalent – as with the introduction of the Winter Games in 1924 (see chapter 3). From 1948 onwards, there were the beginnings of a qualitative shift in philosophy, with appropriation of the Olympic spirit to cover sporting competitions for athletes with disabilities. This development, which culminated in the establishment of the Paralympics as a parallel yet integrated festival, challenged the core notion of the Olympics as a celebration of bodily perfection, while retaining the ethos of participation and competition (Bailey, 2008; Gilbert and Schantz, 2009: also chapter 5). It would also eventually lead to lasting changes for host cities as they became obliged to meet the access requirements of the disability agenda.

Other developments had rather less to do with the founding ideals of the revived Games or the development of the IOC's policies than with the objectives of specific Games' organizers. This substantially reflected the fact that there exists a broad but tacit bargain between the Olympic movement and the chosen host cities that allows the latter to pursue their own agendas as recompense for meeting the heavy burden of organization and material costs incurred in staging the Games. This, itself, evolved over time as the Games developed in scale and complexity. The early festivals saw organizers treat the Olympics as an adjunct to the fairground, employing them as an additional but subsidiary attraction for the programmes of International Expositions (World's Fairs). From the mid-1930s, host nations seized the opportunity to use the Olympics as flagship events that would act as advertisements for their countries and regimes. Berlin 1936, as already noted, served as a platform for Hitler's Germany to put an acceptable face on the Third Reich's political regime and to mask its endemic theories of racial supremacy. Tokyo 1964 was an important medium for conveying Japan's credentials as a modern country and for signifying its re-emergence on to the international stage after the Second World War. Moscow 1980 and Los Angeles 1984 were both overlain with manifestations of late Cold War superpower rivalries. Beijing 2008 provided tangible and lasting proof of China's emergence as an economic superpower.

At times, participating nations also acted *en bloc* to bring political agendas to bear on the Games. Most notably, from the late 1960s through to the 1980s the Summer Games regularly took centre stage in the realm of international relations as competing nations made use of the limelight afforded by the Olympics to mount politically-inspired boycotts. Some indication of the shifting currents of such boycotts was supplied by Guttmann (2002, p. 141), who noted the case of Youssef Nagai Assad, an Egyptian shot putter. Assad qualified for three Olympics but never had the chance to participate in his event. In 1972, his government ordered their competitors home from Munich to show solidarity with the Palestinian cause. Four years later, the team returned to Egypt from Montreal without taking part in the Games in order to support the Non-Aligned Nations' protest against New Zealand's rugby ties with South Africa (even though rugby was not then an Olympic sport).[5] In 1980, Assad again lost his opportunity to compete when the Egyptian government chose to join the American-led boycott of the Moscow Games, mounted in protest at the Soviet Union's invasion of Afghanistan. Ironically, he was too old for selection for Los Angeles in 1984 when Egypt did at last participate, albeit in a Games overshadowed by a Soviet-inspired retaliatory boycott.

Aims

Selection by the IOC as an 'Olympic city', then, invites the host to contribute to a process that is now more than a century old, but in continual evolution. The Olympic city gains the right to stage a festival carefully wrapped in the trappings of historical precedent, but which, as we have seen above, also possesses a remarkable malleability that has allowed the event to survive repeated crises and emerge, by the start of the twenty-first century, as unquestionably the 'World's Games'.[6] Olympic cities are partners in the staging of the Olympics rather than nominees that run a festival crafted by its sponsoring body. The IOC guards the continuing traditions of its festival but each recipient city shapes the Games to greater or lesser extent and contributes to the body of customs and practices associated with the Olympics. In a process of continual adaptation and change, the Olympics and host cities enjoy a symbiotic relationship.

This book explores that relationship, examining the experience of Olympic cities and the balance sheet of success and failure from the revival of the Games in 1896 to the plans for the Summer Games in Rio de Janeiro in 2016. As such, it has three main aims. First, it examines the city's role in *staging* the modern Games, a word that covers the full spectrum of activity from initial selection of sites to final modification of these sites to their post-festival condition. Secondly, it explores the underlying *agendas* that host cities have brought to bear on staging the Games, recognizing the different blends of social, political, cultural and economic aspirations that have emerged over time. Finally, it recognizes that, despite being an exceptional event in the life of a specific city, the business of staging the Games is now commonly related to the wider *planning* process. In this respect, we focus particularly on issues concerned with legacy, including infrastructural development and urban regeneration projects, which are now regarded as central to the process of planning for the Olympics.

Having said this, three points are important in understanding the scope of this book. First, while giving understandable prominence to the Summer Games as by far the largest, most prestigious and visible of the Olympic events, we seek a more comprehensive approach. The Olympics are not a single event. The advent of the Winter Olympics in 1924 and the gradual convergence of the Paralympics with both the Summer and Winter Games have added further strands to the Olympic sporting competitions. In addition, as noted above, the revival of the modern Games predicated a cultural festival to exist alongside the sports events. Each of these strands merits coverage as intrinsic parts of the experience of being an Olympic city.

Secondly, the prevailing focus is historical. This does not mean that we have confined the scope of this book purely to dealing with the past since later chapters deal with Olympics that, at the time of writing, are yet-to-come. What this volume does stress, however, is the value of seeing even these forthcoming Games as the product of a chain of events that reaches back into the late nineteenth century and has been steadily developing since that time. The staging of the Olympics positively invites historical analysis. Continuity between Games arises from each new Organizing Committee scrutinizing the experience of previous Committees, with transfer of knowledge from one to another facilitated by the IOC's own procedures (see chapter 6). In addition, each new host city prepares its Olympic festivals in the sure and certain knowledge that its efforts will be compared to those of predecessors and will, in turn, provide a new point of comparison.

Thirdly, and related, we have endeavoured throughout to counter the trend towards what is sometimes termed 'presentism' – the tendency evinced by some historians to see the past in the light of the present and in support of their current beliefs (see the commentaries by Fischer, 1971; and Bourne, 2006). Seen from the standpoint of the present, two possible meta-narratives emerge. One construes both the general history of the Games and the more specific history of the relationship between the Olympics and their host cities as the inevitable triumph of visionary ideas. The other, heavily influenced by the cultural turn in the social sciences, views the modern Olympics as being at a key moment of reformulation, with the underlying philosophy arguably tending towards some new, postmodern state. Neither view, however, is wholly satisfactory. Any book that views the Olympics through an historical lens inescapably encounters a flow of events quite unlike a strip cartoon moving tidily from frame to frame. Quite simply, the unpredictable highs and lows of the experience of Olympic cities resist the imposition of simple categorizations or single-strand narratives.

Structure

As befits the multi-stranded nature of the narratives that surround the Games, therefore, the ensuing chapters divide into three main sections, each of which offers different perspectives on the Olympics. Part 1 contains four parallel but complementary essays that look chronologically at the progress of the individual Olympic festivals from inception to the early twenty-first century. Chapter 2 provides an overview of the relationship between the Summer Olympics and their host cities, acting as a general framework for the case studies of selected cities found in Part 3 as well as adding coverage of Summer Games, particularly from the early years, which are not tackled there. After examining the circumstances behind the revival of the Olympics, it traces eight phases in the history of staging the festival from the opening Games in Athens 1896 to the most recent manifestation in 2008. In a similar vein, Chapter 3 identifies a five-phase framework for analysing the role of the Winter Olympics in changing and modernizing the built environment of its host cities. Chapter 4 examines the cultural dimension of the Games and its attachment to both the Summer and Winter Games. Recent developments have seen the cultural festivals growing in scale, particularly in response to the economic interests of host cities. Chapter 5 examines the Paralympic Games. It charts their development from small beginnings as a competition for disabled ex-servicemen and women in England in the late 1940s to the present day ambulatory international festivals for athletes with disabilities, which now take place in the Olympic city immediately after both the Summer and Winter Games.

Part 2 provides surveys of five key aspects of activity involved in planning and managing the Olympics. Chapter 6 examines finance, adopting a business-historical perspective to identify past growth and potential trends in development of income streams and the major sources of expenditure. Chapter 7 deals with city marketing, recognizing the importance of the Olympics in global place promotion and particularly in securing the bid in the first place. The ensuing chapter (chapter 8) switches attention to the question of security, which has rapidly become one of the key parameters for site organization. It discusses the gradual but inexorable increase in the securitization of Olympic sites, offering a perspective on London 2012 as the 'Security Games'. Chapter 9 then reviews the association between the Olympics and urban renewal and regeneration. After surveying the regenerative impact of Summer Olympics on host cities between 1896 and 1980, it highlights the development of holistic and citywide models of regeneration adopted from 1992 onwards, along with recent concerns about the environmental implications of the Games for the host city. The final chapter in this section (chapter 10) adds the important dimension of Olympic tourism. It outlines a range of Olympic tourism products, before outlining how the Summer and Winter Games can be leveraged to generate tourism.

Part 3 offers nine portraits of Olympic Cities, arranged in chronological order. Chapter 11 discusses the various phases in development of the Olympic sports complex in Berlin and its subsequent problematic history in light of the postwar division and eventual reunification of the city. Chapter 12 recalls the first occasion that the Games were held in a developing nation, analysing the way that the bid was won and the economic and political consequences of the 1968 Olympics for Mexico City. Chapter 13 deals with Montreal 1976, widely recognized as a watershed in modern Olympic history for the scale of its financial mismanagement and the lasting burden upon the city. By contrast Barcelona 1992 provides perhaps the most celebrated example of employing the Olympic Games as part of successful urban development strategy. The account in Chapter 14 provides a detailed picture of the planning of the Barcelona Games, showing how calculations about the Olympics as place promotion strategy and as catalyst for urban regeneration preoccupied planners as much as the conduct of the Games themselves.

The next chapters deal with the first three Summer Games held during the twenty-first century. Chapter 15 focuses attention on cultural policy and planning, exploring the way that the cultural programme was organized at Sydney 2000, the way in which the city was experienced during the Olympic fortnight, and the types of images that the city projected to the rest of the world prior to and after the Games. The ensuing chapter (chapter 16) analyses the Games' return to Athens in 2004, discussing the serious delays incurred by belatedly switching from a nucleated to a dispersed locational policy for Olympic facilities. It also highlights the lip-service paid to the much heralded goal of environmental sustainability before the event and the continuing desolation of the Olympic sites in their transfer to post-Games usage. Chapter 17 examines the astonishing expenditure and associated spectacle that was part and parcel of Beijing 2008. In doing so, it recognizes not only the urban dimension of this Games but their significance within wider processes of development taking place within the People's Republic of China.

The remaining chapters look ahead to Games that are yet to be held. Chapter 18 focuses on London 2012, a Games in which the prospect for regeneration of a deprived and environmentally blighted area of East London was as much part of the bidding process as the image of an inclusive and spectacular Olympic festival. Chapter 19 looks somewhat further ahead to Rio de Janeiro, the latest addition to the family of Olympic Cities and the first city in South America to have received any Olympics, Summer or Winter. The chapter places the emphasis on the process of bidding that led to Rio's successful candidacy and examines the evolving thinking behind its plans for the Games. Finally, chapter 20, the Afterword, comments on the Olympic movement's continuing protection of the Olympic brand and its further development as now carried forward into two new Olympic festivals – the Summer Youth Olympic Games (to be first scheduled for Singapore in August 2010) and the Winter Youth Olympic Games (Innsbruck, January 2012).

Notes

1. The opening part of this chapter is based on Gold and Gold (2009). We are grateful to the London Journal and to Professor Matthew Taylor, the Editor of the special issue in which it appeared, for permission to reproduce it here.

2. Further dimensions of this issue in terms of the political relationship between the IOC and host city regimes lie beyond the scope of the current discussion.

3. For further information and contrasting perspectives, see Swart and Bob (2004), Vigor *et al.* (2004), Shipway (2007) and O'Bonsawin (2010).

4. Based on http://gladstone.uoregon.edu/~caer/ej_definitions.html. Accessed 25 March 2010.

5. Rugby union, however, did feature in Olympic Games before 1924 and will appear again in its seven-a-side form at Rio 2016.

6. It is important to distinguish this commonly applied aphorism for the Olympics from the 'World Games', a multi-sport event staged at four-yearly intervals since 1981 by the International World Games Association and covering sports not represented in the Olympics, such as billiards, netball, surfing and body-building. These aspire, as yet unconvincingly, to equal or even exceed the importance of the world championships that are organized individually by each individual participant federation.

Part I

The Olympic Festivals

Chapter 2

From A to B: The Summer Olympics, 1896–2008

John R. Gold and *Margaret M. Gold*

Yet let us all together to our troops,
And give them leave to fly that will not stay;
And call them pillars that will stand to us;
And, if we thrive, promise them such rewards
As victors wear at the Olympian games

William Shakespeare[1]

Knowledge about the Olympic Games and its significance for ancient Greek society had never faded from the European consciousness, notwithstanding the centuries that had elapsed since the prohibition of the festival by the Christian Emperor Theodosius I in 393 AD. Shakespeare's matter-of-fact reference to the Games illustrates the point that the Olympic idea 'was a shared, not isolated reference' in the arts throughout Western Europe (Segrave, 2005, p. 22); indeed, as Littlewood (2000, p. 1179) observed, the Olympics were 'probably the one' among the 'incalculable influences of the Greeks in the modern world ... of which the general public [were] the most aware'. Much the same applied to Olympia, the place with which the Games were associated. As the English theologian Richard Chandler (1766, p. 308) remarked, its name would 'ever be respected as venerable for its precious era by the chronologer and historian', for whom:

> [it] had been rendered excessively illustrious by the power and reputation of its ancient princes, among whom were Œnomaus and Pelops; by the Oracle and temple of the Olympian Jupiter; by the celebrity of the grand *Panegyris* or general assembly held at it; and by the renown of the *Agon* or Games, in which to be victorious was deemed the very summit of human felicity. (*Ibid.*, p. 303)

Yet despite its reputation, no one was certain as to Olympia's exact whereabouts. Despite being indicated on maps since 1516, when the Venetian cartographer

Battista Palnese referred to it as 'Andilalo',[2] the passage of time meant that 'Olympia has since been forgotten in its vicinity' (*Ibid.*, p. 308).

Matters changed in the 1770s when travellers ventured to the Peloponnesus on the west coast of Greece, then an obscure corner of the Ottoman Empire, in search of this important place. For example, towards the end of a trip in 1776 sponsored by the Society of Dilettanti, Richard Chandler and his companions took local advice as to where Olympia might have been. There was little immediately apparent on arriving at the spot that had been indicated. Two earthquakes had levelled the buildings, already in ruins, in the sixth century AD (Fellmann, 1973, p. 109). Periodic flooding by the two rivers (Cladeos and Alpheios) that meet there had subsequently deposited a layer of alluvium several metres thick. Yet despite the site appearing 'almost naked', closer inspection revealed some wall footings and a massive capital from a Doric column that had recently emerged from the river mud. The latter, Chandler correctly inferred, was a fragment of the Temple of Jupiter (Zeus). He made further deductions about a depression occupied by a pestilential pool: 'At a distance before it was a deep hollow, with stagnant water and brickwork, where, it is imagined, was the Stadium' (Chandler, 1766, p. 308). From these fragments, Chandler provided a mind's eye account of classical Olympia, drawing on ancient descriptions to outline the grandeur of buildings, temples and stadium that had made this 'no inconsiderable place'.

Chandler attached no special significance to these observations within his travelogue, but the rediscovery of the site brought new waves of visitors. Surveys carried out for Lord Spencer Stanhope in 1807 revealed an imposing complex replete with temples, gymnasia, stadium, hippodrome and accommodation (Stanhope, 1824). Noticeably, Stanhope's account extended to the ruined city of Elis, the prime settlement of the *polis* in which the festival site was situated, and recognized the links between the two. Adopting a similar approach to his subject matter, William Leake (1830, I, pp. 23–44) described Elis as the 'place of ordination and preparation for the *athletæ* of the Olympic Games' (*Ibid.*, II, p. 220) and the point from which participants set out in procession to traverse the distance (36 kilometres) to Olympia. The journey, complete with ceremonies of ritual purification *en route*, took place before the start of each Games (see also S.G. Miller, 2003, p. 9). The complex of permanent structures at Olympia also contained buildings that served the Elis-based civil government's need for political administration rather than having religious or sports functions (Crowther, 2003; see also Drees, 1968). These were early and intriguing recognitions of the close relationship between host city and Games.

Understandably, discovery of the ruins prompted campaigns for archaeological work since, as Leake (1830, I, p. 44) observed, 'there is every reason to believe that the most interesting discoveries in illustration of the arts, language, customs and history of Greece, may yet be made by excavations at Olympia'. The first fruits of those campaigns were small-scale digs by English and then French archaeologists in the early nineteenth century, but these encountered Greek sensitivities about removal of artefacts. The third set of excavations, however, proved decisive. Licensed by the Greek Parliament after negotiations between the Greek and German governments to ensure that artefacts did not leave the country, the excavations between 1875 and 1881 by a team from the Imperial German Archaeological Institute provided systematic analysis of the core of the site and vital insights as to its usage (Kyrieleis, 2003). Progressively, a picture emerged of a site sufficiently intact to evoke not just the layout of a complex with a 210 yard (192 metre) running track and associated buildings but also to allow free rein to the imagination as to the activities associated with this place (Perrottet, 2004).

The reports coming from the excavations aroused excitement beyond archaeological circles. Historians and other scholars eagerly devoured news emerging from Olympia and reflected on the mystique of the Games and the place of sport in classical Greek society. Their interest was not simply antiquarian. Some saw the achievements of the past as offering parallels for the modern age. For example, in a public lecture Sidney Colvin, the Director of Cambridge University's Fitzwilliam Museum, enthused over the new archaeological findings, but wistfully remarked that:

> It has been said that Englishmen and ancient Greeks are much like one another in two respects. One is their ignorance of all languages except their own, and the other is their love of physical sports. We have our Epsom and our Grand National, our games of cricket and football, our rowing and our running matches, and we despise Frenchmen and foreigners, generally, with the most impartial disdain; but somehow we don't make of our athletic sports so much as these ancient Greeks did. (Colvin, 1878, p. 7)

Colvin primarily had in mind the link between sport and art, seeing the Games as bridging the sacred and secular and creating a vital exemplar for contemporary cultural life. Others also felt that the ancient Games *per se* had an important ethos that might be revived and recaptured. Their model was that of a peaceful yet competitive sporting festival that brought nations together notwithstanding the pressures of a turbulent external environment.

This chapter provides a review of the principal phases in the development of that festival, as expressed in the evolution of the Summer Games. It opens by discussing the revival of the modern Olympics, before providing an overview of the intricate history of cities staging the Summer Games from Athens 1896 through to the most recent Games in Beijing in 2008 (see table 2.1). We then identify eight phases in the development of the relationship between the city and the Games. The first (1896–1906) traces the way that the nascent Olympics narrowly survived negative associations with the fairground, with two sets of Games held in Athens a decade apart offering a more positive path forward that intimately involved city and stadium. The next phase (1908–1936) saw local Organizing Committees devote mounting resources to preparing stadia and associated facilities. By the time of the 1936 Berlin Games, the Olympics had started to gain a consensual content with ingredients broadly replicated by each succeeding festival, although remaining an event that gave the home nation scope to mould the associated spectacle according to its own needs. After the war and a brief series of lower-

Table 2.1. Cities bidding for the Summer Olympic Games, 1896–2016.

Games	Year awarded	Host city	Other candidates
1896	1894	Athens	London
1900	1894	Paris	
1904	1901	St Louis★	Chicago
1908	1904	London†	Berlin, Milan, Rome
1912	1909	Stockholm	
1916	1912		Berlin, Alexandria (Egypt), Budapest, Cleveland, Brussels
1920	1914	Antwerp	Amsterdam, Atlanta, Brussels, Budapest, Cleveland, Lyon, Havana, Philadelphia
1924	1921	Paris	Los Angeles, Atlantic City, Chicago, Pasadena, Rome, Barcelona, Amsterdam, Lyon
1928	1921	Amsterdam	Los Angeles
1932	1923	Los Angeles	
1936	1931	Berlin	Barcelona, Buenos Aires, Rome
1940	1936		Tokyo, Helsinki, Rome
1944	1939		London, Athens, Budapest, Lausanne, Helsinki, Rome, Detroit
1948	1946	London	Baltimore, Lausanne, Los Angeles, Minneapolis, Philadelphia
1952	1947	Helsinki	Amsterdam, Chicago, Detroit, Los Angeles, Minneapolis, Philadelphia
1956	1949	Melbourne	Buenos Aires, Chicago, Detroit, Los Angeles, Mexico City, Minneapolis, Montreal, Philadelphia
1960	1955	Rome	Budapest, Brussels, Detroit, Lausanne, Mexico City, Tokyo
1964	1959	Tokyo	Brussels, Detroit, Vienna
1968	1969	Mexico City	Buenos Aires, Lyon, Detroit
1972	1966	Munich	Detroit, Madrid, Montreal
1976	1970	Montreal	Los Angeles, Moscow
1980	1974	Moscow	Los Angeles
1984	1978	Los Angeles	Tehran
1988	1981	Seoul	Nagoya (Japan)
1992	1986	Barcelona	Amsterdam, Belgrade, Birmingham, Brisbane, Paris
1996	1990	Atlanta	Athens, Belgrade, Manchester, Melbourne, Toronto
2000	1993	Sydney	Berlin, Beijing, Manchester, Istanbul (Brasilia, Milan, Tashkent withdrew)
2004	1997	Athens	Buenos Aires, Cape Town, Istanbul, Lille, Rio de Janeiro, Rome, San Juan, St. Petersburg, Seville, Stockholm
2008	2001	Beijing	Bangkok, Cairo, Havana, Istanbul, Kuala Lumpur, Osaka, Paris, Seville, Toronto
2012	2005	London	Paris, Madrid, Moscow, New York
2016	2009	Rio de Janeiro	Baku, Chicago, Doha, Madrid, Prague, Tokyo

★ The nomination was originally to Chicago.
† The nomination was originally to Rome.

Source: Partly based on Buchanan and Mallon (2001).

key events framed by Austerity (1948–1956), the Olympics witnessed growing acceptance of the economic importance and general promotional significance of the event for the host cities. The years from 1960–1976 saw host cities view the Olympics as a catalyst for initiating major infrastructural and related works; a period that ended with the misfortunes of Montreal 1976. After an interlude when the Games became dominated by late-Cold War ideological issues with rather less attention to regeneration (1980–1984), the success of the strategies introduced at Los Angeles 1984 and Barcelona 1992 heralded a new phase of commercialism and regeneration programmes (1988–1996). The Games of 2000 and 2004 found cities actively competing to host a festival justified in terms of sustainable legacy, albeit with varying degrees of plausibility. Finally, we deal with Beijing 2008; a Games that rivalled any predecessor in terms of its elaborate spectacle and impact on the physical fabric of its host city.

Revival

The idea of appropriating the title 'Olympic' had long appealed to organizers of sporting events (Redmond, 1988; Buchanan and Mallon, 2001). Robert Dover, described as an 'English captain and attorney' (*Anon*, 1910, p. 453), established a 'Cotswold Games' on his estate in 1604, largely as a protest against Puritan proscriptions of sporting pastimes and other frivolities (Mandell, 1976, p. 29). The festival that contemporary writers described as 'Mr Robert Dover's Olimpick Games upon the Cotswold Hills' included 'cudgel-playing, wrestling, running at the quintain, casting the ball and hammer, hand-ball, gymnastics, rural dances and games, and horse-racing, the winners in which received valuable prizes' (*Anon*, 1910, p. 453). The Cotswold Games lasted until 1644, although they were briefly revived during the reign of Charles II, with a separate 'Olympics', largely devoted to dog racing, occurring at Hampton Court Palace in 1679.[3]

During the first half of the nineteenth century, a series of separate initiatives consciously sought to use Olympic sport to cement nationalist or pan-national aspirations. The Scandinavian Olympic Games of 1834 and 1836, founded at Ramlösa (Sweden) by the sports educator Gustav Johan Schartau, were designed as national festivals for the 'strong sons of Scandinavia' (Øresundstid, 2003). The Anglophone community in Montreal staged an Olympics in 1844 to assert their identity against the Francophone majority. The influential Much Wenlock Games, founded by Dr William Penny Brookes, grew from an initially limited affair to subsequent grander aims. Founded in October 1850 and still held annually, they aimed 'to promote the moral, physical and intellectual improvement of the inhabitants of the Town and neighbourhood of Wenlock' (WOS, 2006). Gradually, Brookes's vision expanded, most notably assisting the establishment of a National Olympian Association (NOA) in the 1860s. This eventually foundered, particularly due to opposition from the Amateur Athletic Club – an aristocratic and elitist group founded in 1866 to counter the NOA. Nevertheless, during its brief lifespan the NOA stimulated a brief flowering of athletics events in British cities, including the London Olympics – which attracted 10,000 spectators to Crystal Palace between 31 July and 2 August 1866.

Understandably, there was considerable interest in reviving the Olympics in Greece. Having achieved political independence in 1830, groups within the country campaigned to restore the Games as a symbol of their re-emerging nationhood (see chapter 16). In 1859, an Olympic sports festival took place in Athens, assisted by sponsorship from Evangelis Zappas, a wealthy expatriate Greek landowner living in Romania (figure 2.1). The so-called 'Zappas Games', held again in 1870 and 1875, constituted a different scale of competition and spectacle than other events previously styled as 'Olympian'. The 1870 meeting, for example, attracted 30,000 spectators to watch Greek athletes compete in the partially restored Panathenian stadium.

Historians, however, show considerable selectivity in relation to these events. Official versions of Olympic history typically styled them as 'pseudo-Olympics' (Redmond, 1988); interesting as expressions of the desire to create prestige sporting competitions, but not representing progenitors of the revived Games as developed by the IOC under Baron Pierre de Coubertin's leadership.[4] This selectivity had an ideological purpose since, by emphasizing the originality of Coubertin's vision and downplaying the contribution of others, it privileged the IOC's claims for

Figure 2.1. Statue of Evangelis Zappas, situated outside the Zappeion, the building named in his honour and used for the fencing competitions at the Athens 1896 games.

ownership of the Games. The traditional treatment of the personal relationship between Pierre de Coubertin and William Penny Brookes is a case in point. Historical accounts recognize that the two men actively corresponded and that Brookes had staged a special Autumn version of the Wenlock Games in Coubertin's honour when he visited England in October 1890, which featured award ceremonies and pageantry that greatly impressed Coubertin (Young, 1996, p. 78). The 1866 London Olympics, by contrast, received no mention in official Olympic histories; nor do Brookes's speeches in which he proposed an international basis for the Games and advocated that they should have a permanent home in Athens (Young, 1998, p. 31; Toohey and Veal, 2000, p. 29). Brookes, therefore, emerged as the organizer of a small rural sporting festival rather than one of the lynchpins of the Games' revival.

The ideological dimension was even stronger in the disparagement of Greece's attempts to reinstate the Games. Downgrading the significance of the Zappas Games denied approval to any proprietorial claims by Greece to the revived Olympics, even though they were clearly based on a classical festival held on Greek soil for almost 1,200 years. In one sense, this ran counter to the mood of the times which favoured folk revival and saw collectors scouring the margins of Western nations in a nationalistic search for the 'authentic' roots of folk culture (Gold and Revill, 2006). Instead, the founders of the Olympics perceived their task as resuscitating an event that represented the quintessence of ancient cultural achievement to which Western civilization in general, rather than the late nineteenth-century Greek state, was heir. That outlook, in turn, imbued the modern Olympics with an internationalist stance, able continually to move to new host cities without loss of purpose, rather than needing to return permanently to Greece as a geographic hearth that would give the revived Games authenticity. Ceding control to the Greeks would have interfered with the freedom of action to pursue that policy.

Yet recognition of alternative precursors scarcely detracts from the importance of Coubertin's role in campaigning for the revival of the Olympics and, subsequently for his formative influence on the Games' early development. Commentators (e.g. Mandell, 1976; MacAloon, 1981) rightly identify Coubertin's contribution as a reformer who gradually moved beyond specific concern with promoting sports education within France as a medium for fostering national regeneration to addressing the 'democratic and international' dimension of sport. On 25 November 1892, his speech at the Sorbonne in Paris exhorted a somewhat sceptical audience to aid 'this grandiose and salutary task, the restoration of the Olympic Games' (quoted in Müller, 2000, p. 297).[5] Coubertin repeated his exhortation, with greater success, at an international Sports Congress that he organized in 1894, which supported the re-establishment of the Games and laid down key principles for organizing them.

To summarize its recommendations, the revived Olympics would reintroduce the ancient Games' four-yearly cycle, but would be ambulatory rather than based at a permanent site. They would be open to amateur sportsmen and should comprise modern rather than classical sports, although there was no definitive list of which sports to include or exclude. The Congress initiated the process of constructing a Charter of 'fundamental principles, rules and by-laws' to run the Games, normally known as the Olympic Charter. Central to its outlook was the notion of 'Olympism', the humanistic philosophy that mediated the cultural construction of the revived Games and guided the development of the supporting ceremonial content that steadily accumulated in subsequent years (see chapter 4). Finally, it founded the IOC to control the movement and to select the host cities, although local Organizing Committees would plan the Olympics,[6] with the first two Games scheduled for Athens in 1896 and Paris in 1900. Both locations were pragmatic choices (Young, 1987, p. 271). The Congress accepted the inevitable by recognizing that Athens's symbolic associations made it the only city that could effectively launch the modern Olympics, in spite of wanting to resist Greek claims to ownership of the Games and having given serious consideration to London in view of its advantages regarding access and venues. The choice of Paris for 1900 reflected Coubertin's hope to capitalize on the International Exposition taking place that year and to draw spectators to the newly established Games.

Surviving the Fairground (1896–1906)

The first distinct phase of development saw a sequence of four Summer Games, in which the fortunes of the Olympics fluctuated profoundly. Athens 1896 proceeded against a difficult political and economic background that made preparations problematic and led to the first airing of a perennial question: should money be spent on the Olympics as a prestige project in light of competing needs? In this instance, one side, led by Prime Minister Charilaos Tricoupis, argued against the Games for economic reasons; the other, led by Opposition leader Theodorus Delyannis and supported by the monarchy, sympathized with the Games as a prestigious project that might reflect well on Greek identity and international standing (MacAloon, 1981, p. 182). The latter camp won the day, with the necessary finance raised through a mixture of public funds, appeals for subscriptions, private sponsors and the first special issue of Olympic postage stamps (*Ibid*., p. 196; see also chapter 6).

Athens 1896 set an early pattern of low expenditure, pressing into service the existing Zappeion Building and the restored Panathenian stadium, with new construction restricted to a velodrome, shooting gallery and seating for the swimming events (Davenport, 1996, pp. 4–5; Gordon, 1983). This policy posed some problems. The Panathenian stadium, for instance, successfully held crowds of more than 50,000 and accommodated a modern running surface, but its traditional elongated horseshoe shape with accentuated curves at each end, hindered athletic performance (figure 2.2). Nevertheless, the revived festival worked well. The Games, symbolically opening on Greek Independence Day (6 April), attracted 245

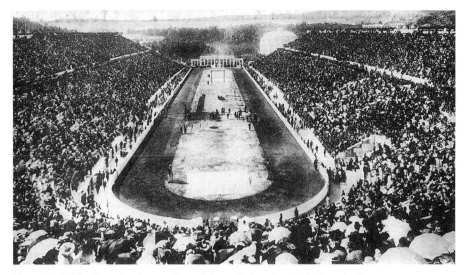

Figure 2.2. The Panathenian stadium, Athens during the 1896 Olympic Games.

athletes from fourteen countries to compete in forty-five events. The Opening Ceremony filled the stadium, with the spectators who occupied the surrounding hillsides and streets swelling the audience to an estimated 80,000–120,000.

The city beyond the stadium readily embraced the Games. The Athenian authorities decorated the streets, illuminated the Acropolis and arranged an entertainments programme that included torchlight processions, parades, fireworks, an orchestral concert by the Athens Philharmonic Orchestra and a performance of Sophocles's *Antigone* (Mallon and Widland, 1998). The marathon, introduced for the first time, added spectacle, provided a link with tradition[7] and supplied an important, if invented, symbol. Spectators lined the route through the Greater Athens region and filled the stadium to see the finish. Its popularity, enhanced by the victory of a local man, Spiridon Louis, not only brought a new fixture to the athletics calendar,[8] but also served to provide a focus that stressed the unity of city and Olympics.

Although small scale by contemporary standards, the 1896 Games showed that the modern Olympics had considerable potential as a coherent framework for a new international festival. By contrast, the two succeeding Games came perilously close both to derailing the Olympic movement and to downgrading the relationship between host city and Games to inconsequentiality. In both cases, the reason lay in the conflict between the nascent Games and larger, more important International Expositions. At Paris 1900, the connection between the events was the conscious, if misguided policy of associating the second Games with the 1900 Paris Exposition Universelle. Coubertin believed that the Olympics could capitalize on the Fair's many visitors and festive backdrop and, in particular, wanted to build a replica of Olympia, with temples, stadia, gymnasia and statues and an archaeological display.[9] The organizers, however, remained unmoved by this idea. Disputes over the control of the sporting element resulted in the Olympic movement effectively withdrawing, with a new committee appointed to plan the Exposition's Games (Mallon, 1998, p. 6). The Olympics became an International Games rather than a true Olympics. They were of indeterminate length, given that they lacked Opening or Closing Ceremonies and that the organizers haphazardly added events to the programme, some of which, like fishing in the River Seine (Harlan, 1931, p. 88), did not conform to Olympic standards. Indeed some competitors in tournaments connected with the Exposition never realized that they had entered Olympic competitions. For example, Michel Theato, the marathon winner, only learned in 1912 that he was the 'gold medallist' at the 1900 Olympics (Mallon, 1998, p. 9).

Compared with the considerable impact that the Exposition had on Paris – with a 543 acre (219 hectare) fairground located in the heart of the city in the Avenue Alexandre III and the Bois de Vincennes – the Olympics scarcely registered a presence. There was no stadium or running track. The track and field events were staged at the Racing Club of France's grounds in the Bois de Bologne, but the owners refused permission to remove any trees. As a result, discus and javelin throws often landed in wooded areas. The 500 metre (546 yard) grass running track sloped and undulated. Rigid former telegraph poles served as hurdles. The organizers hastily constructed a grandstand, but a row of trees obscured the track from spectators (Howell and Howell, 1996). Wholly overshadowed by the Exposition, the movement that had shown 'so much promise in 1896 seemed to have collapsed by 1900' (*Ibid*., p. 17).

The next Summer Games at St Louis proved equally inimical to the revival of the Olympics. The IOC had strongly backed selection of a North American city and chose Chicago in May 1901 to stage the 1904 Games. Spoiling tactics by the organizers of St Louis's Louisiana Purchase International Exposition, however, led the IOC reluctantly to revise that decision even if it was inevitable that the Olympics 'would only be a sideshow attraction to the much larger international exposition' (Barnett, 1996, p. 19). Their fears had justification. The Exposition itself brought considerable kudos to St Louis, created an extensive fairground from the wooded Forest Park, and allowed much needed improvement works to the erstwhile heavily polluted and flood-prone Des Peres River. By contrast, the Olympics left little trace. There was at least a stadium, capable of seating 10,000 spectators, although with a one-third mile (536 metres) track instead of the standard quarter-mile circuit of the time, and 'something approaching' an Opening Ceremony on 14 May 1904 (Mallon, 1999a, p. 11). The programme, however, supplied little sense of continuity, with sporting competitions held at irregular intervals through to November, with scarcely any distinction between 'Olympic' sports and other competitions. The organizers added sports of their own choosing such as college football (gridiron), local cross country championships, professional events, the national championships of the American Athletic Union of the United States, and 'automobiling' (Anon, 1904, pp. 3, 48). In addition, the festival was tarnished by the infamous 'Anthropology Days' (12–13 August 1904) when African, Asian and

Native American competitors competed in racially motivated athletic contests that denigrated their performances and gave succour to theories of white supremacy (Brownell, 2008). Following hard on the heels of the 1900 debacle, St Louis 1904 threatened the continuance of the modern Olympics (Barnett, 1996, p. 23).

In the event, it took a sporting festival not usually reckoned as part of Olympic history – the 1906 Intercalated Games held in Athens – to secure the future (Young, 1996, p. 166; Mallon, 1999b, p. 5). This was the first, and only, product of a tactical compromise made in 1897, when a Coubertin-inspired initiative offered Greece the opportunity to hold a series of Intercalated Games at four-yearly intervals in non-Olympic years. Greece's defeat in the first Greco-Turkish War (1897) had left the country bankrupt (Davenport, 1996, p. 10), but improved economic circumstances allowed the staging of an Intercalated Games by 1906. This returned to the Panathenian stadium, with more extensive and eye-catching rituals and accompanying festivities than those staged in 1896. The sporting festival once more spilled over into the city, in a manner that contrasted with the experience of Paris and St Louis. The streets and buildings of Athens were again decorated, the city's squares staged evening concerts and there was a sustained programme of entertainments. The international press was more in evidence than at previous Games, although the eruption of Mount Vesuvius (4 April) and the San Francisco earthquake (18 April) detracted from the coverage that the Games received (Mallon, 1999b, p. 6). Nevertheless, the Intercalated Games effectively rescued the Olympics from its disastrous flirtation with the fairground and initiated a period in which host cities actively welcomed the Olympic Games as a premier and prestigious sporting event that merited purpose-built facilities.

Olympics by Design (1908–1936)

Just as the eruption of Vesuvius in April 1906 detracted from the coverage of the Athens Intercalated Games, so, arguably, did it put paid to its successor as the severe strains that recovery from the devastation placed on the Italian economy led to Rome abandoning its attempt to hold the 1908 Games.[10] In November 1906, the IOC formally confirmed the transfer to London (Mallon and Buchanan, 2000, p. 3). With just 20 months in which to prepare the Games, the OCOG decided to use existing venues in the London region wherever adequate facilities were available. Hence, *inter alia*, the tennis competitions were held at Wimbledon, polo at Hurlingham and shooting at Uxendon School Shooting Club and Bisley Rifle Range. Nevertheless, the organizers also decided to seek a purpose-built stadium where most of the Olympic competitions and ceremonies could take place; a strategy that broke with the practice of the previous Games.

Its construction was facilitated by developing a partnership with the Franco-British Exhibition of Science, Arts, and Industry, held to celebrate the recent Entente Cordiale between the two nations, which was due to open in the summer of 1908. This arrangement seemed at first glance to pose precisely the same threat of eclipsing the Games as at Paris 1900 and St. Louis 1904. That this did not happen was due largely to the 1908 Games being both organizationally and spatially separate from the International Exhibition. Organizationally, they were firmly under the control of sports interests, in the shape of the newly-formed British Olympic Association. Spatially, they gained distinctiveness from having a separate stadium. The Franco-British Exhibition, then under construction on a 140 acre (56 hectare) plot of former agricultural land and brickfields at Shepherd's Bush (West London), had included plans for entertainments to be staged at a small stadium with spectators standing on a surrounding mound. Under the new agreement, the Exhibition Organizing Committee agreed to develop this prototype into a full-blown stadium in return for 75 per cent of the Olympics' proceeds.[11]

The largest stadium of its day, its enormous concrete bowl enclosed athletics and cycle tracks, a 100 metre swimming pool, platforms for wrestling and gymnastics and even archery. Dressing rooms, restaurants and emergency services were located under the stands (figure 2.3). The foundation stone of the White City stadium, so-called because the Exhibition Buildings were finished in gleaming white stucco, was laid on 2 August 1907 and the stadium was inaugurated on the opening day of the adjoining Exhibition (14 May 1908). It held 93,000 spectators, with 63,000 seated. A newly opened station at Wood Lane, on an extension of the Central London Railway from its terminus at Shepherd's Bush, supplied both the Exhibition and Olympics with direct connections to central London.

London 1908 left a considerable positive legacy for the Olympic movement by developing the spectacle of the festival and supplying the basis for 'a compact and independent Olympic festival' (Wimmer, 1976, p. 22). Yet while it allowed the Games to prosper as an event in its own right, London 1908 also provided the less desirable physical legacy of a huge and largely unwanted stadium. Although the

Figure 2.3. The White City stadium, Shepherd's Bush, London, 1908.

initial intention was to demolish the stadium and provide 'no permanent addition to the athletic grounds of London' (*Anon.*, 1907), its continued existence after 1908 made it arguably the first instance of the 'limping white elephants' associated with the Olympics (Mangan, 2008). It remained scarcely used for two decades before passing to the Greyhound Racing Association in 1926. The stadium was then renovated, with its capacity reduced from 93,000 to 80,000, installation of a greyhound track over the existing running track, and removal of the cycling circuit and the defunct swimming tank (Hawthorne and Price, 2001, p. 7; Jenkins, 2008). In 1932, the reconfiguration of the running track to a new 440 yard (402 metre) circuit allowed the stadium's use for national and international athletics events. On occasions, the White City did stage large-scale sporting festivals, such as the 1934 British Empire Games and the 1935 International Games for the Deaf, and provided a base for British athletics from 1933 onwards. However, when the athletics events moved to their new home at Crystal Palace in 1971, the stadium languished before eventual demolition in 1985 to make way for offices for the British Broadcasting Corporation and housing.

The 1912 Games in Stockholm saw the Olympics move to a far smaller city.[12] Partly as a result, the Stockholm Organization Committee found it easier to create a festival that integrated city and stadium. The design of the latter, built in the grounds of the royal Djirgaden (Zoological Gardens), assisted that aim. More modest than the White City, it seated 22,000 people, with stands arranged around a 400 metre running track (figure 2.4). From the outset, it was intended to be multipurpose, a decision that Coubertin applauded:

> The Gothic Stadium ... seemed to be a model of its kind. You could see it turned into a banquet hall, a concert hall, or a dance hall, and yet on the following morning always ready once again for carrying on with the contests. You could see how in a single night it got covered with ready-made squares of lawn, how hurdles were being put up, and how it decked itself with blossoming brushwood for the riding tournaments. All this was achieved without any ado, any delay, any blunder. While in London it had proved impossible for the life of the great city to be in any way affected by the proximity of the Olympic Games, Stockholm turned out to be thoroughly imbued with them. The entire city participated in its efforts to honour its foreign guests, and one had something like a vision of what the atmosphere must have been like in Olympia in the ancient days ... (quoted in Wimmer, 1976, p. 27)

The stadium's evening entertainments included military concerts, displays of Scandinavian sports, gymnastic displays, fireworks and illuminations. The city provided street decorations, opera, theatre, a two-day aquatic festival, the usual round of receptions and banquets, and played reluctant host to the artistic competitions that were a cherished part of Coubertin's vision of linking sport and the arts. For the first time, too, the organizers took steps to publicize the Games internationally, through the Olympic movement, the Swedish diplomatic service

Figure 2.4. The American team entering the stadium during the Opening Ceremony of the Olympic Games, Stockholm, 1912.

and advertisements in national newspapers of other countries. The makings of the promotional activity that typified later Olympic Games had started to emerge.

The next Games took place 8 years later. Hidebound by its observance of the four-year cycle of Olympiads despite the inconvenient reality of the First World War, the IOC retained the fiction of a sixth Olympiad in 1916. Although six cities in the, as yet non-belligerent, USA (Chicago, Cleveland, Newark, New York, Philadelphia and San Francisco) had offered to act as hosts to avoid disrupting the series, the IOC maintained that it had awarded Berlin the right to stage the 1916 Olympics and could not withdraw a nomination without that city's agreement. As the German Olympic Committee remained adamant that Berlin held the nomination, the sixth Olympiad was never held and the Games resumed their four-year cycle with the seventh Olympiad in Antwerp in 1920.

Awarded at an IOC meeting in Lausanne in April 1919 as much as a political act of moral support for Belgium than as a sporting event, Antwerp 1920 used the quickly renovated Beerschot stadium. Shortage of resources and materials meant that the standard of facilities was much poorer than at Stockholm, with constant rain leaving the running track pitted and rutted. A canal at Willebroek near Brussels, used for the rowing events, provided an industrial setting so ugly that Coubertin called it 'anti-Olympic' (Renson, 1996, p. 57). There were few associated festivities in the city. Yet despite the austerity, Antwerp 1920 recorded a deficit of 626 million Belgian francs, prompting accusations of acute financial mismanagement and leaving the organizers accused of treating the event as 'a symbol of conspicuous consumption' (*Ibid.*, p. 59).

The responsibility of consolidating the progress made at London and Stock-holm therefore passed to the Organization Committees of the two ensuing Games. Paris 1924 represented the first occasion on which the growing prestige of the Olympics led to serious international competition among cities to act as hosts. Four American cities (Los Angeles, Atlantic City, Chicago and Pasadena) and five European (Rome, Barcelona, Amsterdam, Lyons and Paris) expressed interest in staging the Olympics (Welch, 1996, p. 61). The return to Paris proceeded with assurances that, unlike 1900, the organizers would treat the Olympics as an important international event. Rather than employ the Pershing stadium, which staged the 1919 Inter-Allied Games,[13] the Organization Committee decided in June 1922 to construct a purpose-built stadium at Colombes. The Stade Olympique Yves-du-Manoir had seating for 20,000 spectators, standing room for an additional 40,000 (*Ibid.*, p. 64) and would remain the main venue for national soccer and rugby matches until the opening of the Parc des Princes in 1972. Paris 1924 saw the birth of the concept of the Olympic Village at Rocquencourt, although the barrack-like accommodation with few services had 'very little to do with what was to be the first Olympic village' at Los Angeles 1932 (Muñoz, 1997, p. 30). Paris also witnessed the first significant dissatisfactions about the growing size of the Games, given that the scatter of the Olympic venues around the Paris region necessitated long bus journeys for most competitors.

The 1928 Amsterdam Games favoured the now familiar idea of clustered Olympic sites. Although the athletes were housed on ships in the harbour rather than in a specially constructed Village (Goldstein, 1996), the Dutch employed the 'Cité Olympique' idea of bringing the stadium and associated facilities together in a sporting complex. The new athletics stadium, built on reclaimed marshland,

Figure 2.5. Water polo competition in progress, the Olympic Pool, Amsterdam, 1928.

had seats for 40,000, with the other venues having a capacity of a further 30,000. The open-air swimming pool was located next to the main stadium (figure 2.5), with adjacent gymnasia for boxing, wrestling and fencing. Concerns were again expressed about the growing size of the Games, although the target was now the 'excessive festivities', with proposals that there should be reforms to allow only those that 'the reception of authorities and officials demanded' (Organizing Committee, 1928, p. 957).

The two final interwar Games completed the Summer Olympics' development into a high-status international festival that would play an important part in the lives of host cities. Los Angeles 1932 was an Olympiad conceived in the American boosterist tradition, resolutely advancing the city's economic and cultural interests against rivals. The city gained the right to stage the 1932 Olympics in 1923, but faced severe funding problems in the wake of the 1929 Wall Street Crash, with the federal government refusing to contribute. The Games' survival rested on the city issuing bonds and capitalizing on connections with the private sector, most notably the film industry which actively promoted the Olympics. Yet perhaps the key to encouraging participation lay in making the Games affordable to competitors by assisting travel and in constructing the first true Olympic Village, an innovation that combined economy with the spirit of Olympism.[14] The Official Report of the Games (TOC, 1933, pp. 235, 237) waxed lyrical about the symbolism of the Village and intermixing of peoples, to the extent that the observers recommended the Organizing Committee for the Nobel Peace Prize for their work in promoting the fellowship of the Games through the nations' athletes living peacefully side-by-side (Stump, 1988, p. 199).

With the assistance of substantial subsidies for food and accommodation, 1,500 athletes from thirty-four nations competed at Los Angeles 1932 despite the vicissitudes of the international economy. Apart from the auditorium for the indoor competitions, most of the stadia were at Olympic Park (the former Exposition Park). The Memorial Stadium, the last Olympic arena to use the old-fashioned modified U-shape (Wimmer, 1976, p. 39), was created by refurbishing and enlarging the Coliseum into a venue with a seated capacity of 105,000. The swimming stadium and the State Armoury, which staged the fencing competitions, were built nearby. The Olympic Park also housed the Los Angeles Museum of History, Science and Art, which held more than 1,100 exhibits from the thirty-two countries that supplied entries for the Olympic Art Competition. The organizers added another important innovation by coordinating the decoration of the Olympic venues and the city using streamers and bunting in the official colours of blue, yellow, black, green and red. Flags of the competing nations, Olympic banners and large insignia hung across the main streets. The organizers also encouraged the owners of buildings and businesses to buy specially manufactured materials to embellish their buildings.

Despite the economic situation, the Games achieved an enviable operating surplus, with 1.25 million people paying $1.5 million to watch events over the 16 days of the Games. Tourist agencies put together packages featuring the Olympics and the scenic attractions of Southern California. Sixty-two conventions were attracted to Los Angeles, enabling their delegates to enjoy the Games and further boosting the local economy at a time of continuing economic depression (TOC, 1933, p. 215). A visiting journalists' programme dealt with several hundred reporters from around the world in the 3 years leading up to the Games (*Ibid.*, p. 211); a strategy that maximized the possibility of favourable coverage. Not surprisingly, the 1932 Games left the city eager to repeat the exercise, with repeated candidacy before the Olympics finally returned in 1984 (see below).

Berlin 1936, the final Summer Games before the Second World War, was a landmark in political as well as sports history. The background to the Berlin Games, as chapter 11 shows, resonates with the history of Germany in the interwar period. Berlin, the host city, bid unsuccessfully for both the 1908 and 1912 Games, had seen the cancellation of the 1916 Games for which it held the nomination, and saw its further ambitions placed in abeyance until Germany was readmitted to the Olympic movement in time for the 1928 Games in Amsterdam. In May 1931, the IOC awarded the 1936 Games to Berlin as an act of reconciliation, but the choice proved problematic with Hitler's rise to power. The Nazis' initial hostility to the financial burden and avowed internationalism of the Games seemed likely to bring rapid cancellation, but subsequent reappraisal of the classical origins of the Games to align them with National Socialist ideas of German origins[15] quickly brought enthusiastic support. This led to concern within the Olympic movement that the Games would be hijacked by the Nazi leadership for propaganda purposes (Hart Davis, 1986).

Certainly the creation of the stadium, the surrounding complex and other Olympic venues proceeded with wider ideological and propaganda goals in mind. As chapter 11 shows, the regime vetoed Werner March's original plans for expansion of the 1913 stadium, already approved by the IOC, favouring instead a proposal for a 110,000-seater stadium with a steel- and stone-clad structure. The stadium would lie at the heart of the Reichssportsfeld, soon to become the world's largest sports complex, complete with swimming and diving pools (with seating for 18,000), facilities for lawn tennis, hockey, equestrian sports, the House of German Sports (Deutschland Halle) for boxing, fencing, weightlifting, wrestling, the Reich Academy of Physical Education, accommodation for female competitors and the Maifeld Parade Ground (figure 2.6). Located in a peripheral area of Berlin but well connected into the city's U-bahn rail system, the site became the focus of attention throughout Germany in the period leading up to and including the Games for a regime that appreciated and mobilized the opportunity for powerful spectacle. Berlin was specially decorated throughout the Games and codes of behaviour issued to present the best possible impression to visitors, with careful concealment of explicit aspects of racial policies. After the Games, the city and state gained the infrastructural legacy of a sports complex and parade ground that could be used for military purposes and for future National Socialist celebrations.

Figure 2.6. Aerial view of the Reichssportfeld, Berlin, 1936.

Austerity (1948–1956)

The bidding process after 1945 revived the pattern set in the interwar period. American cities, with their ingrained city rivalries, featured prominently, with formal bids for the 1948 Games from Baltimore, Los Angeles, Minneapolis and Philadelphia as well as informal interest from several other potential US contenders. There was a feeling, however, that the United States was too far away for affordable travel in these austere years (Voeltz, 1996, p. 103). Therefore, after conducting a postal ballot, in 1946 the IOC officially awarded the Fourteenth Summer Olympics to London.[16]

The next 2 years proved far more difficult economically than the British had anticipated when agreeing to host the Games, with few surplus resources available (Holt and Mason, 2000, pp. 27–29). The organizers quickly abandoned any idea of laying on stunning spectacle and custom-built stadia in favour of existing sports facilities. Instead, mild renovation of existing facilities saw the Empire Stadium at Wembley, originally built for the 1924 British Empire Exhibition, become the Olympic Stadium, with the adjacent Empire Pool staging the swimming events. Although both venues needed conversion and repair, along with a new approach road to link the stadium to Wembley Park railway station, the costs were borne by Wembley Stadium Ltd rather than by the state – as with 1908 for a share of the proceeds (Hampton, 2008, p. 29). Royal Air Force accommodation at Uxbridge, a convalescents' camp in Richmond Park, Southlands College in Wimbledon, and convenient school premises provided bargain basement substitutes for an Olympic Village. Other venues pressed into service included the Herne Hill Velodrome (cycling), Bisley (shooting), Henley-on-Thames (rowing) and the more distant

Torbay (yachting). The organizers borrowed sports equipment from the Armed Forces or from manufacturers on a lend-and-return basis. The Board of Trade adjusted rationing regulations for participants and new Tourist Voucher Books made it easier for foreign visitors to spend money in British shops.

Despite the difficulties, there were tangible and intangible non-sports legacies from London 1948. The city was not *en fête* as Berlin or Los Angeles had been, but the Games undoubtedly lifted the mood of postwar Britain and recorded a profit of £30,000. Visitor numbers to London in 1948 were a post-war record, with the city's hotels enjoying bumper receipts (Holt and Mason, 2000, p. 31). The nation also received a temporary respite from the unrelenting greyness of Austerity and gained the morale-raising experience of hosting a premier international event. Yet the main legacy from London 1948 was again for sports. Admittedly, there were few tangible outcomes given the lack of purpose-built facilities or associated infrastructural improvement. By contrast, in intangible terms, London 1948 successfully relaunched the Games after the traumas of war, drawing the highest-ever attendance figures for an Olympics. In return, the Games sowed the seeds of important change for British society through sports development. They eroded the long-established notion that participation in such sports was the preserve of gentlemen amateurs (Hampton, 2008, p. 318). In addition, they indirectly played a catalytic role in developing disability sport. As chapter 5 shows, the archery competition held on the front lawns of Stoke Mandeville Hospital on 28 July 1948 – the same day as the Opening Ceremony of the London Olympics – is widely accepted as the first competitive sporting event for seriously disabled athletes. This symbolic event also marked the start of the process of convergence that would see London 2012, like other aspirant twenty-first century host cities, bidding to stage the Olympic *and* Paralympic Games rather than just the former.

The two succeeding Games followed London's low-key approach. Helsinki had held the nomination for the Twelfth Summer Olympics in 1940, after the Japanese withdrew, and had built a stadium, swimming and diving arena, and a competitors' village in anticipation of that event. The organizers renovated and expanded the sporting facilities for the 1952 Games (figure 2.7), with the aid of a $1.25 million grant from the Finnish government, but the Olympic Village posed greater problems. The one originally constructed at Käpylä, 3.7 miles (6 kilometres) from the city centre, had long since been converted to public housing. The increased size of the Games required new accommodation not just at Käpylä, but also at two new sites, Otaniemi and Töölö. The situation was further complicated by the Soviet Union's demands for a separate village for the socialist bloc's athletes (Hornbuckle, 1996, p. 117). In response, the organizers allocated the Otaniemi site to the USSR and its allies, placing competitors literally as well as figuratively into two ideological camps.

Melbourne 1956 was the last Summer Olympics developed under conditions of postwar financial stringency. The city's bid document for the Games (MIC, 1948) projected an image of a prosperous, developed and well-equipped 'city of

Figure 2.7. Olympic stadium, Helsinki, 1952.

culture', with the promise of a new Olympic stadium complex on the banks of the Yarra River east of the Melbourne Cricket Ground (MCG). Once Melbourne won the Games, the organizers decided to reduce costs by modifying the MCG and restricting construction of major new buildings to the swimming pool and velodrome. Available spaces at the local university, museum, art school and public library were employed to display the four associated art exhibitions – on architecture, painting, graphics and literature. The Olympic Village was built as a cheap housing project in the suburb of Heidelberg, using the existing system of government loans. These buildings, however, presented so many subsequent construction and social problems that the Games might well have been 'a force for urban degeneration rather than regeneration' (Essex and Chalkley, 1998, p. 194).

Catalyst (1960–1976)

Although important for their host nations, the financially straited 1948–1956 Games made little lasting impact on the Olympic cities. By contrast, Rome 1960 threw off the pall of Austerity and propelled the Games into the modern era. The city's Olympian aspirations stretched back many years. Rome, as noted above, initially held the nomination for the 1908 Games and, under Mussolini, had lobbied hard for the right to stage the 1940 Olympics. Indeed, Rome 1960 effectively capitalized on two districts developed by the Fascist regime with international festivals in mind. The first, the Foro Italico in the north of the city, already offered two imposing arenas: the Stadio dei Marmi, built in 1932, and the Stadio Olimpico, built in

1936. The second district was EUR, so-called because it was initially designed to supply a spectacular setting for the (cancelled) 1942 Esposizione Universale di Roma. Located to the south of the city, it was only partially developed before the Second World War, but its monumental and spacious qualities made it an ideal place for the core of the Olympic facilities. These included the Palazzo dello Sport (Sport Palace), the Velodrome, the Piscana delle Rose (swimming pool) and the Fontane Sports Zone training area. Ten other venues were scattered throughout the city, with several using sites with classical associations to underline the Games' pedigree. The vaults of the Basilica of Maxentius built in 303 AD, for instance, housed the Greco-Roman and free wrestling contests, while the Caracalla Baths (217 AD) staged the gymnastics.

These 'Olympic areas' made a permanent contribution to the city's sporting and cultural life. The Village at Campo Paroli provided private sector housing (Wimmer, 1976, p. 202; see also Muñoz, 1997) and the city also gained from infrastructural improvements undertaken with the Games in mind. These included new roads and bridges built to connect the Village to the main Olympic sites, modernization of the airport, improvement of the telephone, telegraph and radio networks, and initiatives to expand hotel accommodation. The Rome Olympics also had a major impact on financing the Games. Core funding came from the Italian soccer pools, the Totocalcio, but now supplemented for the first time by sales of television rights. Broadcasters had refused to pay for rights at Melbourne, arguing that covering the Games was akin to televising news and should be similarly free to the broadcaster. The organizers of the Rome Olympics, however, managed to convince the major television networks that the Games were a proprietorial commodity for which payment was necessary. The American Columbia Broadcasting System (CBS) paid $600,000 for US television rights, with Eurovision subscribing another $540,000. It marked another significant step towards realizing the economic potential of the Games and ensured that, when leaving aside wider infrastructural improvements, the Rome Olympics ran at a profit.

Tokyo 1964 followed Rome's example by embarking on major redevelopment projects before the Games, merging the specific proposals for the Olympics into the city's 10-year development plan. Aiming to cater for Tokyo's infrastructural needs up to the year 2000, the combined works cost $2.7 billion and included housing, hotel developments, harbour improvements, a monorail system, water supply, sewage disposal and a public health programme (Essex and Chalkley, 1998, p. 195). The city had thirty Olympic sites, with thirteen major facilities concentrated into three districts: the Meiji Olympic Park, which contained the Olympic Stadium; the Yoyogi Sports Centre, which housed the swimming competitions; and the Komazawa Sports Park. Accommodating participants in six Olympic Villages ensured, at least in principle, that competitors and officials had no more than a 40-minute journey to reach their venues (Organizing Committee, 1964, p. 114). Hoteliers received grants to remodel their premises for Western tourists, with a further 1,600 visitors lodged on ships in Tokyo harbour.

Importantly, Tokyo saw the introduction of an approach concerned with the 'look' of a city during the period of the Olympic festival. This represented more than the old approach of simply decking the city in flags, but instead saw conscious attempts to unify the disparate sporting and Olympic infrastructure into a cohesive whole through design of signage, dressing the venues and decorating the streets. As a result of an open competition, the Japanese designer Yusaku Kamekura won a contract to provide visually consistent designs for all the ephemeral elements of the Games – symbols, signs, pamphlets, posters, tickets, decorations and even the colour scheme used for the city and at Olympic venues (Yew, 1996, p. 176).

The 1968 Games in Mexico City saw Latin America, and more specifically a developing nation, host the Olympics for the first time. Set against a background of political tension and sports boycotts, the Olympics stretched Mexico's resources and contributed to domestic unrest in the months leading up to the Games. The organizers' approach was to use existing sports facilities and blend them with new venues by means of a common 'look', in the manner pioneered by Tokyo, to supply a sense of visual unity (see chapter 12 for details). Despite troubled beginnings, the Mexico City Games finished with a favourable balance sheet. Costing $175 million, much of which was expended on facilities with a lifespan that extended well beyond the festival, the Olympics were considered to have covered their costs. For some observers, the 1968 Games represented an important moment of achievement and harmony for the Mexican nation that fully justified the cost (e.g. Arbena, 1996), but others argued that money diverted into the Olympics had exacerbated the divide between Mexico City's rich and poor. Before the Games, for example, the city chose to transfer $200 million from the social services budget to city improvement projects in an elaborate urban and national re-imaging campaign. Not only did this have a detrimental long-term impact on the city's provision for the poor; it also prompted protest demonstrations that left no less than 325 dead (Lenskyj, 2000, pp. 109–110).

The ability of the Olympics to polarize opinion would escalate steadily over the next decade. In their different ways, Munich 1972 and Montreal 1976 created crises for the Olympic movement: the former due to problems over security and the latter finance. Initial planning for both events, however, proceeded unproblematically with an upbeat view that emphasized the Olympics' apparently risk-free character; seemingly guaranteeing host cities advantageous international attention and endless prospects for undertaking urban development. Partly because of this mood, the 1970s Games were lavish affairs, with huge expenditure on iconic facilities and distinctive urban quarters.

The return of the Olympics to Germany in 1972 inevitably raised the spectre of 1936. The powerful militaristic and nationalist images still associated with that Olympics encouraged the Munich organizers to stage a 'Carefree Games' (Organizing Committee, 1972, p. 28). Their bid to the IOC emphasized Munich's claim to embrace international and modern cultures; a rich hearth of 'the arts and Muses' that offered four orchestras, twenty-three museums and seventeen theatres (*Ibid.*, pp. 24, 28). At the same time, Munich in the early 1970s was in the throes of rapid economic and demographic growth, with severe pressures on services and physical infrastructure. Preparation for the Games, therefore, also addressed the host city's broader planning goals, fitting Olympic developments alongside schemes designed to restore and pedestrianize Munich's historic centre, to improve and extend public transport, construct 145 miles (233 kilometres) of expressways, provide underground parking, and build new retail and hotel accommodation (Essex and Chalkley, 1998, p. 195).

The location for the new Olympic Park in the north of the city was a derelict area long earmarked for redevelopment. Originally flat, its surface was bulldozed into a gently rolling landscape, with a hill created from wartime rubble and a small lake formed by damming the Nymphenburg Canal. The organizers then placed the athletes' warm-up facilities, the swimming pool, many smaller sports venues, restaurants, a theatre, the Olympic Village, press centre and stadium around the lake. The 80,000-seater Olympic stadium was an innovative tent-roofed structure designed by Gunter Behnisch and Frei Otto. The Olympic Village, which housed 10,000 athletes, was designed for conversion into a 'self-sustaining' community for single people and middle- and lower-income families – groups who found it difficult to find accommodation in the city (Essex and Chalkley, 1998, p. 195; Organizing Committee, 1972, p. 125). Trams, an underground rail line and a rapid transit provided physical links between the complex and the city centre. Symbolic links were again added by attention to the 'look' of the city. Coordinated by a German designer Otl Aicher, the city adopted a holistic design policy towards decorations for the city, venues and orientation of visitors. Besides choosing colours felt to resonate with Olympic values, the dominant colour of blue was chosen to symbolize peace with the 'aggressive' colour red deliberately avoided (Organizing Committee, 1972, p. 269; Yew, 1996, p. 213).

Viewed in organizational and financial terms, the Twentieth Summer Games were critically regarded as a success. They generated a working profit, with marketing and television rights producing over $12 million for the IOC and international federations. Munich and Bavaria gained lasting publicity benefit (Brichford, 1996, p. 151). Other aspects of their legacy proved more difficult. Despite the efforts to promote the 'carefree' theme, Munich 1972 brought the Olympics face-to-face with the realities of security. The massacre of the Israeli athletes and officials on 5 September effectively destroyed the OCOG's attempts to stage a light-hearted, non-nationalistic Olympics. It also ensured that future host cities faced a bill for security measures of a wholly different order, recognizing the Olympics' new, and unwanted, status as a prime target for international terrorism (see chapter 8).

The ensuing Games were a landmark in Olympic history for being ill-conceived and poorly planned. Although intended as a 'modest Games', Montreal 1976 produced a final shortfall of $1.2 billion, primarily caused by cost overruns on over-ambitious buildings. Admittedly, the times were not propitious. The Games took place against a background of severe world recession and inflation that profoundly affected costings, especially those concerning the surfeit of transport infrastructural projects associated with the Olympics. Nevertheless, as chapter 13 makes clear, a large measure of the blame rested with the counterproductive machinations of the political regime led by Jean Drapeau and the flawed architectural design of the Olympic complex, particularly the stadium. The organizers ditched the notion of providing an orthodox open-air Olympic stadium in favour of a design that might be used all-year round. As the Olympic movement would not countenance a covered stadium for athletics, it was decided to build a new stadium with a retractable roof – understandably at much greater cost (Killanin, 1983, p. 123). The chosen design by the French architect Roger Taillibert, architect of the critically acclaimed Parc des Princes in Paris, exacerbated the problems by embracing an unmistakeable monumentality. Most notably, it featured an innovative system for opening and closing the roof involving a 575 foot (190 metre) tower, inclined at 45 degrees, which supported the roof on 26 steel cables (figure 2.8). This radical conception produced problems that plagued construction. In fact, the infamous

Figure 2.8. Olympic stadium, Montreal 1976 (architect Roger Taillibert).

roof was not completed until 1987 and quickly became unusable. It was an episode that led, in the fullness of time, to a stadium with an impressive observation tower and a non-retractable roof.

Other buildings contributed their share of problems. Difficulties with subsoil meant the velodrome needed new foundations to support its roof (Organizing Committee, 1976, pp. 16–17). The adjacent Olympic Village lodged participants in four architecturally innovative ziggurat structures, around 19 storeys high at their tallest points, which proved difficult to service. Among the infrastructural investment projects was the remote, expensive and unnecessary international airport at Mirabel, which closed three decades later without ever achieving any useful function. In addition, labour problems caused the loss of 155 working days in the 18 months leading up to the Games. Lack of proper operational planning and failure to sequence the construction process led to delays and bottlenecks. Round the clock working was introduced at great expense to meet the Games deadline, but it still proved impossible to complete all the facilities. In May 1976, emergency work began to erect temporary installations for several sports rather than continue with the intended venues. It all contributed to an event that inevitably presented a 'kaleidoscope of contradictory narratives and outcomes' (Kidd, 1996, p. 153).

Ideological Games (1980–1984)

The 1980 and 1984 Summer Games were essentially rival Olympics, staged by two superpowers as indicators of the superiority of their ideological systems, but which left less mark on their host cities than the Games of the previous two decades. Moscow and Los Angeles were the only candidates for the 1980 games and, after the withdrawal of a half-hearted bid from Tehran, Los Angeles was the sole formal bidder for 1984. With an eye to the lessons of the Montreal Games, both sets of organizers made virtues out of economy and pragmatism. Both OCOGs would also have to cope with political boycotts orchestrated by their superpower opponents. In 1980, the USA led a boycott of Moscow 1980, as part of a package of measures taken in response to the Soviet intervention in Afghanistan. This reduced participation to eighty competing nations compared with 121 at Munich and even ninety-two at boycott-hit Montreal, with many other nations sending weakened teams. Not surprisingly, a Soviet-led tit-for-tat boycott of the subsequent Los Angeles Games, ostensibly over the security of athletes and officials, saw fourteen socialist countries miss the Los Angeles Games in 1984. These Cold War gestures, however, only materialized in the final weeks before these Games and, therefore, had little effect on the plans made by the host cities for staging their respective Olympics.

The OCOG for Moscow 1980 made much of rejecting the recent trend towards gigantism, leaving behind expensively maintained and underused sports facilities. Rather they 'sought efficiency', building only 'essential' installations that would 'not remain monuments to vanity' but would be 'in constant use for the benefit of the Soviet People' (Organizing Committee, 1980, p. 43). They therefore planned to use Moscow's existing sports facilities wherever possible, employing temporary grandstands and ensuring that any new structures would be designed as multi-purpose venues. The main ceremonies and the track and field competitions, for example, centred on the renovated Lenin Stadium (built originally in 1956).

Given the nature of the command economy, the authorities subsumed prparations for the Olympics into the city's planning strategy (the General Plan for the Development of Moscow 1971–1990) and the state's tenth Five-Year Plan for Economic and Social Development. The former adopted decentralist principles, dividing Moscow into eight functional zones, each with a population of between 600,000 and 1.2 million and their 'town public centres' and subsidiary centres, to achieve a 'balance between labour resources and employment opportunities' (Lappo *et al.*, 1976, pp. 138–140). The Olympics provided the opportunity to improve access to sporting, cultural and entertainment facilities for those living within these zones by designing new venues for use once the Games were over (Promyslov, 1980, p. 230). The main Olympic facilities were distributed into six main areas, with the Village in a seventh. Located in the south west of the city, the Village comprised eighteen blocks, each 16 storeys high, arranged in groups of three with associated communal catering facilities, entertainment, shopping and training facilities. After the Games, the Village would become a self-contained neighbourhood complete with cultural and sporting facilities (*Ibid.*, pp. 245–246). This dispersal posed logistic problems, but there was little need for new road construction given the low levels of private car ownership at this time. Infrastructural improvement was primarily confined to building new media centres and renovating the city's three airports, with a new international air terminal added to Sheremetyevo International Airport. The authorities also renovated historic buildings (especially churches), planted trees, and commissioned new hotels, cafés and restaurants. In a distant echo of Berlin 1936, Moscow was unusually free of banners expressing party slogans, posters and even the legendarily flinty guides working for Intourist desisted from propaganda during the Games (Binyon, 1980).

Notwithstanding the rhetoric of virtuous utilitarianism, the regime could not resist the urge to display Soviet technological expertise in designing large structures. This contributed to the organizers commissioning the world's largest indoor arena in north Moscow for the basketball and boxing competitions. Capable of seating up to 45,000 spectators, it could be used either as a single space or divided into two separate auditoria, allowing it to serve as a multipurpose space for sports, political and cultural events after the Games (Promyslov, 1980, pp. 236–237).

Like Moscow, Los Angeles sought economy in staging the Games, with the organizers' commitment to funding the Games without the public funds available in the USSR resulting in an event that added fine-tuned commercialism to cost-consciousness. This meant using volunteers wherever possible and making maximum use of existing facilities. The Los Angeles Memorial Coliseum was refurbished as the Olympic stadium, with just four new venues required – for rowing, cycling, swimming and shooting. Each attracted high levels of sponsorship. The McDonald's Swim Stadium, for example, was built in Olympic Park for the University of Southern California. The Southland Corporation, parent company of the 7-Eleven chain of convenience stores, funded the velodrome on the California State University site. Fuji Film sponsored the shooting range. The three Olympic Villages used sites on university campuses (University College at Los Angeles, University of Southern California and the University of California at Santa Barbara), with the accommodation later available for students (Burbank et al., 2001, pp. 76–77). This emphasis on named sponsorship and private finance introduced a measure of commercialism that the Olympic movement felt powerless to resist at that time. Rather more serious perhaps was the lack of intimacy caused by using existing facilities scattered around the sprawling, car-based Los Angeles city region rather than creating a nucleated Olympic Park. Some effort to create a sense of place came from decking the city in standardized colours to create a 'festive federalism' (Yew, 1996, p. 288), although it was recognized that only so much could be achieved by design.

Where Los Angeles 1984 scored most heavily was its success in changing ideas about Olympic finance. Los Angeles's commercial approach dramatically altered the prospects for other prospective host cities. The Games made a profit of $225 million that was channelled into American sports bodies and programmes. Local universities gained major new facilities. The event injected an estimated $2.4 billion into the Southern Californian economy.[17] After the events of the 1970s, the act of being host to the Olympics was fully restored as the pinnacle of ambition for cities with global aspirations.[18]

Shifting Horizons (1988–1996)

Seoul's decision to seek the 1988 Games was less inspired by the thoughts of financial benefit – which had yet to re-emerge when the city gained the nomination in 1981 – than by the success of Tokyo 1964, which the Koreans believed had altered perceptions of the Japanese and helped Japan join the ranks of the developed world in the cultural, social, diplomatic and economic fields. The Games would provide a positive context for international scrutiny, show the economic transformation and political progress within Korea, and establish dialogue with Communist and non-aligned nations, even though there was a real risk of terrorism or international conflict from continuing tensions with North Korea. It also provided an opportunity to regenerate Seoul. The South Korean capital faced severe environmental, economic and demographic problems for which staging the Olympics seemed to offer a means to short-circuit the process of replanning and reconstruction.

The organizers concentrated the Olympic facilities in the Seoul Sports Complex, built in the Chamshil area on the south bank of the Han River around 13 kilometres south of central Seoul, with another six venues at the Olympic Park, just over 3.5 kilometres to the east. The South Korean government had originally commissioned the Seoul Sports Complex in 1977, when the country lacked the facilities even to host the Asian Games. The 59 hectare site contained a major stadium, which became the 100,000 capacity Olympic stadium, as well as a 50,000-seater venue for the exhibition sport of baseball. The complex was linked to the Olympic Expressway, which connected the airport with Seoul's downtown. The Olympic Park provided the venues for the cycling, weightlifting, fencing, tennis, gymnastics and swimming events. The Athletes' Village comprised blocks of flats of various heights (6–24 storeys) clustered in groups around common open spaces. In total 5,540 units were built, which were sold after the Games as private housing for upper middle-income families (Kim and Choe, 1997, pp. 197–198). During the construction of the Park, the discovery of the earthen walls of a fortress from the Baekje Kingdom (18 BC–660 AD) led to the designation of a historic park within the masterplan (*Ibid.*, p. 208; also see Yoon, 2009).

Beyond the Olympic Park, the authorities conducted a programme of repairing historic monuments, including palaces and shrines, tree planting, and improvements to streets, drainage and power supply. Two new urban motorways linked the airport to the Olympic sites and improved east–west traffic flows in the city. The authorities built new Metro lines and expanded the airport. Seoul's planners instigated the Han River Development Project, which combined anti-flood measures, water treatment for the heavily polluted river, habitat regeneration and the creation of a series of recreational areas. Temporary measures that applied for the duration of the Games included encouraging dust-producing firms along the marathon route and around Olympic venues to switch to shorter working hours or night-time operation, and advising public bath houses to take holidays on days of key events.

The strategies chosen to improve the city's built environment and infrastructure, however, drew international criticism for paying greater attention to urban form than social cost. Ideas of improvement centred on the removal of slums and the creation of modernistic, often high-rise, developments for high-income residential or commercial use. Traditional walking-scale urban forms (*hanoks*), built at high density with narrow streets and passageways, were bulldozed for commercial redevelopment. Laws covering preservation and conservation were not introduced until 1983 and, even then, only the oldest historic buildings with connections to the Yi dynasty benefited. Clearance continued in areas without that historic cachet (Kim and Choe, 1997, pp. 209, 212).

Barcelona 1992 would take the regeneration theme further and supply a model that is a benchmark for prospective Olympic cities. Although still facing significant domestic security threats from Basque separatists and other groups (see chapter 8), the Games took place against a political background of brief-lived optimism about the world order, with no boycotts and lowered security problems. In conditions that allowed the potential of the Olympics to act as a vehicle for urban development to shine through, Barcelona launched a challenging package of regenerative measures that countered years of neglect under the Franco regime (Maloney, 1996, p. 192). This was not an entirely new strategy. The city had used earlier international festivals to address urban planning goals, with the 1888 Universal Exhibition in the Parc de la Ciutadella to the east of the old medieval centre and the International Exhibition of 1929 on Montjuic to the west both resulting in urban improvements and enhancements to the city's cultural institutions, open space and transport (Hughes, 1996; see also chapter 14).

The Olympics were seen in a similar light. Barcelona had previously bid to host the Games for 1924, 1936 and 1972. Selected at the IOC meeting in 1986 over Paris, the only other credible candidate, Barcelona's bid claimed that 88 per cent of the necessary facilities for the Games *per se* were already 'available'.[19] The Olympic Stadium was an updated and renovated version of that used for the 1929 International Exhibition. Ten other venues came from refurbishments to existing facilities, with forty-three other facilities used very much in their existing state (Essex and Chalkley, 1998, p. 198). The promoters emphasized that only fifteen new venues would be required. Altogether, less than 20 per cent of the total expenditure for the 1992 Games went on sports facilities (Varley, 1992, p. 21), with the lion's share of the investment devoted instead to urban improvements. Barcelona's planners concentrated the Olympic facilities in four areas located in a ring around the city, roughly where the outer limits of the nineteenth-century city met the less structured developments of the second half of the twentieth century. These were: the Vall d'Hebron in the north (cycling, archery, and accommodation for journalists); the Diagonal (football, polo and tennis); the Montjuic (the major Olympic site including the 60,000-seater stadium, the Sant Jordi Sports Palace, and the swimming and diving pools); and Parc de Mar, which housed the Olympic Village (figure 2.9). Large-scale investment in the city's transport systems,

Figure 2.9. The Olympic Village, Barcelona 1992.

substantially stimulated by the Olympics, served to link sites together. The Metro system was extended, the coastal railway rerouted, the airport redesigned and expanded, and the telecommunications systems modernized (see also Brunet, 2009).

Barcelona 1992 codified the changing nature of the criteria by which to judge whether or not a Summer Games had been a success. The spectacle of the Games delighted the Olympic movement and television audiences were captivated by images from the outdoor pool, showing divers performing against the panoramic backdrop of the city beyond. Economically, the Olympic festival *per se* performed less well. Cost overruns ate into the projected $350 million surplus such that the Games barely broke even (a mere $3.8 million surplus). The innovative Sant Jordi Sports Palace, for example, may have supplied stunning architecture but cost $89 million rather than the estimated $30 million. Construction costs on the ring road were 50 per cent more than the estimated $1 billion. The Cultural Olympiad also spawned heavy losses, despite trading on Barcelona's rich heritage in the arts and architecture (Hargreaves, 2000, p. 106).[20] Inflation and adverse movements in foreign currency rates also severely increased costs. Unemployment rose by 3 per cent in the city immediately after the Olympics, prices soared and business taxes rose 30 per cent (Maloney, 1996, p. 193). Nevertheless, critical opinion remained highly positive with regard to the wider regenerative impact on Barcelona. The city had deployed the Games as part of a conscious long-term development strategy that existed before obtaining the nomination to stage the Olympics and continued afterwards. It represented a major transformation in the fortunes of Olympic cities just 16 years after the debacle of Montreal.

Atlanta 1996, by contrast, would renew questions about staging the Games, particularly regarding commercialism. Unusually for Olympic practice, a private consortium undertook the organization, with heavy representation of and deference to business interests. Funding came from sponsorship, broadcasting rights and merchandizing which, when combined with ticket sales, raised $1.72 billion (Burbank *et al.*, 2001, p. 94). In addition, the Federal government expended nearly $1 billion on infrastructure, housing, safety and security, with smaller amounts spent by the state of Georgia and the city (*Ibid.*, p. 116). Most of the spending on the Games and on infrastructure took place in central Atlanta's 'Olympic Ring' – an area around 3 miles (5 kilometres) in radius that contained sixteen of the twenty-five Olympic facilities and most of the urban improvements. The Atlanta Committee for the Olympic Games (ACOG) made use of existing facilities such as the Georgia Dome and Omni Arena, coupled with facilities at Atlanta's universities. The Georgia Institute of Technology, for example, provided sites for the Olympic Village, a new aquatic centre (swimming, diving and water polo) and boxing. ACOG commissioned a new but temporary Olympic Stadium in the Summerhill district in the south of the Olympic Ring. This was tied in with a longer-term plan to develop baseball in the city. The Olympic Stadium was located next to the Atlanta Fulton County Stadium, which was used for the baseball competition. Built to seat 85,000 spectators, the Olympic Stadium was scheduled for partial demolition after the Games to create a new 47,000-seater stadium (Turner Field) for the Atlanta Braves, with the Fulton County Stadium demolished to provide parking space (Larson and Staley, 1998, p. 281). Neighbourhoods near Olympic sites experienced beautification, with projects designed to improve central city streets and upgrade twelve pedestrian corridors that linked the venues. This work included widening pavements, burying power-lines, installing new street furniture, tree planting, history panels, signage, and the redesign of five parks and plazas.

Atlanta disappointed those who looked for more from the Games that marked the centenary of the modern Olympics. The conduct of the Games and the quality of ceremonial content led Tomlinson (1999, p. 69) to describe it as 'an elongated event of tattiness and tawdriness'. Concentrating so many facilities at the centre of the city placed pressure on the transport systems. Traffic congestion, slow journey times, and long queues to use the shuttle buses added to the difficulties for athletes, officials and spectators reaching venues (Larson and Staley, 1998, p. 278). The organizers' claims that Olympic sites were within walking distance of one another proved meaningless given the excessive summer temperatures. The repeated systems failures of the results service, the arrogance of officials, poor relations with the press, the large numbers of unauthorized street vendors, aggressive sponsorship and rampant commercialism undermined Atlanta's desire to stage a modern and efficient event. The city's policy towards regenerating two areas close to the Olympic sites encountered particular condemnation. One, the Techwood and Clark Howell public housing district to the south of the Georgia Institute of Technology, was demolished and replaced by a mixed gated community, effectively replacing poorer tenants with more affluent residents. The other, a rundown housing and industrial area near the Georgia World Congress Centre (GWCC), was cleared to create Centennial Park as an area where visitors and spectators could congregate during the Games and where entertainment could be provided (figure 2.10). Clearance here and in nearby Woodruffe Park removed more than 16,500 of Atlanta's poorest inhabitants to make way for the stadium. The additional loss of a hostel and three shelters displaced around 10 per cent of Atlanta's homeless (Burbank et al., 2001, p. 112). Aggressive use of city ordinances that criminalized anti-social behaviour and measures to remove the homeless resulted in the physical eviction of 'undesirables' from the vicinity of the Games (Lenskyj, 2000, pp. 138–139).

The passage of time has eroded the force of some of these criticisms. For example, Atlanta's policy towards the stadium fully acknowledged the realities of post-Games use and spared the city from being saddled with expensive and underused venues, as was subsequently the case with Sydney, Athens and Beijing. The central area was remodelled and Centennial Park stands as a memorial to the Games. The Olympics raised Atlanta's profile as a sporting venue, even if it failed to enhance its broader image as a cultural centre. Nonetheless, the distaste for

Figure 2.10. Centennial Park, Atlanta 1996.

commercialism persisted, with the IOC stating that the Games would never again be entrusted to an entirely privately-run organization (Whitelegg, 2000, p. 814; also Poynter and Roberts, 2009). Even a century after the revival of the modern Olympics, the formula for staging a successful event remained downright elusive.

Towards Sustainability

Although chosen as Australian nominee for candidate city in March 1991, Sydney's bid for the Olympics had actually been in gestation since the late 1960s (see chapter 15). The city drafted feasibility plans for both the 1972 and 1988 Games, with the latter envisaging an Olympic Park at Homebush Bay, approximately 9 miles (14 kilometres) upstream from Sydney's city centre. Originally tidal wetlands and scrub, Homebush Bay at different times had housed Sydney's racecourse, a saltworks, the country's largest abattoir, the state brickworks and a naval munitions store. In the 1930s, the bay had regularly spawned algal blooms through contamination from waste products from the slaughterhouses and from depositing household and industrial waste in landfill sites. Work had begun in the 1980s to clean up and redevelop the area, but a successful Olympic bid would help regenerate the remainder of the site, tackle its severe environmental problems, supply the city with a replacement for the Royal Agricultural Society's outmoded Showground at Moore Park, and provide a cluster of modern world-class sports facilities. Any bid would involve the state and federal governments as funding agencies and as the owners of the land, as well as the city of Sydney.

Sydney gained the nomination for the 2000 Games in September 1993 against competition from Beijing, Manchester, Berlin and Istanbul, with a key element in its candidacy being the promise to concentrate the Olympic venues in one central park, which would eventually have a built core surrounded by parkland. The main Olympic venue, named Stadium Australia, was built using public funds, sponsorship and sale of corporate packages. Designed to hold 110,000 spectators during the Games, its capacity would be reduced to 80,000 for its subsequent life as a rugby and Australian Rules football stadium. The other major stadia at Homebush were the Hockey Centre, Superdome (basketball and artistic gymnastics), International Athletics Centre (warm-up facilities), Tennis Centre, the Aquatic Centre (swimming and diving) and the Archery Park. The adjacent Olympic Village would accommodate all participants at a single centre for the first time. It comprised a mixed development of apartments and town houses, arranged into three precincts and designed to ecologically sustainable guidelines. Provision of a school and commercial precinct looked ahead to the area's post-Games future as a residential suburb of Sydney. The other Olympic facilities, particularly those associated with rowing and sailing, were located within the Sydney city-region at a maximum distance of 60 miles (100 kilometres) from Homebush Bay.

Planning for the Games embraced different agendas. First, responding to the growing mood of environmentalism the bid claimed these would be a 'Green Games' expressing environmental responsibility in use of resources and design of facilities. Secondly, the Sydney Games were a national project, celebrating the 'entire continent of Australia' rather than just the host city: a strategy also adopted at Melbourne in 1956. Thirdly, capturing the Games would allow the organizers to highlight the profound changes that had taken place in the 44 years since Melbourne, in particular the need for explicit recognition of the multicultural identity of Australia. The organizers of the Sydney Olympics in 2000, for example, were mindful of problems that arose at the Australian Bicentennial in 1988, when the celebration of European conquest had led to severe inter-communal frictions. Part of the adopted solution was to broaden the constituent basis of support for the Olympics, making efforts to gain the involvement of community leaders. Another element lay in seeking to change modes of representation, particularly with regard to tackling prevalent negative and stereotypic representations of Aboriginal peoples. Most notably, the Olympic Opening Ceremony commenced with an enacted encounter between indigenous and white Australians, emphasizing the antiquity of indigenous culture, its diversity, myths, legends and spirituality. The Aborigines emerged as environmentally-wise managers of the land, in contrast to the approach of what the Official Report described as the European period of 'vitality and violence' (SOCOG, 2000*b*). Later in the ceremony, the Aboriginal athlete Cathy Freeman was selected to receive the relay-run Olympic torch to light the cauldron of the Olympic flame in the stadium.

One indication of the IOC's sense of relief at the success of the resulting Games came with the IOC President Juan Antonio Samaranch, resurrecting the statement that 'these have been the best Games ever', a description that he had pointedly omitted at the Closing Ceremony of Atlanta 1996. An early study of impact by the Australian Tourist Commission revealed that 75 per cent of the Americans surveyed had seen pictures and stories concerning Australia as a holiday destination as part of the Olympic coverage and half reported that they were more interested in Australia as a destination (Morse, 2001, p. 102). Locally, the Games passed off well. Potential demonstrations about homelessness, the plight of Aborigines, ticketing, and the claimed misuse of public funds did not occur. An economic analysis (Haynes, 2001) argued that the total cost of the Games at A$6.5 billion was roughly neutral in that it was covered by an equivalent amount in extra economic activity in Australia between 1994–1995 and 2005–2006, of which A$5.1 billion would accrue in New South Wales. For this price, Sydney had achieved the regeneration of a severely blighted industrial region, gained significant improvements to infrastructure, improved its tourist standing, and gained world-class sports facilities. For the Olympic movement, it again showed the value of a festival largely held at a central venue rather than the dispersal of Atlanta.

The experience of Sydney 2000 continues to influence subsequent OCOGs, albeit sometimes in complex ways (Cashman, 2009). The Sydney Games retain a positive aura in terms of organization, friendliness and raising the profile of the city, but specific questions have arisen about cultural legacy (see chapter 15) and certain aspects of the Olympic Park. Environmentalists have continued to question whether the decontamination of the toxic waste site had been fully tackled (Berlin, 2003). Critics note the lack of the promised affordable housing. The main stadia have had a chequered post-Games usage. The Superdome, latterly rebranded as the Acer Arena, had a post-Games history that parallels London's O2 Arena. Initially languishing and lacking a viable legacy plan, it eventually developed into a thriving and internationally recognized entertainments venue on the basis of a successful private-public partnership (Jefferies, 2006). By contrast, Stadium Australia, first renamed the Telstra stadium, operated consistently at a loss from the moment that it was handed over for post-Games use. In November 2006, the group running the stadium defaulted on its debts and was taken over by its bankers (Askew, 2006). Subsequently rebranded as the ANZ stadium, the venue continues to struggle against competition from the pre-existing modern stadia clustered in the Moore Park area of east Sydney (Searle, 2002, p. 857).

Similar uncertainties cloud the legacy of Athens 2004, although any Games involving Greece inevitably involves circumstances unique to that country. As chapter 16 shows, the reconstruction of Athens and the return of the Olympics were parallel themes in the consciousness of the Greek people during the nineteenth century and continued to have resonances in the late twentieth century. The city's successful bid in 1997 for the 2004 Olympics claimed that most of the competition venues and almost all the training venues were already in place, with the makings of an Olympic Stadium and Park in the complex already constructed for the 1982 European Athletics Championships. The subsequent decision to revisit the plans and make drastic alterations, in particular exchanging the nucleated Olympic centres for a more dispersed approach, undermined the timetable to the point where completion on time hung in the balance.

The immediate impact of the Games was a profound psychological boost for the country and agreement that tourism had benefited from transformation of the city centre, creation of pedestrianized routes interlinking Athens's major archaeological sites, and investment in the city's hotels, cultural sector and, especially, public transport. Yet, as with Sydney, wider questions about *sustainability* quickly surfaced. In the narrower sense, critics focused on the way in which the environmental guidelines for the Olympics were, at best, perfunctorily observed. In the more general sense of sustainable development, profound doubts surround the potential use of the Olympic facilities. Despite its architecturally sophisticated buildings being intended as a symbol of the new Athens, the Olympic Sports Complex at Maroussi remains heavily underused (figure 2.11), with the stadium only open to the public when concerts or soccer matches are being staged. The Faliro and Helleniki complexes have also struggled to find alternative uses. All have continued to lose money as borrowing and maintenance costs have still to be met. The evidence suggests that pre-Games plans for post-Games use of Olympic facilities contained a strong dose of wish fulfilment; a product of a lingering wish to have a comprehensive set of facilities available whenever the opportunity arose to stage further sporting mega-events.

Figure 2.11. The Olympic Stadium and Park for the Athens 2004 Games, June 2009.

The Highwater Mark?

Questions of how to turn the lavish and large-scale facilities required for the Summer Olympics into sustainable legacy, however, did not in any way daunt the organizers of Beijing 2008. Rebuffed by just two votes in 1993 in its candidacy for the Millennial Games, largely due to the recent memories of the 1989 Tiananmen Square Massacre and concerns over environmental issues (Poast, 2007, p. 76; also Gartner and Shen, 1992), Beijing decided in November 1998 to launch its candidacy for the 2008 Games. This time, its bid gained overwhelming support, achieving an absolute majority on just the second round of voting against opposition from Istanbul, Osaka, Paris and Toronto. The ease of its victory partly reflected memories of 1993, in which Beijing had led the voting in all rounds apart from the final run-off with Sydney, but the first bid had also served as a valuable learning process. The Chinese team carefully crafted a message that recognized 'the importance of considering what others might think of China and making adjustments to be sure that nothing offended' (Guoqi, 2008, p. 243). The bid team deftly promised an environmentally-friendly but 'high-tech' Games that would promote cultural exchange, act as 'a bridge of harmony' between peoples and embody the 'unique integration of sport and culture' intrinsic to Olympism (*Ibid.*, pp. 243–234). It effectively addressed key areas of dissatisfaction with the first bid and allowed the attractions of the site plan and other elements of the proposal to shine through.

Within days of the city's success in the bidding process, Beijing's municipal government unveiled an ambitious five-year plan to modernize the city's infrastructure, carry out urban regeneration and improve the environment (Broudehoux, 2004, pp. 200–201). While some of the estimated 180 billion yuan ($22 billion) expenditure would have been incurred anyway as part of the city's development plans, there is no doubt that the Olympics acted as a catalyst for a substantial part of this investment. In addition, a total of $14.25 billion was officially earmarked as funding for developing the sites for the Beijing Games, although as Brunet and Xinwen (2009, pp. 166, 169) note: 'the total investment catalysed by the Games is likely to be much larger – between $20 and $30 billion dollars – especially when the private sector contribution is added'. Modernization and development, however, rested substantially on urban clearance, with estimates in 2007 that at least 1.5 million people had been displaced to make way for Olympic-related developments (COHRE, 2007*c*).

In total, the Games required thirty-seven venues, of which thirty-one were in Beijing and the rest scattered elsewhere within the People's Republic of China (particularly for soccer and sailing) and Hong Kong (equestrianism). Of the venues within Beijing, twelve were newly built, eleven were renovated or extended from pre-existing structures, and eight were temporary sports facilities or related installations (such as the Media Centre). The main examples of architectural spectacle were among the seventeen venues clustered in and around the Olympic Park in the north of the city (He, 2008, pp. x–xiii). The new National Stadium served as the Olympic stadium and the setting for the Opening and Closing Ceremonies. Designed by the Swiss firm of Herzog and de Meuron in association with the Chinese office of Arup Associates, this oval-shaped arena seated 91,000 during the Games, with post-Olympics reduction to 80,000. Its nickname, the 'Bird's Nest', derived from its open lattice structure of interwoven steel trusses, which exposed glimpses of the interior to the outside (*Ibid.*, pp. 2–7). The National Aquatics Centre, situated to the east of the 'Bird's Nest', provided an equal measure of spectacle. Widely known as the 'Water Cube', its exterior covering of 3,000 irregularly-shaped, translucent, blue 'air pillows' provided a highly distinctive panorama when set against the background of the adjacent National Stadium (*Ibid.*, pp. 20–26).

In most respects, Beijing 2008 was a Games for the television audience, without the now customary carnival atmosphere in the streets provided by live entertainments and giant screens. The pre-Games Olympic torch relay proved a public relations disaster when it passed through countries willing to allow protests and occasional disruption by Free Tibet activists and other demonstrators. Once the relay came within the control of the Chinese authorities, however, such incidents disappeared. Viewers around the world joined the spectators in the stadia in witnessing the stunning and intricately choreographed Opening and Closing Ceremonies, albeit with television viewers of the former witnessing effects that were partly enhanced by overlayering of computer graphics.[21] Summarizers and analysts were routinely seen against the backdrop of the Bird's Nest and Water Cube – two of the most iconic structures ever produced for an Olympic Games. After the Games, these facilities have remained very much on the tourist trail, even if the initial signs suggest that their post-Games use is likely to be sparse enough to join the 'white elephant' category.

The instant punditry maintained that Beijing 2008 had established a new yardstick for the Olympic movement; leaving behind a hard legacy of magnificent facilities and memories of spectacular ceremonies that might never be equalled. Yet however plausible that view might seem at a subsequent time of severe financial stringency, the hairshirt principle rarely persists when dealing with the staging of the Olympics. The Games invite indulgence in architectural spectacle and grand gestures intended to leave a lasting favourable impression with visitors. No matter how much attitudes might currently tend towards downscaling facility and infrastructural provision, such ideas have a habit of seeming mean-spirited once prosperity returns. They might also prove counterproductive to subsequent place promotional ambitions.

It would be a foolhardy analyst who would make long-term predictions about Beijing 2008 representing the highwater mark for Olympic spectacle and expenditure.

Notes

1. Spoken by Prince George, later Duke of Clarence, in William Shakespeare (1593) *Henry VI*, Part 3, Act II, Scene III, lines 53–56.

2. Although there was a nearby village called Andilalo – the name means 'village of the echo' – it is just as possible that the name simply relates to the spot where the remarkable reverberating echo found at Olympia occurs (see Leake, 1830, I, p. 31).

3. The event was mentioned in a letter dated 30 April 1679, written by Colonel Edward Cooke in London and addressed to the Duke of Ormond, Viceroy of Ireland, in Dublin (Source: Notes and Queries, Tenth Series, X (22 August 1908), p. 147).

4. Baron Pierre de Coubertin (1863–1937), a French educational reformer, was the key figure behind the movement that founded the IOC (see note 6).

5. This came at the end of a speech made at a Jubilee event to celebrate the fifth anniversary of the founding of the Union of French Sports Associations.

6. At the outset, the IOC was a small, conservative and entirely male-dominated body, heavily under the sway of Coubertin, comprising prominent sportsmen and titled individuals whose social status might lend weight to the embryonic organization. The first committee comprised fifteen members from twelve countries. By 1904, this had increased to thirty-two members, of whom seventeen had aristocratic or civil titles (eight counts, three barons, two princes, a knight, a professor, a general and a bishop). To Coubertin, that social background seemed to suggest people whose impeccable pedigree and private means would insure their impartiality. To later commentators, it would provide the recipe for cronyism and an unrepresentative self-perpetuating oligarchy (e.g. Simson and Jennings, 1992; Sheil, 1998; Lenskyj, 2000).

7. The marathon made connection with ancient legend, with the story of the runner who brought news of the Greek victory over the Persians from Marathon to Athens in 490 BC. In reality, however, the race had no parallel in ancient Greek practice, where races rarely exceeded 5 kilometres. For other suggestions as to the martial connotations of the original Games, see Rustin (2009. p. 11).

8. Athletes returning from the Athens Games established the Boston Marathon the following year (Lovett, 1997, p. xii).

9. Mallon (1998, p. 5) points out that Coubertin had previously suggested a recreation of Olympia for the 1889 Universal Exposition in Paris, with some sporting events.

10. There may well have been an element of pretext here: it is now suggested that the Italians were preparing to withdraw from the Games before the eruption occurred (Mallon and Buchanan, 2000, p. xxxvii).

11. British Olympic Association, Minutes of Council Meeting, A7/3, 18 February 1907.

12. With a population in 1900 of 300,624 compared with Greater London's 1901 figure of 6.5 million.

13. Named after General John Pershing, the Commander-in-Chief of the American Expeditionary Force, the Pershing stadium was built by the Americans on land donated by the French.

14. This prefabricated encampment was for male athletes and was demolished after the Games. Female athletes were housed in the Chapman Park Hotel as it was thought they required a rather more permanent type of residence (TOC, 1933, p. 292).

15. It was suggested, for example, that ancient Greece was partly settled by early Germanic migrants during the Neolithic period (Arnold, 1992, p. 32).

16. The Games of the Twelfth and Thirteenth Olympiads were not celebrated because of the war.

17. Accusations of commercial excesses galvanized the IOC into taking control of sponsorship through TOP (The Olympic Programme). For all the disdain of commercialism, the IOC now found itself in the position of inviting corporations to pay tens of millions of dollars to become worldwide Olympic sponsors.

18.   Discussion of the televisual portrayals of the Games and their implications is found in MacAloon (1989).

19.   Financial Times, 15 October 1986.

20.   This was partly through facing the competing attractions of Expo 92 in Seville and having Madrid as 1992 European City of Culture.

21.   Notably for a sequence that involved a set of twenty-nine footprints in the sky (Spencer, 2008).

Chapter 3

The Winter Olympics: Driving Urban Change, 1924–2014

Stephen J. Essex

The delay in establishing a separate Winter Olympic Games until 1924, almost 30 years after the revival of the Summer Games, reflected the fact that winter sports were not included in the original conception of the Olympics. Pierre de Coubertin objected to their inclusion partly because of Scandinavian fears that to do so would have possible detrimental effects on their traditional sports festivals, such as the Nordic Games and Holmenkollen Week.[1] However, as the popularity of winter sports spread, the movement to include them in the Olympic programme gathered pace. Some of the early Summer Games included figure skating (London 1908, Antwerp 1920) and ice hockey (Antwerp 1920) in their programmes. In 1924, a separate winter sports week was held at Chamonix six months before the Summer Games in Paris. In light of the success of this winter sports week, the IOC amended its Charter in 1925 to establish the Winter Olympics, with Chamonix retrospectively designated as the first Winter Games. Until 1948, the country hosting the Summer Games also had the opportunity to stage the Winter Games. Thereafter, the selection of the host for the Winter Games was subject to a separate competition decided by a vote of IOC members, but the event was staged in the same year as the Summer Games. From 1992, further change occurred, with the Summer and Winter Games now held alternately every two years in order to maximize the profile of the Olympics and the television revenue (Borja, 1992).

This chapter reviews the role of the Winter Olympics in changing and modernizing the built environment of its hosts, together with consideration of the changing organization and funding of the event over time. Certain features, of course, remain relatively fixed. The construction or refurbishment of sports facilities has been a constant requirement on hosts throughout the history of the Winter Games, albeit with different outcomes based on local circumstances. The range of sports facilities required for the event is normally standard, although the detailed specifications may change. The main sports venues for the Winter

Olympics include a stadium, slopes for slalom and down-hill ski runs, cross-country ski-trails, bob-sled and luge runs, and an indoor ice arena. The scale of provision of the associated infrastructure, such as the Olympic Village, Media Centre, hotels and transport, reflect the increasing popularity and interest in the event. The impact on host cities, however, involves greater degrees of change. In this respect, there are inevitable comparisons to draw with the Summer Games, which have witnessed a progression from the minor impact of the early Games to a more substantial, entrepreneurial and business-led approach to urban planning through Olympic-led development (see also Essex and Chalkley, 1998, 2002; Chalkley and Essex, 1999). The key questions addressed here are whether the Winter Olympics have had the same trajectory of development impacts on host centres and whether the role of the public sector in the planning and management of the event has contracted in deference to the emergence of more entrepreneurial approaches.

To answer these questions, this chapter draws on the Official Reports of the Organizing Committees and identifies five phases in the development of the event and in the changing scale of impacts (Essex and Chalkley, 2004). These phases, respectively, are characterized as ones of minimal infrastructural investment (1924–1932), emerging infrastructural demands (1936–1960), a tool of regional development (1964–1980), large-scale transformations (1984–1998), and sustainable development and legacy planning (2002–present). While business interests have always been instrumental in galvanizing a desire to stage the Games throughout the period under consideration here, the public sector has traditionally organized and funded much of the infrastructural investment for the Winter Olympics, as well as accumulating the main debts. Moreover, although private sources of capital, such as television rights and sponsorship, have emerged since 1984, the public sector remains pivotal for the organization of the event.

Minimal Infrastructural Investment (1924–1932)

The first three Winter Olympics (see table 3.1 and figure 3.1) were characterized by relatively low levels of interest and participation. The events were staged in settlements with populations of about 3,000, with less than 500 athletes competing in each of the Games. Nevertheless, the motivations of the hosts in staging the Games signify some interest in the development prospects, especially given the emerging interest in winter sports tourism. Chamonix, in the Haute-Savoie department of eastern France, appears to have been volunteered as the host by the French Olympic Committee, which was no doubt cognisant of the need to have world-class facilities to develop winter sports. Similarly, the local Chamber of Commerce was not slow to recognize the economic advantages for the town created by the popular interest in the Games (see figure 3.2). Funding of the first Winter Olympics appears to have been shared equally between the public and private sectors. In 1928, the Games in the Swiss resort of St Moritz were led by

Table 3.1. Winter Olympic Games, 1924–2014.

Games	Host city	Host nation	Other candidates
1924	Chamonix	France	–
1928	St. Moritz	Switerland	Davos, Engelberg (Switzerland)
1932	Lake Placid	USA	Montreal (Canada), Bear Mountain, Yosemite Valley, Lake Tahoe, Duluth, Minneapolis, Denver (USA)
1936	Garmisch-Partenkirchen	Germany	St Moritz (Switzerland)
1948	St Moritz	Switzerland	Lake Placid (USA)
1952	Oslo	Norway	Cortina (Italy), Lake Placid (USA)
1956	Cortina	Italy	Colorado Springs, Lake Placid (USA), Montreal (Canada)
1960	Squaw Valley	USA	Innsbruck (Austria), St Moritz (Switzerland), Garmish-Partenkirchen (Germany)
1964	Innsbruck	Austria	Calgary (Canada), Lahti/Are, (Sweden)
1968	Grenoble	France	Calgary (Canada), Lahti/Are (Sweden), Sapporo (Japan), Oslo (Norway), Lake Placid (USA)
1972	Sapporo	Japan	Banff (Canada), Lahti/Are (Sweden), Salt Lake City (USA)
1976	Innsbruck	Austria	Denver (USA), Sion (Switzerland), Tampere/Are (Finland), Vancouver (Canada)
1980	Lake Placid	USA	Vancouver-Garibaldi (Canada): withdrew before final vote
1984	Sarajevo	Yugoslavia	Sapporo (Japan), Falun/Göteborg (Sweden)
1988	Calgary	Canada	Falun (Sweden), Cortina (Italy)
1992	Albertville	France	Anchorage (USA), Berchtesgaden (Germany), Cortina (Italy), Lillehammer (Norway), Falun (Sweden), Sofia (Bulgaria)
1994	Lillehammer	Norway	Anchorage (USA), Östersund/Are (Sweden), Sofia (Bulgaria)
1998	Nagano	Japan	Aoste (Italy), Jaca (Spain), Östersund (Sweden), Salt Lake City (USA)
2002	Salt Lake City	USA	Öestersund (Sweden), Quebec City (Canada), Sion (Switzerland)
2006	Turin	Italy	Helsinki (Finland), Klagenfurt (Austria), Poprad-Tatry (Slovakia), Sion (Switzerland), Zakopane (Poland)
2010	Vancouver	Canada	PyeongChang (South Korea), Salzburg (Austria)
2014	Sochi	Russia	PyeongChang (South Korea), Salzburg (Austria)

Source: Compiled by the author from IOC (2009).

the local authority and assisted the consolidation of the resort as an international winter sports destination.

Although the initial idea to stage the Winter Olympics in Lake Placid (USA) in 1932 came from the American Olympic Committee in 1927, it was the Lake Placid Club, which owned existing sports facilities in the area, which had investigated the feasibility of the event. The decision to bid for the Games was only made after a representative of the Lake Placid Club had visited a number of European resorts and the St Moritz Olympics of 1928 to convince himself, on behalf of the community, that Lake Placid could match the highest standards abroad and secure longer-term benefits from the investment required. The Lake Placid Chamber of

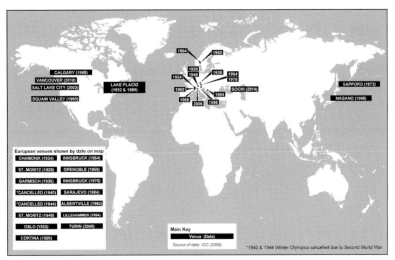

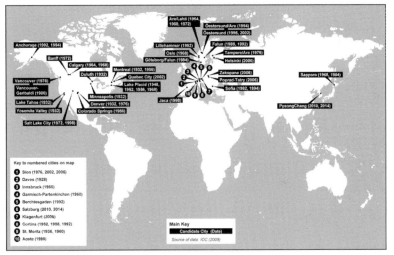

Figure 3.1. Host and bid centres for the Winter Olympic Games, 1924–2014. (*Source*: International Olympic Committee, 2009)

Figure 3.2. The stadium for the Winter Olympics in Chamonix in 1924. (*Source*: IOC/Olympic Museum Collections. Photograph by Auguste Couttet, used in Comité Olympique Français (1924) *Rapport Officiel, Les Jeux de la VIII Olympiade Paris*, COF, Paris, p. 648)

Commerce set up a guarantee fund of $50,000 to support the bid in July 1928, but it was the State of New York that provided the main funding for infrastructural requirements for the event (see figure 3.3). The involvement of New York State eased the concerns of some local residents about the magnitude and responsibility of the task (LPOOC, 1932, p. 43). The organization of the event was a partnership between New York State, Essex County Park Commission, North Elba Town

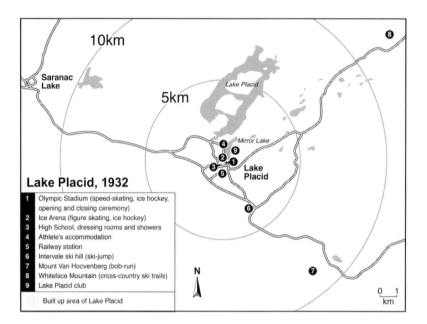

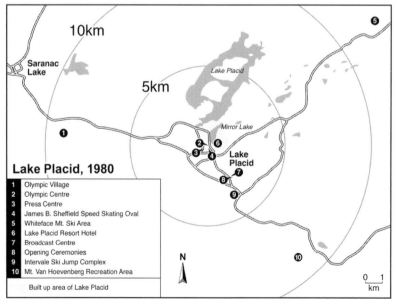

Figure 3.3. Comparison of the Olympic facilities provided for the Winter Olympic Games of 1932 and 1980 in Lake Placid, USA. (*Source*: III Olympic Winter Games Committee, 1932 and Lake Placid Olympic Organizing Committee, 1980)

Board, North Elba Park Committee and Lake Placid Village Board (*Ibid.*, p. 74). In 1932, substantial funding from New York State led to the establishment of the New York State Olympic Winter Games Commission to ensure that the money was spent wisely (*Ibid.*, p. 60), which is a model that has been followed in subsequent Games.

Many of the hosts of the early Winter Olympics were especially aware of the long-term viability of facilities when deciding whether to stage the event, mainly because of the settlement's small size and limited capacity to sustain expensive, high-order facilities. The skeleton[2] run constructed at St Moritz for the 1928 Games proved to be an expensive and non-viable legacy. Less than thirty people used the facility after the Games. As a result, the organizers of the subsequent Games at Lake Placid 1932 questioned whether the cost ($25,000) of a similar facility could be justified.[3] The event was subsequently eliminated from the programme at Lake Placid in light of the expected high costs and low post-Games use[4] and was not re-introduced until Salt Lake City (Utah) in 2002.

In contrast to this prudence, the Lake Placid organizers were criticized for the extravagance of building an indoor ice rink very late in the preparations. The plan was not supported by the State of New York because of the proposed costs ($375,000). The organizers were responding to a suggestion by the IOC President that such a facility would provide an alternative venue for events in the case of bad weather (which had so badly disrupted St Moritz 1928) and would also be a tangible and physical memorial to the event. The required finance was eventually raised by forcing the hand of the town authorities. The site for the rink was already cleared and, with the prospect of a derelict site in the middle of town, the authorities were forced to fund the construction via a bond issue (Ortloff and Ortloff, 1976, p. 77). According to the organizers, the indoor ice rink proved its worth by providing an alternative venue for skating events affected by the unseasonably warm weather and so prevented the programme from being disrupted (LPOOC, 1932, p. 154).

The construction of Olympic Villages or new hotels was certainly not justified in this phase because of fears of over-provision. Instead, existing accommodation within a wide geographical catchment area was used and, if necessary, 'winterized'. Hotel and cottage owners in the vicinity of Lake Placid were urged by the organizers of the Games of 1932 to 'winterize' their summer accommodation to house the expected 10,000 visitors. Eventually accommodation in Montreal, which was three and a half hours from Lake Placid, had to be used to cater for the demand (Organizing Committee, 1932, p. 112).

Despite their small scale, some Olympic-related developments proposed for early Winter Games could still raise environmental protests. In March 1930, a local action group (the Association for the Protection of the Adirondacks) brought a successful legal action against a proposed Olympic bobsleigh run for the Lake Placid Games on environmental grounds and because building on state land was unconstitutional. As a result, a less sensitive site was found at South Meadows Mountain, later renamed Mount Van Hoevenberg (*Ibid.*).

Emerging Infrastructural Demands (1936–1960)

The second phase bears many of the hallmarks of the first: host centres were generally small (normally less than 13,000 residents) and had been offered as hosts by a combination of National Olympic Committees, Sports Federations and local authorities. The funding of the infrastructural investment was predominantly public sector. The key difference was that by 1936 there was substantial growth in the number of participating countries and athletes. Investment in Olympic-related infrastructure continued to be constrained by the same factors of long-term viability as in the first phase, but with the added pressures created by the temporary influx of larger numbers of competitors and spectators. Initial plans for an Olympic Village at Cortina d'Ampezzo in northern Italy for the Winter Games of 1956 were abandoned after opposition from local hoteliers who feared the effect of an increase in the town's accommodation capacity on their businesses (CONI, 1956, p. 267). The award of the 1960 Games to Squaw Valley, according to the organizers, had transformed a remote mountain valley into a 'throbbing city' (California Olympic Commission, 1960, p. 27). The development of the Olympic Village for Squaw Valley 1960 was out of scale with the small local community, but was considered necessary because of the number of athletes now requiring accommodation and because local hotel capacity was required for officials and journalists (Chappelet, 1997, p. 83). Yet it was only a temporary construction, as the town's small population (*c.* 4,000) meant there was no viable post-Olympic use.

The main exception in this phase was the Norwegian capital Oslo, which hosted the Winter Olympics of 1952. With a resident population of 447,100, the city was by far the largest centre to have accommodated the Games by that date. The larger population created new opportunities for the type of facilities provided, as the post-Olympic viability and future use was more assured. In the period before 1960, Oslo was also the only host to have built an Olympic Village, albeit dispersed in various locations around the city with planned post-Olympic uses such as student halls of residence, a hospital and an old people's home (Organisasjonskomiteen, 1952, pp. 23, 42). However, new infrastructural requirements were also created by the increased size of the host settlements. For example, larger urban centres were often at some distance from competition sites. Large numbers of athletes and spectators had to be moved considerable distances to isolated locations in difficult terrains and within limited timeframes, sometimes compounded by adverse weather conditions. Investment in transport infrastructure, such as new roads, bridges and skilifts, became essential to the operation of the Oslo Games of 1952 and subsequent events.

Tool of Regional Development (1964–1980)

The third phase was characterized by a number of definite shifts: an expansion of the number of athletes, appreciably larger host centres and the emergence of regional development and modernization as a key motivation for staging the Games. Four of the five hosts during this period had populations of more than 100,000, with the other having more than one million. Only Lake Placid in 1980 had a level of population comparable to those of previous phases. Both private development companies and local authorities recognized the potential of the Winter Olympics for justifying major infrastructural investment as part of broader modernization programmes. Television revenue was also emerging as an important source of income during this phase, which began to shift the onus of the funding from the public sector to the private sector, although the local public sector remained central to the organization of the event. Innsbruck 1964 received $597,000 from television rights, while Lake Placid 1980 received $15.5 million.

Partly because of their increased size, the Winter Olympics were recognized as a tool of regional development from the 1960s. Innsbruck 1964 was used as a showcase for Austrian businesses, especially those related to ski equipment (Espy, 1979, p. 90). The modernization of the Isère Department was accelerated by Grenoble 1968 (Borja, 1992) and as a means of remodelling its planning system after a period of rapid growth (1946–1968) (COJO, 1968, p. 46) (see figure 3.4). Sapporo 1972 was viewed by the Japanese government as a unique economic opportunity to invigorate the northern island of Hokkaido (Borja, 1992). Most of the spending was on investment in the urban infrastructure, with less than 5 per cent of capital improvements for these Games expended on sports facilities (Hall, 1992, p. 69).

With the choice of host centres with larger populations after 1960, the post-Games viability of a purpose-built Olympic Village became more assured, usually as a residential area of the host settlement or a student hall of residence for a local

Figure 3.4. The Olympic Village constructed for the Winter Olympics in Grenoble in 1968. The event was used as a tool of regional development. (*Source:* IOC/Olympic Museum Collections)

university or college. For example, the Olympic Village at Grenoble was built in a Priority Urbanization Zone and subsequently was used as an 800-room university hall, a 300-room hostel for young workers and a tower block with fifty-two apartments (COJO, 1968, p. 71). In Innsbruck, which staged the Games of 1964 and 1976, the organizers were forced to build an Olympic Village for each event. That built for the Winter Games of 1964 was not available for the Games of 1976 as it had become a residential suburb of the town in the interim. The new Olympic Village was built on an adjacent site. The 1976 organizers later reported that having to build a Village was, perhaps, rather extravagant, as not all the athletes wished to stay there, some preferring to be closer to event sites. In retrospect, they felt that accommodating athletes in hotels might have been preferable from cost, security and transport perspectives (HOOWI, 1967, p. 400).

Olympic-related investment in transport infrastructure was often central to regional development objectives. Road construction accounted for 20 per cent of the total investment for Grenoble 1968 (COJO, 1968, p. 46), and was designed to decentralize the region and facilitate economic growth. The investment included a motorway link from Grenoble to Geneva, which acted as a catalyst for the regional economy and transformed the host town into a major conference and university centre (Chappelet, 2002a, p. 11). The city's old airport at Grenoble-Eybens was closed to make way for the Olympic Village and was replaced by two new airports at Saint-Etienne-de-Saint-Geoirs and Versoud (COJO, 1968, p. 290). For Sapporo 1972, transport investments included extensions to two airports, improvements to the main railway station, forty-one new or improved roads (213 kilometres) and the construction of a rapid transit system (45 kilometres). This last project had already been started by the City of Sapporo, but was completed for the Winter Games using government funding.

With the increasing scale of the Winter Olympics, the risks associated with staging the Games became greater. First, the changing scale of the event affected the character and operation of the Games. One of the consequences of the Winter Olympics being staged in larger cities and across whole regions was that the focus and impact of the event became dissipated. Critics claimed that the size and dispersed geography of the Games had detracted from the camaraderie of the event and increased transport problems. Secondly, warnings about the long-term limitations of the event as a tool of regional development began with the debt accumulated by the organizers of Grenoble 1968, together with the abandonment or demolition of some of its venues. It was also during this third phase that the award of the Winter Olympics of 1976 to Denver had to be reassigned – the only time in Winter Olympic history that this has happened (Olson, 1974). The reason was local concern about the rising cost of the event and about how the organizers, led by business interests, were ignoring environmental considerations. An action group, 'Citizens for Colorado's Future' was successful in placing the issue on the State and City ballots in November 1972. The citizens then had a vote on whether the Games should be staged using state funding. The turnout was high (93.8 per cent) and 60 per cent voted against the Olympics, which meant that neither state nor federal funding for the event would be forthcoming. Denver was therefore forced to withdraw its candidacy for the Winter Games of 1976, which were then staged in Innsbruck at short notice.

There was also growing consideration of environmental factors elsewhere, though in different ways. For the 1972 Sapporo Games, the only mountain close to the host city and suitable for downhill ski events was Mount Eniwa, within the Shikotsu-Toya National Park. The National Park Council gave permission on condition that all related facilities were removed and the terrain in the affected area restored to its original state. A comparable instance concerned the 1980 Games at Lake Placid, where the town itself lay within Adirondack Park, designated in 1971 and regulated by Adirondack Park Agency. The park's public lands were directly administered by the State Department of Environmental Conservation, which also operated bobsled and luge runs, the biathlon and cross-country trails and the Whiteface Mountain Ski area (LPOOC, 1980, p. 18). The extensions of the ski jumps, originally built for the 1932 Games, had to comply with standards set by the Adirondack Park Agency and the Federal Environment Agency (*Ibid.*, p. 38).

Large-Scale Transformations (1984–1998)

The fourth phase is characterized by the most significant increase in participation in the Winter Games. By 1994, the ratio of support staff to athletes was 6.5 times bigger than in 1956. Numbers of athletes were also growing, with over 2,000 athletes at Nagano in 1998 (Chappelet, 2002b). The accommodation of athletes, media and spectators became a substantial infrastructural challenge in itself. After 1988, two or more Olympic Villages became necessary to accommodate athletes closer to their event venues. Separate Villages for the media were also necessary. These demands have favoured centres with larger populations. Perhaps more significantly, television revenue rose from $91.5 million in 1984 to $513 million in 1998, with the additional revenue partly funding ever larger and more ambitious urban redevelopment.

These various changes intensified the advantages of placing the Games in host centres with larger populations. In this phase, the Games were staged in centres with an average population of about 298,000, although three of the five hosts have been substantially larger and two smaller. The role of the Winter Games as a means to secure major urban infrastructural change and modernization has intensified. Sarajevo 1984 was taken as an opportunity to modernize the city by the government. The motivation for Calgary 1988 and Lillehammer 1994 was to act as a stimulus to revive the local economies (e.g. COWGOC, 1988, p. 5). At Calgary, the Organizing Committee moved some venues originally selected by the Calgary Olympic Development Association to make them more viable after the Games (*Ibid.*) and the Games also caused some facilities to be provided much earlier than would otherwise have occurred. For example, the construction of the Olympic

Saddledome (20,000 seats, C\$7 million), home for a professional ice hockey team established in 1980, was fast-tracked to show the city's commitment to its bid (Hiller, 1990, p. 124). Large investments required to stage the 1992 Albertville Games appear, however, to have made more difficulties for other northern French Alpine resorts seeking finance for restructuring (Tuppen, 2000, p. 330). This case shows that Olympic investment has 'opportunity costs' which may postpone or eliminate other forms of investment.

Given the changing circumstances, smaller hosts in this phase faced problems in justifying investment in permanent purpose-built Olympic Villages. Albertville 1992, which had a population of only 20,000 at the time, renovated a small spa at Brides-les-Bains as the Olympic Village rather than constructing a purpose-built facility. However, the village proved to be too far from the sports facilities, so seven smaller Olympic Villages were established in existing hotel accommodation closer to the event sites. After this experience, the IOC stated that it favoured the use of a single Olympic Village in future Games in order to promote contact between athletes from different countries (Charmetant, 1997, p. 115), although this aspiration has not proved possible in more recent events. At Lillehammer 1994, which had a population of 23,000, a temporary Olympic Village consisting of 200 wooden chalets, was constructed. These examples were significant departures from the trajectory of large-scale infrastructural investment.

The increasing scale of the event has also necessitated more formal recognition of environmental issues in the planning and development of related infrastructure (May, 1995). The intrusion of built structures into fragile environments, as well as the use of chemicals to create the appropriate snow conditions, have become a major issue in the preparations for the Winter Olympics. Most notably, the preparations for the Lillehammer Games of 1994 incorporated, for the first time, the principles of sustainable development. The proposed location of one of the main indoor arenas was moved to protect a bird sanctuary, while its heat circulation operated from excess heat from its refrigeration unit. Contracts with suppliers and contractors included environmental clauses. The approach influenced the IOC to add an environmental commitment to its Charter, with the candidates for the Winter Games of 2002 being the first required to describe their environmental plans in their bid documents (IOC, 1999a, p. 5; see also chapter 1).

Sustainable Development and Legacy Planning (2002 Onwards)

During the fifth phase (2002 onwards), the trend for the event to require large-scale infrastructural investment has continued, but with a greater emphasis on the protection of the environment, sustainable development and legacy planning. As a consequence, the Games have begun to be staged by large metropolitan cities together with their surrounding mountain communities, essentially making them multicentred events (Chappelet, 2008, p. 1897). There have also been other significant pressures which have altered the character of the Winter Olympics, such as the threat from international terrorism and reforms to the host city selection process following corruption over the award of the 2002 event.

As noted earlier, Salt Lake City was the first host city elected after being required to outline environmental plans in the bid process. However, the Winter Olympics of 2002 are likely to be better remembered for the corruption scandal that tainted the city's election as host and for the heightened security threat following the terrorist attacks in New York on 11 September 2001. The Salt Lake Bid Committee, making their second bid and determined to secure the event, allegedly made payments to IOC members for holidays, medical treatment and members' children while at university or working in America, in return for support (Booth, 1999; Lenskyj, 2000; Toohey and Veal, 2007, p. 232). The allegation emerged in December 1998 and was followed by an *ad hoc* IOC Commission of Inquiry and a US Olympic Committee Special Bid Oversight Commission (Mitchell Commission) in 1999. The Mitchell Commission concluded that the IOC's lack of accountability had contributed directly to the gift-giving culture, which had fostered the actions of the Salt Lake City organizers (Kettle, 1999; Sandomir, 1999). The IOC's own inquiry excluded six members (in addition to four who had resigned and one who had died), issued warnings to ten members and exonerated three (IOC, 1999b). The President/Chief Executive Officer and Senior Vice President of the Salt Lake City Organizing Committee left the organization in January 1999. The controversy led to reforms in the host city selection process, including the elimination of member visits to candidate cities and the creation of a permanent Ethics Commission, as well as amendments to the composition of the IOC itself. These changes were relevant to the future selection and conduct of both the Summer and Winter Olympics.

Similarly, the 9/11 terrorist attacks made the security risk associated with the Winter Olympics much greater. Salt Lake City was staging the Games only five months after the attacks, so the security measures were enhanced and placed centre stage. Strict constraints were introduced for local air space as well as access to zones within the city (Warren, 2002, p. 617). The organizers spent $200 million on security and public safety measures and deployed 9,750 security-related personnel during the Games (SLOC, 2002, pp. 114 and 490). Although security had been a major concern and source of expenditure since Munich 1972, the Salt Lake City Games set a new benchmark for the implementation of security plans and measures at the Olympic Games in an era of global terrorism.

The development of infrastructure and facilities for Salt Lake City 2002 was based on three Master Plans: for Downtown, the University of Utah and Park City. In total seven permanent venues were constructed, with only three requiring investment by the Organizing Committee itself. The other four venues were built by public-private partnerships, with a further twenty temporary venues or overlays (*Ibid.*, p. 187).[5] There was significant investment in transport infrastructure, involving ten Olympic-related roads and highway projects and four non-Olympic related regional projects, including the reconstruction of two interstate routes and two light rail transit lines (*Ibid.*, p. 179).

All Salt Lake City developments were subject to environmental management systems to minimize adverse environmental impacts. The Environmental Plan contained four 'aggressive objectives', which were all achieved. First, 95.6 per cent of all waste was recycled or composted to achieve the objective of 'zero waste' (*Ibid.*, p. 26). Second, the Games succeeded in its goal of 'net zero emissions' by offsetting its carbon footprint of 122,936 metric tons of hazardous and greenhouse gas emissions as well as 243,840 metric tons of pollutants in Utah, the US and Canada (*Ibid.*, p. 196). The event was certified as climate neutral by the Climate Neutral Network. Third, the event's advocacy programme for urban forestry resulted in 100,000 trees being planted in Utah and 15 million trees planted worldwide (*Ibid.*, p. 26). Fourth, zero tolerance for environmental and safety compliance errors was successful (*Ibid.*, 195–198). The environmental and sustainable development agenda had been clearly cemented as part of the organization of the Winter Olympic Games following those in Salt Lake City.

The award of the Winter Olympics of 2006 to Turin, with a population of 1.4 million, represented the use of the event as part of a strategy to transform an old industrial city into a modern post-industrial city, a scenario which is normally associated with the Summer Games. Turin had been almost totally dependent upon the motorcar manufacturer Fiat for a century, and had become known as the 'Italian Detroit' (Rosso, 2004, p. 5). With the contraction of Fiat in the city in the 1980s, involving the loss of 110,000 jobs by 2001 (Winkler, 2007, p. 16), there was a need to forge a new urban identity to attract tertiary businesses and improve its tourism potential.

In order to modernize the city's infrastructure, innovations were first required in the city's governance structures. When Fiat had been dominant in the city, a tradition of industrial conflicts and strong economic interests inside the Municipal Council had prevented the creation of an overall vision or strategy for the city (Pinson, 2002, p. 483). Instead, town planning interventions had only been allowed to act in a pragmatic and opportunistic way. Following the corruption scandals that led to the collapse of both national and local government in Italy in 1992, national political reforms were introduced involving the directly elected mayors with increased executive powers and resources (Winkler, 2007, pp. 18–19). In 1993, the election of Valentino Castellani as Mayor, with backing from the Chamber of Commerce, the University and the Catholic voluntary sector, emphasized the importance of the internationalization agenda to the city's revitalization and long-term future. This focus created a space for dialogue and an opportunity for organizational and entrepreneurial capacity to develop. A new ethos slowly began to evolve which placed the municipality at the centre of collective governance as facilitator with an emphasis on open regional partnership, collaboration and networks rather than centralized, secretive confrontation and conflict dominated by Fiat (Pinson, 2002, p. 489). Implementation of the emerging vision was assisted by over 15 years of political continuity achieved by the re-election of both Castellani and his successor (Chiamparino) (Winkler, 2007, p. 23).

An urban Master Plan had been prepared by architects Cagnardi and Gregotti in 1995 to alter the city's urban structure and create opportunities for regeneration. The Plan focused on the improvement of transport access and private-led investment on brownfield sites within clear land use zoning and regulation. The organizing principle of the plan was the 'Spina Centrale', which was a north–south avenue along the railway line, which had fractured the city into two. The railway line was taken underground, as a means of increasing its capacity fourfold, which enabled the surface to be transformed into a 12 km, six-lane arterial road (*Ibid.*, p. 28). The change reconnected the two halves of the city and established a new urban centrality and image along the central backbone (see figure 3.5). Along the route, four disused industrial areas totalling over 2.1 million square metres and owned by the public sector and major private companies (such as Fiat and Michelin) would be redeveloped as mixed-use developments. A new cross-rail system, the 'Passante Ferroviao', was introduced. Key functions such as libraries, theatres, regional government offices and higher education were developed on brownfield sites adjacent to the railway stations, often in iconic landmark buildings. A programme to improve the quality of neighbourhoods, public spaces and cultural and leisure attractions throughout the city was implemented (Falk, 2003).

The award of the Winter Olympics to Turin on 19 June 1999 therefore enabled the scope and importance of the new vision for the city to be integrated (Rosso, 2004, p. 17), prioritized (Pinson, 2002, p. 485) and above all to be implemented. The Strategic Plan for Turin was formulated through a highly participatory process and signed by all relevant agencies in February 2000. It outlined six overall strategies and twenty objectives, which would be achieved by eighty-four specific projects (see table 3.2). Implementation was overseen by Torino Internazionale Association, the 'Invest in Turin and Piedmont' inward investment agency and Turismo Torino (Pinson, 2002, p. 485; Rosso, 2004, p. 18; Winkler, 2007, p. 28). The Olympics was perceived as an opportunity to modernize the city's infrastructures (Pinson, 2002, p. 485) and galvanize the longer-term vision for the city.

The staging of the Winter Olympics was also organized as a means of regional integration between the urban centres (Turin, Grugliasco and Pinerolo), which provided venues for the ice competitions, an Olympic Village, Media Village, Press Centre and International Broadcasting Centre, and the surrounding mountain communities, which provided venues for the snow competitions and two Olympic Villages (Torre Pellice, Pragelato, Bardonecchia, Sauze d'Oulx, Claviere, Cesana-San Sicario, Sestriere). This strategy sought to extend the benefits of Olympic investment beyond the city to the whole region through opportunities to upgrade ski facilities and structures and to extend the tourism season (Dansero *et al.*, 2003). Substantial improvements were made to the local road networks to increase the area's tourism potential, as well as to benefit daily life for its citizens. The transformation of Turin as a European metropolis was also signalled with

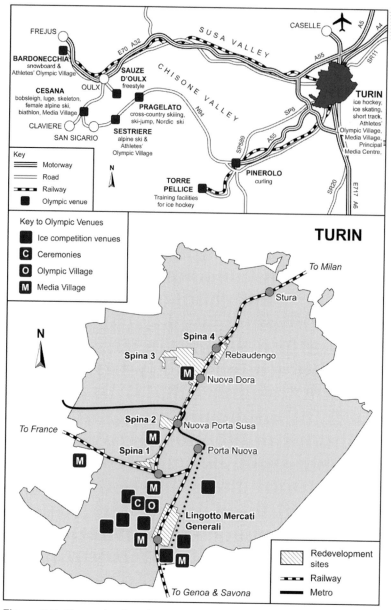

Figure 3.5. The regional setting of the 2006 Winter Olympics in Turin and the Urban Master Plan for the city's redevelopment devised in 1995. (*Source:* Winkler, 2007)

plans to connect to the high-speed rail lines to Milan (2009) and Lyon (2011), thus positioning the city in the dynamic Mediterranean arc of technopoles in southern France (Sophia-Antipolis and Montpellier) through to Barcelona (Falk, 2003, p. 213).

As with the other recent Winter Olympics, the Turin Games were notable for their emphasis on environmental protection and sustainable development. A strategic evaluation assessment (the so-called 'Green Card') was adopted by the

Table 3.2. The Strategic Plan for Turin, 2000.

Six lines of strategy	20 objectives (examples)	84 actions
To integrate the metropolitan area into the international system	• To develop international cooperation networks • To facilitate access to Turin • To improve mobility within the city	• A standardized, integrated communication plan for the international promotion of Turin • Privatization and expansion of – and improved access to – Torino-Caselle airport • Participation in the creation of the Turin-Milan and Turin-Lyon sections of the high-speed railway • Construction of an underground rail network linking the various Turin mainline stations • Construction of a metro line between Collegno and Lingotto via Porta Nouva
To construct metropolitan government	• To create new forms of governance • To construct services for the metropolitan area	• To institute a Metropolitan Conference • To constitute the Torino Internazionale Association to monitor the strategic plan • To create a Metropolitan Transport Agency
To develop training and research as strategic resources	• To strengthen a university centre of international level and appeal • To foster the development of research in tandem with economic initiatives • To promote vocational training and work-training integration	• To build new university sites • Enlargement of the Polytechnic • To involve research centres in international collaboration networks • To establish links between research and business • To create two business incubators within the city's two universities
To promote enterprise and employment	• To develop the innovative potential of the production system • To create conditions favourable to the development of new enterprise • To promote local development and active employment policies	• To upgrade 'technology districts' by setting up shared services in the fields of training, quality assurance and the environment • To create a structure for technology transfer • To develop an aerospace centre around the Alenia company • To develop an Internet Exchange at the Environment Park

Table 3.2 continued on page 72

Table 3.2 continued from page 71

Six lines of strategy	20 objectives (examples)	84 actions
		• To develop an Information and Communication Technology Centre around the Telecom Italia and Motorola research centres • To develop an insurance and financial services centre • To create a new body to assist business start-up activity • To support the 'territorial pacts' launched by the Province of Turin
To promote Turin as a city of culture, tourism, commerce and sport	• To enhance and develop the city's cultural heritage • To coordinate cultural activities and to schedule events of international standing • To develop the tourist industry • To position Turin/Piedmont in the national and international tourist markets • To support growth and innovation of the region's commercial network • To use the 2006 Winter Olympic Games as a driver for development and international promotion	• To rethink the city's system of museums and relocate the Egyptian Museum • To promote Turin as a 'Cinema City' centred around the National Cinema Museum in Mole Antonelliana • To improve and develop hotel facilities for the 2006 Winter Olympic Games • To develop tourist activities linked to sport • To build an Olympic village to contribute to urban regeneration • To build new sports infrastructures
To improve the quality of the city	• New 'centres' providing focal points for local facilities; urban renewal and social integration as a strategy for spreading prosperity, cohesion and urban regeneration • Local Agenda 21, sustainable development and environmental innovation as the guide and foundation for the city's strategies	• To regenerate depressed and/or outlying districts on the model of the 'Special Project for Peripheral Areas' • To develop 'centres' of urban development and local identity in outlying districts • To create an Urban Centre • To promote Turin as a centre of excellence in the non-profit sector and to attract the European Third-Sector Authority to locate in the city • To reclaim the city's rivers and riverbanks • To revive public spaces

Source: Pinson (2002, pp. 486–487).

Environment Department of the Turin Organizing Committee (TOROC) to assess the environmental consequences of proposed developments and to monitor environmental impacts. This environmental management system was awarded ISO 14001 status.[6] All plans and projects were assessed by the Consulta Ambientale (Environmental Council) before implementation so that recommendations about environmental sustainability could be instigated. An 'Ambiente 2006' logo was awarded to companies who manufactured goods for the Olympics in compliance with predetermined environmentally sustainable criteria (TOROC, 2005, p. 122), and local hotel accommodation was awarded an 'Ecolabel' for adopting sustainable practices (*Ibid.*, p. 124). The Games themselves offset 100,000 metric tons of greenhouse gases through the HECTOR programme (HEritage Climate TORino) (*Ibid.*, p. 122). The Turin Winter Olympics was noteworthy for its achievements in transforming the city's structures for governance and in mobilizing the city's long-term redevelopment plan. In this respect, Turin is the closest that the Winter Olympics have come to replicating the transformational effects of the Summer Olympics in Barcelona. Turin also secured advances in the minimization of the environmental impact of the event – an example for future Games to emulate.

The Future

The Winter Olympics in 2010 were held in Vancouver, Canada, which also emphasized its credentials in sustainable development (Holden *et al.*, 2008). The urban centre of Vancouver acted as the venue for the ice competitions and the neighbouring winter resort of Whistler provided the venues for the snow competitions. New and upgraded facilities were constructed, together with a rapid transit link between the airport and central Vancouver and an upgrade of the 'Sea-to-Sky' highway between Vancouver and Whistler. The 'performance goals' of the organizers focused on accountability, environmental stewardship and impact reduction, social inclusion and responsibility, aboriginal participation and collaboration, economic benefits from sustainable practices and sport for sustainable living (Chappelet, 2008, p. 1896). The provincial government set up an independent not-for-profit company called '2010 Legacies Now' to ensure that each region in British Columbia benefited from the Games, through maximizing social and economic opportunities, building community capacity and expanding volunteer resources (2010 Legacies Now, 2009). The agency is funded by grants from various levels of government, contributions by the private sector and investment income and has undertaken various programmes in schools education, sport and recreation, the arts, volunteerism and literacy to achieve its goals (2010 Legacies Now, 2008). It has created a new model for securing 'softer' Olympic legacies related to people, skills and employability rather than simply the 'hard' legacies related to the built environment.

Despite the apparent concern for securing a positive post-Olympic legacy, the organizers in Vancouver have faced criticisms. The onset of a worsening global recession in 2008 threatened to jeopardize the financial viability of many developments, including the Olympic Village where the city government has had to subsidize the project in order to ensure timely completion (O'Connor, 2009). Social impacts resulting from the effects of land speculation and reversals on promises of affordable housing have produced substantial concerns about increasing homelessness in the city. During the pre-Olympic development boom, single-room accommodation for low-income tenants was converted into high-cost condominiums or boutique hotels, resulting in increased evictions and homelessness (CTV, 21 September, 2006; AMSUBC, 2009). Indigenous peoples objected to their political groups being co-opted onto the local Olympic organization as a means for their artists, cultural performance groups and symbols to be used in Olympic events (No 2010, 2009). Indeed, the use of an inutshuk as the symbol of the 2010 Olympics was disputed by some groups. Environmental protests against the construction of the 'Sea-to-Sky' highway through Eagleridge Bluffs resulted in twenty arrests and two jail sentences. It is feared that the cost of the Vancouver Olympics will rise to over $6 billion (O'Connor, 2009). The staging of the Winter Olympics has become as contested as their summer equivalents.

The award of the Winter Olympics of 2014 to Sochi in Russia may represent the start of a new phase or even a step backwards in the trajectory of the event (Chappelet, 2008, p. 1897). The decision by the IOC in 2007 to award the Winter Olympics to Russia appears to have been a mixture of political gesture and commercial opportunity to extend Olympism into the former communist world, along the lines of the Summer Olympics of 2008 in Beijing. It is also a symbol of a resurgent Russia. The bid proposed to develop the small mountain village of Krasnaya Polyana in the Caucasus Mountains from almost nothing into a new winter sports resort to be used for the venues of the snow competitions together with the existing seaside resort of Sochi as the venue for the ice competitions. Sochi is located in a sub-tropical coastal region, while Krasnaya Polyana, 30 miles (49 kilometres) away, is part of an alpine mountain range (see figure 3.6). Besides eleven new Olympic sports facilities and over 19,000 new hotel rooms (IOC, 2007b, pp. 18 and 24), substantial investment is required in power and gas lines, telecommunications, water supplies and transport. No less than seven power stations (some thermoelectric and some hydro-electric) are planned to be constructed or refurbished to increase the capacity of the region's energy network by 2.5 times and secure a stable power supply for the event and beyond (SOOC, 2009). A new terminal will be built at Sochi airport, together with a new offshore terminal at Sochi seaport. A light railway will be constructed from the airport to the Olympic Park. Transport between Sochi and Krasnaya Polyana will be enhanced by the reconstruction of the railway to a double track line and a new motorway (IOC, 2007b, pp. 25–26). While the construction of a winter sports resort to state-of-the-art Olympic standards represents an unparalleled opportunity to advance regional development, winter sports and tourism, the IOC Coordination Committee overseeing the 2014 Games warned Russia not to delay on major

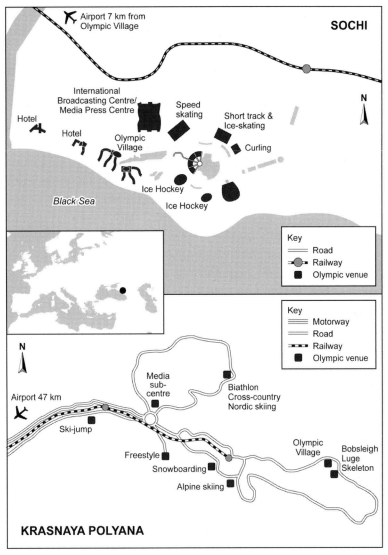

Figure 3.6. The geography of the Winter Olympic Games to be staged in Sochi, Russia in 2014. (*Source*: Sochi Olympic Organizing Committee, 2009)

construction work during an inspection visit in May 2009 (Harding, 2009). The estimated costs associated with these developments range from $12 billion to $20 billion (Kasparov, 2008) and appear to be at odds with the IOC's concern to reduce the cost and scale of Olympic events.

Serious environmental concerns also exist over the preparations since some the venues were planned to be located in the Sochi National Park and the Caucasus State Biosphere Reserve (a UNESCO World Heritage Area). Initially, the National Park was to be rezoned to allow the construction of an Olympic Village in Krasnaya Polyana and the bobsleigh and luge runs in a buffer zone of the Reserve. In July 2008, the Russian Prime Minister, Vladimar Putin, ordered the Olympic facilities noted above to be relocated. He is reported as having stated that 'in setting our priorities and choosing between money and the environment, we're choosing the environment' (Finn, 2008). It later emerged that the Master Plan for Sochi (to 2032) did include plans for development in the National Park (RIA Novosti, 2009). An appeal by Greenpeace Russia to the Russian Supreme Court about these environmental concerns was rejected (IOC, 2007b, p. 14; GamesBids.com, 2006).

There are also human rights issues related to these environmental concerns. A law has been introduced to allow public agencies to acquire land required for Olympic-related developments at a fair market price, but with no right of appeal (Kasparov, 2008). Homes and businesses are threatened, especially in beachside locations which have the greatest real estate value (BBC, 2008). A group of local protestors who attempted to publicize their plight using 'SOS' banners during an IOC inspection visit in 2008 were physically attacked by police (Kasparov, 2008). Other sources have suggested that properties and businesses acquired for Olympic-related development are being treated with sensitivity and fairness, involving appropriate compensation, land or housing exchange (or both) and even a telephone hotline (RUVR, 2008). Indeed, information available on the preparations for these Olympics indicate clear biases in content and message depending on the source – not least related to political affiliation.

Security concerns have also been voiced over the 2014 Winter Olympics because Sochi is located close to the disputed region of Abkhazia (Georgia). A website (RevoketheGames.com) has been set up to draw attention to Russia's attack on Georgia in 2008 and to campaign for the 2014 event to be moved from Sochi to another host. In November 2008, the Georgian National Olympic Committee requested that the IOC reconsider its decision to award an Olympics which would be staged close to a conflict zone. The IOC rejected the request because security was the responsibility of the Russian organizers. A number of challenges are therefore posed by the event in Sochi, which might affect the future trajectory of the Winter Olympics, particularly related to the IOC's concerns to control financial and environmental costs.

Conclusions

The infrastructural implications of staging the Winter Olympic Games have grown in line with the increasing participation and interest in the event. The average number of athletes participating in the Games has increased from 325 in Phase I to 2,508 in Phase V. Television rights for the event now amount to about $833 million. As a consequence, the size of host centres has also increased to accommodate the infrastructural demands: from an average resident population of 3,122 in Phase I to an average of 635,900 for the Games between 2002 and 2014. It is now common for the host city of the Winter Olympics to be a large urban centre together with surrounding mountain communities rather than a single winter resort. The event has begun to emulate the Summer Olympics in its ability to modernize and stimulate urban regeneration. Nevertheless, the scale of investment can still represent a challenge to the hosts in ensuring that the post-Olympic legacy is positive and facilities are sustainable. Indeed, the increasing scale of the event has introduced new infrastructural demands, such as major improvements to transport systems, enhanced security measures and projects integrating sustainable development. In some cases, the athletes' demand to be closer to competition venues has required the Winter Olympic Villages to be fragmented into smaller units. The extent to which the Winter Olympic Games therefore represent a cost-effective and positive force for sustainable legacies and urban revitalization policies is much contested.

In economic terms, legacies appear mixed, with the impacts often experienced as an 'intermezzo', that is a short dramatic interlude yielding a poor long-term return on investment (Spilling, 1998). In Spilling's research into the effects of Lillehammer 1994, new business start-ups were substantial immediately after the Games were awarded, but many did not survive. The tangible economic impacts might be short-lived but intangible impacts, such as the creation of new networks, skills and images, can have longer-term importance. Research into the effects of the 1988 Games on Calgary's image in twenty-two centres in America and Europe between 1986 and 1989 showed an increased awareness immediately before and after the event but tended to dissipate after a few years (Brent Ritchie and Smith, 1991). The impact of the event can also be uneven across different sectors. During the 2002 Winter Olympics in Salt Lake City, hotels and restaurants prospered (experiencing a combined estimated $70.6 million net increase in taxable sales), while retailers suffered (with a larger net loss of $167.4 million) (Baade *et al.*, 2008).

Other preparations have had damaging impacts on the daily lives of local people in host cities of the Winter Olympics. These implications usually appear in sources other than the Official Reports. As an example, Victoria Park in Calgary shows how an area used as a venue for several proposed and actual mega-events, including the 1988 Winter Games, has changed from a living community into an area of residential obsolescence. Uncertainty about whether proposed mega-events would actually take place impeded investment. Consequently, residential rehabilitation has ceased, being replaced gradually by tourism and entertainment land uses (Hiller and Moylan, 1999). The emergence of local action groups opposing bids for Winter Games in several potential hosts shows some local perceptions of the negative impacts (for example, Helsinki 2006 Anti-Olympic Committee; Nolympics!, Turin, 2006; No 2010 Network and Native Anti-2010 Resistance, Vancouver, 2010).

Despite the emergence of more entrepreneurial approaches to the urban management of the Olympics, the role of the public sector appears to remain central to the organization and, to a certain extent, the funding of the event. The private sector does appear to be assuming more responsibility in urban governance, especially in terms of the initial motivation to stage the Winter Olympics emanating from business coalitions and the generation of income through corporate sponsorship and television revenue. However, public-sector expenditure remains high and often pivotal to the success of the event. The French government treated Grenoble 1968 as an *affaire nationale*, met 80 per cent of the basic sports installation costs and provided a subsidy of 20 million francs for operational expenses (COJO, 1968, p. 39). The Albertville Games of 1992 were originally conceived as a means of regional modernization by local businessmen, but it was the French government that funded the project. Similarly, the Norwegian government covered the huge costs and debts of Lillehammer 1994. The staging of Turin 2006 was pivotal in the city's transformation from an industrial to a post-industrial centre and the Sochi Winter Games in 2014 will create a new ski and winter sports resort in Russia.

The debate about the increasing size of the Winter Olympics has been a long-running affair. Preparations for Oslo 1952 included consideration of a proposal to reduce the number of events. It was feared that the increasing size of each Winter Games would detrimentally affect their character and make it impossible for any town to undertake the necessary arrangements.[7] There is no record of the response to this proposal but, in practice, the Games continued to grow. Avery Brundage, the IOC President from 1952 to 1972, criticized the huge expenditures at the Grenoble Games of 1968. He wrote: 'the French spent $240 million in connection with these Grenoble Games and when you consider that this was for ten days of amateur sport, it seems to be somewhat out of proportion. With that kind of money involved there is bound to be commercialization of one kind or another' (quoted in Espy, 1979, p. 136). As a result of related controversies, Brundage hoped that the whole Winter Olympics would receive a 'decent burial' at Denver, the original host of the Winter Games of 1976 (Espy, 1979, p. 135).

Nevertheless, the Winter Games has survived and, in terms of its scope and size, it has continued its upward trajectory. Although the Winter Olympics have received much less attention from both the media and from academics, they do have an interesting story to tell. Their inputs and legacies are on a smaller scale than the Summer Olympics but, for the host centres and regions affected, can be no less profound and no less controversial. While the Summer Games focus on the comprehensive regeneration of a specific part of the host city, the Winter Games have a wider regional development focus with an emphasis on the potential of winter sports tourism. Since 1984, the Winter Games have been hosted by centres with populations from 20,000 (Albertville 1994) to 1.1 million (Turin 2006) and averaging about 400,000. By contrast, over the same period, the Summer Games have been hosted by cities with populations from 394,000 (Atlanta 1996) to 12 million (Beijing 2008) averaging about 4.5 million. Overall, the mean size of host centres for the Winter Games is only one-eleventh of that for their summer counterparts. As a result, justification of the Olympic infrastructure of the Winter Games is more difficult because of problems concerning the long-term viability of more specialized facilities dispersed around remote and mountainous rural regions. The infrastructural demands and financial costs of staging the Olympics are felt much more acutely by the hosts of the Winter Games, which is reflected in the substantial levels of public sector support. Carefully integrated and realistic strategies for all aspects of Olympic-related development can produce beneficial legacies for host cities of the Winter Olympics, although these effects are not necessarily experienced equally across social groups within the host communities.

Notes

1. The Nordic Games, founded in 1901, were organized by the Swedish Central Association for the Promotion of Sports. The Holmenkollen Week is a leading Norwegian winter sports event.

2. 'Skeleton' sees competitors drive a one-person sled in a prone, head-first position down an ice track. The availability of the run at St Moritz meant that the event was held there as part of the 1948 Winter Olympics, although it was generally referred to as 'tobogganing'.

3. Olympic Museum Archive, Lake Placid General file 1928–1991. Letter, G. Dewey, Chairman of Lake Placid, to M. Le Comte, President of the International Federation of Bobsleigh and Tobogganing, Paris, 9 November 1929.

4. Olympic Museum Archive, Lake Placid General file 1928-1991. Letter from IOC, 29 March 1930.

5. Overlays are temporary structures such as walkways, which are required for the Games but might be removed after the event itself.

6. A quality benchmark 'first published as a standard in 1996 and it specifies the requirements for an organization's environmental management system. It applies to those environmental aspects over which an organization has control and where it can be expected to have an influence' (BAB, 2010).

7. Olympic Museum Archive, Oslo Correspondence COJO, 1947–1953. Undated draft of suggestion of the Special Committee regarding the reduction of the sports' programme of the Olympic Games, Jeux Olympiques de 1952 Oslo Correspondence COJO, 1947–1953.

Acknowledgements

The author wishes to acknowledge use of the IOC Archives, Olympic Studies Centre, Lausanne for some of the material presented in this chapter. Thanks also to Professor Brian Chalkley for his comments and advice on an earlier draft of this paper and for his collaboration in previous papers. Credit also to Brian Rogers, Tim Absalom and Jamie Quinn in the School of Geography, University of Plymouth for the cartography.

Chapter 4

The Cultural Olympiads: Reviving the Panegyris

Margaret M. Gold and *George Revill*

The process of creating this project has been demanding, full of tension, creativeness and passion, just as when preparing for a sport competition. Our reward will be the emotions sketched on tourists' faces as they discover a land of many contrasting nuances, constantly poised between past and future, nostalgia and innovation. (TOROC, 2005, p. 3)

The Olympic revival in the nineteenth century incorporated a cultural dimension from inception. As noted in chapter 1, the modern Games were always intended by Pierre de Coubertin and his collaborators to be more than a collection of sporting competitions. Rather, they would take up the ethos of the *panegyris* from the classical festival – a festive assembly in which the entire people came together to participate in religious rites, sporting competitions and artistic performance. To recreate this characteristic in a modern idiom represented a considerable challenge, but Coubertin felt that much could be done, first, by adding ceremonies to dignify the Games and so provide some continuity with the past, secondly, by creating festivities to accompany the Games and, thirdly, by introducing artistic competitions as part of the Olympic programme.

This chapter examines the cultural dimension and its growth to embrace not just the Summer but also the Winter Games and the Paralympic Games. It recognizes that while key Olympic rituals and the spectacle of the Opening and Closing Ceremonies are familiar from global media coverage, the other cultural components of the Games are much less well known. Indeed, even in the academic literature, the epithets 'neglected' or 'forgotten' are often used in relation to the cultural programme (Good, 1999; Stanton, 2000). After briefly discussing the nature of the classical heritage, the chapter explores why the founders of the modern Olympic movement gave prominence to the arts and how this was expressed in the Games between 1912 and 1948, with Olympic cities staging competitions in music, literature, painting, sculpture and architecture. Thereafter, as subsequent sections show, the cultural dimension has had a chequered history. The abandonment of artistic competitions in favour of exhibitions took place after 1948, with subsequent reinterpretations of the nature and duration of the associated festivals. The Olympic Charter limits the sporting festival to 16 days, but the only stipulation about the Cultural Festival is that it must run while the Olympic Village is open (IOC, 2004*b*, p. 80) – there are no specific limits about its maximum duration. This has permitted the Olympic Arts Festival to grow in scale, so that since 1992 the summer hosts have planned four-year Cultural Olympiads, with the cultural elements of the Olympics starting to mesh with the wider agendas that interest cities and governments. These agendas, as the above epigram from the organizers of the Turin 'Cultural Olympiad' in 2006 implies, suggest a legacy for cultural tourism, identity building or culture-based urban regeneration strategies.

Reviving the Classical Heritage

Knowledge of classical Greece pervaded Western European thought from the Renaissance onwards. Certainly scholars in the nineteenth century were fully conversant with the works of Homer, Herodotus, Euripides and Sophocles, all of whom explicitly alluded to the harmonious association of art and sport (Nikolaou, 1986, p. 78). There was familiarity with the representation of athletes in Greek art, who were held to embody ideals of beauty. In classical Greek culture there was also widespread appreciation of the importance of sporting competitions (*agones*), with sporting and artistic contests an integral part of religious ritual and ceremonial. The most important sporting events were the four festivals that had emerged as prestigious Pan-Hellenic gatherings by the sixth century BC, attracting Greeks from around the Mediterranean world. These were the Olympic Games at Olympia which honoured Zeus and Hera, the Pythian Games at the oracular shrine at Delphi (Apollo), the Isthmian Games in the Isthmus of Corinth (Poseidon) and the Nemean Games near Mycenae (Zeus). Of these, the Olympic and the Pythian took place every four years, while the Isthmian and Nemean took place biennially. These were *stephanitai* or crown games awarding symbolic prizes, normally wreaths, whereas the numerous other festivals were *chrematitai* or money games with valuable prizes (Golden, 1998, p. 33).

The Olympics were the oldest and most prominent of the four cycles of Games, with the first victors' list dating from 776 BC. They grew from a simple festival involving foot races to incorporate other athletic and equestrian events. By the fourth century BC, for example, they included running races, the pentathlon, wrestling, boxing, pancration (a form of wrestling), hoplites (a race in armour), chariot racing and horseracing with competitions for boys as well as men. Sport itself was encapsulated by ritual supervised by the religious authorities, with athletes and trainers bound by oaths and a truce to enable people to assemble freely at the appointed time. The festival spread over five days with a set programme of sporting competitions, prayers, parades, singing, music, orations, animal sacrifice, feasting, a ceremony on the last day for crowning victors, a final banquet and celebrations (Golden, 1998, p. 20; Toohey and Veal, 2007, p. 10).

In reality, the conditions at Olympia probably presented athletes and visitors alike with a 'notoriously squalid experience' (Spivey, 2004, p. 84), characterized by 'noise, congestion, smell, blood, slaughter, flies and heat'. However, historians favoured a romanticized vision; a picture of athletes, artists and scholars, coming together in an Arcadian setting surrounded by the glory of classical architecture embellished by great art. It was this vision that inspired Coubertin's ideas of beauty, harmony and the arts and their combination in the modern Games. In 1904 he announced that it was time 'to restore the Olympiads to their original beauty' and bring art and sport together (cited in Müller, 2000, p. 612).

The widespread circulation of these ideas, expressed in articles, speeches and memoirs over some 50 years, has ensured that the philosophy of the Games is seen very much as one man's vision – an impression that the IOC and related institutions have done much to perpetuate. Coubertin's writings, in particular, are treated with a reverential mystique, although frequent ambiguities in language mean that it is no straightforward matter to unpick his philosophy (Loland, 1995, p. 63). Moreover, there is a tendency to see Coubertin's views as a revivalist attempt to recreate ancient Olympia rather than to place the project firmly within the movement for social and moral reform or as part of aesthetic modernism, which sought through fusion of sport with genres of experimental performance to create 'new and homogeneous aesthetic spectacle' (Brown, 2001, pp. 96–97). Coubertin, for example, was one of many individuals engaged in creating open-air spectacle intended to unite performer and spectator in a shared experience. He also succeeded in getting figures from the peoples' theatre movement and modern dance to speak at meetings, write in the *Revue Olympique* and cooperate in arranging festivals to celebrate IOC events. They included Maurice Pottecher, founder of the People's theatre in Bussang, the writer Romain Rollard, the poet and playwright René Morax, and Jacques Delacroix, the pioneer of the system of movement known as eurhythmics (Brown, 1996*a*, 1996*b*). Collectively, their ideas had links to the Volkstheater movement in Germany (Bradby and McCormick, 1978, pp. 11–12) and the pageant movement in England (Readman, 2005). So while an alliance between 'athletes, artists and spectators' (Müller, 2000, p. 612) and attempts to create spectacle marrying together drama, music, physical movement and sport may strike an odd chord in the twenty-first century, they meshed squarely with the spirit of their day.

Coubertin encapsulated his concept of the renovated Games in terms of Olympism, which the Olympic Charter defines as:

> a philosophy of life, exalting and combining in a balanced whole the qualities of body, will and mind. Blending sport with culture and education, Olympism seeks to create a way of life based on the joy of effort, the educational value of good example and respect for universal fundamental ethical principles. (IOC, 2010, p. 11)

'Olympism' mediated the cultural construction of the revived Games. Coubertin had realized that restoring the outward form of the Games was comparatively easy, since it only involved restarting the four-year cycle of Olympiads, but re-establishing their deeper meanings was more difficult (Müller, 2000, p. 569). For the ancient Greeks, these meanings centred on the power of religious observance and athleticism to honour the gods (*Ibid.*, p. 566). Coubertin had a utopian belief in the significance of athleticism,[1] but recognized that giving the modern Games a spiritual component was difficult in a world of competing religions. Instead, he suggested inculcating the idea of 'modern patriotism', symbolized by the national flag 'being raised on the pole of victory to honour the winning athlete … would keep the faith alive at the newly rekindled hearth' (*Ibid.*, p. 573).

Olympism would imbue the nascent Games with notions of beauty and harmony, which Coubertin referred to as eurhythmy. This required suitable ceremonial expressions to communicate its essence both to spectators and participants. The diverse array of elements shown in table 4.1, intended to lend dignity to the Games, evolved over time with that objective in mind. Certain elements, like the release of pigeons or doves were part of the ceremonial from the outset; others, such as the judges' oath, did not appear until 1972. Some aspects, such as the Hymn or Anthem, were developed specifically for the Olympics; others, such as the Creed or competition motto, were assimilated from elsewhere.[2]

Classical precedent played an important part in shaping these practices, although more from inventive adaptation of ancient Greek custom than from direct attempts at replication. Perhaps the most revealing conflation of a classical precursor with invented tradition was the physical relaying of the torch to the host stadium and the lighting of the flame, probably the most evocative aspect of the Opening Ceremony. Certainly, the flame had an ancient forerunner that burned on the altar of Zeus at Olympia for the duration of the Games, and torch races, staged at night with winners needing to complete the course with their torches still

Table 4.1. Key aspects of Olympic protocol.

Item	When Introduced
Opening ceremony	1896
Motto: *Citius, Altius, Fortius*	
Pigeons (doves)	
Hymn (anthem)	
March of Nations	1906
Competitors' oath	1920
Olympic flag	
Closing Ceremony	
Olympic flame	1928
Olympic Creed	1932
Olympic torch relay and flame lighting	1936
Informal entry of athletes in closing ceremony	1956
Adoption of the 1896 Olympic Hymn adopted as the official Hymn	1960
Judges' oath	1972

alight, were features of classical Greek sporting competitions (Harlan, 1931, p. 34). Yet although members of the IOC often referred to the 'Olympic flame', initially they used the expression metaphorically, as being akin to the Olympic spirit. It was only at Amsterdam 1928 that the practice of having a physical flame reappeared and the torch relay from Olympia was a wholly invented addition to the ritual, instigated at Berlin 1936 on the suggestion of Carl Diem, General Secretary of the German Olympic Committee.

In the 1960s and 1970s host cities (Tokyo, Mexico City, Munich and Montreal) began introducing folkloric elements into the Opening and Closing Ceremonies to soften the Western military tradition and add some local distinctiveness. The advent of live television transmission turned the ceremonies from a stadium event into global entertainment, providing a vehicle for cities quite literally to perform on a world stage. Moscow 1980 provided no less than an hour of artistic programming in their Opening Ceremony and a further 30 minutes in the Closing Ceremony to reflect the 'multi-faceted life and culture of the Soviet people' (Organizing Committee, 1980, p. 280). Los Angeles responded with a show intended to make Moscow's efforts 'look like chopped liver' (Ueberroth, 1986, p. 301).[3] From this point, organizers employed an ever-increasing vocabulary of choreography, music, dance, aerial ballet, lights, lasers and pyrotechnic effects to create spectacle culminating, in the case of Athens 2004, with the creation of a lake in the centre of the stadium, and at Beijing 2008 with the dramatic precision of 14,000 performers representing the antiquity of China's inventiveness and civilization. Spectators too are drawn into these performances by giving them cards, lights, masks, bells, pipes, whistles and even clothing to create special effects.

The idea of festivities beyond the stadium to accompany the Games was willingly adopted by the organizers of Athens 1896. The 'Receptions Committee', charged with accommodation and hospitality for athletes and visitors, initially came up with grandiose plans to recreate the ancient Panathenian festival. While lack of funds and fears over creating a 'parody of Antiquity' led to the abandonment of these schemes, the organizers provided music, theatre and torchlight processions (Georgiadis, 1996, pp. 83, 90). In that sense, the Greeks did not need Coubertin's advice about the value of festive accompaniments to the Games, since they already regarded such festivities as an integral part of how such events should be staged (*Ibid.*, p. 90). The same formula was repeated on a larger scale for the 1906 Intercalated Games (see chapter 2), with illuminations, processions, concerts, performances of 'Oedipus Rex' in the Panathenian stadium, a Venetian festival in Piraeus, and tours of the Acropolis.

The 1906 Congress

The idea of incorporating arts competitions into the Games required the approval of the IOC. To this end, Coubertin organized an Advisory Conference on the 'Incorporation of the Fine Arts in the Olympic Games and Everyday Life' at the

Comédie-Française in Paris (23–25 May 1906). Its purpose was to complete the Olympic project by discussing the development of art competitions as part of the programme. In particular, it sought to establish a dialogue between sports administrators and the arts world, with the aim of studying 'the extent to which and in what form the arts and literature could be called upon to participate in the modern Olympic Games and, in general, to be associated with the practice of sports in order to benefit from them and ennoble them' (Müller, 2000, p. 608). While only five IOC members attended,[4] the conference attracted around sixty participants mainly from France, of whom half were artists, writers, architects, actors, arts managers and the rest sports administrators. The conference covered architecture, theatre, dance, decoration, literature, music, painting and sculpting, including the subject of music and literature competitions (see table 4.2). Its recommendations favoured establishing competitions in 'the pentathlon of the arts' – architecture, sculpture, painting, literature and musical composition – on an equal footing with the sporting events. The submitted works would need to have been created in the previous four years and inspired by the spirit of sport. They would be judged by an international jury with the winning works performed or exhibited during the Olympic Games (Müller, 1994, p. 74). The conference also agreed that the IOC should encourage artistic and literary performance at sporting events generally, including athletics meetings, automobile shows, horse races and regattas (Brown, 1996b, p. 3). Agreement was also reached over the aesthetic presentation of sports festivals including questions of building design, stadium decoration, ceremonies and parades. In his role as President of the IOC, Coubertin sent a circular conveying the wishes of the Conference to heads of universities, sports federations and clubs in October 1906 urging them to ensure that all major sports events:

> include a literary or artistic component through the addition of poetry competitions or appropriate drama productions, and above all outdoor choral music – stressing, moreover,

Table 4.2. Programme for the Advisory conference circulated by Pierre de Coubertin, 2 April 1906.

	Conference Programme
Dramatic art	Outdoor productions; essential principles; recent writings; sports on stage
Choreography	Processions; parades; group and coordinated movements; dances
Decoration	Stands and enclosures; mats, badges, garlands, draperies, clusters; night festivals; torchlight sports
Literature	Possibility of setting up Olympic literary competitions; conditions for these competitions; sporting emotion, source of inspiration for the man of letters
Music	Outdoor orchestras and choirs; repertoire; rhythms and alternation; fanfares; conditions for an Olympic music competition
Painting	Individual silhouettes and general views; possibility of and conditions for an Olympic painting competition; photography as an aid to the artist
Sculpture	Athletic poses and movements and their relationship with art; interpretation of effort; objects given as prizes; statuettes and medals

Source: Müller (2000, pp. 609–610).

the numerous advantages that sports clubs would enjoy by creating choral sections within them. (Quoted in Müller, 2000, p. 619)

Notably, however, the Congress did not follow the classical precursors in one respect. The ancient festivals contained competitions that involved performance in music, drama and recitation. At first glance, this would have seemed perfectly acceptable, since music competitions were long established by the early twentieth century (e.g. Vaubel, 2005), but this type of competition was not favoured by some of the Congress's participants. For delegates such as the French composer Louis Bourgault-Ducoudray, the aesthetic experience of singing in great choral ensembles was not just about the beauty of the music or the joy of participation but the 'disinterested' nature of the performance where great art alone was the reward. Writing in the *Revue Olympique* in July 1906, he expressed the view that this purity and beauty of purpose would be destroyed by choral competition as 'gold medals or sums of money' would generate 'rivalries and antagonism' – a wholly undesirable state of affairs (Brown, 1996b, p. 6).

Art Competitions and City-wide Festivities

The most celebrated legacy of the Advisory Conference was the art competitions. The Advisory Conference expected that the first art competitions would be introduced at the 1908 Games. The London Organizing Committee, with the help of the Royal Academy, formulated rules and subjects for two classes of painting, two of sculpture and an architecture competition (Cook, 1909, p. 179). The subjects were narrowly defined; for instance, for one of the painting and one of the sculpture categories there was a choice between a triumphal procession or the battle between Greeks and Amazons. For the other painting and sculpture categories, contestants had to select from a modern football match, classical discus throwers, or Hercules and Antaeus. The architecture competition set three briefs: for a swimming bath of given dimensions; a town house containing a gallery for works of art and a private gymnasium; and a sports club for a small town of 20,000 inhabitants (Müller, 2000, p. 624). The intention was to display the entries to all the competitions in a 'gallery attached to the stadium during the games' but, despite this effort, the competitions were 'abandoned' when time ran out (Cook, 1909, pp. 179–181).

The first competition successfully staged by the IOC was for architecture and organized through the College of Architecture in Paris in 1910. The brief was to design a 'modern Olympia' to include 'buildings, porticos, arenas, tracks etc. required for athletic and artistic events included in the programme of the modern Olympic Games, the structures required for spectators, the buildings or spaces required for ceremonies associated with the Games and facilities for administration, athletes etc' (Müller, 2000, p. 625). The competition received nine entries and was won by the Swiss architects Eugéne-Edouard Monod and Alphonse Laverriére

(Müller, 1994, p. 78; Lennartz, 2006a, p. 10). Their achievement is normally counted under the medal-winners for the Stockholm Games in 1912.

The remaining competitions were held in Stockholm, although not without difficulty. The challenge now facing Organizing Committees was how a group of sports administrators could organize art competitions, something deemed outside their expertise. This was invariably solved by involving the local arts establishment in the arrangement of the competitions but, in the case of Stockholm, there was little enthusiasm from the main arts institutions. The Royal Academy, in particular, objected in principle to the idea of competitions with such constricted subject matter, arguing that the results would be merely 'illustrations' rather than works of art (SOC, 1913, p. 807). Their opposition led the organizers to drop the art competitions from their Olympic Programme in February 1912 and allocate 5,000 francs towards their organization should the IOC wish to organize the competition themselves. Coubertin assumed personal responsibility, collecting the competition entries and organizing the judging (although the basis on which this was done is unclear). After the carefully crafted topics of 1908 and 1910, the rules now simply stated that entries had to have some direct connection with sport and should not have been previously published, exhibited or performed (Mallon and Widland, 2002, p. 24; SOC, 1913, p. 808).[5] There were still relatively few entries: four in the painting competition, eight for sculpture and eight for literature (Lennartz, 2006a, p. 10; Masterson, 1986, p. 105). The winning entries went on display in Stockholm during the Games.

The festivities and cultural activities accompanying the games also slowly began to take shape. Given that the White City stadium was adjacent to the spectacular grounds of the Franco-British Exhibition, the organizers of London 1908 did relatively little to arrange entertainments other than plan receptions, balls and banquets for the Olympic family, excursions to places of interest in and around London and provide free tickets for theatres and concerts (Organizing Committee, 1908, pp. 394–398). By contrast, Stockholm 1912 created a substantial cultural programme. The main focus, as noted in chapter 2, was the multipurpose stadium, which featured cultural and sporting displays in the evenings. Elsewhere, the organizers encouraged institutions to offer attractions in the hope of developing Sweden as a tourist destination in the longer term (SOC, 1913, p. 283). The Royal Opera House, normally closed during the summer, was reopened for a programme of opera, music and dance, and the four principal theatres staged a varied season of plays, operettas and comedies (Ibid., p. 827). Museums exhibited traditional Swedish handicrafts, with the open-air Museum of Skansen also hosting theatre productions for visitors during the Games. The Royal Library held an exhibition of manuscripts and books charting the development of sport in the region over five centuries – one of the first examples of a sport-related exhibition staged for the Games (Ibid., p. 829).

The same formula of art competitions and associated city-wide festivities continued for the six summer Games between 1920 and 1948. During this period, the arts competitions attracted growing numbers of entrants to a steadily expanding set of art categories. The organizers of Antwerp 1920 actively promoted the art competitions, but the short time scale available for organizing the first post-war Games led to concern that there would be insufficient entries. They, therefore, organized two art exhibitions at the Royal Museum of Antwerp to run concurrently with the exhibition of competition entries: a retrospective of Belgian art since independence (1830); the other celebrating the emergence of Belgian art from the Great War and documenting the impact of war on contemporary art (Guillain, 2005, p. 27; Lennartz, 2006b).

Paris 1924 saw the arts competitions receive 189 entries from twenty-three countries, with an increasing number from outside Europe including South Africa, Australia, Brazil, Egypt, the United States and Uruguay (Stanton, 2000, p. 78). The organizers publicized the competitions through foreign embassies in Paris, the international press and the personal efforts of the Marquis de Polignac, President of the Commission for Arts and External Relations. Large and eminent juries were assembled to judge the entries. The music competition, for example, had forty-three judges, including Fauré, Ravel, Stravinski, Bartók and Honneger. These far outnumbered the seven entrants, to whom they declined to award any medals (Guillain, 2006, p. 23; Organizing Committee, 1924, p. 604). The artwork was displayed in the Grand Palace between 16 May and 27 July. The organizers complemented the art exhibitions with an international festival of the performing arts, offering mass choirs and instrumental groups, music, folk ballets and plays (Guillain, 2006, p. 22).

Amsterdam 1928 saw 1,150 works submitted from eighteen countries. The organizers re-divided the five art categories into thirteen new categories (three each for music, literature and painting; two each for sculpture and architecture) – the original intention being to display the art work in the planned Cité Olympique complex, which would cater for all the sporting competitions, integrated transport and visitor amenities. It was initially intended that this should include an exhibition hall and a sunken sculpture garden easily accessible from the main stadium (Organizing Committee, 1928, p. 179). For reasons of cost, this plan was abandoned and, instead, the exhibition was staged in the Municipal Museum of Amsterdam – a solution much preferred by the Art Committee who felt a 'well-equipped museum with quieter surroundings' was more suitable despite its distance from the sporting competitions (Ibid., p. 180). Over 10,000 people visited the exhibition during the two months it was open (Bijkerk, 2006, p. 29).

Los Angeles 1932 offered nine competitions (three for painting; two each for sculpture and architecture; and one each for literature and music). Entries were received from twenty-four nations and exhibited in the Los Angeles Museum of History, Science and Art in Exposition Park, augmented by works of art from American Museums (Stanton, 2000, p. 41). Taken together, this produced a substantial exhibition occupying fifteen galleries, the foyer, rotunda and main hall with over 1,100 items on display. Being easily accessible to athletes, officials and spectators, a record number of 384,000 visitors was recorded between 30 July and 31 August.

Berlin 1936 had fifteen art competitions, the most ever held, despite political difficulties which meant that a number of countries, including Britain and France, refused to participate. The exhibition of the submitted work attracted 70,000 visitors (Organizing Committee, 1936, p. 1127). A major innovation was a performance of the medal-winning music compositions during the Games by the Berlin Philharmonic, conducted by the composers. This took place in the 20,000-seater Dietrich Eckart open-air theatre (see chapter 11). Berlin was also noteworthy for the extent of the auxiliary cultural programme. It was not the first Olympic city to stage exhibitions, live performance, folk culture or mass displays during the Games, but it provided a new scale of offering. The extensive programme gave the regime an opportunity to express its cultural ideology in terms of the subject matter and art forms exhibited and to indulge in the spectacular mass displays and epic productions that were hallmarks of its propaganda. Classical music and theatre featured strongly. The German Opera House offered a Wagner Festival and the Dietrich Eckart staged large-scale productions such as Handel's 'Heracles', with 2,500 performers, and a performance of Hamlet with the Prince of Denmark being accorded 'a first class Party funeral', with marching soldiers, trumpets and displays of weapons (Rürup, 1996). By contrast, the dance programme was curtailed on the instructions of Joseph Goebbels, who disapproved of Rudolf Laban's epic 'Von Tauwind under der neuen Freude'.[6]

The largest associated exhibition was 'Deutschland', a propaganda exercise aimed primarily at the 1.3 million German visitors who attended. This, in the words of Goebbels, was intended to show 'a reawakened, reborn nation, pulsating with the desire to create … the eternal Germany'. Besides this, the exhibition programme included two exhibitions with classical themes: 'Sport in Hellenic Times' and an exhibition of casts and reproductions of finds from German archaeological work at Olympia (Organizing Committee, 1936, p. 1132; see also chapter 2). Another exhibition, 'Great Germans in Contemporary Portraits' drew 63,700 visitors to a display of portraiture that featured the 'pioneers of German civilization in foreign countries' – including, ominously, countries soon to be incorporated into the Greater Germany (Ibid., p. 1135).

The Reichssportfeld and particularly the Olympic stadium (see chapter 11 and figure 11.1) were the focus for the associated festive entertainments. The stadium staged spectacular performances during the period of the Games, including the Kraft durch Freude[7] movement's presentation 'Music and Dance of the Peoples', a military concert involving over 2,000 musicians and a festival play entitled 'Olympic Youth' (figure 4.1). This was conceived as 'an artistically constructed echo of the Opening Ceremony' and in many ways presaged the cultural content of contemporary Opening Ceremonies. Organized by Carl Diem, it was performed in the Olympic stadium after the Opening Ceremony and again two days later as a para-Olympic event. Diem used 10,000 performers,

Figure 4.1. 'Festival of Youth', Berlin 1936.

each of whom had signed a declaration claiming their Aryan descent, international celebrities, light, sound, and a musical score written by Carl Orff and Werner Egk to create an imposing spectacle. It presented a series of tableaux weaving Olympic, mediaeval and modern themes: 'Children at play', 'Maidenly Grace', 'Youth at Play in a Serious Mood' and 'Heroic Struggle and Death Lament'. The last of these contained a celebration of sacrificial death for the fatherland, ending with the 'Ode to Joy' from Beethoven's Ninth Symphony, at which point searchlights created a dome of light above the arena and flames of fire leapt up around the edge of the stadium (Organizing Committee, 1936, p. 577).[8]

The Demise of the Art Competitions

After an interval of 12 years, London staged the Summer Games in 1948 and organized fourteen art competitions with National Olympic Committees from the competing nations selecting three entries per class (Organizing Committee, 1948, p. 96). The painting, sculpture and crafts were displayed at the Victoria and Albert Museum in Kensington for a month, but plans for a concert featuring the musical entries were abandoned (Barker, 2006, p. 65). On the basis of this experience, the British Fine Arts Committee made recommendations for future Games, covering the categories of entries, subject matter, and marketing. It was not anticipated at this point that the 1948 arts competitions would be the last (Organizing Committee, 1948, pp. 197–198).

Numerous reasons have been given for the demise of the art competitions (Masterson, 1986; Bandy, 1988; Good, 1999; Guillain, 2005), including organizational problems, the poor quality of the entries, and fundamental conceptual opposition. Certainly the logistics of organizing truly global competitions in the time available had taxed many Organizing Committees, a problem compounded by the challenge of embracing different artistic traditions from around the world, different languages in the literature competitions, and a wide range of subject matter within categories. Olympic Organizing Committees could delegate the running of the competitions to arts administrators, but they still had to work through the National Olympic Committees with their memberships dominated by sports enthusiasts. The Olympic movement rarely succeeded in involving the worldwide artistic community and the number of participating nations remained low – never more than twenty-five. The quality of the competitions, too, was of longstanding concern. They were shunned by the day's leading artists, resulting in incongruence between excellence in the sporting arena and the quality of the work in the artistic competitions. Tellingly, juries often refused to award medals. Over the seven Olympiads, only 145 of the possible 198 medals were awarded (73 per cent). In the case of music, awards were made of only seventeen out of the possible thirty-nine medals.

Two more fundamental factors were also at work. First, analysis by Stanton (2000) of the correspondence, minutes and memoranda produced by the IOC between 1949 and 1954 suggests that the specific reason for the IOC deciding to abandon the arts competitions was due to entrants being professional artists. The view was expressed that the professional status of artists went against the Olympic Charter and that artists would use success in the Olympics to promote their reputations and profit from the increased value of their work. Secondly, it was increasingly recognized that the basic concept was fatally flawed. On the one hand, twentieth-century Western art had moved away from the figurative work beloved by Coubertin and the philhellenes of the modern Olympic movement. On the other hand, it had become clear that there was no longer that engagement between artists and sport that was so central to classical Greek artistic culture. No amount of rhetoric on the union of body, mind and beauty could reverse that trend (Guillain, 2005, p. 29).

The first signs of change came at a small IOC sub-committee meeting in New Orleans in January 1949, which was called to revise the IOC Charter. It recommended that medals no longer be awarded for art competitions and that exhibitions of art be held instead. Although approved at the next full IOC meeting, the decision produced an outcry from those fiercely loyal to Coubertin's original vision for the arts and those convinced that exhibitions would fail without the incentive of medals to encourage participation. This, in turn, led to the appointment of a committee to reconsider the matter. Its report led to the reinstatement of the arts competitions at the IOC meeting in May 1951.

This *volte-face* left the Helsinki Organizing Committee in an invidious position. They had earlier campaigned for the retention of the art competitions, but now had to request permission to continue with the art exhibitions because there was insufficient time to revert back to organizing competitions (Stanton, 2000, pp. 234–236). In practice, however, there was little material difference since the exhibition model used at Helsinki 1952 was identical to the old competitions. The organizers requested that the National Olympic Committees collect contemporary work and submit it for display. Twenty-three countries responded and 181 works were submitted, but the resulting exhibition was deemed disappointing with only 5,000 visitors. The organizers awarded artists a diploma as a memento of their participation (Organizing Committee, 1952, p. 110).

The issue of the art competitions was raised at the next IOC meeting in April 1953. The IOC President Avery Brundage repeated his views on the evils of professionalism in the arts, but admitted that the exhibitions in Helsinki had met with 'relatively little success' (Stanton, 2000, p. 242). The meeting commissioned another inquiry into the art competitions but, before it reported, Brundage circulated a powerfully worded letter to IOC members in favour of exhibition programmes but suggesting a new model. These would be 'special exhibitions of outstanding works of art dealing with sport from the museums of the country where the games are being staged, or even borrowed from other countries' (*Ibid.*, p. 245). The IOC meeting in Athens in May 1954 supported this suggestion, which the commission of inquiry also recommended, although the link with sport was dropped. Brundage concluded the discussion by saying that this 'new formula' would ensure exhibitions of the highest standard and that if the Games went to Vienna there would be the best music in the world, in Russia the best ballet, in 'Italy or, when we add Greece, we have the possibility to see the most marvellous works of classical art in the world' (quoted in Stanton, 2000, p. 256). The Olympic Charter was then amended to read:

> The Organising Committee of the Olympic Games shall arrange exhibitions and demonstrations of the host country's art (architecture, literature, music, painting, sculpture, photography, and sport philately) and fix the dates during which these exhibitions and demonstrations shall take place. The programme may also include theatrical, ballet, opera, performances or symphony concerts.
>
> This section of the programme shall be of an equal standard and held concurrently and in the same vicinity as the sports events. It shall receive full recognition in the publicity released by the OCOG. (Cited by Masterson, 1986, p. 108)

Olympic Arts Festival, 1956–1988

The Olympic Charter now gave Organizing Committees greater flexibility in devising the artistic programme for the Games. There was no longer a requirement for the art content to have a specific sports connection – although this remained a recurrent theme over the years – but rather placed emphasis on the Olympic principle of excellence. Host cities and nations would put the best of their arts and artists on display, which in turn opened up a new role for the Olympic Arts Festival as a showcase for the host city and nation and as an event that meshed well with urban policy goals of host cities. In particular, the Olympic Arts Festivals contributed to urban and national agendas in four respects.

The first, present since the earliest Games, found Organizing Committees using the Olympics as an opportunity to show the cultivated nature of the host society. This invariably gave prominence to high art, with visitors offered a programme that included opera, symphony concerts, ballet and classical theatre. This expanded over time to incorporate programmes intended to show the vibrancy of the contemporary arts scene in music, visual arts, sculpture and new media. For non-Western countries with different artistic traditions, there was the added concern that their culture was undervalued, misunderstood or simply ignored by Western audiences. Therefore, for example, the Organizing Committee for Tokyo 1964 carefully crafted their Art Festival to introduce their culture to an international audience (Aso, 2002, pp. 18, 33). Tokyo also saw attempts to reinforce a 'particularistic Japanese national identity' and sense of community in the aftermath of war, occupation and economic change by means of a powerful portrayal of traditional arts and culture for the *domestic* audience (*Ibid.*, pp. 19, 33)

Secondly, the Olympic Arts Festival could also serve the goals of political ideology. Mexico City 1968, for example, sought to advance the interests of the developing world by making the Cultural Festival more inclusive, particularly embracing nations that did not traditionally perform well in the sporting competitions. This would, in the words of the Chairman of the Organizing Committee, 'promote mutual understanding and respect, brotherhood and friendship between nations and genuine international accord'. The IOC congratulated Mexico City 'for expanding the cultural programme … in such a significant manner' (Organizing Committee, 1968, p. 272). These aims were subsequently incorporated into the Olympic Charter (IOC, 2004b, p. 70) to encourage host nations to broaden the content away from the purely 'national' character stipulated in 1954. The new rule 44 stated:

> The OCOG must organise a programme of cultural events which shall be submitted to the IOC for approval.
>
> This programme must serve to promote harmonious relations, mutual understanding and friendship among the participants and others attending the Olympic Games.

During the 1980s, a succession of Olympic Arts Festivals had openly ideological goals. The intent behind the Moscow Olympic Arts Festival in 1980 was to acquaint the visitor with 'the heritage and achievements of the Soviet multinational culture' (Organizing Committee, 1980, p. 402). The Cultural Festival at Los Angeles 1984 was accused of being 'part of a wider entertainment and tourist programme with strong profit-making elements' (Nikolaou, 1986, p. 17). Seoul 1988 saw South Korea use the Arts Festival as an exercise in cultural diplomacy by forging links with states that had previously refused them diplomatic recognition. The presence of the Moscow Philharmonic and the Bolshoi Ballet, for instance, was of singular importance to the Koreans (Organizing Committee, 1989, p. 429).

Thirdly, the Arts Festivals could address economic development and urban regeneration. There was acceptance by the 1980s of the idea that the cultural sector had a role to play in the urban economy and could contribute to solving economic and social problems. The Olympic Art Festivals provided the catalyst to develop the cultural infrastructure by building or refurbishing exhibition and performance spaces, usually accompanied by measures to upgrade the urban environment to provide the basis for developing cultural and business tourism in the longer term. The first signs of this activity were witnessed in 1968 when both Mexico City and Grenoble gained new arts infrastructures, but by 1990s the expectation was that cities would make major investments in their arts sectors in preparing for the Games.

Finally, the Olympic Arts Festivals addressed the growing arts agenda that developed after the Second World War. From the 1950s, governments increasingly intervened in the arts sector with regard to audience development, access, and inclusion. These concerns, in turn, began to permeate the Olympic Arts Festivals. Moreover, policies to support traditional culture or intangible heritage could also be accommodated within these festivals. A re-evaluation of indigenous cultures, often previously denigrated and disregarded, can be seen developing within the Arts Festivals in Mexico (1968), Canada (1976, 1988 and 2010), and Australia (2000).[9] The Olympic Arts Festivals also offered opportunities to develop the cultural sectors within cities and nations through developing skills and expertise, consolidating art networks, developing partnerships – particularly with arts organizations in other Olympic cities – and establishing further arts festivals which could be continued after the Games. The results often left their mark not only in Olympic terms but in terms of museum and curatorial practice.[10]

Table 4.3 shows the considerable variation in the Olympic Arts Festivals between 1956 and 1988. They could run from a matter of weeks to a year. Content might be predominantly national (as at Melbourne 1956, Tokyo 1964 or Montreal 1976) or international, as with Mexico City 1968 or Seoul 1988 where ninety-seven and seventy-three nations, respectively, participated (Organizing Committee, 1968, p. 275; 1989, p. 429). The Festival might be confined to the Olympic City or spread to other locations, an idea that has gained ground since being pioneered by Mexico City 1968. The range of art forms included reflects the host nation's interests and agendas, with the ever-present content of elite art steadily being complemented by expressions of folk and popular culture. Open-air street entertainments have steadily become an important element in animating the city around the Olympic venues (as at Munich 1972, Montreal 1976 or Seoul 1988). Some cities have tried to retain the link between art and sports (including Rome 1960, Mexico City 1968 and Los Angeles 1984), while others ignored it (Tokyo 1964 and Montreal 1976). The one trend universally apparent was that the scale of the offering steadily increased in the period between 1956 and 1988. By the 1980s, the gigantism of the Cultural Festival had become established with the audience numbers being counted in their millions.

Table 4.3. Olympic Arts Festivals, Summer Games 1952–1988.

Olympiad	Length of Cultural Festival	Content and Themes	Highlights
Helsinki 1952	4 weeks	International exhibitions of architecture, painting, graphic arts, sculpture, literature, music	Submitted musical compositions performed in a concert
Melbourne 1956	4 weeks	National culture	Exhibition: *Showcase of Australian Art*
Rome 1960	6 months★ 3 weeks	National culture with an emphasis on history; sporting references in exhibition programme	Exhibition: *Sport in History and Art*; Medieval historical pageants
Tokyo 1964	7 weeks	Japanese high art and traditional culture.	Exhibition: *Ancient Japanese Art Treasures*
Mexico City 1968	1 year	International; high art and indigenous culture Nation-wide celebration of culture	World Folklore Festival Ballet of the Five Continents; *International Exhibition of Folk Art Exhibition of selected works of world art*; New Fire ritual at Teotihuacán
Munich 1972	3 months★ 6 weeks	*Olympic Summer* International; high art and folk culture	Exhibition: *World Cultures and Modern Art*; International folklore festival; Avenue of Entertainment: live performance in the Olympic Park
Montreal 1976	4 weeks	National – showcase for Canadian provincial culture	Exhibition: *Mosaicart* – Canadian visual arts; *Artisanage* – craft demonstration; Canadian festival of popular arts; The Celebration – live outdoor performance
Moscow 1980	1 year★ 5 weeks	National, mass participation, high art and folk culture: national art of the peoples of the USSR	Exhibition: *One hundred masterpieces from the Hermitage Collection*; Exhibition: *Moscow in Russian and contemporary art*; Exhibition: *Sport – Ambassador of Peace*; Opera and classical music
Los Angeles 1984	10 weeks	7 weeks: international festival for domestic consumption 3 weeks LA and US culture for international Olympic audience	Exhibition: *A day in the country: impressionists in the French landscape*; Performing arts programme; Art commissioning programme
Seoul 1988	7 weeks	Korean high culture and traditional culture for an international audience; international artists and companies; contemporary culture for domestic audience	International festivals in folk culture, dance, theatre, music, song; The Olympiad of art – contemporary sculpture park; International modern art competition; Street festivals and Han River Festival

★ Length of cultural festival including exhibition runs and pre-Games programme.
Source: Compiled from official reports of Organizing Committees.

The Cultural Olympiads, 1992–2004

This era came to an end at Barcelona 1992, where the organizers changed the cultural agenda for the Summer Games by introducing a four-year Cultural Olympiad that culminated in an Olympic Arts Festival to coincide with the Games. For Barcelona, the official reason for the innovation was to develop the cultural infrastructure, demonstrate the richness of its cultural heritage and to make the city more attractive for visitors (COOB, 1992, I, p. 287). From this juncture, all the Summer Games staged Cultural Olympiads, although these longer festivals pose challenges for cities in terms of creative programming. The Cultural Olympiad starts well before the Olympic infrastructure is in place and only three years after the successful bidding process – a relatively short time horizon by the standards of the cultural sector. Moreover, it is difficult to maintain the Olympic connection in the cultural events throughout the four-year period particularly in the light of perennially poor marketing (García, 2001, p. 198). Funding has also been problematic with Organizing Committees tempted to retrench by cutting the cultural budget, and art events have greater difficulty attracting sponsorship compared with the sports competitions. Barcelona 1992, Atlanta 1996 and Sydney 2000 suffered badly in this respect, with Atlanta having its cultural budget cut from $40 million to $25 million, offset only in part by $8 million from sponsorship (Good, 1999, p. 165; García, 2001, p. 156). The goals of the Olympiads tend to mix a strong domestic arts-related agenda of audience development and capacity-building in the arts sector with the desire to have an international dimension that promotes the city's Olympic and cultural role outside the host nation. The four-year format allows cities to take the Cultural Olympiad out to the participating nations with events and exhibitions staged abroad.

By and large, cities have tended to develop themed annual festivals (see table 4.4), although both Atlanta 1996 and Athens 2004 modified their programmes after the bidding process. In the case of Barcelona 1992, the series of annual festivals leading to the Olympic Arts Festival was said to have increased the local arts audience and introduced them to more challenging work (COOB, 1992, I, p. 323). The 1992 Olympic Arts Festival was designed for the Games' audience and had three main themes, mixing historical heritage with contemporary and performing arts.[11]

Atlanta's four-year Cultural Olympiad had the twin aim of celebrating Southern culture while including a major initiative to develop a proper recognition of African American art. It presented both traditional and contemporary work and brought international artists to Atlanta from the five continents – symbolizing the Olympic rings. The organizers hoped that Atlanta would ultimately be 'recognized as an international centre for innovative arts, culture, and entertainment' (Organizing Committee, 1996, p. 146). In the years leading up to the Games, a series of multi-year projects and international festivals covering film, drama, and international culture under the title of 'Arts Atlanta: Preludes to the Centennial

Olympic Arts Festival' was presented (*Ibid.*, p. 148). The Olympic Arts Festival itself, with its themes of Southern celebration and international connections, lasted 64 days and attracted over 2.6 million visitors: an attendance figure assisted by concentrating the programme in the Olympic Ring (where thirty-seven of the forty-one venues were located). In particular, two million visitors attended the 'Southern Crossroads Festival' in Centennial Park (figure 4.2), where 1,114 performers entertained the crowds on three stages and a demonstration area was provided for local artisan craftsmen (*Ibid.*, p. 152).[12] Although the press grumbled that the cultural dimension had been neglected, seemingly confirmed by a leaked letter from a member of the Cultural Olympiad Advisory Board complaining of lack of support for his committee (Yarborough, 2000, p. 130), the festival's success in attracting visitors seemingly belied that view. The exhibition 'Five Rings of Passion' at the High Museum of Art remains a landmark in Olympic Arts Festival planning, despite only receiving approval to proceed nine months before the Games. Organized around five themes – the emotions of love, anguish, awe, triumph and joy – and with works from around the world, it managed to combine an Olympic theme with important artworks in a readily accessible location.

The Cultural Olympiad planned for Sydney 2000, as chapter 15 makes clear, was at pains to stress Australia's multicultural character. Four major festivals were staged whose themes ranged from considering Australia's place in the world at the Millennium, to showcasing the way that its environment has impacted on culture and the arts, to highlighting Australian artistic and cultural achievements and celebrating indigenous culture (SOCOG, 2000*b*, p. 303). The first of the festivals, 'The Festival of the Dreaming' was in many ways the most ground-

Figure 4.2. Centennial Park, Atlanta 1996. Olympic rings.

breaking. Staged over six weeks in Sydney in the autumn of 1997, it was Australia's first major celebration of Aboriginal art and it involved more than 700 indigenous artists. These came principally from Australia, but contributions from other nations (New Zealand, Canada, Greenland, the United States, Korea and Oceania) made connections with indigenous experience. In the light of Australia's previous treatment of Aboriginal peoples, this opening festival of the Olympiad assumed great symbolic importance, particularly as it was held at the Sydney Opera House – a cathedral of Australian high art. By contrast, the subsequent annual festivals were hit by budget cuts and fell so far short of their desired impact that Cashman (2006, p. 82) considered them 'second or even third-tier'.

The six-week Olympic Arts Festival at Sydney 2000 presented a range of national, international and indigenous culture. It attempted to reconnect art with sport with, for example, the exhibition '1000 Years of Olympic Games' featuring artefacts loaned from Greece. Overall, the festival attracted criticism for its elite art emphasis in contrast to the *LiveSites!* programme of popular entertainment, run by Sydney City Council, that animated the city streets and Olympic venues and had a more immediate impact and appeal (see chapter 15).

Greece was anxious to leave a cultural legacy to the Olympic movement arguing that while for other host cities the Cultural Olympiads were secondary to the sport, for Greece it was 'part of its essence'. To this end, in 1988 an agreement between the IOC, UNESCO and the Hellenic Ministry of Culture established an International Foundation of the Cultural Olympiad with its headquarters at Olympia. This would promote understanding and respect between cultures and promote global values by developing links with participating nations. However, the subsequent absence of any substantial references to this organization either within the IOC or beyond shows that little has yet occurred that represents concrete outcome from this initiative.

The four-year Cultural Olympiad, which adopted the title of 'For a Culture of Civilizations', succeeded in commissioning new work, staging performances including classical drama in historic settings, exhibitions and conferences throughout Greece and internationally. This culminated in 'Athens 2004 – Culture' which ran from March to September 2004. The renovation of museums, the creation of new contemporary art spaces and the beautification of central Athens, including the restoration of classical heritage sites and a large-scale pedestrianization programme, have left Athens with a legacy on which to build cultural and conventional tourism (see chapter 16).

Beijing initiated its Cultural Olympiad in September 2003 within two months of winning the bid. This was subsequently a series of three-week festivals, each with a particular theme (see table 4.4), which were staged from June 2004 onwards; timed to start on 23 June (International Olympic Day) and finish on or around 13 July the anniversary of the day Beijing won the Games. They comprised performances, exhibitions, film, competitions, symposia, sport, Opening and Closing ceremonies. These festivals were aimed principally at a national audience. They had a strong educational element through developing knowledge of the Olympic Games and its history, launching various aspects of the Games (such as the slogan and Olympic Songs) and generally building up public expectation and participation. The final Cultural Festival in 2008 ran from 23 June to 16 September 2008 and boasted a 200-page programme showcasing the 'special charms and wisdom of the ancient Chinese culture, modern cultural innovation and the colourful diversity of its ethnic cultures' but with over 300 performances, involving 20,000 artists from over eighty countries, exhibitions and historic sites in Beijing and the co-host cities this was by no means confined to Chinese culture (BOCOG, 2008, pp. 4–5). In addition the programme included twenty-four live sites (referred to officially as 'Cultural Squares') around the city with big screens for sports coverage but also providing live entertainment, exhibitions and refreshments, with eighteen of these continuing during the Paralympic Games.

For the overseas visitor to Beijing during the Games, the Cultural Olympiad was less visible. The cultural programme was readily available on the Beijing

Table 4.4. Thematic annual programmes of the Cultural Olympiads: Barcelona 1992 to Beijing 2008.

Barcelona 1992	Atlanta 1996	Sydney 2000	Athens 2004	Beijing 2008
1988 Cultural Gateway 1989 The year of culture and sport	1993 Olympic wonderland: encounters with Norwegian culture; Salute to Lausanne; Mexico! A cultural tapestry	1997 Festival of the Dreaming	2001 Man and space★	2003: Charming Beijing, Cultural Olympics 2004: From Olympia to the Great Wall 2005: Launch of the Olympic slogan: One World One Dream
1990 The year of the arts	1994 Celebrate Africa 1994–1995 One hundred years of world cinema	1998 A Sea Change	2002 Man and the earth★	2006: Experience the Civilization and Enjoy the Olympic Games
1991 The year of the future	1995 Nobel Literature Laureates gathering	1999 Reaching the World	2003 Man and the spirit★	2007: One World One Dream: I participate, I contribute, I enjoy
1992 Olympic Arts Festival	1996 Southern Connections; International Connections	2000 The Harbour of Life: Olympic Arts Festival	2004 Man and man★ Olympic Arts Festival: ATHENS 2004-Culture	2008: Rendezvous in Beijing 6th Beijing Olympic Cultural Festival
3 months	9 weeks	6 weeks	7 months	12 weeks

★ Athens Bid Document, Vol III, p. 4.

Source: Compiled from Official Reports of Organizing Committees and Bid Documents.

2008 website and a published version was distributed inside the Olympic Green and the Olympic Village. Beyond these areas, the guide was not on offer at city information points and indeed many volunteers were not familiar with the concept of a Cultural Olympiad (García, 2008, p. 27).[13] The Cultural Squares programme, although much larger in scope than in Sydney's 2000 programme, did not succeed in animating the city to the same extent. A combination of dispersed locations, cultural difference and the inability of foreign tourists to obtain the free tickets and find the sites seem to have conspired to leave them 'deserted' for most of the day. García (*Ibid*., p. 28) contrasts this with the unofficial animation of Tiananmen Square and other tourist centres where athletes, visitors and Chinese gathered to celebrate in traditional Olympic style.

Winter Games Olympic Arts Festivals, 1956–2006

As the previous chapter showed, the Winter Games started as relatively small sporting festivals in ski resorts where the emphasis was on sports facilities and accommodation. Organizing Committees routinely offered programmes of receptions, dinners and the occasional concert for the IOC and officials, but there were no expectations or requirements that competitions, exhibitions or arts festivals would be staged. The first winter host to provide an artistic programme was Cortina d'Ampezzo 1956 where lectures, concerts and exhibitions, including an exhibition on the history of winter sports, were held in the Circolo Artistico 'for those in search of more intellectual amusements of an artistic nature' (CONI, 1956, p. 255). Grenoble 1968, however, was the first occasion on which a Winter Olympic Arts Festival developed along the lines of the Summer Festivals and addressed a similar agenda. Here, the organizers offered a programme that embraced ballet, theatre, classical music, popular music and film during a 19-day festival and used the event as a catalyst to build a Civic Cultural Centre. Sapporo 1972 featured a 19-day festival concentrated on Japanese culture. Innsbruck 1976 staged a 'simple Games' in an effort to counteract the escalation of previous years, but the following Games at Lake Placid 1980 laid emphasis on the performing arts, particularly newly commissioned work. Sarajevo 1984 boasted the 'most versatile and richest programme of this kind that had ever accompanied the Winter Olympic Games' (Organizing Committee, 1984, p. 138).

Table 4.5 provides details of the Olympic Arts Festivals from Calgary 1988 to Turin 2006. Calgary was the largest city to host a Winter Games to that point and staged the most comprehensive programme using its wealth of theatres, concert halls, galleries and museums (COWCOG, 1988, p. 273). It covered all the arts including literature and its Native Participation Programme was designed to involve Canada's Aboriginal peoples by presenting aspects of their traditional and contemporary culture (*Ibid*., p. 271). By the 1990s it was the norm to have an international dimension in the programming so that even cities like Salt Lake City 2002, with its emphasis on American and Western culture, had international

Table 4.5. Olympic Arts Festivals, Winter Games 1988–2010.

Olympiad	Length of Cultural Festival	Content and Themes	Highlights
Calgary 1988	5 weeks	Canadian high arts; Canadian artists; indigenous traditional and contemporary culture	Native participation programme; Exhibition: *The spirit sings: artistic traditions of Canadian First Peoples*; dance; Literature; Wintershow'88 winter carnival; rodeo
Albertville 1992	1988–1992 Youth of the World Festival 5 months	French cultural tradition: contemporary art; international artists; events held throughout Rhône-Alpes and W Europe with the theme of breaking down international barriers	Performing arts; contemporary dance; music; fringe theatre
Lillehammer 1994	2 years OAF 5 weeks	National and regional Norwegian culture and international art; traditional and experimental art, high arts and informal Winterland festivals held in past Olympic cities	Cultural programme surrounding the torch relay; Informal cultural programme; Sami cultural programme; classical music; popular music exhibition *Slowly we won the land*; Winterland; *Edvard Munch's monumental projects 1909–1930*
Nagano 1998	1 year OAF 3 months	*One heart – one world* Japanese traditional culture, high arts, events taking place throughout Japan International artists and repertoire	Classical music, orchestral, opera, traditional; Children's art and performance; Traditional drama
Salt Lake City 2002	5 weeks	*Light the Fire Within* National art and culture; the American West International artists	Newly commissioned performing arts, new commissions e.g. *Here .. Now* tribute to Florence Griffith-Joyner; Exhibitions: *Declaration of Independence; Discover Navajo: people of the fourth world; Chihuly 2002*
Turin 2006	6 months	'Open to change and exchange'; Italian high art, traditional art and culture of the alps; international artists	Contemporary art and performance; Italian film; museum collections; Exhibitions: *Leonardo da Vinci masterpieces on show; Inuit and people from the ice*
Vancouver 2010	2008: 7-week Cultural Festival February–March 2009: 7-week Cultural Festival February–March 2010: 9 weeks: January–March	'Touch the soul of the nation; inspire the world'; Celebration of the contemporary imagination: *Find It, Live It*	CODE Cultural Olympiad's Digital Edition *Fiddle and the Drum* (contemporary ballet based on Joni Mitchell's folk and rock songs); Neil Young tribute concert; opera *Nixon in China*; exhibition – Leonardo da Vinci's artistic and scientific investigations; First Nations art forms

Source: Compiled from Official Reports of Organizing Committees and TOROC (2005).

artists in its festival. The length of the festivals varied considerably from Calgary's five weeks to Lillehammer's two years. A number of hosts tried to make a wider geographical impact as in the case of Albertville 1992 with events throughout the Rhône-Alpes, and further afield including Paris, Barcelona, Lausanne and Antwerp (Organizing Committee, 1992, p. 476). Lillehammer 1994 staged Winterland Exhibitions in the Olympic cities of Atlanta, Tokyo, Barcelona and Munich presenting Norwegian music, theatre, literature, film and Sami culture. Nagano 1998 staged a year-long festival with events nationwide.

The Winter Games in Turin saw full convergence with the strategies adopted for the cultural programme by host cities of the Summer Games. With a population of over 850,000 and some two million in its urban region, Turin was the largest city yet to have hosted the Winter Games. It also staged the most dispersed Games given the distances between Turin, where the ice events were held, and the snow sports venues in the mountains 35–50 miles (55–80 kilometres) distant. The city aimed to rebrand itself as the 'Capital of the Alps', an ambitious description given the potential competition and its abiding reputation as an industrial city. It also sought to assert its role as a centre for culture, leisure, cultural tourism, business tourism, recreation and higher education, to capitalize on its existing cultural facilities, and to promote an urban regeneration agenda in the face of the dramatic restructuring of the car industry. The Cultural Festival – Italyart – fitted that agenda. Its organizers sought to 'promote, together with the historic heritage, the contemporary image of a territory open to experimentation, innovation and research' (TOROC, 2005, p. 3). The official programme (TOROC, 2005) listed twenty-five visual art exhibitions, seven dance and theatre productions, ten music productions, a festival of Italian cinema, a series of literary dinners, and eleven historical and social events. In addition there were 126 events listed under the title 'Dedicated to Turin 2006', the result of an invitation to cultural organizations to contribute events and performances to the programme. These included exhibitions, performances, lectures, thematic tours and traditional culture. The sweep of the festival included Italian and international artists, the Occitan culture of the Alpine valleys and the Inuit of the Arctic, life in ancient Egypt and masterpieces of Leonardo da Vinci, 'La Bohème', and Nordic myth.

Vancouver in its bid document for the 2010 Winter Games promised to host the first four-year Olympiad. In the event financial considerations reduced this to three festivals, with two seven-week winter festivals in 2008 and 2009 and a 60-day festival in 2010 – still the longest winter Cultural Olympiad to date. The cultural programme combined community arts with higher-profile events that featured national and international stars. There were numerous specially commissioned works, with particular attention given to representations of Canadian identity. One project indicative of this approach was CODE (Cultural Olympiad's Digital Edition) – a project that invited Canadians to submit photographs that would create 'a grassroots portrait of the country' but also aimed to harness the power of digital technology to allow audiences to interact with artists with the slogan: Connect.

Create. Celebrate. It also acted as a portal to live entertainment, visual artists and filmmakers (Vancouver2010, 2010). In terms of attendance, the Vancouver Art Gallery achieved the highest visitor figures in its history (95,000 visitors over 17 days) by means of free admission and two blockbuster shows: 'Leonardo de Vinci: the mechanics of man' showing works on loan from the Royal Collection; and 'Visions of British Columbia: a landscape manual', displaying paintings mainly from museum collections (BC Arts News, 2010).

London 2012

London promised a four year nation-wide celebration of innovation and inspiration and a 'world cultural capital celebrating youth and world culture' (LOCOG, 2004, p. 171). It was launched in September 2008 within two weeks of the Closing Ceremony of the Paralympic Games in Beijing. The Cultural Olympiad was conceived in terms of a series of aims, values and themes (see table 4.6) whereby

Table 4.6. The aims, values and themes of the London Cultural Olympiad 2008–2012.

Aims	Values – for everyone	Themes – bring culture and sport together
Encourage and welcome involvement from communities across the UK including London	Celebrating London and the UK and inviting the world to share the event with us	Encourage audience participation
Leave a lasting legacy that improves cultural life	Inspiring and involving young people to unlock their creativity	Make public spaces exciting through street theatre, public art, circus skills and live big screen sites
Showcase excellence in the performing arts and creative industries as well as sport	Using cultural and sports participation, audience development, urban regeneration, tourism, international links and other key strands of the cultural Olympiad to build a meaningful legacy	Raise environmental sustainability, health and well-being issues through culture and sport
Introduce young people to the UK's many artistic communities and those from around the world Promote London as a major cultural capital		Honour and share the values of the Olympic and Paralympic Games Create unique collaborations and innovations between communities and cultural sectors
Heighten economic regeneration and encourage tourism in the UK through the work of creative industries		Support the learning, skills and personal development of young people through links to our education programme
Incorporate the Olympic values of 'excellence, respect and friendship' and the Paralympic vision to 'empower, achieve, inspire'.		

Source: London 2012 (2010) http://www.london2012.com/get-involved/cultural-olympiad/values-and-themes/index.php.

individual projects are to address all three values and at least three of the themes. The programme has two distinct strands – a series of major projects offering world-class cultural events with public funding and a nationwide festival with an emphasis on the local and regional, co-ordinated by Creative Programmers appointed in the regions during 2008. These projects need to find their own funding streams. The launch of the 'Inspire Mark' in 2008 introduced a way of identifying and branding cultural events that would form part of the Olympiad (LOCOG, 2008, p. 3). To date there has been a range of cultural events taking place around the United Kingdom and two weekend festivals; one during the launch weekend in 2008 and a second in July 2009, with further festivals in 2010 and 2011. These are designed to raise awareness and encourage mass participation.

London is not a city that needs much additional arts infrastructure or major refurbishments as has been the case with many other cities preparing to host the Cultural Olympiad. Similarly, a modicum of extra pedestrianization or façade-painting will not make much of a difference to a city of London's size. Rather, the aim is to emphasize innovation, creativity, participation and new ways of working. One example of this is the Museums, Libraries and Archives Major Project: Stories of the World. This programme, which will run from 2011 to 2012 and involve fifty-nine museums across the United Kingdom, will mount exhibitions curated by young people – many from the cultures that are represented in Britain's museums – in a project that reconnects objects with the communities from which they come (MLA, 2009). This fits very clearly within the museum world's agenda of connecting with its audiences and breaking down traditional relationships between experts in museums and their visitors.

The evolution so far of London's Cultural Olympiad has not been smooth. Dogged by resignations, charges of inertia, concerns about funding and public ignorance, and less-than-enthusiastic media, the winter of 2009–2010 saw the appointment of Tony Hall as Chair of the Board and Ruth Mackenzie as Artistic Director, who initiated an editing and reshaping process. One of its first results is the announcement that the summer 2012 programme will focus on a 12-week summer festival running from 21 June to 9 September (Brown, 2010).

Conclusion

This chapter has traced the circuitous path by which a cultural dimension has been incorporated into the modern Olympics. The Arts Festivals have absorbed the more haphazard festivities and cultural programmes of earlier times, and exhibitions have replaced the competitions. There has been a measure of convergence between the Summer Games and the Winter Games as winter hosts have taken on the organization of Olympic Arts Festivals and in some cases attempted longer festivals. Sochi 2014 intends to be the first winter host to stage a five-year Cultural Olympiad with a series of art-themed festivals: 2010 the year of cinema; 2011 the year of theatre; 2012 the year of music; 2013 the year of museums; and the final festival in 2014 during the Games themselves (Sochi2014, 2010). The Arts Festivals now extend past the Olympic Games to embrace the Paralympics, whose athletes, officials and spectators can now benefit from the Olympic ambience of the host city as never before.

Despite this apparent success, the cultural dimension of the Games still struggles to gain significant international or even public recognition. For most people the Games remain essentially a sporting festival and they are unaware of the cultural aspect. The ideal of uniting art and sport has not been achieved and they remain separate entities. García (2002*a*, p. 13) blames this on the poor integration of the cultural programme in the overall organization of the Games and its consequent inability to attract the attention of Olympic sponsors who are naturally taken with the opportunities afforded by the ceremonies, torch relay and sporting events (*Ibid.*, p. 12). Yet research also suggests a deeper problem, as epitomized by the fact that journalists at the Main Press Centre and the International Broadcasting Centre in Sydney 2000 were either unaware or uninterested in the cultural information that these centres distributed (García, 2002*b*, p. 11; see also chapter 15). Sydney set up a Non-Accredited Media Centre that could more easily deal with non-sporting material but this simply reinforced the idea that the cultural programme was set apart from the sporting event (*Ibid.*, p. 12).

For the host cities themselves, the Cultural Olympiad and Olympic Arts Festivals now take their place alongside other strategies in efforts to rebrand the Olympic city, create a platform for growth in cultural tourism and improve the quality of life for residents. Certainly many of the Games now leave a legacy of cultural venues and improved urban infrastructure that benefits residents and visitors alike but, in terms of rebranding, it is the Opening and Closing Ceremonies with their artistic segments that have far greater impact in projecting the image of city and nation to the world than the largely overlooked arts offering.

As far as the arts community is concerned, Cultural Olympiads have provided opportunities to stage high-quality exhibitions and performances, commission new work and develop partnerships. While the high art origins of the festivals are still much in evidence, there has been a broadening of the art forms on offer and the animation of the city by means of live performance has created an atmosphere of inclusiveness. This has been achieved despite the fact that such festivals remain particularly vulnerable to budget cuts, when the inevitable escalation of expenditure on the Olympic infrastructure results in the need for cost savings elsewhere.

For arts organizations, these festivals can be a risky business. They bring visitors to town, but the competition for their time and money is intense. All benefit if cultural tourism is raised by the exposure of the city, region and nation in the long term but evidence of the short-term impact of the Arts Festivals on their operations is mixed. Scott (2004, p. 36) found some pessimism among arts managers in Australia and New Zealand about the impact of sporting mega-events on the arts sector prior to the Games. Against that, anecdotal evidence from Barcelona suggested that while local audiences stayed away from museums and galleries, this was compensated by a rise in the number of inbound visitors. Atlanta's High Museum of Art exhibition 'Five Rings of Passion' attracted large numbers of visitors because it was located close to the Games venues, had a theme with an Olympic connection and operated a joint ticketing scheme with Olympic events. Scott's own study of two Sydney museums (Powerhouse and the National Maritime Museum) during the Games found similarly that proximity to the site of a sporting event, location on the transportation route to that site and a thematically linked exhibition programme raised attendances (*Ibid.*). Inevitably, the many venues that failed to combine these attributes fared less well.

As the Cultural Festivals have got bigger, the sport references have necessarily become relatively less important. The original concept of the Olympic celebration of the arts as an integral part of sporting culture was always a romantic notion borne of a particular reading of classical Greek culture and embodied in a number of the early classically-trained sportsmen at the end of the nineteenth century. The Olympic movement has remained committed to a Cultural Festival that at best reinforces the idea of harmonious relations between the peoples of the world but, in reality, signally fails to demonstrate the connection between sports and the arts – for the simple reason that they inhabit separate spheres in the twenty-first century.

Notes

1.   One of Coubertin's earliest surviving writings on the subject, dating from 1908 (cited in Müller, 2000, p. 543), talks about an ideal world where sport is so embedded within society that all young men practise physical exercise to perfect their health and increase their strength.

2.   This dates back to the 1908 London Olympics where Coubertin was inspired by the sermon in St Paul's Cathedral delivered by Ethelbert Talbot (Bishop of Central Pennsylvania) to participants in the Games: 'In these Olympiads, the important thing is not winning, but taking part'.

3.   The Americans could not match Moscow's card stunts where 4,500 athletes manipulating cards, flags, shirtfronts and caps were able to create a backdrop of 174 giant images. Instead they used all spectators in the stadium to create 'one giant card trick' that would 'blow them away'. Each seat had a coloured card attached that, when held aloft, created the flags of all the competing nations (quoted by Ueberoth, 1986, p. 301).

4.   The reasons for the poor IOC attendance was that Coubertin did not start to inform members about the Conference until the end of March and many of the members were attending the Intercalated Games in Athens (22 April to 2 May 1906). Coubertin himself in his memoir of 1931 (Müller, 2000, p. 621) states that the timing of the Congress was deliberate on his part to give himself a reason not to travel to Athens to an event with which he profoundly disagreed.

5.   Among the gold medal winners was Coubertin himself with 'Ode to Sport' submitted under the pseudonyms of Georges Hohrod and M. Eschbach.

6.   After seeing the dress rehearsal with its 1,000 performers at the Dietrich Eckart Theatre in June, Goebbels cancelled the project and the professional dancers involved were sent on vacation for the duration of the Games. After the Games, Laban was sent to Franconia under house arrest from which he escaped to Paris in early 1937, finally joining Dartington Hall in January 1938 (Green, 1986, pp. 111–112).

7.   Literally meaning 'Strength through Joy', KdF was a state-controlled workers' leisure association, established in 1933.

8.   This glorification of sacrificial death was echoed in the final months of the war when Diem addressed the Hitler Youth in March 1945. He lectured them on the men of Sparta and appealed to them not to shrink from sacrifice for the fatherland, even if they were conscious of possible defeat (Rürup, 1996, p. 219). Just over a month later many of these boys, and the Peoples Reserve Battalions troops fighting with them, were killed trying to regain control of the Reichssportfeld from Russian troops.

9.   See chapter 1 for discussion of the contrast between Melbourne 1956 and Sydney 2000.

10.   Rome's 'blockbuster' exhibition 'Sport in History and Art', for example, ran for six months in the EUR Olympic complex. Spanning 3,000 years of Italian sport history with over 2,300 exhibits brought together from over a hundred collections and over thirty libraries across Italy, it represented a major achievement in exhibition planning and archival work that was four years in the planning (Organizing Committee, 1960, pp. 313–316).

11.   These were: 'Two Thousand Years of Barcelona' which explored Barcelona's past from its Roman heritage to contemporary art; 'Art and Sport', which recalled the original purpose of the cultural dimension of the Olympic movement; and 'The Olympic Festival of the Arts' which included high art, street performance, modern work and incorporated the WOMAD (World of Music, Arts and Dance) festival.

12.   Centennial Park, itself part of the transformation of central Atlanta, would provide the desired space for visitors, conventioneers and office workers that the city's business leaders had long wanted albeit, as chapter 2 showed, at the expense of the underclass.

13.   One visitor found that he was unable to obtain any information about the Cultural Olympiad from information points or volunteers during the Games. In fact the volunteers did not understand what he meant by the Cultural Olympiad and assumed he wanted to know where the theatres and museums were (Information courtesy of Chuck Little).

Chapter 5

The Paralympic Games

John R. Gold and *Margaret M. Gold*

The Paralympics is becoming a truly worldwide event … we want it to be the same as the Olympic Games.

Tanni Grey-Thompson

Speaking to an academic audience, Dame Tanni Grey-Thompson (2006), the leading medal winner in the history of the Paralympic Games, noted the remarkable convergence of the Paralympic and Olympic movements. From pragmatic beginnings as part of the treatment of spine-injured ex-servicemen towards the end of the Second World War, disability sport has developed so rapidly that it now supports sport-specific national squads of elite athletes participating in international competition. As the summit of disability sport, the Paralympic Games have played a major part in changing social attitudes by emphasizing achievement rather than impairment and by accelerating the agenda of inclusion. They have also forced changes in official attitudes in countries where disability was ideologically problematic, if only to accommodate international opinion when bidding for the Olympics – given that Paralympics are now closely linked to that process (Gold and Gold, 2007).

This chapter considers the development of the Paralympics from small beginnings as a competition for disabled ex-servicemen and women in the grounds of Stoke Mandeville Hospital to the present day ambulatory international festival held in Olympic cities immediately after the Summer or Winter Games. It traces their origins to the work of Dr (later Sir) Ludwig Guttmann at the National Spinal Injuries Unit at Stoke Mandeville Hospital in Buckinghamshire, who used sport as an integral part of the treatment of paraplegic patients. The sports competition held at the hospital to coincide with the Opening Ceremony of the London Games in July 1948 became an annual event attracting the first international participation in 1952, after which it became the International Stoke Mandeville Games. From 1960 onwards attempts were made to hold every fourth Games in the Olympic host city, although the path towards acceptance by host cities proved difficult. As will be seen, it was only from 1988 onwards that a process of convergence began that brought the Paralympics into the central arena of the Olympics, both literally and figuratively, leading to the host city being required to include a bid for the Paralympics as part of its bid for the Olympics.

The later parts of this chapter discuss the relatively modest ramifications of this requirement for prospective host cities, given that Paralympians make use of many of the same facilities as their Olympian counterparts. Although unlikely ever to drive major infrastructural or regeneration projects, the Paralympics have repercussions for the host city in the need to accommodate a group of athletes and officials with different requirements and in promoting the cause of a barrier-free urban environment. The implications of these provisions are discussed in relation to the Paralympics of the twenty-first century, particularly in relation to the emphasis placed on the disability agenda in the successful bid made by London for the 2012 Games.

Origins

The first stirrings of disability sport emerged in the late nineteenth century, primarily through the work of activists in the deaf community. The first Sports Club for the Deaf was founded in Berlin in 1888 and by 1924 national sports federations for the deaf had emerged in Belgium, Czechoslovakia, France, Great Britain, Holland and Poland. Collectively, these six federations sent 140 athletes to Paris in 1924 to participate in the First International Silent Games – the gathering that marked the birth of a four-yearly cycle of 'World Games for the Deaf' (Séguillon, 2002, p. 119). Subsequently divided into Summer and Winter festivals after the pattern of the Olympics, these were later recognized by the International Olympic Committee (IOC) as the Deaflympics.

The Deaflympics were important as an indicator of possibilities, but the deaf community retained a separate existence as a disability group rather than participating in the movement that would create the Paralympics. Instead, the latter stemmed from the treatment of severely injured servicemen at the end of the Second World War and particularly the work of Ludwig Guttmann – a figure whose role is comparable to that of Baron Pierre de Coubertin in reviving the modern Olympics (see chapter 2). Guttmann, a prominent Jewish neurosurgeon, had arrived in Britain as a refugee from Nazi Germany in 1939. After appointment to a research post at Oxford University's Department of Neurosurgery and then at the Wingfield-Morris Orthopaedic Hospital, he became director of what would become the National Spinal Injuries Centre at Stoke Mandeville Hospital (Aylesbury, Buckinghamshire). Guttmann later commented that paraplegia was the 'most depressing and neglected subject in all medicine' at this time (quoted in Goodman, 1986, p. 96), characterized by poor patient survival rates, low morale amongst nursing staff, and difficulty in recruiting specialist physiotherapists. His approach instituted a programme of 'total care', having patients turned physically every two hours day and night to prevent pressure sores and improving standards of bladder hygiene to help tackle problems of infection. Physiotherapy assisted limb flexibility and, for some patients, increased mobility. A pre-vocational work regime and various forms of recreation including concerts, visits and *competitive* sports, designed to keep patients busy and create a sense of purpose, complemented the medical regime.

In this context, therefore, sport transcended mere leisure. Not only was it 'the most natural form of remedial exercise' restoring physical fitness, strength, coordination, speed, endurance and overcoming fatigue, but also had the psychological impact of restoring pleasure in life and contributing to social reintegration (Guttmann, 1976, p. 12). Developing these ideas, Guttmann formulated the concept of a sports festival for the disabled that would promote contact with other patients and address attitudes about the capabilities of the disabled. On 28 July 1948, an archery competition took place on the front lawns of the hospital, involving sixteen competitors arranged into two teams: one from Stoke Mandeville and the other from the Star and Garter Home for disabled ex-servicemen in Richmond-on-Thames. The event was consciously chosen as a demonstration of potential, symbolized by being held on the same day as the Opening Ceremony of the London Olympics, with archery seen as second only to swimming in its 'physiotherapeutic value … for the paralysed' (Special Correspondent, 1948). In 1949, Stoke Mandeville hosted a larger competition, involving sixty competitors from five hospitals participating in what became a steadily widening group of sports (table 5.1). During the meeting, Guttmann gave a speech in which he expressed the hope that the event would become international and achieve 'world fame as the disabled men and women's equivalent of the Olympic Games' (Goodman, 1986, p. 150).

The Stoke Mandeville Games quickly acquired an international dimension, particularly by drawing on institutional connections that the Hospital had developed through training visiting staff, through staff moving to other hospitals and spreading Stoke Mandeville's characteristic approach to sport, and through ex-patients who pioneered paraplegic sport in their own countries. In 1952, another Olympic year, the involvement of a group of Dutch war veterans presaged wider European participation. In 1953, teams from Finland, France, Israel and the Netherlands appeared, along with a Canadian team. The Americans first participated in 1955, followed by the Australians in 1957 – by which time the Stoke Mandeville Games had commonly gained the nickname 'Paralympics' (Carisbroke *et al.*, 1956, Brittain, 2010, pp. 24-25).[1] The word 'Paralympics' at this stage was clearly a pun combining 'paraplegic' and 'Olympic' (IPC, 2006a), effectively confronting Olympian traditions of celebrating excellence and the perfectly formed body with the realities of disability. It was only over time that reinterpretation occurred. In part, this was driven by the Games embracing participants with forms of disability other than paraplegia. Equally, it resulted from a process of convergence that closely allied the Paralympics with the Olympic movement. With an ingenious revision of the etymology, the approved version of the term asserted that the first syllable of 'Paralympics' derived from the Greek preposition 'para', meaning

Table 5.1. Paralympic Sports.

Summer Games	Year included in the full Paralympic Programme
Archery	1960
Athletics	1960
Boccia	1984
Bowls	1968–1988, 1996
Cycling	1988
Equestrian	1996
Football 5-a-side	2004
Football 7-a-side	1984
Goalball	1976
Judo	2004
Powerlifting/Weightlifting	1964 men
Powerlifting/Weightlifting	2000 women
Rowing	2008
Sailing	2000
Shooting	1976
Swimming	1960
Table Tennis	1960
Volleyball – standing volleyball	1976–1996
Volleyball – sitting	1980
Wheelchair Basketball	1960
Wheelchair Fencing	1960
Wheelchair Rugby	2000
Wheelchair Tennis	1992
Winter Games	
Alpine Skiing	1976
Ice Sledge Hockey	1994
Nordic Skiing – Cross Country	1976
Nordic Skiing - Biathlon	1994
Wheelchair Curling	2006

Source: IPC (2006a).

'beside' or 'alongside'. Viewed in this way, the Paralympics constitute a festival that exists alongside and operates in parallel with the Olympic Games, while retaining a separate identity (*Ibid.*).

Building Connections

As the Games grew, demands for greater professionalism towards the organization, funding and management of international sport for the disabled saw the establishment in 1959 of the International Stoke Mandeville Games Committee (later Foundation, hence ISMGF). This ran and developed the annual Stoke Mandeville Games and oversaw the organization of a parallel four-yearly 'Olympic' competition until 1972 (see table 5.2).

The process of building links with the Olympics, however, proved long and torturous despite highly promising beginnings. In 1956, during ceremonies at the Melbourne Olympics, the IOC had awarded the Fearnley Cup to Guttmann for 'outstanding achievement in the service of Olympic ideals' (Goodman, 1986, p.

Table 5.2. Summer Paralympic Games.

Year	Aegis	Location	Number of countries	Number of athletes	Number of sports for which medals awarded	Disability Groups
1952	Stoke Mandeville Hospital	Stoke Mandeville★	2	130	6	SI
1960	ISMGC	Rome	23	400	8	SI
1964	ISMGC	Tokyo	21	357	9	SI
1968	ISMGC	Tel Aviv, Israel★	29	750	10	SI
1972	ISMGF	Heidelberg, West Germany★	43	984	10	SI
1976	ISMGF ISOD	Toronto, Canada★	38	1657	13	SI, A, VI, LA
1980	ISMGF ISOD	Arnhem, Holland★	42	1973	12	SI, A, VI, LA, CP
1984	ISMGF	Stoke Mandeville★	41	1100	10	SI
	ISOD	New York★	45	1800	14	A, VI, LA, CP
1988	ICC	Seoul	61	3013	18	SI, A, VI. LA, CP
1992	ICC	Barcelona	82	3021	16	SI, A, VI.
		Madrid★	73	1400	5	ID
1996	IPC	Atlanta	103	3195	19	SI, A, VI, LA, CP, ID
2000	IPC	Sydney	122	3843	19	SI, A, VI, LA, CP, ID
2004	IPC	Athens	136	3806	19	SI, A, VI, LA, CP
2008	IPC	Beijing	150 expected	4000 expected	20	SI, A, VI, LA, CP
2012	IPC	London	150 expected	4200 expected	20	SI, A, VI, LA, CP, ID
2016	IPC	Rio de Janeiro	tbc	tbc	tbc	SI, A, VI, LA, CP, ID (tbc)

★ Years in which the Paralympic Games did not take place in the Olympic location.

Guide to abbreviations: *SI* Spinal Injury; *A* Amputee; *VI* Visually Impaired; *LA* Les Autres; *CP* Cerebral Palsy; *ID* Intellectual Impairment.

Sources: various and Scruton (1998).

157), a remarkable degree of recognition less than a decade after the foundation of the Stoke Mandeville Games. The next stage was to take the Stoke Mandeville Games to the Olympic host city itself and, when the Games were held in Rome 1960 and Tokyo 1964, the convergence of the two sets of Games seemed assured. Such arrangements, however, depended on the goodwill of the host city, sponsorship and public funding to cover the cost. The Rome Games, for example, had the cooperation of the Spinal Unit at Ostia, gained sponsorship from INAIL (*Istituto nazionale per l'assicurazione contro gli infortuni sul lavoro* – the Italian National Insurance Institute against Accidents at Work), and had the support of the Italian Olympic Committee (CONI). The 400 disabled athletes used the Olympic Pool and Village, but last minute changes meant that those parts of the Village equipped with lifts were unavailable. Moreover, withdrawal of an offer to use nearby Olympic facilities meant that competitors were perforce conveyed by a 40-minute bus ride to the Tre Fontane sports ground (Scruton, 1998, p. 308). The Tokyo Games followed on from the Summer Olympics, accommodated competitors in the Athletes' Village, and shared facilities recently used by the Olympic athletes. Its Opening Ceremony, with the Crown Prince and Princess acting as patrons, attracted 5,000 spectators.

From this point, problems with the host city seriously affected further progress. It was another 24 years before disabled athletes again competed in an Olympic host city (Seoul 1988), with a succession of cities refusing to host the Paralympics. The IOC, in its role of handling the bidding process for the Olympics, was only interested in the candidate cities' ability to meet the costs and needs of elite athletes. There was no stipulation that the Olympic city must host parallel games for athletes with disabilities. Admittedly, the Paralympics became a greater challenge to hosts as they grew in size (see table 5.1), especially with admission of a wider range of disability groups after 1976. The increasing scale of the Games, coupled with prevailing building standards that failed to accommodate the disabled, shortage of available funds and lack of any inclusive philosophy regarding athletes with disability proved obstacles for further collaboration with many Olympic cities.

For example, despite having sent three observers to Tokyo, Mexico City declined the Games in 1968 because of 'technical difficulties'. They were held instead at the sports centre of the Israel Foundation for Handicapped Children in Ramat Gan near Tel Aviv. In 1972, the University of Heidelberg staged the Games rather than Munich, as plans for the post-festival use of the Olympic Village had meant transferring the site to developers for conversion into private apartments immediately after the Olympic Closing Ceremony (Scruton, 1998, p. 320). Lack of suitable accommodation, real or claimed, plagued subsequent events. In 1976, Toronto acted as hosts rather than the Olympic city of Montreal, with the athletes housed at Toronto and York Universities. These two Paralympic Villages were located some distance from each other as well as from the competition venues. When the Moscow Olympic Organizing Committee failed even to respond to a request to stage the Games, the 1980 festival took place at Arnhem in the Netherlands. Here, too, the available accommodation (an army barracks) was inconveniently located for access to the sports venues. In 1984, the Americans agreed to host the Games for all disabilities, but not in the host Olympic city (Los Angeles). Instead, they were to be split between New York and the University of Illinois (Champaign); an arrangement that foundered when the latter withdrew through funding problems just four months before the Games. As a result, 1,800 amputee, cerebral palsy, visually impaired, and Les Autres[2] athletes competed at the Mitchel Park athletics complex in Uniondale, New York, with 1,200 athletes participating in the wheelchair events that were hurriedly rearranged at Stoke Mandeville (*Ibid.*, pp. 184, 202). Ironically, these were the first Games that the IOC officially recognized as the Paralympics (figure 5.1) although the first full Games to use this title was in Seoul 1988.

Figure 5.1. Stoke Mandeville stadium (Aylesbury, Buckinghamshire).

The early Winter Paralympic Games for the disabled fared little better (table 5.3). Established in 1976, initially they too did not take place in Olympic cities or even in the same countries. The first Winter Games took place in Örnsköldsvik (Sweden) rather than at Innsbruck (Austria). These were followed in 1980 by Games at Geilo (Norway) rather than Lake Placid, at Innsbruck in 1984 rather than Sarajevo (although an exhibition event was held in the Winter Games there), and Innsbruck again in 1988 rather than Calgary, which declined to hold the Paralympics.

This retreat from the positive pattern seemingly established in the early 1960s greatly disappointed the Paralympic movement. Guttmann (1976, p. 174) denounced the thinking that had prevented Mexico City 1968 or Munich 1972 holding the Games, commenting on 'the lamentable lack of appreciation of the place thousands of disabled sportsmen and women have earned for themselves in the field of international sport'. Chiefly as a result of this, a new complex of

Table 5.3. Winter Paralympic Games.

Year	Aegis	Location	Participating countries	Number of athletes	Number of sports	Disability Groups
1976	ISOD	Örnsköldsvik Sweden★	17	250	2	VI, A
1980	ISOD ISMGF	Geilo Norway★	18	350	2	VI, A, SI, CP, LA
1984	ICC	Innsbruck Austria★	21	457	2	VI, A, SI CP, LA
1988	ICC	Innsbruck Austria★	22	397	2	VI, A, SI, CP, LA
1992	ICC	Albertville France	24	475	2	VI, A, SI, CP, LA
1994	IPC	Lillehammer Norway	31	492	3	VI, A, SI, CP, LA
1998	IPC	Nagano Japan	32	571	4	VI, A, SI, CP, LA
2002	IPC	Salt Lake City USA	36	416	3	VI, A, SI, CP, LA
2006	IPC	Turin Italy	39	477	4	VI, A, SI, CP, LA
2010	IPC	Vancouver Canada	45 expected	650 expected	4	VI, A, SI, CP, LA
2014	IPC	Russian Federation	tbc	tbc	tbc	VI, A, SI, CP, LA, ID (tbc)

★ Years in which the Paralympic Games did not take place in the Olympic location.

Guide to abbreviations: *SI* Spinal Injury; *A* Amputee; *VI* Visually Impaired; *LA* Les Autres; *CP* Cerebral Palsy.

Sources: Various; Scruton (1998).

Figure 5.2. Cauldron for the Paralympic flame, Paralympic Games, Stoke Mandeville, 1984.

buildings was constructed at Stoke Mandeville (figure 5.2), comprising a Stadium for the Paralysed and Other Disabled (opened in 1969 and later renamed the Ludwig Guttmann Sports Stadium for the Disabled) and an 'Olympic' Village in 1981 (Goodman, 1986, p. 164). Thus the sporting facilities were finally separated from the hospital itself and from the notion of 'illness', reflecting the fact that disabled athletes were now achieving elite status with an emphasis on performance.

Institutional Convergence

The problem, however, was not simply the resistance of Olympic cities and their Organizing Committees, since the definition of disability and competing jurisdictions of relevant organizations also affected progress. The Stoke Mandeville Games originally confined entry to medically controlled paraplegics, but the organizers felt impelled to respond when other groups pressed for participation in internationally organized sports festivals. The foundation of the International Sports Organization for the Disabled (ISOD) in 1964 created opportunities for the blind, amputees and individuals with other locomotor disabilities (de Pauw and Gavron, 2005, p. 39). ISOD collaborated with ISMGF in broadening the scope of the 1976 Toronto Games to include amputees, visually impaired and Les Autres. Competitors with cerebral palsy joined the 1980 Games.

The expanding scope of disability sport quickly generated new international disability organizations. The need to coordinate their activities and eliminate duplication of events required further institutional arrangements, leading in particular to the foundation of the ICC (International Coordinating Committee of the World Sports Organizations) in 1982. This brought together nominated senior representatives from the four major International Sports Organizations: ISMWSF (the International Stoke Mandeville Wheelchair Sports Federation, previously the ISMGF), ISOD, IBSA (the International Blind Sports Federation), and the CP-ISRA (Cerebral Palsy International Sport and Recreation Association). These were later joined by CISS (International Committee of Sports for the Deaf) and INAS-FID (International Sports Federation for Persons with Mental Handicap – later changed to Intellectual Disability). Thus constituted, the ICC gave the disabled sports movement a single voice for the first time. It also allowed greater clarity in developing relations with the IOC and Olympic Games Organizing Committees, which found immediate expression in the geographical convergence of the Summer Games at Seoul 1988 and the Winter Games at Albertville 1992.

The ICC oversaw the Games held in Olympic cities in 1988 and 1992, with the exception of the Winter Games in Calgary in 1988. The 1988 Seoul Olympics and Paralympics had separate Organizing Committees, but with sufficient coordination to allow the sharing of venues, equipment and key personnel. With the Olympic Village unavailable after the Olympics, a specially designed Village was constructed for the Paralympians. They also received the same spectacular

Opening and Closing Ceremonies as the summer Games, watched by capacity crowds of 75,000.

Barcelona pioneered the organizational integration of the two sets of Games by giving overall responsibility to the Organizing Committee of the Barcelona Games (COOB), with a separate Division charged with overall responsibility to plan the Paralympics. This ensured explicit attention to the needs of disabled athletes and comparable treatment with Olympians. The Paralympic Games now had their custom-designed Opening and Closing ceremonial spectacles (Rognoni, 1996, p. 264). Free admission to Paralympic events ensured large numbers of spectators and there was substantial television coverage. At the same time, COOB imposed its own decisions, cutting the number of sports to fifteen and refusing to allow the mentally impaired to participate in the Paralympics. Instead INAS-FID held an officially recognized Paralympic Games in Madrid in which 1,400 athletes from seventy-three countries competed. This took place after the Barcelona Paralympic Games. The subsequent inclusion of INAS-FID athletes in the Paralympic Games between 1996 and 2000 was ended abruptly after an investigation showed that ten of the twelve Spanish basketball team were not intellectually disabled. After two years of negotiations between INAS-FID and the IPC, the IPC General Council voted in November 2009 to admit athletes for the London 2012 Games in four disciplines: athletics, swimming, rowing and table tennis. The aim is to progress further with inclusion in the Sochi Winter Games 2014 and extend the Rio participation to basketball and futsal (a form of indoor football).[3]

The final stage in the evolution of the institutional basis for the Games came with the establishment of the International Paralympic Committee (IPC) in 1989: an organization similar in structure to the IOC itself. Based in Bonn, it serves as the umbrella organization for 165 National Paralympic Committees, five regional bodies, and ten international disability-specific sports federations. It also acts as the international federation for nine of the twenty-five Paralympic sports (IPC, 2010). Its vision is to enable 'Paralympic athletes to achieve sporting excellence and inspire and excite the world' and professes an eleven-point mission which includes sport development 'from initiation to elite level' (IPC, 2006c, p. 3). Crucially, since 1992 it is now the sole coordinating body for Paralympic sport recognized by the IOC.

As the IOC and IPC moved closer together, there was identification of areas that had produced conflict, notably, the use of the term 'Olympics' (which the IOC regard as their copyright), and the Paralympic Logo. The IPC Logo, originally introduced at the Seoul Games, comprised five traditional Korean decorative motifs (Tae-Geuks) in the Olympic colours (blue, black, red, yellow and green). Given that the IOC felt this was too close to their five-ring symbol, the IPC reduced the five Tae-Geuks to three in 1994 and replaced them completely as part of a rebranding exercise in 2003. The new logo, comprising three 'agitos' (from the Latin *agito* meaning 'I move'), was first used at the 2004 Athens Games, along with the new motto 'Spirit in Motion' (IPC, 2005, p. 6).

Four agreements between the IOC and IPC signed between 2000 and 2006 clarified the relationship between the two organizations, set out the principles for further cooperation and provided financial support for the IPC. An agreement in October 2000 brought the workings of the two organizations closer by co-opting the IPC President to the IOC and including an IPC representative on eleven of the IOC Commissions, including the Evaluation Commission – the body that examines the competing bids from cities seeking to host the Olympic Games. The IOC also undertook to pay an annual subvention towards IPC administration costs ($3 million per annum), annual sums for development projects, and specific assistance to help athletes from developing countries attend the 2002 Salt Lake City Winter Paralympic Games and the 2004 Athens Summer Paralympics (IOC, 2000a). An agreement in June 2001 elucidated the organization of the Paralympic Games, confirming that the location would always be the Olympic host city and would take place 'shortly after' the Olympic Games using the same facilities and venues. From the 2008 Summer Games and 2010 Winter Games onwards, there would be full integration of the two Organizing Committees (IOC, 2001). An agreement on revenues for broadcasting and marketing the Paralympics (August 2003) guaranteed IOC payments to the IPC of $9 million for the 2008 Games and $14 million for 2010 and 2012 (IOC, 2003a). The final agreement (June 2006) extended these arrangements through to 2014 and 2016, increased funding for the IPC and set out the respective roles of the IOC and IPC in the planning, organization and staging of the Paralympics, the use of technical manuals, the sports programme, and the number of accredited individuals (IOC, 2006a).

Accommodating the Disability Agenda

The move towards a 'one city, one bid' approach for selection of Olympic host cities was of vital importance to the IPC. It meant that the two festivals came into line as part of an overall package that prospective host cities would put together. Cities bidding for the 2008, 2010, 2012 and 2014 Games had to show complete organizational integration between the Olympic and Paralympic Games, with details of the Paralympic Games fully articulated in the bid documents. Indeed, the speed of integration was more rapid than these agreements stipulated, with both Salt Lake City 2002 and Athens 2004 establishing a single Organizing Committee (IOC, 2003a) and information on the Paralympic Games appearing in the official Reports of the Olympic Games since Sydney 2000 (e.g. SOCOG, 2000a, pp. 47–49).

This development, of course, needs to be set in proper perspective. On the one hand, it was never likely that this smaller festival, held in the wake of the main events, would assume the same significance as the Olympics or preoccupy the thinking of city planners to the same extent. For many cities, the right to stage the Olympics is a prize aggressively won, whereas 'they inherit the Paralympic Games as an obligation' (Cashman, 2006, p. 247). As such, the Paralympics tend to be fitted into the package offered for the Olympics – a pragmatic strategy given that they produce little demand for additional facilities, other than for a few sports such as boccia and goalball that have special requirements[4] and for modifications to transport and stadia to allow free access for competitors, officials and spectators. It is also scarcely conceivable that the Paralympics *per se* would ever act as a catalyst for major infrastructural investment or urban regeneration.

Yet, on the other hand, their significance for the host city is far from negligible. A city's Olympic bid that features a lukewarm or ill-considered approach to the Paralympics may well suffer regardless of the strength of its proposals for the Olympics. In addition, the act of staging the Paralympics impacts on host cities through the way that they confront questions of disability, most notably with respect to creating a barrier-free environment.[5] Although, as noted, the requirement to integrate the two sets of Games only became binding with the 2008 Beijing Games, hosts with an established record of upholding disability rights and with legislation enshrining rights of access already in place have enjoyed an advantage in the bidding and preparation of the Games. Hence, cities such as Sydney, Turin and London could build on their existing practices which were already enshrined in legislation, whereas the Games in Athens and Beijing were the catalysts for initiating the disability agenda. In October 2008, the Russian State Duma passed new legislation embedding IOC and IPC standards in Russian law in anticipation of Sochi's hosting of the 2014 Winter Games (IPC, 2008).

In the case of Sydney, for example, efforts were made to address problems seen at Atlanta 1996, such as the lack of visibility of the Paralympic Games and poor coordination between them and the Olympics. As host for the Eleventh Paralympic Games, the city achieved a good working relationship between the bodies responsible for the two Games (SOCOG and the Sydney Paralympic Organizing Committee), which had shared departments, and with other Games-related organizations. The Games themselves took place in the Olympic Park, with the (Paralympic) Village home to 6,943 people, comprising 3,824 athletes, 2,315 team officials and 804 technical officials (BPA, 2007). The design of the Olympic Park also represented a drastic improvement in accessibility over previous Paralympics, with Australia able to capitalize on the country's longstanding active involvement in disability sport. The improved access provided in the Olympic Park, however, was 'only as good as the city and suburban network which fed into it' (Cashman, 2006, p. 254). For example, only 5 per cent of railway stations facilitated easy access for wheelchair disabled, and relatively few buses had low-floor access (*Ibid.*).

The Winter Games in Turin 2006 similarly sought to boost the visibility of the Paralympics. The Italians treated the staging of the Paralympic Games in Italy as a welcome reminder of history, given that Rome in 1960 had been the first Olympic city to welcome the Stoke Mandeville International Festival (BPA, 2007). Continuing the themes adopted by the Winter Olympics (e.g. as in figure 5.3), the Paralympics used the same accommodation and facilities (figure 5.4). The major innovation was worldwide coverage of all sports of the Paralympic Winter

Games, with over 100 hours of coverage provided through an internet television channel owned by the IPC (paralympicsport.tv), narrowcast free-to-air. Seen as a way of overcoming the resistance of the larger broadcasting networks, the service was relaunched in 2007 and provides coverage of all Paralympic sport in addition

Figure 5.3. Welcoming slogan, Turin Airport, March 2006.

Figure 5.4. Turin Esposizione, venue for the sledge hockey, Paralympic Games, Turin, March 2006.

to full coverage of the Paralympic Games themselves. Over 240 hours of coverage was provided during the Beijing Games (IPC, 2009, p. 40) and with the use of Youtube and Facebook, the Games are employing social networking sites to engage with a broader audience.

By contrast, there was little tradition of disabled sport in Greece. This was addressed in the years leading up to Athens 2004 by developing an accessible sports infrastructure for athletes with disability that could be used in the preparation of Greek athletes and to permit training by other Paralympic teams (ATHOC, 2005, p. 178). Eighty-five per cent of the venues used were the same as for the Olympics, with additional ones for the Paralympic-specific sports. Nevertheless, while it was possible to plan for disabled access in new Olympic investment (including public transport, venues and the public spaces around venues), the wider environment posed challenges. The Official Report of the Games went so far as to call Athens 'unfriendly' to the disabled community and requiring 'drastic measures' to make the city accessible (*Ibid.*, p. 177).

The Organizing Committee (ATHOC) produced design guidelines and accessibility information for the municipalities making up the Greater Athens area, where much of the Olympic infrastructure was located, to encourage them to upgrade their public spaces, particularly along key routes it identified (see chapter 16). Furthermore, it urged private businesses to promote accessibility in their own premises and to raise awareness among their staff. To this end, ATHOC and the Chambers of Commerce of the four cities participating in the Olympics (Athens, Thessaloniki, Heraklio and Volos) developed the Accessible Choice Programme (ERMIS). Businesses compliant with this programme earned the right to display a symbol indicating that they welcomed customers with disabilities and their details were included in a directory issued to all Paralympic delegations on arrival in Greece. Although attendances were less than at Sydney (850,000 compared with 1.1 million) and some venues were less than half-full, part of the value of the festival was considered to lie in its pedagogic impact. As in Australia, the organizers had developed an educational programme to promote greater understanding of the Paralympics and a large proportion of the audience were children. An accident that killed seven students who were travelling to watch the Paralympics cast a shadow over this strategy, leading to cancellation of the artistic and entertainment sections of the Closing Ceremony out of respect. The ceremony continued, but with only the protocol elements required for the completion of the Games (*Ibid.*, p. 511).

Beijing's plans for 2008 also reflected significant shifts in attitude. China's own participation in the Paralympic Movement is relatively recent. When invited to the Rome Games in 1960, the official statement declared there were no disabled in China (Lane, 2006). Relaxation of this ideological stance saw the establishment of the Chinese Sports Association for Disabled Athletes in 1983 (de Pauw and Gavron, 2005, pp. 127–128). Chinese athletes started to compete in international competition, with a small group entering the 1984 Games held in New York. No Chinese team participated in the Winter Paralympic Games until Salt Lake City in

2002. The increasing seriousness with which the Chinese then took sport for the disabled is reflected in the spectacular improvement in the performance of their athletes – rising from ninth in the medal table in 1996, to sixth in 2000, first place in Athens 2004 with 141 medals and 211 medals in 2008 (89 gold, 70 silver, 52 Bronze).

This new priority reflects China's characteristic use of sporting investment as an adjunct of foreign policy (see chapter 17), as much as any root-and-branch change in prevailing attitudes. Nevertheless, the requirements of provision for 2008 focused attention on the challenge of creating a barrier-free Games in a city where access has only been on the agenda for a short time and where much of the infrastructure was anything but barrier-free. The Beijing Municipal People's Congress adopted the country's first local legislation relating to physical accessibility when passing the 'Beijing Regulation on Construction and Management of the Barrier-free Facilities' in April 2004. The regulations applied to public transport, hospitals, banks, public toilets and parks. As a result, for instance, underground stations had ramps installed, disabled toilets, tactile paths for the visually impaired and public telephones for wheelchair users, with disabled seats provided on trains (CIIC, 2004).

However while reshaping the built environment proved relatively straightforward, the challenge of changing public attitudes towards the disabled was highlighted in May 2008 when the *Manual for being Olympic Volunteers* was published (BOGVWCG, 2008). Chapter 6 dealt with 'Volunteering Skills' and in attempting to provide the volunteer with information on how to engage with visitors from different cultural backgrounds revealed some disturbing attitudes towards people with disabilities:

(2) Physically Disabled

Physically disabled people are often mentally healthy. They show no differences in sensation, reaction, memorization and thinking mechanism from other people, but they might have unusual personalities because of disfigurement and disability. For example, some physically disabled are isolated, unsocial, and introspective; they usually do not volunteer to contact people. They can be stubborn and controlling; they may be sensitive and struggle with trust issues. Sometimes they are overly protective of themselves, especially when they are called 'crippled' or 'paralyzed'. It is not acceptable for others to hurt their dignity, so volunteers should make extra efforts to assist with due respect. (*Ibid.*, pp. 6–7).

The guide was hastily withdrawn and 'poor translation' blamed. Dame Tanni Grey-Thompson's reaction to the guide was to observe that the Paralympics themselves would change attitudes and Mike Brace, chair of the British Paralympic Association, called it 'a clumsy attempt to override years of limited awareness' and observed that this was in fact progress given that up to seven years before, disabled people were often not recognized at all (O'Connor, 2008).

Paralympic Legacy

As their history shows, Paralympic Games have a very different relationship to their host city when compared to the Olympic Games. In the early years, the Paralympics went to places best able to accommodate athletes with disability and organizers worked round any shortcomings in the facilities or the wider city. Once the Paralympics started sharing host cities with the Summer Games in 1988 and the Winter Games in 1992, athletes were able to enjoy environments designed principally for the Olympics but adapted for Paralympic use. The requirement that cities bid for both sets of Games requires them to think through Paralympic provision from the outset, but it does not follow that the two festivals receive equal treatment throughout the planning and consultation stages for it is the Olympics that drive the desire to host the Games and the legacy agenda.

Laura Keogh (2009, p. 9), in her study of London 2012 legacies, poses the question as to whether Paralympic legacy is different from Olympic legacy and whether the Paralympics generate 'distinct legacies'. With that in mind, it is possible to identify five broad categories of Paralympic legacy. These are:

♦   The hard legacy of accessible sports facilities, accommodation and environment often concentrated in and around the main Olympic venues;

♦   Greater accessibility in the wider urban environment including buildings, leisure facilities (including museums, galleries and the arts), accommodation and transport;

♦   Sports provision for the disabled community;

♦   The soft legacy of public awareness of disabililty; improving the position of the disabled community in society generally; and

♦   Providing a legacy for the Olympic movement in terms of relations between the IOC and IPC media coverage of the Games.

The exact agenda that a city adopts depends on the position of the disabled community in that society, the level of inclusion in decision-making processes and the degree to which disability has already been accommodated in the physical environment. The long-term impact of a Paralympic Games also depends on how embedded new thinking becomes and how vigilant society is in monitoring provision and maintenance of facilities and continuing with education programmes. Evidence from Athens suggests that it is all too easy to relax vigilance once the Games are over (see chapter 16).

London 2012

In the case of London's bid for the 2012 Games, there is no doubt that, perhaps for the first time, the quality of that portion of the Olympic bid which concerned the

Paralympic Games was seen as constituting a major positive factor for the entire candidature. The location of Stoke Mandeville in London's Home Counties meant that there was a sense of the Paralympics 'coming home'. From the outset, Paralympians were part of the group responsible for organizing and drafting the bid and attended the vital IOC meeting in Singapore in July 2005, when the outcome was decided.

Under the new rules agreed in 2001, the candidate cities for the final phase of the Olympic selection procedure had to complete a questionnaire with seventeen themes. Theme 9 related exclusively to the Paralympic Games and contained nine sets of questions covering the structural integration of the organization of the Paralympics within the Organizing Committee, the dates and the competition schedule, the venues, accommodation, transport operation, travel times, disability awareness (including staff and volunteer training), media facilities, vision for the Games, finance, and the Games' legacy (IOC, 2004a). In its bid, the London Committee capitalized on the heritage of disabled sport in the United Kingdom, a tradition of volunteering for Paralympic events, anti-disability discrimination in service provision dating back to the 1995 Disability Discrimination Act, and a good record in disability awareness training. The London Bid Book promulgated three goals: to strengthen the Paralympic Movement; to deliver accessible and inclusive designs for all facilities; and to maximize media coverage (LOCOG, 2004, p. 173). The bid contained eight specific commitments for the Paralympics (*Ibid.*, p. 191):

- Creating an Olympic Village that is fully accessible to all from the outset;
- Maximizing media coverage and exposure, as pioneered by the BBC;
- Integrating Olympic Games and Paralympic Games planning;
- Training all Games workforce in the principles of inclusion;
- Establishing operational policies that encompass Paralympic values;
- Recruiting suitably qualified disabled people;
- Promoting the Paralympic Games nationwide;
- Creating a cultural programme featuring disabled artists.

London plans to stage eleven Paralympic sports in the Olympic Park, seven in the 'River Zone' (ExCel in Docklands and Greenwich), road racing in Regents Park and sailing at Weymouth. Housing the athletes in the Olympic Village will mean that 95 per cent are accommodated within 15 minutes travel time from competition venues, linked by what are described as 'environmentally friendly and fully accessible' buses. Ticket holders for Paralympic events would travel free by public transport, with a Games Mobility Service for disabled spectators (*Ibid.*, p. 185).

In its assessment, the report of the IOC's Evaluation Committee was highly complimentary with regard to the bid's coverage of the Paralympics. There was praise for the degree of integration between the Olympic and Paralympic Games in terms of organization, management and physical planning. There was also acknowledgement of the rich history of Paralympic sport in the United Kingdom, the nation's reputation in television coverage and public support for disability sport, and recognition that capacities for United Kingdom Paralympic sport were 'among the best in the world' (IOC, 2005a, p. 73). In particular, the report noted the proposal for a 'Paralympic legacy for all' including 'social, educational and sport legacies with a focus on improving society' (Ibid.).

However, much of the subsequent documentation coming out of official agencies tended to concentrate on the legacy aims for the Olympics with scant reference to the specifics of the Paralympics. The five legacy promises for example were: to make the United Kingdom a world-leading sporting nation; transform the heart of East London; inspire a generation of young people to take a part in local volunteering, cultural and physical activity; make the Olympic Park a blueprint for sustainable living; and demonstrate the United Kingdom is a creative, inclusive and welcoming place to live, visit and for business (DCMS, 2007a, b). While projects for the disabled were being developed and were referred to in these documents the main thrust was the Olympics themselves. Even the 'inclusive' goals in the fifth promise were interpreted in the introductions to those documents as being about employment, skills and workforce capacity – getting people into work and long-term employment rather than inclusion of the disabled.

In December 2009, with 1000 days to the opening of the London Paralympic Games, Tessa Jowell, then the Minister with responsibility for London 2012, announced a sixth legacy promise for the London Games, namely: 'to bring about lasting change to the life experiences of disabled people' (Office for Disability, 2009). This finally gave greater visibility to Paralympic outcomes and lent weight to claims that the two games are part of the same project. This was followed in March 2010 with a legacy document *London 2012: A Legacy for Disabled People* which finally set the Paralympic project in the context of the government's wider disability agenda: 'Our goal is not only to host the most accessible Games ever, but also to ensure that we harness the full power of London 2012 to help realise progress towards achieving equality for disabled people by 2025' (DCMS, 2010, p. 2).[6] The document identified three 'areas of change', within each of which were a further four objectives (see table 5.4).

This legacy document focuses on people rather than physical places and spaces. The Olympic venues by this point had already been planned as barrier-free environments and the Olympic Delivery Authority had won a Royal Town Planning Institute Planning Award for their accessibility strategy (Ibid., p. 29). The hard legacy issues identified in this strategy related to 1,000 sports and leisure facilities to improve access (under objective 2b); to encourage more hotels to adopt improvements in accessibility (under 3c); improve infrastructure of the London Transport system (164 stations) and 145 main line stations by 2015 (although Olympic related stations within that group would be upgraded by the Games under 3d).

Table 5.4. Legacy vision for the Paralympic Games.

Aims	Objectives
1 Influence the attitudes and perceptions of people to change the way they think about disabled people	(a) Ensuring comprehensive media coverage (b) Providing an accessible and inclusive London 2012 Games (c) Connecting the UK with London 2012 (d) Engaging children at home and abroad
2 Increase the participation of disabled people in sport and physical activity	(a) Encouraging disabled people to be more active (b) Widening sports opportunities for disabled adults (c) Widening sports opportunities for disabled children and young people (d) Increasing the supply of accessible facilities
3 Promote and drive improvements in business, transport and employment opportunities for disabled people	(a) Opportunities for business (b) Access to jobs and skills (c) Accessible tourism (d) Improved public transport

Source: DCMS (2010) pp. 4–7.

The real emphasis here is on soft legacy. The first aim concerns social attitudes (including the role that the media play in shaping those attitudes) and deals with the support necessary for people to participate in the Games and Cultural Olympiad as volunteers, employees, spectators, or active contributors in the ceremonies and torch relay. The second aim concerns participation in sport for all age groups – within and beyond educational institutions covering leisure sport and elite participation. The third aim is about inclusion more generally in the economy for businesses owned by disabled people, access to employment and skills training, and greater customer provision and care in tourism and transport. The document also demonstrates how many of the existing Olympic programmes feed into these goals: Cultural Olympiad-Unlimited; Access to Volunteering Fund; Get Set Programme; Lets Get Moving; Be Active Be Healthy; Playground to Podium; CompeteFor; Access Now; and Personal Best.

Conclusion

The success of the Games in Beijing 2008 and Vancouver 2010 and the plans for London 2012 show the progress over the last half-century as the Paralympics have developed since the first competition between 130 British and Dutch athletes in 1952. Notwithstanding a chequered history and the characteristic dissonance between bid promises and final realities, the Paralympic Games have spread geographically, have moved into new sports, have encompassed a wider range of disabilities, and have helped give credence to the belief that access to sport is available to all. The growing scale of the Games provides relatively little challenge given that they primarily use facilities and accommodation provided for the rather larger sporting festivals that occur immediately before the Paralympics.

Nevertheless, there are important qualitative changes. As the Games came progressively closer to the heart of the Olympic movement, they have ensured that the disabled community had to be accommodated, figuratively and literally, within the planning, design, and cultural and educational programmes of Olympic cities. Cities could avoid those obligations in the 1970s and 1980s, but the bidding process now ensures that they must provide not only barrier-free Olympic facilities, but increasingly also a wider environment and society that welcome diversity. As such, attention to issues of access and discriminatory practices undertaken in relation to an Olympic host city at one point in time have a demonstration effect that may well have implications for that city, and the wider society, at all other times.

Notes

1.   Nomenclature has varied. Other terms used in the 1940s and 1950s included 'Paraolympics' and 'Paraplegic Games' (Brittain, 2010, p. 15). The first use of the term Paralympic was traced by Brittain to the *Bucks Advertiser and Aylesbury News* in 1953. He also has found a number of papers from the *New York Times* to the *Dublin Evening Herald* using the term in 1960 (Brittain, 2008, pp. 21, 247).

2.   Les Autres athletes have 'locomotor conditions such as Arthrogryposis, Arthrosis, cerebral palsy (some types), spinal cord conditions (e.g. polio), multiple sclerosis and muscular dystrophy [and] are allowed to participate in events under the Les Autres classification. Les Autres also incorporates dwarf athletes under its classification. The locomotor conditions may be congenital or as a results of an injury or accident' (BALASA, 2007).

3.   For a full discussion of the issues involved, see *inter alia* Howe (2008), Bailey (2008), Cashman and Darcy (2008) and Brittain (2010).

4.   'Boccia' is similar to petanque (French bowls) played individually or as a team game by people with cerebral palsy and other locomotor disabilities. 'Goalball' is a three-a-side gymnasium team game for the blind or visually impaired played on a special court of the same size as that used for volleyball. It involves trying to propel a heavy sound-enhanced ball past the backline of the opponents' half of the court.

5.   For more general thinking on planning and disability, see Imrie (1996), Gleeson (2001) and McCann (2005).

6.   See the Prime Minister's Strategy Unit's *Improving the life chances of disabled people: Final Report* published January 2005, which sets out the strategy for independent living, support for families of young disabled children, transition to adulthood, support and incentives for getting and staying in employment (PMSU, 2005).

Part II

Planning and Management

Chapter 6

Financing the Games

Paul Kitchin

The relationship between the Olympic Movement and commercial forces extends back to the first staging of the modern Olympics in 1896 (IOC, 2008). Today the Olympic Family – the complex network of organizations responsible for the development, administration and management of Olympic sports and their athletes (see table 6.1) – is funded by television revenues and corporate partnership programmes that are seen as jewels in many organizations' commercial portfolios. Never before has the Olympic Movement been as financially stable. Organization Committees for the Olympic Games (OCOGs) have a wide range of financing options at their disposal and the government support that is now vital for bid cities sees many additional costs being borne by local and national communities. Nevertheless it was not always this way. The International Olympic Committee's relationship with commercialization started as a troubled experience (Magdalinski and Nauright, 2004). Since the emergence of television and myriad sponsor deals associated with the Games the stakeholders of the Olympic Family have vied for power, repositioning their levels of interest in the Olympic Games as a tool to achieve their individual goals. In recent years, the IOC's actions have reduced the conflict to create a more symbiotic link with commerce.

The purpose of this chapter is to survey how an OCOG finances the Games, while at the same time recognizing that the current finance situation is framed within its historical context. The shifting position of the IOC, the International Federations (IFs), the OCOGs, the National Olympic Committees (NOCs), broadcasters and sponsors can be mapped through stakeholder analysis, and in particular Mendelow's (1991) power/interest matrix. By examining the changes in the levels of stakeholder power and their interest in the Games over time, it is possible to arrive at a better understanding of not just the key finance options but in what context they support the Games. This discussion then serves to complement the more detailed discussion of the experiences of individual Olympic cities in later chapters.

The first part of this chapter examines the use of stakeholder analysis as a strategic management tool. The second section applies stakeholder mapping, a form of stakeholder analysis, to demonstrate how changing stakeholder relationships within the Olympic Movement have positioned the OCOG over time and explores the ramifications for their ability to finance the Games. The analysis of stakeholders is itself based on accounts of personal experiences within the IOC's management structure (e.g. Miller 1994; Payne, 2006; Pound, 2006), with additional insights provided from a range of scholarly sources (in particular Barney *et al.*, 2004; Preuss, 2000, 2002, 2004). In doing so, this chapter illustrates the principles of stakeholder analysis. As such, this analysis provides greater insight into the implications of finance issues for the OCOG. Later sections of the chapter analyze the finances of the host city through a discussion of sources of revenue and expenditure, ending with a survey of indirect sources of revenue.

Stakeholder Analysis

The growth of literature on stakeholder analysis has coincided with the realization that the organization is a part of an extended network of interests. Freeman (2006, p. 40) defined a stakeholder as 'any group of individuals who can affect or is affected by the achievement of the organisation's objectives'. When assessing who stakeholders are and how they may support or block a chosen strategy, Frooman (1999) has suggested the following three questions as a way of providing a framework for analysis;

1. Who are they?

2. What do they want?

3. How are they going to try to get it?

In relation to who they are, Mitchell *et al.* (1997) proposed that stakeholders could be identified by their possession of any of the following attributes: power to influence the organization; the legitimacy of the relationship with the organization (level of power); and the urgency of the stakeholder's claim on the organization (level of interest). As applied to the Olympic Family, for which table 6.1 provides details on internal and external stakeholders, we may note that an organization such as the OCOG should seek to classify its stakeholders by these attributes. To manage the relationships with its stakeholders the IOC must use communication, negotiation, leadership and compromise to balance the wide variety of needs and claims that the network would produce (Chinyo and Akintoyee, 2008). For instance, the IFs are responsible for the management of a number of sports within the Olympic programme. An IF may feel that it provides the technical support for hosting integral components of the event. In addition, the IF aims to generate interest in the sport outside the Games themselves which is important for encouraging talented individuals to consider that sport in the future. One method of determining the second and third question is by performing a stakeholder analysis using one or more of a number of analytic tools.

Table 6.1. Who are the stakeholders of the Olympic Games?

The Olympic Family

This group consists of a number of internal stakeholders such as:

1. The IOC: The International Olympic Committee is responsible for a number of functions. Primarily the IOC is responsible for the international governance of the Olympic Movement through an Executive Board and a General Assembly of IOC Members that manages the Olympic Charter. The IOC is responsible for the management and marketing of the intellectual property (IP) of the Olympic Movement and awarding the Summer and Winter Olympic Games to host cities. The IOC members represent the IOC at the national level within the National Olympic Committees ensuring that the NOC represents the Olympic movement effectively.

2. The OCOG: The Organizing Committee for the Olympic Games is the organization that is responsible for staging the Summer or Winter Olympic Games each Olympiad. In recent Olympic Games this organization has also been supported by government Delivery Agencies which have handled the construction of the event facilities in preparation for the Games. Once the Games has been staged this organization disbands.

3. The IF: The International Federations of Sport are the bodies responsible for the coordination and global promotion of their respective national sporting bodies. The primary difference between the IF structure and the structure of the IOC is that the former uses a delegate structure where the international body is managed by national representatives. This style of management can lead to continental rivalries and block voting to influence the outcome of presidential elections and executive board composition (Shilbury and Deane, 2001).

4. The NOC: The National Olympic Committees represent the Olympic Movement in each of the 202 member nations of the Olympic Family. NOCs are responsible for managing national representative athletes, support staff and officials that take part in the Olympic Games. Within this stakeholder group there is vast disparity in resources between powerful nations such as the United States of America (USOC) and Great Britain and Northern Ireland (BOA) and smaller nations such as Western Samoa and Vanuatu.

9. The Athletes: Fêted always by the Olympic Family the athletes have increased their power in the management of the movement through a number of events, some unplanned others planned. The Munich massacre led to increased security precautions being taken in all subsequent Olympic Games that now places athlete security first amongst operational procedures. The highest profile athletes are now professional and their willingness to participate has never been in doubt. However a collective union of athletes, especially the highest profile in each sport, could see this group gain substantial power in years to come.

Commercial Partners:

This group consists of a number of external stakeholder groups such as:

5. Broadcasters: The primary broadcasters to have a significant impact on the operations of the IOC were the US television networks that realized the value of sports programming to generating advertising revenue for their stations. The US television networks for many years paid the bulk of the global television rights fees compared with their European and international counterparts (Pound, 2006). Since the 1990s however the global television rights have been more evenly spread across the international market.

6. TOP Sponsors: The Olympic Partnership (TOP) is a partnership programme between the IOC and some of the most successful multi-national companies in their respective businesses. The TOP sponsors support the Olympic Movement through the payment of sponsorship fees and the provision of value-in-kind assistance at the staging of Olympic Games. Each TOP sponsor has exclusive global rights to the Olympic IP that can be used in their marketing, promotion and communications activities during their partnership.

7. OCOG Partners, Sponsors, Suppliers: The OCOG offers a tiered platform of domestic partnerships, sponsorships and supplier relationships to provide services to the staging of the Games in turn for the right to communicate their association within the market where the Games are held. These sponsors cannot conflict with the TOP sponsors.

8. Local and National Governments: These public sector organizations are responsible for supporting the OCOG and its partners in the delivery of the Olympic Games. Government support is extremely important for cities wishing to win the bidding for the Games; however this level of support is generally dependent on the government's wider direct or indirect role in society.

Mendelow (1991) provides a good example of how this might be done. His power/interest matrix classifies stakeholders by determining the bases of their power (to initiate action, or influence strategy) and the level of interest they have in the operations of an organization (Bryson, 2004). Stakeholders are divided into four groups on the basis of scores derived for each criterion. *Key Players* are stakeholders that are both moderate-to-high in power and interest and can have significant impact on organizational strategy. *Keep Satisfied* is a class where stakeholder power is moderate-to-high but interest in current activities and strategy is low-to-moderate. The third category, *Keep Informed*, is characterized by moderate-to-high levels of interest but low-to-moderate levels of power. The final grouping is rather contentious as few organizations would publicly group any of its stakeholders in the *Minimal Effort* category where levels of power and interest are low-to-moderate. However, if managing each stakeholder is important in rationalizing resources, it is feasible that certain stakeholders may be classified as such. By assessing stakeholder analysis over time the rise and fall of stakeholders' interest and power can be determined and predicted for future strategy recommendations.

Period 1: 1960 to 1978

The 1960s brought a sea change to the staging of the Games. Although worldwide television rights fees of $1.6 million (Tokyo) and $9.8 million (Rome) (IOC, 2008) may pale in comparison to current Olympic broadcasting rights, in a historical context these rights fees placed considerable strain on the relationship within the Olympic Family (Barney *et al.*, 2004). Moreover, the Olympics were no longer simply a sporting event but a vehicle to showcase nations. The use of the Summer Olympics from 1960 to 1972 for example gave countries a chance to present a new face to the international community as three of the hosts (Rome 1960, Tokyo 1964 and Munich 1972) highlighted their post-war societies. Furthermore the awarding of the Summer Olympics to Mexico City in 1968, the first to a non-developed country, gave the hosts the stage to demonstrate their economic development. Central to the realization of these goals was the staging of an increasingly expensive Olympic festival.

During this period, Article 49 of the Olympic Charter stipulated that the OCOG would be responsible for negotiating the television rights for their events. The IOC signed its approval on all deals but only took a passive advisory role. Barney *et al.* (2004) noted that the in-fighting between the members of the IF and the NOC over their allocations of television money, with each wanting a greater share, placed pressure on the IOC. Meanwhile the OCOG became a significant stakeholder within the Olympic Family through their Charter-directed ability to negotiate television rights.

Coerced by members from the IF and NOC, the IOC decided on a new distribution method for the broadcasting rights. The Rome Formula, established in 1966, divided the revenues through a set method. The OCOG would receive none of the first million dollars, a third of the second million, and two-thirds of every subsequent million over $2 million. This handed the initiative to the OCOG, in that it would see increasing returns if it could negotiate a substantial fee (*Ibid.*). With hindsight, it is clear to see that the creators of the Rome Formula did not expect the significant increases in broadcasting rights (see figure 6.1) that would be realized after 1966. This actually highlighted the lack of commercial knowledge within the IOC at that time (Pound, 2006).

$US Millions

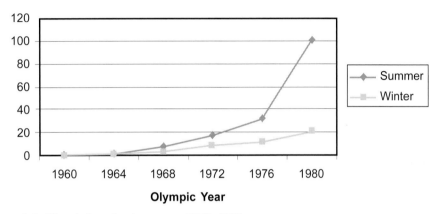

Figure 6.1. Olympic broadcast revenues (1960–1980).

Despite the generous allocation of funds the perspective of the OCOG differed from that of the IOC. The OCOGs were the bodies responsible for the financial risk of staging the Games and therefore saw these allocations as redistributions of their money (Barney *et al.*, 2004). As the payee of all related costs the OCOG ensured that the costs of broadcast production – 'service facilities' (Miller, 1994, p.102) – should be separated from the overall broadcasting rights fee before the remainder was returned to the IOC for redistributive purposes. Therefore the OCOGs of the 1970s saw an opportunity to reduce the slice of funds available for redistribution through the Rome Formula. In 1979 the Los Angeles Organizing Committee claimed nearly half ($90 million) of the negotiated $200 million broadcast deal for service facilities fees (Miller, 1994).

In sum, the key feature of this period in Olympic history was the influx of television money and the search for an equitable distribution method palatable to each member of the Olympic Family. The importance of Article 49 in determining the right of the OCOG to negotiate broadcasting deals, coupled with the structure of the Rome Formula, allowed the OCOG to operate from a position of significant power in securing resources for the host city. Further increases in OCOG power were achieved by the selective re-focusing of the guidelines determining rights fees and the fee for technical assistance. It is clear that from this support the OCOG were the most powerful of the *Key Players* during this period (see figure 6.2). The infighting between the IF, NOC and the IOC over commercial revenue sharing resulted in a lack of attention and assertiveness from the IOC in dealing with commercial realities placing them in a weaker position. Additionally the reliance on television revenues alone to cover the majority of costs for the Olympic Family placed the entire Movement in an uncertain position.

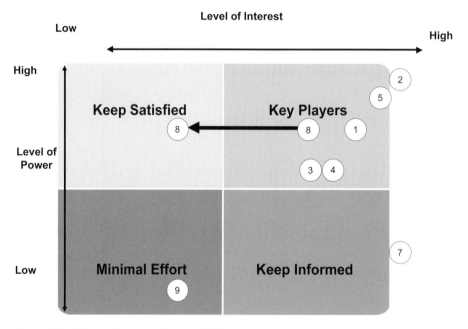

Figure 6.2. Stakeholder mapping pre-1979.

Period 2: 1979 to the Present

After Los Angeles 1984, organizers had secured significant broadcast funding to help finance their Games, the advisory role of the IOC was altered to allow them a more 'active role in the process' (Pound, 2006, p. 170). This was a key moment in the IOC's financial history and initiated a re-alignment of the Olympic stakeholders. Although this took 20 years to come to fruition, it saw the IOC become the most powerful member of the Family. Nevertheless, a number of authors all placed great emphasis on the establishment of the TOP marketing programme as the factor that turned the Olympic Family's fortunes around (Payne, 2006; Miller, 1994).

Horst Dassler and his company International Sports and Leisure (ISL) persuaded the IOC to embark on an ambitious marketing programme that sought to exploit the Olympic intellectual property internationally (Magdalinski and Nauright, 2004; Toohey and Veal, 2007). The use of brand categories by Los Angeles in 1984 showed how a sophisticated marketing programme could work.

The organizers of Los Angeles 1984 guaranteed sponsoring companies exclusivity so that their competitors would not be able to associate with the event. This exclusivity allowed them to increase the value of each deal while reducing the total number of sponsors. In effect, fewer sponsors gave more funds and also provided value-in-kind assistance to the operations of the Games.

The structural design of the fledgling TOP (The Olympic Programme) was very similar to the model applied at Los Angeles 1984, with the exception that while Los Angeles only had to fund the 1984 Games, the TOP programme would last four years and apply to both the Summer and Winter Olympic Games. From 1988 onwards, it also included the Paralympic Movement. To that point, the sole source of revenue had been broadcasting rights, but since this was prone to political arguments between the stakeholders, it could not supply all the IOC's funding needs. The real importance of the TOP revenues was that they allowed the IOC to reduce its reliance on broadcasting rights and supplied a more robust financial platform for future activities. Barney *et al*. (2004) highlight the difficulties experienced by ISL in starting up the TOP programme. However, over a period of three Olympiads revenue increased from $96 million in 1985 to $279 million by the end of 1996, establishing it as a key aspect of Olympic financing (IOC, 2008). The combination of the TOP fees and the broadcasting revenue created what is currently known as the Olympic Marketing Programme.

Payne (2006) highlights the proposal by Channel 7 of Australia to bid for two summer events in the one negotiation as the catalyst for the IOC to achieve true independence in the financial affairs of the Olympic Movement. When negotiating Games broadcasting fees the effort expended by the IOC not only incurred time and effort but failed to achieve medium-term stability from broadcasting sources. In 1995 NBC offered a $2.3 billion deal to acquire multiple Games from 2000 to 2008 (Roberts, 2003; Payne, 2006). While the deals would be signed later, the general principle was that within a period of three months the IOC was able to secure medium-to-long term financing from this source. By obtaining revenues in advance of the bidding decisions the IOC could tell the candidates the exact figures that would assist them in financing their Games.

The implications of these deals for members of the Olympic Family were significant. The NOC and IF each received increasing amounts of revenue from the total marketing contribution, rising from $86.6 million and $106.9 million in 1993–1996 to $319.5 million and $472.4 million in 2001–2004, respectively. From 1992 to 2004 the OCOG received the significant share of all distributed funds (60 per cent of all revenues), which increased the certainty of being able to budget for their event with predetermined figures. In 2004 the IOC decided to lower the OCOG share from 60 per cent to 49 per cent, arguing for a larger portion of the proceeds in order to fund the wider Olympic Family. The justification for giving the OCOG a smaller percentage was that, with increased television rights fees, the real value remains on an upward curve. Hence, despite the lower percentage, the OCOG is likely to receive increasing revenues from these sources.

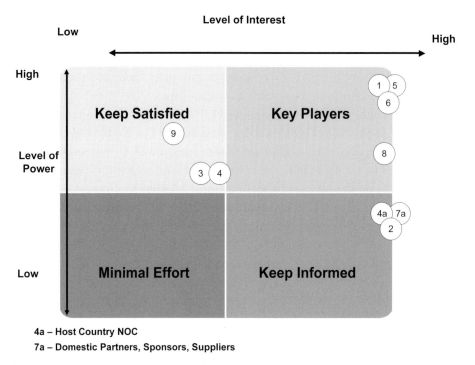

4a – Host Country NOC
7a – Domestic Partners, Sponsors, Suppliers

Figure 6.3. Stakeholder mapping post-1979.

From these changes the IOC is in a stronger, more powerful position (see figure 6.3) in which it can distribute 92 per cent of all revenues to its stakeholders and still manage its activities and stand financially secure (IOC, 2008). The OCOGs have lost involvement in television negotiations and forgone their ability to determine the total sponsorship packages for the Games. Nevertheless, the establishment of the TOP programme produces significant resources of which the OCOG gets a significant share. Therefore the OCOG has lost power but gained relative security over their financing arrangements from two key sources of revenue.

Analysis

By examining the power/interest maps in figures 6.2 and 6.3 it is clear that over time stakeholders have been repositioned in accordance to their power and interest over Olympic finances. Turning to analyze the significant shifts in or out of power, one begins by noting that some stakeholders have increased their power/interest status since 1960. The IOC has repositioned itself to become *the* Key Player within the Olympic Movement. Although this may appear logical, it was arguably not the strongest of the stakeholders prior to 1979. This turnaround can be attributed to two key decisions: the move in 1979 to take an active role in television negotiations; and the establishment of a commercial sponsorship programme that would provide an alternative to over-reliance on broadcasting fees. Furthermore, the decision in 1995 to offer multiple Games television packages to NBC was important as it bought the television rights negotiations forward before a future OCOG was appointed, thereby reducing the ability of any OCOG to be involved in the process.

Broadcasters' interest in the Games had steadily increased since the 1960s. The growing television revenues from 1960 to 2010 increased the power of this group of stakeholders over the Olympic Family. Since the decision by the IOC to involve themselves directly in television negotiations the broadcasters have become more of a partner than simply a financier. The power of NBC was apparent at the 2008 Beijing Olympics where the swimming heats and finals were reversed from their traditional timetable in order to position the medals races for the US prime time audience. While Olympic rhetoric is dominated by an athlete-centric ideology it was clear in this case that the broadcaster was granted its request despite the objections of the swimmers.

The creation of TOP acted to formalize and simplify the commercial relationships of Games sponsors. Not only did TOP provide control over the management of Olympic-related sponsors but it also offered greater value to these commercial interests. Although outside the scope of this chapter, the ability of the TOP sponsors to have an influence on the IOC agenda after the Salt Lake City bribery scandal demonstrated that, with broadcasters, these sponsors are now significant partners in the Olympic Movement. Nevertheless, the number of organizations involved in TOP reduces the level of power that the broadcasters can enjoy unless they act collectively.

As a result of the TOP programme, domestic sponsorship arrangements also received greater management attention. Coordinated in a fashion not to conflict with TOP sponsors the domestic offerings still provide exclusivity for the partner. This has allowed domestic sponsors to form another stakeholder group (numbered 7a in figure 6.3) and although lower in power than TOP sponsors they still wield power over the OCOG. However this segmentation under the TOP programme ensures that they are classed as *Keep Informed*.

The level of OCOG power has decreased over time due essentially to the same actions that have increased the IOC's power. Although this is not a directly inverse relationship, the management of television rights and the creation of TOP sponsors have seen its power decrease. Since Los Angeles 1984, when the organizers wielded such financial muscle, the OCOG has taken a backseat on certain aspects of Olympic financing. It is important to note however that this does not imply that the OCOG is worse off in financial terms. The increased revenues from the broadcasters and the share of global sponsorship rights mean that the OCOG has a sounder financial footing to stage its games and at the same time the IOC is not exposed to short-term financing options. While the OCOG has benefited from the growing revenues, raised expectations for the *best games ever* have led to equal or more-than-equal rises in expenditure.

An interesting observation from comparing the second stakeholder map is the formation of stakeholder clusters. In figure 6.2 each of the stakeholders could arguably occupy many distinct positions, whereas in figure 6.3 two distinct sets of clusters have appeared. These two clusters are essentially separated by their bases of power. The IOC, in partnership with the broadcasters and TOP sponsors control the revenues into the organization and distributions out to the Olympic stakeholders. The OCOG, with its domestic sponsorships and its host NOC, has the power to raise Games-related revenues but does not have the final say on key aspects of Olympic financing, as the host has to coordinate facility design with the relevant IF.

The remaining stakeholder groups have also been repositioned over time. The IFs, originally a source of discontent on finance issues (Barney et al., 2004), are now satiated by the revenues distributed by the IOC. While still holding some measure of power, their interest in Olympic finances has arguably decreased as they focus now on the World Championship events, significant tournaments in their own right.

Government involvement in the Olympic finances peaked, slumped and peaked again between 1960 and the present. Initially government involvement in financing the Games decreased after the budget over-runs of Montreal 1976. After the success of Los Angeles 1984, government involvement again grew on the conviction that there was not only an economic case for bidding but also a rationale for achieving non-Games related benefits including increased tourism, economic development and regeneration. Given the significant funds required to stage the modern Olympics, governments are still key players in the management of Olympic finances, despite fluctuating levels of interest over the past 40 years.

Another notable feature is the rise in the status of athletes as Olympic stakeholders. The distinction between amateur and professional was abolished in the Olympic Charter in 1986. It is now fully accepted that Olympic and Paralympic bodies can assist their athletes in securing resources and opportunities for their careers, such as in sports media and marketing. The ability to earn a living from sport combined with heightened event-security concerns could imply that the power of athletes, as Olympic stakeholders, is increasing but is not yet absolute. Their lack of collective organization – possibly because the tradition of the event sees the Games as the peak of athletic achievement and prevents such action – means that they have not significantly increased their level of interest and power over Olympic financing. Should they ever do so, the results might well have implications for stakeholder management.

From the above analysis, the OCOG is in a good position to draw down significant funding from the IOC's Olympic Marketing Programme. Although OCOG power has been reduced over time, the number of cities willing to bid for the Summer and Winter Games makes it evident that interest is still high. Despite now occupying a more subservient position, the OCOG still has a substantial range of revenue sources available, notwithstanding the range of expenditure items that needs to be met.

Financing the City

Domestic Sponsors and Suppliers

As discussed previously, while certain categories under the TOP programme are restricted for domestic sponsoring organizations, many other categories exist in which sponsorship deals can be created. The value of these sponsorships varies depending on the domestic conditions of the host city but, importantly, the revenues flow directly to the OCOG. Taking London 2012 as an example, the domestic programme is structured into tiers as it seeks to raise approximately £450 million to assist in financing the 2012 Games (see figure 6.4). For London the domestic commercial programme will be tiered with categories termed Official Partners (Tier One), Official Supporters (Tier Two) and Official Providers and Official Suppliers (Tier Three). Organizations will contribute in the region of £40–80 million for Tier One, £20 million for Tier Two, and £10 million for Tier Three status. Once again, a key feature is the provision of in-kind services from these partners. For example, LOCOG has appointed Adeco as their partner to be responsible for human resource services when recruiting staff for London 2012.

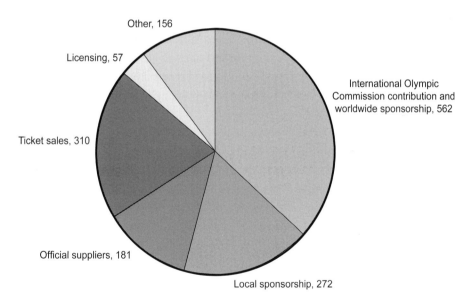

Figure 6.4. Proposed revenue for London 2012 est. (£m – 2004 prices).

Similarly, with the rise in security and logistical concerns after 9/11, LOCOG has appointed specialist firm Airwave to handle their organizational communications. Of particular interest is the fact that this company specializes in secure radio networks for the emergency services and public safety users. The fact that the OCOG is able to capitalize on this assistance by allowing potential suppliers to gain benefit over rivals works to the advantage of the sponsor, the OCOG and the Olympic movement. Nevertheless with the recent global economic recession, it has become more difficult for organizers to secure such partners. In July 2009 Nortel, a Tier One Partner, filed for bankruptcy causing LOCOG to terminate the contract. While a suitable replacement was found in Cisco Systems, this firm only agreed to be a Tier Two partner, leading to a shortfall in funding from this category. Although the opportunity to attract another Tier One place remains open, it demonstrates that under the TOP system the search for sponsors and partners can be a complex procedure.

Ticketing

Income from ticket sales has been present in every Olympics since 1896 and is the most traditional of all OCOG revenue sources. Fine-tuning tariffs according to the events on offer frequently leads to a complex structure of ticketing arrangements that ensures maximum resources for the OCOG, which has sole rights to the revenue raised through this method. Within any given Olympic venue, there is a limit to the number of the tickets available for spectators; hence the ticket prices are determined to a considerable degree by the demand for any given event. Generally, the Opening and Closing Ceremonies and the 100 metres finals are the premier events on the athletics programme and the tickets sold for those sessions can command higher prices. By contrast, the qualifying rounds for other, lower-profile sports command less public support and can only justify lower ticket prices. Each event within the Olympic programme has its own level of demand, which, if interpreted properly, can yield a ticketing strategy designed to maximize possible revenue streams.

Los Angeles 1984 revealed the potential of capitalizing on ticket sales, which generated between $90 million and $150 million. This equated to 45 per cent of all facility costs and was equivalent to the amount that the OCOG donated to the Amateur Athletic Foundation of Los Angeles (AAFLA) as a legacy payment (Hill, 1996; IOC, 2008). With the increase in the IOC coordinated commercial rights, the overall value of ticketing has decreased since the mid 1990s. The $12–15 billion cost of Athens 2004 was not supported well by ticket sales, in fact both Athens and Turin 2006 suffered from poorer than anticipated ticket sales (Nguyen, 2009). For Beijing 2008, despite commentators stating that the OCOG thought that ticket sales were poor (Bristow, 2008), the official report from the IOC claimed that 99 per cent of tickets had been sold (IOC, 2009a).

Developments in the way that consumers purchase tickets now present challenges to the OCOG that previous host cities did not face. The collapse of Beijing's online ticketing system on the day of launch created embarrassment for an OCOG boasting about a technologically advanced event. In addition, the security of online transactions for ticketing gives cause for concern. Customers around the world were victims of a ticketing scam set up by fraudsters posing as official Beijing ticketing sites. Nevertheless, the complexity involved in ticketing has presented opportunities for host cities to secure *Official Suppliers* in this field, such as Ticketmaster in the case of London 2012.

A revenue-maximization strategy available to event organizers is the use of corporate hospitality areas that offer exclusive service and benefits. Due to the importance of the sponsorship funds in the staging of the Olympics, these value-added tickets are usually included in a bundled deal. This form of ticketing enables the OCOG to receive higher revenues for the seats within the stadium, although problems can occur if organizers fail to plan appropriately and make inadequate estimates of demand. The Sydney 2000 organizers made headlines for overestimating consumer demand, with the launch of an Olympic Club scheme designed to tap into the perceived pre-Olympic demand by offering consumers a Stadium Australia Gold Pass that secured a seat at the stadium for the entire Games. This scheme proved a failure, with the sales of tickets allocated through this method being significantly below the 72,000 that were expected. Other initiatives such as the Premium Packages designed to allow consumers to purchase category 'A' tickets (for the best seats) was ineffective, illustrating the point that special ticket categories need specialized planning and promotion in order to be effective (Thamnopoulos and Gargalianos, 2002).

Managing ticketing operations involves the OCOG in the challenging task of balancing the needs of the Olympic Family, corporate partners, citizens of the host country, and Games tourists. For example, despite the post-event accolades (Barney *et al.*, 2004; Haynes, 2001), the Sydney 2000 organizers faced harsh criticism for their role in managing the allocations of tickets to specific events (Thamnopoulos and Gargalianos, 2002). The popularity of specific sports in the host country brings unique qualities to the local market. For instance, swimming is an important part of Australian culture and one of the best opportunities for the Australian team to win gold. The sheer size of the Sydney International Aquatic Centre (20,000 seats) as prepared for the Olympics in 2000 was testament to the likely demand for tickets to the swimming events.

Licensing

Licensing involves owners of intellectual property passing over the right to use trademarks, logos and symbols to a third party for revenue generation. Its importance for the Olympics cannot be overstated. The organizers of Athens 2004 raised $61.5 million from the sale of licensed goods, while Turin 2006 produced $22 million from this source (IOC, 2008). Licensing deals are also intended to reflect the host city's cultural and symbolic characteristics. The use of mascots linked to the host city is one of the primary communication tools at the OCOG's disposal. The introduction of Waldi, for Munich 1972, as the first official mascot, was a key feature of the IOC marketing programme for children. A further driver of licence and merchandise is the 'collectability' of Olympic mementos. Outside the Olympic financing model, pin collecting has been a pastime of many

Olympic enthusiasts around the world and is an activity in which the athletes and the spectators can both engage. In Beijing, Coca-Cola hosted the pin trading area which was an important aspect of their on-site experiential marketing tactics (IOC, 2009c). Outside the Olympic events the growth of online auction houses has made it possible for collectors in many parts of the world to continue this practice between Olympic events. The emotional value of merchandise is strong for event consumers as it provides them with tangible evidence of the intangible experiences of the event (Shank, 2005). The greater the emotional value of the event, the greater the consumer demand for event-related merchandise. Hence although not a direct source of revenue for the OCOG pin trading could be seen as a significant indicator of the market demand for certain types of licensed products.

Other Sources

The use of lotteries to raise revenues for governments has been a key feature of general economic policy for the past 15–20 years. In Australia and the United Kingdom, lotteries have proved one of the main sources of finance for the establishment of new sporting facilities. The IOC itself has encouraged host cities to use special lotteries as financing tools for Olympics. Moscow 1980 and Seoul 1988 adapted existing lotteries for Olympic financing, while Montreal used a lottery to help reduce the debt burden incurred by the 1976 Games. Lotteries, however, have the socially regressive habit of redistributing income from lower classes, attracted by the large prizes and undeterred by the small chances of winning, into projects that generally advantage the middle class. Moreover, the creation of an Olympic lottery may take funds away from other worthy lottery-funded causes, which can include non-Olympic sport. For London 2012, the establishment of an Olympic lottery is a major contributor to the finance model, being employed to generate £750 million in funds. Careful examination of this proposal though, reveals that the existing lottery funds for sport and other good causes will be diverted into Olympic channels, favouring the elite end of sport to the possible detriment of sports with wider participation. Taking these factors together with increased competition from the establishment of new lotteries means that the overall estimate may be optimistic, leaving a potential shortfall in revenues.

Philatelic and numismatic programmes are long-standing revenue sources for the Olympic movement (IOC, 2008). For stamp sales, the revenue comes from adding a surcharge on the face value of the stamp. The numismatic programme was established at Helsinki 1952. Coins cast in Olympic editions contribute directly to OCOG revenues. Similar to the stamps, a surcharge on each coin that is minted goes to the OCOG (Preuss, 2004). Although not of the same magnitude as other sources of finance, the numismatic programme can provide useful revenues for the host city. An example of this is the A$12 million made by the Sydney Organizing Committee (SOCOG) for the sale of Olympic Commemorative coins in 2000. When placed in perspective, this income equated to half of the initial bid costs to win the Games. Figure 6.4 highlights the potential revenue sources for London 2012 as indicated in the Candidature File.

Expenditure

Fluctuations in Games-related expenditure have occurred through the building and refurbishment of venues and facilities. Generally, host cities employ at least some refurbished and existing facilities, which are usually more cost effective than new purpose-built facilities. The use of a refurbished or existing stadium can keep costs down dramatically, as shown by contrasting Montreal 1976, which spent $2 billion on new sporting facilities, against the $242 million expended on refurbished venues at Los Angeles 1984. Increasingly, OCOGs design temporary stadia that can be taken down once the Games are completed; a strategy that meets better the long-term leisure demands of the local area. For their part, IFs play a role in the technical specifications for the facilities, sometimes adding substantial costs to their design. In September 2009, for example, moves by London's Lord Mayor to rationalize facility provision were met with opposition from LOCOG stakeholders determined to ensure that the OCOG did not offend either the IOC or the relevant IF. Non-sporting construction, especially in the technologically advanced and sophisticated facilities now required for the media and for Athletes' Villages, will impact differently on balance sheets according to whether or not they can be converted to effective post-Games use. Finally, event operations costs – the costs incurred through running the event – have a marked tendency to change over time. Sydney 2000, for example, cost a fraction of the security costs spent

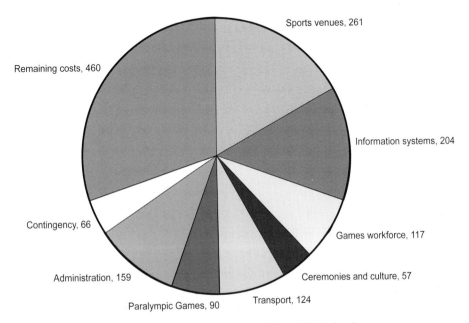

Figure 6.5. London 2012 Games Related costs est. (£m – 2004 prices).

at Athens just four years later due primarily to the new circumstances posed by 9/11 (Nguyen, 2009; also see chapter 9). Operational costs can be largely met by the OCOG and, compared to facility and infrastructure costs, have relied less on public funds. Games-related expenditure for London 2012 from the Candidature File can be seen in figure 6.5. Regardless of these increasingly expensive items, however, the Olympics generate economic activity for governments and increase tax revenue. The promise of these indirect benefits assists proponents for the Games in justifying their quest to become Olympic hosts.

Indirect Financing: Economic Impact

Apart from Los Angeles 1984 and Atlanta 1996, few Games have balanced their direct costs with revenues. To a greater or lesser extent, the equation is tempered by the fact that staging the Olympic Games often serves a wider political agenda. Once this decision has been made, the boundaries between the sums allocated to the staging of the Games and non-sports goals are often blurred. As mentioned earlier these goals require public funds in order to come to fruition, but the *indirect* benefits generated may be seen as sufficiently desirable to compensate for the expenditure. Such arguments have invariably aroused controversy but, without acceptance of the principle that associated indirect revenue flows to the host city from this initial expenditure, it might well be difficult to gain public support for this scale of project. The difference can been seen in comparing the expenditure items for staging the London 2012 in figure 6.5 with the total expenditure on all London Games activity as seen in figure 6.6.

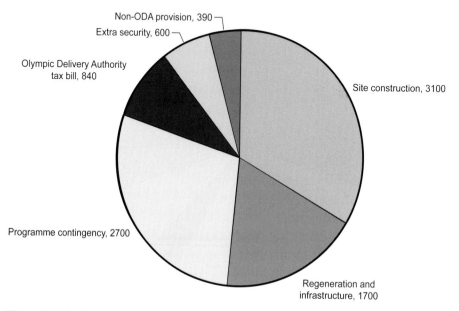

Figure 6.6. London 2012 total costs of hosting est. (£m – 2007 prices).

The confusion in assessing Games costs applies particularly to political arguments surrounding legacy and regeneration (see also chapter 1), but conclusive evidence is perennially difficult to obtain. The key parties in the bidding process, for example, will commission reports to investigate the potential economic impact of the Games in order to influence public opinion. Baade and Matheson (2002) observed that a key consideration is whether an economic impact study is prospective *(ex ante)* or after the fact *(ex post)*. Games proponents often use economic impact studies carried out *ex ante* to assist in highlighting the benefits that can be obtained through the staging of the event. This serves their purpose but is not always as rigorous as those carried out *ex post*. Unfortunately however, there have been few *ex post* studies to measure the final economic impact of the Olympics. Therefore with the Games significantly expanding in year-on-year cost and with economic impact assessment being questioned, it is time to query the sustainability of the event. The Games can always be sold to the public, despite a history of cost overruns and shattered budgets, but notions of 'can do' management, associated particularly with host countries' NOCs, continually pressurize other potential stakeholders to join them in bidding for the Games. In many ways, a new logic of 'must we do?' is needed to counterbalance such tendencies.

Chapter 7

Promoting the Olympic City

Stephen V. Ward

We will never know the true significance of French President Jacques Chirac's widely reported casual denigration of Finnish cooking in securing the 2012 Summer Olympic Games for London instead of the longstanding favourite, Paris. According to a secretly recorded restaurant conversation with the German Chancellor and the Russian President in July 2005, he said of the London bid that, '[y]ou can't trust people who cook as badly as that. After Finland, it's the country with the worst food' (Barkham, 2005*a*). The following day the story appeared in the French newspaper, *Libération* and was widely picked up by international news media. It was variously presented as a huge insult to British and Finnish cookery, a sign of French arrogance or, simply, a colossal error of judgement. Two days later the IOC met in Singapore to make its decision (Campbell, 2005). When successive rounds of voting had eliminated all other candidate cities, only Paris and London remained, with London winning by just four votes. Finland had two of these, so its delegates' choices (which remain entirely anonymous, of course) could hypothetically have swung the result in London's favour.

It can readily be conceded that other, equally unverifiable, theories about the reasons for London's 2012 success in this unusually close final vote also have their advocates. The real importance of this anecdote is, however, the insight it gives on the world's most extraordinary process of competitive city marketing. In one incident it captures the unique mixture of high politics, the expectation of good living, intense media interest and moments of complete farce that descend on the process of trying to win the Olympic prize. Many commentators have noted the rivalry between cities across the world for all kinds of mobile investment and consumption (e.g. Hall and Hubbard, 1998; S.V. Ward, 1998). They have also observed that this competition has become ever more intense in recent years, as traditional city economies have faltered and capital has become more mobile. In turn, this has put growing pressure on city leaders to engage in place marketing and promotion. This serves as a means both to achieve tangible physical and economic change by attracting new investment and activity and, in a deeper sense, to facilitate symbolic reconstruction.

The tangible prizes for the city marketers are no longer the manufacturing plants that were once the economic bedrock of cities. Nor has this traditional imperative simply shifted into the producer services that have replaced manufacturing in a post-industrial age. The process now goes much further, as cities compete to be centres of cultural and leisure consumption. To this end, many cities have invested heavily in new or extended cultural and other leisure investments such as museums, galleries, performance venues and sports facilities (Bianchini and Parkinson, 1993). Part of this move into the cultural marketing of cities also embraces major events and spectacles that can animate the new cultural investments and intensify the process of cultural consumption. In a crude sense, all these changes attract more tourists and increase consumption. In the longer term, however, these investments and the activities they contain contribute to raising the quality of urban life which, it is thought, will make cities into magnets for the new movers and shakers of the global economy – the entrepreneurs and the creative people from whom new innovations will flow.

These changes in the physical character and economic activities of cities also play an important part in the process of symbolic reconstruction. New buildings, structures and places, particularly those with iconic potential, play an important part in the re-branding of cities. So too, albeit in a more transitory fashion, do the major events and spectacles staged by cities (Gold and Gold, 2005; Smith, n.d.). New physical icons and spectacles provide images that can be deployed to point to a changing city. As well as being a way of attracting new investment and consumption, city marketing is also a way of manipulating the signs, real and promised, of change and integrating them into a new brand identity for the city. This is self-evidently important in promoting the idea of a changing city to investors and consumers. It is also extremely important as a way of selling the idea of change to those who actually live in the city and have to bear many of the costs of that change, financial and otherwise.

At the pinnacle of this most recent phase of city marketing is that associated with the Olympics. This applies particularly to the Summer Games which are a truly global affair (Miller, 2003); somewhat less so to the Winter Games, although they have the compensatory marketing benefit of reaching the world's most affluent countries. Given their scale, it is perhaps surprising that these mega-events continue to be awarded to just one city, rather than to a country as, for example, with major soccer events such as the FIFA World Cup. For their part, despite persistent questioning of financial and other benefits, many cities remain eager to compete for the Olympic prize. As of the early twenty-first century, the chosen city gets a large injection of funds from the IOC ($1.1 billion in the case of Sydney in 2000), paid for from world broadcast rights, sponsorship and merchandizing deals (Lee, 2005). It also receives a huge boost to tourism and other consumption, substantial new investment (funded from multiple but usually government sources) and an enduring boost to property values (Halifax plc, 2004). Staging these Games signals to outsiders and citizens alike that the host city really is a world city, well placed in other respects to become, or remain, a key hub in the global economy. Even being a serious contender confers real marketing benefits, showing that a city is ambitious for international attention (Hiller, 2000).

The result is that no other variant of city boosterism even approaches the extraordinary series of events now associated with the bidding for these events. This begins at the national level, as candidate cities are chosen, and proceeds through a shortlist as the IOC decides which city's bids should go forward to the final selection. The city eventually chosen as host is then presented with a colossal media opportunity to show itself to the world, to market its brand to anyone, anywhere. This builds up as the Games approach, culminating with the event itself. In 2008 the IOC reported that 2.1 billion viewers in 160 countries had watched the 2002 Winter Games in Salt Lake City and 3.9 billion viewers in 220 countries had watched the 2004 Athens Summer Games (IOC, 2008, p. 31). All this media exposure, provided it is reasonably positive, influences many tourist decisions at the time of the Games. This tourism impact will focus on, but extend beyond, the city to the country and the wider global region. More importantly, there is also huge long term potential for both tourism and investment (Kasimati, 2003).

No other city marketing opportunity achieves this global exposure. At the same time, provided it is carefully managed at the local level, it also gives a tremendous opportunity to heighten and mobilize the commitment of citizens to their own city. The competitive nature of sport and its unrivalled capacity to be enjoyed as a mass cultural activity gives it many advantages from the marketing point of view (S.V. Ward, 1998, pp. 231–232). In a more subtle way it also becomes a metaphor for the notion of cities having to compete in a global marketplace, a way of reconciling citizens and local institutions to the wider economic realities of the world. The notion of competition *in* sport can be elided, fairly smoothly, to embrace competing *for* sporting events, to the idea of cities having to compete with each other more generally.

Who Promotes the Olympic City?

It follows from the foregoing discussion that marketing the Olympic city in the later stages itself becomes a mass activity. Seemingly everyone from heads of government downwards takes part. Particularly important are the media, especially television, radio and newspapers, which play a key part in widening the commitment. They may also play a questioning or critical role but usually, at least for cities whose Olympic bid aspirations progress to the short-list and the final play-off, the net effect will be positive. Yet this mass media involvement normally only becomes critical after the bandwagon has begun to roll, reaching a peak during the Games themselves. More important therefore is the question of who actually starts the more difficult process of getting it moving in the first instance.

The detailed answer has of course varied, but one or a small group of individuals have normally been involved (Hill, 1996, pp. 90–238). The national sporting and Olympic organizations are in evidence, but these are rarely powerful enough on their own to provide the primary leadership for such a complex undertaking that cuts across so many aspects of city and national life. In some cases, the key actors have, not surprisingly, operated mainly within the sphere of government, whether at city or wider level. It is not difficult to appreciate why this has been so in cities with nations within Communist regimes at the time of the Games. Although only two, Moscow and Beijing have actually hosted the Summer Games, in 1980 and 2008, other communist cities – Budapest, Belgrade, Tashkent and Havana – have entered short-listed bids (Gold and Gold, 2005, pp. 179–180).

The government role has also been central in the promotion of Olympic cities under other authoritarian regimes, notably Seoul 1988 – awarded in very controversial circumstances in 1981 (Hill, 1996, pp. 189–217). The best known Games staged by a totalitarian state, Berlin 1936, were not primarily instigated by government (Hart Davis, 1986) although here the special circumstances of interwar Germany need to be taken into account (see chapter 11). Awarded to the city in 1931, before the Nazi state was created, their initiator had to persuade a suspicious Hitler (who saw them as promoting dangerously internationalist sentiments) that they were worth backing. Once he had been persuaded however, the Führer's Games set new standards in Olympic marketing, albeit with overtly propagandist motives that transcended the city itself to promote the Nazi regime.

Yet the centrally-planned, totalitarian and authoritarian examples have been the exceptions. The most typical Olympic bidders have been cities within capitalist and more or less democratic countries, although even here there are important examples of key actors being essentially political figures holding some kind of governmental office. Most typically in such cases, though, the impetus has usually been more genuinely city-based, with Mayors or their nominees often playing a critical part. A very notable example was Montreal, which bid for the 1972 Summer Games and staged the 1976 Games, thanks to the drive of its Mayor Jean Drapeau (Organizing Committee, 1976; see also chapter 13). More recently, successive Mayors of Barcelona, Narcis Serra and Pasqual Maragall, were directly responsible for Barcelona's successful bid for the 1992 Summer Games (COOB, 1992, I). In 2005 the bids of both New York and Moscow for the 2012 Summer Games were led by their cities' Deputy Mayors.

Even where city government leaders have been the driving force, this does not mean that Olympic bidding and marketing simply becomes a special municipal department. The most common feature amongst the individuals or small groups, who have promoted most of the successful recent city bids to stage the Olympics, has been the prevalence of what has come to be termed 'regime politics' (Stone, 1993; Painter, 1998). This kind of urban action involves relatively few key figures who might well include city government leaders but would be likely also to involve local and regional business leaders, national government appointees or relevant Ministers. The resultant partnership thus has an unusual status, in which the limits of governmental and private action become difficult to define.

The exact composition of these interests has not been the same in all would be

Olympic cities. However, most differences in the source of promotional effort are ones of degree. The usual pattern of recent years, certainly for successful bids, has involved a mix of national, city government and entrepreneurial effort and there has not even necessarily been a consistent pattern in the same countries. Birmingham's 1986 bid for the 1992 Games and Manchester's first (1990 for the 1996 Games) bid were advanced by city and local entrepreneurial effort without any effective central government backing (Hill, 1996, pp. 90–119). Yet Manchester's second bid (1993 for the 2000 Games) had significant material and symbolic central government backing (Law, 1994). Finally, central government support of all kinds for London's successful 2005 bid for the 2012 Games was very substantial.

In part, these differences reflected the changing political character of national government, under successive Prime Ministers Thatcher, Major and Blair. It is also highly likely that national government, whatever its complexion, had little inclination to back bids that had only a small chance of success. All politicians prefer to associate themselves with winners and may lose face if they make the wrong judgement. Barack Obama discovered this when his unprecedented Presidential support for his home city of Chicago did not stop it being eliminated at the first round of the voting to choose the host city for the 2016 Games (Gibson, 2009b; see also chapter 19).

Much of the original push in most bids to stage the Olympics has come from the middle ground between the public and private sectors. Yet there have been cases where the impetus has been predominantly private. This has been especially so in the United States where national government, except in 2009, did not involve itself to any great extent in Olympic bidding (Andranovich et al., 2001). Partly because of this, there have been few of the constraints on city boosterist ambitions that have operated in other countries. Just as they have explored every other conceivable way of promoting themselves, American city business-led coalitions were remarkably quick to see the city marketing potential of the Olympic Games. The result is that an astonishing number and variety of American cities have advanced short-listed bids (for both Summer and Winter Games) (Gold and Gold, 2005, pp. 141, 179–180; Essex and Chalkley, 2004). In part this was possible because, until 1955 when the host city for the 1960 Summer Games was decided, the United States Olympic Committee allowed multiple American cities to bid against each other for the same Games. Thus four US cities were candidates in 1946 (for the 1948 Games), and five in each of the 1947 and 1949 decisions for the 1952 and 1956 Games. This somewhat farcical process meant that the competition to stage the Olympics was to a considerable extent just another means for American cities to assert themselves over their domestic rivals.

Los Angeles, the history of which has been built more completely than that of any other large American metropolitan city on promotional puff, appropriately holds the record with two hostings (1932 and 1984) and seven other short-listed bids (Andranovich et al., 2001). Had the domestic bidding rules not changed in 1955 it would also have notched up an extra five bids, the last for the 2012

Games (SCCOC, 2010). Behind all its post-1945 bids has been a private business organization, the Southern California Committee for the Olympic Games. This had been formed in 1939 by a group of Los Angeles businessmen with the intention of bringing the Games back to the city after its earlier hosting of them. Eventually, in 1978, with Jean Drapeau's financially ruinous Montreal Games fresh in everyone's mind, they were successful in regaining the 1984 Games against only one other, very half-hearted, contender (Tehran). To both the IOC on the one hand, and local and state interests on the other, the promotional language and the eventual reality of the Games were the same – frugality and commercialism (Hill, 1996, pp. 156–162). Existing facilities and infrastructure were to be used, commercial sponsorship aggressively sought.

Although the 1984 Games had many perceived weaknesses that reflected this ethos, the approach proved highly profitable (especially so for Los Angeles and the United States) with the result that it both saved and changed the Games. The Los Angeles experience paved the way for the resurgence in competition to stage both Summer and Winter Games. However, no subsequent Games have been quite as completely privatized in their approach. It was, predictably, another American city with a long record of boosterism which most consciously modelled its own bid on Los Angeles (Andranovich et al., 2001; Whitelegg, 2000). Atlanta's bid for the 1996 Games was led by a local lawyer, Billy Payne, who played the central role in advancing the city's bid. Once again the model was highly privatized though a key difference was that, unlike Los Angeles, city government soon sought active involvement once the Games had been secured. This added regeneration and wider city objectives, causing some confusion about the promotional message. Not surprisingly the Games, whose organization remained private throughout, failed to deliver these muddled objectives. It was the widespread criticisms of Atlanta 1996 that have drawn subsequent bids back in the direction of public initiative, albeit without neglecting the methodologies of private business. These, embracing the full range of marketing and branding arts, remain absolutely central to the Olympic story.

How is the Olympic City Marketed?

In a very formal sense the key marketing material produced by would-be Olympic cities is the so-called candidature file. This is the official bid document, in recent years running to several volumes, submitted by short-listed candidate cities to the IOC. It is prepared by the bidding organization to set out the case for their particular city. The file will first be assessed by technical adjudicators (who may weed out unsatisfactory bids) and then forms the basis for the final voting by IOC members. At its core are technical details about the projected budget and how the various sports events and participants are to be accommodated in an effective and secure fashion. Although much of the file is thus very specific, it also has to display the wider city's capacity to host a large international event successfully. Thus the need to deal with logistical considerations, about how the movement of people associated with the Games will be handled, involves broader scale matters such as transport. The report will also include a general volume or section that markets the city and its wider setting. This part of the submission tends to showcase the city's attractiveness and openness in a way that also tries to communicate a more general sense of a wide and deep local commitment to sports and to hosting a successful Olympics.

Central it may be, but a city's candidature file is generally reckoned to be less a vote winner than a vote loser if it reveals any significant deficiencies relative to other cities. Real doubts about financing, organizational and technical competence have invariably scuppered bids by cities from the less affluent world. It was therefore absolutely vital if its hopes were not to go the same way that Rio de Janeiro did not falter on these aspects in the bidding for the 2016 Games. In the event, despite continuing insinuations from some competitors, it actually excelled in the technical assessment (Gibson, 2009a). Yet, having passed this initial test, Rio's team, like that of any other aspirant Olympic city, could not then rely on it to any major extent.

In all bidding cities, therefore, many marketing approaches and methods have to be deployed around this technical core element, many coming into play long before the IOC even becomes involved (e.g. McGeoch and Korporaal, 1994). Building the wide and deep commitment within the city and beyond is itself a major task. It involves a great deal of public and media relations work by the group initiating the bid first to win support from newspapers, television and radio. Media executives, editors and journalists all need to be briefed and persuaded. Business leaders, politicians and other prominent figures will similarly be schmoozed and convinced of the benefits of making a strong bid (and of contributing to it in money or other material ways to raise awareness). A typical wider marketing output at this stage would be a special issue or supplement of the local newspaper that would also carry considerable amounts of advertising expressing business and public agency backing.

Provided they can be convinced that the candidature will be competently advanced, many companies associated with a bidding city are likely to see benefits in the wider exposure that will result. The experience of Atlanta 1996 suggests that bidding for the Olympics (and, once awarded, the preparation period for the Games themselves) can shift business contributions away from more routine city marketing campaigns (S.V. Ward, 1998, p. 207). Overall, however, the total amount of business contributions to city marketing tends to increase. If, of course, the bid should eventually prove successful, then the benefits of early support in gaining an inside placing for any business opportunities during the Games themselves will be even more palpable. Yet this perception of benefits seems often to hold true even if the bid eventually turns out to be unsuccessful. Thus, despite their city's ignominious defeat in consecutive final IOC voting to decide the locations of the 1996 and 2000 Games, much of Manchester's business community would certainly have been happy to see a third bid to host the Summer Olympics. It was this support which also underpinned what became the city's successful bid to host the 2002 Commonwealth Games.

Alongside all this wooing of business, there will be an increasing engagement with the community, locally and more widely, to win the backing of key individuals and gain at least the semblance of widespread popular support. Any local organizations or individuals with sporting links, especially Olympic sporting links, are almost certain to be harnessed in some way to the bid. Typically the bidding organization will sponsor local sports and cultural events that will raise awareness and often involve the distribution of personal marketing items such as tee shirts, flags, balloons, pens and key-rings that bear its logo. Sale of these and the fees to enter mass events are often a way of raising funds for the campaign. Sydney's bidding team, for example, organized a mass community walk across the Harbour Bridge, charging two dollars per participant and thereby raising A$300,000 (SOCOG, 2000b, pp. 15–17). These approaches have the added benefit of enabling mass voluntary identification with the city's bid. In recent years, bid teams have become more adept at marshalling this, recruiting volunteers at an early stage to help spread the word and provide a tangible sign of the level of popular support. Barcelona, for example, had an army of over 100,000 volunteers to call upon by the time the bid campaign was transformed into the Games Organizing Committee (COOB, 1992, I, pp. 207–208).

The logo itself forms a key identifier for the bidding campaign. This would usually embrace a combination of Olympic imagery and various signifiers of the bidding city. In cases such as Sydney, these would be iconic buildings or structures, in others more symbolic associations (McGeoch and Korporaal, 1994, pp. 67–70). A key requirement, however, is that it has to be capable of being reproduced in many different media. The publicity officers of the bidding organization would typically try to ensure that this appeared around the city and beyond, and especially in major media and at airports. Another promotional device that has occasionally been used at this stage has been the Olympic mascot. In most cases mascots have appeared after the award of the Games, with Moscow's 1980 bear cub mascot, Misha, being perhaps the most celebrated. An exception was Barcelona's bid team who launched a competition to design a mascot to build youth involvement (COOB, 1992, I, pp. 299–300).

These and other marketing devices form part of a widening promotional campaign. Business and community commitment provides marketing assets which can actually be used in the successive encounters with the National Olympic Committee (NOC), especially so if there are other bidding cities from the same country, and the IOC. Governments will be similarly aware that overwhelming local support is fundamental for a credible bid. For Rio's bid, the highly visible backing of the President of the Central Bank of Brazil was very important, addressing IOC anxieties about the city and country's financial capacity to stage the Games (see chapter 19). Manifestations of such support appear in the formal bid. Commonly, for example, the more general sections of the candidature files include portraits and brief statements of support from key individuals from business and the wider community, along with figures from politics and government and those with an international profile. In its bid, Atlanta, for example, secured the endorsement of film star Kim Basinger. Sydney, which borrowed many of Atlanta's marketing tactics, had the support of Nicole Kidman and her then husband, Tom Cruise (Burroughs, 1999; ACOG, 1990; McGeoch and Korporaal, 1994, pp. 141, 286). Although Cruise was American, there would usually be some local connection between the star and the place. Occasionally though, some bidders make serious mistakes in claiming celebrity endorsement. Berlin's generally mishap-prone bid for the 2000 Summer Games suffered when they publicized the endorsement of tennis stars Steffi Graf and Boris Becker without actually having asked them (McGeoch and Korporaal, 1994, p. 108).

From the beginning the bidding organization requires a team well versed in the promotional arts. It is quite common for key individuals to move on to advise subsequently bidding cities. Thus Mike Lee, who worked at the centre of the London 2012 campaign, played an important role in adapting the London template to Rio's successful campaign for 2016 (Gibson, 2009b). All successful campaigners understand that opportunities for personal meetings with people of influence are critical. Any possibilities of encountering IOC delegates, such as in meetings of other sports organizations, are seized upon and frequently planned in great detail (SOCOG, 2000b, pp. 17–18). Similarly, IOC gatherings ostensibly unrelated to the Games for which bidding is taking place become major opportunities to promote would-be Olympic cities. Hence meetings to decide the location of Winter Olympics are also significant marketing occasions for later Summer Games. Still more important are the Olympic Games which precede the fateful decision. The festival atmosphere which prevails at these times is particularly helpful to the bidding teams of intending future Olympic cities.

The potential demands on bidding teams' time and effort, therefore, are huge. Successful bidding cities appear to be those which can field a larger number on such occasions, especially of very senior individuals. London's 2012 bid certainly benefited from having Lord (Sebastian) Coe and Keith Mills able to share the burden (Campbell, 2005). As well as following the course of the sporting event itself, the bidding teams will be drawing lessons from how the Games are staged. They need to be fully attuned to perceived successes and failures to which they can respond in their own bid. Stamina is essential for the many events (including those hosted by opponents) that provide multiple opportunities for persuasion (McGeoch and Korporaal, 1994, pp. 148–168).

The official hotels occupied by delegates usually become the key arenas for this activity. While bidding organizations will have their own hotel suites, the more open meeting places of the hotels are highly significant locations because of their public nature. Here they literally have the opportunity to lobby any passing IOC delegates. Members of bidding teams will often try to station themselves in strategic positions in lobby areas where they can engineer 'chance' encounters, spy on opponents and generally see who is talking to whom. Some bid teams have tried to use more novel settings for these occasions. At the Barcelona Games of 1992, for example, the Milan team, bidding for the 2000 Games, moored a large yacht in the harbour, until it was ordered out by a senior IOC official.

Until 2002, a key marketing episode was presented whenever IOC delegates exercised their rights to inspect prospective host cities. Not all IOC delegates would visit all places, though those who did would usually come in several waves, amounting to another extraordinarily demanding period for bidding teams. In preparation, the bidding teams prepared very detailed dossiers on the individual delegates, listing their various interests and personal details. This information was sometimes traded by members of previous bidding teams and cities, who themselves had bid several times and were able to draw on their own previous experiences. Invariably delegates were very well looked after, in a fashion that approached the care lavished on official visits by leading heads of state. Sydney, for example, ensured that all traffic lights encountered by visiting IOC groups were changed to green on their approach, to avoid delays or any sense of traffic congestion (McGeoch and Korporaal, 1994, p. 196).

The ostensible purpose of these visits was to show delegates the city, its sporting credentials and its capacity to stage the world's biggest sporting event. In reality, however, they were very much more than this and the technicalities were only a small part of these occasions. Lavish entertainment was usual, along with expensive and carefully selected gifts for all the visiting delegates. In case this luxury might appear too shallow, many bidding cities also tried to introduce a more personal dimension, involving parties in the homes of leading members of the bidding team or other prominent citizens of the host city. Great care would be taken to ensure that language and cultural affinities, so far as possible, matched on these occasions, thereby underlining the openness of the city to visitors from all parts of the world.

Such visits were not without their risks. Few bids to host the Olympics are entirely without a local opposition. All successful bids have managed this process effectively, so that opposition was from an early stage marginalized. Yet there have certainly been cases where the IOC visits presented local opponents to the bid with a prime opportunity to market their own viewpoint. Unsuccessful bids by Toronto for the 1996 Summer Games and Berlin for 2000 both suffered in this way (McGeoch and Korporaal, 1994, p. 107; Kasimati, 2003). Their rivals were quick to exploit any such public expressions of opposition in their own marketing efforts. Bidders from more authoritarian countries were naturally at an advantage, though action outside the country by dissidents could have the same effect. It was used, for example, to damage Beijing's first bid (for the 2000 Games), when memories of the crushing of the democracy movement in Tiananmen Square were still fresh (McGeoch and Korporaal, 1994, pp. 225–227).

Yet there were altogether more serious problems beneath the surface of this part of the choice process. As the competition to host both Summer and Winter Games intensified in the 1990s, it is clear that the proper limits of legitimate marketing and promotional activity during these encounters were becoming very blurred. In part this may have reflected genuine cultural differences in expectations about how promotional activity should be conducted (Booth, 1999). Gifts such as alcohol, tobacco, perfume, luxury products associated with the bidding cities or other personal gifts to delegates were routine (Jennings and Sambrook, 2000, pp. 115–130). There had been growing unease for many years, with allegations of improper favours granted in response to outright or coded demands from delegates in the desire to obtain precious votes. Moreover, since votes in the final selection process remained secret, delegates could not be called upon to justify their voting decisions by their NOCs.

The Olympic movement began to prohibit the most extravagant forms of hospitality by bidding cities in 1991–1992. It was not, however, until 1998 that sufficient evidence emerged to cause the practice to be comprehensively changed (Jennings and Sambrook, 2000, pp. 115–130; D. Miller, 2003, pp. 321–329). The occasion was the IOC delegate visit prior to the selection of the location for the 2002 Winter Olympics, which were hosted by Salt Lake City. The Utah city's Mormon heritage had scarcely endowed it with a reputation for venality. Yet during the visit several delegates and their families were allegedly bribed with holidays, medical treatment and other favours. When allegations from a Swiss IOC member came to light, there was an IOC investigation that saw six members excluded, ten received warnings and only three exonerated. Following this scandal, the IOC decided to ban delegate visits. Instead it has strengthened the demands for technical and financial information from bidding cities, to provide a more evidence-based rationale for decisions.

Another consequence has been that the final IOC selection meeting has taken on even more importance because this is now the most significant opportunity for bidding organizations to meet rank and file delegates. Despite the new strictures, there remain differences of opinion as to how much lobbying is proper. Bidding teams constantly strive to find new ways to do some last minute promotion. On the eve of the 1990 IOC decision in Tokyo, Atlanta's bid team somehow managed to recruit chambermaids at the hotel where the IOC delegates were staying (McGeoch and Korporaal, 1994, p. 292). The latter thus went to bed to find their pillow cases had been changed to bear a message urging them to sleep 'with Georgia on their minds', a timely linking of Hoagie Carmichael's famous song with Atlanta's home state. Sydney's campaign took a flavour of the city to Monte Carlo where the IOC held its selection session in 1993. Celebrity lunches of the glitterati, sporting and otherwise, were familiar enough fare to Monaco's super rich but the street theatre, koala and kangaroo costumes struck a more exotic note (*Ibid.*, p. 285). Despite meticulous planning and securing of permits, however, some of their efforts were reined in by the city authorities.

Lobbying tactics were also a sore point following the 2005 IOC meeting in

Singapore where the 2012 Summer Games venue was determined (Campbell, 2005). In contrast to the Paris bid team, which deployed the already gaffe-prone President Chirac in the main presentation, London used the then British Prime Minister and his wife in person only in the pre-presentation lobbying. Over a quarter of the IOC delegates were individually subjected to a full Blairist charm offensive in a two day series of brief interviews that went on far into the night. These 'unfair' Anglo-Saxon tactics profoundly annoyed the French, a fact lovingly recorded in the British media.

London's successful deployment of political charisma in 2005 also shaped the tactics adopted by all the candidate cities bidding for the 2016 Games. At the Copenhagen meeting where the IOC made its decision in 2009, Rio and Chicago were supported in person respectively by Presidents Lula and Obama, Madrid by King Juan Carlos and Tokyo by Prime Minister Hatoyama. But this was no rerun of the 2005 Singapore meeting. If it had been, Barack and Michelle Obama would have won the votes for Chicago. This time it was Lula, actively and very visibly involved in the Brazilian city's bid almost from the outset, who played the ace. Ultimately, real commitment at the top of national government trumped an eleventh hour blast of charisma.

The final selection event itself is the great marketing set piece of the competition. Depending on the number of final bids, each presentation might last thirty or more minutes. In recent years, successful bids have combined charismatic individuals, technical wizardry and pure theatricality. Each candidate city uses individual speeches, not usually of any length, promotional videos, computer-generated simulations of intended Olympic venues, elements of cultural display and political campaigning. In theory, all the work ought to have been done by this stage. Nevertheless the presentation can certainly make a difference. For this reason, they are very carefully constructed and rehearsed, often over a long period. Every word and inflection is carefully judged. Sydney's successful bid, for example, was planned by a television producer with speeches written by a former Prime Minister's speechwriter (McGeoch and Korporaal, 1994, pp. 277–278). All those making speeches were trained and coached by a communications consultant.

For all this attention to detail, however, there are some common pitfalls. The videos are often a weak point, usually because they try to say too much. Explicit details of a city's infrastructure, cultural assets, love of sport or visual charms are important to get across but not necessarily very engaging unless done with imagination. There is also a temptation to use video clips to present too many talking heads. As well as subtly reminding delegates of the important people who were not able, or could not be bothered, to make it to the presentation, this can have the effect of making the presentation disjointed. Nor are there very many people, important or otherwise, who have a sufficiently strong screen presence to engage an audience.

This is not to say that the videos are not made to the highest professional standards and aspire to a celebrity quality of their own (Barkham, 2005b; BBC

News 24, 2006). There has been a recent tendency to use well known film makers to create them. Thus in the 2005 IOC selection meeting for the 2012 Summer Games, Steven Spielberg prepared the New York video and Luc Besson that for Paris. Even so, neither escaped the 'travelogue' and 'talking heads' tendencies already noted. Besson's film, for example, showed an extraordinary technical virtuosity in its opening animated scenes with the Olympic Rings dancing happily through the landmarks of Paris. A truly beautiful city was presented at its most engaging. Within a few minutes, however, Parisian charm and Besson's virtuosity were squandered. There followed an essentially dreary succession of middle-aged men (including, for example, several trades union leaders) expressing their support to camera. It mirrored the style of Paris's overall presentation.

By contrast, London's effort had no celebrity film maker to direct it. Instead two comparative unknowns with almost no feature film experience, Daryl Goodrich and Caroline Rowland, directed and produced its short and, in the circumstances, rather low budget video (Johnston, 2005). It contained no talking heads or touristic scenes. It focused instead on four children from different parts of the world seeing the Olympics and being inspired by a particular moment of sporting achievement. In time, they grew up to become world class sportsmen and women themselves. Yet the children were from Nigeria, Mexico, Russia and China, rather than the United Kingdom. Absolutely nothing that was place-specific about London appeared in the film. The idea was instead to associate it with deep-rooted Olympian ideals. Despite taking much from London's experience, Rio's successful use of video in 2009 differed in some significant ways. The well known director, in this case Fernando Meirelles, was back and the city itself was again the 'star'. Yet, like the London video, Meirelles's video, 'Passion unites us' played on the emotions, with Rio the sparkling embodiment of a diverse world united by a love of sport.

Another source of weakness can sometimes be in the very senior government figures who now normally play a part in these presentations. The problem is often the result of their only fleeting engagement with the campaign. This perception undoubtedly contributed to the abject failure of Obama, despite an eloquent speech, to rally IOC votes for Chicago in 2009. Even more, Chirac's 2005 speech supporting Paris at Singapore, delivered shortly after his arrival, was generally judged to be unfocused (Campbell, 2005). Nor were the political rivalries between the Gaullist French President and the Socialist Mayor of Paris sufficiently subordinated to the overall objective. By contrast, Barcelona's 1986 handling of the highly combustible mix of competing Spanish, Catalonian and city affiliations and sensitivities at the Rome IOC meeting showed consummate political dexterity (Hill, 1996, pp. 218–230). Australian city, state and national politics might have been less genuinely explosive but Paul Keating's prime ministerial intervention in 1993 on behalf of Sydney was nonetheless a powerful and meticulously prepared contribution (McGeoch and Korporaal, 1994, pp. 276–278).

Leading sportsmen and women, preferably Olympic medallists, with some charisma or star quality are common elements in these final set-pieces. In a hand that turned out to be full of aces, one of the most effective elements in London's final presentation for 2012 was the presence of the globally recognizable footballer, David Beckham. The legendary Brazilian footballer, Pelé, performed an even more important role for the Rio 2016 bid. There has also been a growing tendency to exploit the winsome potential of children and young people in the final presentations, either *en masse* in flag-waving or similar roles or as individual speakers. Atlanta had its 'dream team' of fifty-eight youngsters and Sydney used an 11 year old school girl as one of its individual speakers (Organizing Committee, 1996, pp 13–14; SOCOG, 2000*b*, p. 20). The latter is a particularly risky tactic, given the greater possibility of a child being either overawed by the occasion or conversely so nauseatingly self-possessed as to irritate the audience.

Yet, alongside such strong presences, the key figure in the final presentation will always be the leader of the bidding team. The necessary qualities of conviction, persuasion and self confidence that will have been well tested in the earlier stages of the bidding process now have to face their ultimate test. Before the world's and, perhaps more searchingly, their country's and city's own media, these figures have to capture in their words and body language the essence of their city's case. They also have to make it look easy, which it certainly is not. However effective and relaxed these people may have been in making off the cuff speeches or in lobbying conversations over the bid's course, the final speech is on a different level. Like the rest of the presentations, these final speeches are normally honed and rehearsed over a long period, every word and nuance carefully judged. Rod McGeoch reckoned to have rehearsed his speech for Sydney at least sixty times so it was deeply imprinted on his memory (McGeoch and Korporaal, 1994, p. 277). It seems unlikely that his was an unusual experience.

The Promotional Message

Marketing methods and presentational style are very important in promoting aspiring Olympic cities. So too are the technical details and the sense of strong backing from business, governments and communities. Yet even taken together, these are not enough. There has to be an overarching marketing proposition around which the bid can cohere in an intellectual sense. To be successful, this will first involve a simple and easily grasped idea of the intended event as it will be delivered at that particular time and in that particular city. In addition, and very importantly, it must also demonstrate that the event will be a historically momentous realization of the internationalism and altruism of the Olympian ideal.

One might reasonably question how far the contemporary Olympic movement itself, with its extraordinary commercialism and luxury hotel lifestyle, may be squared with this lofty ideal (Simson and Jennings, 1992; Barney *et al.*, 2004). The record of IOC delegates in choosing the locations of Summer and, increasingly, Winter Games certainly suggests a strong preference for highly sophisticated cities. This is a material reality that certainly needs to be addressed in the marketing message. So too do elements that relate very directly to competitive sports and, in a more subtle way, to the higher purposes of the Olympian ideal.

The result is that there are many common features in the marketing messages of Olympic candidate cities. Almost all will have spoken to the internationalism of the movement by portraying themselves in some sense as cities of the world. A good example of this is Barcelona's bid which stressed its international connectedness, the amount and quality of its hotel accommodation and visitor attractions, and its cultural sophistication (COOB, 1992, I, p. 303). Culture has been a theme of increasing importance in the Olympic movement. Barcelona, for example, was able to stress its own high cultural reputation, mentioning legendary figures with strong associations such as Gaudi, Miró and Picasso (COOB, 1992, I, p. 303). Living testimony was provided by the Catalonian opera singer, Monserrat Caballé, a powerful ambassador for the city's Olympic hopes.

Another way of signifying culture is to stress the multiculturalism of the city, a feature especially of Atlanta, Sydney, London and Rio's successful candidatures (ACOG, 1990; SOCOG, 2000b, pp. 15–17; LOCOG, 2004). Also important is a general openness and welcoming attitude, a theme first emphasized by Melbourne's 'friendly Games' in 1956 and which Sydney sought to revive in its 1993 bid (McGeoch and Korporaal, 1994, p. 138). Cities that were less obviously multicultural, such as Barcelona (at least in 1986) or Beijing, tended to portray themselves as conduits through which a major cultural group might be claimed for the Olympic movement. Barcelona thus linked itself to its wider linguistic community in Latin America (COOB 1992, I, p. 312; BOBICO, 2001, I, p. 3). For Beijing, the vastness of the world's Chinese population scarcely needed any labouring of the point.

Alongside these elements of the message that emphasize the city, there are also others that focus more specifically on sports. Candidate cities, certainly those in the most highly developed parts of the world, are virtually obliged to argue that their populations are keen participants in and spectators of all types of sport. They will also try to show that their climate will be particularly conducive to sporting attainment when the Games are held. In keeping with all claims of this type ever made by city promoters, considerable scepticism must be exercised (S.V. Ward, 1998). Atlanta, for example, averaged its night and day temperatures to reach the claimed figure. Similarly Barcelona's claimed mild climate proved stiflingly hot during the actual Games.

In recent years, several campaigns have also sought to claim that theirs will be an 'Athletes' Games', most explicitly by Sydney which used these exact words (SOCOG, 2000b, p. 20). By this, cities usually mean that they do not want to allow commercial considerations to swamp sporting ideals. Close proximity of proposed athletes' accommodation and sports venues is often associated with this claim. In part this emphasis has emerged as a reaction to the most highly commercialized Games, notably those of Los Angeles 1984 and Atlanta 1996. There may also be a specific need for the marketing message to rebut potential criticisms of the bidding city. For example, the 1963 Mexico City team that successfully bid for the 1968 Summer Games devoted much attention to countering its own, rather serious, weak points, namely, that its altitude and poor air quality would prejudice a successful sports occasion (Organizing Committee, 1968, II, pp. 11–13).

Normally this kind of operation would be done in a less overt manner that stresses positives rather than overtly acknowledging negatives, at least in presentational set-pieces. Thus all post-Munich Olympic candidates have stressed the safeness of their cities, sometimes against compelling counter-evidence. Even Barcelona's confident campaign experienced a serious wobble when the Basque terror group ETA launched an attack and murdered a policeman in the centre of the city on the eve of the critical IOC meeting in 1986 (COOB, 1992, I, p. 310). In 2005, London's team did not have to face the far more serious atrocities on London's public transport system until the day *after* they had secured the 2012 Olympics. Had these events been transposed that would surely have been a terrible testing of even the most well-conceived promotional campaign.

The Olympic movement's fear about terrorism has since 2001 morphed into a more general global paranoia, with the result that safety can be represented in odd ways. Rio was able to use Brazil's comparatively low terrorist risk to its advantage in bidding for the 2016 Games. This was plausible enough but it overlooked the city's daily experience of violent criminality which had brought around 6,000 murders in 2008 and made its streets far less safe than any of the other candidate cities. Just two weeks after it won the Games, Rio's drug gangs launched a major assault on the police, bringing many deaths and the shooting down of a police helicopter (Phillips, 2009).

Safety, however perceived, was one of several very widely occurring aspects of the promotional messages employed by all aspiring Olympic cities. The examples used have been drawn from those cities that won their bids to host the Games. Yet it would be possible equally to document broadly similar elements within the marketing messages of those that lost. In 2009, the unsuccessful bidding teams from Chicago, Tokyo and Madrid stressed their cities' cultural qualities, accessibility, attractiveness to visitors and safety every bit as much as Rio. So it has been in all recent Olympic contests. This tendency to a generic message begs the question: does the marketing *message* itself really make a difference? Perhaps the role of marketing and promotion is simply to prove commitment, a matter more of method and persistence than of what is actually said.

If the message is important, we can be sure it is not because a city says essentially the same thing as everywhere else. The decisive aspect and, it can be argued, the thing that does sometimes differentiate the winners from the losers, is the presence in the marketing message of a compelling 'big idea'. As Tony Blair remarked in 2006, reflecting on London's success in winning the 2012 Games, it was not simply a case of saying that yours was the sleekest, smartest city (BBC News 24, 2006). To work, the 'big idea' in the marketing message has to connect to the Olympic ideal in more than a superficial sense. The rhetorical ambition of the ideal itself, based on an altruism and purity of purpose that transcends the ordinary selfishness of humanity, is important here. So too is the associated vanity that lies within the Olympic movement's self image, that it is a portentous and positive force that anticipates the tides of global history. Candidate cities, if they really want to succeed, do well to flatter this vanity in their promotional rhetoric.

In this vein, we can note how many successful bids have sought to position themselves and their message, sometimes almost subliminally, as part of a momentous transition or movement. Barcelona's bid, for example, was portrayed by Pasqual Maragall as part both of 'plucky little Catalonia' and the 'great Spain which is awakening' (COOB, 1992, I, p. 312). In this view Spain was finally moving beyond the sterile centralist Franco dictatorship to become a fully democratic and culturally diverse entity, a progressive influence on its neighbours and its linguistic realm. The significance of this proposition was acknowledged when the IOC President, Juan Antonio Samaranch, himself Barcelona-born, pointedly chose to pronounce its winning name not in Castilian Spanish but in the long suppressed but lately reborn regional language of Catalan.

The 'big idea' within Beijing's successful bid in 2001 for the 2008 Summer Games was that it represented a China that was now ready to emerge from its own economic and political isolation, '… to speed up its modernization and integration into the international community' (BOBICO, 2001, I, p. 1). The references were highly coded, so much so as to be almost invisible in the case of moving towards democracy and better standards on human rights. Yet after the city's rebuff largely because of this issue in 1993, helped by some subtle negative campaigning by Sydney and other cities, it definitely had to be addressed if the city's candidature were to succeed (McGeoch and Korporaal, 1994, pp. 226–227). Interestingly though, in 2001, Paris's attempt to use human rights arguments against Beijing rebounded, damaging the French rather than the Chinese bid (D. Miller, 2003, pp. 340–341).

Brazil's economic and political emergence as a new global player with democratic credentials was a powerful theme in Rio's 2009 bid. The Brazilian capital, Brasilia, had sought the 2000 Games (though had then withdrawn) and Rio the 2004 Games (Gold and Gold, 2005, pp. 179–180). The difference by 2009 was, however, that the nation's position and status in the world had grown. Rio's grandiose appeal that '[h]istory's first Games in a new continent, in a city with a global image, will open new horizons … [a] compelling new story is ready to be told' now seemed to be plausible (ROCOG, 2009, I, p. 19). Having been convinced on the technical assessment, the IOC was prepared to give in (and on an impressive scale) to the emotions to which Rio's 'big idea' appealed.

Other cities have addressed different aspects of the Olympic ideal. The language of Atlanta's black civil rights martyr, Martin Luther King, permeated its message of a brave city that was realizing his integrationist vision and would use the 1996 Olympics to show this to the world (ACOG, 1990). A key word throughout all Atlanta's promotion was 'dream', a direct reference to King's most powerful speech. The prominence in the bid campaign of a black former Atlanta Mayor and Ambassador to the United Nations, Andrew Young, also provided vigorous testimony to the reality, playing a key role in swaying African IOC members. Sydney linked its bid to environmental sustainability, setting a new benchmark for the Olympic movement (SOCOG, 2000b, p. 19). It used the Executive Director of Greenpeace International, himself Australian, to substantiate the claim (McGeoch and Korporaal, 1994, pp. 139–141).

We have noted how many cities make use of youth in their message. London was unusual in making youth its big idea. It spoke of the city as 'a beacon for world youth' with a 'voice that talks to young people' (LOCOG 2004; BBC News 24, 2006). A London Games would inspire the young people of the world to become involved in sport and grasp the opportunities for self-improvement and social betterment that it offered. It was a theme that was consciously echoed throughout its presentation, most obviously in the video mentioned above. The team's leader, the double Olympic gold medallist Lord Coe, told what was essentially the same story, of how as a boy he too had been inspired by Olympians of an earlier generation (Campbell, 2005). David Beckham brought in the theme of childhood, referring to his boyhood home in heart of the area where London's Olympics were to be located. His presence, despite then being one of Real Madrid's *galacticos*, also underlined his 'real' loyalty, to his birthplace rather than his adopted city which in 2005 was London's strongest rival after Paris for the 2012 Games. London also used large numbers of real children on the stage, living testimony to the city's multi-ethnic, multicultural character. Most commentators, including many in France, agreed that London's final presentation did make a difference.

Conclusion

Marketing is then a key part of the Olympic selection process. While it is no substitute for a competent bid that is technically and financially convincing, it can make a difference. For those centrally involved in that promotional process, it may well be the pinnacle of their careers. If they win, they are likely to be fêted by an ecstatic city and a grateful nation. They will be the new gods, literally Olympians, of the marketing profession, likely to command, if they so choose, high fees to address business gatherings throughout the world. They may well become advisers to subsequent bidding cities or find lucrative roles in the Olympic movement. The intelligence they collect about IOC delegates and the mechanics of the bidding process will be a tradable commodity. Even the runners up will be able to cash in on some of the bidding assets they have accumulated.

Yet, paradoxically, winning the right to be an Olympic city is only a prelude to the real marketing event, the actual Games themselves (Barney et al., 2004; Lee, 2005). Once the host city has been selected, the promotional devices invented to advance the bid immediately become commodities that can henceforth be sold to enhance the products of sponsors. The symbols that originated as an image to disseminate a speculative proposition now become the basis for a carefully controlled market brand. Branding is essentially about the ownership of an idea that is then transferred to an actual product, which is quite literally what happens. The big idea of the successful city's vision of its Games is now expressed in an increasingly tangible product. Naturally, a burgeoning brand marketing department is needed within the organizing body to police the use of such images and symbols. All this will have been carefully planned and forms a mandatory part of the candidature file. To ensure this plan is properly implemented, cities will find powerful and experienced allies in the IOC, anxious to extract every last scintilla of monetary value from the Games. In the end, therefore, many of the great Olympic ideals resolve themselves into material matters. For all the lofty ambitions of Olympicism, it is perhaps appropriate that it falls to the marketers to compete in what has become the greatest Olympic challenge of all.

Chapter 8

Olympic Security

Jon Coaffee and Peter Fussey

The 2012 Olympic and Paralympic Games will require the largest security operation ever conducted in the United Kingdom. The success of the Games will be ultimately dependant on the provision of a safe and secure environment free from a major incident resulting in loss of life. The challenge is demanding; the global security situation continues to be characterised by instability with international terrorism and organised crime being a key component. (Metropolitan Police Authority, 2007)

The International Olympic Committee (IOC) make clear in guidance to host cities that it is *their* responsibility to provide a safe environment for the competitors, officials and dignitaries attending the Olympics and Paralympics, while ensuring that such securitization does not get in the way of the sporting activities or spirit of the Games. As Thompson (1999, p. 106) observed, 'the IOC has made clear that the Olympics are an international sporting event, not an international security event, and while Olympic security must be comprehensive it must also be unobtrusive'. However, since 2001, given the escalation and changing nature of the terrorist threat 'securing' the Olympics is increasingly difficult and costly to achieve (Coaffee and Murakami Wood, 2006). Certainly if the risk of terrorism remains at its present critical level, there is the possibility of seeing core notions of Olympic spectacle replaced by dystopian images of 'cities under siege' as organizers and security personnel attempt to deliver an Olympics, in maximum safety and with minimum disruption to the schedule.

As has been well documented, as a result of increased fears of international terrorism catalysed by the events of 9/11, the cost of security operations surrounding, in particular, Summer Olympic Games has increased dramatically since Athens 2004. A large proportion of this increased cost arises from the need for extra security personnel as well as an array of temporary security measures, especially those which are effective at stopping or minimizing the impact of vehicle borne improvised explosive devices (Coaffee, 2009). For most Olympic organizers, preparations for the Games necessarily include attempts to equate spectacle with safety and to 'design-out' terrorism, often by relying on highly militarized tactics and expensive and detailed contingency planning.

The Olympic Games have become an iconic terrorist target, which imposes a burden of security on host cities well beyond what they would otherwise face. Security planning is now a key requirement of bids submitted to the IOC by prospective host cities, and has become a crucial factor in planning the Games. There is now a broadly accepted security management 'model' for Olympic Games, which is modified according to local circumstances of place, and which comprises elements of governance and organization which seek to forge a relationship between the numerous public safety agencies and the local Organizing Committee. This follows the example set by the successful use of a dedicated Olympic police force at Lillehammer 1994. As well as the planned deployment of police and military personnel, and the co-option of private security and safety volunteers, a typical Olympic security regime also employs the latest technology in an attempt to plan for and deter terrorist attack. For example, recent Games, as well as other major sporting and cultural events, have become highly militaristic at certain geographical locations through the construction of large-scale bunkers and barriers, secure fencing around the key sites, as well as almost ubiquitous closed circuit television (CCTV) camera coverage. Pre-Games and Games-time monitoring of key sites also commonly occurs, for example, through the use of underwater surveillance by scuba divers, by helicopter reconnaissance and by recourse to advanced technology such as biometric identifiers and remote detection.

Such exorbitant levels of security also transform the cityscape into a series of temporary 'spaces of exception' (Agamben, 2005) with displacement of the policing by consent as special regulatory regimes are brought to bear so as to control behaviour and maintain order. Browning (2000) observed during the period immediately before the 2000 Games that 'Sydney in September will be under siege'. Athens 2004 continued this trend, with widespread deployment of technology and human resources that was intended as much to assuage the fears of the outside world as to create necessary levels of security (Samatas, 2004, p. 115).

Securing the Olympic Spectacle

In light of these circumstances, the scrutinizing committees and delegates of the IOC will carefully examine bids to ensure that host cities provide the necessary safety and security for the smooth running of the games. This is particularly the case with regard to international terrorism, which since the early 1970s, has become a crucial factor in planning the Games.

The imperative to address the phenomenon of international terrorism began with the so-called 'Munich Massacre' in 1972 when, as seen in chapter 2, members of the Israeli Olympic team were killed after being taken hostage by the Palestinian terrorist organization Black September. This event, widely considered to have launched a new era of international terrorism (Reeve, 2001), saw the security bill for future Games soar.

In particular, the events at Munich 1972 stimulated a period of reactivity, continuing to this day, whereby organizers have prioritized security to avoid hosting a repeat tragedy. Sharply contrasting Munich's 'low-key' approach to security (reflecting contemporary German sensitivities over conspicuous public displays of social control), little expense was spared on securing Montreal 1976. The fallout from Munich and the global condemnation levelled at the IOC and German authorities also led protection from terrorism to become *the* key security concern for Montreal's Organizing Committee (COJO). This manifested itself in the first of many 'total security' approaches alongside the inauguration of several core principles informing the protection of subsequent Olympiads. These incorporated a strong emphasis on preventative strategies, a conspicuous security force presence, enhanced integrative practices (a failure at Munich) and intensive surveillance measures. Within these general principles, specific measures included isolated secure transport corridors between sites, accommodation and transportation hubs; enhanced accreditation requirements for site workers; and probably the first widespread and systematic deployment of CCTV to feature at an Olympics (Organizing Committee, 1976). Montreal's reaction to the Munich massacre became a blueprint for future Olympic security operations.

These themes were embraced and consolidated at the next Olympic event at the geographically proximate Lake Placid 1980. Augmenting the Olympic site's geographical isolation were a number of strategies aimed at strengthening and surveying its perimeters, including 12 feet high touch sensitive fencing, voice analysers, 'bio-sensor' dogs, ground radar, night vision and CCTV (LPOOC, 1980). Together, these measures drew inspiration from strategies deployed to secure military sites and airports. Such was the level of securitization that the post-Games legacy of the Olympic Village saw its conversion into a correctional facility (*Ibid.*). A further feature of note was the unprecedented scale of private security deployment, a feature that has since become central to almost all subsequent Olympic security operations.

Although seen by some as isolated and distinct from other Olympic operations (Sanan, 1996), the components of Moscow's Olympic security strategy illustrate how these standardized principles may cut across geographical and ideological barriers. For example, the deployment of US-made security apparatus including metal detectors and x-ray scanners used at previous Games, including at Lake Placid during the same year, demonstrates continuity between Moscow and its predecessors. Additionally, the extensive use of zero-tolerance style policing approaches and exclusion orders have also featured at subsequent games, notably Sydney (Lenskyj, 2004) and Beijing (Peng and Yu, 2008) (albeit with variations of scale). Although the contemporary form and function of social control in Brezhnev's Russia may have allowed these strategies to be applied with an intensity unacceptable elsewhere (Sanan, 1996, argues that 120,000 people were displaced by Moscow's security strategy), many of the underlying principles informed both previous and subsequent Olympic security programmes.

According to estimates (Anon, 2004), the average cost of security at the Summer Olympics Games rose from around $80 million to $1.5 billion over the 20 years between Los Angeles 1984 and Athens 2004. When viewed on the basis of cost per athlete, this equates to rise from $11,627 per capita to $142,857 per capita (see table 8.1). Security for Los Angeles 1984 was organized by the private sector, but successfully launched a relationship between the numerous public safety agencies and the OCOG that has been adopted in subsequent Games. At Los Angeles, the arguments to spend large amounts of finance on security were largely premised on heightened tensions emanating from the Cold War. Notably, less than three months before the Opening Ceremony, the Soviet Union announced that it was boycotting the Games, blaming not only the overt commercialization of the Olympic spectacle, but crucially a lack of adequate security measures. This, they argued, amounted to a violation of the Olympic Charter.

Table 8.1. Security Costs of Olympic Games 1984–2004.

Games	Total security cost (US$)	Cost per Athlete (US$)
Los Angeles (1984)	79.4 million	11,627
Seoul (1988)	111.7 million	13,312
Barcelona (1992)	66.2 million	7,072
Atlanta (1996)	108.2 million	10,486
Sydney (2000)	179.6 million	16,062
Athens (2004)	1.5 billion	14,2857

Source: Adapted from the *Wall Street Journal*, 22 August 2004.

By contrast, Seoul 1988 witnessed the South Koreans engage in a large-scale security operation, their major concern being North Korea's use of Japanese proxies to bomb Korean aviation in the run-up to 1988 and the spectre of further attacks on the Games. This involved over 100,000 security personnel drawn from the police, military and private security forces – the largest in Games history at the time. The organizers also drafted thousands of volunteers in to help with security. The Korean question became further involved in Games' security when riot police were sent in to break up demonstrations by student protestors seeking unification of the two countries. Additionally, North Korean hostility to the Seoul Olympiad led the IOC to adopt a new and unprecedented international diplomatic function. For many, the security operation is what captured the headlines of the news media rather than sporting spectacle.

Barcelona 1992 saw the deployment of over 25,000 security personnel due to fears expressed over reprisal terror attacks linked to the recently ended 1991 Gulf War, coupled with recent action from the Basque separatist movement (ETA), Catalan separatists (Terra Lliure) and left wing extremists Grupo de Resistencia Antifascista Primo Octobre. Although this operation used fewer security personnel than employed in Seoul, security was highly militaristic at certain sites. The security forces, for instance, constructed large-scale bunkers around the perimeter of the main Olympic Village, with tanks situated at strategic locations.

This complemented secure fencing and numerous CCTV cameras within the Village, as well as a highly visible police presence at the sporting locations.

Prior to Atlanta 1996, terrorism was not considered the major risk facing the Games despite serious terrorist attacks on American soil at the World Trade Centre (1993) and at Oklahoma City (1995). As the *Wall Street Journal* emphasized (Anon, 2004), terrorism ranked behind heat-related illness and the possibility of soccer violence on the official lists of 'potential worries'. That said, more than 20,000 military and law enforcement personnel were assigned to monitor security measures, supplemented by 5,000 unarmed volunteer security personnel in an operation that, for some, was seen as the most hi-tech and measured in Olympic history. On the eve of the Games, for example, Macko (1996), argued that:

> When it comes to the security of these games, nothing has been left to chance in Atlanta and the other venues that will be used by the athletes. An army of law enforcement officers will outnumber the athletes themselves. The security for the 1996 games is said to be the tightest ever in history. Security planners for the Olympic Games have tried to cover every angle possible – from cops on patrol to scuba divers and helicopters and high-tech devices such as ID badges with computer chips.

Despite these intensive preparations, the small-scale bomb blast that occurred at an unsecured public space designed for the Olympics, killing one person and injuring over 100, rekindled anxieties about further attacks.

Fears of the alternative spectacle of violence (Gold and Revill, 2003) led to even tighter measures to protect the official Olympic spectacle at Sydney 2000. The cost and sophistication of security rose steeply from that incurred in Atlanta and involved nearly all Australia's Special Forces plus 30,000 security personnel (drawn from the police, private security and volunteers) who were also called to duty. Even though the national Australian government considered, in public at least, that the risk of attack was unlikely, the media began highlighting connections between Osama Bin Laden, the most wanted on the CIA's terrorist hit list, and Australia.

Although no major terrorist incident took place during Sydney 2000, the spectre of terrorist violence took on unparalleled concern for Athens 2004, particularly in view of the security situation in both Greece and internationally (see chapter 16). The cost of security increased dramatically. As table 8.1 reveals, despite being the smallest nation to host the Games since 1952, the Greek authorities spent well over five times more than the amount spent by the Sydney organizers and deployed over 70,000 specially trained police and soldiers as well as another 35,000 military personnel to patrol the streets. Military hardware used for security was the most expensive used for the Olympics. It included a network of 13,000 surveillance cameras, mobile surveillance vans, chemical detectors, a number of Patriot anti-aircraft missile sites, NATO troops specializing in weapons of mass destruction, AWAC early warning surveillance planes, police helicopters, fighter jets, minesweepers, and monitoring airships (see Smith, 2004). The airships themselves became icons of the Games and attracted much media interest. Indeed the Security Airship patrolling above the Olympic sites was joined by a second Skyship that broadcast images for US television networks and gave spectacular aerial footage of the Games.

The Olympic stadium in Athens, always likely to constitute the most spectacular target, received the heaviest fortification. According to Peek (2004, p. 6) Athens was 'supposed to be one of the most secure places on earth, impenetrable to terrorists plotting a possible attack on this summer's Olympics'. Significantly, the Olympics forced the Greek state to speed up the modernization of its state security system. For the duration of the Games, Athens became a 'panoptic fortress' to give assurances to the rest of the world that the city was safe and secure to host the world's greatest sporting spectacle (Samatas, 2004, p. 115). However, the retrofitting of such security systems is envisioned as a long-term project that will be maintained after the Olympics and which critics have argued will become a menace to privacy and civil liberties (*Ibid.*, p.117; see also chapter 1). Moreover, the technological centrepiece of the strategy, Science Applications International Corporation's 'C4I' ('Command', 'Control', 'Coordination', 'Communications' and 'Integration') system was a colossal failure. Unable to host the large numbers of potential users, the fabled communications system never operated to capacity and, on still failing to establish the system in time for the Summer Games, its manufacturers were forced by the Greek courts to compensate the Athenian authorities (*Ibid.*).

As chapter 17 highlights, the IOC's award of the Twenty-Ninth Olympiad to Beijing in July 2001 stimulated large-scale development of the city. Coupled with China's hosting of the 2010 World Expo in Shanghai and the 2010 Asian Games in Guangzhou, the Beijing Games catalysed a monumental security programme across the country both within these epicentres of tourism and beyond. Embedded within this programme has been an emphasis on technological and surveillance-based approaches and has included use of Radio Frequency Identification (RFID) tags in tickets to some Olympic events (such as the Opening Ceremonies) to enable their holders' movements to be monitored. Despite such headline-catching technologies, however, the principal emphasis has been on developing and inaugurating CCTV networks. These include the 'Grand Beijing Safeguard Sphere' (developed between 2001 and the start of the Games) which, according to some claims, has cost over $6 billion and provided the city with 300,000 networked and highly capable public CCTV cameras (Magnier, 2007). Nationally, China's hosting of sporting mega-events has also coincided with the 'Safe Cities' programme aimed at establishing surveillance cameras in 600 cities (Bradsher, 2007). As elsewhere, these technological approaches were combined with more traditional 'low-tech' forms of policing. In particular, the state's capacity to mobilize security manifested in the deployment of 100,000 personnel whilst policing strategies adopted 'sand-pile' techniques (Peng and Yu, 2008), vernacular interpretation of zero-tolerance strategies adopted at other Olympiads (notably

Seoul 1988 and Sydney 2000). Moreover, security hardware often found itself centre stage in television coverage. As Boyle and Haggerty (2009, p. 64) observed: '… the conspicuous placement of ground-to-air missile launchers near the Bird's Nest stadium formed a striking backdrop for the many televised reports from the Games beamed around the globe'.

The Security Games 2012

Securing Olympic spectacle and protecting against the spectacle of terrorist violence remains an *overriding* concern for Olympic organizers. This has become increasingly stark in the United Kingdom as London gears up for hosting the 2012 Games. Security concerns and responses not only played a critical part in the bidding process, with the IOC in 2004 arguing that London was uniquely placed to offer a secure venue for the Olympics given its many decades of experience of coping with Irish terrorism (LOCOG, 2004, p. 31). However serious security concerns also dominated media discussion after the host city was announced, especially after the terrorist bomb attacks on London's transport network on 7 July 2005 – the day after London was confirmed as host city. These attacks led to a massive increase in perceived security needs and prompted organizers to draw up ever more detailed plans, with an Olympic Security Directorate (OSD) created to address threats related to 2012.

By November 2009 this has led to the initial security bill quadrupling from £224 million to over £1 billion; the planned adoption of advanced biometric security systems to monitor crowds, officials and athletes, special 'measures' to track suspects across the city; and, of increased importance, a series of efforts to 'design-in' counter terrorism features to the physical infrastructure of the Olympic venues and environs (Coaffee, 2009). These measures may well achieve the Olympic Delivery Authority's stated aim of creating an 'Island Site' (ODA, 2007).

As briefly highlighted in this chapter, in recent Summer Olympiads a host of *temporary* security solutions have literally swamped the host cities and in particular the sporting venues. However, *permanent* design and architectural features intended to counter such threats have, to date, been largely absent from Olympic security preparation, only becoming a key strategic issue during the ongoing redevelopment of sites and venues for London 2012. The bid team (LOCOG, 2004, p. 27) argued in their candidacy file that surveillance and security operations would begin at the start of construction or adaptation of every venue and would continue throughout the Olympic Games. This interest in how planners, architects, developers and designers, alongside security specialists, design-in counter-terrorism features for Olympic facilities in London, is a function of not just the supposed threats faced by sporting venues but also the longer term regeneration vision for the areas in the post-Games period, where issues of safety and security will be paramount within 'legacy' community facilities (Marrs, 2003).

For effective security planning it is clear that solutions need to combine managerial co-ordination *and* innovative design approaches to physical security to ensure the host city, and in particular the Olympic Park area containing the main venues, does not become 'siege-like' but is resilient to possible attack. In this sense, counter-terrorist security must be comprehensive, but also as unobtrusive as possible (Coaffee, 2009). As the then Head of 2012 Olympic security noted in 2007:

> This is a celebration of what London is about and of the Olympics… It's not about security or safety. Making the games as accessible as we can without security being obtrusive, is the trick we have to pull off. (Cited in Culf, 2006)

In terms of the design and construction of stadia, it is clear that 'Secure by Design' approaches employing vehicle access restrictions will be deployed in a similar manner to that adopted elsewhere in London, for example, at Heathrow Terminal Five, the Millennium Dome, Wembley and Lord's Cricket Ground. This will involve the embedding, at the concept stage, of design features such as access control and integrated CCTV, as well as the designing-in of 'stand-off areas' for hostile vehicle mitigation and the use of more resilient building materials. There has also been talk of setting up advanced screening access points around the main venues – the so-called 'tunnel of truth' which can check large numbers of people simultaneously for explosives, weapons and biohazards – and which could use face recognition CCTV which can be compared against an image-store of known or suspected terrorists (Coaffee, 2009). Such an approach might also serve to restrict the need for queuing and hence reduce vulnerabilities although, in the case of face recognition, CCTV has proved of limited worth when deployed at previous sporting events (ACLU, 2001).

The stadium-specific security is strategically aligned with that of the Olympic Park in which the facility sits – a large expansive area that is undergoing securitization in preparation for 2012. The site for the main Olympic Park in Stratford, East London, has already been partially securitized. It was 'sealed' in July 2007 and nearby public footpaths and waterways closed for public access. The encircling 11 mile blue fence – 'cordon blue' which was put in place for 'health and safety' reasons (see figures 8.1 and 8.2) – has been likened by some to the Belfast peace walls (Beckett, 2007). Biometric checks are routinely carried out on the construction workforce within the sealed site.

Security planning for the Olympic Park – explicitly termed the 'Island Site' in the documents and thus semantically emphasizing the geographical isolation of this space – saw resources disseminated towards addressing the themes of 'access control systems' (ACS), 'searching and screening', command, control and integration', and 'security guarding' (ODA, 2007). To achieve this, policy guidance was given towards provision of technological solutions for these problem areas including the implementation of 'ACS comprising RFID token and biometric[s]', a 'combination of technology and physical searching' and 'CCTV, security lighting systems and intruder detection systems to be [established,] integrated with, and form a part of, the perimeter security' (*Ibid.*). Analysis of such proposals raises the argument that the emphasis for suppliers to offer strategies that 'create an integrated security environment that is effective, discrete and proportionate' (*Ibid.*) creates a

Figure 8.1. The security cordon, known as the 'Blue Wall', round the Olympic Park site, East London (November 2009).

Figure 8.2. Checkpoint for the 'island site': Olympic Park security (November 2009).

climate that elevates the likelihood of particular strategies being deployed. Indeed, this echoing the IOC's longstanding (and often abandoned) aim of projecting the Games as an athletic event and not an exercise in security is significant, since 'discretion' and 'proportionality' have normally translated into distanciated forms of control, especially in the form of technological surveillance.

What is clear though is that security at Games time will be significantly heightened with an undoubtedly imposing and visibly policed security cordon encircling the site. Inside the cordon, landscaped security and crime reduction features, infrastructure strengthening on bridges and other structures, and electronic devices that scan for explosives are being embedded, seeking to push threats away from the Olympic site. Likewise, concealment points – areas where explosives might be hidden – have been scrutinized and where possible removed (for example bird boxes or litter bins) or sealed (for example, drains). These features, if implemented, would be designed to be as unobtrusive as possible, and with a view to being kept in place post-Games for legacy purposes in order to deter activities such as joyriding, ram raiding, drug dealing, prostitution, and general anti-social behaviour. This means that features that are 'designed in' specifically for counter-terrorist purposes must, wherever possible, have a crime prevention capability in the legacy period when the park will be fully open to the public. Embedded safety and security features must also be as 'invisible' as possible and be *proportional* to the threat faced.

Physical security will also need to be strategic and extend beyond the Olympic Park sites, as fears of the 'displacement' of possible terrorist attack to other key sites in London persists. As such, London authorities will be using advanced surveillance to track suspects across the city, including London's ever expanding system of Automatic Number Plate Recognition cameras (Fussey, 2007). This is seen as a soft-touch approach and preferable to having a police officer on every corner, although an extra 9,000 officers are expected to be on duty in London at peak time (despite concern about leaving other parts of the United Kingdom vulnerable to attack if police officers are drafted in from other forces). As the then Head of Olympic security noted in 2007, Olympic security is a pan-London operation:

> The whole rhythm of life in London will change as a result of these events and for 60 days we will have to take charge of that and make it safe in a way that people can enjoy themselves … 9000 officers at the peak is a heck of an ask. (Cited in Culf, 2006)

In the build up to the Games, different scenario table-top tests will be played-out for dealing with major incidents, including terrorism, to allow logistics such as cordon placement and evacuation routes to be planned in advance. The aim of all the security preparations and testing is to allow 'customer-sensitive' security to prevail which will provide the highest possible levels of security without resulting in having to 'lock down' the entire city (Coaffee, 2009), as has happened with other

Olympiads. This will apply to the sporting venues as well as other key locations such as transport hubs and tourist areas and is in line with the wider objective as outlined in the *London 2012 Olympic and Paralympic Safety and Security Strategy* published in July 2009: 'To host an inspirational, safe and inclusive Olympic and Paralympic Games and leave a sustainable legacy for London and the UK' (Home Office, 2009). Such a legacy will include the upgrading and expansion of London's already impressive security infrastructure and is promoted as being central to everyday community safety. As the Chief Inspector of Police noted in 2006:

> We want the security legacy to be us leaving a safe and secure environment for the communities of East London after the Games, on issues such as safer neighbourhoods, lighting and crime prevention. We want a Games legacy that will reduce crime and the fear of crime. (Cited in Boyle and Haggerty, 2009, p. 267)

Most recently, Rio's successful candidacy to host the 2016 Olympic and Paralympic Games also draws on these continuities of mega-event security. Although security practices are likely to be accented towards localized criminality rather than international terrorism (ROCOG, 2009), security is likely to be a major concern. These concerns can be more specifically related to the city's murder rate (that annually stands at triple that of the entire United Kingdom), and fears of robberies against tourists. Indeed, a statistical increase in robberies against foreign visitors to the 2009 Carnival has also attracted particularly poor publicity (although such statistical variations may also reflect changing policing priorities (see Crowther-Dowey and Fussey, 2010) and mask the fact that Cariocas bear the brunt of criminal victimization in their city). Nevertheless, such issues are likely to elevate the attention afforded to security, particularly given that in the IOC's pre-ballot review of all 2016 candidate cities, Rio scored poorly in this area, trailing Chicago, Tokyo, Madrid and Doha while only marginally ahead of Baku and Prague. To mitigate these risks, a familiar plan to that being developed in London is being formulated:

> A comprehensive security overlay will be implemented to ensure the integrity of all Games facilities and prevent unauthorized access. This will include perimeter security, integrated access control and alarm management, coupled with technical surveillance... The security overlay will be based on Crime Prevention through Environmental Design (CPTED) principles, to be incorporated into the design of all venues. (ROCOG, 2009, p. 27)

Such imperatives connect international standards of Olympic security with Rio's tradition of delineating 'high-value' spaces from their urban context. Coupled with the prior location of prestigious sporting sites within an existing urban milieu, it is likely that continued re-bordering of the city may risk further splintering of Rio's divided spaces and provide a significant challenge to its regenerative aspirations.

Standardization and Olympic Security

The numerous security vernaculars which inevitably penetrate the IOC's governance, given the exceptionality of security need experienced by hosts, enables standardized forms of security to prevail. Indeed, these consistencies easily extend beyond vastly different social, cultural and political settings as the Mayor of London, Boris Johnson, made clear to a recent Culture, Media and Sport Committee hearing:

> … broadly speaking, there will be quite substantial security and protection around the main Olympic venues of the kind that you would expect, and you will be seeing more detail about that nearer the time, but it will be not unlike what they did in China. (DCMS, 2008)

Together, the exceptionality of Olympic security coupled with the transference of its strategies across time and place culminates in standardized approaches that map on to the uneven terrain of diverse host cities. Borrowing from Bauman (2000), such transferable paradigms operate as a form of 'liquid security' where a shared *lingua franca* of defensible motifs coalesces into spaces that become disassociated from their geographical contexts. In turn, these spaces of exception, once constructed, generate a particular vision of order, a dislocated uniformity, owing to, as Bauman (*Ibid.*, p. 103) suggests, 'the lack of overlap between the elegance of structure and the messiness of the world'.

What we can gauge from a study of securitization utilized by host Olympic cities is a series of normalized event security features which combine temporary physical elements and the aggressive management of spaces with the aim of projecting an air of safety and security for both visitors and potential investors. First, there is intense pre-planning involving the development of control zones around the site, procedures to deal with evacuation, contamination and decontamination, and major incident access. Technical information is also scrutinized for all structures and ventures so that any weakness and vulnerabilities can be planned-out in advance. Secondly, there is the development of 'island security' involving the 'locking down' of strategic (vulnerable) areas of host cities with large expanses of steel fencing and concrete blocks surrounding the sporting venues. This combines with a high visibility police presence, backed up by private security, the security services, and a vast array of permanent and temporary CCTV cameras and airport-style checkpoints to screen spectators. Thirdly, to back up the intense 'island security', peripheral buffer zones are often set up in advance containing a significant, visible police presence. This is commonly reinforced by the presence of law-enforcement tactics such as police helicopters, a blanket 'no-fly zone', fleets of mobile CCTV vehicles, and road checks and stop and search procedures. The result of these measures is that access to apparently 'public' spaces such as roads or footpaths is often restricted due to 'security concerns'. Fourthly, the enhanced resilience that, in theory, is delivered by such security planning is actively employed as a future selling point for urban competitiveness – in that the ability to host such an event in a safe and secure fashion and without incident is of significant importance in attracting future cultural activities and in branding a city as a major events venue. Fifthly, there is increased evidence from major sporting events that a lasting benefit of hosting events is the opportunity for the retrofitting of permanent security infrastructure linked to a longer-term crime reduction strategies and 'legacy'. This post-event inheritance of security infrastructures is a common Olympic legacy. Indeed, the legacy of retained private policing following Tokyo 1964 and Seoul 1988 and the continuation of zero-tolerance style exclusion laws after the Sydney 2000 Games are cases in point. Likewise in Athens 2004, the retrofitting of such security systems was envisioned as a long-term project to be maintained after the Olympics and which has been condemned by civil libertarians (Athens Indymedia, 2005).

In London 2012 the major emphasis on a regeneration legacy for the people of East London also extends to the machinery of security. Indeed, in 2009 the tenders for Olympic Park security providers encouraged companies to supply 'security legacy', thus bequeathing substantial mechanisms and technologies of control to the post-event site. Here, questions remain over the security priorities of a high-profile international sporting event attended by millions of people and the degree of infrastructure that will remain afterwards in order to police a large urban parkland (the future incarnation of the Olympic site).

Bidding to host an Olympics is also, in many cases, considered a strong enough stimulus to develop robust security planning procedures. For example, the unsuccessful bid by Cape Town for the 2004 Games required the city to be seen as secure enough to host the Olympics. As a result an extensive security infrastructure was introduced into areas posited as likely venues and visitor accommodation centres (Minnaar, 2007). After their bid failed, the CCTV systems were not removed. Instead they were justified as part of a general programme to combat crime; the threat of which was seen as likely to discourage foreign tourists, investors and conference delegates (Coaffee and Murakami Wood, 2006).

Conclusion

In terms of the relationship between security and Olympic spectacle, the IOC regulations and guidance for host cities make clear that there is a responsibility to provide a safe environment for the 'Olympic Family', while ensuring that such securitization does not get in the way of the sporting activities or the spirit of the Games. This, increasingly, is a difficult scenario for host cities to achieve. Certainly if the risk of terrorism remains at its present critical level, there is the possibility of seeing core notions of Olympic spectacle to some extent replaced by dystopian images of cities under siege as organizers, security personnel and the media attempt to deliver an Olympics, in maximum safety and with minimum disruption to the schedule.

Chapter 9

Urban Regeneration and Renewal

Jon Coaffee

Increasingly, the Olympic Games are being viewed as a once-in-a-lifetime opportunity for the host city (and sometimes country) to embark on a series of major development or redevelopment projects that have the potential to change the way in which the city operates, the feeling local citizens have for their city, and the perception of the rest of the world toward the host city and country. (Chernushenko, 2004)

Since the 1960s the importance of what has been termed urban regeneration and renewal has risen in prominence within public policy circles as a result of the attempts made at post-industrial restructuring of cities and their economies in the face of urban degeneration. While there is no single agreed definition of the term 'urban regeneration', it might be seen as 'a comprehensive integrated vision and action which leads to the resolution of urban problems and which seeks to bring about lasting change in the economic, social, physical and environmental condition of an area that has been the subject to change' (Roberts and Sykes, 2000, p. 17). Equally, while 'urban renewal' still carries connotations of 1960s comprehensive redevelopment, it retains currency as a term that implies the rebirth of a faded or deteriorating area.

In recent years the relationship between sport and strategic urban regeneration has grown in importance, largely attributed to the perceived economic and social benefits of hosting major sporting events, developing sporting infrastructure, and creating opportunities for the development of sustainable communities (Coaffee and Shaw, 2005). In particular, much has been written about the potential for cities to improve and develop urban infrastructure and to stimulate widespread urban revitalization by hosting the Winter Olympics (e.g. Teigland, 1999; Richie, 2000; Essex and Chalkley 2004) or their Summer counterparts (e.g. Essex and Chalkley, 1998; Olds, 1998; Tufts, 2001; Burbank *et al.*, 2001; Searle, 2002). Similarly, much has appeared on the impact of Olympic hosting on the marketability of place, with the Olympics seen as offering an unparalleled shop window for inward investment and private sector land development. Both these impacts have developed in significance and magnitude over time. Indeed, given the continuing effect of economic globalization, associated socio-cultural flows and, currently, recession, cities hosting Olympics gain a unique opportunity simultaneously to regenerate and to project themselves on the global stage.

Paralleling the rise in importance of the promotional opportunities associated with hosting the Olympic Games has been a reconceptualization of what planners and other built environment professionals view as 'regeneration and renewal' and their assessment of the current value of mega sporting and cultural events to achieve this end. Whereas at the beginning of the modern Olympic movement regenerative benefits, when they accrued, were associated with physical infrastructure projects, more recently regeneration has been viewed as a holistic intervention targeting a variety of interrelated physical, social, environmental and economic problems in a coordinated fashion linked to ideas of sustainability and 'legacy'. As such, Olympic-led regeneration is now associated not just with large-scale physical development schemes but also with local and national intervention programmes which target health, education, employment, local economic development, community cohesion, housing needs, crime reduction and environmental cleansing.

Within this changing context, this chapter provides an overview of how urban regeneration and renewal opportunities have been associated with the modern Olympic movement, and in particular the Summer Games. It does so first by considering a historical perspective that highlights the regenerative impact of Summer Olympics on host cities between 1896 and 1980; then by examining more contemporary perspectives that emphasize a more economically rational and private sector-led model of Olympic regeneration management; next by considering the development of more holistic and city-wide models of regeneration adopted initially in relation to Barcelona 1992; and finally by discussing attempts made since 1992 to adopt the normative Barcelona model for Olympic city regeneration whilst paying attention to the environmental implications of hosting the games.

Olympics and Urban Impact

The broad trajectory of the urban impact of the Olympics is outlined in chapter 2, but a brief summary is helpful here. When considering the early games, it is instructive to use the categorization suggested by Chalkley and Essex (1999), who divided the period before 1936 into two segments. The first comprised the Games between 1896 and 1904, which had minimal urban impact. In essence, the organizers of the early Games made little attempt to think about the possibilities of using the Olympics to stimulate urban development. The Summer Games at Paris 1900 and St Louis 1904, for example, were small-scale events run as 'side-shows' to more prestigious International Expositions (Matthews, 1980; see also chapter 2).

The second period (1908–1932) saw the Games better organized, larger in scale, and using facilities constructed specifically for the Olympics. Admittedly, London 1908 was still associated with a Fair (the Franco-British Exhibition), but was the first time that the organizers supplied purpose-built venues and facilities as well as greatly improving the organization and planning of the Games (Organizing Committee, 1908; Essex and Chalkey, 1998). When the decision was made to award London the 1908 Games, it was planned that the Franco-British Exhibition should be 'more than just a trade fair' (Mallon and Buchanan, 2009, p. 4), with the addition of the Olympics as a key element (*Ibid.*, p. 16) instead of an added attraction. Those responsible for organizing the Olympics managed to persuade the Exhibition organizers to build the required stadium (the White City stadium) in return for three-quarters of the gate receipts. The stadium was considered to be the finest in the world at that time and provided a partial blueprint for future Olympic venues. Transport improvements were introduced specifically to cope with the crowds attending the Exhibition and Olympics, with a new underground railway station added to the network at Wood Street.

Many commentators judged that the combined event was a great success that had legacy effects for both the host city and the Olympic movement. As Levin (2001) noted 'the fair grounds, and Olympic stadium, remained and served as the site for future exhibitions and events. White City became a pleasure/amusement park, and the stadium's functions ranged from training Olympic athletes to the site for greyhound dog races until the stadium was demolished' (see also Grose, 2001). London 1908 appeared to create a new model for the development of sports facilities, which was adopted four years later at Stockholm 1912, and in subsequent Games at Antwerp 1920, Paris 1924 and Amsterdam 1928. Los Angeles 1932 also adopted the model of developing a purpose-built sports facility for the Games, but also for the first time constructed a purpose built Athletes' Village that was auctioned for housing needs in the post-Olympic era (Chalkey and Essex, 1999, p. 377).

Berlin 1936 provided a watershed as far as expenditure on the Games was concerned, although the question of the impact on Berlin was secondary to the incumbent Nazi regime's desire to present a façade to the outside world. The Games developed facilities and infrastructure of a scale and grandeur far in advance of previous games, intended to display Germany's architectural prowess and cultural history. The nature and significance of its difficult legacy are discussed in chapter 11.

In stark contrast to Berlin, the first Games after the Second World War gave organizers less opportunity to carry out major works. London 1948, held with Britain in the grip of Austerity, required considerable improvisation to provide the necessary facilities, with Helsinki 1952 and Melbourne 1956 concentrating their activities on sporting facilities and associated Athletes' Villages. It was from Rome 1960 onwards that substantial investment in city infrastructure, particularly transport, began to be planned hand-in-hand with new sporting facilities. This changed the way in which municipal authorities perceived the task of hosting the

Summer Olympics. Chalkley and Essex (*Ibid.*, p. 379), for example, noted that in addition to the sporting facilities, the city of Rome:

> developed a new municipal water supply system, new airport facilities, improved public transport, street lighting and the illumination of monuments and numerous decorative improvements to the city. Interestingly, the changes produced by the Olympic Games led to calls for the next Games to be cancelled because of the scale and complexity of the related urban developments.

The scale of sporting facilities and associated urban regeneration for host cites was taken to new levels at Tokyo 1964. Although motivated by a political agenda connected to Japan's re-emergence on the world stage after the Second World War, the Japanese government saw the Games as an opportunity to invest as much in public transport and utility infrastructures as in sporting stadia, and to modernize Tokyo. The city authorities developed many new highways, metro-lines, monorail, airport and port facilities, along with improvements in the city's water supply and waste management systems. The areas immediately adjacent to the main stadium (see figure 9.1) were also rejuvenated with landscaping and the addition of new subway stations. Subsequently this newly accessible district became a centre of commerce.

Entrepreneurialism and Short-Term Urban Upgrading

The strategy adopted at Rome and Tokyo would presage the future, although the trend towards the regenerative approach was by no means a linear path. Mexico City 1968, for example, saw a far less lavish and expensive Games than Tokyo, with

Figure 9.1. The main Olympic Stadium for the 1964 Games in Tokyo.

many critics arguing that investment should be prioritized towards serious socio-economic issues in the country, rather than on updating existing infrastructures or building anew. Although Munich 1972 and Montreal 1976 invested in both sporting facilities and associated urban and infrastructure elements, neither competed with Tokyo in terms of sheer investment in urban development projects. Moscow 1980, by contrast, made little effort to invest in facilities not directly related to sport, other than a new airport terminal, media centres and hotels (Chalkley and Essex, 1999, p. 384).

Los Angeles 1984, as noted in chapter 6, provided a watershed in the financing of the Summer Olympics and stimulated a boom in the number of cities that aspired to be Olympic hosts for subsequent Games. Its approach to urban regeneration, however, was to limit costs while still maintaining spectacle. The prevailing strategy reflected the fact that the Organizing Committee ran the Games as a commercial enterprise along private sector lines, given the refusal of taxpayers to foot the cost. The overall approach was to update and use existing sporting and utility infrastructure. The campuses of the University of Southern California and the University of California at Los Angeles provided accommodation to serve as the Olympic Village, which was then passed back to the universities after the Games. The International Airport was also hurriedly upgraded (Burbank et al., 2001).

For Peter Ueberroth, the leader of the Los Angeles Olympic Organizing Committee, the Games reversed a worrying trend for host cities of financial deficit by showing it was possible to run the event profitably. The $225 million profit generated by Los Angeles 1984 helped to subsidize a youth sports programme across Los Angeles in subsequent years. Although not necessarily obvious at the time, the Olympics also stimulated the development of a regional fibre-optic telecommunications system in Southern California, which provided an advanced regional telecommunications infrastructure that reflected and helped to boost the intense communications activities of the Los Angeles area at a crucial time (Moss, 1985). Equally significant were the attempts by the organizers to integrate a community regeneration element into their plans although, cynically, this might also be interpreted as a way of 'encouraging' volunteerism. For example, schemes such as the 'Olympic neighbour programme', run in 1983, introduced youths in south-central Los Angeles to Olympic athletes and served as an impromptu orientation session for those working, or thinking of volunteering to work, at the 1984 games. Over time such volunteer programmes have become an integral part of Olympic preparation and Games time activity, with (Burbank et al., 2001, p. 80) commenting that:

> Overall despite being heralded – or in some quarters derided – as the 'capitalist' Olympics, the Games were seen as 'great for the city' and 'contributed to a sense that LA was the place to get things done. It also put the lustre back on the Olympics as the mega-event of choice for cities wishing to achieve world-class status'.

This notion of the Olympics as a catalyst for urban boosterism was also fully exploited in 1988 in Seoul where the Games were seen as an ideal opportunity to improve urban infrastructure (particularly transport), revalorize and refurbish the city, and clean up water systems, parks and open space through pollution abatement programmes and air pollution controls. For example, the OCOG's official report of the Games drew attention to various aspects of 'government support and people's participation' such as environmental beautification programmes, improvements in health and hygiene standards, realignment of traffic systems and tourism promotion and the expansion of cultural facilities. It also laid great emphasis on identifying the future legacy of the games, but this was expressed in terms of promotion rather than regeneration and urban development impact:

> The successful staging of the Seoul Olympic Games provided a momentum to bring Korea close to the ranks of advanced countries on the strength of bolstered national development and the enhancement of general level of awareness among the people. The economic growth and enhancement of sprit of the public bolstered Korea's stature in the international community. (Organizing Committee, 1989, p. 798)

However, many analysts expressed concern that the Korean authorities had focused on spatial form rather than social process. As Gold and Gold (2005, p. 203) noted:

> the methods chosen to improve the city's built environment and infrastructure ... attracted international criticism for paying greater attention to urban form than to social cost. Ideas of improvement centred on the removal of slums and the creation of modernistic, often high-rise, development for high income residential or commercial use.

The Barcelona Model

The key moment for thinking about the regenerative impacts of hosting Summer Olympics was undoubtedly Barcelona 1992 (see also chapter 14). Indeed, it is now the 'Barcelona Model' of regenerating through the Olympics that provides the blueprint for other cities bidding for Summer Games, as well as offering the conviction that the Olympic legacies can be positive in terms of urban planning and regeneration rather than simply making short-term profits for organizers (Monclús, 2003; see also Marshall, 1996; DETR, 1999).

For many observers, the Olympic Games were more concerned with bringing about an urban rejuvenation (and an associated tourist boom) in Barcelona than about the sporting event, with significant investment required due to a growing population, high levels of unemployment and severe deprivation in particular neighbourhoods. Indeed, the expenditure on infrastructure accounted for 83 per cent of the total budget, compared with just 17 per cent being spent on sport. Clusa (2000) identified the wide array of infrastructural projects developed, which included:

- Stadium renewal
- Construction of a new Sports Palace
- Ring Road
- Additional main roads
- 4,500 new flats in the four Olympic Villages
- Two communication towers
- Five new centrality areas (offices)
- Airport enlargement (offices and housing)
- Leisure port improvement
- Cultural facilities (especially museums)
- 5,000 new hotel rooms
- Five kilometres of new beaches: Barcelona opens to the sea

The Barcelona 'model' encompassed a number of key features that other countries have subsequently attempted to replicate. These include strong and long-term strategic visioning, excellence in urban design, and the importance of well-funded social programmes. Perhaps the most significant aspect of the model with regard to urban regeneration was its focus on long-term and strategic planning rather than piecemeal and area-specific interventions that had been associated with many of the previous Summer Games. Within the Olympic planning process the city was envisioned as an accumulation of its distinct neighbourhoods rather than as a number of different districts. The aim was to construct a spirit of shared identity and a sense of ownership of the urban restructuring process – as such, interventions were linked to local priorities as well as overall city aims. For example, the locations of new public buildings were chosen specifically to stimulate or 'pump prime' regeneration in adjoining areas, retail development was spread around the city, and mixed-function land uses were encouraged.

Underpinning this strategic vision was the strong political and local leadership required to drive the process forward and to develop a flexible approach to regeneration programme management, which allowed the infusion of significant private finance to help fund the renewal projects and alleviate some of the financial risk that Olympic cities faced. The municipal authorities in Barcelona also focused on good quality urban design and public realm work. Important historic buildings and monuments were refurbished and preserved, innovative architectural thinking was encouraged, green and open space were designed so as to maximize the opportunity for social mixing, and an emphasis was put on high quality refurbishment for which tax incentives were given. The pre-Olympic preparations focused on social programmes as well as morphological alterations. The governing authorities also employed holistic approaches to tackling the problems of poorer neighbourhoods, focusing on the interrelated problems of poor education, high crime rates, poor health, unemployment and poor leisure facilities, and a lack of social mixing in disadvantaged neighbourhoods.

The success of Barcelona in linking wide-scale and strategically orientated urban regeneration with the hosting of the Olympics has had profound implications for urban planners worldwide. The greatest impact has probably been in the United Kingdom, where the rhetoric surrounding contemporary *urban renaissance* draws strongly upon the Barcelona experience. Indeed, this 'driver' of urban policy owes much to the architect Lord Richard Rogers who master-planned the Barcelona sea-front developments (see figures 9.2 and 9.3) and was largely responsible for the influential British policy document *Towards an Urban Renaissance* (DETR, 1999).

Figure 9.2. The newly regenerated Barcelona Seafront.

Figure 9.3. Torre Calatrava communication mast.

This broad policy narrative uses the example of Barcelona and its Olympic experience to promote the virtues of a particular style of regeneration design and management. Pasqual Maragall, the Major of Barcelona at the time of the Games, returned the favour by writing the Foreword to the *Urban Renaissance* report, where the emphasis was strongly focused on improvements in urban quality rather than quantity, and the 'marriage between City Hall and the School of Architecture and alliances made with the public and private sectors' (Maragall, 1999*b*, p. 5). As he (*Ibid.*) noted:

> The 1992 Olympics were not the cause of Barcelona's design fame. For example, the prestigious Harvard University Prize was specifically given for the quality of urban design up to 1987. A commitment to develop networks of new plaza, parks and buildings was the cause of our success. The Olympics helped multiply the good works.

Towards an Urban Renaissance supported this assertion by highlighting the long-term re-imaging attempts undertaken in Barcelona and consolidated and showcased by the Olympics:

> The Catalonian capital re-invented itself throughout the 1980s and 1990s with a series of urban design initiatives that improved the quality of the public space in the city and radically enhanced its infrastructure. Under Major Pasqual and architect Oriol Bohigas, the city created 150 new public squares at the heart of urban communities. The city succeeded in winning its bid for the 1992 Olympics and coupled this with a strategy of urban regeneration that has paid long term dividends to the citizens of Barcelona, rather than making a short term profit for event organisers. (DETR, 1999, p. 72)

In contrast to the profound transformations in Barcelona, Atlanta 1996 returned to the model of Los Angeles 1984 and focused investment on sporting facilities. Lack of public funding and primary reliance on private finance resulted in a lack of lasting and strategic regeneration, with Atlanta's dream of hosting 'the best Olympics ever', whist stimulating the social regeneration of the city, turning sour. As Burbank *et al.* (2001, p. 118) remarked:

> Mayor Jackson's dream was to scale the twin peaks of Mount Olympus (*sic*) by staging the best games ever and uplifting the people of Atlanta. In the end, however, the politics of image building and downtown revitalization displaced neighbourhood redevelopment, as well as the needs and dreams of central city residents.

Nevertheless, the longer-term impact of the Olympics was not wholly negligible. Significant investment for infrastructural improvements flowed into Atlanta, with $371 million of federal money being spent on road, transit and sewer construction, and housing projects (*Ibid.*, p. 118). The airport received a further runway capable of accommodating international flights at a cost of around $450 million.

Environmental Sustainability vs. Commercialization

For more recent Games of the new millennium, the IOC has laid the requirement on Organizing Committees to adopt more environmentally and socially responsible approaches to planning, which, in turn, has influenced how commentators view and evaluate the regenerative legacy of the Olympics. Both Sydney 2000 and Athens 2004 provided tangible examples of attempts by city authorities to follow the model of regeneration through Olympic hosting that was successful in Barcelona and to project themselves to the world as vibrant 'global cities'. At the same time, these cities also focused on aspects of the experience of Los Angeles 1984 and Atlanta 1996, in particular the concept of developing public-private partnerships to organize the Games.

The twenty-first century has indeed seen host cities focusing on delivering the associated spatial planning and regeneration gains now associated with the Olympics with a new emphasis on creating an environmentally-friendly Games. Sydney received the standard plaudit from Olympic President Juan Antonio Samaranch in his closing speech as 'the best Olympic ever', but was also heralded by the organizers as 'the sustainable games'. The rhetoric employed in the media leading up to Sydney 2004 revealed great optimism that the Games would leave a lasting and sustainable legacy. Large areas of disused industrial and military land at Parramatta in Western Sydney underwent significant transformation to provide the main location for the sporting venues, showgrounds and Olympic Village. As Dunn and McGuirk (1999, p. 25) commented:

> This part of western Sydney has been undergoing a profound and symbolic restructuring. The prior land use ... can be fairly described as noxious industrial. The area was dominated by an industrial complex of chemical manufacturers, brickworks and abattoirs. The Olympic village will be sited over what were a landfill garbage tip and an Australian Navy ammunition dump. The area was, and still is badly contaminated by industrial, chemical and household wastes.

They continued by noting the importance of regeneration being 'clean and green' (*Ibid.*, p. 27). As Weirick (1999, p. 77) further noted, 'Sydney decided to promote an environmental image, and the idea of the "Green Games" captured the imagination of the world'. This included a series of innovative designs for the Olympic Village, although many of these ideas were dropped from the preparations after the bid was won:

> A consortium of young designers developed the concept of an eco-village which was incorporated into the bid books. The eco-village was to be aligned so as to maximize solar energy. Water would be recycled through the wetlands so as not to create pollution, and the Village would be linked to public transport. (*Ibid.*)

Although the eco-village was never built, other commentators emphasized the changes in building design that had been implemented – notably the introduction of 'green criteria' for individual construction projects (Prasad, 1999). Having said that, other observers argued that, in the period before the Games, the significant investments in transport infrastructure that was occurring for air, road and rail were not being built to facilitate travel for the Olympics. They also argued more negatively that Sydney's planners had pressed ahead in pursuit of commercial gain and opening up new sites for commerce rather than attempting to address the inherent problems of environmental pollution and transport congestion faced by the city (Weirick, 1999, p. 74).

After the event, critical reflection on the regenerative impacts of Sydney 2000 differed markedly from the rhetoric of the 'Green Games' that had preceded the Olympics. Many observers drew attention to the legacy of underused stadia and facilities. Searle (2002), for instance, noted how post-Games analysis of the Sydney Olympic stadium legacy showed the lack of profitability of the underused facilities and argued that, during their construction, the true extent of the financial risks associated with their construction was kept from the public eye. Lenskyj (2002) also indicated how the reduction of funding to non-Olympic planning projects was concealed in the run up to the Games. The Olympic Park, designed to be Sydney's showcase venue after the Games and the heart of significant and lasting urban transformation, closely resembled a 'ghost town' with little of the planned post-Games construction completed (Mahne, 2004). As chapter 2 shows, these medium-term assessments have retained much of their force a decade after the Games.

In a similar manner to Sydney, Athens 2004 was seen as an opportunity for the city's authorities to display the Greek capital to the world, to modernize its substandard transport infrastructure, and to leave a tangible legacy of regeneration for the city (see chapter 16). Here, too, environmentalist rhetoric suffused the initial plans for the Games. The organizers claimed that: 'Athens 2004 would be the first Olympiad using 100% green energy' and that 'all projects will be realized with the use of environmentally friendly technologies and materials, and this will be a prerequisite in all relevant tenders' (cited in Videl, 2004).

In one sense, Athens 2004 heralded a construction boom and offered a new model for urban development that was an alternative to the fragmented and *ad hoc* development of neighbourhoods of past Athenian attempts at regeneration. Planners, architects and urban designers were forced to think of citywide initiatives not just in terms of the development of new and expanded transport infrastructure and impressive sporting facilities, but also in the construction of large-scale residential communities. The Olympic Village was transferred after the Games for use as private residencies. The lower densities, greenery, open spaces, safety considerations, and appropriate car parking and access marked out these neighbourhoods as quite distinct from traditional Athenian residential landscapes.

More problematically, the potential of Athens for regeneration was badly affected by delays in construction, which dogged the schedules of work before the Games and led to a familiar scenario of builders working around the clock to complete the venues. The apparently 'green' construction technologies that, it was claimed, would be employed were largely absent. An environmental audit of the Games by Greenpeace argued that, in construction of the Olympic Villages, nearly all environmental recommendations were ignored and energy conservation, product recycling, the use of solar energy and natural cooling systems were all dropped from final plans. A spokesperson claimed:

> Instead of moving forward, the Athens 2004 Games have gone way back as far as environmental issues are concerned. The International Olympic Committee has called the environment the third pillar of the Olympics, behind sport and culture. Right now, it seems all but invisible. (Cited in Videl, 2004)

A report on BBC television in June 2005 about the impact of the Games on Athens (see also Anon, 2003) recognized that the city has gained a positive legacy from staging the Olympics. It noted, for example, the benefits associated with the widening of existing highways and the addition of two extra metro-lines, which have contributed to lessening the city's atmospheric pollution problem as well as providing greater accessibility to the revamped beaches. However, this report also drew attention to the increases in the price of basic goods such as food and petrol, which local people had had to suffer, as well as the substantial costs of maintaining the thirty Olympic venues (see chapter 16). Many venues have had a post-Games history of being redundant, locked, or out of bounds. Some were guarded by the police to prevent vandalism. Lacking concrete plans of their own, the Athenian authorities are engaged in attempts to encourage the private sector to take over the venues and turn some of them into sporting and cultural theme parks. As one local resident interviewed on the BBC programme had noted: 'we had a fantastic Games but no plan for the day after'.

Holistic Regeneration and Urban Remodelling

Infrastructure upgrading and regeneration for Beijing 2008 and planned urban change for London 2012, make it clear that the agendas of host cities must now pay attention to combining lasting regeneration with environmental sustainability – at least at the outset. In China central and municipal governments aimed, and in many ways succeeded, in transforming Beijing into a world-class global city through major regeneration programmes intended to solve the city's inherent environmental and infrastructural problems and leave a lasting legacy (Ness, 2002, p. 1). As Chernushenko (2004) has noted:

> Sydney took a huge step toward building for and hosting a 'greener Games'. Beijing has now committed to doing so. But in order to host the Olympics in a cleaner, greener city, Beijing must find solutions to some significant and unique challenges, notably in such areas as air and water quality, wastewater and solid waste management and transportation. With these challenges come tremendous opportunities: for the city and country, and for

domestic and international suppliers of innovative technology, as well as planning and management skills.

Such challenges, however, took their place alongside other perceived needs that the Organizing Committee sought to balance. *Inter alia*, these include showcase architecture and property development in order to create a 'modern high tech metropolis' (RICS, 2004). The argument was that 'the commercial, residential and infrastructure developments that will accompany the Games will effectively act as a catalyst to change the entire physical structure and planning of the city' (Van de Berg, cited in RICS, 2004). The plans envisaged, and delivered spectacular stadia in the north of the city and elsewhere with the aim of stimulating further regeneration of the adjoining areas, aided by significant upgrades in existing water recycling, parkland and transport infrastructures including new subways, urban railways and a new international airport terminal (see chapter 17). Construction, and use of facilities, where possible, was also undertaken with 'green' standards in mind. For example, the Athletes Village was a 'zero emissions' zone exclusively utilizing electric or fuel cell buses and cars with all buildings constructed to high energy efficiency standards.

Some of the venues also used the latest technology to inculcate greater energy conservation measures. These occurred most notably in the iconic Water Cube where 'the "air pillows" constructed from ETFE plastic for the outer walls permit natural lighting through their adjustability. They provide passive heating for the pool and allow pre-heating or cooling to ensure optimum energy conservation' (McCarthy, 2008). We should, however, remember that the regeneration of Beijing that has occurred as a result of hosting the Olympics, despite some 'green credentials', has been incredibly resource and energy intensive. Moreover, as with previous Games, the opportunities for regeneration led to the demolition of housing deemed to be substandard on sites key to redevelopment efforts (Gold and Gold, 2008).

Launching London's 2012 bid in January 2004, the British Prime Minister also highlighted the urban change mantra of the bid in that 'as well as being a wonderful sporting and cultural festival, the Games would drive the environmentally friendly regeneration and rejuvenation of East London' (Blair, 2004, p. 1). More specifically, the bid organizers (LOCOG, 2004) noted, 'the key catalyst would be the development of the 500 acre Olympic Park ... containing the main sporting facilities, would be set in 1,500 landscaped acres – one of the biggest new city centre parks in Europe for 200 years'. In addition, they stressed that:

London 2012 ... would form part of the most extensive transformation of the city for generations ... and its legacy would transform one of the most underdeveloped areas of the country... All development would form part of an enormous and tangible legacy, ranging from sport and cultural venues through to infrastructure and environment. London 2012 would change the face of the capital forever. (*Ibid.*)

London officials also pledged to make 2012 'the greenest games in history' (Townsend and Campbell, 2005). The Major of London in 2005, Ken Livingstone, reiterated that commitment when launching a set of design rules after London was officially awarded the Games. It was argued that sustainable regeneration would not accrue automatically and must be planned for properly. As such, it was noted that the organizers aimed to combine the environmental achievements of the 2000 Games in Sydney with the holistic and in particular inner-city, physical regeneration of Barcelona 1992 (see Weaver, 2005).

Conclusion

This chapter has shown that urban regeneration, as either a minor physical element or as part of dramatic transformations of the host city, has for many years been a key element of the Olympics and central to the decision of urban authorities and national government to bid to host future Games. The Summer Games in particular continue to offer an unrivalled opportunity for a host city to propose, plan and deliver major regeneration work over a 5–7 year period. Whereas, in previous decades, regenerative impact focused almost exclusively on physical urban development, latterly the emphasis of regenerative impacts has shifted away from purely physical construction or renovation towards more holistic notions of renewal and environmental sustainability becoming *de rigueur*. These have been seen to focus on the economic, social, cultural and environmental benefits and legacy that hosting Olympic Games can bring to cities and surrounding regions. There is, however, a growing body of evidence to suggest that regeneration legacy is now used by bidding cities as an important, if not the most important, criterion by which they develop their proposals. Whether the actual impacts ever meet those promised, of course, is open to conjecture.

Chapter 10

Olympic Tourism

Mike Weed

It is regularly claimed in justification for the hosting of the Olympic and Paralympic Games that Olympic cities can generate considerable inward tourism, both as tourism destinations in their own right, and as gateways to wider regions surrounding the host city. This chapter draws on the author's previous work (Weed, 2008) to examine the role of Olympic cities in the generation of tourism. As context for this analysis, the early part of this chapter outlines a range of Olympic tourism products, before briefly outlining the ways in which the Olympic and Paralympic Games might be leveraged to generate tourism. The two subsequent parts of the chapter then examine, first, the ways in which Winter Olympic Cities can be tourism gateways to the wider region surrounding the host city and, secondly, the contribution of the Summer Olympic Games to the development of the host city's tourism product and image.

Olympic Tourism Products

Broadly speaking, it is possible to identify six Olympic tourism products, five of which relate to sports tourism, and one of which relates to more general tourism (Weed, 2008; Weed and Bull, 2009). These are as follows:

Event Sports Tourism

This refers to the provision of event sports tourism opportunities, both for participants and spectators. Obviously, it includes the Olympic and Paralympic Games themselves, but also the myriad of other events that take place in the years before and after the Games in and around Olympic cities. In this respect, even previously inconsequential competitions can become significant international events as athletes seek to experience and acclimatize to local conditions, providing an increased media and spectator sports tourism attraction.

Sports Participation Tourism

The most obvious sports tourism product, this refers to active participation in sports tourism activities, such as skiing, cycling, golf or sailing, or at multi-activity centres such as Centre Parcs or various outdoor activity and education centres. For some activities, participating at Olympic venues, or at Olympic winter sports resorts, can be an attraction.

Sports Training Tourism

Sports training camps are often talked about as being a generator of Olympic tourism, but the sports training tourism product also incorporates 'learn to play' courses, and also elements of advanced instruction. As such, it can overlap considerably with sports participation tourism in Olympic sports such as sailing and skiing.

Luxury Sports Tourism

Uniquely, this product type is not defined by reference to the sports tourism activity, but to the wider aspects of the experience relating to the nature of the attendant facilities and services. It therefore overlaps with the other product types, and may often use associations with the Olympic and Paralympic Games to add to the feeling of a premium product.

Supplementary Sports Tourism

The broadest of the sport tourism products, supplementary sports tourism refers to the provision of sports tourism activities as a supplement to the providers' main product. Examples include a range of water sports on beach holidays or the opportunity to hire a cycle for a day. It may also include trips to past or prospective Olympic sites, venues or museums as a supplementary part of a broader city visit.

Generic Tourism

The Olympic Games can be used as part of strategies to generate future non-sports tourism related visits. Such tourism may be generated among those who have visited the Olympic city for sports tourism related products, but who later return for a more general tourism trip, or among those who have been exposed to the city though various Olympic-related written and audio visual media and, as a result, believe it may be an attractive place to visit.

Drawing on the range of Olympic tourism products outlined above, Weed (2008, p. 22) suggests that Olympic tourism should be defined as, 'tourism behaviour motivated or generated by Olympic–related activities'. This definition covers both pre- and post-Games tourism activity, including 'aversion tourism', in which people leave or avoid Olympic cities as a result of the Olympic Games or Olympic-related activities. It also covers the generation of tourism to Olympic cities and their surrounding regions stimulated by exposure to either corporeal (live) or mediated Olympic-related activities.

Leveraging Strategies

The Olympic Games is the resource with which to leverage the six Olympic tourism products outlined above, where leveraging is regarded as the principle of using something as a mechanism by which to pursue other beneficial consequences. However, the potential impacts of the Olympic Games do not just occur during the Games period, but for several years before and after. As such, the Olympic Games as a leveragable resource provides a wide range of potential opportunities to develop Olympic tourism products, potentially over a 15 year period in the run up to and beyond the Games.

Two 'opportunities' for leveraging the Olympic Games are identified in table 10.1. Firstly, direct Olympic tourism trips may be leveraged by the Olympic Games. Secondly, Olympic media may be leveraged, either by capitalizing on Olympic-related media coverage of the host city, surrounding region or country, or by

Table 10.1. Strategies for Leveraging the Olympic Games for Tourism. (*Source*: Weed, 2008, adapted from Chalip, 2004)

Leveraging opportunities to stimulate Olympic tourism trips	*Leveraging Olympic-related media coverage to raise awareness of the host city as a tourism destination*
Entice Olympic tourism spending	Benefit from Olympic-related reporting and event coverage
Retain local resident spending	
Lengthen Olympic-related visits	Use of Olympics in host destination advertising and promotion
Maximize Olympic-related visits	

incorporating Olympic-related material into host city, region or country advertising and promotion. The strategic objective in leveraging Olympic media is to enhance the image of the Olympic host destination, which in turn will help to generate further future tourism business. As the strategic objective of leveraging Olympic tourism is to optimize Olympic-related tourism benefits, the opportunities to leverage Olympic tourism and Olympic media have very similar long-term goals. Perhaps a crude way of looking at the two leveraging opportunities is to view the leveraging of Olympic tourism as referring to immediate strategies to generate tourism business related to the Olympics, whereas the leveraging of Olympic media is part of a longer term strategy for host destination image enhancement that is aimed at stimulating more generic tourism business in the future.

Gateways to Tourism Regions – The Winter Olympics

Unlike some other sport mega-events, such as the football, rugby or cricket World Cups, the host for an Olympic and Paralympic Games is a city rather than a country.

This presents a range of challenges for the country in which the host city is located, one of which is the way in which the Games can be leveraged for tourism, not only to the host city, but also to the surrounding regions and to the country as a whole. In this respect, a useful way to analyse Olympic tourism is to regard Olympic cities as tourism generators. Olympic cities can be divided into those that largely act as a gateway for tourism to the wider region in which they are situated, and those that largely generate Games-related tourism to the Olympic city itself. While these two areas are obviously not mutually exclusive, the respective structures, histories and requirements of the Winter and Summer Olympic and Paralympic Games mean that Winter Olympic cities, although destinations in their own right, can also act as tourism gateways, whereas tourism generated by Summer Olympic cities tends largely to be to the Olympic city itself.

Dealing first with the Winter Games, it is important to note here that the tourism generated by these Games is not dominated by any one Olympic tourism product. Given that the Winter Games focus on skiing and a range of other winter sports, it can be very effective in generating sports participation tourism. However, it can also contribute to the generation of event sports tourism related to ice and snow-based winter sports, to luxury sports tourism products associated with the après ski experience, and, of course, to sports training tourism in relation to learning the basic skills for winter sports, to advanced instruction to improve technique, and to the provision of training opportunities for performance athletes.

Given that Winter Olympic tourism opportunities are spread across the sports tourism-related Olympic tourism products, it would appear that the greatest leveraging opportunities for tourism in relation to the Winter Games are those that are associated with the direct stimulation of Olympic tourism trips, rather than long-term image enhancements for general tourism. To a certain extent this is because Winter Games host cities are dwarfed by the size of hosts for the Summer Olympics. Despite the trend towards major city hosts, Winter Games hosts still need to be located near mountainous terrain to provide for the snow events. Therefore, although there has been a continuous growth in the size of Winter Games hosts, the average population size of Winter Olympic cities is still less than one-tenth (236,000) of the average size of Summer Games hosts (2,840,000). There are several implications that emerge from this. While the cost of the Summer Games since 1984 has always been higher than that for the winter event, the Winter Games are far more costly on a per-capita basis (Preuss, 2004; see table 10.2). Furthermore, because Winter Games host cities, notwithstanding their growth over time, tend to be smaller with less capacity to attract commercial funding for development (Essex and Chalkey, 2002), the burden of investment tends to fall on the public sector (although as noted below, there is a long-standing link with the ski industry). While the Summer Games have increasingly attempted to follow the commercial model adopted by Los Angeles 1984, only Calgary 1988 has had any success in following this approach.

The staging of a Winter Olympics, therefore, can yield varying benefits, with

Table 10.2. Respective costs of Summer and Winter Games. (*Source:* Preuss, 2004)

Olympiad	Host cities	Total cost (US$ million)	Cost per capita (US$)
XIV	*Winter:* Sarajevo, 1984	179	400
	Summer: Los Angeles, 1984	412	121
XV	*Winter:* Calgary, 1988	628	981
	Summer: Seoul, 1988	3,297	326
XVI	*Winter:* Albertville, 1992	767	38,350
	Summer: Barcelona, 1992	9,165	5,578
XVII	*Winter:* Lillehammer, 1994	1,511	65,695
	Summer: Atlanta, 1996	2,021	5,129
XVIII	*Winter:* Nagano, 1998	3,412	9,451
	Summer: Sydney, 2000	3,438	929
XIX	*Winter:* Salt Lake City, 2002	1,330	7,628
	Summer: Athens, 2004	–	–

gains often being specific to host cities and to the stage of development of the city/region at the time. Preuss (2004) reinforces this, noting that a city's unique characteristics and the economic conditions at the time are largely responsible for relative successes. However, that is not to downplay the potential opportunities of the Winter Games for which, as they are hosted in much smaller cities than the Summer Games, 'effects can be proven much more easily because the economic impact to the host city is comparatively larger' (*Ibid.*).

Chappelet (2002*a*) singled out Calgary 1988 as the point where the emphasis shifted from tourism promotion to economic development. The fact that Calgary was able to follow the Los Angeles model can be attributed to the fact that the petrochemical industry in Alberta subsidized the Games in an effort to attract inward investment, and the city grew to a population of almost 700,000. Notwithstanding the continued presence of tourism promotion as a goal of the Winter Games, not least at Lillehammer 1994 where the portrayal of the small Norwegian ski resorts in the region on the world stage as worthy competitors with Alpine countries was significant, such promotion is now but one among a number of goals for Winter Olympic host cities.

Salt Lake City 2002

Prior to the Nineteenth Winter Olympic Games in 2002, Salt Lake City and Utah were very much domestic tourism destinations – of the 17.8 million visitors to Utah in 2000, 96 per cent were residents of the United States (IVC, 2002), and Travel Utah's 1000-day plan reflected this fact. The plan, seen as long-term, covered the 150 days leading up to the Games and the 850 days after the Games. In doing so, it appears that opportunities to capitalize on the Olympics in the pre-

Games period may have been missed as Travel Utah considered that the 'window of opportunity' was only two years. One of the main goals of the 1,000 day plan was to capitalize on the 'awareness bonus' of the Winter Olympics. This involved, on the one hand, trying to improve awareness among Europeans while, on the other hand, focusing on the link between Utah's brand values of 'Discovery and Recovery' and Olympic values and memories when addressing the core American market.

Salt Lake City 2002 attempted to draw on lessons from Calgary in building a strategy for Olympic-related economic development and tourism. In taking this and the experiences of other past Winter Olympics, Travel Utah (2002) discussed the six key lessons that they had drawn from former Olympic hosts:

1. *Context*: Each Games is unique and has its own political, social and economic circumstances which, combined with external events, greatly influence future tourism activity in an Olympic region.

2. *Post-Games Marketing*: Increases in tourism are not a direct function of hosting the Games or of Olympic media; such increases need to be effectively leveraged.

3. *Economic Returns are Uneven*: Tourism growth is most likely in areas directly involved with the Games; outlying areas should consider ways in which they can associate themselves with an Olympic area.

4. *Focus Strategies*: Leveraging strategies are most likely to be successful if they are targeted; holistic approaches can dilute resources and messages.

5. *Sustainable Development*: Normal (i.e. 'without Olympic') growth patterns should guide expectations and development to avoid excess capacity which can destabilize the host region in the post-Games period.

6. *Preserve Networks*: The people and organizations responsible for the presentation of the Games should also be those involved in leveraging the post-Games environment.

In seeking to examine how useful these lessons had been, Travel Utah (2002) conducted an immediate post-Games analysis of the winners and losers in an Olympic year (see table 10.3).

In relation to the impact of Olympic media, Travel Utah (2002) estimated that the value of print media that focused on tourism-related themes during the Games was $22.9 million. This comprised:

- $22 million – National and syndicated stories
- $89,100 – Features from *Sports Illustrated* 'dailies'

* $89,800 – *USA Today* stories
* $420,300 – US daily newspapers from major markets
* $367,600 – Southern Utah stories

Table 10.3. Winners and losers from the 2002 Salt Lake City Winter Games. (*Source*: Travel Utah, 2002)

Winners	*Losers*
• Hotels	• Business services
• Restaurants	• Finance, insurance and real estate
• Retailers (particularly Olympic vendors and 'Made in Utah' products)	• Ski resorts
	• Transportation
• Olympic travellers	• Construction
	• Business and ski travellers

Hotspots: Olympic Venues, Park City and Downtown Olympic District

Empty: Businesses outside Downtown Olympic District

Given the Travel Utah strategy of focusing on the US tourism market, this represents a very useful return. What is not clear, however, from the Travel Utah report, is what leveraging strategies (if any) were employed to generate these stories, and how 'tourism-related themes' are defined. Nevertheless, the generation of $22.9 million worth of print media alone is a significant achievement given the problems of attempting to get tourism/destination themes media coverage (Chalip and Leyns, 2002).

Turin 2006

A clear feature of Olympic cities' outlook in the twenty-first century is a desire to learn from previous hosts. Turin attempted to apply more recent knowledge from both Summer and Winter Olympic cities to its specific modern European city context. Table 10.4 shows the complex range of lessons that Turismo Torino (2004) had attempted to draw from previous Olympic Games, both summer and winter, in the bidding, pre-Games, Games and post-Games periods.

Indeed, if there was a 'role model' for Turin, it was Barcelona 1992 (Bondonio and Campaniello, 2006). Turin, like Barcelona, sought to increase its ranking as a tourist destination not just on the world stage, but also within its own country:

> [Torino] ... envisions a tourist Mecca that would finally marry its historic centre – and all of its elegant cafes and museums – with the rustic Alps. 'When people think about northern Italy, they think Milan,' said Cosmo Perrello, a manager of the Amadeus Hotel, a 26-room local fixture just off the grand Piazza Vittorio Veneto. 'Torino has been a last stop in Italy. It has always been a town of working people. We hope now that it will become a first stop for Italy'. (USA Today, 2006)

Table 10.4. Turin 2006: Lessons Regarding Impact and Benefits for Tourism. (*Source*: Turismo Torino, 2004)

	Bidding	*Pre-Games*	*Games*	*Post-Games*
Investments	Advertising	Infrastructure Media Interest	Visitor services	Promotion and avoiding the 'intermediate effect'
Effects	Image positioning Increase in popularity	Peak in market interest Creating new "cathedrals" Increase in infrastructures	Customer satisfaction Media publicity Increase in number of tourists	Avoiding drop in occupation Increase in business tourism Long-term image growth
Examples	Sion 2006 Andorra 2010 Salzburg 2010 Beijing 2008	Salt Lake City 2002 Sydney 2000	Sydney 2000	Barcelona 1992 Sydney 2000

Given that Turin, like many other major city Winter Games, was a two-centre Games, with Turin itself only able to host the 'arena' ice events, many venues were located outside the city in the 'Olympic Valleys' at distances of up to 60 miles (96 kilometres) away. This generated high costs for transportation, road construction, communication networks and two Olympic Villages in the valleys (Bondonio and Campaniello, 2006), but it has also left an infrastructure that links the Alpine areas with the city, and thus allows the city to develop as a gateway for not only winter sports tourism, but also for summer sports such as canoeing, rafting, cycling and hiking, and for general 'lakes and rivers' tourism.

Turismo Torino, unlike Travel Utah which developed only a 1,000 day plan for tourism, considered the tourism impacts of its Winter Olympic Games from bidding to well into the post-Games period. In doing so it noted that, particularly in the pre-Games period, there was potential to displace and crowd out tourism, and that strategies were needed to address this, both in terms of general tourists, who may have felt that the city would be a 'building site' and business tourism organizers, who may have felt that the Olympic Games would have caused price rises for conferences and meetings (Turismo Torino, 2004). This is reflected in the objectives for the Turin Games as laid out in their Olympic tourism strategy, which covered the pre-Games (2002-2005), Games (2006) and post-Games (2006–2008) periods:

• Avoiding a decrease in the tourist flow in the years preceding the celebration of the Olympic Games;

• Projecting the image of a city and an area under transformation as evolving thanks to the Olympic Games;

◆ Achieving perfect co-ordination to promote both the Turin 2006 Winter Games and Turin itself before, during and after the Games;

◆ Promoting Turin 2006 so as to create internal support and awareness, attracting the widest audience and the support of the tourist sector.

Among the strategies that Turin employed was an 'Olympic Turin' promotion programme that focused on generating positive stories about Turin in the non-sports media in the pre-Games period, thus seeking to leverage the image benefits of Olympic media. While the success of this programme does not appear to have been evaluated, it is a clear attempt to move towards the leveraging approach outlined in the early part of this chapter.

In February 2007, Turismo Torino reported on 'Turin 2006: One Year On' in which they noted that Turin's Olympic facilities have already hosted twenty sports events, including the Winter University Games and the World Fencing Championships (showing that Winter Olympic arenas need not exclusively be used for winter sports) as well as over forty non-sporting events (such as rock concerts and exhibitions). Turismo Torino's estimated figures claim an increase of 100,000 to 150,000 tourists per year to the Olympic area following the Games. A local guidebook, *Turin: a Local's Guide to the Olympic City* (Sajo, 2006) provided for such visitors is itself a nice touch in leveraging the post-Games Olympic effect. Organizationally, the Fondazione XX Marzo has been established to run seven of the former Olympic sites and to optimize the legacy of the Games – an indication that Turin recognizes that legacy benefits, like most other Olympic impacts, need to be leveraged.

Vancouver 2010

A leveraging focus was a key part of Vancouver's preparations for the 2010 Winter Games from the very start of its bid. Eight years before the Games, Inter Vistas Consulting (IVC) were commissioned by British Columbia to report on the economic impacts of hosting the 2010 Winter Olympics in Vancouver, and a central part of this study was a recognition that:

> In order to achieve the higher tourism growth scenarios and capitalize on long-term opportunities, British Columbia's tourism industry will require significant marketing resources and a co-ordinated effort. (IVC, 2002)

Vancouver was fortunate in that it was able to draw on the recent experiences of a Winter Games in North America, namely that in Salt Lake City in 2002. However, like Turin 2006, Vancouver considered that the potential tourism impact of the Games extended beyond the 'two-year window of opportunity' that Salt Lake City sought to capitalize on. The IVC study (2002) for Vancouver 2010 drew up four 'visitation scenarios': low, medium, medium/high and high. In all but the fourth scenario, pre-Games Olympic tourism was assumed to commence in 2008 and the 'tail' of post-Games tourism was assumed to end in 2015. However, in recognizing that the lessons from Salt Lake City did not 'represent the best outcome that British Columbia can achieve', largely because Salt Lake City's marketing efforts did not start until five months before the Games, the 'high visitation' scenario assumed that pre-Games Olympic tourism would be induced prior to 2008, but noted that this was dependent on pre-Games marketing efforts commencing seven years in advance of the Games. Similarly, the 'high visitation' scenario for post-Games tourism included post-Games tourism through to 2020, but once again this assumed that tourism marketing organizations used the Olympics as part of a long-term growth strategy and, more importantly, that the funds and the will existed to develop a marketing programme that had a positive impact on international visitors both before and after the Games. IVC's scenarios for incremental (i.e. additional) economic impact of Games visitors and tourists were as shown in table 10.5.

Table 10.5. Visitation scenarios for Vancouver. (*Source*: IVC, 2002)

Scenario	Expenditure (C$ million)	Expenditure (US$ million equivalent)
Low	920	787
Medium	1,295	1,108
Medium/High	2,228	1,906
High	3,145	2,690

In providing a composite estimate of these numbers for the more concentrated two years before and two years after period, Jane Burns, the Director of British Columbia 2010, claimed that there would be approximately 1.1 million additional international (including US) visitors to British Columbia between 2008 and 2012 (Burns, 2005). Her estimate was given to a US Senate sub-committee hearing on the potential impact of Vancouver 2010 on Oregon and the Pacific North West. Submissions to these hearings showed that regions around British Columbia – in this case, those in another country – had been considering the range of Olympic tourism products they could offer and the nature of Olympic tourism flows. Todd Davidson, the Director of the Oregon Tourism Commission, identified four opportunities for Oregon arising from Vancouver 2012:

• Acting as a training site for Olympic athletes seeking to acclimatize;

• Reaching out to non-accredited media that attend Olympic Games to generate lifestyle stories;

• Exploring the potential to develop travel packages to bring athletes and spectators through Oregon and to encourage the extension of visits to include time in Oregon

⬩ Promoting Oregon at Olympic venues to build awareness.

Similarly, Dave Riley, the General Manager of Mount Hood Meadows Ski Resort in Portland, Oregon, but only 75 miles (120 km) from Vancouver, noted that a key opportunity for his resort, and for Oregon more generally, would be to capitalize on the numbers of skiers and snowboarders that would be avoiding Vancouver and Whistler during and in the run up to the 2010 Games (see discussions of Olympic tourism flows in chapter 3). He identified the key opportunity as 'taking advantage of the displaced visitors who would otherwise have gone to Whistler by developing the amenities on Mount Hood between now and 2010 that are necessary to influence their destination choice' (Riley, 2005).

Planning for Olympic tourism in and around Vancouver, therefore, appeared well in advance of the 2010 Games and, by comparison, far ahead of what had been seen for previous Winter Games. In particular, the explicit recognition that investment and co-ordination in terms of tourism marketing were the keys to leveraging the tourism potential of the Games was a core part of the planning process even before the Games were awarded to Vancouver. The recognition of this in the IVC study commissioned by British Columbia is a lesson for all future Olympic hosts: '[Tourism] benefits will not materialize automatically. They must be earned by a focused, adequately funded and skilfully executed marketing programme' (IVC, 2002).

Tourism Destinations – The Summer Games

As noted earlier, while the Winter Games generate tourism volumes across Olympic tourism products, sports tourism related to the Summer Games is most significant in relation to events sports tourism. While governments may attempt to claim that sports training tourism (training camps), sports participation tourism and supplementary sports tourism (particularly post-Games) are important products, undoubtedly events sports tourism is the major Olympic sports tourism product. However, the major tourism-related justification for investing in the Summer Olympic and Paralympic Games is the image benefits that hosting the Games bring, and the related future generic tourism numbers that such an enhanced image are likely to generate. As such, the greatest leveraging opportunity to develop tourism from the Summer Games is the leveraging of Olympic media for tourism image benefits. Due to the much more concentrated focus of the Summer Games, such image benefits will be largely reaped by the Summer Olympic city itself, rather than by surrounding regions, or by the country in which the host city is situated. The generation of tourism in Summer Olympic cities is now explored in relation to the first three Summer Games of the twenty-first century.

Sydney 2000[1]

While successive Olympic cities since 2000 have been keen to draw lessons from previous Games, tourism planning for the Olympics in Sydney had to be developed without the benefit of prior experience as at the time there were few examples of how Olympic cities had previously planned for tourism. A review by the Australian Tourism Commission (ATC) concluded that Seoul 1998 had left a legacy of new railways and an upgraded airport but public relations had been oriented internally, to Korea's domestic population, rather than to an audience in the rest of the world. The development of tourism infrastructure and Barcelona's enhanced credibility as an international tourist destination were noted as outcomes of the 1992 Games in the Catalan capital (ATC, 1998). Tourism impacts in Barcelona have been recognized to a greater extent more recently, as certain trends have become more apparent. A review by the Director General of Turisme de Barcelona concluded that the Games 'provided the impulse for Barcelona to become a leader in many respects, but especially in tourism' (Duran, 2005, p. 89). He noted that Barcelona had been named as the best world urban tourism destination in 2001 by *Condé Nast Traveller* magazine and described the dramatic growth in the number of cruise ships that now called at the port and of product launches, particularly for new car models, that had been held in the city. These developments were attributed to the way Barcelona's image had been positively affected by the Games (*ibid.*).

In contrast to the benefits gained by Barcelona, an assessment of Atlanta's performance judged that

> the city missed out on a golden opportunity for future tourism. Local attractions suffered substantial downturns in visitors, day trips were non-existent, and regional areas suffered. Neighbouring states took out ads telling people to stay away from Atlanta and the city suffered. (ATC, 1998)

These findings served to reinforce what needed to be done in Sydney to ensure different outcomes.

Within the city of Sydney, proximity to certain routes and sites that attracted the largest number of Olympic visitors determined the type of impacts that were experienced (Brown, 2001). Some of the impacts spread beyond Sydney to other areas of New South Wales (NSW) which were able to host Olympic visitors. However, some areas experienced a decline in tourism demand. The dominance of the Games served to capture the attention and resources of visitors to the detriment of attractions that were effectively competing with the event. This situation was compounded when tour operators were unable to offer their normal services in the absence of buses that had been committed to the Games. A desire to present the 2000 Olympics as a national event for the whole of Australia was contingent upon a sense of engagement by people throughout the country. Strategies were thus developed to spread tourism benefits. These included attempts to encourage visits by international teams for pre-Games training and to stage events, as celebrations, to coincide with the arrival of the Olympic torch.

Accurate post-Games measures of the impact of the Sydney Olympic Games on tourism are not available as little research specifically examining this issue has been conducted. As is the case with most major events, considerable effort was spent to gain support for and to justify the bid and to ensure that the event could be staged successfully. As such, while considerable research informed the planning stages, post-Games impact analysis received less attention as people with relevant knowledge move on to work on the next event.

Research was conducted by the ATC (2000) to track awareness of the Olympics in overseas markets and to monitor community attitudes towards the Games in Australia. In 1999, the highest level of awareness about the Games was recorded in New Zealand (92 per cent) followed by China (75 per cent), Korea (71 per cent), Germany (70 per cent) and England (58 per cent). Significant increases in awareness had occurred between 1998 and 1999 in Korea (from 47 per cent to 71 per cent), Malaysia (from 34 per cent to 43 per cent), Taiwan (from 28 per cent to 38 per cent) and England (from 38 per cent to 58 per cent). Nearly half of potential travellers in India (45 per cent) were found to be more likely to consider going to Australia as a result of the Games. The likelihood in China and Malaysia had increased between 1998 and 1999 from 30 per cent to 37 per cent and from 33 per cent to 41 per cent, respectively. Between 1998 and 2000 there was a steady increase in the perception of the host population that the Olympics would boost the image of Australia (1998: 25 per cent; 1999: 27 per cent; 2000: 29 per cent). However, there had also been a fall in the perception that the Games would bring economic benefits to the country (from 25 per cent in 1998 to 19 per cent in 2000).

Data from the Australian Bureau of Statistics reveal that there was a 15 per cent increase in the number of international arrivals to Australia in September 2000, the month of the Games, compared to the previous year, with changes from markets closely associated with the Olympics being particularly noticeable. The number of tourists from the United States nearly doubled. Within the city, locations that housed *Olympic LiveSites!*, such as Darling Harbour, were crowded throughout the Games and retail sales for businesses in the Harbourside complex increased considerably (see chapter 15 and especially figure 15.2). This contrasted with the situation in regional areas of Australia where a 10–15 per cent decrease in normal visitor levels was recorded (Brown, 2001).

Indications immediately after the Games suggested that Australia would gain the anticipated tourism benefits. There was a 9.7 per cent increase in visitor arrivals in October 2000 compared to October 1999 and tour operators throughout Europe and North America reported unprecedented interest in and bookings to Australia (*Ibid*). A record 565,700 international visitors arrived in December 2000, a 23 per cent increase on 1999; the highest number ever for a single month (ATC, 2001). These increases helped arrivals for the year 2000 to reach a record 4.9 million but everything changed in 2001. The combined impact on demand from the terrorist attacks in New York on 9/11, the outbreak of severe acute respiratory syndrome (SARS) in Asia, and the collapse of Ansett Australia meant that visitor numbers to Australia declined for the next two years. This was the first time this had happened in Australia. Visitor numbers to Australia have increased since 2003 but it is now impossible to determine the role played by any residual Olympic effect. This is disappointing but it does not minimize the lessons that are offered to other host countries by the strategies developed by the tourism industry in Australia that sought to maximize the benefits offered by the Sydney Olympic Games.

Athens 2004

Like many other Olympic cities, Athens expressed a desire to follow the Barcelona model to inform its development planning (Poulios, 2006). However, Beriatos and Gospodini (2004) claim that the Athens approach was very different to that used in Barcelona, and that it lacked focus in terms of a coherent urban development strategy. In fact, there were a number of worries among local businesses and policy-makers not only about the escalating costs of the Games (not an unusual thing for Olympic cities), but also about the lack of planning. In 2002, *Sports Business* carried an interview with the President of the Athens Hotel Owners Association, Sypros Divanis, who claimed that while local hotel owners had invested over €500 million ($437 million) in modernizing and expanding hotels, they were being let down by the government which had failed to produce a plan for tourism linked to the Games. Divanis claimed that:

> The Olympics are the most positive event that could happen to the Greek tourism industry, but while there's over-activity on the part of the hotel community, the state … seeks sloppy solutions which will not offer the infrastructure needed.

One such 'sloppy solution', proposed by the head of the Organizing Committee, Gianna Angelopoulos, was to accommodate visitors on islands or other tourist hotspots and to watch events on day trips to Athens. The lack of tourism planning for the Games was further highlighted in 2003, when the formal co-operation agreement between ATHOC (the OCOG for Athens 2004), the government, and private enterprises was launched. At the launch, in August 2003, it was claimed that the focus needed to be on the development of business and tourism after, rather than during or before, the Athens 2004 Games (Yannopoulos, 2003). However, this approach was severely criticized by George Drakopoulos, Managing Director of the Greek Association of Tourism Enterprises (SETE), who stated (quoted in Yannopoulos, 2003, p. 24):

> Tourism is the principal sector where the economic benefits from hosting the Olympics are obvious, even to a child. And yet, neither the government nor EOT [the National Tourism Organization] have done anything all these years to formulate a marketing strategy that

would make the Olympics the pole of attraction for millions of foreign visitors to Greece. Let's face it, we have forsaken the chance to make the Olympic theme the linchpin of our tourist publicity drive prior to the Games.

While Athens is by far Greece's most important city, Petrakos and Economou (1999) note that within the wider European context, it represents a large peripheral city with low-level influence in the region. This is a result of a range of historical factors (see chapter 16), as well as spatial disadvantages, including unplanned peripheral residential developments, obsolete infrastructure, degraded built fabric, traffic congestion and environmental pollution, caused by unregulated rapid economic and physical growth due to rural immigration between 1950 and 1980 (CEC, 1992). Consequently, Athens 2004 presented a major opportunity to redevelop and rebrand the city. However, despite the city's expressed aim to follow the 'Barcelona Model' (Poulios, 2006), the development of Athens bore little resemblance to Barcelona's approach, and this might be seen as a planning shortcoming that has failed to leave the city with an infrastructure legacy that best provides for future tourism and inward investment. Specifically, some of the failings of planning were:

• *Lack of integrated planning* – partial spatial interventions were not integrated into a strategic plan for Athens as a whole, especially in relation to the post-Games period (Beriatos and Gospodini, 2004).

• *Failure to re-develop brownfield areas* – Barcelona focused on the redevelopment of run-down areas whereas Athens largely developed green spaces on the outskirts or undeveloped sites in the city. Beriatos and Gospodini (2004, p. 198) express surprise that Eleones, 'a large declined area with light industrial uses centrally located in Athens' was not considered for development.

• *Architects and urban designers not given a central role* – Barcelona incorporated architects and urban designers on the bidding and organizing committees for the 1992 Games, whereas Athens only consulted a few 'big name' architects, and did so much later in the process.

• *Lack of spatial concentration* – perhaps the key failing in creating a long-term legacy for urban tourism was the failure to concentrate spatial interventions and landscape transformations in a limited number of strategic sites. Unlike the approach taken in Barcelona, development and redevelopment projects in Athens were scattered 'all over the plan of the city without a focus' (Beriatos and Gospodini, 2004, p. 192).

Despite these deficiencies, there was a clear intention to create an urban legacy as around 95 per cent of Olympic projects were permanent structures. There were also projects that sought to enhance the city's historic sites, in particular those carried out by the Agency for the Unification of the Archaeological Sites of Athens, which sought to link together a geographically disparate range of historical sites and to enhance the city's 'historic physiognomy' (*Ibid.*, p. 199). The intention, therefore, to link the historic local with the modern global existed, but was poorly implemented in practice.

Business File (2004) reported at the end of 2004 that tourism to Athens and Greece was 'lacklustre' during the Games and in the Olympic year, and that Olympic ticket sales were much lower than expected. None the less, there remained hope in the Athens tourism sector that the tourism benefit would occur in the post-Games period, with a Gallery owner in Athens oldest neighbourhood commenting that despite lower than expected tourism in 2004, 'Next year will be better. We don't know, we just hope. It happened in other places and we think it will happen here too' (*Ibid*).

Evidence in the period since the Games suggests that, despite the *laissez-faire* approach to planning for Olympic tourism, the Athens Games have had a positive effect. A study by Alpha Bank, published at the end of 2004 estimated that the Games added €9 billion to Greece's Gross Domestic Product between 2000 and 2004 (as against the country's total GDP of €163 billion in 2003). However, the most optimistic estimates remained predictions: namely that foreign visitors to Greece 'may reach 19–20 million by the end of the decade', from *c*.13 million in 2004 (Alpha Bank, 2004). It is perhaps worth noting, though, that Alpha Bank was a major sponsor of the Athens Games, and thus had a vested interest in demonstrating a positive outcome from the Games.

Beijing 2008

A key goal of both the municipal government of Beijing and the national Chinese government for the 2008 Games as stated in the Beijing Olympic Action Plan (BOCOG, 2003) was to harness aspects of traditional Chinese culture in presenting the city and the country to the world in the run up to and during the Beijing Olympics. Elsewhere in the plan, the role of traditional Chinese culture in such an 'opening-up' strategy, as part of the humanistic 'people's Olympics' promotional theme, was clearly stated:

> … we will take the hosting of the Olympic Games as an opportunity to … promote the traditional Chinese culture, showcase the history and development of Beijing as well as the friendliness and hospitality of its citizens. We will also take the Games as a bridge for cultural exchanges in order to deepen the understanding and enhance the trust and friendship among the peoples of different countries. (*Ibid.*, p. 2)

Yet there were no discussions of the strategies by which this was to be achieved, and there was certainly no stated plan to leverage Olympic media, which was a key requirement for Beijing's Olympic tourism strategy. Furthermore, the lack of such a strategy cannot be blamed on the need to concentrate on ensuring that the facilities and infrastructure were ready as, four years prior to the Games, Ritchard (2004, p. 2) noted that:

> Beijing will be supported by world-class facilities and logistics planning. The city is well underway in developing its Olympic-related facilities, including a new airport, magnificent stadia, convention centre and a much-improved transport network. Construction is reported to be on time and, in some cases, ahead of schedule.

Such efficiency in construction might have been expected in a country that has only relatively recently undergone a transition from a planned 'state socialist' political system to what is still characterized as a 'socialist market economy'. Given that the construction and infrastructure projects were well ahead of schedule, the need to turn attention to media concerns might be seen as even more pressing. Ritchard (*ibid.*, p. 3) claimed that the efficiency of infrastructure development and construction provided Beijing with a world-class tourism product to serve the 2008 Olympics and, as such:

> the greatest potential of the Beijing Games will be the marketing opportunity which will instantly create global consumer awareness of 'China – the brand'… Beijing – like no other previous Olympic city – has a fascinating extra dimension: the unveiling of what China really is and what it can achieve, showcased to a global audience which, generally, knows little about the country. Beijing 2008 will be the source of many 'first impressions'. The Games will be the most comprehensive [and nicely packaged] up-close look at China in half a century, and history will judge the event as the vehicle for demystifying the world's image of the country.

The key question, though, was whether the 2008 Games, and the coverage of the city and country in the years before the Games, would be sufficient to 'convert public curiosity into travel bookings for conferences, leisure tours, city breaks, and business' (*Ibid.*). In this respect, China did not have such an easy ride, and it was not really the case that an Olympic media leveraging strategy was all that was required. Despite reforms, politically Beijing remains a society strikingly at odds with Western liberalism (Wei and Yu, 2006). Furthermore, one of the key aspects of this difference is the Chinese state's perceived attitude to, and record on, human rights, with organizations such as Amnesty International, Human Rights Watch and the Centre of Housing Rights and Evictions commenting both on the state's previous record and on alleged human right violations specifically linked to the preparations for the 2008 Games. The existence and coverage of such issues can increase perceptions of difference and distance from China and Beijing as a desirable tourist destination and, consequently, reduce travel propensities in the key Olympic tourist markets, virtually all of which are liberal democracies with a distaste for human rights violations.

Specifically, it was alleged that, alongside censorship of the press, the 2008 Games led to the exploitation of construction workers and the use of child labour, and the enforced displacement of families and communities from their homes, which have been demolished to make way for Olympic infrastructure developments. Against this background, Ritchard's (2004, pp. 2–3) comments that 'China is absolutely committed to ensuring the success of the Olympic Games – whatever it takes' and that the Games will be 'nicely packaged' become much more insidious. Of course, the displacement of residents to facilitate Olympic development is not a new phenomenon. Many of the criticisms of Barcelona 1992, which is often held up as the best example of the positive effects of the Olympics on long-term trade and tourism development (Sanahuja, 2002), highlighted the displacement of 624 families (approximately 2,500 people) to facilitate the redevelopment of the waterfront area (COHRE, 2007a). Nevertheless, this is a mere drop in the ocean against COHRE's estimates that almost 1.25 million people were displaced in Beijing by 2007, and that this figure was set to rise to 1.5 million by the time the Games commenced in 2008 (Ibid.).

With the glare of the global Olympic media spotlight concentrated on Beijing and China in the run up to 2008, these issues continued to feature in Olympic (and other) media, and could not be addressed by a media strategy without addressing the underlying human right issues themselves. As the Beijing 2008 torch relay progressed around the globe in the months preceding the Games, it was subject to considerable disruption by protesters seeking to highlight a range of human rights issues in China. This became a major global story in the run up to the Games, although its long-term impact on 'China – the brand', given that Beijing undoubtedly hosted a largely successful and spectacular Games in 2008, remains to be seen.

Conclusion

A theme running throughout the discussions of the six Olympic cities in the first ten years of the twenty-first century has been their stated desire to learn from the experiences of previous hosts. However, the discussions often note planning failings in relation to the way in which the various cities have attempted to generate tourism. Such failings serve to highlight the very different contexts of the Games hosted by the Olympic cities discussed. The differences between the potential tourism implications of and the resultant strategies that might be employed in Winter and Summer Olympic cities have been highlighted. In particular, notwithstanding the ambitions and aspirations of national governments responsible for Summer Olympic cities, Winter Olympic cities appear to have a much greater potential to act as a tourism gateway to the wider regions in which they are situated as a result of the resource needs of the Winter Games (i.e., ski and other winter sports provision) that cannot be provided for in cities. Summer Olympic cities, however, have a much greater potential to capitalize on the image benefits that the Games can bring as they are much larger cities than their Winter counterparts, and therefore have an infrastructure and a range of city resources and icons that can be leveraged for tourism image benefits through Olympic-related media.

In closing this chapter, a final comment is perhaps appropriate in looking forward to London 2012. This, already the most planned-for Games in history, will see an attempt to buck the general trend of Summer Olympic cities as destinations rather than gateways in order to extend Olympic tourism benefits throughout the United Kingdom. Undoubtedly, the success or failure of the extensive planning for London 2012 will face considerable scrutiny, both in the United Kingdom and around the world, as London has benefited from a decade of research and knowledge transfer in relation to the opportunities that an Olympic Games can present. As such, in comparison to the Sydney Games of 2000, which are widely recognized as having set the benchmark for leveraging the benefits of the Olympic Games, there is, quite rightly, a higher expectation across a range of policy areas that, most certainly, includes tourism.

Note

1.   The discussions of Sydney 2000 are drawn from a guest chapter contributed by Graham Brown to *Olympic Tourism* (Weed, 2008).

Part III

City Portraits

Chapter 11

Berlin 1936

Monika Meyer

The sports venues of the 1936 Olympic Games left Berlin a significant but difficult legacy. The grounds of the former Reichssportfeld, especially the Olympic Stadium, are important reminders of the history of the city of Berlin and the German state. They show us that sport cannot be non-political. In a staged spectacle the image of a tolerant and open regime was played to the world, but behind the illusion Jews and political dissidents were persecuted systematically and preparations were made for World War II, which had devastating effects on Europe and beyond.

This chapter analyses the construction history of the Berlin Olympic Stadium and its surroundings up to the present. Observations on aspects of National Socialism (Nazism), with which the 1936 Olympic Games are always associated, are touched upon and presented only to the extent that they are significant to the topic. Nevertheless, the focus would be too narrow if the history of the Olympic facilities concentrated only on the period around 1936. The history of the sports facilities began at the start of the twentieth century during the formation of the German Olympic Movement. The various phases of stadia and sports field development were closely tied to Germany's efforts to host the Olympic Games, with the movement first becoming successful during Germany's Weimar Republic. Since 1946 the stadium and other former Olympic facilities have repeatedly been the setting for great national and international events. Especially noteworthy are the games of the 1974 FIFA World Cup that presented the opportunity for the first fundamental renovations. Berlin's renewed bid for the 2000 Olympic Games was controversial both in the city and nationwide, and provoked a lengthy discussion about the future of the stadium: should it be torn down on the basis of cost or kept as a historical building complex? The final decision favoured the Olympic Stadium, which was adapted for contemporary sport in preparation for the 2006 FIFA World Cup.

Becoming an Olympic City

Since the founding of the IOC in 1894, German sports officials had argued seriously about whether holding an international sports competition would comply with the

Olympic tradition of ancient Greece and whether German participation would be sensible. This discussion remained active in Germany into the Nazi period. Between 1896 and 1904, independent committees were formed for Germany's participation in the Olympic Games, and each time they had to discuss this issue with the public, sports associations and government authorities. In 1904 the first successful German national committee for the Olympic Games was formed out of the committee for the Games in St. Louis: the Deutscher Reichsausschuss für die Olympische Spiele (DRAfOS). The goals of DRAfOS were to organize national games, to have German teams participate in international games, and to bring German sports clubs together in a unified association for physical fitness.

Efforts to bring the Games to Berlin in 1908 and 1912 failed because there was no suitable stadium available. After financing had been secured in 1911 and the start of stadium construction had been set for September 1912, the IOC at their meeting in Stockholm in July of 1912 decided to grant Berlin the Games for 1916. In 1913 Carl Diem[1] became the General Secretary of the Organizing Committee for the Berlin Games. The Deutsches Stadion (German Stadium) was inaugurated that same year.

Due to the outbreak of the First World War in 1914, the 1916 Olympic Games were cancelled without an official declaration by Germany, the city or the IOC.[2] In the period following the First World War, sports officials, notably from France, pressed for the exclusion of German athletes from the international arena. This prevented German participation at Antwerp 1920 or the 1924 Games in Chamonix and Paris, with the IOC no longer including German members in its lists.[3] However, Pierre de Coubertin and Carl Diem made efforts to find ways to lead Germany back into the Olympic Movement. In 1924, German members were again appointed, and Germany received an invitation to Amsterdam 1928.

The thought of a renewed candidacy of Berlin seemed logical and so, at their meeting on 29 January 1927, the DOA (German Olympic committee – Deutscher Olympischer Ausschuss)[4] decided that Berlin should bid for the 1936 Games. The official bid was announced at the 29th IOC Session held in Berlin in May 1930. A year later Berlin was chosen at the 1931 Session in Barcelona. On 24 January 1933, the Organizing Committee held their founding meeting. Theodor Lewald,[5] who was voted president, presented the committee's goals: conversion of the Deutsches Stadion, the composition of an Olympic anthem, the organization of an art exhibit and the presentation of an Olympic festival. Six days later on 30 January 1933, Adolf Hitler was appointed Reichskanzler and the National-Socialist dictatorship began in Germany.

Sport during the Third Reich

The position of the Nationalsozialistische Deutsche Arbeiterpartei (NSDAP) was strengthened again in March by the elections for parliament (the Reichstag). The streamlining of sport with the regime began when the Interior Minister appointed

SA-Gruppenführer Hans von Tschammer und Osten as Reichssportkommisar and Reichssportführer. The National Socialists quickly liquidated the Deutscher Reichsausschuss für Leibesübung (DRAfL).[6] The guidelines passed on 24 May 1933 for creating the Deutscher Reichsbund für Leibesübungen established a sports organization according to the Führerprinzip. The Reichssportführer was also the head of the DOA and a member of the leadership of the Organizing Committee of the Olympic Games.

For a long time the Nazis had mounted anti-Olympic campaigns. During the period of the Weimar Republic, these efforts were generally unsuccessful but, after Hitler became Reichskanzler, many in the NSDAP saw a chance to prevent the Olympic Games from being an international event and to hold Germanic or German combat games instead. The Kampfring gegen die Olympischen Spiele, an organization of National-Socialist student groups, demanded on 6 February 1933 that 'the 1936 Olympic Games must not be held in Germany' (Schmidt, 1992, p. 219). Just six days after winning the Reichstag election, however, Hitler received Lewald, with Joseph Goebbels[7] also present, and declared that he would support the Games (*ibid.*, p. 220).

Hitler and Goebbels had recognized very early on the opportunities for Nazi propaganda in hosting the Olympic Games in Germany with its international presentation and the appropriation of the classical Olympic ideal. On 15 January 1934, Goebbels founded a propaganda committee within the Organizing Committee and thereby created an instrument to manipulate the Games to his liking (see Hoffmann, 1993, pp. 12ff).

After Hitler's appointment as Reichskanzler, the world, and especially the United States, raised concerns that the Games could be misused by the new German rulers. On 3 May 1933, IOC President Count Henri de Baillet-Latour wrote to the German IOC members, saying that 'they must bring proof to the upcoming session in Vienna that the government of the Reich does not oppose the Olympic rules' (quoted in Schmidt, 1992, p. 12). The misgivings continued and there were repeated attempts during the preparation period of the Games to create an international boycott (Hoffmann, 1993, p. 12). These efforts increased further as the Nazi system was consolidated and the persecution of Jews became more and more obvious from actions such as the 'Nuremberg Laws' of 1935. In June 1936, after many failed attempts to come to an international decision, the congress of the 'International Committee for the Defence of Olympic Ideals' in Paris called for a boycott of the Games. The same congress proclaimed an 'Olympiad of the People' in Barcelona for 19–26 July 1936. However, due to Franco's coup which started on 17 July 1936, these games could not begin and the boycott did not occur.

Olympic Facilities

The location of the Olympic Stadium and the sports facilities is in the western part of the city in a hilly and wooded area. This area had been used for military purposes since the early nineteenth century and was accessed from an army road leading west. At the beginning of the twentieth century the Kaiser indicated his intention to turn this site over to the public for recreation and leisure. In 1906 the Prussian Federation of Horse-Breeding and Horseracing Sports was able to lease a plot of land to build a horse racecourse and for general sporting purposes. Between 1907 and 1909, Rennbahn Grunewald was built here to the plans designed by Otto March[8] and Albert Brodersen while taking the utmost care to preserve the existing Grunewald pines on site. The racecourse was demolished in March 1934 for the new construction of the Reichssportfeld. The area was a peripheral location, but always had well-developed access to transport. Two roads, two commuter train lines (S-Bahn) built at the beginning of the twentieth century, and an underground (U-Bahn) line connected the sports grounds with the centre of Berlin.

After the unsuccessful bid in Rome to host the 1908 Olympic Games, the DRAfOS and committed athletes attempted to secure financing for an Olympic stadium from 1906 to 1911. In February 1906 the first stadium proposal by Otto March was published in the press, and commentaries even then were printed with regard to future Olympic Games. As the discussions on the financing were drawn out, the stadium was not opened until 1913 after nine months of construction:

> The stadium [was] in a dug-out hollow in the interior space of the horse racecourse in Grunewald. In order to not block the view of the back straight, only low stands [could] be built [50,000 spectators]. In the otherwise large interior space there [was] a 600 m long track and a 666⅔ m long bicycle course… The spectator seating across from the stand side [was] left out as space for a 100m-long swimming pool. Under the swimming pool stands there [were] rooms for a stadium laboratory. (Borges *et al.*, 1995, p. 122)

At the prompting of Carl Diem, further expansion took place after the founding of the Deutsche Hochschule für Leibesübungen in 1919. As a result, the Deutsches Stadion was expanded according to the plans of architect Johannes Seiffert. The Hochschule opened on 15 May 1920 and Diem commissioned Seiffert in 1924 to propose sites for its enlargement. Seiffert chose a 20 hectare area north of the racecourse, where the Deutsches Sportforum was built in three phases between 1926 and 1936. It was designed by Seiffert as well as by Werner and Walter March, with the Nazis beginning to influence matters in 1933. Up to then, Werner March had designed open, interconnected spaces and had pursued a modest but prominent effect. Instead, the map of the area in 1936 revealed a monumental site – 300 metres long and 220 metres wide – with an interior field of honour referring to an oversized hall of pillars. The college became an academy, the Reichsakademie für Leibesübung.

Meanwhile, plans for changes to the stadium were under way. In 1925 the DRAfL began considering a modernization of the stadium and commissioned Werner March[9] to create a draft proposal, which he produced in 1927. The stadium was to be adapted for the latest hygienic standards and expanded for an audience of 80,000. The design proposed by March was presented to the IOC at its 1930 Berlin Session. It called for deepening the stadium and expanding the stands to hold 70,000 spectators. The swimming pool would also be relocated to the narrow eastern end of the stadium where it would be accessed from a prominent plaza. At the Deutsche Bauausstellung 1931, March displayed a model for the conversion of the stadium. A few months later, he presented his proposals to the DOA. When the approval was given for hosting the 1936 Olympic Games, March was commissioned to plan the stadium.

On the day the Olympic Organizing Committee was founded, one week before Hitler was appointed Reichskanzler, the committee decided to avoid costly new construction and to expand the existing stadium instead. That strategy, however, did not meet with the approval of the National Socialists. Their influence led to a complete alteration of the plans in favour of a new stadium. In the spring of 1934 the Deutsches Stadion was torn down to make way for the construction of the Olympic Stadium.

From earliest conceptions, the Deutsches Stadion was intended to be the central sports venue of the Olympic Games. Until October 1933, considerations were attention centred on the modernization of the stadium, but Hitler then decided that the core of the events would be the Reichssportfeld,[10] with an Olympic stadium built on the site of the Deutsches Stadion itself.[11] A tour of the construction site by Hitler on 5 October 1933 accompanied by Frick, the Interior Minister, and Lewald marked the beginning of a phase in which Werner March's construction and urban planning design were broadly overhauled in line with the Nazis' demand for symbolic presence. Hitler ordered the demolition of the horse racecourse and the generous expansion of the sports sites. He wanted the 'largest stadium, the largest assembly field, the largest open-air theatre' (Schmidt, 1992, p. 30). He also intended to relocate the traditional May festival from the field in Tempelhof to the Reichssportfeld.

In the newspaper *Vossische Zeitung* for 6 October 1933, Hitler explained, 'German sport needs something gigantic' (Schäche, 1991, n.p.; Schäche, 2001). After DRAfL was disbanded and the racecourse was acquired, the German Reich was the sole owner of the land and developer of the sports facilities. By 9 October 1933, Werner March[12] had revised his designs, but they did not yet contain the large assembly field that Hitler wanted. Therefore, the meeting on 10 October 1933, at Hitler's offices with Frick and Goebbels as well as Lewald and Diem, did not lead to the desired approval but instead to further planning decisions by Hitler on the construction and layout of the stadium. He demanded an assembly field for 500,000 people (Maifeld) and an open-air theatre for 200,000 spectators (called the Dietrich-Eckart-Bühne).

By December 1933, March had created three variants that differed particularly in the layout and size of the assembly grounds. All designs assumed that the racecourse would be abandoned, but the existing buildings and the surrounding park-like facilities would remain intact. Furthermore, March maintained the development of the Sportforum, the Graditzer Allee, the Schwarzbergallee (as the main entrance to the grounds), and the S-Bahn train line as the southern boundary of the grounds in all his alternative designs. Invariably, the assembly field was west of the stadium and the open-air theatre was in the Murellen ravine (Murellenschlucht).

At another meeting with Hitler on 14 December 1933, Werner March presented a solution using modified plans and a scale-model. They showed the double-axis plan that was finally implemented: an east-west axis which emerged from the Schwarzbergallee containing the sequence of Olympic Plaza (Olympischer Platz), the stadium, the Maifeld and the Fuehrer Tower (Führerturm); and a north-south axis that integrated Rennbahnstrasse and led to the central stadium (figure 11.1). This proposal had an assembly field of 107,000 square metres and was estimated to hold 150,000 people.[13] Werner March received approval to start construction according to this solution. The estimated costs had since increased from 2.6 million Reichsmarks to more than 36 million.[14]

The Reichssportfeld was opened on 23 and 24 May 1936 with the central complex of the Olympic Stadium, Maifeld (figure 11.2) and swimming stadium (figure 11.3), as well as the riding arena, the hockey stadium, the Sportforum with a number of sports and training areas, the open-air theatre, a tennis stadium with various tennis courts, a dance space, a firing range, residence halls, parking lots and areas for small businesses. With the Reichssportfeld, March had effectively designed the first Olympic park complex in history (Wimmer, 1976, p. 192).[15]

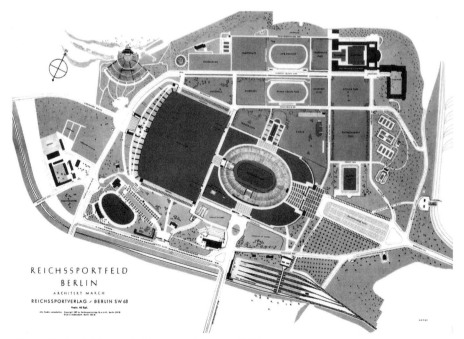

Figure 11.1. Reichssportfeld, map of the area, 1937.

Figure 11.2. Maifeld, 1936.

Figure 11.3. Swimming pool, 2005.

He included the spatial design and the landscaping considerations of earlier developments, the existing usable facilities, optimal transport access for the entire facility and for individual sports venues, and the 'construction plan elevated to a gigantic level by the developer' (Eckert and Schäche, 1992, n.p.). Moreover:

> March's overall design presents a clear arrangement of space and a dominant east-west axis that the broad spaces and expansiveness of the facilities are arranged along. The grounds are differentiated by the staggered height contours of the accompanying sports facilities that are adapted to the available situation on site. The integration of the *Reichssportfeld* into the landscape is accomplished on one hand with the natural effects of plants on the scarce areas available between the sports sites and on the other hand with the expansion of the green belt leading around the grounds to achieve the desired bridging effect into the adjacent wooded areas. (*Ibid.*)

Instructed to abandon the planned renovation of the German Stadium in favour of building a new Olympic stadium, Werner March looked for inspiration to the historical models of Antiquity, such as the Coliseum in Rome, and to contemporary stadium structures, such as the Olympic stadium in Amsterdam. In addition, the basis for his design was also formed by considerations of view and of organizing how to empty the stadium.[16] March proposed an oval stadium, the longitudinal axis of which would run along an east-west line. As in the Deutsches Stadion, the interior space would be a sunken area. This made it possible to place the middle level of the stadium at the level of the surrounding terrain, which significantly improved the development of the stadium. The tiers of seating towards the west were non-continuous so that the marathon gate opened to a view of the bell tower on the Maifeld and created a monumental entry into the stadium.

Though the stadium's shape was obviously a matter for debate, there were serious arguments about the exterior between Hitler and Speer[17] on one side and Werner March on the other. After Hitler toured the stadium grounds and viewed a test section of the façade on 31 October 1934, he expressed his irritation about the thin abutments and the missing stone coverings. The contrasts between March's contemporary architectural perception and Speer's powerful and forceful views could no longer be bridged, and so in February 1935 March was relieved of his decision-making responsibilities for the styling of the stadium.[18] Despite this interference into his designs, Werner March received the gold medal for the Reichssportfeld and the silver medal for the stadium in architectural competitions in 1936, the 'Grand Prix' of the Paris World Exhibition in 1937, as well as other honours and medals abroad.

The Maifeld was west of the Olympic Stadium and was laid out as an assembly field, measuring 395 metres by 295 metres, that could accommodate 180,000 people. A set of stairs separated the lower field from the level of the stadium. Four towers and four large sculptures emphasized the spatial differentiation. Banks of earth formed the boundaries on the north and south sides of the field. On the west side, the monumental east-west axis of the Reichssportfeld reached its end point at the stands with the Führer and speaker stand and the bell tower. In the middle of the stands, the bell tower rose over the three-storey structure that provided access to the field and the tower as well as the Langemarckhalle on the middle storey. Construction of this 50 metres by 10 metres hall of honour for athletes who died in the First World War is attributed to Carl Diem who himself participated in the battle at Langemarck as a soldier and brought soil from the German soldiers' cemetery back to Berlin.

The open-air Dietrich-Eckart-Bühne theatre,[19] which Goebbels demanded, represented an 'important instrument for fulfilling cultural duties of the people and mental and political promotion to the nation' (Schmidt, 1992, p. 60). He wanted 'to fill the German people ... with a national will in the sense of National Socialism' (*Ibid.*). As in many other locations in Germany, a large theatre was to be created here for Germanic festivals of song and dedication and other political events. Goebbels wanted the theatre to hold 500,000 to 1,000,000 people. However, March never proposed a structure that even approached such numbers. His first proposal was for an arena for 35,000 spectators; in the end, it was built for 20,000 people. In the

30 metre-deep natural basin of the Murellenschlucht, March created an open-air theatre in the image of the Theatre of Epidauros from Antiquity.

In the final designs, the swimming stadium was along the cross axis on the north side of the stadium. Two grandstands, facing one another with a total crowd capacity of 17,000, were fitted with two watchtower-like staircases and framed the pool for swimming and diving. In contrast to the Olympic stadium, the swimming stadium remained largely free of interference from Hitler and Speer.[20] Noticeably, there was no Führer or speaker podium in this stadium. Elsewhere, Werner also integrated a hockey stadium for 18,000 spectators into the sports sites of the Sportforum.

A number of the other sports venues in Berlin are also worth mentioning. The Deutschlandhalle (Germany Hall) on the Berlin trade fair grounds (Messegelände), near the Eichkamp S-Bahn station, was built for 20,000 spectators and was the first hall ever built for Olympic Games. For the rowing competitions, the existing facility on the Langer See in Berlin-Grünau was expanded and a stage was added. At the Avus automobile racecourse, the Münster architect Clemens Schürmann built a velodrome.

The Olympic Village

During the first discussions of the spatial organization of the Olympics, Werner March had intended that the military grounds in Döberitz, about 15 kilometres west of the Olympic Stadium, should become the site of the Olympic Village. This huge area was located between Spandau and Wustermark, Falkensee and Potsdam. There were large barracks on the avenue Hamburger Chaussee and a parade ground further south. On 28 March 1933, the Organizing Committee asked Reichsminister General Field Marshal von Blomberg to make the Döberitz Barracks available for use as the Olympic Village. There were 280 rooms available in the officers' barracks. However, the head of the Wehrmacht Office, General von Reichenau, who was himself interested in sport and the Olympic Games, made the further suggestion to use part of the training area north of the Hamburger Chaussee to build a separate Olympic Village. This suggestion was accepted at the site tour that took place on 7 November 1933.

On 26 April 1934, the Organizing Committee gave the Reichswehr the public memorandum entitled 'Olympic Village' with the request to begin the necessary measures. From that point, the Reichswehr acted as the developer of the Olympic Village. It commissioned Werner March to propose a draft scheme for building the facility. He then founded a consortium of architects including Dr Georg Steinmetz, who was responsible for the residential buildings, Walter March, in charge of the shared facilities, and Heinrich Wiepking-Jürgensmann, responsible for landscaping. The implemented design had an organic urban quality (figure 11.4). There was an entry plaza along the Hamburger Chaussee that enabled traffic to flow freely underneath the freeway. The reception halls that formed

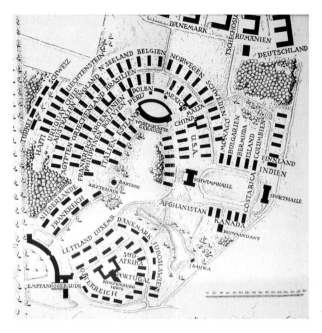

Figure 11.4. Olympic Village, Döberitz, general layout, 1936.

almost a quarter-circle bordered the area on the northwest. The Village extended from this entry area along streets that followed the edges of a valley floor. The individual residential buildings followed the natural contour lines and enclosed green 'village commons'. At the end of the valley, the businesses and dining halls were housed in the Haus der Nationen (House of Nations). The grounds were marked by the existing trees, as well as a hilly topography, brooks and a small lake. In addition, the Village had a swim hall and a sports hall, as well as a Finnish sauna at the lake. The scattered settlement of one-storey bungalows in an almost idyllic and attractively set landscape met with general approval.[21] In February 1936 the Village had to be expanded to the neighbouring Flak barracks in order to house the surprisingly high number of athletes registered. The completed Village was handed over on 10 April 1936.

Ceremonial Aspects

The Berlin Olympic Games were characterized by an unprecedented level of ritualization. This change originated not only with the Nazi rulers but also with the German sports officials who were in contact and agreement with the IOC during their preparations. In this spirit Carl Diem had the idea in 1931 of a torch relay from ancient Olympia to each location of the Games – a ritual that has been a permanent part of the Opening Ceremony of the Olympics since Berlin 1936. In 1932 there was a competition for an Olympic anthem. On 31 July 1933, Pierre de Coubertin met Carl Diem and determined that Beethoven's chorus on Schiller's ode 'An die Freude' would be an element of the opening ceremony. The performance of the 'Olympic Youth' festival written by Carl Diem was planned (see also chapter 4). On 20 October 1934, Richard Strauss finished composing his Olympic anthem with lyrics by Robert Lubahn. This was presented to Hitler on 29 March 1935.

The opening day of the Games was designed as a day-long stage production about Adolf Hitler, Nazi Germany and the Olympic Games. The day began with a reveille concert for the IOC in front of the Hotel Adlon, on the avenue Unter den Linden. After a celebration by the National-Socialist Youth in the Lustgarten, the arrival of the Olympic flame was celebrated by 28,000 members of the Hitler Youth, participants of the international youth camp and a group of student athletes. At the same time, there were school sports events at seventy playgrounds and sports facilities throughout Berlin. Hitler held a reception for the IOC in the Reichskanzler-Palais and rode from there with members of the IOC, the Organizing Committee and representatives of the government and the NSDAP party to the Reichssportfeld. In an unprecedented ceremony, this group entered the Olympic Stadium through the marathon staircase, processed together and took their place in the honorary boxes to the sounds of Richard Wagner's 'Huldigungsmarsch'. As noted in the *Deutsche Olympiade Kalender*: 'In this way Hitler held the attention of the spectators for several minutes. He also benefited from the form of entry into the stadium for officials and honoured guests that was already used at previous Games' (quoted in Borges *et al.*, 1995, p. 273).

Subsequent Usage

The fate of the Olympic complex at Berlin makes a fascinating story in light of current interest in legacy, with its destiny inextricably interwoven with the advent and aftermath of war, the partition of the city and its eventual reunification. In the plans for 'Berlin, the City of Colleges', the Reichssportfeld represented the central assembly and sports grounds. The urban area on both sides of the Heerstrasse was to have a complete re-configuration with large ring roads and spokes, but these plans were never implemented (see also Matzerath, 1984, pp. 308–311). In 1938, parts of the tunnel system were converted to bunkers and a manufacturing facility for anti-aircraft weapon fuses. In the period before and during the war, various large athletic and political events were held on the grounds and in the Olympic Stadium. The International Olympic Institute under the direction of Carl Diem moved into the buildings of the Deutsches Sportforum. Most of its activities ended after it was severely damaged by bombing in 1943.

On 26 June 1945, Diem composed a public memorandum in Berlin for the continued use of the Reichssportfeld. He described it as a 'People's park, symbolic German sports site, central German place of learning, practice grounds for greater Berlin and a central seat of administration of sport'. Essentially, it should continue to be used as it had been previously, but the administrative area was reduced and the settlement of the Friedrich-Wilhelm-Universität was suggested (Schmidt, 1992, p.

331). In June 1945, the stadium was again being used for practical purposes, with the swimming stadium in operation and available for the general public. This short phase of opening the grounds ended in July 1945 when the British Army requisitioned the Reichssportfeld. Henceforth, the facility was made accessible to the public only partially and in phases, transferring the Olympic Stadium, the swimming stadium with the Frauenplatz, the riding grounds and the hockey area to the Magistrat (city council) of Greater Berlin on 22 June 1949. From 1963 onwards, the stadia came under the administration of the Land (region) of Berlin.

The main facilities of the Reichssportfeld have been registered landmarks since 1966, but there have been numerous changes to meet changing needs. The Olympic Stadium has undergone a series of renovations and conversions since 1949; the most extensive being its partial covering, to a design by the architect Friedrich Wilhelm Krahe, for the 1974 FIFA World Cup. The swimming stadium also underwent a series of modernizations and structural changes. The most comprehensive were the measures for the 1978 World Swimming Championships when more pools were built in the surrounding green spaces. The theatre, known today as the Waldbühne, saw the installation of an open-air movie theatre in 1951, with the war-destroyed stage area rebuilt in 1961. In 1982 a tent roof structure designed by Wolfgang Noack was constructed over the stage, making it a venue for large concerts. Public access to the Maifeld, as well as the eastern entry zone of the stadium, was only granted for specific events. Initially after 1945 the shrine to the fallen soldiers and the bell tower lay in ruins, with the remains of the bell tower blown up for safety reasons in 1947. Both were rebuilt between 1960 and 1962, again under the direction of Werner March, although a lively debate broke out about the use of the Langemarckhalle. From 1988 to 1990, a sports centre (Horst-Korber-Sportzentrum) was built along the Glockenturmstrasse according to plans devised by the architectural firm of Langhof, Hänni and Meerstein. It contains a regional performance centre for various types of sport such as handball, hockey and volleyball.

The British Forces installed their Berlin headquarters in all other areas, covering the entire Sportforum and the tennis stadium. These areas were inaccessible to the public and lay outside the authority of any German planning body. In 1956, the Haus des Deutschen Sports, the Friesenhaus and the gymnastics hall were rebuilt. The rebuilding preserved the outward appearance, but adapted the buildings' interiors to meet the needs of the British administration. Various buildings of the British Army, unconnected with sports, were also erected on the grounds.

Berlin's Bid for the 2000 Olympic Games

In 1990, the treaty among the Allies, the reunification of the two German republics and the reuniting of the two halves of Berlin, provided the opportunity for a comprehensive use of the former Reichssportfeld. In Berlin, support quickly grew among the public for the idea of celebrating the beginning of a new epoch in world history by hosting the 2000 Olympic Games. They also recognized the opportunity of renovating the stadium with the financial means that would no doubt be made available for hosting the Games.

For the Olympic bid, the FPB (Freie Planungsgruppe), was commissioned to draft a spatial design. By October 1990, the Berlin Senate had defined the basic principles of the plan. These included the idea that the Reichssportfeld and the Olympic Stadium would be the location for the Opening and Closing Ceremonies and the competitions in track and field, football, baseball, hockey, modern pentathlon and water polo. The Olympic Village would be built in a neighbouring wooded area in Ruhleben. The unique feature of these plans was their inclusion of other existing sports facilities in the western and eastern parts of the city. In its bid, the FPB linked its proposed expansion of the northern line of the S-Bahn ring into an Olympic Express with its scheme for modernizing the sports venues near the northern line for the Olympic Games. This scheme would have been the first time in the history of the Olympics that a decentralized layout for the Games would be tied effectively to the building of a public transport system usable after the Games. These plans, however, were shelved in 1993 when the IOC awarded the 2000 Olympic Games to Sydney (see also Alberts, 2009).

The failure to gain the nomination completely changed the outlook facing both the Land of Berlin, which held the rights of use of the Reichssportfeld, and for the German state, the landowner. By losing the bid for the Games, they also lost the opportunity to finance at least part of the significant renovation work with a profitable event. After the British forces left Berlin according to the Treaty of 1994, Berlin had the additional burden of having the Haus des Deutschen Sports and the Sportforum again available for other uses.

The essential aspect of all thinking about using the Reichssportfeld and the stadia was the restoration and conversion costs as well as the historical significance of the facilities. The costs of renovating the Reichssportfeld were estimated at about €5 billion, but the financial situation of the City of Berlin and the German state was extremely strained. From that perspective, restoration without financing from revenues was almost inconceivable. Possible plans for public facilities included a recreational area, a historical park or a sports facility, but none of these could be financed. Officials and politicians then considered how commercial uses might improve returns. Basic uses under consideration, such as an amusement park, hotel, shopping centre, residential area or office space, would increase the frequency of visitors, but additional music events were complicated due to the noise problems. As almost all the buildings and a large part of the open spaces were registered landmarks, it would be more difficult to promote the grounds to private investors.

The Olympic Stadium posed particular problems. Complaints from international sports associations about its shabby and insufficient facilities and its structural condition meant that its long-term use could no longer be guaranteed. However, the award in 1998 of a different mega-event, the 2006 FIFA World Cup, to the German national football association provided an opportunity for a full review, given that the Olympic Stadium in Berlin would be its most important venue. On the basis of various appraisals and an architectural competition, Berlin and the German Federal government decided to renovate the Olympic Stadium according to the plans of the Hamburg-based practice gmp (Architekten von Gerkan, Marg und Partner). Construction work was completed in 2004 at a cost of €242 million, of which Berlin funded €46 million (figure 11.5).

With regard to other major installations, the Deutsches Sportforum was again placed under the administration of the Federal government in September 1994, and was open on a limited basis for sports clubs. Today, the fields and facilities of the Sportforum are used for professional and amateur sports alike, and the diverse activities of a wide variety of clubs define the grounds. For its part, the Olympic Village was shaped by its long association with military purposes. As originally intended, the Wehrmacht used the Olympic Village after the Olympic Games. The Soviet Red Army requisitioned the facilities from 1945 to 1991 and used them to house Soviet soldiers and their families. Very few of the athletes' residences remained. Instead, a large number of concrete tower blocks of up to five storeys were built, although integration into the landscape remained largely intact. The community building, the Hindenburghaus, the sports and swim halls and the original buildings intended for athletes from Switzerland, Turkey and the USA were all still maintained and used. When the Russian troops left in 1991,

Figure 11.5. Olympic Stadium, View from Olympischer Platz, 2005.

the Village was empty and succumbed to disrepair, looting and vandalism. The swimming hall was destroyed by arson in 1993.

Since 1994, the regional development society of the Land Brandenburg has attempted to develop the entire 120-hectare barracks area into a residential neighbourhood, albeit with little success. There was discussion of using the Haus der Nationen as a hotel or office space, but no definite use is in sight for the Hindenburghaus, which was the cultural centre of the Olympic Village. The lake also has mostly been filled in, although plans exist for its re-creation if circumstances allow.

Conclusion

The facilities in Berlin are some of the most impressive structures of the Olympic Games of the modern era, although the area had only a limited effect on the development of the city.[22] The choice of location for the Games was determined by personal relationships and financial problems, not urban design or overall considerations of city interests. The chosen site, however, was satisfactory in many ways for implementing a sufficient area, quality of development and a uniquely designed sports venue for the politically symbolic intentions of the time. The Reichssportfeld was designed as a venue for mass events in such a way that different events could be held separately and simultaneously at different points on the grounds.

Werner March's designs had significant urban and landscaping qualities. It is an urban planning accomplishment still recognized today that he integrated a facility capable of holding almost 400,000 people at a time into the pastoral landscape of Grunewald between the Havel and Spree rivers while overcoming issues concerning travel by large numbers of people to and from the site. The extension of the plans into monumental proportions has its basis in Hitler's intention to create the prototype of a venue for National Socialist assemblies. Such abuse of the Games, the athletes, the spectators and the Olympic ideal for the propagandistic goals of the Nazi government was indissolubly linked to this kind of forceful architecture.

The Olympic Village is also unique in the history of the Olympic Games, as it was built by the military and was intended for military purposes after the Games. The layout and use of the Village are contradictory. The almost idyllic setting is still recognizable today, with the Haus der Nationen strongly resembling the organic architecture of Alvar Aalto. This is in direct contrast to the monumental architecture of the Olympic grounds and the intentional use of the Village after the Games as barracks. It is distressing in retrospect to see the similarities when comparing the Village entrance and the Olympians' housing with the barracks at Dachau, Auschwitz and Majdanek. Just as unsettling is the knowledge that the peaceful co-existence of nations took place in such barracks.

The thought of holding the Olympic Games for 2000 at the former

Reichssportfeld seemed logical but still provoked widespread protest. Issues of dealing with and re-using the architectural legacy of Nazism proved to be a significant problem for the public. There was also the concern that the necessary investment for both parts of Berlin to grow together again would instead be used for symbolic building projects. However, part of the bid's designs was completed. The northern line of the S-Bahn ring was made operational again which significantly improved the infrastructure and traffic connections for the northern part of Berlin. Individual sports facilities were modernized or rebuilt and the planned Olympic Village on the inlet in Rummelsburg (Rummelsburger Bucht) was partially completed as a waterfront housing development with a mixture of residences and services.

Notes

1. Carl Diem (1882–1962) was organizer and patron of German athletics from 1903 onwards. He was the General Secretary for the 1916 Olympic Games; a co-founder of the German College of Physical Education (Deutsche Hochschule für Leibesübungen) in 1929; the General Secretary of the Organizing Committee for the 1936 Olympic Games from 1933 to 1937; the director of the Reichssportfeld in 1936; director of the International Olympic Institute in Berlin from 1938 to 1945; founder of the German College of Physical Education (Deutsche Hochschule für Leibesübungen) in Cologne in 1947; and secretary of the newly founded German National Olympic Committee from 1950 to 1952. From 1906 onwards, Diem composed reports and wrote books about the Olympic Games. At the end of July 1912 Carl Diem's book *Die Olympischen Spiele 1912* was published as the first Olympic book in German (Diem, 1912). Three decades later, in 1942, he published his three-volume work *Olympische Flamme* (Diem, 1942).

2. A winter sports festival which had been planned for February 1916 in the Black Forest and Berlin was not held. As a substitute for these games, there were national Olympic Games in Amsterdam from 24 June to 3 September 1916, and an international sports festival was staged in Stockholm on 8 July 1916 for Scandinavian athletes.

3. During this time the idea of holding national Olympic Games was formed. Such games were held in Berlin in 1922, in Cologne in 1926, in Breslau in 1930, in Nuremberg in 1934, and in Breslau again in 1938. The Breslau games in 1938 were also the first German gymnastics and sports festival (Deutsches Turn- und Sportfest).

4. The German Olympic Committee (DOA) was constituted in February 1926 as a sub-committee of the national committee for physical fitness (DRAfL – Deutscher Reichsausschuss für Leibesübungen), which originated in the DRAfOS.

5. Theodor Lewald (1860–1947) was the Secretary of State in the Interior Ministry and was the acting National Commissioner (Reichskommissar) in 1903 for the World's Fair of 1904 in St. Louis. Starting in 1919, he was the president of the DRAfL and by 1933 he was the president of the Organizing Committee for the 1936 Olympic Games. In 1924 Lewald was appointed to the IOC at the wish of Coubertin and, in 1925, he was appointed to the Executive Board of the IOC. In 1938 he resigned from the IOC. Lewald was publicly reviled by the Nazis as a 'half-Jew' and was forced in 1933 to give up the head of the DRAfL.

6. The National Committee for Physical Fitness (DRAfL – Deutscher Reichsausschuss für Leibesübung) originated in the DRAfOS in 1917 (see also note 4 above).

7. Director of the newly created ministry for 'People's Enlightenment and propaganda' (Reichsministerium für Volksaufklärung und Propaganda).

8. Otto March (1845–1913) lived and worked in Berlin. After his studies at the Berlin Academy for Construction (Berliner Bauakademie), he began a career as an independent architect in

addition to his job in the public sector. His proposals influenced his contemporaries and later architects such as Ernst May, Walter Hegemann and his son, Werner March.

9.   Werner March (1894–1976), son of architect Otto March, became well-known due to his proposals for the Reichssportfeld in Berlin for the 1936 Olympic Games. After his studies in architecture in Dresden and Berlin, he worked as an independent architect starting in 1925. In 1936 March became director of the Technical Institute for the Construction of Practice Venues (Technisches Institut für Übungsstättenbau) at the National Academy for Physical Fitness (Reichsakademie für Leibesübungen). In Germany, he performed various tasks of urban planning and construction of large structures until he volunteered for military service in 1940. In 1946, March worked as a planner for urban history in Minden. In 1953, he became Ordinarius of the professorship for urban planning and housing at the Technische Universität Berlin. In the 1950s and 1960s he received international contracts for the construction of stadia in places such as Egypt and Greece.

10.   March's plans for the Reichssportfeld and especially the influence of Hitler, Goebbels and Speer are described comprehensively in Schmidt (1992). Wolfgang Schäche (1991, n.p.) holds a significantly different opinion regarding the disagreements between Hitler and Speer on one side and March on the other. 'To that extent, the almost bizarre thesis of interpreting the Olympic Stadium with its architectural contradictions as documentation of rivalling ideologies (contemporary architect versus regressive position of Hitler and Speer) is therefore to be approached with extreme scepticism'.

11.   Other sites for the Olympic events were dispersed throughout the city, with the sailing competitions held in Kiel.

12.   As the architect, he was responsible for the urban planning and the architecture of the grounds; Heinrich Wiepking-Jürgensmann was responsible for the landscape architecture.

13.   It is worth noting that despite the enormous pressure placed on him, March knew how to create the dimensions of the Reichssportfeld facilities so that they still maintained a human scale.

14.   On 15 December 1933, Hitler was quoted in the newspaper *Völkischer Beobachter* as saying: 'On this day I have given my final approval for the start and the completion of the structures on the stadium grounds. Germany will thereby have a sports venue unequalled by any other in the world' (cited in Hoffmann, 1993, p.17).

15.   Eckert and Schäche (1992, n.p.) on this topic wrote: 'The Reichssportfeld facility in this design presents a sports complex designed by function and purpose that already was developed in the 1920s. In this context, note the following path-breaking facilities: the Müngersdorf sports complex in Cologne by Fritz Encke (1920–1923), the Zentralsportpark in Frankfurt am Main by Max Bromme (1921–1925), the Volkspark with the "Rote Erde" stadium in Dortmund by city planning commissioner (Stadtbaurat) Strobel (1925–1927) or the Sportpark Tempelhof by Ottokar Wagler in Berlin'.

16.   See also the text by Werner March as published in Schmidt (1992, pp. 42 ff and 64 ff).

17.   Architect Albert Speer (1905–1981) was one of Hitler's closest confidants which placed him in an exceptional position. The dictator appreciated Speer's unconditional loyalty and the ability with which he created large construction projects in short amounts of time. Hitler saw Speer as the artist and visionary that he himself would like to have been. Beginning in 1932 Speer received construction contracts from the Nazis and in 1934 became the most influential architect in the Third Reich. In 1938 he was appointed as the general building inspector (Generalbauinspekteur) for the capital city of the Reich, Berlin. Among his most important projects are the monumental structures and productions for the Reich party conventions in Nuremberg, the chancellery (Reichskanzlei), the German pavilion for the Paris World Exposition in 1937 and the plans for the conversion of Berlin into 'Germania', capital city of the world, with numerous monumental structures. In 1942 Hitler appointed him to be the Minister for Weapons and Ammunition (Reichsminister für Bewaffnung und Munition), and in 1943 he became the Minister for Armament and War Production (Reichsminister für Rüstung und Kriegsproduktion). Speer's organizing of

the war economy was based on using forced labour and prisoners from concentration camps. In the Nuremberg Trials in 1946 he was sentenced for war crimes and crimes against humanity. After his release he published his memoirs (Speer, 1969), in which he attempted to portray himself as a 'respectable Nazi' and 'misled citizen'. However, more recent publications reveal his role as one of the most brutal leaders of the regime.

18.   Schmidt (1992, p. 46) continued: 'The overall contemporary architectural design for the Olympic Stadium is no longer recognizable today. The stylistic adjustments made by architect Albert Speer during the realization planning continued to alter the outward appearance of the stadium. Almost all of March's intended construction elements and wall surfaces made of nidged concrete were covered with shell limestone. The natural stone material was intended to express the values of simplicity, durability, hardiness, being down-to-earth, greatness and power that were propagated by the National Socialists'.

19.   Naming the theatre after the founder of the anti-Semitic newspaper *Auf gut deutsch* and the first editor of the *Völkischer Beobachter* was an indication of the Nazi orientation of the theatre. See also Schmidt (1992, p. 60).

20.   Hitler admitted in 1935 that: 'He was certainly not satisfied with everything happening at the Reichssportfeld, but he did not have enough time that year to attend to such matters' (quoted in Schmidt, 1992, p. 62).

21.   From today's perspective, the history of the Village's origins and its intended use after the Olympic Games as a military facility are irreconcilable with the Olympic message of peace. The entrance buildings of the facilities and athletes' barracks are macabre, as they appear in an only slightly adapted form of the Nazi concentration camps.

22.   A comparative evaluation of the urban planning effects of large events on the locations where they are held is explored by the author in her work *Der planbare Nutzen: Stadtentwicklung durch Weltausstellungen und Olympische Spiele* (Meyer-Künzel, 2002). The urban planning for events is documented and evaluated in the context of each political, social and cultural situation. The work therefore compiles a cross section of the planning goals of large events, their realization and their long-term use after the Games and explains them with extensive pictures and planning materials.

Chapter 12

Mexico City 1968

Michael Barke

The torch for the 1968 Games was lit at Olympia in mid-August 1968. It then began a journey that moved from Greece and circulated to European sites with Olympic and Mexican connections. These included Genoa (Italy), the birthplace of Christopher Columbus, Palos (Spain), where Columbus's expedition started in 1492, and Barcelona, a major seat of the Spanish empire. From Europe the relay conveyed the torch by sea to San Salvador, the site of Columbus's first landing in the Americas, then on to Vera Cruz where four additional torches were lit. The five torches, echoing the five Olympic rings, then made their way to Mexico City by different routes. On 11 October, they arrived at the pyramid of the Moon at Teotihuacán to the north of Mexico City, where a ceremony imitating the Aztec ritual of New Fire – celebrating the resurgence of life and the triumph of light over darkness – was enacted. On the evening of 12 October, Norma Enriqueta Basilio, a 20 year old 400 metre runner from Baja California, lit the Olympic flame; the first woman in Olympic history to be given the honour.

There were thus strong overtones of Mexico's history in the main public ceremony leading up to the Games, but the intention to engage fully with the present was symbolized in the choice of a young female to light the flame. She 'represented a new kind of Mexican, tall, thin and beautiful, contrasting the older generation that she called short and fat' (quoted in Witherspoon, 2003, p. 113). Although Mexico's rich cultural history was not ignored during the Nineteenth Olympiad, it was reinterpreted in a variety of ways, ways that emphasized national unity rather than diversity. More than anything, from the Mexican perspective, the project was about modernity. The President of the Organizing Committee, Pedro Ramirez Vázquez, later commented '... of least importance was the Olympic competition; the records fade away, but the image of a country does not' (quoted in Rivas and Sarhandi, 2005). Despite the efforts of the political elite from the late nineteenth century onwards (Tenorio-Trillo, 1996), the organizers of the Mexican Olympics – both sporting and cultural – were well aware that much of the rest of the world saw the country in Third World terms and their response was driven by the need to counter such stereotypes at almost every turn. Thus, issues of international prestige were never very far from the minds of the chief protagonists (Brewster and Brewster, 2009).

Mexico City 1968 remains one of the most memorable meetings of modern times – and perhaps more because of non-sporting events than some undeniably spectacular sporting achievements. However, along with Berlin 1936 and Moscow 1980, the Mexico City Games demonstrated overtly the political context of the modern Olympics. Whereas the politicization of the Berlin Games could easily be dismissed as an aberration of Nazi Germany, Mexico City was more significant in that no single ideology could be held responsible for events, and that the manifestations of that politicization were apparent in many different ways. Some were obvious; others more subtle. Some were internal to the host country; many others were products of issues and pressures external to Mexico. After 1968, it became impossible to deny that sport and politics were inextricably linked.

The Mexico City Games were also highly significant in terms of the development of the relationship between the Olympics and television (Wenn, 1995). From this juncture, the way that the Games were 'packaged' and 'sold' would be as important as the actual Games events themselves. Indeed, it has been claimed that Mexico City 1968 'sticks in the mind because the originality and cogency of its system of communication converted it into a paradigm of modern graphic and event design' (Rivas and Sarhandi, 2005). Yet with regard to the role of television, the selective framing of events was foreshadowed at the Opening Ceremony, when the cameras studiously avoided the massed ranks of heavily armed security forces surrounding the stadium.

Another notable feature of the 1968 Games was that they were the first held within Latin America or, more significantly, in a 'developing' or 'Third World' country. This, in itself, was a remarkable choice that requires explanation. How did Mexico manage to win the contest to stage the 1968 Olympics? Having done so, how did a relatively poor developing country set about staging the Games in infrastructural terms? This process, itself inevitably immensely complicated and expensive to accomplish, has acted as a deterrent to many cities and countries from even entering the competition to host the Games. In that light, how then did Mexico and its capital city accomplish this feat and at what cost? Part of the answer to the last question raises further questions about how the Games were promoted, not least to the Mexican people and the citizens of Mexico City. Questions of how the country and city presented itself to the outside world are also important here. Finally, with the benefit of hindsight and more than four decades of reflection we can ask what the 1968 Olympics really meant in their wider context, that is, beyond the sports fields and arenas. This series of issues is still debated in the historiography of modern Mexico (Brewster and Brewster, 2009), but it is perhaps insufficiently recognized that the answers may be very different from an 'internal' perspective than from an 'external' one.

Winning the Games

Answers to these questions begin by noting that the Mexican elite had, from the late nineteenth century, sought to portray their country in modern terms and to engage with international cosmopolitanism (Tenorio-Trillo, 1996). Participation in World's Fairs, in the Olympic Games and, eventually, presenting a bid to host those Games represented a natural progression in nation building and representation. Adolfo López Mateos, President of Mexico from 1959 to 1964, took the decision to compete for the Olympic Games of 1968. He continued to be involved after retiring as President, serving on the Committee that organized the Games. Remarkably, López Mateos managed the feat of staying on good terms with the United States whilst refusing to break ties with Cuba's new revolutionary government. Significantly, he was also the first Mexican president to engage in substantial travel abroad (Riding, 1987) in a determined attempt to establish Mexico's international prestige. There is little doubt that he saw hosting the Olympic Games as a major step forward in establishing Mexico as a modern nation on the international stage (Krauze, 1997). Although a very different President and with considerably less charisma, Gustavo Díaz Ordaz, his successor from 1964 to 1970, eventually became no less determined that Mexico should host the Games and in a way that would enhance Mexico's international prestige. His inherent authoritarianism and inflexible perspective led him to interpret the student movement of 1968 as a communist-inspired plot to disrupt the Olympics, an interpretation that was almost certainly inaccurate (Zolov, 1999). Nevertheless, it is clear that, in competing to host the 1968 Olympics, national boosterism was placed on the agenda very early in the process.

There were three important components to this strategy. The first was to establish international legitimacy for what was still a single party state. The second was to generate a stronger sense of nationalism while, third, demonstrating the modernity of Mexico. We shall return to these issues later, but what must concern us first is the international scale and the factors operating at this level that led to what remained, for many years, the only successful Olympic bid made by a developing nation.

Ostensibly, there were considerable objections to Mexico, with doubts being expressed about the country's ability to organize the Olympic Games (Arbena, 1996) and, especially, about the altitude issue. Mexico went to great lengths to counter both these objections, having sponsored numerous scientific studies on the effects of altitude, offering to defray the expenses of athletes while acclimatizing to conditions in Mexico City and hosting a 'mini-Olympics' in 1967 (Wrynn, 2004). Support on the altitude issue eventually came from a somewhat unexpected quarter in the form of Avery Brundage, president of the IOC who observed: 'The Olympic Games belong to all the world, not the part of it at sea level.' (quoted in Guttmann, 1984, p. 123).

One important factor was that the competition to hold the Games, although initially seeming to be formidable, eventually turned out to be not particularly strong. While the bid comes from the potential host city, Mexico City's bid could scarcely be described as emanating solely from the metropolis itself and was about much more. Three other cities competed to host the 1968 Olympics – Detroit, Buenos Aires and Lyons. Detroit had also attempted to host the Games in 1952, 1956, 1960, and 1964 and was to try again – unsuccessfully – in 1972. Despite its long involvement in the bidding process, Detroit's bid in 1968 was lacklustre and revealed weaknesses in the shape of lack of hotel space, failure to mobilize significant local enthusiasm, and shortcomings in financial arrangements (Zimmerman, 1963). The city's bid was not helped by the fact that Los Angeles, only six months before the final vote, had challenged Detroit's bid to represent the United States at the IOC decision-making meeting in Baden-Baden in October 1963 (*Anon.*, 1963). The rival and mutually-damaging campaigns of Los Angeles and Detroit undoubtedly harmed Detroit's ultimate bid in the eyes of the IOC adjudicators, particularly through Los Angeles pointing out previous Detroit failures and publicly airing its continuing weaknesses (Witherspoon, 2003). The bid from Buenos Aires was widely recognized as weak, lacking in detail or any real sense of enthusiasm and, in the event, only received two votes. Lyons probably represented a greater threat with advantages of governmental support, France's record in hosting previous Olympics, the city's accessibility from Africa and the Middle East, and promises to enlarge the airport and expand an existing stadium from a capacity of 60,000 to 95,000 (Daley, 1963.) The fact that Lyons was a much smaller city, however, probably counted against it. The Mexican strategy was skilful, determined and enthusiastic and struck many of the right notes with the voting panel, including dealing effectively with the altitude issue (Wrynn, 2004).

Whether by fortune or subtle appreciation of the international mood, the Mexican bid caught the imagination of the times and presented a distinctive and appealing image, albeit one with a specific national agenda. Thus, in their presentations, Senator Carillo presented the Mexican people as:

> ... simple, humble, hard-working and honest. They were a determined people who had transformed their nation after the Mexican Revolution, and the Olympics would symbolize the success of that transformation.

and Dr. Eduardo Hay, concluded with:

> We seek the Games not for us, not for our business, but for our youth. That is why we are asking for this. Not to have another title. You can be sure that the Mexican public will be with you with the best of them. (Quoted in Witherspoon, 2003, p. 41).

Having said this, the Mexican delegation also exploited Cold War political allegiances to the full with intensive lobbying of the Soviet and related members of the IOC and, of course, its natural allies in the Third World representatives.

Through this means, Mexico won support from Latin American, African and Soviet-bloc representatives in order to defeat the main opponents from North America and Europe. An effective bid from a developing country that could demonstrate its capacity to put on the Games was therefore always going to appeal to a large number of the voters in this new international environment. López Mateos and the Mexican delegation understood this very well. Avery Brundage himself (who had voted for Detroit) commented:

> What helped Mexico was that it is one of the smaller-scale countries, and some members felt they could do more for the Olympic movement by giving encouragement to such a country. (*Ibid.*, p. 44)

Hence, its campaign was highly effective and skilfully managed, and in the final analysis Mexico City won the right to stage the 1968 Games because of geopolitical alignments and the prevalent international atmosphere of the 1960s. This atmosphere worked in favour of a country such as Mexico in a manner not previously seen and, with the ending of the Cold War, is probably unlikely to be repeated.

Yet there was more to Mexico City's bid than politics. Unlike Detroit, Lyons and Buenos Aires, Mexico City could draw on the country's impressive record of accomplishment in hosting major international events, with the capacity to meet most of their accompanying demands. The country had staged the 1926 and 1954 Central American and Caribbean Games, the Pan American Games of 1955 when over 2,000 athletes from twenty-two countries attended, the Modern World Pentathlon Championships of 1962 and the National Children and Junior Sports Games of 1961 and 1962. Mexico City itself had numerous and impressive sports facilities and arenas, many of them built recently and publicly funded (Arbena, 1991; Brewster, 2005), a large number of hotels and other visitor facilities, and an apparently dynamic growth-oriented philosophy, albeit one that had yet to engage with contemporary ideas of city-regional planning (Campbell and Wilk, 1986).

The development of these facilities reflected the profound belief of many of the protagonists of the Mexican Revolution that a process of nation-building was necessary and that sport could be one of the main instruments through which this could be achieved. Although initially reluctant (McGehee, 1993), the Mexican government gradually came to understand the wider significance of sport and participation in international events, especially after the Central American Games of 1926 when 'Mexicans had held what they considered to be their own Olympics' (*Ibid.*, p. 326). Symbolic events, most notably associated with 20 November, 'Revolution Day', celebrating Francisco Madero's call to arms in 1910 against the 34-year rule of Porfirio Díaz, were celebrated with parades at which athletes took a prominent place (over 50,000 in 1934) and 'sports that were perceived as modern and western led the way' (Lorey, 1997, p. 51). 'Gradually Mexican cities and towns began to create a nation by acting it out in countless local and regional exhibitions, parades and gatherings' (Tenorio-Trillo, 1996, p. 245). From 1930 onwards the annual 'Revolutionary Games' were also inaugurated. Sport, and especially international sport, became not only an opportunity to promote the image of the country abroad but also to provide a unifying focus around which, hopefully, different regions, peoples, and sections of society could rally (Brewster, 2005). 'By the late 1920s regional integration became one of the featured themes of sports displays on November 20' (Lorey, 1997, p. 55) and the subservience of the regions to the centre was symbolized by the ritual relay race from Puebla to Mexico City.[1]

The first major physical manifestation of this desire to use sport as a means of national unification after the chaos of the Mexican revolution of 1910–1919 and its aftermath, was the construction of a National Stadium in May 1924 (McGehee, 1993). In the same year Mexico sent its first group of athletes to the Paris Olympics, although they were privately funded. This participation led directly to Mexico hosting the 1926 Central American Games which, although modest, were an important catalyst for interest in sport more generally. However, it was not until 1932 that the Party of the Mexican Revolution (PRM) established the national sport confederation with the specific objective of creating '... an integrated nation [composed] of healthy, virile and dynamic men' (quoted in Arbena, 1991, p. 355).

Interest in sport grew rapidly during the 1930s and especially in the post-war years, although one issue that surfaced at this time was the extent to which Mexico was importing and imitating developed, Western, and especially US sporting activities rather than enhancing or developing an indigenous sporting culture. Inevitably, the former was the preserve – at least initially – of the mainly white middle classes and the meaning of such activities for the *mestizo* and Indian populations was highly contested.

A major boost was provided by the 1955 Pan-American Games, in support of which the government built an Athletes' Village, numerous sporting facilities and distributed over 1.5 million free tickets to the public. Indeed, on an earlier visit to Mexico City, Avery Brundage (1951) had observed 'the second Pan-American Games will be held in Mexico City in 1955 and new facilities of Olympic calibre are already under construction'. The event was a great success in terms of the facilities and organization and it also led to the creation of a generation of athletics fans in Mexico. The combination of popular support and government ideology which '... interpreted participation in the Games as an opportunity to express national identification' (Espy, 1979, p. viii), provided a dual impetus for bids to host the world's major sporting events.

Producing the Games

The process of bidding for, and winning, the right to stage the 1968 Olympic Games was integral to a much larger project on the part of the Mexican government. It was part of a campaign to establish international recognition, to create a stronger sense of nationhood and also to modernize the nation. The

Olympic bid and that for the 1970 FIFA World Cup only make sense within this wider context and it is no coincidence that this agenda was driven forward by one of Mexico's most outward looking Presidents. Not surprisingly, therefore, major investments were made in transport and tourism, but these served to reinforce the position of Mexico City as the centralized hub of the country (Nolan and Nolan, 1988; Clancy, 1999). Indeed, despite various attempts to achieve the opposite (Barkin and King, 1970), with some recent checking of urban population growth rates (P.M. Ward, 1998) most political, social and economic processes since the mid twentieth century have served to highlight the concentration of economic and political power in Mexico City.

The Olympic Games supported this trend. All the sporting events were held within the city apart from sailing which took place at the Acapulco yacht club (Arbena, 1996). In winning the bid, the Mexican delegation had made much of the fact that, in contrast to their competitor cities, considerable infrastructure was already in place. Nevertheless, there was much more that needed to be done. The basic budget amounted to $84 million of federal spending and $75 million from private sources for projects directly related to the Games, especially the building of the Olympic Village with twenty-nine structures varying from six to ten storeys (Witherspoon, 2003, p. 108). However, this excluded other infrastructure deemed to be necessary such as a new six-lane motorway linking the main facilities, improved water supply and sewage disposal systems and, controversially, the new subway system. Although it was supposed to be open for the 1968 Olympics, work on the subway system did not start until 1967 and was still only partially opened by 1969. Thus, while the Olympics and its 'modernization' project were instrumental in promoting this massive investment, the principal catalyst had passed before a significant component of the infrastructure was even partly open.

Ward (1990, p. 217) has argued that in Mexico City, '... the purpose of monuments constructed since the 1960s appears to be one of reinforcement: of the modern, of the abstract, and of the international'. If not precisely beginning with the Olympic Games, this process was boosted by that event and laid Mexico City's cultural environment firmly open to international scrutiny. An important component of the ideological background to Mexico City 1968 was to demonstrate Mexico's engagement with modernity and this was best demonstrated in the 'audacious plan for decentralized facilities that turned the whole city into temporary festival ground' (Gordon, 1983, p. 99). Facilities were deliberately spread around the city in a conscious attempt to integrate the Olympics more widely and encourage participation after the Games. The relationship between the sporting events and urban structure disdained the recent convention of using the former as a regeneration tool. The overall philosophy was expansionist. Emphasis was placed on large-scale transport planning, on freeway building and catering for motor vehicles; trends that inevitably privileged an advance to the periphery rather than a focus on the core. New peripheral motorways were built and the city's public transport system was increased by an additional 1,500 special vehicles to provide access to the new and existing facilities, scattered widely over Mexico City, in an 'unprecedented dispersion' (Muñoz, 1997, p. 35), some being over 30 kilometres apart. Olympic routes were colour coded and marked by streamers while enormous balloons or fibreglass figures indicated the sites themselves.

The main focus was in the south of the city at the Olympic Village, known as the Miguel Hidalgo Village, which contained 5,000 units in several tower blocks – 'more than previous Olympic villages, it was a city' (Gordon, 1983, p. 101). It was the intention after the Games that they would be sold as condominium apartments. A second Olympic Village, the Narciso Mendoza Village, also known as Villa Coapa, was built for the Cultural Olympics with 686 houses and flats, the latter in four-storey blocks (Muñoz, 1997). Both Villages were inspired by the features of mass social housing prevalent in Europe in the 1960s and reflected the *grandes ensembles* tradition (*Ibid.*). The new 25,000-seat Sports Palace for indoor sports, costing $8 million was 9 miles (more than 14 kilometres) to the north-east of the Olympic Village at the Magdalena Mixhuca Sports Park where the velodrome was also located, whilst the new Olympic Pool and Gymnasium was built in the smart southern suburb of Coyoacan. The rowing basin was located still further south at Xochimilco. Although not built with Olympic funds, the Aztec stadium (designed by Pedro Ramírez Vázquez in 1966) was used for Olympic football in 1968 and later for the FIFA World Cup Finals in 1970 and 1986. Among the other renovated buildings was the 12,800 capacity National Auditorium at Chapultepec, used mainly for gymnastics. The main sporting location for the athletics events, however, was also not new, being the renovated University City Stadium built in 1953 but expanded to a capacity of 80,000. Inevitably, there was much scepticism from the 'First World' about whether this entire infrastructure would be ready in time (for example, see Giniger, 1968*a*, 1968*b*).

The main axis for the Games was the so-called Route of Friendship in the southern periphery of the city, a newly built motorway connecting most of the main Olympic locations. This route became famous for one of the most high-profile cultural events associated with the Olympics, with the distinguished architect Pedro Ramírez Vázquez (President of the Organizing Committee of the Mexico Olympics) and the architect and sculptor Mathias Goeritz promoting its iconic status (Goeritz, 1970).[2] In 1966, Goeritz proposed to Ramírez Vázquez that the Olympics should be marked with an invitation to sculptors from around the world to create a sequence of abstract sculptures in concrete, which would be sited along the Route of Friendship (Wendl, 1998). Goeritz's ideology was clear in his speech of welcome to the international sculptors, where he asserted his belief that:

> An art integrated from the very inception of the urban plan is of fundamental importance in our age. This means that artistic work will have to leave its environment of art for art's sake and establish contact with the masses by means of total planning. (Quoted in Wendl, *op. cit.*, p. 115)

In the event, eighteen sculptures were executed along a 17-kilometre stretch of the motorway with the Olympic Village at its centre. The sculptures were initially well signed and illuminated at night and the critical reception was generally favourable but, for a long time, the subsequent fate of the sculptures was less fortunate.

Another dimension of contemporary modernity reflected in the Games was the design of the logo, deliberately psychedelic in inspiration, but also reflecting the Pacific Coast Huichol Indian designs that used stark black and white lines. The number '68' was generated from the geometry of the five Olympic rings with MEXICO set in the middle of a series of concentric swirls and the whole logo was claimed to be a fusion of Mexican indigenous culture with the Op Art movement then spreading over the globe (Brewster, 2005).[3]

The infrastructure of the 1968 Olympics was clearly intended to demonstrate to the world Mexico's advance as a modern nation. This message was also reinforced in other ways. The new buildings did not celebrate Mexico's rich pre-Columbian cultural heritage but rather 'reflect[ed] a technology of rapidly rising sophistication in an economy where labour was still cheap … they were designed by architects and engineers of international outlook – citizens of architecture's world state' (Gordon, 1983, p. 107), and the cultural festival accompanying the Olympics similarly played down indigenous cultural forms and sought to celebrate internationalism. The chief protagonists were emphatic in their desire to break away from the value laden stereotype of Mexico as 'the land of *mañana*' as Avery Brundage had remarked to the Mexican President Díaz Ordaz at an IOC meeting in 1966 (quoted in Zolov, 2004, p. 168). This intention was clear to two foreign artists involved in designing the Olympic logo, Peter Murdoch from Britain and Lance Wyman from the United States, whose only instruction was that 'the sleeping man with the sombrero did not properly represent Mexico' (*Ibid.*, p. 173).

After the excesses of Tokyo 1964, the Mexico City Olympics were perceived as comparatively low cost, but in the context of a developing country this is, of course, a relative concept. Overall, the total cost of building and organization was $175.8 million, of which $53.6 million (30 per cent) was spent on new or remodelled sports facilities, $16.5 million on municipal improvements, $16 million on the Olympic Village and $12.7 million on the Cultural Village. The remaining $77 million was spent on direct outlays by the Organizing Committee, the vast majority of which was spent in Mexico. Nevertheless, there were numerous other, Olympic-related expenditures which never entered the official calculations, not least the wages of the security forces massed outside the key locations. To offset this expenditure, $20 million revenue was received in ticket sales, television rights, and the profits from Olympic souvenirs. In total, the 'official' Mexican government subsidy was about $56.8 million (Gordon, 1983, p. 108). At the peak of the Games, some 14,000 people were employed directly, but the majority only on a temporary basis. Hardly surprisingly, 1968 was a good year for economic growth in Mexico – net tourism receipts increased by 15.5 per cent to $510 million and GNP increased by 7.1 per cent (Hofstadter, 1974).

For the first time, the sporting Olympics were accompanied by a Cultural Festival that went on throughout the Olympic year with the participation of ninety-seven countries (Arbena, 1996). International figures were invited, including Robert Graves, Arthur Miller, Eugene Ionesco, Martha Graham, Evgeny Evtushenko, John Cage, Dave Brubeck, Duke Ellington, and Alexander Calder (who designed the 80 foot high sculpture *El Sol Rojo* outside the re-opened Aztec stadium). Many of the cultural events took place in the Olympic Village and in the extensive Chapultepec Park on the western side of the city, although museums and auditoria all over the city were also used. Overall, there were 1,500 events throughout the Olympic year of which 550 were dispersed through the country (Zolov, 2004)

The Cultural Festival was conceived as an integral part of the whole Olympic experience and was organized by the Chairman of the Mexican Olympic Committee, the architect Pedro Ramírez Vázquez. It has been argued that the main driving force for this was to 're-energize Mexican domestic support for the Olympics following nearly three years of divisions and doubts' (*Ibid.*, p. 168). If this were the case, there was no obvious attempt to appeal to a broad spectrum of Mexican society. Although Mexican folk culture (especially dance) played some part in the Cultural Olympics, each participating nation was asked to bring 'jointly with their athletic delegations two works of art: one representative of any of its brilliant cultural stages of the past; the other the best of its contemporary art' (*Ibid.*, p. 175). In other words, the celebration was international and it seems difficult to imagine how inviting numerous foreigners to come and display their folk heritage could actually enthuse a population as large, diverse and geographically distinctive as that of Mexico. Indeed, an alternative explanation of the significance of the Cultural Festival has been offered, namely that it reflected Mexico's desire to be the 'champion' of the Third World and this explains '… the use of the cultural aspects of the Olympiad as a platform for Third World cultures' (Brewster and Brewster, 2009, p. 719).

Assessing the Games

While it is true to say that the efficiency of organization for Mexico City 1968 took many international observers by surprise it was not an opportunity for unqualified self-congratulation. Rodríguez Kuri (2003) argued that the background to the organization of the Cultural Olympics in particular demonstrated a 'matured modernity' within Mexico. Yet the preceding discussion has demonstrated that the primary engine driving forward the Mexican Olympic project of 1968 was the need to convince the world outside of its capabilities and, as part of that project, no opposition could be tolerated.

The official announcement that Mexico City had been awarded the 1968 Olympic Games was met with almost universal joy within Mexico. For example, as a Mexican student (quoted in Calvert, 1973, p. 316) argued in 1968:

the very fact that this country has been chosen as the theatre for the Olympic games signifies that it has reached a high degree of development and equipment. One can see other signs in the intensity of foreign investment and the level of productivity we have attained here

Within a short space of time, this optimistic view was challenged. The government had certainly hoped that the excitement of preparing for the Olympics would generate an atmosphere of popular support. Although sport was demonstrably being used as an instrument of unity, it has been claimed that Mexicans evidenced an ability to resist such cultural impositions (Brewster, 2005). In this context, the events immediately preceding the Olympics in the summer of 1968 are often cited. For example, Essex and Chalkley (1998, p. 192) observed:

the costs of the Games were such that many ordinary Mexicans questioned whether the money might not have been better spent on dealing with poverty and alleviating the city's severe social problems. This opposition resulted in violent protests which police and army units quelled with force.

However, this is to recycle a common misunderstanding about the student movement of 1968, which was about much more than the cost of the Olympics. Although many Mexicans did question the cost of the Games, most informed views now agree that this was not the primary basis of the civil unrest of 1968 (figures 12.1 and 12.2). Although the savage repression and massacre at the Tlatelolco rally

Figure 12.1. Security forces facing demonstration in Mexico City, October 1968.

Figure 12.2. Detainees being strip searched, Mexico City, 1968.

on 2 October was undoubtedly exacerbated by the fact that Mexico was about to
stage the Opening Ceremony (Preston and Dillon, 2004), the student movement
was intent on reminding the world that Mexico was a one-party state with a history
of corruption and police repression (Zolov, 1999). The Olympics provided the
opportunity for higher profile protest but it was not the object of the protest.

Any sympathy and good feeling that the Mexican government may have won
through its difficulties in the summer of 1968 was quickly eroded by its subsequent
behaviour. According to official figures, the death toll at Tlatelolco was forty-nine.
Foreign journalists estimated the figure at well over 200, later adjusted upwards to
260 deaths and over 1,200 injured (Toohey and Veal, 2007). An Italian journalist,
Oriana Fallaci, had attended the rally and was wounded. Instead of receiving help
from the state security guards, her watch was stolen from her wrist (Preston and
Dillon, 2004). Injured students were indiscriminately tortured in an attempt to
uncover the names of organizers and ringleaders of their movement (Witherspoon,
2003). The government quickly took steps to lay the blame firmly at the door of
the usual suspects – Communists and other foreign agitators – while sentencing
over 100 'ringleaders' to heavy terms in jail, some for 25 years. The Olympic
Games continued but the image of Mexico, so carefully prepared and massaged in
the years leading up to October 1968, was now something much darker than the
planned official representation. Whatever the roots of the student protest of 1968,

most of the benefits of hosting the Olympics – the modern image, the enhanced presence on the international stage and the attempt to create the sense of one nation – were eroded by the repression and the evident lack of political harmony, despite all the efforts to present such an image (Zolov, 2004).

Turning from the political repercussions of the events surrounding the Games, one of the main alleged benefits for hosting the Olympic Games is the prospect of an enhanced city image both nationally and especially internationally. Undoubtedly the level of awareness of the city is bound to rise when its name is repeatedly mentioned in the national and international media. However, increased awareness is not the same as enhanced image and in the case of Mexico City the latter proved to be problematic. The Games themselves went off remarkably well and the organization and staging were generally judged to be good. Yet the dominant and lasting images were of the 'Black Power' demonstration of the American sprinters Tommy Smith and John Carlos during the 200 metre medal ceremony, the police repression of Tlatelolco, and the fact that the Games were on the point of cancellation at least twice – once through the potential boycott of countries objecting to the invitation to participate sent to South Africa (Hill, 1996) and once through the security fears following the 12 October massacre.

The Games also served to highlight some of Mexico City's problems of urban infrastructure, especially those to do with transport. The concept of a decentralized Games with events widespread across the city proved to have many practical difficulties, especially as some aspects of the transport infrastructure had not been completed on time. Contemporary accounts also pointed to the cosmetic nature of some of the alleged urban improvements – 'many of the construction projects taking place within Mexico City were carried out with little or no consultation with the Mayor of Mexico City' (Brewster and Brewster, 2009, p. 795). The gaudiness of displays and liberal use of colour in street decoration could not wipe out the reality, for example on the walls of neighbouring slums, which were painted in shocking pink, purple and yellow, temporarily hiding the deprivation within (Salázar, 1968).

Although seen as an integral part of the modern image of the 1968 Olympics, the sculptures on the Route of Friendship were quickly usurped from their original purpose, adorned with graffiti and used to convey entirely different messages. While there has been some recent renovation (Reyes, 2009), several of them are damaged, stained concrete structures often partially hidden by roadside weeds and disregarded by motorists speeding by. Other elements of the Olympic iconography were also usurped and used as part of the protest campaign. For example, the symbolic white doves of peace used widely in the graphic arts programme in association with the official motto for the Olympics, ('*Todo es possible en la paz*' – Everything is possible in Peace), were ironically spattered with red paint after the October massacre.

Initially, the Olympic Village also had a different fate from that originally intended, which had been to sell the 904 four-room apartments in the private market. Two years after the Games, however, the Village was still half empty with no one on the waiting list (Schmitt, 1971). The city centre is 15 kilometres to the north, there are no shops or supermarkets and no significant places of employment adjacent to the site, so a car is essential. A major deterrent to early rapid sales was that the apartments were severely vandalized by the athletes themselves (*Ibid.*, p. 261). Subsequently, the two Olympic Villages have ended up as 'gated' dormitory commuter areas entirely dependent on private transport (Muñoz, 1997).

One final and possibly significant epitaph on the 1968 Olympics relates to the historiography of Mexico City. In the main English language monograph on Mexico City (Ward, 1990), the Olympic Games warrant only a brief mention (*Ibid.*, p. 217) and in its equivalent by two French authors published in 1979, none at all (Bataillon and Rivière d'Arc, 1979). In the context of the evolution of the modern urban structure of Mexico City, the Olympic Games of 1968 are little more than a footnote. Consequently it is difficult to argue a case for any underlying change in city structure emanating from the Olympics. A more sustained phenomenon is the annual student demonstration held each October in memory of the Tlatelolco massacre. Indeed, the fortieth anniversary of the Games was marked solely with a celebration of the graphic design component of the event but, somewhat ironically given the forward looking ideology that was so prominent in Mexico's winning and presentation of the Games, this exhibition was almost entirely retrospective, celebrating the 1960s (MacMasters, 2008). Nevertheless, in the broader context of the city, its relationship to Mexican governance and the perception of the nation on the global stage, the events of 1968 are of fundamental significance, albeit profoundly different from those originally intended.

Notes

1. Although Spanish is, of course, the official language of Mexico, there are at least ninety indigenous languages, mostly with a regional ethnic basis.

2. Ramírez Vázquez designed the National Museum of Anthropology and the Aztec Stadium in Mexico City and went on to design the administrative buildings of the IOC and the Olympic Museum in Lausanne, Switzerland. Mathias Goeritz had designed a group of high-rise concrete towers in Mexico City called the Torres de Satelite in the suburb of Ciudad Satelite, planned in direct relationship to a super-highway.

3. However, note the exchange between Eduardo Terrazas and Beatrice Trueblood and Daoud Sarhandi in *Eye*, 59, Spring 2006, on the provenance of the Olympic symbol. Available at http://www.eyemagazine.com/opinion.php?id=130&oid=455. Accessed 10 May 2010.

Chapter 13

Montreal 1976

Daniel Latouche

The Montreal Summer Olympics were to be a modest affair, remembered for the harmony they would bring back to the Games and for demonstrating that even a medium-sized city could stage a successful world event. These were to be the Olympics with a human face. In this chapter,[1] we take stock of the fact that three and a half decades later a different legacy has taken hold and the 1976 Olympics are best known for their extravagant cost overrun ($700 million on an inflated $1.2 billion price tag), for the boycott of twenty-six African nations, and for coming close to an abrupt cancellation.[2] Although Montrealers still retain a rather positive image of those three weeks in July, they remain convinced that in the short run the Games proved a catastrophe for the city's economy and its reputation, with very little to show except an over-sized and under-used stadium.

Is this vision of the 1976 Montreal Olympic legacy an unfair one, dictated only by the size of its abysmal deficit, a distortion which prevents us from realizing that the cat is already very flat indeed?[3] Can things be that bad? Is there no silver lining running through this sad script? How are we to judge an event which took place in a context which, although only 35 years ago, seems to resonate from another era? In 1976, the Olympics were still a young affair with the majority of Games having taken place before the Second World War. In Montreal, athletes from the first modern Olympiads were still alive and regularly interviewed. The dominant political perspective was that of 1945 with political divisions inherited from the Yalta Conference. Nuclear deterrence was a household concept and the Cold War a permanent political fixture. In 1976, the Internet did not exist, PCs were unknown, Urban Studies had not discovered consumption-based economic development and Cultural Studies were still years away from deconstructing the tourist gaze.

While the debate still goes on in specialized circles as to whether the Munich, Montreal or Moscow Games should be awarded the prize for the worst-ever Olympics, there is no doubt that the Montreal Games have their place in the triangle of Disappointment Games. Such failures, exaggerated or not, are there to remind us that the worst is always possible and that with each 'successful' Games, the chances increase of seeing the next ones falter, often on the most innocuous detail. There is, however, failure and failure. While it can be argued that both Munich and Moscow were the victims of political circumstances over which they had little control, the failure of Montreal was entirely self-induced.

Nor is the disappointment limited to the financial side of the operation. If one is to look at the 1976 Olympics as the birth of a new elite 'sport', the *Urban Triathlon*, the initial performance of a city which had just come out of a successful World Exhibition (Expo 67), a sort of Pre-Olympic Trial, was far from *éblouissante*. In all three disciplines of this new highly competitive sport, (1) City marketing and promotion, (2) Urban development and mega-event economics, and (3) Local planning and governance, Montreal did not do very well. How could things go that wrong?

City Marketing and Promotion

Marketing and promotion are important components of both a winning candidature and the successful completion of the Games themselves. The tools, techniques and objectives vary depending on the message the organizers want to put forward and successful marketing campaigns make certain not to mix the messages or confuse the audiences. During the bidding war, the sole objective is to convince a majority of IOC voters to support your bid. Contrary to the regular electoral process, this first audience is almost totally irrelevant for the second phase of the operation as the IOC Grand Electors play no significant role during the preparation phase. Nevertheless, what you say and what you do – and not do – to win the minds and hearts of the IOC will come back to haunt you during the preparation phase of the Games.

How Not to Win the Candidature Competition

Until 1976, the fight to hold the Games was principally a national affair pitching country against country, political system against political system. The choice of Tokyo 1964 or Mexico City 1968 can be understood only against a background of 'national' calculus having to do more with the need to move the Games outside of their European/North American confines, confirm the rehabilitation of former enemies or choose a country acceptable both to the West and the USSR rather than the technical and marketing quality of one bid versus the others (Augustin and Gillon, 2004).

The choice of Montreal marked a first in the sense that the IOC, following its own rules, chose a city and only secondarily a country or a continent, a tendency which persisted with the selection of Los Angeles, Barcelona, Atlanta and Sydney. This is not to say that national and geopolitical considerations no longer play any role in the competition to be selected as the 'national' champion or in the final selection process. In fact, in the cases of Beijing and later London, decisions appeared to have been determined by non-city related factors (Martins, 2004).

Even in Montreal, these 'outside' considerations were never too far from the surface, although they rapidly became instrumentalized by a single individual, Mayor Jean Drapeau. As told on previous occasions (and certainly embellished with each new version), the idea of having the Olympics Games in Montreal first came to Drapeau during an impromptu visit to Lausanne in 1963 (Auf der Maur, 1976). Following the last-minute withdrawal of Moscow from arranging a Class A International Exposition in 1967, Montreal gained the nomination from the Bureau International des Expositions in its place. Desperate for fresh ideas, Drapeau visited the team organizing the Swiss National Exhibition, Expo '64 (part of a series held every 25 years). For the practical reason that the headquarters of Expo '64 were located in the same building as the Olympic Museum, the Mayor was 'introduced' first-hand to the Olympic movement and told of the benefits that both Tokyo and Mexico expected to receive as host cities.

Jean Drapeau not only brought back a number of ideas for his exhibition – including its name, Expo 67 – but also the conviction that the Olympics represented the long-awaited solution to a more pressing problem, the need for Montreal to get a decent sports stadium. In 1961, the newly-elected Mayor had surprised everyone by applying for a franchise from the National League, one of the two professional baseball leagues then operating solely within the territory of the United States. For Drapeau, Montreal's future as a tourist destination and economic centre lay in obtaining a professional sports franchise in order to reassure Americans as to the normalcy of this Francophone and somewhat peripheral city. At the time, the answer of the Baseball Commissioner had been a well-publicized: 'First get yourself a stadium and then we will see'.

Two years later, in 1966, Montreal made a bid to the IOC, arguing that the city was simply the best place to stage the 1972 Games. By this time, it was in the final throes of organizing its very successful World's Fair and would soon inherit a large-scale stadium as a result of having obtained an American baseball franchise. In the event, Montreal did not get the 1972 Olympics, in part because it became clear that a reverse promise had been made to the baseball authorities who had been told that a baseball franchise could safely be awarded to Montreal since an Olympic-size stadium was just around the corner.[4] Apparently, the message was better received at the baseball end, as the Montreal Expos began their operation in April 1969.

With the Montreal baseball team operating in a temporary stadium, the pressures on the city to build the much-promised world-class stadium mounted. Following Mexico City 1968, it was decided that Montreal would try again to win the right to stage a Summer Games. Between 1966 and 1970, the Mayor travelled the world and met at least once with each national Olympic Committee to make sure that Montreal was the second-choice of all those whose support had been promised to either Los Angeles and Moscow. Needless to say, IOC delegates from countries whose vote was considered crucial were personally invited and given VIP treatment during Expo 67, with a promise to all those involved that since their Pavilion, although a temporary structure like all Expo exhibits, was among the most significant on the site, everything would be done to preserve it for future generations.

Nevertheless, the Mayor's major problem did not so much lie with the other candidates as with the negative campaigning staged by Vancouver, already hustling to get the 1978 Winter Olympics. Another major obstacle was the lukewarm support of the Canadian government and the Canadian Olympic Association (COA). At the time of the final IOC selection meeting, COA remained unreconciled to the fact that Drapeau had forgotten to consult them before going public with Montreal's campaign. They had always assumed that Toronto, which had no World's Fair and no baseball team to show for its efforts, and not Montreal was the 'natural' Canadian candidate. As for the federal government, it emphatically did not want to appear to support a Montreal initiative to the detriment of Vancouver or Toronto, where its electoral base was in urgent need of reinforcement if it was to be re-elected in the coming 1972 election. In order not to put the federal government on the spot and run the risk of an official rebuff, Mayor Drapeau agreed not to force Ottawa to declare a firm financial commitment.

Following allegations from Vancouver officials which resurfaced during the showdown meeting in Amsterdam as to the absence of any serious financial planning on the part of Montreal, each candidate city was asked to provide financial guarantees and make a detailed presentation.[5] While both Los Angeles and Moscow managed satisfactorily, Drapeau chose to turn the tables and insisted in his presentation that all such talk of money was demeaning to the Olympic ideals and that the entire financial issue was out-of-order and rather insulting in light of Montreal's reputation and since the city had every intention of presenting a 'modest' Games.

This mixture of bluff, shrewd calculus, self-promotion and hard sell would never again produce similar results,[6] but it gained Montreal the maximum return for a very limited investment. In 1972, no major company chose to associate itself with the Montreal bid, nor were they asked to do so; no doubt a wise decision considering the negative fallout from the Nike controversy at the Mexico Games. There was no significant engagement of the local community and no attempt by the Bidding Committee to sponsor events in order to raise awareness and monies for the project. In fact, there was simply no Committee in the first place. No army of volunteers and spokespersons was recruited and none was required as there was little opposition to the whole enterprise. The Olympic Mascot, Amik the Beaver, made only a brief and late appearance on one of the official posters. Instead the Mayor relied on an elaborate intelligence system which allowed him to know everything that could be known on each delegate so as to be able to fine-tune his argument, a task made somewhat easier since there was only one line.

On all issues which were raised as to the city's capacity to host such a large and intense international event, the candidature file and the Mayor had the same answer: Expo 67, the immensely successful World Exhibition organized by

Montreal on three artificial islands in the middle of the Saint-Lawrence River. To the question: 'Would people come to Montreal in the middle of summer?', the answer was inevitably 'They will. As a matter of fact many of the 50 million visitors of 1967 have been looking for an excuse to come back to Montreal'. 'What about security?' 'Montreal is the safest metropolis in North America. In 1967, even the Queen of England and Lyndon B. Johnson could visit the city'.[7] 'What about transportation?' 'Montreal already has the world's most efficient metro system, one which will be expanded. And a brand new airport will also be built'.

Promoting an Olympic City in a Worst Case Scenario

Present in Munich, Drapeau saw at first-hand the devastating effect of the terrorist attack on the unfolding of the 1972 Games. In subsequent working visits, Montreal officials were told of a 30 per cent drop in the number of tourists visiting or planning to visit the Bavarian capital. Having gone through what he considered the De Gaulle ordeal of 1967 – when the French President made use of the ceremonial balcony at City Hall to proclaim his support for Quebec sovereignty – and subsequently the FLQ crisis of 1970, the Mayor came back from Munich determined that nobody, especially not the Quebec sovereignty movement, was going to derail 'his' Games. Eventually, he would face the reverse problem as nobody wanted to be associated with such a colossal failure.

Although unforeseen at the time, Munich 1972 had a direct impact on both the planning and the promotional model used to prepare for the Montreal Games. Not inclined by nature to delegate or to share authority, Drapeau made clear from the beginning that all decisions concerning the Games were to be taken by his office. Until very late in the process, he effectively resisted all attempts to have the Official Organizing Committee run the operations. His suspicion was directed at all those who did not recognize his absolute leadership and did not agree to act as grateful foot soldiers in his Grand Project. This group included the Labour movement, suspected of working hard to destabilize his Administration, and even the Federal and Provincial governments, the latter being suspected of being both too nationalist and too soft in its dealings with community and progressive groups.

As the months passed, the increasingly paranoid Mayor made sure that no one even closely associated with the intellectual and cultural effervescence prevalent in the Quebec of the 1970s was even indirectly associated with the promotional and marketing efforts necessary to stage such an endeavour. Only one person was found to be acceptable, French architect Roger Taillibert, who was given a free hand to propose a concept for a new 'revolutionary' stadium. As doubts rose as to whether or not the facilities could be built in time, not to mention their cost, the promotion campaign turned into a 'public relations' one, whose sole purpose was 'damage control'. On occasion, the obsession with detail was pushed to extremes as when the Mayor insisted that all documents and materials made extensive use of the colour red, a colour associated with Canada, the Federal government and generally 'les Anglais', and as little as possible of blue, considered too French and too nationalist.

The transfer of the flame from Greece to the host city is usually the occasion of a symbolic appropriation of the Olympic ideal by the population and much thought usually goes in figuring out the itinerary as well as choosing the 'correct' runners. In 1976, for the first time the transmission of the Olympic flame from Greece to Montreal came by way of an electronic signal which landed not in Montreal but in Ottawa, the Federal capital. A Montreal official objected to this technological hijacking but, for the Federal government, it was imperative that the flame travelled electronically so as to show off Canadian telecommunication *savoir-faire* (Canada was then desperately trying to sell a communications satellite to Greece). For a moment, it was suggested that the 'flame' could land electronically at the tip of the Gaspé Peninsula and then travel along the banks of the Saint-Lawrence, following in the footsteps of the early French explorers. In the end, this itinerary was considered too risky politically as it was pointed out that a similar path had been followed in Mexico and only served to reanimate long subdued ethno-cultural tensions. Instead, it was decided that the flame would bypass Quebec as much as possible and arrive in Montreal from the west and not the east, a decision tantamount to bringing the Olympic flame to Cairo through the Libyan Desert, in order not to cross the Nile.

More was still to come on the saga of the flame. Located 200 kilometres west of Montreal, in the neighbouring Province of Ontario, the Federal capital is linked to Montreal by the Ottawa River (Rivière des Outaouais) which also separates the two Provinces. Thus the flame could have arrived at Montreal using the waterway or the Quebec side of the river. As later recalled, the reaction of Federal authorities at the idea of a Quebec-only itinerary bordered on hysteria, no doubt because of the vivid memory from 1967 when General De Gaulle travelled from village to village along the old Chemin du Roy and then reached Montreal just in time for his controversial 'Vive le Québec libre' speech.

Instead the flame would follow a 'safe' itinerary crossing only occasionally into Quebec and then coming back on the Ontario side, definitively entering Quebec at the last moment and then reaching the centre of Montreal (Montreal is an island) after going through rich Anglophone suburbs west of the island. It rained for most of the day and especially for the final leg of the Olympic Run through the city of Westmount, the symbol of past Anglo-Saxon domination in Quebec, and where the Olympic flame spent its first night on Quebec soil. At no time did the Olympic flame travel through central Montreal as the Mayor had made sure that the relay did not use Sherbrooke Street where, just days before, he had unilaterally ordered the demolition of the 'Urban Art' exhibition which he disliked so much. Even 35 years later, it is easy to imagine how the local press played such grand manoeuvres.

Three series of posters were produced for the 1976 Games, often after acrimonious and somewhat esoteric debates. For example, the main poster presented a schematic view of the Olympic stadium but ran immediately into controversy as it served to remind all participants of the unfinished status of the central infrastructure. The poster representing Montreal was certainly the least inspiring one. Unable to agree on a pictorial representation of the city and unwilling to use its best known trademarks, the small mountain in the middle of the city or the Saint-Lawrence River, designers came to rely on a sculptured head of a Greek athlete superimposed on part of the Montreal coat of arms. So much for civic identity and pride.

The end product of this constant political interference was a surreal promotional campaign with no central message except to emphasize that everything was indeed under control, an obsession with protocol and the requirement that Montreal be presented as a city with no conflict, no history, and no tensions of any kind. The results were nothing short of catastrophic with probably the most insipid Opening and Closing Ceremonies in the history of the Games, certainly a paradox in the land of Céline Dion and the Cirque du Soleil. One came out from the ceremonies with the image of a city drowning in political correctness and good intentions, a city made up of a multitude of ethnic, religious and linguistic groups coexisting peacefully because of their shared love for gymnastics and folk-dancing.

Tensions with the cultural community, already high from when the Mayor ordered city employees to tear down the 'Corridart' exhibition, evolved into full-scale artistic war around the orientation to be given to the Arts and Culture Programme. Again posters became the centre of attention as their design pitted Quebec and Canadian artists against one another, mainstream versus *avant-garde* clans, and stage against music performers. As the Quebec cultural community became more and more involved in the definition of the Arts Programme, artists from other Provinces insisted that their presence should be equal to that of Quebec. This created interminable discussion as to who would pay for what and for whom, with the Federal government agreeing to pay for English-Canadian artists and even, under certain conditions, for the controversial arts posters.[8] The requirement that artists from all ten Canadian Provinces, as well as from First nations, share equally in the Arts Festival only produced a cacophony of voices and performances, translating into a box-office nightmare and a full-blown cultural war.

Urban Development

Any assessment of Olympic-induced urban development includes the economic spill-over from the Games, especially in terms of tourism, the multiplication of sport and leisure facilities, the post-Games quality of urban design and architecture, the physical infrastructure left behind and the new housing facilities inherited by the city. On all five counts, the performance of the Montreal Olympics, although not as bad as could have been expected under the circumstances, provided numerous lessons for subsequent Games.

The Montreal Games and Urban Economics

The first formal cost-benefit analysis of any Olympiad was prepared for the Montreal Games (Iton, 1977). The fact that it has received so little attention is in part due to the enormity of the financial burden imposed by the Games, which made it impossible for even the most complacent cost-benefit analysis to hide. In addition, the study was but an afterthought to the Games and played no role during the bidding phase of the exercise. Yet the value of the study, *The Economic Impact of the 1976 Olympic Games*, goes beyond what it tells us about the Games. It also illustrates how imaginative economists can be in order to make a point. For example, rather than using the official Quebec input-output econometric model, researchers preferred the less disaggregated Canada-wide model in order to argue that all of Canada and not just Quebec benefited from the Games.

Equally imaginative was the attempt to provide the Games with a progressive image. In order to counter the frequently heard argument that public monies spent on the Olympics, including those coming out of the Olympic Lottery, could have served better purposes, the study makes a valiant attempt to assess the health consequences of the Olympics, going as far as calculating morbidity and premature death rates in and around the Olympic installations. Of course, they were unable to arrive at a precise figure for health savings, but nevertheless concluded that a sizable portion of $129 million annually lost because of premature deaths in this underprivileged part of town could be recuperated if only a fraction of Montrealers made use of their new sport facilities.

Compared with more recent documents, the Montreal cost-benefit analysis is a rather primitive affair with few equations and much approximation.[9] One advantage of producing an *ex post facto* cost-benefit analysis – in 1977 – rather than before the preparation phase is the possibility for its authors to confirm some unpleasant facts, such as the small impact of the Games on tourist flows. For example, the number of American tourists who visited Quebec in the months prior to the Games was actually lower than normally expected, as visitors simply postponed their visit to coincide with the Games. In the following months, the number of visitors also dropped, although this is probably as much due to the economic situation as to the negative image left by the Games.

The study also highlighted some unexpected findings, mostly regarding the economic impact of the Games; findings which would have been more difficult to obtain in any pre-Olympic study. For example, one could have expected that with a final price-tag of more than a billion dollars, spent almost entirely on construction costs, the Montreal economy would have received a lasting boost. Apparently, this was not the case and if there were a boost, it left little trace. For example, in order to prove that inflated labour demands were not the major reason for the ever-ballooning deficit, John Iton, the McGill economist in charge of the study, confirmed that during the year prior to the Games, unit labour costs did not rise more significantly in Montreal than in Toronto. This was for the simple reason that the $1.2 billion investment had very little spill-over in the local economy.

The 1976 Olympic Facilities and the Creation of a Sports Space

Although rarely mentioned, the Antwerp Games of 1920 were nevertheless important inasmuch as for the first time the local business elite, sports enthusiasts for the most part, promoted the candidacy of their city by insisting on the sport facilities which Antwerp would inherit.[10] Since then, cities have always put forward the legacy of Olympic installations as an argument for holding the Games, while juggling their act in order to find the correct mix between existing and new facilities, specialized or multifunctional ones, on a centralized or decentralized site.

Clearly, the functionality of the infrastructure for the events for which they were designed is one major element of any analysis. Their contribution to the city's sport and recreational offering provides a second. Third, the total and marginal costs of the enterprise must also be taken into account, as well as the financing schemes required to pay for them. A fourth set of criteria relates to the image of the city and involves, among other things, the architectural quality of the facilities. Finally, the overall contribution of the sport infrastructure to the urban development and planning process should also be considered.

How well did the Montreal infrastructure perform on these five counts? Having advertised a 'modest' Games, the Montreal bid to the IOC made clear its intention to use existing facilities for most competitions. The only explicit commitment was for a new 70,000 spectator stadium. The stadium was to become the centrepiece of what rapidly became known as the Olympic Park where new facilities for cycling and swimming were also constructed. All in all, 35 per cent of all finals were held within the Park. From a strictly functional perspective, the installations proved a success with all those involved: the athletes, the organizers, the IOC, the spectators and journalists. The proximity of the Olympic Village to the main installations – athletes could walk to their events – and the concentration of events within the Olympic Park was particularly appreciated. All installations directly related to the competition were finished in time and no serious glitches developed following the lack of 'break-in' time for most of the newly built installations.

There was some attempt to relax some of Coubertin's most sacred rules, like the necessity of holding the Finals of the equestrian Olympics in the Olympic Stadium. All other equestrian competitions were held 80 kilometres south of Montreal in what would eventually become a high-class resort community. The promoters of this residential development-in-the-making insisted on having all equestrian events in their town, but eventually failed since one of the Mayor's original arguments had been that temporary stables could be built to accommodate horses and training in a park just north of the Stadium. Nevertheless, the city of Bromont managed to stage the equestrian competition effectively and to this day continues to promote itself as the equestrian capital of Quebec and even Canada, a fact which contributed decisively to IBM's decision to establish one of its major Canadian installations there.

Eight Summer Games later, the debate as to the final costs of the Montreal Games still goes on, this time centring on the pertinence of spending an additional $500 million to tear down the Olympic Stadium in order to make room for an 'urban forest' more in tune with the objectives of sustainable development and healthy cities. As for two professional sport teams (football and baseball) scheduled to use the stadium, they adamantly refused to play in what is generally considered a gloomy and very permeable concrete cavern.[11] Potential users of the motocross racing or commercial fairs variety are still waiting for a permanent roof to replace the retractable one which did not survive even its first Montreal winter. Finally, no one has formulated a plausible use for the Stadium's Leaning Tower – the tallest such tower in the world – while the Velodrome has been transformed into a biological reserve. As for the swimming and diving installations, they aged so rapidly that when Montreal was awarded the 2005 International Water Competition, the city had to lease temporary swimming pools. Only one set of infrastructure passed the test of time, the Claude-Robillard Centre, built for the handball and water-polo competitions and which was used as the major training facility for track-and-field athletes. With all the elegance of a blockhouse, the Claude-Robillard Sport Complex is also home of the Montreal Impact, the much-adored Montreal soccer team. It would seem that in his obsession to make Montreal into a baseball town, Mayor Drapeau had been blind to the multicultural transformation of the city, today more in tune with the *ballon rond* than with its oval counterpart.[12]

Urban Design and Architecture after the 1976 Olympics

The architectural legacy of the Montreal Olympics is difficult to assess with even a minimal degree of 'objectivity'.[13] The fact that the Olympics followed two decades of highly positive architectural (Place-Ville-Marie, Place Bonaventure) and urbanistic achievements (Expo 67, the Metro, the Underground City) in Montreal complicates matters even further. Visually the 56,549 capacity stadium with its fluid and elliptical forms is truly a work of art. Those who see the stadium and the adjacent Velodrome and Swimming Hall as artistic contributions like to point out that in Montreal only one major functional building dared to escape the tyranny of the modular approach dominant since the Renaissance. For Luc Noppen, a well-known architectural critic, temporary difficulties in finding a proper use for such a monument should not obscure the fact that for once an architect had had the Kennedy-like vision to challenge the technological community to achieve what everyone said could not be done. Nonetheless, as Jean-Claude Marsan (1994), later Dean of the Architecture School at the University of Montreal, pointed out, it is difficult to make a lasting contribution and become a famous architect, if the technological innovations on which your future reputation rests fail ever to materialize.

Nothing much is known about the architectural vision of Jean Drapeau who in this case acted very much like the Prince in selecting *his* architect, *his* project, even *his* material (cement). He is known to have profoundly disliked the Buckminster Fuller designed dome built for Expo 67, while being enthusiastic about the French Pavilion which he worked hard to preserve first as a Civilization Museum and later as the site of the Montreal Casino. His only well-known architectural aspiration was to give Montreal a 'Tower-like' signature, much along the lines of the Eiffel Tower which he briefly envisaged asking the French to move to Montreal at the time of Expo 67. When defending the choice of a French architect, he never ceased to praise the non-American quality of this choice and repeatedly mentioned the need for Montreal to inscribe itself in a European monumental tradition where buildings mean something. In the eyes of the Mayor and of an architect more than ready to oblige, the stadium was not to be a simple object for mass consumption, a strictly functional construction like the ones in Mexico City and Munich. The Stadium was to be a statement, not of Québécois identity but the local incarnation of a cosmopolitan world culture where the superior values of the intellect and of human fraternity would prevail. As Drapeau frequently reminded perplexed visitors, Montreal's destiny was to be the Athens of North America, nothing less.

Urban Infrastructures

Montreal 1976 is often considered as standing in the middle between those Olympics where nothing much happened on the urban redevelopment level (Mexico City 1968, Moscow 1980, Los Angeles 1984) and those where redevelopment was a central element of a city-boostering strategy (Barcelona 1992, Sydney 2000). The reality, however, is a far cry for even such a moderate assessment. Except for the extension of a metro line to reach the Olympic Park located 4 miles (6.5 kilometres) from downtown, Montrealers would be hard-pressed to identify any urban infrastructure which could be considered an Olympic inheritance. In at least one case, however, the legacy is certainly there but few are willing to lay a claim to it. To elaborate, in 1969 the Federal government had decided to build a new International Airport, 50 kilometres north-west of Montreal. Having expropriated 80,000 acres (32,375 hectares) of highly productive agricultural land, although the airport only needed 14,000 acres (5,665 hectares) the government rapidly found itself in the middle of a Kafkaesque situation. The Provincial government, which had preferred a site to the south-east, adamantly refused to pay for the high-speed link as well as numerous highways which such a location called for. The successful Olympic bid put an end to all discussion and the airport was built according to the Federal government specifications. In 2002, Mirabel Airport was closed and all flights, domestic and international, were transferred back to Dorval Airport, now renamed Pierre Trudeau Airport, in 'honour' of the Canadian Prime Minister who single-handedly imposed the Mirabel choice. The cost of the entire operation has reached more than $600 million, not including the $300 million needed to rehabilitate the older airport.

Although not directly called for by the Olympics, the Federal government also used the occasion of the Olympics to push through an urban renewal project which meant tearing down 600 housing units in order to build a massive Television Tower in the eastern part of Montreal. One project that, fortunately, did not materialize was the completion of the east-west expressway which would have cut Montreal in two. The expressway was to provide a rapid link to the Olympic Stadium, but was deemed redundant once the metro extension was approved. Except for this indirect, although valuable contribution, the new metro line had little impact on attendance at the many large-scale events since held in the stadium or on future urban and housing development in the eastern part of town. With a 3,000 space underground parking lot, the comparative advantages of taking public transportation are at best minimal.

Housing

To study the evolution of Olympic Villages, according to Francesc Muñoz (1997, p. 28), is to study 'the history of ideas about how to develop the city, how to plan it and how to manage it'. If this is the case, what then can we learn by looking at the Montreal Village?

While the Olympic Villages of the 1960s can be considered as examples of Fordist functionalism and those of the 1990s as personification of the post-modern search for eclecticism, the two Villages of the 1970s (Munich and Montreal) are clearly post-1968 affairs with an emphasis on leisure, autonomy and integration of different functions within the same building. This is clearly the case with the two large-scale pyramids of Montreal where the first floors are entirely occupied by services, convenience stores, cafeterias, medical clinics and pools, serving 980 apartments capable of housing 11,000 athletes and trainers. Like the rest of the Olympic facilities, the construction of the Village went ahead under increasing difficulties, a complete lack of planning and control, much hesitation and consider-able costs overrun. Confronted with rising scepticism as to the estimated costs of the Games, the Organizing Committee (*Comité Organisateur des Jeux Olympiques* – COJO) first floated the proposal of a temporary Village (like Los Angeles 1932). When this idea was rejected, it was then proposed to build not one but five differ-ent Olympic Villages, located within a 3–10 kilometre radius from the Stadium. That idea, first proposed by a group of students and faculty from the Urban Planning Department of the University of Montreal, was uninspiringly defended by the Mayor before the IOC with the result that it was also rejected. For their part, the IOC made it clear that it wanted a full-blown permanent Village, close to the major sites and built, at least, to a specified minimum standard quality.

Within months of this second refusal, the Mayor and the COJO had a new proposal which was officially unveiled in June 1974, with construction beginning the following November. There was no architectural competition, nor even a discussion of possible options as Drapeau simply imposed his own idea, with the result that the Montreal Pyramids closely resemble – some even mention the possibility of plagiarism – those of the Baie des Anges in Southern France. At the press conference unveiling the plans for the Village, he proudly announced the name of the contractor for the project, but failed to mention that there had been no costs estimates and that the financing was still undecided. Unable to produce such estimates, the Mayor simply forced the project upon the COJO in October 1974, not even bothering to inform them that the contractor in charge of realizing the Village had already withdrawn from the project. The Village was officially completed in June 1976 three weeks before the opening of the Games and a bare eight days before the first contingent of 197 athletes was registered. The overall costs went from $22 million in February 1975, the first such estimate, to $43 million in mid-July, and to $80 million in August 1976.

The difficulties encountered throughout the planning and construction phases of the Montreal Olympic Village overshadowed all discussions as to what to do with the Village after the Olympics. The original idea of spreading out the Village in five neighbourhoods was in line with Montreal's long standing tradition of not conforming to the American or French policy of massive 'Public Projects' or 'Barres', but instead of spreading low-cost housing throughout the urban fabric. In order to placate rising criticism, the Mayor came out with the idea of turning the Pyramids into middle-income apartments for retired people. The suggestion proved impracticable as all internal corridors in the Pyramids are in fact located outside and open to the weather, not a genial situation considering the severity of Montreal's winters. Despite this, both buildings have since been fully privatized and are considered a choice location.

Urban Planning and Governance

Olympics are large-scale events which require specialized infrastructures, often spread out through the city and beyond, and the capacity to handle a large and temporary influx of visitors. These infrastructures have to be put somewhere, not an easy task considering that this locational choice may have little to do with the future use of the facilities. During the hectic two weeks of the Games, the activities of the city must go on and the need to accommodate visitors and participants must not interfere with the daily lives of citizens.

As can easily be deduced from the difficulties encountered, Montreal did not fare particularly well on either the planning or the governance side of the exercise. In fact, the Olympic saga contributed more than it benefited from an effective planning and governance system as it showed that a more transparent and rational urban regime was not a luxury for a city with such ambitions.

City Planning in Pre- and Post-Olympic Montreal

Much of the blame for the organizational and financial difficulties encountered by the Montreal Games has been put on the overall planning process (or lack of it), with enough blame available to cover all those involved and not just the Montreal COJO. For example, the COJO is often singled out for having waited until 1973 to present its first global *proforma* budget and for the fact that no cost constraints were ever put on Monsieur Taillibert who was never asked to submit anything more than sketches for the realization of his future masterwork.

Published in late 1980, the detailed report of the Quebec Government Commission of Inquiry on the costs of the Twenty-First Olympics apparently was of some use to the Los Angeles and subsequent COJOs (OCOGs) which have managed to forgo some of the most astonishing excesses of the Montreal managerial experience. Yet there is another aspect to the planning story of the Montreal Olympics, that of the urban and city planning *per se*. If Barcelona is to be considered as the best example of an Olympic city benefiting from a strong urban planning tradition, Montreal 1976 was city planning's worst nightmare. It is not so much that the city planning process was ill-adapted (as in the case of Moscow), too centrally-decided (as in Seoul) or purely elite-oriented (Atlanta), rather that it simply did not exist. In the truly entrepreneurial and 'visionary' style which was his own, Mayor Drapeau had always strongly rejected even the idea of city planning arguing that all his great 'accomplishments' – the Metro, the new downtown, Expo 67 – had been conducted outside any formal planning process. Under no circumstances, he argued, would Montreal limit its own development in order to follow technocratic and bureaucratic constraints.

No one at the IOC complained of the lack of a formal City Plan for Montreal, much less of the lack of a democratic input in this plan or in the entire Olympic process. Indeed, the absence of a City Plan and a City Planning Board came in handy when it was time to decide on the location of core infrastructure or the reassignment of city facilities and, in fact, the *Plan Général des Installations Olympiques* came to be presented by the Mayor as *the* Plan for the Montreal of the future. On a few occasions, when asked to detail his vision of the future of Montreal, the Mayor allowed himself to speculate on the idea of transforming Montreal into a permanent Olympic city by integrating the Olympic ideals, as defined by Pierre de Coubertin, into both the form and the fabric of the city. When a few heroic city councillors – no doubt avid golfers – objected to the elimination of the Municipal Golf Course and its transformation into an Olympic site (north of the Olympic Stadium) the Mayor simply replied that he did not play golf, that it was not an Olympic sport, and that it did not figure in the future plans of the city.

Clearly, the absence of a Comprehensive City Plan had a detrimental impact on the Olympic planning process itself and, by extension, on the entire Olympic operation. It meant that the COJO faced no constraint of any sort and that all city installations were there for the taking. As is often the case in similar situations, since the COJO could do anything, it ended up doing nothing and, in the end, doing anything to catch up for lost time.

Very rapidly, it became clear to many inside and outside the City Administration that this was indeed not the way to prepare for an Olympics and certainly not the way to run a city. Unfortunately, the Mayor, especially during the first few years after Montreal's successful bid (roughly from 1970 to 1974), could count on the blind support of both the Federal and Provincial governments since both levels of government had actively supported the Mayor during the pseudo-terrorist events of 1970. For Pierre Trudeau, the Liberal Prime Minister of Canada and Robert Bourassa, the Liberal Premier of Quebec, Mayor Drapeau, although somewhat difficult to manage, was a staunch ally who had shown strength in his campaign to eradicate the 'separatist' and 'leftist' threat. Since the first criticisms of the Mayor's way of doing things came from the Parti Québécois and associated left wing groups, they carried precious little weight, especially since the Mayor was particularly adept at dividing the two groups. He enjoyed pointing out to the French-speaking population that any criticism of the Olympics and of his stewardship was but an English plot against Quebec while reminding Anglophone citizens that to criticize the Games would contribute to a victory of the 'Séparatistes'. After the Munich incidents, the anti-terrorist argument of the Mayor became particularly convincing following the Parti Québécois traditional pro-Palestinian and leftist stand.

Very rapidly, too, the Olympic debacle reached Olympian proportions and in the 1974 municipal election, the local opposition party gained its first seats and began to harass the Mayor successfully on his almost dictatorial conduct of civic affairs. The absence of a Comprehensive Plan reached almost mythical proportion as the Opposition came to blame all problems, from the most structural – the pre-eminence of Toronto – to the most daily ones – potholes and snow removal – on the absence of a Comprehensive Urban Plan. Montreal, they argued, was apparently the only city in the World without one.[14]

An unexpected aspect of the fallout from the Montreal Olympic experience has been the almost obsessive attention given to citizen involvement in the bids of other Canadian cities for Olympic status. In fact, the preoccupation with community involvement in the planning and staging of Olympic Games originated with the 1988 Winter Games in Calgary whose success was attributed to the 95 per cent rate of satisfaction expressed by citizens, a level of support which translated itself in an unprecedented number of volunteers and the festive atmosphere which characterized the Games (Hiller, 1990). Probably the real impact of the Montreal experience came with Toronto's attempt to stage the 1996 Olympics and the almost perfect scores of that city on both the community involvement and democratic participation level. As celebrated by observers, Toronto's democratic performance was above any reproach and only the fact that other cities were not forced to show the same track record has been said to explain the failure of Toronto. If only this high level of undemocratic attitudes among its rivals could have been detected in time, Toronto it was argued, would have won over Atlanta.

According to Lenskyj (1992), even the decision to award the Games to Sydney was unfair since that country's performance on the aboriginal issue and the quality of the Sydney community involvement was far behind that of Toronto.[15]

Metropolitan Governance in Montreal: The Saga Goes On

All major hurdles in the Olympic drama have an important impact on local governance, that is, on the ways local governments and authorities operate.[16] The impact is compounded in the case of federations (Canada, Australia, Switzerland, and Germany) or quasi-federal systems (Spain) by the multiplicity and the intricacies of the constitutional architecture. The decision to present a city's candidacy and obtain the official support of the national Olympic Committee, selection by the IOC, organizing and holding the Games and, to a lesser extent, organizing the post-Games management of the infrastructure involve complex negotiations between local actors and central authorities, civil society, and interest groups.

As a rule, the ability to work together and to bring everyone aboard the Olympic coalition is an important ingredient in getting selected by both the national and international Olympic structures, probably more so in the latter case since the national selection process is more influenced by political considerations at the national and sub-national levels. In their comparative analysis of the mega-event strategy of three recent American Olympic Cities (Los Angeles, Atlanta and Salt Lake City), Greg Andranovitch and his colleagues provide us with insightful understanding of how the three local governance regimes help shape the candidacy of each respective city and of the management model used by each to organize the Olympics (Andranovich *et al.*, 2001). According to the authors, all three bids were the product of regime politics with the city's business elite in the driving seat but nevertheless seeking the endorsement of elected officials to provide public legitimacy. In all three cases, this business group was successful in incorporating the visions of city leaders and the specific agendas of local stakeholders who felt they had little choice but to go along in order to share in the benefits. Without the active backing of local officials, support from local groups would have been difficult to achieve and in both Salt Lake City and Atlanta this support made the difference when referenda were held. Although they were not entirely successful in imitating the purely private entrepreneurial model put forward by Los Angeles 1984 in running the Games, both Atlanta 1996 and Salt Lake City 2002 came close to it.

By looking at the Olympics through the prism of the urban regime which contributed in shaping its bid and organization, we can move past the usual clichés on the 'capitalist' nature of the Los Angeles Games or the public-private-partnership prevalent in Salt Lake City. The question then becomes: what kind of impact did the local governance regime have on the Games themselves and, indirectly, on the Games' contribution to local development? Clearly, the model used for Los Angeles pushed in the direction of ever-more spartan Games. Paradoxically, the fact that the Games did not benefit from any public funding also made it difficult for the local authorities to obtain satisfaction on certain elements deemed to be politically sensitive as when Mayor Tom Bradley insisted that the Los Angeles Organizing Committee set aside the objections of local residents and install a rowing basin in the San Fernando Valley. Such a decision, which the Mayor had sought to obtain long before the Olympics, would have allowed the city to apply for grants from existing federal programmes and help redevelop part of the area. Since neither the city nor the Federal government was willing to provide additional financial support, the Organizing Committee had little choice but to find a different site and the Mayor was forced to concede defeat.

Yet, what of the other way around: what impact did the Olympics have on these three urban regimes and, indirectly, on the way Los Angeles, Atlanta and Salt Lake City govern themselves? Los Angeles went smoothly and even turned a sizable profit, a majority of which was returned to the development of local youth sport programmes. Four new facilities were built, all privately financed and approximately $145 million went directly to local and state authorities. The construction of the airport was speeded up and the Games are said to have contributed $9.6 billion to the Southern California economy. By contrast, the political fallouts were less impressive. In the very short run, Mayor Bradley benefited from the successful and 'profitable' Games. Unfortunately he had very little to show for his involvement. It takes a substantial amount of 'pork' for 'pork barrel' politics to operate.

Against that background, we can note that, except for a brief interval (1957–1960), Jean Drapeau served as Montreal's Mayor from 1954 until 1986. Up to the end, his urban vision was exclusively made up of large-scale projects of which the Olympics were to be the final step before the 'mother of all projects', moving the United Nations to Montreal, had a chance to materialize. Throughout this period, the tireless Mayor was hard at work to realize his dream of 'One Island, One City' and thus replace the twenty-eight municipal administrations now coexisting on the Island into one powerful city government, capable of standing up to the Quebec government which has full responsibility for municipal administration. Fearful of his autocratic manners and strongly attached to their respective local identity, suburban Mayors always thwarted attempts at amalgamation and prevented Drapeau from realizing his dream. The best that he could achieve was the establishment of the Montreal Urban Community (MUC), where Montreal had a majority of seats (including on its Executive Council) and whose unelected President represented no challenge to Montreal. Responsibilities for territorial planning, the police, food inspection and evaluation were given to the new structure (borrowed from a singular concept in France). The MUC came on line in 1970 and, although clearly a set back for the Mayor, was used by him as a supporting argument to boost the candidacy of Montreal against those of Los Angeles and Moscow. As Mayor Drapeau carefully argued – not always with total respect for the facts – the MUC formula provided Montreal with the best of both worlds, a less decentralized governance structure than in Los Angeles and a less centralized one than in Moscow.

Apparently the argument worked as Montreal's candidacy suffered no local dissenting voice. Worried that Montreal could try to pass along to them some of the spiralling costs of staging the Olympics, suburban Mayors set up the Conference of Suburban Mayors in order to present a united front against the central city. In fact, the Olympic fiasco, by increasing animosity between local municipalities prevented the emergence of any intra-island grouping or even region to settle on the North or South Shore. In short, Montreal came out weaker not stronger from the Olympic exercise.

One important set of collateral damage concerned relationships between Francophone and Anglophone in Montreal and for that matter throughout Quebec. The 1976 Games were regarded as a strictly Montreal affair, a largely French-speaking city, and for many Anglophones the financial fiasco simply confirmed their image of Francophones and heralded what would happen if they were ever put in charge of a country of their own. The fact that the Parti Québécois gained power on 15 November 1976 was considered by many a by-product of the Olympic fiasco. More than 30 years later most of the issues which came to the surface at the time of the 1976 Olympics are still there to be solved, be they those of Anglo-Franco relationships, public housing or the best way to organize local governance of the island of Montreal.

Conclusion

If staging the Olympics were the equivalent of a Triathlon, it is doubtful if Montreal would have accumulated the required number of points in the city marketing, urban development and local governance competition to make it to the finals. In this sense the Montreal experience serves to remind us that some of the clichés regarding human behaviour often have a solid base in reality. It does indeed happen that if something can go wrong, it will and that some cities, like individuals, are known to reach their level of incompetence more rapidly than others.[17]

On a less philosophical level, one lesson from the Montreal Games stands above all others and that is the importance of the strategic campaign orchestrated by cities to win the bidding war. This was a battle of the 'winner takes all' variety and where the 'good guys' do not always win. Nevertheless, the way the war is conducted and the victory achieved often come back to haunt, with a vengeance in the case of Montreal, the organizers of the Games. The Montreal bid was a one-man affair conducted with the secrecy appropriate for a military operation. There were no campaigns to mobilize the local population, no army of spokespersons ready to testify, no business interests willing to lend their know-how in return for 'future considerations'. Montreal was, above all these commercial and often populist considerations, probably closer to the ideal of the Coubertin Olympics than any other set of Games, but when the going got a bit rougher, none of these allies from the first hour could be counted upon. Worse still, having worked hard to make sure that artists, intellectuals and associated progressive forces be arrested at the times of the FLQ crisis of 1970, Drapeau was left with very little support among the very people with whom his appeal for more humanist and universal Games could resonate. Apparently the lesson as to the importance of the Pre-Games manoeuvring has tended to be lost in recent years. For example, one could have imagined the open warfare between Mayor Delanoe and President Chirac if Paris had succeeded in overcoming the respective *faux-pas* of the two leaders and been awarded the Games over London and Madrid.

A second lesson concerns the very idea of an Olympic urban legacy and some of its unintended effects. As expected, there has always been some disagreement as to the 'real' (as opposed to 'imaginary') legacy of specific Olympics. For example, Atlanta is considered by many a good example of low-impact Games (in the same league as the Los Angeles one) with little impact on the city, while others insist that the city performed extremely well in terms of sports facilities and urban amenities (Essex and Chalkey, 1998), while still a third group concludes that the new facilities only serve to deepen the divide between rich and poor as they tended to stay away from the poorest areas of town (French and Disher, 1997). In Sydney and Athens, both Olympic Committees went all out in making sure the urban legacy of 'their' Olympics went unrivalled and that the public everywhere be informed about it. So successful was Sydney that the IOC itself recognized that this issue of legacy was a determining factor in the exponential growth in the number of countries, athletes, journalists and officials participating in the Games and in the willingness of National Committees to submit bids for future Games. However, as recognized by the Pound Committee (Pound, 2006), set up to study the exponential growth of Olympic budgeting, aspiring cities are in a bind inasmuch as competing cities are increasingly judged by the quality of the investments they are willing to make in sport and urban infrastructure, a criterion which not only pushes Olympics up the financial pole but also increases the risk of going overboard. To insist on environmental-friendly Games and even sustainable infrastructures will be unlikely to put an end to a spiral which began in Montreal.

One would have expected the difficulties around the Montreal Olympic Stadium to have prompted an intense debate as to what kind of stadium Olympic cities need. Until Sydney, the stadium question remained a non-issue as all contestants made sure to mention that their own proposal would avoid all the mistakes of Montreal. The Atlanta case is an interesting one inasmuch as it was decided that an entirely new facility was to be constructed while satisfying the requirements of its future use as a baseball stadium.[18] Sydney was awarded the 2000 Games in 1994 and it was decided that what urban planning had done for the success of the 1992 Games, high-quality 'ecological' architecture could do for Sydney. In the end, the success of the Sydney Games seems to have been more favourable to an open debate about the future of sport and Olympic Architecture than the experience of Montreal had proven.[19] Unfortunately that debate came too late for the Athens Games, which again went in for a 'monumental' Olympic Stadium of the 'grand statement' variety.

Finally, there is the uncomfortable question: 'so what?'. True, the Montreal Games were an urban catastrophe which few other cities have had to endure, but apparently, the city survived without too much difficulty. Mayor Drapeau has gone and so have the baseball team and Mirabel airport, but the city's cultural, economic, social and even political scene is thriving and, with four major universities, Montreal has become one of the leading academic and research centres in North America, while the downtown area would be unrecognizable to the 1976 visitors. Anglos and Francos still do not mix much, but are happy to have two cultural scenes to choose from. In fact, none of the positive things now associated with Montreal – its multicultural flavour, its four-month all-out festival period, a vibrant and cosmopolitan artistic scene – can in any way be associated with the 1976 Olympics.

Notes

1. This chapter is part of an on-going research project on 'Architecture and Politics in the New Glocal Age'. Financial support from the Social Sciences Research Council of Canada is gratefully acknowledged.

2. Not to mention that in 1976 Canada attained the dubious achievement of being the first host country not to win a gold medal at its own Games, a feat repeated at the Calgary 1988 Winter Olympics, but rectified in spectacular manner at Vancouver 2010. In passing, it should be stressed that, unlike other chapters of this book, the financial statistics are expressed in Canadian dollars.

3. In fact most of the 1900 'laws' found on the 'Murphy's Laws and Corollaries' site (http://rooso.epfl.ch/dm/murphy.html) can be said to apply to the Montreal Olympics – a telling fact in itself – including the less known 'Enough Already Law' which postulates that the more you run over a dead cat, the flatter it gets.

4. The competition included Madrid, Detroit, Montreal and Munich, which was selected in the first round. Later on the Mayor was to acknowledge one serious mistake in his first Olympic campaign, his last minute promise to provide free meals and lodging for all athletes, a promise which was judged 'so shocking' and contrary to the spirit of the Olympics.

5. Bad memories rarely die. In May 2006, much of the role of Vancouver in the years before the 1976 Olympics resurfaced in Montreal newspapers when it was revealed that Vancouver had asked both the Federal and Provincial government for a minimum additional grant of $90 million to stage the 'modest' and 'self-financing' Winter Games of 2010.

6. In the end, the Mayor's calculus proved correct. In the first round Moscow obtained twenty-eight votes, Los Angeles seventeen and Montreal twenty-five. In the second round, Montreal managed to attract all seventeen LA votes (Purcell and McKenna, 1980).

7. Luck and timing are also important ingredients in any successful bid. In May 1970, it was still possible to argue that Montreal was free from the political and social tensions which affected the rest of the world. Six months later, an improvised commando unit belonging to the so-called *Front de Libération du Quebec* kidnapped James Cross, a British diplomat stationed in Montreal, and murdered Pierre Laporte, Minister of Labour in the Quebec government.

8. The posters were finally produced by a group known as the 'Artists Athletes Coalition' set up precisely to counter the overwhelming Québécois overtone of the Arts Programme. As reported

by Bruce Kidd, a Canadian runner turned academic, the Canada Council director had only one condition: 'We love your proposal and we're prepared to give you twice as much money as you've asked for, as long as you agree to one condition – Canada and not Montreal has got to go on top' (Kidd, 1992a, p. 161.)

9.   See, for example, the early economic impact analysis prepared for another Canadian Olympics – the Vancouver Winter Olympic and Paralympic Games – by Intervistas (2002).

10.   See Renson and den Hollander (1997). The Antwerp games initiated numerous other traditions including arguments as to who should pay for the infrastructure upkeep and the overall deficit.

11.   In 2004, the baseball team, the Montreal Expos, folded and moved to Washington, DC, where they became the Washington Nationals.

12.   This rather austere complex is named after Claude Robillard, the first Director of City Planning of Montreal, who died in 1968 and was known to stand up to Mayor Drapeau.

13.   For a spirited defence of this 'unfinished cathedral', see Morin (1997). For a more technical attack on the Stadium, see COCO (1980). The rebuttal from the architect in charge of the project is to be found in his memoirs (Taillibert, 1977).

14.   A Development Plan was finally adopted in 1992, 4 years after the Municipal Opposition had finally replaced Mayor Drapeau and his Civic Party.

15.   If Mayor Drapeau were still alive, he would surely point out that good guys often finish second and that too much democracy does not always carry the day. Competition for mega-events has now become so intense and of the 'winner takes all' variety – a very un-Coubertin attitude – that cities that 'lose' are quick to suggest that they are also 'winners'. On 'failed' bids, inter alia see Kidd (1992b), Cochrane et al. (1996), Hiller (2000) and Alberts (2009).

16.   This section will not consider what was perhaps the most dramatic and direct governance impact of the 1976 Olympic Games, the election in November 1976, of the Parti Québécois.

17.   See note 3.

18.   Times are changing. In Atlanta the main controversy has not been the stadium which was entirely built with private support, but whether or not the baseball team should abandon its name of 'Atlanta Braves', a reference to American Indians, in favour of a more politically-correct one.

19.   Even the Sydney Stadium has come under some scrutiny, although in a subdued and polite manner – not particularly Australian qualities. See, among others, Searle (2002).

Chapter 14

Barcelona 1992

Francisco-Javier Monclús

The trick in Barcelona was quality first, quantity after…
Pasqual Maragall[1]

The profound urban transformation experienced by Barcelona over the last 20 years is linked, to a large extent, to the 1992 Olympic Games. The case of Barcelona has been the focus of international attention and has been specifically analysed from different perspectives by economists, geographers and town planners. On many occasions, its 'exemplary' nature has been referred to as the 'Barcelona model', which 'for urban transformation … has been a reference for other cities since the mid-'80s – the outstanding example of a certain way of improving cities' (Marshall, 2004, p. 1). It must be said that this has been a common theme in most of the existing literature, particularly that originating locally and prepared by the leading figures of the Olympic experience (Barcelona City Council, 1983, 1987*a*, 1987*b*, 1996, 1999*a*, 1999*b*). To these viewpoints are added those of international critics, who have interpreted this unique experience as one of the most successful in the history of the Olympic Games (e.g. Chalkley and Essex, 1999). The 'Barcelona model', a much discussed and indiscriminately used expression, has been characterized in several ways, depending on the period and the aspect which is considered to be most representative of town planning in Barcelona (Monclús, 2003). For some, it would be a way of acting in accordance with the proliferation of specific interventions in public areas, which were undertaken from the beginning of the 1980s. For others, the most outstanding element would be the rebirth of the city with the implementation of a series of strategic urban projects linked to the 1992 Olympic Games.

The reclassification of public spaces and the new urban architecture of Barcelona have attracted the attention of many international critics. Different authors have highlighted the formal dimension of these transformations and the high quality of the public spaces (Buchanan, 1984, 1992; Rowe, 1991, 1997; Sokoloff, 1999; Gehl and Gemzoe, 2001, 2004). From a more strategic perspective, linked to the rebirth of cities and to the significance of events in a growing context of deindustrialization and 'spectacularization' of urban politics, the ability to administer an extraordinary event such as the 1992 Olympic Games, of turning it into a 'lever' and a strategic instrument of urban renewal and recovery, has been highlighted (Borja, 1995; Marshall, 1996; Portas, 1998; Ward, 2002). In any case, the opinion appears to be widespread that the true success of the Barcelona Olympic Games was the transformation experienced by the city, through a series of actions that would normally have taken decades and which were introduced in just 6 years. In these perceptions, the enterprise of the political class, as well as the 'creative planning' of the experts and the spirit of citizen cooperation, is particularly noteworthy.

In this chapter, Barcelona's Olympic experience will be looked at from a perspective associated with the debate on the impact of major events. The first part refers to the background, origins and criteria that were the basis of the candidature from the 1970s; the second, the development of the Olympic programme and the associated urban actions during the 1980s; and the third, its subsequent impact in the urban sphere including the catalysing effects in other urban projects. The final section considers the benefits and limitations of the Olympic operation, as 18 years after the Games it is possible to have a historical perspective, although it is not easy to assess an urban strategy which still represents the foundations of present actions in the city.

From *Reconstruction* to Urban *Marketing*

An important question is that of continuity and change in urban strategies. According to some interpretations of the Olympic Games, the methods of 'progressive' intervention, of the first years of democratic recovery (in the first half of the 1980s), would have continued. Other more 'continuist' viewpoints regard the Olympic Games as a period in which many of the plans and projects designed in the 1960s and 1970s took shape. What is important to point out is that the profound modification of the urban structure of Barcelona associated with the Olympic Games is not just a result of the new proposals arising in the preparatory process of the Games.

The '92 programme' can be understood as a bid to re-launch the city in the context of economic and political crisis which Barcelona experienced from the mid-1970s until the mid-1980s; a context in which strategies adopted by other European cities, affected to a different degree by deindustrialization and economic globalization processes, were also placed. Some interpretations recognize two differentiated stages: prior to and following the Olympic nomination in 1986. In the first period (1979–1986), the 'progressive' nature of 'recovery' planning of a city with large urban deficits is stressed. In the second (1986–1992), 'strategic' urban planning would have been imposed with greater emphasis on determining factors of returns and less interest in urban improvement actions (Montaner, 1990; Montaner and Muxí, 2002).

Although to a certain degree these stages correspond to a change in the economic and urban cycle affecting many European cities, in the case of Barcelona – as in many other Spanish cities – the recovery of democracy must also be taken into consideration, particularly following the municipal elections in 1979. In any case, the debate on these stages and the different versions of the so-called 'Barcelona model' is not merely a formal debate, but expresses different interpretations of its profound nature. Compared with those who associate the experience with changes induced by globalization and covering a longer period of history, some see a greater continuity between the different historical stages. For example, the anthropologist Manuel Delgado (2005) suggests that 'the vision of Barcelona as a stage', as characterized particularly by the Olympic Games, began with the first Universal Exhibition of 1888. To some extent, it seems clear that the Olympic Games initiative can also be recognized as part of a long tradition in the pragmatic use of major events: the Universal Exhibition of 1888 (García-Espuche *et al.*, 1991); the International Exhibition of 1929; and, possibly, the failed Exhibition project for 1982.

Without going back too far in time, it is possible to find some continuity with previous projects. The attempt to hold an International Exhibition in 1982 is particularly noteworthy (presented in 1973). To a certain extent, this would be the case of the Greater Barcelona Project which was defined in the 'Barcelona 2000 Project' led by Josep Porcioles, the Mayor who determined the destiny of the city

Figure 14.1. Plan de la Ribera, 1964.

for more than 15 years during the Franco regime (from 1957 to 1973)[2] and who launched a strategy aimed at obtaining state investment for Barcelona (Barcelona City Council, 1971). The proposal had been approved in 1970 by the Council of Ministers and was developed during the following three years with the support of Juan Antonio Samaranch (then a lawyer but later the influential president of the IOC). The intense criticism of the Expo 82 project, 'Porcioles' favourite municipal project in the final stage of his mandate', condemned what was seen as its speculative nature, compared with the central argument and *leitmotiv* put forward by its defenders: 'that the Expo will be a driving force in the resolution of our urban development problems' (Alibés *et al.*, 1975). Although the proposal for this International Exhibition never came to fruition – among other reasons, because of its origins in the period of political conflict at the end of the Franco regime – 'it gave way to important urban transformation proposals and the design of important road networks' (*Ibid.*). Therefore, it is not unreasonable to relate this strategy to the different attempts to promote key projects through international events, even going back to the Greater Barcelona discourse, formulated at the beginning of the twentieth century (Monclús, 2000) and redrafted at the beginning of the 1970s (Moreno and Vazquez-Montalbán, 1991).

Without considering the profound differences of this 'pre-democratic' project for an Exhibition in 1982 with that of hosting the Olympics of 1992, it is important to stress that in the 1970s diverse hypotheses of urban transformation were formulated that would later be key parts of the 1992 programme. This not only affected infrastructural improvements that would contribute to the modernization of the road network but also more aesthetic urban projects, such as those aimed at 'opening the city to the sea'. Among the latter, the so-called 'Riverside Plan', devised in 1966 with the objective of revaluing the waterfront, stands out. It was frustrated due to powerful opposition from the citizens of Barcelona (although designed by Antonio Bonet Castellana, a prestigious modern architect with works in Barcelona and Argentina).[3] The fact that it was decided 20 years later to locate the Olympic Village in this area is at the heart of the debate presented here: to what extent was it that these plans rather than other, very different plans that became a reality in the democratic period during the 1980s (Moreno and Vazquez-Montalbán, 1991, p. 101)?

It must be remembered that Barcelona has experienced a profound crisis in its urban growth model since the 1970s. The failure of the Greater Barcelona idea is relative, although it is true that an agreement between different visions and interests was imposed. This agreement was translated into the new urban development plan for the city, the PGM (*Pla General Metropolità* – General Metropolitan Plan) of 1974–1976. The situation in Barcelona in the mid-1970s matched the explosive urban growth and 'modernization' experienced in Spain during the years of Franco's dictatorship and 'economic development policy'. The industrial city, which in 1930 had one million inhabitants, had become a metropolitan region of more than four million, in which extensive industrialization experienced a profound crisis.

Figure 14.2. Barna Harbour, 1965.

This was the period of 'Grey Barcelona' – the city of 'development policy', of 'informal' growth, of 'peripheral' developments, and shortfalls in urban facilities, all set against a background of growing speculation (Guárdia *et al.*, 1994).

With the return to municipal democracy, but in direct response to these circumstances, the City Council began to consider solutions to the problems created by the absence of strict urban development policies, with overcrowding and shortage of land for infrastructure and facilities in the city. It is important to point out that the profound political and social transformation following the death of Franco in 1975 coincided with an economic crisis that seriously affected the industrial foundations of Barcelona. The fact that many of the technicians who had been working in public institutions since the 1960s were assuming key positions was also influential. In short, the superimposition of the economic, political and urban development crisis enabled the PGM to be approved in 1976.

This plan was the framework on which actions for the recuperation of public spaces and facilities were defined over the following years. At this time, there was a conflict of interests centred on two aspects: reclaiming land for green areas and amenities; and proposals for changing road layouts. With the approval of the PGM, an important land reserve was obtained (critical for the 1992 Olympic operations) and more than 56 hectares, freed by former industries, were acquired. In fact the change in the PGM enabled areas dedicated to Olympic projects to increase fivefold and for parks and green areas to expand by 250 per cent. The development of the road system (ring roads) prompted new growth, although thoroughfares were also common. The PGM involved an important agreement between, on the one hand, the more 'pro-development' visions – with large-scale road layouts – and those of 'local movements', on the other, which were joined by the 'progressive technocrats'. From here, some consider there to be certain continuities between the urban development of the 'development policy' years and that initiated at the end of the 1980s. In any case, it seems evident that the democratic City Council continued with this policy of responding to the serious urban development shortfalls in a climate that continued to be characterized by widespread economic crisis (Esteban, 1999; Calavita and Ferrer, 2000).

During the 1980s, a series of economic, political and urban development processes coincided. The first, as noted, was that of economic crisis. The second was the democratization of the municipal government with the advent of a left wing majority in the elections of 1979, 1983, 1987 and 1991. The third was the adoption of new urban development strategies, backed by the PGM and new urban projects. In this context, a programme for the creation of public spaces and small local amenities was established. The availability of land occupied by former industries, railways or port installations enabled their re-use for new leisure facilities, parks or amenities. It is not difficult to find similarities between the ideas that dominated Barcelona's most distinctive schemes in the 1980s and those of other cities, particularly Paris's 'Grand Projects' and those linked to the IBA in Berlin (Rowe, 1997; Sokoloff, 1999; Monclús, 2003).

The so-called 'culture of the urban project' was highlighted in the City Council's first publications, albeit being presented empirically. However, it is in the well-known book by Oriol Bohigas,[4] Director of Planning between 1980 and 1984, significantly titled *Reconstruction of Barcelona*, in which the principles of a new architectural and contextualized form of urban planning are put forward (Bohigas, 1985). In this book, the efficacy of small-scale projects of urban reform as an alternative to the abstraction of conventional planning was vindicated. The message was simple but strong: to overcome the limitations of planning, one has to give way to architecture. At the same time, the public spaces of the historic city, the squares and streets are recovered. It is not necessary to think in literal terms about the adoption of the principles of the 'reconstruction of the European city'. However, a number of convergent elements are clear. Above all, understanding the city to be essentially architecture is required, as well as an extraordinary emphasis on its morphology. This conception also struck a chord with the visions of the fragmentary construction of the city or 'collage city' put forward by Colin Rowe (Rowe and Koetter, 1978), or with the ideas that dominated the transformation of other cities during the 1980s. Bohigas himself cited Berlin as the clearest reference: a city in which 'a reconstruction of the centre starting from the absolute respect for the road and the traditional form of the street' (Bohigas, 1985, p.118). It was a strategy based on the relative effectiveness of the specific project compared to the abstraction of the traditional general plan.

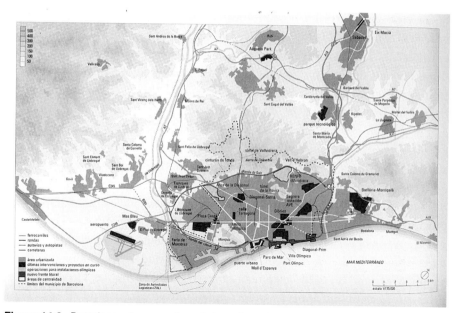

Figure 14.3. Barcelona urban growth and strategic projects (1980–1992).

Based on these principles, development in Barcelona focused on a series of schemes that sought to recover public spaces. These schemes, developed within areas in continuity with the existing neighbourhoods, involved more than 150 projects in parks, squares and amenities during the 1980s. However, it comes as no surprise that a 'reconstruction' model was promoted in these years of scarce resources, with modest interventions of a public nature with regard to open spaces and amenities (Barcelona City Council, 1983).

This entire experience led the School of Urban Design at Harvard University to award Barcelona the 1991 Prince of Wales Prize for architecture in recognition of the modernity and rationality which had guided the planning of the new spaces created during the first years of municipal democracy. Prior to this, in 1987, the city had achieved the Harvard Prize for its good design. In 1999, the Royal Institute of British Architects' Gold Medal for Architecture was given to the politicians and professional architects of the City Council, for their 'commitment to planning', including 'the combination of spectacular urban projects and of small-scale improvements to squares and streets'. In addition, the widely publicized report *Towards an Urban Renaissance* (DETR, 1999; see Hebbert, 2000), prepared by a group of experts and co-ordinated by Richard Rogers at the request of the then newly-elected Labour government, contained significant references to the case of Barcelona (see also chapter 9). In the report, attention is focused on two types of planning intervention: the capacity to regenerate or treat central spaces through small operations of urban reform; and the 'strategic' projects that characterize later intervention. Of particular significance is the fact that Pasqual Maragall, the former Mayor of Barcelona (between 1982 and 1997), was asked to provide the Foreword to that publication (Maragall, 1999a). The message was clear: 'It is critical to understand that improving public spaces is relevant to solving social and economic problems'. However, Maragall stressed the leap to a more ambitious strategy in the mid-1980s, when the initial small-scale operations were followed by large-scale strategic urban planning projects: 'The trick in Barcelona was quality first, quantity after' (see the epigram at the start of this chapter).

From Quality to Quantity

In this context of economic crisis and 'strategic urban development', the candidature of Barcelona to host the Olympic Games was launched in 1981. The shift 'from quality to quantity' evolved at that time, with the Games as a pretext. It was a strategy to attract public and private investment (therefore, not so different to the Expo 82, although now in a democratic version), but also an instrument capable of generating consensus and action in a depressed economy. All this in a few years in which the transition to a service-based, rather than an industrial-based, economy was assumed to be inevitable.

In 1981, the Mayor of Barcelona, Narcís Serra, and the Deputy Mayors (Josep Miquel Abad, Josep Maria Cullell and Pasqual Maragall), began to carry out a study of the possibility of holding the Olympic Games in the city. From the debate which took place on 30 June 1981 among the representatives of these parties, the first agreement was adopted unanimously by the new democratic council: namely, to present the Barcelona Olympic Candidature again.[5] Work began on the ideas and dossiers for the first Candidature and by 1982, the 'Cuyas Report' or the Preliminary Project had already been drafted. Over the following four years, the '92 Programme' was drawn up.

The choice of Barcelona in October 1986 emerged against intense competition. Eight years earlier, Los Angeles had been the sole candidate. For the 1988 Games, Seoul only had to compete with Nagoya. By contrast, there were six candidates for the 1992 Games, among them cities of importance such as Paris, Amsterdam and Brisbane. The Olympic nomination marked the difference between Barcelona and other Spanish and European cities, which were then also experiencing a change in their urban dynamics as a result of widespread economic recovery. However, when Barcelona obtained the nomination, the economic circumstances had already changed, with full integration in the European Economic Community (which reached completion in 1993) and a climate favourable for the rebirth of the city. The Olympic euphoria was soon unleashed with an exhibition of projects under way.[6] By 1986, it was not difficult to realize that the urban development strategies that characterized the early 1980s were giving way to others with similar, but more ambitious, criteria. As Bohigas (1999) later explained 'the new urban development programme corresponded to simple and rapidly applied premises'. Deep down, they were the same conditions that had been applied in the specific actions at the beginning of the 1980s. With reference to the planning of the four Olympic areas, three fundamental criteria were used. First of all:

locate the four main Olympic areas within the municipality of Barcelona, in strategic points – the edges of the consolidated city and the first periphery – which will directly affect the problematic areas and at the same time accelerate the surrounding osmotic regeneration processes. Secondly, apply the same methods in this area as those which had been used in the specific actions of the neighbourhoods; in other words, the formula for urban projects. Thirdly, ensure that all the buildings and public spaces constructed have a clear use following the Games and represent fundamental pieces in the transformation of the city. (*Ibid.*)

The four Olympic areas were therefore designed and presented, with qualitative criteria similar to those of the previous small projects, but incorporating objectives corresponding to the new scale of the Olympic urban development interventions. One such objective was to contribute to continuous urban promotion and the creation of new centralities through these four areas.

In reality, two key areas were considered for the sporting facilities (with a third of less importance) and a strategic location for the Olympic Village. The main venue was planned in the Montjuïc Mountain. In 1929, a park with cultural and sporting facilities had been planned here. The second Olympic area was that of 'Valle de Hebrón', which was planned in a semi-developed area of the first periphery, surrounded by diverse amenities, a strategy in which the wish for urban regeneration was clearly shown.[7] In addition to these two venues, and in contrast

Figure 14.4. Olympic Ring (M. Guárdia, 2002).

to the aforementioned, another was reorganized around the most prestigious route of the city – the 'Diagonal' – with the objective of taking advantage of the existing installations. Finally, the Olympic Village was located on the waterfront, with the objective of its regeneration and of 'opening of the city to the sea'.

The Preliminary Project listed the venues for the competitions and described the Barcelona Olympic Games. In the first phase, the general criteria had to be developed and the process of transformation of the city to host the event specified. The Candidature Preliminary Project took six months to draft, and during that time a team of specialists outlined the matters that would have to be dealt with: the sporting and technological requirements, town planning, residences and financing. Experiences from previous Olympics and contacts with the organizers of Los Angeles 1984 were a primary source of information and comparison. The conclusions of the Preliminary Project followed the line traced in *Primeres Aproximacions.* It was stressed that the figures for the budget were merely indicative, corresponding to detailed estimates based on data from previous Games. They were therefore a useful reference point for the administration when it came to estimating the finance for the infrastructure required to organize the Games. There was also an analysis of the cost to the city in comparison with that of previous host cities and the conclusion reached was that it was within its means. The Preliminary Project defined fundamental questions for the later development of the Candidature and the organization of Barcelona 1992: the demarcation of the four Olympic areas (Montjuïc, Diagonal, Vall d'Hebron and Parc de Mar); the participation of other cities as venues for sports competitions; the establishment of a mixed model of financing, which included contributions from public administrations and the support of private enterprise; and the programming of a cultural Olympiad lasting four years (COOB, 1992, p. 237).

The 'areas' were an attempt to concentrate a series of activities at sites which, in the tradition of Olympic parks, would provide suitable conditions for holding the great festival of the Games. At the same time, the intention was to avoid packing all the sports facilities into a single place, which would have meant that they were useful for the sixteen days of the Olympic competition, but would have been of little social value afterwards. Another consideration was ease of access to all the venues, which were located at reasonable distances to avoid transport problems and other inconveniences for the Olympic Family and spectators. The competitions in nineteen of the twenty-four planned sports would be held in the four chosen areas. The areas were all near junctions with main city thoroughfares and easily accessible by public transport. All four were in a circle with a radius of five kilometres and travelling time between them would not exceed twenty minutes, either by public or private transport. The Dossier stated that of the thirty-seven competition venues required for the Games, twenty-seven had already been built (of which five would need to be converted and seven adapted for the occasion), five were under construction and five more at the planning stage (*Ibid.*, p. 271).

The most ambitious and innovative urban project associated with the Olympic

Figure 14.5. Olympic Village and Parc de Mar area (M. Guárdia *et al.*, 2004).

Games was the regeneration of the 'seafront' or 'maritime façade' which, under the slogan of 'opening the city to the sea', was the prime sector for attracting investment (with housing for the Olympic Village through VOSA [Vila Olímpica Societat Anonimà] as part of the Olympic Holding). The aim of the town planning initiatives in this area was to provoke a radical reshaping of the city's entire seafront; not just the Olympic Village sector but also six kilometres of coastline immediately to the north. It is important to point out that the decision to locate the Olympic Village on abandoned industrial land was part of a much wider operation, namely, the regeneration of the whole coastline or 'seafront' of Barcelona in line with other international experiences of *waterfronts*. In this way, continuity with previous initiatives can be better understood. In 1987, the redevelopment of the Bosch and Alsina wharf – popularly known as the Moll de la Fusta – and its connection to the area of the old city was the first step in the renovation of the central area of Barcelona's seafront and the beginning of an extensive redevelopment of the old port with the object of turning it into a recreational and sporting area. This process of renewing the city's seafront was complemented by improvements to the district of Barceloneta and the conversion of the old industrial and warehousing zone of Poblenou into a residential area.

Within the strategic plan for the location of the Olympic installations proposed in the Barcelona Candidature, two options were considered for the Olympic Village.

In keeping with the aim of building all the facilities on the periphery, somewhere in the suburbs, Vallès would have been the safest and the cheapest bet. In the end, however, it was the opportunity for the city to benefit from the Olympic Village that effectively determined the decision. As McKay (2000, p. 5) noted:

> The site chosen was a practically abandoned industrial triangle, between the curve in the railway line bordering the Parc de la Ciutadella and the diagonal of the Bogatell storm water channel, which meant that the city could finally be opened to the sea. The reward was that, after the Games, Barcelona would have 4.5 kilometres of beaches with an urban front open to the Mediterranean.

The Parc de Mar, the proposed location for the Olympic Village, was undergoing a process of deindustrialization; the beaches were in an extremely degraded state and railway lines separated the district from the sea. The redevelopment of the area changed all this. An alteration in the route of the railway was already envisaged in a project to reorganize the Barcelona railway system, with two new stations planned on the outskirts of the city. The design for the residential area was to follow the pattern of streets in the Eixample, something which would also allow the Diagonal to be extended as far as the sea and would integrate the new area of the Olympic Village into the fabric of the city. Finally, the development of the Poblenou seafront and the construction of the coastal ring road entailed the redesign of the main drainage system. A plan was drawn up in 1988 which covered the municipality of Barcelona and its entire hydrographic area and provided for a 100 kilometre extension of the sewer network.

The Parc de Mar was the district of Barcelona that underwent the greatest change as a result of hosting the Games. The Olympic nomination made it possible to recover more than 100 hectares of industrial land for residential use and public facilities through a large-scale redevelopment project. The Parc de Mar area contained the Olympic Village, with 2,400 housing units for more than 15,000 people, both athletes and officials, and the Parc de Mar Village, for referees and judges. Competitions for four of the sports in the Barcelona 1992 programme were held there: yachting (based in the Olympic harbour), badminton (in the Pavelló de la Mar Bella), table tennis (in the Polisportiu Estació del Nord, two kilometres from the Olympic Village, in the Eixample district) and some events of the Basque pelota competition (in the Frontó Colom, in the lower part of the Rambla). The Olympic Village, as noted, was built in an area which shortly before had been occupied by declining industries, separated from the rest of the city and from the sea by two railway lines. This, in turn, restricted access to beaches affected by pollution, caused by an industrial sewer outflow as well as a less polluted ground water drain. The Special Town Plan,[8] approved in June 1986, provided the instrument that made it possible to turn the Olympic Village into a new district, integrated into an urban fabric graced with public spaces and endowed with sports facilities.

The complex operation of transforming the whole of this large area of the city and integrating it into the urban structure implied the execution of a large number of projects, which can be summarized as follows:

◆ Regeneration of the coastline and the restructuring of the sewage network.

◆ Restructuring the railway network, with the elimination of the two lines that crossed the area.

◆ Construction of the semi-covered stretch of the Ronda del Litoral which passes through the area, so that parks could be laid out over it and the streets of the Eixample district could be extended to the sea.

◆ Widening the Passeig Marítim to 30 metres.

◆ Building a new marina, the Olympic Harbour.

◆ Construction of hotel, commercial and leisure facilities between the Ronda del Litoral and the Passeig Marítim.

◆ Continuation of the morphology of the Eixample district, with the creation of 'super-blocks'. These super-blocks include commercial spaces, a sports hall and cultural, religious and health care centres.

◆ Provision of a network of green spaces throughout the area, with the Parc de Mar Area covering 130 hectares, of which 45 hectares are occupied by the Olympic Village.

The town planning operation made it possible to recover 5.2 kilometres of the coastline for the use of the people of Barcelona and of all the inhabitants of the metropolitan area.[9]

The Olympic Village represented the flagship of the new urban development in Barcelona and the culmination of the previous discourse on the reconstruction of the city. In its architectural and urban development configuration, the influence of some historical models of modern urban development can be observed (especially that of south Amsterdam). The 'reconstruction' discourse turned out to be particularly appropriate for an updated version of the traditional morphologies of the Ensanche (Solá-Morales, 1992).

The jump in scale involved in the strategic or major urban projects linked to the Olympics was in keeping with the extension of the new strategies based on the so-called 'new areas of centrality', although the principles of the 'new strategic planning' were as simple as in the first phase of 'pragmatic planning and public spaces'. These projects were now developed and formalized as part of the new category of 'strategic urban projects' (Barcelona City Council, 1987b; Busquets, 1992) and included the so-called 'areas of new centrality', the interventions in the city road system and other projects centred on major infrastructure, highlighting the implementation of the ring roads and road accesses.[10] The four Olympic areas were promoted by the public sector. The rest relied on private initiative, were

Figure 14.6. Forum of Cultures 2004 (Barcelona City Council).

under the management of the public sector, or were funded according to mixed formulae, determined by the rate of private investment.

Catalyst for Strategic Urban Projects

Analysing the nature of the urban development strategy at the time of the Olympic nomination one needs to consider international progress in 'city entrepreneurialism', which was being developed in association with the proliferation of strategic urban projects in the United States and later in diverse European cities. This urban planning transformation which Peter Hall identified in the 1970s also occurred in Barcelona, although some years later. As Hall (1988, p. 355) observed:

> Planning turned from regulating urban growth to encouraging it by any and every possible means. Cities, the new message rang loud and clear, were machines for wealth creation; the first and chief aim of planning must be to oil the machinery.

In the first volume of the Official Report, published just prior to the start of the Games, Josep Miquel Abad made the significant point that the sixteen days of competition would merely be:

> the climax of a process which has taken years and that many of our objectives – the reactivation of the city and the country, the town planning works, the boost to the economy – will have already been more than accomplished before the magic date. (COOB, 1992, p. 1)

However, as was seen later, the development of the Olympic Games took place at a time when clear priority was given to the economic promotion strategy. In this way, the main sources of urban policy in Barcelona centred on the attempt to become a more competitive and dynamic city, using the Olympic Games as the agent for the strategic projects.

The level of continuity between the Olympic initiative and the projects developed at the beginning of the 1970s is questionable. However, it is not difficult to see how new more strategic approaches were imposed compared with the visions of conventional urban development, based on zoning and control of urban growth. Although the Expo 82 initiative could now be registered in these visions, it was in the mid-1980s when Barcelona definitively absorbed the message of 'leverage' – the reorientation of urban policy towards 'entrepreneurial urban development' based on the use of public capital to stimulate private capital investment.

After the 1980s, the leaders of Barcelona understood the need to adapt the city to the pressures and opportunities arising from economic globalization, a process from which the city could not opt out. From here came the implementation of strategic plans designed as part of a new urban impulse for the economic re-launch of the city. The experience of the North American strategic plans, particularly San Francisco in 1984, contributed to the preparation of the 'Barcelona 2000 Economic and Social Plan', a document produced from the consensus between the different urban agents (including institutions, companies and trade unions). This took place in 1987, when 'strategic' decisions were under way for the important urban projects associated with 1992 (Barcelona City Council, 1999a). The strategic plans approved in the 1990s were less characterized as 'antidotes' against a situation of crisis and urban stagnation, than tools to ensure urban growth beyond the Olympic event (Santacana, 2000). Barcelona was less original with regard to the aims and objectives of the Games: place promotion and urban regeneration. The Barcelona 2000 Plan identified three goals: improving communications; improving the quality of life with reference to the environment, training, research, social opportunities for housing and cultural infrastructure; and supporting industry and advanced services to business with particular reference to telecommunications and technological innovation. It was a long-term strategy for modernization, aimed at regenerating the city's economy and more generally its central urban fabric. In relation to the city's strategic modernization process, there was continuity in the developments connected with the Olympics (Roche, 2000, p. 144).

With the Olympic programme already developed, the picture presented in the post Olympic situation raised the need to agree on a new set of actions which would enable the continuation and extension of the initial strategy of 'extracting investment from the central government'. The promotional objectives were becoming increasingly more explicit, *city marketing*. It was no longer just a case of guaranteeing state public funds (as with the Expo 82 or in the first versions of the Olympic programme, when this was justified to finance the infrastructural work that the city had pending since the 1960s). Rather, it was a case of using them appropriately, together with advanced business management formulae, with a view to increasing the city's prestige and image at an international level and hence attracting private investment for the 'new Barcelona' (Borja and Castells, 1997; McNeill, 1999).

Analysing the effect of the Olympic Games, the fact that the majority of operations had been considered an adaptation of previous projects to the specific needs of the event has already been mentioned. Therefore, the improvement of the road network was connected to the need to link the different Olympic areas appropriately, but it served as a driving force to a project which had been planned much earlier. The construction of the new ring roads (planned since the beginning of the twentieth century) produced a decisive impact on urban structure. Similarly, the burying and remodelling of railway lines and the modernization of the sanitation network can be considered as important infrastructure projects arising from investment associated with the Olympics. Likewise, new sports facilities and large-scale telecommunications works were the main actions carried out courtesy of the Games.

In this respect, a key aspect which is not easily quantifiable is the relative importance of projects which were not directly linked to the Olympic areas. Indeed, the most important investments were generated in parallel and outside these areas, with investments strictly related to the event representing a mere 15 per cent of the total cost of 'approved' investment (Clusa, 1999, p. 93). This is probably the most relevant aspect of the Barcelona experience and helps to explain the scope of other schemes linked, to a greater or lesser degree, to new infrastructure, such as ring roads and the remodelling of the railways. It is not easy to measure the economic impact of the Games, as their planning and preparation coincided with Spain joining the European Community (1986). However, between 1986 and 1991 employment rose by 20 per cent in the municipality, 45 per cent in metropolitan Barcelona, and 30 per cent in the rest of the metropolitan region. The economic impact was most notable: between 1986 and 1992 'Barcelona would go from depression to economic boom'. Finally, the impact of other operations linked even less directly to the Olympic project has to be taken into consideration, including the remodelling of the port, the airport, the 'Diagonal Mar', the high-speed train and the Sagrera area (Barcelona Regional, 1999). In this process, public and private investment associated with the Olympic Games was a determining factor – almost $10 billion – which contrasts with the costs of $1.3 billion strictly associated with the event (Brunet, 1995).

No less decisive were other repercussions in the sense of new ways of running the city, which became increasingly business-like and less controlled by the traditional city council departments. New methods of intervention and management of urban planning were introduced, as with the creation of Olympic Holding (1987–1993, managed by Josep Acebillo, transformed in 1994 into the Agencia Metropolitana Barcelona Regional, SA). This was a 'joint venture' between the local administration and central government that would not have been possible without exceptional circumstances such as those arising from the Olympic Games. It is well known that cooperation between institutions is usually more difficult than between companies.[11]

Perhaps above all else, it seems evident that the most important effects were related to the so-called 'map effect'– the repeatedly expressed wish 'to stamp Barcelona's image on the map'. It is not an exaggeration to suggest a direct relationship between the Olympic Games and the notable increase in tourism: from 4.1 million tourists in 1991 to 6.3 million in 1995. The adoption of 'cultural urban development' strategies, with the construction of museums and cultural facilities, must also be noted in this respect. In fact, the centrality of the cultural strategies was reinforced a few years after the Olympic Games, with the decision to organize a new international event, the Forum of the Cultures 2004. This event, unique in the field of large-scale urban celebrations, adopted the 'dialogue between cultures' as an excuse for intense urban renewal in a problematic and strategic area of the city. Once again, Barcelona placed its trust in the use of international celebrations as the engine of important urban development transformations – a formula used repeatedly here, as in many other cities (Monclús, 2006).

Epilogue

'When the Olympic flame has been quenched, everyone, and particularly the generations to come, will be left with a city transformed, with a new urban weft and a new loom'. In the Foreword to the Official Report (COOB, 1992), Mayor Maragall summarized the main achievements of the Olympic programme, prior to the celebration of the Games, with references to the extraordinary urban transformation of the city. However, following the enormous success of Barcelona 1992, the city's ability to organize the Games also contributed to improving the image of the city, another fundamental objective although somewhat less explicit. Linked to this new urban image, the use of the 'leverage opportunities' (see also chapters 6 and 10) also shows the success of the Olympic bid, as mentioned in relation to the economic impact of the Games and its multiplier effect on the tourist industry.

As with other major events, assessment of Barcelona 1992 must be undertaken in accordance with the level of compliance with the main objectives, both officially stated and those which were not so explicit, but also in accordance with the eventual costs and social and cultural benefits. This is where the limits of the 'Barcelona model' are shown. Among the most important criticisms are the references to the excessive, almost obsessive, concern to improve the image of the city, with the resulting trivialization process of urban methods and a certain loss of its historic identity. Rem Koolhaas (1995) pointed out that a unique city like Barcelona could become a 'generic city', by oversimplifying its identity',[12] sentiments echoed by other noteworthy critics (Tello, 1993; Delgado, 2005; Capel, 2005).

This concern contrasts with the necessity of interventions in areas as essential as public transport and housing. As far as the former is concerned, it seems that the main advances have been in private rather than public transport, with repercussions for the new road networks in the restructuring of the metropolitan area of Barcelona. Admittedly, however, it is also true that the responsibility for the suburban and metropolitan dispersion processes cannot be attributed solely to the Olympic projects rather than other factors (Monclús, 1998). As far as the weakness in housing policy is concerned, the urban land revaluation and the property boom that coincided with the 'Olympic years' made the consequences more serious and negative. In addition to the rise in housing prices, the excessive importance given to hotels and offices and the 'over-development' of real estate markets have been criticized. Here, the strong dependence on short cycles of the economy shows one of the limits of this type of event, with the high revaluation of central areas resulting in the displacement of public sector housing and the young towards the metropolitan periphery.

Nevertheless, the Barcelona Olympic Games were extraordinarily successful in catalysing plans and projects and stimulating the urban economy. There was decisive and consensual public intervention and the event was used to improve extensive areas of the city. The project for 'Greater Barcelona' – thought about for decades but developed in the 1980s – became a reality in the 1990s. The city is now an international point of reference for architects and international investors alike and the Olympic Games were the instrument used for private-led developments. There is a 'before' and 'after' effect of the Olympic Games, although for some, the change produced in the 1990s would have involved greater importance of private capital in urban development – a principle far from the thinking behind the initial 'Barcelona model' (Montaner and Muxí, 2002; Bohigas, 1999). Although it may seem contradictory, Barcelona may have become a victim of its own success. As in other cities, the success of the strategic urban development in the city may have been the root of problems arising from the revaluation of certain urban areas. The quickening of decentralizing tendencies and the exponential increase in metropolitan mobility correlates with considerable costs in energy, land and commuting times, in other words, the quality of urban life.

Perhaps it could be concluded that the 'new urban development' of Barcelona, following the Games, has decisively opted for quantity, taking the quality of the interventions for granted – although this conclusion may not be so clear, if one includes other parameters associated with urban development quality: for example, housing characteristics (price and quality), reasonable mobility, and environmental aspects. The Olympic Games, however, have a limited responsibility for these trends, if they are considered, first, as a logical conclusion to a process initiated far earlier than the celebration of the event and, secondly, as a Barcelona version of 'international global urban development', which here had greater support and was more 'domesticated' than in other cities affected by the phenomenon of globalization.

Notes

1. Maragall (1999*b*, p. 5).

2. Josep Porcioles was appointed Mayor of Barcelona by the Franco regime in 1957, a post he did not leave until 1973.

3. The 'Riverside Plan' – which had the poetic sub-title 'Barcelona. A city which can no longer live with its back to the sea' – was a project promoted by a group of important companies with land and factories in this sector. In 1968, the City Council approved the project, made up of a strip separated from the old 'Poble Nou' by a ring road. Local resistance paralysed the project in 1973.

4. Oriol Bohigas was born in 1925. He became an architect at the Barcelona School of Architecture (Escola Técnica Superior d'Arquitectura de Barcelona – ETSAB) in 1951, Town Planner in Madrid in 1961, Professor at the ETSAB in 1966, and its Director from 1977 to 1980. In 1980 he was appointed Planning Director at the Barcelona City Council, a position he held until 1984 when he became Personal Advisor to the Mayor.

5. The City Council, democratically elected for the first time in forty years, had councillors from five parties: PSC, PSUC, CiU, UCD and ERC (COOB, 1992, I, p. 219).

6. Exhibition held in October 1988 in the Edifici de les Aigües under the title *Barcelona, the City and 92*. It was a comprehensive account of the town planning projects in progress which were related directly or indirectly to the organization of the Games. The exhibition was an unprecedented success and received over 350,000 visitors (COOB, 1992, II, p. 347).

7. The objective of the action was to structure an urban space located in an under-privileged area. In the Vall d'Hebron Area, the Candidature Dossier could point to an Olympic venue completed well before the city was nominated to host the 1992 Games: the velodrome, which had been inaugurated for the World Cycling Championship in 1984. The area, which occupies 160 hectares, has other facilities, such as the Llars Anna Gironella de Mundet, the Club Esportiu Hispano-Francès and the Unió Esportiva d'Horta (COOB, 1992, II, p. 247).

8. Drawn up by the team of architects: Josep Martorell, Oriol Bohigas, David MacKay and Albert Puigdomènech.

9. In contrast, what happened in Barcelona's Old Harbour (Port Vell) was the generalized renovation of port and industrial facilities into something approaching a thematic park. This was done by the Port Authority, outside the control of the City Council. Indeed, the remodelling of the Port Vell reflects these influences: the conversion of former port facilities for recreational, leisure and tourism uses in the 'Rouse style' (after the developer of Baltimore and Boston). It is now a part of a new city image. Some similarities can be found with the 'Baltimore model' (Ward, 2006).

10. From the twelve new 'poles' or 'areas of centrality' four were for the Olympics, four for the waterfront, and four for other places. There were two main objectives: 'decentralizing central land uses' (tertiary uses: offices); and regenerating the seafront. If we look at the seafront, we can understand that those objectives were complementary. These areas benefited from special planning conditions in order to attract the new types of directional and tertiary uses corresponding to the services and facilities sectors, in spaces with obsolete uses but with good accessibility (Barcelona City Council, 1987*b*; Esteban, 1999).

11. This formula allowed 40 per cent of public investment from the central administration, 32 per cent from the regional government and 18 per cent from Barcelona City Council to be managed (Brunet, 1995, p. 103).

12. 'Sometimes an old, singular city, like Barcelona, by oversimplifying its identity, turns generic. It becomes transparent, like a logo' (Koolhaas, 1995).

Chapter 15

Sydney 2000

Beatriz García

This chapter studies Sydney's experience as an Olympic city from the perspective of cultural policy and planning. In previous work I have argued that culture and the arts play a critical role in defining the Games' symbolic dimensions and are determining factors in the sustainability of event legacies (see García, 2002*b*, 2003, 2004; Moragas 1992). In this context, interpreting Sydney's cultural discourse is fundamental to understanding how the city was experienced during the Olympic fortnight and the kinds of images that it projected to the rest of the world in its lead-up and aftermath.

Sydney's cultural discourse offers a good example of the internal contradictions that underpin many examples of city-based events that try to be everything for everyone: locally meaningful, nationally engaging and globally impacting. The problem of such a multi-layered approach is that it tends to lead to overly simplistic and tokenistic cultural representations, an issue best reflected in the often confused narratives of Olympic Opening and Closing Ceremonies (see Tomlinson, 1996). Despite claims to the contrary (Cashman, 2006), Sydney 2000 was no exception as its ceremonies failed to depart from established narratives about Australia dominated by a white and Western sense of aesthetics where indigenous and multicultural cultures are an exotic addition rather than a core component (García and Miah, 2000). However, Sydney promised a comprehensive programme of cultural activity over four years and presented an unprecedented programme of street activity during the Olympic fortnight, which provided additional opportunities to explore and demonstrate the worth of its cultural discourse.

This chapter offers a detailed analysis of how Sydney's cultural discourse came about and influenced its profile as an Olympic city. It builds on the current debate about event-led cultural regeneration in urban environments (Chalkley and Essex, 1999; Burbank *et al.*, 2002; Monclús 2004; Richards and Wilson, 2004; Gold and Gold, 2005) to provide critical scrutiny of existing definitions and guidelines for cultural engagement within the Olympic Movement. Its key argument is that the positioning of the Olympic Games as a city-based, nationally-framed and globally embracing cultural event presents important challenges for those that make cultural policy, yet has rarely resulted in sustainable cultural legacies. Sydney had an opportunity to question established practices and overcome the trend towards using cultural activity as a platform for global media spectacle at the expense of meaningful local representation. However, existing Olympic structures, particularly media and sponsorship agreements, prevented this ambition from coming fully to fruition.

Bringing the Games to Sydney

Sydney was the third consecutive Australian city to present a candidature for hosting the Olympic Games between 1992 and 2000. Brisbane, capital of the state of Queensland and host city of the 1988 World Expo, had bid for the 1992 Games, while Melbourne, capital of the state of Victoria and host of the 1956 Olympic Games, bid for 1996. Farrell (1999) argued that Australia's continuing interest in staging the Games cannot be explained on the grounds of expected economic benefits and international exposure alone. Rather, there is a rooted passion for sports manifested by the day-to-day practices of most Australians and a widespread acceptance and interest in the Olympic Movement, as shown by Australia's uninterrupted participation in the Games despite its geographical isolation (*Ibid.*). Sydney's Olympic promotional material claimed that, with Greece, Australia is the only other country to have participated in every Olympic Games since their revival in 1896 (see SOBL, 1992; SOCOG, 1999a, 2000a).

The Sydney Olympic Bid Limited (SOBL) emphasized these cultural factors to show the deep commitment and support of Australians for the Olympic Games (McGeoch and Korporaal, 1994). Further, SOBL (1992) argued that in Australia there was no organized group opposed to the Games. Tony Veal noted that not even Aboriginal communities, initially feared for the threat of boycotts, were strongly opposed to the Olympics as the opportunity to participate and win Olympic medals had converted many of their members into national heroes.[1] Despite some opposition from academics and community leaders (Frankland, 2000; Waitt, 2003, 2004), the notion of a nationally and culturally cohesive Olympic proposal was to emerge as a key selling point in the bid, particularly at an international level. As such, once key operational arguments, such as sound infrastructural and environmental strengths, had been won among national stakeholders, two cultural arguments became a distinctive factor of Sydney's bid discourse among IOC members and the global media: the celebration of Sydney's and Australia multiculturalism, and the advancement of Aboriginal reconciliation (Hanna, 1999; García, 2002b).

The Australian bid organizers realized that the multicultural composition and, most importantly, the presence of Aboriginal cultures, made Australia a unique place to explore exemplary ways in which the Olympic ideals of universal understanding could foster and promote respect of human rights (Hanna, 1999). Accordingly, the Sydney bid incorporated references to Australia's indigenous cultures and emphasized the advances made by the Australian government in supporting them. An example of the centrality given to Aboriginal cultures is found in the social component of the bid presentation during the last night preceding the IOC final vote in Monaco. McGeogh and Korporaal (cited in Hanna, 1999, p. 28) observed that 'indigenous musicians played outside the Hôtel de Paris' with 'the haunting sounds attracting [IOC] members to [the Sydney 2000 Bid Committee's] hospitality suite'. This cultural presentation was criticized by Australian scholars Booth and Tatz (1999, pp. 6–7), who considered that the SOBL 'flooded Monaco with black dancers and performers, but … they were tourist curios like koalas and kangaroos'. By contrast, Hanna (1999, p. 28) claimed that 'although used tokenistically, the significant inclusion of Indigenous culture created the impression of a national culture that values the contributions of its minority groups' and resulted in renewed debates about this issue throughout Australia.

Furthermore, McGeoch and Korporaal (cited in Hanna, 1999, p. 29) argued that Sydney presented its official cultural programme as an important part of the bid strategy and noted that 'it was promoted at the July 1993 opening of the Olympic Museum in Lausanne [while] other cities, by contrast, focused primarily on the sporting festival'. Reinforcing this argument, Donald McDonald, chairman of the Cultural Committee for the Bid and subsequent chairman of the Olympic Cultural Commission, emphasized the unique characteristics of the Sydney proposal by claiming that:

> Sydney was the only city to have produced a special publication on the Cultural Olympiad and presented an extensive programme of activities to be held in the four years leading to the Games. (McDonald, 1994)

In his words, the use of the Sydney Opera House as the main cultural venue and the emphasis given to Aboriginal reconciliation were considered 'issues crucial' to the success of Sydney's bid (*Ibid.*).

International Expectations and Brand Images

Sydney's emphasis on Aboriginal issues and multiculturalism must be understood within a particular climate of international expectations strongly concerned with human rights abuses. The Sydney bid was in close competition with that from Beijing, with the latter being the favourite. An important limitation of the Beijing bid was China's dubious human rights record, a factor accentuated by the killing of pro-democracy demonstrators at Tiananmen Square in 1989, only three years before the IOC vote. In order to gain some advantage over Beijing, Sydney and Australia needed to address areas likely to raise similar international concern. Accordingly, the promotion of a harmonic and progressive view of the Aboriginal and multicultural composition of the country became a top priority.

The emphasis on reconciliation and multiculturalism was also a response to the pressures faced by the promoters of the bid to present an image of the host city and country that is distinctive and easy to understand. The use of simplified cultural themes to define the idiosyncrasy of a given place has been widely discussed within events and Olympic-specific literature. Berkaak (1999, p. 68) argues that 'an Olympic event is an opportunity to be focused on – with an assured benefit' and an opportunity for the host city or nation to 'choose which aspects [it wants to] showcase to the world'. Moragas (1992, p. 32) adds that it is necessary that the Olympic city or nation 'synthesize[s its] complex reality in an image [or] brand image' in order to suit global media production processes, thus maximizing its communication impact and avoiding misunderstandings. This makes the Games 'a laboratory of incalculable value to understand the logic behind the commercialisation of nowadays culture' (*Ibid.*, p. 34). The use of Aboriginal reconciliation and multiculturalism as Australia's international brand images were well adapted to the requirements of mass media during the bid period and thus received extensive publicity worldwide (García, 2002b).

In order to strengthen its cultural case, Sydney decided to follow the example of Barcelona 1992 and present a four-year Cultural Olympiad fully engaged with these themes. However, as discussed below, at the time of winning the bid, the celebration of multiculturalism and Aboriginal reconciliation was not as established and clearly defined in Australian cultural policy terms as the chosen brand images of previous Olympic cities, notably Mediterranean culture in Barcelona 1992 and Southern and African-American cultures in Atlanta 1996 (see Australian Democrats, 2001; Bottomley, 1994; NSW Ministry for the Arts, 1997). This would be a cause of conflict and disagreement over the management and implementation of the cultural programme and was, arguably, a reason for the inconsistent support that the programme received over the years.

Reviewing Sydney's Chosen Brand Images

Despite the apparent strengths of multiculturalism and reconciliation as brand images, a closer look at these motives reveals a contradiction between their cultural potential and their essentially problematic political dimensions. The emphasis placed on the concept of 'multiculturalism' or 'multicultural society' was aimed at acknowledging the diverse first or second generation migrant communities composing Australia's and, particularly, Sydney's population. However, Jakubowicz (1981, 1994) discussed the uses and abuses of the term multiculturalism within the Australian government rhetoric, questioning its promotion as an official state ideology. In line with this, Cunningham argued that the multicultural discourse in Australia has never been taken from a cultural policy perspective but only from the perspective of social policy:

> this discourse is focused on solving the social problems of immigration in terms of language, education, jobs, health services etc. but not in consistently promoting a presence of ethnically and culturally diverse people in the media or the arts world. [Thus], it is unlikely that relevant multicultural components are included within the Games cultural programme beyond a token presence in the event promotional or marketing discourse.[2]

Accordingly, it can be argued that the use of a multicultural discourse in Sydney's cultural programme was not an effect of the host city or Australia's priorities in cultural policy but rather a strategic decision associated with the country's policies in communication and international relations (see also Wilson, 1996).

At a different level, the promotion of Aboriginal culture was shaped around the term 'reconciliation'. Reconciliation was meant to signify the commitment of Australian society to a full acceptance and acknowledgement of Aboriginal and Torres Strait Islanders cultures within its national discourse and sense of self. However, Tatz (1999) has contested the use and meaning of the term reconciliation and has accused the Olympic organizations and those government bodies supporting them of masking an extremely delicate and largely unsolved issue behind a public relations game. For Tatz, this game 'has always been conceived from a white sense of aesthetics' which prevents the public from genuinely understanding the situation (*Ibid.*). In support, Aboriginal film-maker Frankland (2000) states that the way Aboriginal questions were dealt with in Olympic discourses tended to be superficial and tokenistic. He argues that they were aimed at exploiting their most appealing side for both governments and the media to present a harmonious Australia to the world, but were not consistent in the process to create truly significant cultural projects and offer Aboriginal peoples a representative voice.

The suspicion arising over the Olympic bid's brand 'images' within the Australian academic and arts communities did not prevent Games' promoters and organizers from using the terms as core elements of their Olympic discourse for the edification of foreign audiences. Nevertheless, in common with previous Olympic bids, the key words that were used to attract the investment of national stakeholders and promote the key benefits of the Olympic project were terms such as 'trade' and 'tourism', which had little to do with pursuit of cultural identity.[3] This is indicative of a conflict between the image that was projected abroad and the beliefs or aspirations of the Australian population, in particular, the stakeholders that were to fund the Olympic experience.

There remained a contradiction between what was 'sold' or promised to international audiences and the interests of national audiences and stakeholders. This resulted in the planning of a remarkably ambitious cultural programme which was to be produced almost without any formal support from Australian organizations that, ultimately, had a marginal role within the Olympic city atmosphere.

Managing Culture at the Olympics

The Sydney Organizing Committee for the Olympic Games (SOCOG) was established in 1993 with responsibility to prepare and present the Games and work in close coordination with the Olympic Coordination Authority (OCA). The latter was in charge of managing infrastructures and the overall Games legacy, while SOCOG retained control of all aspects of the Games implementation, including both the sporting competitions and the IOC-required cultural and educational programmes. In previous Games, this programme had been subject to varied policies and strategies, as some cities feel that the mission of an Organizing Committee does not necessarily respond to the priorities and agendas of the host city or country but rather the established IOC global regulations and the demands of other global partners such as sponsors and media. Consequently, cities such as Barcelona and Athens retained control of their cultural programmes through separate organizations.[4] Sydney's decision to keep its cultural programme within SOCOG meant that it was integrated within the main Olympic structures and, theoretically, able to benefit from common resources. Yet, it also ran the risk of losing visibility within the highly demanding and multi-faceted Olympic project.

Sydney's official cultural programme took the form of four annual 'Olympic Arts Festivals' and was located within SOCOG's division of Marketing and Image, which incorporated a wide range of programmes including marketing, design and special events. Despite its positioning within an influential division, the Festivals' management team was rather marginal within SOCOG structure (García, 2002b; SOCOG, 1999b). Beyond the lack of interaction within their own overarching marketing division, the Arts Festivals were isolated from other programmes with a clear focus on cultural matters and an emphasis beyond sport, such as the torch relay, the education programme, community relations and the ceremonies programme. Furthermore, there was no direct interaction with the committees in charge of addressing and collaborating with Aboriginal and multicultural communities at a local or national level.[5] Ultimately, the cultural programme missed an important association with one of the most relevant Olympic programmes in 'city' terms, based at the same division. This was the 'look of the Games', a programme with a major impact on the feel of the city during the Olympic fortnight through the creation of banners and other decorative devices dedicated to locating key venues and embellishing urban public spaces.

A further negative effect of this managerial isolation was the lack of strong strategies to approach and lobby external stakeholders. SOCOG had specific programmes to approach government, sponsors and the media. However, the Festivals were not a central part of their agenda and rarely benefited from established agreements. The lack of clear and convincing strategies to approach stakeholders indicates that the cultural programme was not in a strong position to secure the full accomplishment of all its objectives. Instead, it relied on the willingness and particular interests of specific partners (see section on stakeholders, below).

In sum, nothing indicates that SOCOG's management structure responded to or supported a defined cultural policy. The organization's top decision-making was based on economic imperatives with a view to supporting tourism, business and sporting achievements rather than guaranteeing a coherent cultural strategy. The most evident effect of this situation was the lowering of standards in Sydney's Olympic cultural discourse, with generic entertainment and branding devices dominating over the more distinctive and representative messages devised at the bid stage. Some clear examples are found in the merchandise and 'look of the Games' design which, although effective in media terms, failed to establish a clear message about contemporary Sydney and instead used similar techniques to previous and subsequent Games – a clear case of global standards dominating over place-specific trends.

Designing the Games' Cultural Dimension

Despite its marginal position, Sydney's culture team decided to go ahead with its original proposal of a four-year Cultural Olympiad, following the example of Barcelona and Atlanta. The programme manager argued that it was important to

Figure 15.1. Olympic Games design: global branding vs local representation.

use the Olympics to project ambitious cultural events regardless of the subsequent difficulties in implementing them. In her view:

> a four-year period is better than just three weeks, and national and international presentations, exhibitions and collaborations are more challenging and stimulating for the arts in Australia than a short Sydney-based festival.[6]

However, the cultural programme suffered a radical budget cut in the first year after winning the bid, from A$51 million to A$20 (SOCOG, 1999c, 1999d) and many of the early proposals for implementation had to be cancelled or reframed, which limited their impact on Sydney and Australia. Furthermore, the lack of resources led to reallocating the responsibility for some of the designed Olympic cultural activities to other departments, including the plan for an Olympic Village Cultural Programme and liaisons with the Olympic Youth Camp.[7]

The final programme of activity retained the original concept of Australia-wide and international Arts Festivals. In this context, all generic and festival-specific cultural references were about Australia as a nation rather than Sydney as an Olympic city, as detailed in table 15.1.

The overly ambitious nature of the Festivals, combined with limited resources and a marginal structural position made it very difficult for this cultural discourse to have a direct impact on the city, the rest of Australia and, indeed, the world, as was originally intended. As noted below, the final Olympic communications strategy focused on a generic Olympic discourse that celebrated the Games and Australia's way of life but was not finely tuned to the original bid discourse of multiculturalism and aboriginal reconciliation – and did little to advance the cause for greater cultural understanding and direct representation of cultural minorities, as reflected in reports of racial violence in the city (Greer, 2005, pp. 12–13). Arguably, the decision to focus on the representation of Australia as a nation rather than Sydney as a city was an additional challenge, limiting the programme's ability to make a difference, as its purpose became too vague and difficult to implement.

Promoting the Games, Promoting the City

As discussed earlier (see chapters 6 and 7), Olympic marketing and communications is a priority for the IOC and respective Olympic organizers. The IOC is in charge of the worldwide dimension of Olympic communications by retaining direct control of global sponsorship programmes such as The Olympic Programme (TOP), the negotiation of television rights, worldwide merchandizing and the distribution of generic advertising campaigns about the ideals of Olympism. Contrasting with the global dimensions of the Olympic brand, the design and management of local campaigns to promote particular messages about a specific Games – and, indeed, the host city – is the sole responsibility of respective OCOGs.

The structure of marketing and communications at SOCOG exemplified the need to reconcile the global aspirations of the IOC with the locally based needs

Table 15.1. Olympic Arts Festivals length, themes, objectives and main components.

Year, Name, Length and Location	Theme/Mission	Objectives	Programme Components
1997 The Festival of the Dreaming, September to October (Sydney)	Celebration of the world's indigenous cultures, in particular those of Australian Aborigines and Torres Strait Islanders	*General*: expand a greater awareness and appreciation of Australian indigenous heritage *Specific*: ensure indigenous authorship and control of the work presented	Thirty exhibitions, fourteen dance and theatre productions, eight performance troupes, fifty films, a literature programme, three concerts and special commissions involving overseas indigenous artists. Every state and territory of Australia was represented
1998 A Sea Change, June to October, (Australia-wide)	A 'snapshot' of Australia's diverse migrant cultures	*General*: Create a time capsule of Australian culture in the end of the Millennium for generations to come *Specific*: Help people across the nation learn more about the arts in their country and demonstrate the importance of its geographic and cultural diversity	Ninety-two presenting companies and 122 dance, theatre, visual arts, literary, music and education events. *Highlights*: lighthouse and harbour concerts; touring exhibition *Sculpture by the Sea* *Publications*: 1998 Anthology of Australian writing and photography
1999 Reaching the World, November 1998 to January 2000 (five continents)	Events by Australian companies and artists touring to countries in each of the five regions represented by the Olympic symbol	*General*: bring Australian arts and culture to the international stages *Specific*: establish collaboration with foreign governments and arts organizations	Seventy events travelling to fifty countries and 150 cities or towns including dance, music, theatre, visual arts, literature, films, architecture and design. Publication of *Australia on Show*, a guide to Australian Arts Broadcasting
2000 The Harbour of Life, August to October (Sydney)	The culmination of the Olympiad, 'a festival on a scale to match the grandeur of the Olympic Games'	*General*: define the finest elements of Australian culture; present a number of works on grand scale, unlikely to be seen again in a lifetime; establish artistic legacies	Seventy-five day event focused in the harbour and Opera House – opera, theatre, dance and classical concerts; thirty visual arts exhibitions in key galleries and museums

Source: Information extracted from Olympic Arts Festivals fact sheets (SOCOG, 1997–2000).

of an Olympic host (see Wilson, 1996). Within its sponsorship programme, SOCOG had to address the needs of TOP partners at the same time as the needs of domestic partners. Furthermore, the marketing programmes had to reach local audiences while securing a worldwide impact that was coherent with established IOC strategies. Finally, within its diverse communications programmes, SOCOG had to cover the needs of a wide range of local communities while, at the same time, integrating all Games communications into a joint Olympic promotional plan (SOCOG, 1998).

There is insufficient space here to offer an in-depth study of Sydney's communication plans, but it can be argued that SOCOG's main priority was to ensure the success of the Games rather than Sydney's projection as an Olympic city. Accordingly, it is possible to observe certain imbalances in the levels of support provided to different Olympic dimensions. While programmes such as the torch relay, the Opening and Closing Ceremonies and naturally the sports competitions were placed centrally on the agendas of marketing and communication divisions, the Arts Festivals and educational programmes were rarely mentioned in the mainstream communication and marketing strategies and were excluded from the coverage of the official media centres – the Main Press Centre and International Broadcasting Centre (García, 2001, 2002b).

Arguably, the global aspirations and commercial needs of the IOC resulted in a strong emphasis on marketing imperatives at the expense of communication policies that could have leveraged the meaning and implications of the Olympic cultural programme for the city. This situation forced the Olympic cultural programme to develop its own communication strategy, practically in complete isolation from mainstream Olympic marketing. The strategy involved the creation of a new logo for the final Festival in 2000, and the positioning of the Festival within an emerging phenomenon within the Games hosting process, the non-accredited media centre (see García and Miah, 2004) in coordination with a new arts information service, *ausarts2000*, funded by the Arts Council (National Library of Australia, 2000). These factors helped the 2000 Festival gain more visibility within the cultural sector, but also contributed to disassociating it from previous Festivals and the notion of a four-year Olympiad (García, 2002b). Given that the final Festival was focused on the celebration of world class artists in 'world class venues' such as the Sydney Opera House, this also meant that the original themes of reconciliation and multiculturalism, explored at length in 1997 and 1998, were ultimately lost (*Ibid.*).

Overall, the main limitation of Sydney's Olympic communication strategy in cultural policy terms was the focus on entertainment rather than cultural representation. The main problem was the lack of interaction between the more sophisticated cultural (arts) messages and generic Olympic marketing. As such, overall Games promotions went back to established image stereotypes that marginalized many ethnic communities, while the Arts Festival promotion was limited to the cultural sector through minority or specialized media outlets.

Involvement of Key Stakeholders

Following the practice of most Olympic cities since Los Angeles 1984, the Sydney Games were managed via a public-private partnership led by SOCOG and OCA. Key Olympic stakeholders included the Australian government at local, state and federal levels; corporate sponsors and supporters at national and global levels; and the media at international and Australian local and national levels. The involvement of different stakeholders in Sydney's cultural programme evolved throughout the four-year period of the Olympiad. For the most part, stakeholders who showed interest in the first Festival, became vague or reticent to support the two central ones, but increased their contributions in time for the Olympic fortnight in 2000 (García, 2002b).

Overall, there is no evidence to suggest that the support provided by the average cultural stakeholder led or contributed to strengthening a coherent cultural policy for the event. Stakeholders' interests were often ambiguous or contradictory and so were their strategies for involvement, which combined the search for spectacle and media appeal with the often overstated ambition to guarantee local representation. In general, it can be argued that Olympic stakeholders were unable to prevent the imbalances and limitations provoked by the weak position of the official cultural programme within SOCOG.

Public Sector

Government bodies were fully supportive of the Olympic programme but were divided in their interests and expectations towards the Games' cultural dimension. Local and state bodies viewed the Games – and indeed, the associated Arts Festivals – as an opportunity to expand tourism and trade opportunities. In this sense, their Olympic cultural policy was dominated by a rationalist and market-oriented approach, in line with overall trends in Australia (Caust, 2003; DCITA, 1994; Radbourne and Fraser, 1996; Wilson, 1996) and their priority was to support those activities most likely to have an international impact. In contrast, federal bodies such as the Arts Council were committed to revisiting notions of Australian culture and fighting established stereotypes of white colonialism. Their emphasis was on exploring and supporting the notions of multiculturalism and Aboriginal reconciliation that had been presented as Australia's brand images since the bid stage and, with them, an image of tolerance and pride in diversity that was best represented by the *ausarts 2000* programme. Both approaches had common goals and used similar techniques but the first welcomed the use of pure entertainment and spectacle while the second placed an emphasis on maximizing representation and a shared vision of Australia's and Sydney's cultural discourse.

Until 2000, public support for the Olympic cultural programme was vague and limited. Several observers explain this by pointing to the conflict over government 'ownership' of the Games.[8] The Games had been awarded to Sydney, so they were the responsibility of the state of New South Wales (NSW), with federal government having only a secondary role in terms of decision-making and resource allocations. This resulted in a lack of coordination between state and federal bodies and a certain sense of competition between states wanting to benefit from the Games with priorities and interests differing from those of Sydney and NSW. SOCOG and NSW often reacted to the situation with defensive or protective measures, as was the case in their relationship with Queensland over its contribution to the cultural programme, which was lower than the figure which state agencies had wished. The limited contributions of federal arts funding bodies during the first three years of the Olympiad could also be understood as a measure to avoid conflicts among states.

However, in preparation for the Olympic fortnight, local, state and federal bodies joined their efforts in a common initiative that became one of the greatest catalysts for the promotion of the Olympic cultural programme. This was the creation of a non-accredited media centre, the Sydney Media Centre (SMC). This complemented the established Main Press Centre and International Broadcasting Centre and was managed according to IOC regulations. The SMC had the mission to serve all media, regardless of their access to official IOC accreditation, by providing stories about Sydney and Australia not related to the sporting competitions. The SMC was managed by Tourism NSW and the Department of State and Regional Development (state bodies) in conjunction with the Sydney Harbour Foreshore Authority (local government), the Australian Tourism Commission and the Department of Foreign Affairs and Trade (federal government). Tourism, trade and culture were the focal points of most press conferences at the SMC. Accordingly, the final Arts Festival became a key beneficiary and gained a strong SMC presence with regular press conferences. Furthermore, the Festival had its own media information office in partnership with the Arts Council-funded *ausarts2000*.

Beyond these generic government programmes, in the context of the Olympic city it is of particular relevance to consider the involvement of the main local authority, the City of Sydney. The City had a direct association with the Arts Festivals: the Lord Mayor was a board member of the Olympic Cultural Commission and the City became official presenter of the 2000 Festival, which resulted in the operational authorship of all outdoor arts and entertainment programmes for that year.[9] In addition, the City of Sydney offered A$2.25 million value-in-kind support by presenting Arts Festival banners, bus advertising and brochure placement in official booths and all main city streets and squares. This suggests that local government used the Festival as part of the city's cultural policy strategy.

However, the City of Sydney's interest in the Olympic period went well beyond the official arts programme. The City created a year long Olympic project including an ambitious programme of city beautification, service upgrading and the provision of entertainment during the Olympic fortnight. The latter was aimed at coordinating the efforts by the City, SOCOG, OCA and the Olympic Roads and Transport Authority (ORTA), which only functioned during the Olympic fortnight. The objective was to provide a mechanism for crowd management during all major events in 2000 including the New Year's Eve celebrations and the Sydney Festival. During the Olympics, the project was named *Olympic LiveSites!* (figure 15.2). This was an entertainment programme distributed at six popular locations in the city centre 'at times when Olympic venues were filling and spilling simultaneously and transport would be at its most stressed'.[10] *LiveSites!* offered simultaneous coverage of the sporting competitions via giant screens and also included concerts, acrobatic shows, and street theatre. However, these activities

Figure 15.2. Olympic LiveSites.

were not linked to the 2000 Arts Festival. In fact, the popularity and visibility of *LiveSites!* overshadowed the indoor and somehow elitist nature of most official Olympic cultural activities that year. This led many journalists, tourists and Sydneysiders to believe that the Games cultural programme was the former and not the latter (García, 2002*b*).

Overall, the City of Sydney's involvement in the final Olympic Arts Festival must be understood in the context of other plans and activities for year 2000, where the Olympics and the arts programme were not the only priority. The City's interest in the 2000 Festival was not the exploration of Sydney's cultural values, but rather the projection of a contemporary and lively image of the central business district (CBD) to attract foreign visitors and corporations. This affected the nature and emphasis of *LiveSites!* outdoor activities which, though highly entertaining and widely popular, were poorly related to the bid promise of a multicultural, all embracing and representative cultural celebration.

Sponsors

The corporate sector plays a key role in funding the Games and is also an important element in the look and feel of any Olympic city. Due to the strict IOC ban on any commercial advertising inside the Olympic sport venues, sponsors tend to focus their investment on alternative Olympic activities within outdoor spaces, from the route of the torch relay, to key host city locations involving, typically, the covering of buildings with Olympic-themed corporate messages. In Sydney, the main sponsorship programmes were the IOC-led worldwide TOP programme and, at a national level, the Team Millennium partners, Sydney 2000 Supporters and Sydney 2000 Providers which, together, generated over $492 million (IOC, 2002). The distribution of funding is linked to negotiations over 'core properties', that is, direct associations with specific Games components. Many of these corporate-owned 'core properties' have particular significance at a local rather than global level and thus have a strong impact on the workings of the Olympic city. Table 15.2 lists cultural and entertainment programmes either funded or organized, or both, by specific Olympic sponsors in 2000, most of which took place in Sydney exclusively.

An interesting aspect of table 15.2 is the emphasis on youth programmes. Children and youngsters are a priority in the Olympic context due to the specific connotations of the Olympics as a 'youth movement' (IOC, 2004*a*). Indeed, this approach also has a lucrative appeal, as it provides good opportunities to reach out and engage with potential consumers at an early stage. The other notable element is the emphasis on entertainment over cultural activities – including standard popular activities such as light and sound shows, or pop concerts – over city-specific offerings. Only 20 per cent of the activities in table 15.2 presented the work of locally based artists or performers or stories or work representative of Sydney's diverse communities. As such, even at a local level and for the benefit of mainly

Table 15.2. Olympic sponsors involvement in cultural and entertainment programmes in year 2000.

TOP Sponsors (Worldwide)	Cultural/Entertainment Programme	Description
Coca Cola McDonald's	Coca Cola Olympic Club Sydney & POWERADE Training Camp Olympic Youth Camp	300 teenagers from around the world experience the Games 400 teenagers from around the world share two weeks of cultural exchange in Sydney and Australia
Panasonic Samsung UPS Visa	Olympic LiveSites! World of entertainment at the Olympic Rendez-vous@Samsung Aqua Spectacular Olympics of the imagination	Six giant screens displayed in six popular city locations to showcase Games coverage Cultural performances by traditional folkloric groups at Samsung tent, Olympic Park Nightly laser and water show in Darling Harbour A world-wide arts contest for kids between nine and thirteen years old from twenty-five countries. Thirty-six winners attend the Games

Team Millennium Partners	Cultural /Entertainment Programme	Description
Swatch	Olympic LiveSites!	Six countdown clocks, one at every site
AMP	Torch Relay Official Sponsor	Funding and promotional support for the relay
Energy Australia	Energy of Australia by Marc Newson	Nightly light show over the sails of the Opera House (Olympic Arts F.)
Fairfax	Olympic Arts Festivals, Education Programme, Volunteer Programme	Regular brochures highlighting key arts, education and volunteer activities; special events for programme participants
Holden	Hospitality Community Project Concert at the Domain (2000)	Assistance to the Chinese community Sydney Symphony Orchestra open air free concert
News Corp	Ticketing programme presenter Torch Relay presenter	Regular paper inserts following the Torch route and listing torch bearer names, support to the torch bearer selection scheme; regular brochures highlighting ticketing promotions
Telstra	National Aboriginal and Torres Strait Islanders Art Award	Australia's most prestigious prize for indigenous art, presented at Sydney's Customs House
Westfield	The Olympic Journey (1997–1999) Hosting the Kids 2000 Olympic Arena	Olympic-related activities, focus on children
Westpac	2000 Pacific School Games Westpac Olympic Youth Programme National Education Programme The Olympic Journey (1997–1999)	Youth-oriented educational Olympic programmes

Sydney 2000 Supporters	Cultural /Entertainment programme	Description
Nike	Kids interactive sport park Radio Free Sydney	Entertainment park at the Domain and Fox Studios Underground radio station featuring athletes' interviews combined with youth-oriented house, techno, acid jazz and World Beat music

Source: Extracted from sponsors' media news releases.

local audiences, Olympic sponsors saw more value-for-money and thus focused on supporting global entertainment rather than local cultural representation.

Interviews with Sydney sponsors indicated that current Olympic regulations did not make it worth investing in the official cultural programme. Part of the reason is the high cost compared with the limited profile and visibility of Olympic cultural activities. In Sydney, the ambiguous and, at times, elitist character of the cultural programme also diminished its corporate appeal. Olympic sponsors such as Swatch, Telstra and the Seven Network suggested that the programme – particularly in 2000 – was not able to engage with general audiences in the way that ceremonies and free street entertainment could. Thus, as seen in table 15.2, they saw greater benefit in developing an association with the sporting competitions, Olympic rituals or their own specially designed community fun programmes.[11]

Additional factors limiting potential corporate investment in cultural activity are the IOC exclusivity agreements (only one product category per sponsor, thus excluding brand competitors) and the strict protection of the Olympic rings, which can only be used by official Olympic sponsors. While these regulations have increased the lucrative value of sponsorship agreements, they have had a negative effect on cultural programming as it prevents non-Olympic sponsors from contributing to the Arts Festivals. Furthermore, it prevents existing arts companies and cultural groups from establishing an official and branded association with the Games if they receive funding and intend to acknowledge the support of any non-Olympic corporate sponsor (see also chapter 6).

Media

Together with Olympic sponsors, the media are the other key determinant of the Games' success at a global level. Moragas *et al.* (1995) argue extensively about the Games being first and foremost a 'media event' – their size and global impact being the direct result of the involvement and daily following of media networks representing more than 200 nations and reaching a potential global audience of 2–3 billion people (*Ibid.*; see also Dayan and Katz, 1994; Wilson, 1996). The Sydney 2000 Games presented the unique situation of two competing publishing companies (Fairfax and News Ltd) being Team Millennium Partners simultaneously. SOCOG's marketing negotiations with both groups secured the publication of special supplements on their respective 'core properties'. News Ltd owned the right to associate its national paper, *The Australian*, with Olympic ticketing and the torch relay. Fairfax owned the right to describe the *Sydney Morning Herald*, Sydney's main paper, as the 'official presenter' of the four Olympic Arts Festivals and owned the right to present official information about the Education Programme and the Volunteer Programme through its national tabloid, the *Sun Herald* (figure 15.3). The Olympic official broadcaster was the Seven Network, which did not establish any special outlet for the coverage of Olympic cultural

Figure 15.3. Sydney 2000 Volunteers.

activity and instead focused almost exclusively on the sporting competitions and most popular symbolic dimensions of the Games.

During a series of personal interviews, journalists, press editors and broadcasters representing a range of Australian media expressed the view that, although the official Arts Festivals might be an interesting addition to the Games, they lack the public appeal and uniqueness that characterizes other Olympic elements, from infrastructure developments to the sport competitions.[12] In their view, the only exception was the 1997 Aboriginal Festival, which was viewed as a key point of reference for future festivals all over Australia (Eccles, 1997). All interviewees agreed that the concept of an indigenous festival impacted on and was relevant to Australia, but they thought subsequent festivals lost that momentum, a factor accentuated by the growing presence of more easily recognizable Olympic news stories. Despite the wide coverage offered by major papers such as the *Sydney Morning Herald* and *The Australian*, the 2000 Festival was not seen as a distinctive event capable of engaging the average Olympic fan and was generally excluded from Olympic stories and specially-designed Olympic sections.

Living the Games

Helen Wilson (1996, p. 603) has asked the question, 'what is an Olympic city?' and noted the required 'dual function' that any Games host city must perform, is as a 'stand-in for the nation' and as a 'worldly city'. Wilson claims that 'the Games are as much about the "city as spectacle" as they are about sport' which 'emphasiz[es] the way that television manipulates and "theatricalizes" their urban sites' (*Ibid.*). The latter reflects the notion of the Games as a media event, which ultimately transforms the Olympic city into a space that is essentially understood through its representations in the media. Wilson stresses the impact of the Games experience on urban centres that must become 'sites of cultural consumption' (*Ibid.*, p. 607) according to international standards. This argument is consistent with the findings discussed in previous sections: in Sydney, like many other Olympic cities, the emphasis of key stakeholders was on image rather than representation. Wilson claims that this trend often leads the Olympic city to be 'similar looking' to all its predecessors, with 'world class com[ing] to mean just the standards of facility and kinds of entertainment that affluent international travellers expect anywhere' (*Ibid.*, p. 608).

Olympic versus Public Spaces

One of the most notable aspects of Sydney's Olympic urban planning was its emphasis on environmental sustainability. After various attempts at promoting the 'Athletes' and 'Millennium' Games, SOCOG focused on the promotion of the 2000 Olympics as the 'Green Games', and used its approach to remodelling formerly derelict Homebush Bay into the official Olympic Park as its most iconic environment-friendly development (SOCOG, 1999e; see also chapter 2). Sydney's emphasis on its green policies and credentials was accentuated by the IOC's decision in 1994 to make the 'environment' the third main strand of Olympism, after sport and culture (IOC 2000b, see also chapter 1).[13]

The promotion of a Green Games came not without controversy, as local activists denounced what they saw as an opportunistic top-down strategy that failed fundamental environmental standards but succeeded in creating a perception of success thanks to the 'questionable' or bought-in support of media partners (Waitt, 2004, pp. 398–397). McManus (2004, p. 164) corroborated the view of Sydney's environmental strategy as flawed by referring to what he considered a direct negative effect of becoming an Olympic city:

> [T]he concept of an Olympic city influenced many parts of Sydney. While it was visible in the beautification of routes from the airport and the motorway to the Homebush Olympic facilities, the notion that an Olympic city could not be a 'place of shame' was most noticeable in the decision to relocate the cycling road races from Bankstown in the south-west of Sydney to the more affluent eastern suburbs... In the case of Rozelle Bay, it was possible to appeal to the discourse of the Olympic city in order to gain support for a project such as a 'temporary' super-yacht marina that otherwise may have been considered unnecessary or politically sensitive. The text, in this case plans showing the 'temporary' moorings and even the proposed uses beyond the Olympic Games, were embedded in

a frantic haste to prepare Sydney to become the Olympic city... Approval was likely to be more forthcoming under such circumstances.

Despite these concerns, the 'Green Games' became the strongest line of communication by SOCOG and continued to be used within official documentation and government funded post-Games evaluation reports (PriceWaterhouseCoopers, 2002). However, during the Olympic fortnight itself, the environmental debate was progressively confined to the walled and ticketed official Olympic areas and lost prominence in the perception of what the Olympic city was really about. While a privileged few had access to the new facilities and environmental transformation of the Homebush Olympic Park and other sporting arenas, most Sydneysiders experienced the Olympics simply by living the street. In this context, a fourth, unofficial line became prevalent: the notion of the 'Friendly Games', which had been the most recognizable by-line to the Melbourne Olympics in 1956. It is interesting to consider the implications of the 'Friendly Games' tag over the official denominations as it emerged, rather spontaneously, out of the city's atmosphere and can thus be considered more representative of the sort of Olympic city that Sydney became for those experiencing it first hand.

This situation suggests that despite the many arguments concerning the overarching 'media-space' inhabited by any mega-event (Dayan and Katz, 1994; Wark, 1994; Wilson, 1996), the lived experience of the Games offers an added value and is a fundamental element in understanding how an Olympic host city operates. There are many interesting examples of Olympic street experience prior to year 2000, yet Sydney was able to advance the case further and set a precedent for subsequent Olympic hosts. This came courtesy of a combination of established Games practices (open air and free sport competitions such as the marathon; Olympic decorations or 'look of the Games') and the introduction of unprecedented interventions with the aid of new technologies (*LiveSites!*).

Traditionally, the role of the street and other urban public spaces during the Olympic fortnight is to offer a distinctive experience, rooted in the culture of the local host but supported by world-class services and entertainment. In this aspiration, Olympic cities must balance the tension between offering a culturally meaningful and representative experience and satisfying the expectations of international visitors with global standards. Sydney was particularly successful with its 'world-class' entertainment provision, using both public and private spaces in its CBD to present a wide range of food, drink, accommodation, shopping and related entertainment, both through free and paying programmes of activity. The Olympic city's core spaces were concentrated in two main areas: the spectacular Circular Quay, home to the Sydney Opera House and Sydney Bridge, and the recently developed Darling Harbour, presenting the range of services characteristic of festival marketplace developments (see Stevenson, 2003, p. 101). The latter was also home to key cultural venues such as the Maritime Museum and the Powerhouse Museum, the Sydney Media Centre and several Olympic National

Houses. The Olympic city feel was at its core the result of the combination of the 'Look of the Games' programme, managed by SOCOG, and the innovative *LiveSites!* by the City of Sydney. However, the emergence of alternative and often unplanned manifestations was also central to its success. These ranged from the unofficial creation of Olympic-themed shop motifs (see figure 15.4) to the extreme popularity of some Olympic National Houses such as The Netherlands House, sponsored by Heineken and host to some of the loudest all-night parties in the city.

However, the buzz and vibrancy of the city centre was not equally distributed throughout Sydney and did not extend to the suburbia surrounding key Olympic venues. The town of Parramatta, at the outskirts of Homebush, can be considered the only notable exception, as the authorities supported the setting up of large tents for Olympic pin-trading, which had emerged as one of the most popular hobbies of Olympic fans around the world. Other neighbouring communities were largely deprived of special activity other than the isolated efforts of local authorities to welcome the torch relay on the final days leading to the opening of the Games.

Impacts on Local Creative Communities

At this point, it is relevant to understand the reactions of Sydney's creative communities. Even though general opinion polls reveal high levels of satisfaction from average Sydneysiders (Waitt, 2003), research into the impressions of special interest groups suggests a different picture. Previous work on the cultural dimensions of the Sydney Olympics indicates that some of the strongest levels of dissatisfaction are found within the city's diverse creative communities, in particular, ethnic minorities including Aboriginal groups (García, 2002b).

As is often the case with any mega-event hosting processes and the Olympics in particular, a relevant section of Sydney's creative community felt that the Olympics were a threat to innovative and representative cultural manifestations. This feeling was expressed when Sydney won the bid in 1993 and was accentuated after learning about the existence of an official Olympic cultural programme that was underfunded and unable to guarantee open access and participation (García, 2002b, 2004). In 2000, the worst impressions were found amongst multicultural arts representatives and small companies from suburban Sydney. The latter claimed to be doubly disappointed: first, as they could not become an active component of a festival 'exclusively designed to showcase high art' and, secondly, for their exclusion as potential venues of the event.[14] Cases deserving special consideration were the suburbs of Auburn (which administratively incorporates Homebush, site of the Olympic park), Parramatta (adjacent to Homebush) and Liverpool (host of sporting competitions). Despite their geographical proximity to the principal sporting events, none of these suburbs hosted Olympic Arts Festival events. Another remarkable case was that of Rosehill, an area adjacent to Olympic Park and home to some sporting competitions, which was supposed to

Figure 15.4. The Feeling of the Street.

host 'Australians All', the only Festival event 'taking place out of the city centre' (SOCOG, 1999f). After a year of promoting the commitment to reach suburban Sydney with Olympic arts activities, the initiative was cancelled and the concert was transferred to a popular park in the heart of the CBD, where all other events were taking place.

Sydney's multicultural arts representatives denounced the lack of a genuine interest by SOCOG to embrace the existing diversity of the city despite its being a focal point of the Games' mission statement. To substantiate this impression, representatives of Carnivale, the most comprehensive multicultural festival in Sydney which takes place annually in September and was expected to coincide with the Olympic fortnight, repeatedly denounced the barriers placed in the way of integrating Carnivale into the 2000 Olympic programme.[15] After unclear discussions, it was decided to delay the start of the 2000 Carnivale until the end of the Games. The Festival was finally held in parallel with the Paralympic Games without being allocated any special Olympic funding.

Interestingly, the Premier of NSW proposed the creation of a street festival during the Olympic period with the aim of reflecting aspects of Sydney's multicultural society at a grassroots level. The NSW Ethnic Council obtained a grant for this project and local ethnic councils were invited to present proposals (McMill, 1999). In the event, neither Carnivale nor the Olympic Arts Festival team were included in the negotiations. The Street Festival project was thus designed independently of established ethnic and multicultural arts groups to focus instead on populist events without the direct input of local artists or grassroots cultural organizations. The frequent confusions and misunderstandings between different factions of Sydney's ethnic arts community and government bodies suggests a poorly devised multicultural arts policy which led to noticeable shortcomings within the Olympic programme and prevented the establishment of clear legacies.

Sydney's mainstream cultural institutions had a greater role within the Arts Festivals and insisted on the value of including an official cultural programme as part of the Olympic hosting process. One of the main benefits identified was potential national and global media exposure. In contrast, very few established cultural institutions expressed a belief in the long-term legacy and sustainability of the experience. In their view, the Olympic extravaganza was made for bold and spectacular statements rather than the more subtle or complex cultural messages that would have been required to represent contemporary Sydney or indeed Australian cultures properly.[16]

The Sydney Opera House was one of the main venues presenting Olympic artwork in August 2000 and the sole official performing arts venue during the Games (figure 15.5). To maximize exposure, the management team created 'Opera House 2000', a public relations programme starting on New Year's Eve with an acrobatics show and a large fireworks display on the building's rooftop. The 2000 programme continued throughout the Sydney Festival in January with a roof light design show every night in addition to the established performance programme. These activities were enhanced during the Games in order to emphasize the key role of the building in Sydney's lifestyle. In fact, most of the limited range of Olympic art outdoor events in 2000 took place in the Opera House forecourt, including a Torch Relay Opera Gala; a free performance by New Zealand Maori dancers, and the nightly lighting of the Opera rooftop.

According to the Sydney Opera House's Media Relations Officer, these events, combined with the international dance, music and opera programme taking place indoors, ensured the prominence of the venue throughout the

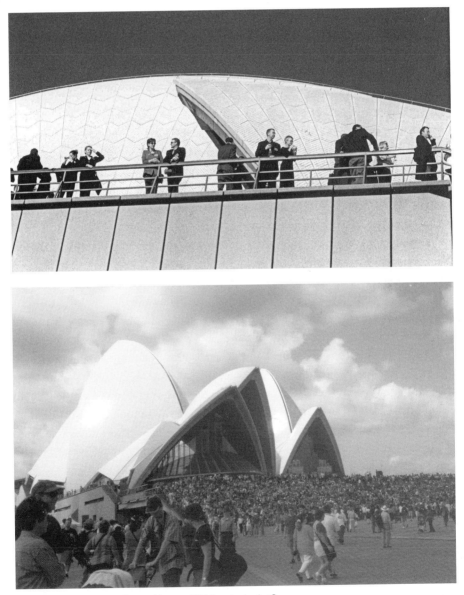

Figure 15.5. Sydney Opera House. Elitist or inclusive?

Games and provided great opportunities for national and international media coverage.[17] Nevertheless, the interest of the international media was focused on its role as an architectural icon of Sydney, rather than its sophisticated indoors cultural programming. While the building was often used as a backdrop to media reporting, references to the Arts Festival programme were practically non-existent, particularly within broadcast media.[18] Furthermore, the levels of coverage of the building as a background to outdoor sporting competitions, from the sailing to the men's and women's triathlon and marathon, clearly outstripped any coverage of outdoor arts events. The only events to rival the sports competitions were the arrival of the torch to Sydney and the Closing Ceremony fireworks spectacular.

The involvement of the Opera House in the official Olympic cultural programme also had some negative consequences, such as a significant increase in ticket prices that, arguably, prevented the average public from attending events during the Games (Morgan, 1999, p. 15). Many shows were sold out but, off-the-record, observers have suggested that it was due to Olympic sponsor functions and other pre-arranged Olympic family evenings, rather than public interest. Indeed, this brings into question the extent to which the Sydney Opera House played a relevant role for the general public during the Olympic period other than as an emblematic background.

Besides the Sydney Opera House, the only arts venues with a strong presence during the Olympic fortnight were Sydney's public arts galleries and museums, which offered one of the most extensive visual arts programmes ever presented alongside the Games. The Art Gallery of New South Wales and the Powerhouse Museum were particularly committed to the Olympics and agreed to finance hallmark exhibitions responding to both local and international demands.[19] As such, they combined the presentation of Australian work[20] with prestigious world collections.[21] Venues such as the Australian National Maritime Museum saw the Games as an opportunity to attract extra revenue and complemented its exhibition programme with rent deals for sponsor and athletes' functions, which proved to be the most lucrative strategy (Scott, 2004). An interesting addition to their involvement in the official cultural programme was the development of an ambitious visitor research project by the Powerhouse Museum and the Australian National Maritime Museum. As mentioned earlier, these institutions are located in the surroundings of Darling Harbour, which became an Olympic sports site and entertainment location, so both museums were interested in assessing whether the Olympic experience brought any change to their visitor profile. The visitor research project compared qualitative and quantitative visitor data from September 1999, 2000 and 2001 and provided evidence of the benefits (e.g. visitor increase) of having cultural institutions physically near the site of hallmark sporting events and presenting event themed exhibitions (*Ibid.*). This was one of few initiatives promoting the Games' impact on host city cultural venues and has contributed to a better understanding of the role and potential of the Games cultural programme.

Successes and Failures

Ten years on, Sydney is still remembered with fondness by the general media and Sydneysiders in particular and criticism remains muted compared with either Atlanta 1996 or Athens 2004. Even though Homebush has not become the environmental hallmark promoters tried to sell, and despite growing references to the 'white elephant' syndrome in Olympic Park (see Searle, 2002), the complaints, outside strict academic circles (see Lenskyj, 2002; Waitt, 2003, 2004), have not been particularly loud. London, host of the 2012 Games, is relying on Sydney's experience over any other previous host city, which probably indicates that, despite inevitable failings, Sydney managed the Games in the right way (see also chapter 2).

Official Reports emphasize Sydney's success in financial terms, claiming that the city managed 'the most comprehensive business development program ever held in association with an Olympic Games' with a clear focus and unprecedented benefits for 'industry development, investment attraction and national tourism' (PriceWaterhouseCoopers, 2002, pp. 1–6).[22] The IOC corroborates this impression of success by claiming that SOCOG established the 'most financially successful domestic sponsorship programme to date' (Ibid., p. 40), and 'the largest television broadcast operation in history' reaching an unprecedented 3.7 billion viewers (Ibid., p. 11). Beyond the positive business impacts, it can be claimed that the Games have left a significant image legacy through presenting contemporaneous Australia, and making the case for Sydney as a 'world city' in the sense argued by Sassen (1994, pp. 85–89), that is, with the ability to attract foreign investment in real estate and finance. The official Arts Festivals, with assistance of the *ausarts2000* programme and, particularly, the popular *LiveSites!,* contributed to the establishment of such images and further strengthened the city's leisure and business tourism markets in areas such as Darling Harbour.

However, the claim that the Games helped the cause of Aboriginal reconciliation and multicultural understanding is harder to prove. This is because it is difficult to dispute Wilson's (1996) claim that the Games were not used to advance the cultural case beyond image terms. As such, many of the groups that were struggling to get their voices heard before the Games, despite brief appearances at ceremonial and entertainment programmes, are still struggling today. Notably, the reputed Carnivale multicultural festival ceased to exist in 2004, with only one of its elements, Café Carnivale, coincidentally inaugurated during the Paralympic Games, surviving to this day.

So what kind of city is Sydney today, and what is the main cultural legacy of having hosted the Olympics? Regardless of the limited progress towards 'reconciliation' in political terms, an unquestionable cultural legacy is the dramatic growth in demands and expectations about Aboriginal arts and culture both nationally and internationally. The 1997 Olympic Arts Festival established an important precedent to ensure that all future festivals and events in Australia include Aboriginal work and that this is presented in mainstream venues with corresponding levels of funding rather than just as fringe activities.[23] Furthermore, Hinkson (2003) argued that, in terms of tourism, Sydney now has a marked 'Aboriginal' profile, which has obliged Tourism NSW to revise its generally outdated promotion of Aboriginal culture as 'traditional' and non-metropolitan and start highlighting urban Aboriginal sites and contemporary cultural expressions to satisfy visitors' demands. Beyond the Aboriginal case, the Festivals also contributed to the long-term sustainability of other cultural initiatives. One of the most successful examples is the 'Sculpture by the Sea' programme, an open air sculpture circuit connecting Bondi and Tamarama Beaches which started in 1997 with minimal funding. This became a core component of the 1998 Festival and, ten years on, is one of Sydney's most popular annual events with regular spin-offs across Australia. At another level, the Olympic cultural programme helped make the case for City of Sydney to invest in a more ambitious and relevant public art programme in the city, which now counts as the Games' most important cultural physical legacy (see Best, 2000).

Overall, the main limitation of Sydney's Olympic cultural dimensions was the emphasis on succeeding at a global rather than local level. This is a fundamental tension that remains unresolved within the Olympic hosting process and requires much more careful attention in the future. As such, while Sydney is presented as the most successful Games host to date by the IOC and Australian government, the question remains: how is success measured in the Olympic city? Should the priority be satisfying the demands of global partners or addressing the concerns of local communities? Sydney opted for the first and reaped important business benefits for local stakeholders as well. However, for the general public, the main benefit was a feeling of pride and renewed confidence in their city and nation. How these elements are taken forward will depend on the vision of current and future opinion leaders. It will be up to them to recover the original bid promises of multiculturalism and Aboriginal reconciliation and to try to embed them further in the day-to-day practices of the post-Olympic city, this time not for the sake of global spectacle but as a regular practice which is perhaps less glamorous but more meaningful and empowering to all.

Notes

1.   Interview with Tony Veal, Associate Professor, Department of Sport, Tourism and Leisure Studies, University of Technology of Sydney, 15 April 1999; see also Thompson (2000).

2.   Interview with S. Cunningham, Head of School, Media and Journalism, Queensland University of Technology, 25 August 2000.

3.   At a local level, the promoted and perceived strengths of Sydney's candidature were a compact Olympic plan guaranteeing minimal travel to the venues for athletes, the Australian climate, the country's political stability and security, the large community support, the fact that it was Australia's third consecutive bid and, overall, 'a government with a strong commitment to sport, as evidenced by the fact that around 70 per cent of the required sports facilities would be available prior to the IOC vote in 1993, regardless of winning the Games' (McGeoch and Korporaal, 1994, p. 38). None of these arguments were directly related to culture.

4.   In the case of Barcelona, this was 'Olympiada Cultural Sociedad Anonima' (OCSA), a private society separated from the Games Organizing Committee but associated with it through the shared responsibilities of board members representing key public agencies. In Athens, this was the Hellenic Culture Company, a sub-branch of the Hellenic Ministry of Culture acting independently from the Organizing Committee, and remains committed to trying to establish itself as a permanent Cultural Olympiad Foundation.

5.   Interview with L. Marinos, Director, Carnivale and member SOCOG Multicultural Advisory Committee, 13 September 1999.

6.   Interviews with K. Brown, Olympic Arts Festivals Programme Manager, SOCOG, 15 May and 6 August 1999.

7.   The Youth Camp is an optional requirement described under Rule 58 of the Olympic Charter. It is aimed at bringing together young people in the host city from each participating country. The Charter recommends that they are accommodated together during the duration of the Games in order for them to learn about the Olympic movement and the host city Culture (IOC, 2004b).

8.   Interviews with E. Louw, Senior Lecturer in Communications, University of Queensland, 25 August 2000 and G. Turner, Department of English, University of Queensland, 25 August 2000.

9.   These included, 'The Sculpture Walk', a permanent public art project featuring outdoor sculptures at Sydney Botanic Gardens and other popular city locations; 'Sunscreen Sydney 2000', an open-air film festival produced in collaboration with Tourism NSW and the corporate sector, and the 'Olympic Park Exhibition', a miniature display of Olympic venues held at Sydney's Customs House Exhibition Centre (SOCOG, 2000b).

10.   Interview with B. Powell, General Manager of Major Projects, City of Sydney, 8 October 2000.

11.   Interviews with A. Jeffrey, National General Manager, Special Events and Olympics 2000, Telstra, 2 September 1999; L. Bits, Public Relations Manager, Swatch, 2 October 2000; and F. Hammond, Olympic Sponsorship Officer, Seven Network, 2 October 2000.

12.   Interviews with J. Christey, Olympic Sponsorship Manager, *Sydney Morning Herald*, 23 August 1999; K. Lyall, Olympic Editor, *The Australian*, 28 September 1999; K. Strickland, Arts Editor, *The Australian*, 13 September and 5 October 2000.

13.   Previously, the three main dimensions of Olympism had been termed 'sport, culture and education' but with the arrival of the environment as a top priority, education has been placed under the generic umbrella of 'culture' (IOC, 2004b).

14.   Interview with C. Gouriotis, Director, Casula Powerhouse Regional Arts, 14 September 1999.

15.   Interviews with J. Díaz, NSW Multicultural Music Coordinator and Carnivale Musical Coordinator, 15 November 1999; and L. Marinos (see note 5).

16.   Interviews with B. Barnes, General Manager, State Theatre, 18 August 1999; J. Dyer, General Manager, Bangarra Dance Theatre Company, 16 September 1999; and E. Capon, Director, The Art Gallery of New South Wales, 22 February 2000.

17.   Interview with G. Coste-Paul, Olympic Media Relations, Sydney Opera House, 5 October 2000.

18.   Interview with F. Hammond, Olympic Sponsorship Officer, Seven Network, 2 October 2000.

19.   Interview with E. Capon, (see note 16) and C. Scott, Manager, Evaluation and Visitor Research, Power House Museum, 4 October 2000.

20.   National Art Gallery: *Papunya Tula,* a highly praised Aboriginal exhibit; *Australian Icons* an exhibition presenting some of the greater Australian names in painting; Powerhouse: display of items from the Opening Ceremony and other Sydney Olympic memorabilia.

21.   National Art Gallery: *The Dead Sea Scrolls* a rare and internationally renowned collection;

Powerhouse Museum: exhibition of the first-ever overseas import of Greek antiquities; Korean art works exhibit; exhibit of the *Codex Leicester* by Leonardo da Vinci.

22.   PriceWaterhouseCoopers (2002, pp. 1–2) pointed out 'some $3 billion in business outcomes', 'injection of over $6 billion in infrastructure developments' and 'over $1.2 billion worth of convention business for NSW between 1993 and 2007', 'over $6 billion in inbound tourism spending during 2001', 'greatly enhanced business profile for Sydney, NSW and Australia through the equivalent of up to $6.1 billion worth of international exposure', 'greater expertise and confidence in tendering, both domestically and overseas, on large-scale projects', 'new and improved business programs including strong collaboration with the private sector'.

23.   Indeed, many Aboriginal and Torres Strait Islanders still prefer to act independently from the mainstream and keep engaging in grassroots alternative or marginal work, but having a 'mainstream' option is generally regarded as an important step forward (interview with J. Diaz: see note 15).

Chapter 16

Athens 2004

Margaret M. Gold

In 2004 the Olympics will return to the place where they were born, where they were revived and where they will be renewed. The ATHENS 2004 Olympic Games are more than an opportunity to participate in the greatest celebration of humanity. They are an opportunity to be part of a story as old as history itself. And when it comes to making history, there is really no place like home.

ATHOC (2004, p. 31)

The relationship between Greece and the Olympic Games is like no other. The slogan 'There's no Place like Home', used in all the advertising for the 2004 Games, resonated with Greek identity, collective memory and historical experience. As home to the classical Olympics, the Games go to the very heart of Greek culture. Indeed, from the point at which Greece regained its independence in 1830, the possibility of reviving the Games, along with the drive to rebuild Athens as a worthy successor to the grand city of Antiquity, became key themes for those seeking to restore Greek values and identity. While not inseparable, there would always be a close link between staging the Olympics and the regeneration of Athens – the most likely host city whenever the Games returned to Greece.

This chapter looks at the 2004 Summer Olympic Games against this background. Its early sections briefly chart the growth of the Olympic movement in Athens alongside attempts to regenerate the city, a period that culminated in the first Olympiad of 1896 and the 1906 Intercalated Games. The subsequent sections analyse the decision to bid for the centenary 1996 Games and its failure, the successful bid made in 1997 to stage the 2004 Games, and the urban planning strategy associated with that event. Finally, there is an assessment of the urban legacy bequeathed by Athens 2004.

An Immature Metropolis

Athens at the start of the nineteenth century was far from the grand city of classical imagining, as 'filtered through European scholarship and imagination' (Waterfield, 2004, p. 29). The handful of more adventurous visitors that made their way to this corner of the Ottoman Empire were confronted by a small provincial centre with a population of around 10,000. The upper town on the Acropolis contained the Turkish garrison with barracks, housing, shops and a mosque intermingled with the remains of the Parthenon and other classical structures. A lower town on the northern and eastern slopes of the Acropolis housed the Greek, Albanian and Turkish civilian populations. The city itself fared badly in the fight for independence (1821–1830). Although Greece gained its independence after the signing of the London Protocol in February 1830, the Turkish garrison did not leave finally until 1833. By this time the population had fallen to 6,000 and the city was described by the traveller Christopher Wordsworth in 1832 as: 'lying in ruins. The streets are almost deserted: nearly all the houses are without roofs. The churches are reduced to bare walls and heaps of stones and mortar. There is but one church in which the service is performed' (cited in Bastéa, 2000, p. 10). At this time, it was not even the Greek capital, with Nauplion, a strategic Venetian fortress on the east coast of the Peloponnesus, serving that function until 1833.

Understandably, thinking soon turned to finding readily recognizable symbolic strategies through which to reassert a sense of nationhood, of which the two that most readily came to the fore were the reconstruction of Athens and the revival of the Olympics. Two German-trained architects Stamatios Kleanthes and Eduard Schaubert, for example, had visited Athens in 1830–1831 and produced a plan for a city of 35–40,000 people. It featured a baroque-inspired layout based on radial axes (meeting at present day Omonia Square) where the Royal Palace, Parliament and Senate would be placed, and a series of grids creating nodal points for other key buildings (Travlos, 1981, pp. 393–394). The opposition to the necessary demolitions to implement the plan, the lack of resources to carry it through and the immediate pressure of population influx as the functions of government were established in Athens and exiles returned, meant that the plan needed almost immediate amendment. Instead, the new Athens developed gradually rather than by radical reconstruction, with an approach that sought to respect the classical archaeology, while creating a new neo-classical townscape.

The idea for the revival of the Olympic Games developed around the same time as the initial schemes for replanning Athens, although not without fierce debate between those that believed their restoration was essential for reviving Greek culture, values and identity and those who saw the Games as a cultural irrelevance and practical impossibility. The Greek poet Panagiotos Soutsos, for instance, launched a campaign in 1835 based around a series of poems that featured figures from the past calling on present-day Greeks to reinstate the Olympic Games. As early as January 1837, a Royal Decree established a 'national gathering' with competitions in agriculture, industry and athletics, with the specified athletic events being those associated with the ancient Games – discus, javelin, long jump, foot races, wrestling, and chariot racing (Young, 1987, p. 273; 2004, p. 141). The ancient Panathenian Stadium formed a natural focus for such activity and was restored to serve as the setting for two of the three Zappas Games (1870 and 1875;

see chapter 2).[1] Various attempts were made to revive that series, notably in 1892, but they were thwarted by financial difficulties. The initiative of the Coubertin-led IOC in reviving the Olympics and choosing Athens as the site for the 1896 Games, therefore, served the interests of both Greece and the Olympic movement. Athens gained a new Olympic Games with international recognition and participation, whereas the revived Games benefited from the imprimatur of being held on Greek soil. However, the IOC's preference for an ambulatory festival and fierce resistance to giving the Games a permanent home in Greece meant that, apart from the Intercalated Games of 1906, Athens would not receive another Olympic festival until the twenty-first century.

Bidding

By 1990, when the city next formally sought the Games, Athens was a byword for problems characteristic of many Mediterranean cities (Wynn, 1984; Leontidou, 1990). A plethora of further plans commissioned from foreign architects and planners had come and gone in the face of military conflict and political and economic problems, with none adopted (Sonne, 2003, p. 146). Athens experienced rapid growth in the 1960s and 1970s, driven by industrial investment, rural-urban migration, a building boom and spontaneous development at the urban fringe – much of it illegal and unplanned. Public transport was poor and the city suffered severe environmental pollution and congestion. Although a capital city, Athens was not competitive with other major centres in Europe (Leontidou, 1990, p. 263) and was unable to offer inducements to counteract its relatively isolated position. Certainly, the idea of seeking the modern Olympic Games, with its inevitable financial burden, appeared implausible before Los Angeles 1984 established the new financial model.

Athens's first, and unsuccessful, bid campaign for the return of the Games between 1987 and 1990 should be seen against this background. The city's reasons for bidding reflected a mixture of the general and specific. Like most potential host cities, there was a broad place promotion message that sought to offset negative features (such as stereotypes about the Greek economy and culture) with positive images of a 'new face for Greece, outward looking and ready to take-up the challenges of globalization'.[2] The city looked to the mega-event to make Athens ready to compete in a world market for jobs and investment, while simultaneously enhancing Greek sporting infrastructure and helping to solve urban problems. As Vissilis Harissis, Director of the Organization for Athens, the body responsible for coordinating the Athens city plan, noted forcefully: 'Getting the Olympics is the best chance we'll ever have to save Athens. It'll be like fighting a war: there will be money and an incentive' (Hope, 1990).

Yet behind these broader objectives lay another set of ambitions that emanated from Greece's special relationship with the Olympics. The Greeks looked to the Olympics to help the nation recapture its soul; linking the ancient and modern in a meaningful and contemporary way for the twenty-first century. At the same time the Greeks wanted to reassert traditional values, especially as a reaction to the politicized and commercialized Games of the 1970s and 1980s when calls periodically surfaced that the Games might be able to regain their core values by returning to their geographical roots (Pound, 2004, p. 4). There was a strong sense that Greece wanted to 'correct the course' of the Modern Olympic Movement (ATHOC, 2005, I, p. 63). While talk of a permanent home for the Games had subsided, there seemed an incontestable logic in a Greek bid to host the Twenty-Sixth Olympiad in 1996 to celebrate the centenary of revival.

The bid achieved Parliamentary approval in April 1986, with the Bid Committee presenting Athens's candidacy to the IOC in 1988 and the final Bid File in March 1990 for the IOC meeting in Tokyo the following September. The case was put that 70 per cent of the sports facilities were already in place or would be completed for the planned Eleventh Mediterranean Games in 1991. The documentation trumpeted Athens's experience in organizing international sporting competitions, listing twelve events hosted between the European Athletics Championships of 1982 and the Men's World and European Weightlifting Championship in 1989. Three of these, it was noted, had won awards from the International Press Association for the best organized press facilities. However, its publicity tactically overlooked the twin disasters of 1982 – the IAAF Golden Marathon when police failed to close the last 5 kilometres of the course to traffic, with runners encountering rush hour traffic, or the fact that the track in the new Olympic Stadium had not been laid by the time athletes were arriving for the European Athletics Championships (Payne, 2006, p. 258).

The strategic plan sought to concentrate the sports facilities in two centres. The first, the Athens Olympic Sports Complex (AOSC), would be at Maroussi, a suburban municipality 9 kilometres north-east of central Athens. This would build on existing facilities, most notably the stadium constructed between 1980 and 1982 for the European Athletic Championships, which was always seen as providing Greece with a facility of international standing that would allow Athens to compete for international events. AOSC would feature the stadium, velodrome, swimming complex, multi-purpose sports hall, an indoor hall and tennis centre, the Press Village, Main Press Centre and International Broadcasting Centre. The second complex, on the coast south of Athens at Faliro Bay and the nearby Karaiskaki Stadium,[3] would make use of the existing Stadio Erinis end Filias (Peace and Friendship Stadium) and new facilities to accommodate basketball, wrestling, judo, boxing, handball, baseball and yachting. Existing facilities in Athens would be used for sports such as archery and shooting, while the city centre would be the focus of the cultural festivities, making use of the classical legacy such as the Panathenian Stadium and Herodeion. The centre would house IOC members, the Olympic Family and official guests, with the Olympic Village scheduled for construction on the northern fringes of the Athens Metropolitan Area on the slopes of Mount Parnitha. The Olympic Ring promised travel times of only 12 minutes between the Olympic Village and stadium and 18 minutes to Faliro Bay. Road projects, new metro lines, a new tram line, improvements to the existing Helleniki International Airport on the coast east of Faliro Bay and a new international airport at Sparta were also planned.[4]

The eventual decision to award the centenary Games to Atlanta came as a shock. Melina Mercouri, the Greek Culture Minister, protested that 'Coca Cola won over the Parthenon' and the Prime Minister, Andreas Papandreou, called it 'an injustice against Greece' committed by the international community (Senn, 1999, p. 250). Rather later, the official Report from Athens 2004 (ATHOC, 2005, I, p. 65) placed part of the blame for the bid's failure on the perception of political instability that was created by the three general elections in eight months leading up to the IOC decision – a factor noted in the IOC Evaluation Commission's report. The Athens team was also accused of taking an arrogant approach towards endorsement, but the real stumbling block was the size of the task needed to provide the required infrastructure and setting for the Games. Even the Mayor of Athens had recognized in 1987 that a radical transformation was required to deal with the city's atmospheric pollution, traffic congestion, noise, lack of parking, shortage of open space and new sports facilities, outmoded media facilities and deficiencies in the public transport network. Such was the scale of the problems that although he supported the government's plan to host the Games, he stated that 'if we are in danger of looking ridiculous, I will not go along with it, and I will stand up and tell the public the truth' (quoted in *Anon*, 1987).

Greece's wish to stage the Games quickly resurfaced after the disappointment of the award to Atlanta. In 1995, the government toyed with the idea of seeking the 2008 Games outside the customary bidding procedure by requesting 'a direct award' of the Games as 'an honour' recognizing the special status of Athens. This was pursued for a while but the impracticality of obtaining the support of two-thirds of the IOC for the necessary change in the IOC Charter led the Hellenic Olympic Committee, in December 1995, to canvass vigorously for a conventional bid for the 2004 Games. Athens's candidature was submitted on 6 January 1996, five days before the official deadline, joining a group of cities already well ahead with their preparations. These comprised Rome, regarded as the favourite, along with Buenos Aires, Cape Town, Istanbul, Lille, Rio de Janeiro, St Petersburg, San Juan (Puerto Rico), Seville and Stockholm (ATHOC, 2005, I, pp. 67–68).

Not wholly surprisingly, Athens's final bid document for the 1997 IOC decision bore similarities to the failed 1990 bid, but with a less strident tone in the presentation (AOBC, 1997). The accompanying statements from politicians and officials now stressed the profound economic changes in Greece and Athens, particularly in the context of membership of the European Union. The Mayor, Dimitris Avramopoulos, wrote about the need to:

> give renewed impetus to the Olympic Ideal and to help the Olympic Movement start afresh
> at the beginning of a new century. Athens is ready, and we Athenians – all of us – are

sensible of the responsibility that stems from the supreme and noble honour that, we hope, awaits us.

The Minister of Sport, Andreas Fouras, assured the IOC that the:

long-term programme of construction and installation of equipment which will ensure that long before 2000 – and regardless of whether Athens is awarded the Games – the city will have made good the few shortcomings it still displays in the facilities necessary for all the Olympic sports.

The Master Plan sought to concentrate the Games in a small number of locations while making use of existing sport infrastructure. Indeed, the bid claimed that 75 per cent of the competition venues and 92 per cent of the training venues were already in place. The backbone of the strategy remained to use the locations identified in the earlier bid: the Olympic Village on the slopes of Mount Parnitha; AOSC at Maroussi to host seven events (athletics, basketball, cycling, football, gymnastics, swimming and tennis); central Athens (Cultural Olympiad and accommodation for Official Visitors); and the Faliro Coastal Zone, designated as a major regeneration project for Athens's 'Riviera', which would house baseball, boxing, fencing, handball, hockey, judo, wrestling, softball, taekwondo and volleyball.

The plan envisaged four further sites within the Athens conurbation: the Nikaia indoor hall for weightlifting and the Peristeri indoor hall for badminton (both in the west); in the north the Galatsi gymnasium for table tennis; and in the east, Goudi for the modern pentathlon. Beyond the conurbation, the equestrian and archery events were located at Tatoi in the north on Mount Parnitha; rowing, canoeing and kayaking at Schinas on the coast north-east of Athens near the ancient battlefield of Marathon; shooting at Markopoulo south-east of Athens; and sailing and the triathlon along the coast at, respectively, Kosmas and Glyfada. The Olympic Ring project remained as before to link the conurbation sporting venues. Investment in roads and in metro, tramlines and suburban railways would improve movement throughout the metropolis and provide access to the other venues. A new international airport at Sparta had become a central part of the planning strategy, although for the period up to and including the Games it would work in conjunction with the existing airport at Helliniki. The latter was proposed for closure in late 2004 (AOBC, 1997). A four-year Cultural Olympiad was planned, with events taking place in Greece and abroad to 'restore the Olympic Ideal' in the opening years of the new Millennium. The estimated budget was $1.607 billion with the principal sources of income being television rights, sponsorship, licensing, official suppliers, donations, ticket sales and lotteries (*Ibid.*, p. 162). The non-OCOG budget, however, was $7.35 billion, which included expenditure on roads, airport construction and landscaping.

Planning Athens 2004

The IOC's decision in September 1997 to award the 2004 Games to Athens reflected the quality of the campaign run by the Greek bidding team led by Gianna Angelopoulos-Daskalaki. Despite assurances that the same team would lead the planning and organization of the Games, they were replaced on return to Athens (Payne, 2006, p. 259). Moreover, instead of immediate implementation of the Master Plan, the government instigated a review in early 1998 'to eliminate potential problems that might arise during the implementation phase due to the existing zoning and town planning legislation' (ATHOC, 2005, I, p. 143). These considerations, coupled with community views on site decisions and rethinking about the logistics of the festival, led to considerable and time-consuming changes to the original strategy.

The final scheme that emerged retained the AOSC complex at its heart, but the government decided to concentrate less activity in the Faliro area while retaining it as a 'pole' of the Games and maintaining the goal of urban regeneration for the area. After exploring the idea of moving some events to Aspropyrgos, west of the Athens conurbation – which proved unacceptable to both the IOC and the International Federations (*Ibid.*, p. 144) – it was decided to use the site of the much criticized Athens International Airport at Helleniki.[5] Faliro was now to stage only four rather than eleven sports (volleyball, beach volleyball, handball and taekwando), Helleniki would handle baseball, fencing, hockey, softball, basketball, some of the handball matches from Faliro and, after a court case (see below), the canoe and kayak slalom centre (*Ibid.*). Boxing and badminton were moved to, respectively, Peristeri and the Goudi complex. Two sports were moved to sites with classical connotations to assert the sense of Greek ownership of the Games: archery to the Panathenian Stadium and the shot put to Olympia. The decision on Olympia was controversial. The first suggestion was to stage the javelin or discus there because these were events that featured in the Ancient Games. This encountered opposition from the archaeologists due to potential damage to the site (see chapter 2). The shot put was finally selected as likely to create fewer problems, but the Archaeological Service insisted that no electronic equipment could be used, the throwing circle was to be portable, and that 15,000 free tickets could be issued for spectators to sit on the grass, obviating the need to build a temporary grandstand.[6]

These changes to the original strategy set back the timetable. Some locations needed planning from scratch, with the transport strategy requiring revision to take into consideration the new sites and relocated sports. The process of rethinking, with associated debates, contributed to the now infamous delays in the completion of venues and infrastructure that Payne (2006, p. 261) called the 'three lost years'. Although it was claimed that 75 per cent of the venues already existed, the renovation work envisaged for some was ambitious; for example, amounting to demolition and rebuilding of the swimming complex and tennis centre at AOSC. Additional problems arose from the presence of multiple and often conflicting agencies (Beriatos and Gospodini, 2004, p. 193), the difficulties of gaining cooperation from officials from different political parties, the bureaucratic planning system, and from archaeological discoveries made during construction that required excavation and recording before work could continue. In some instances plans had to be adjusted in order to preserve structures, such as the re-siting of the Olympic Village site to avoid archaeological remains (see below). Matters were not helped by the increased security concerns that inflated costs and caused a review of the layout of sports facilities.

The resulting delays in finalizing venues or in sites becoming available for development caused alarm at the IOC, with Samaranch warning Greece in April 2000 that they might lose the Games if action was not forthcoming. The sense of crisis was fanned by the press, although some observers (e.g. Waterfield, 2004, p. 372) felt that there was insufficient recognition of the complexities of operating in an ancient city such as Athens. The government reacted by bringing Gianna Angelopoulos-Daskalaki back to the development team (Payne, 2006, pp. 261–262), making available emergency funds and introducing new legislation and mechanisms to speed up the development process (Pyrgiotis, 2003, p. 417). This all added substantially to the cost of the Games, with 'speed bonuses' offered by government as an incentive to improve completion, coupled with threats of loss of licences to contactors that failed to complete on time.

This final plan for the Games was described by Beriatos and Gospodini (2004, p. 197) as a 'scattered model' suggestive of a strategy for promoting 'multi-nucleus urban regeneration and development' (*Ibid.*, p. 192), in contrast to cities like Barcelona which focused investment on a few key locations. The plan diluted the original logic of concentrating development in major nodes by spreading the benefits of Olympic investment geographically to include poorer neighbourhoods lacking leisure facilities. However, there was no proper strategic planning for the period after 2004, and the plan contained apparent contradictions. Despite espousing the desire to protect and create open space, development focused primarily on greenfield sites and overlooked possible brownfield locations. Emphasis was placed on gaining spectacular buildings and monuments to create a sense of place and to signify the 2004 Games, yet these structures are outside the main tourist areas.

Broadly speaking, the plan proposed three approaches to preparing the city for the Games. The first concerned the permanent structures: the sports venues, transport infrastructure, city renovation and arts infrastructure that were designed to be a physical legacy for the city. The second involved a series of temporary interventions designed to house additional sports capacity, visitor accommodation and traffic movements. These also included measures to shape the 'look' of the city in order to provide it with a festive atmosphere that clearly identified it with the Olympics. The third comprised attempts to encourage volunteering and change the behaviour of the population by tackling issues such as litter and smoking.

Olympic Facilities

AOSC was the spectacular centrepiece of the Olympics, eventually developing into a focus that went far beyond simple renovation of the complex created for the 1982 European Athletic Championships. Having decided that it wanted an 'architectural landmark of international recognition', the Ministry of Culture approached the Spanish architect Santiago Calatrava in March 2001 to submit a Master Plan. The result was a series of projects, including equipping the Olympic stadium with an innovative two leaf, laminated glass roof to protect spectators from the fierce sunlight, roofing the velodrome, bringing about the aesthetic unification of the various structures and plazas of the site by means of landscaping and an installation – the sinuous 'Wall of Nations' – that could also double as a giant video screen (Tzonis, 2005). The stadium roof in particular was a complex design and was only moved into position on the day that the IOC set as a deadline for the project to be either in place or abandoned (Payne, 2006, p. 269). Even so, shortage of time meant that only 9,000 of the projected 17,000 trees were planted around the stadium.

In the original plan, Faliro Bay was recognized as a prime candidate for regeneration. This area had developed in the 1870s as an elegant resort serving the Athenian middle class but a century later, cut off from adjacent residential districts by the coastal highway, it had declined into a virtual no man's land, degraded, polluted, and an illegal dumping ground. The nearby low-lying housing districts of Moschato and Kallithea were also subject to flooding. The Olympics provided a unique occasion for upgrading this area, again opening Athens to the sea and supplying much needed public open space. The downgrading of Faliro from the second most important Games complex to one staging just four events, none of which had any great importance within Greek sporting culture, meant there would be no legacy of specialized sports facilities here. Most construction work involved renovation of the two existing stadia – the Peace and Friendship Stadium for volleyball and the Karaiskaki for part of the football competition.

Having said this, the area did receive a moderate amount of remodelling. The racecourse at the east end of the site was moved and the land cleared. The Illissos River was canalized as part of the flood protection works, a marina was constructed in the east of the site and the area landscaped. An 800-metre-long esplanade was built from the old racetrack over the coastal highway to the new indoor sports hall and marinas. This connected the residential area with the renovated coastal zone, with walkways radiating westwards towards the beach volleyball arena. Improvements to roads and a new tram network linked the site to the centre of Athens and to the other Olympic venues. This was to be a prelude to planned post-Games projects intended to continue the anti-flooding work and move the coastal highway into a cutting allowing new bridges to the park beyond.

Of the two new buildings constructed for the Olympics, the beach volleyball centre was intended to become an open-air theatre and the indoor sports hall for handball and taekwando was to be converted into a Metropolitan Convention Centre taking advantage of its proximity to major hotels, the city centre and the coast (Romanos et al., 2005, p. 6). Landscaping the area to the west of the theatre would create a 'green zone', with an environmental centre and communal sports facilities. The old racetrack would become open space with water sports at the end of the esplanade. More tentative plans foresaw an Opera House on the racecourse site, an archaeological park to display classical structures from the regeneration project (Ibid., pp. 4–6) and a heritage park including the Military Museum in the Syngrou villa, the Naval Museum and a new contemporary art museum (Sykianaki, 2003, p. 21). In total, the Coastal Leisure Park would provide 100 hectares of accessible open space (Sykianaki and Psihogias, 2006, p. 12).

The principle of coastal revitalization was continued further south with the redevelopment of the airport site at Helleniki. This entailed conversion of hangars to create indoor halls for fencing and basketball as well as provision of facilities for softball, baseball, hockey, canoeing and kayaking (ATHOC, 2005, p. 144). Not surprisingly, conversion of this site tended to produce a sports centre with a ground plan dominated by the existing geometry of the airport. Suggestions for post-Games usage hazily envisaged the conversion of the East Airport Terminal, designed by Eero Saarinen in 1960, into a Conference and Exhibition Centre and luxury hotel, with the surrounding area touted as the largest metropolitan park in Europe. The question of how many Convention Centres Athens actually required scarcely entered the equation.

The retreat from the original concentrated approach led to a scattering of other centres throughout the region. These included sailing at Aghios Kosmas, the modern pentathlon at the Goudi Olympic Complex at the foot of Mount Ymittos, weightlifting at Nikea, and the equestrian centre at Markopoulo (a significant archaeological site). Perhaps the most difficult location was the Schinas Rowing Centre, which attracted international controversy. Originally a wetland area, this coastal site had been partly drained for agriculture in the 1920s and had been used for civil and military aviation since the 1950s. The official viewpoint was that this was a degraded wetland in need of protection and the removal of existing installations. The 2.25 kilometre rowing course would be on the line of the old runway, along with practice facilities, an adjacent 400-metre slalom course for canoes and kayaks, grandstands for 10,000 spectators with space for 40,000 more along the course, associated start and finish towers, car parks, boathouses and visitor facilities. By contrast, environmentalists saw it as a rare ecological habitat with a delicate freshwater wetland area used by 176 bird species, and with a rare stone pine forest on the coastal dunes. Archaeologists and historians saw it as the site of the battle of Marathon and an important cultural landscape. The Greek government was criticized for removing the area from a list of sites to be submitted for Natura 2000 status – the European Union's initiative to guarantee the maintenance, or reestablishment, of important habitats (Metera et al., 2005, p. 7).

When the Greek government ignored the European Commission's request for it to be reinstated, four environmental groups took the government to court.[7] Archaeological and heritage groups joined the protest, arguing that the Battle of Marathon had raged through the area and the development was akin to building a sports complex on the battlefield at Gettysburg. The government countered by saying that the area was previously under the sea and that there was no evidence of archaeological importance. The outcome did not prevent use of the site for the Olympics, but did produce concessions. The area received National Park status, the facilities were moved to the western end of the site, provision of visitor facilities were curtailed, and the slalom course was re-sited at Helleniki (see above). There was also a commitment to restore the wetlands and create an environmental zone and archaeological park.

The site of the Olympic Village was chosen partly because the government already owned half of the site, thereby reducing the need for compulsory purchase, and partly because the development, with its associated services, would 'upgrade the neglected area of the north-west section of the Greater Athens area' (AOBC, 1997, p. 26). The bid document had claimed the housing would be built to the highest environmental standards using solar energy, water management systems, planting of indigenous species and landscaping to create an ecological park. It was designed to accommodate 17,428 participants, with the maximum occupation level during the Olympics being 14,243 and 7,166 during the Paralympics (ATHOC, 2005, II, p. 49). In addition, the Village development was intended to be self-financing, with the accommodation sold after the Games to middle-income families (*Ibid.*, p. 26).

From the outset, the authorities were criticized for lack of progress, although discovery of the remains of Hadrian's aqueduct on the site caused delay for excavation and redesign to protect the archaeology. Rather more criticism came from environmentalists, initially because the development encroached into an environmentally sensitive area and later due to the failure to implement the environmental elements as originally planned. The World Wildlife Fund, for example, criticized the lack of inbuilt water-saving measures, the irrigation of plantings in the surrounding areas from tap water, the lack of photovoltaic cells or solar heating systems in the design, and the failure to use environmentally friendly materials such as certified timber or ozone friendly cooling systems (WWF, 2004, pp. 8, 9).

Infrastructure

The Olympics provided an opportunity to take a fresh and comprehensive look at transport within Greater Athens, with its attendant problems of congestion, parking, slow travel times, pollution and the unpopularity of the public transport system (comprising bus, trolley bus, metro and suburban railway networks). The metro consisted of a single line dating back to the 1860s which by 1957 ran from Piraeus to Kifissia. By this time, however, the city had long since expanded into Attica, with large swathes reliant on trams (until 1961), trolleybuses (from

1949), diesel buses and the private car. Investment in improving public transport and creating an integrated transport system for the first time, therefore, was paramount.

A proportion of the investment was scheduled before gaining the Games; for example, contracts for two new metro lines were signed in 1991. Nevertheless, early progress was extremely slow due to bureaucratic problems, geological difficulties and delays for archaeological excavations ahead of station construction. Lack of progress on Line 3, which connected with the airport, particularly concerned the IOC, with one observer commenting in 2002 that 'there are plans to extend this line all the way to the airport, but work has yet to start on this' (Dubin *et al.*, 2002). It remained incomplete at the time of the Games but, in reaching Doukaissia Plakentias by July 2004, it was possible to run services to the airport using a suburban rail line. Concerns over pollution led to replacement of the aged bus fleet, with environmentally-friendly vehicles that also offered greater accessibility for the disabled. Developments specifically for the Games included a new tram network that connected central Athens with the coastal Olympic venues – with one branch serving the Faliro Coastal Zone and the other heading south to Helleniki, Agios Kosmas and ending at Glyfada. The route was not a rapid mode of transport however, given that traffic lights, frequent stops and vehicles obstructing the lines caused it to be 'strangely sluggish' (Sales, 2005, p. 29). The road network received investment to improve connections between Athens and other major centres and to create an outer ring road interlinking the Olympic venues, the international airport and the city. AOSC gained a ring road that operated during the Games as a clockwise one-way system reserved for Olympic traffic (ATHOC, 2005, p. 173). Elsewhere, a new Traffic Management System meant that traffic flows could be managed to prioritize Olympic traffic, with appropriate signage and dedicated lanes. In the final event, the free-moving traffic was a public relations coup for a city where congestion and traffic jams were regarded as endemic.

Cultural infrastructure also benefited from the Olympics. Major Athenian museums such as the National Archaeological Museum, Byzantine Museum and the National Gallery were renovated for the Games, although in the case of the National Archaeological Museum the task was made more challenging by damage from the 1999 earthquake (it was not fully opened until 2005). The Olympics were also a vehicle for developing contemporary art. This led to the foundation of two complexes, both housed in former industrial premises: Technopolis, an arts and performance space that also houses a small Maria Callas Museum; and the Athinais, a restored silk factory that contains a theatre, cinema, music space, museum space, restaurants, bars and cafés, and conference facilities. These have acted as exemplars for further developments, most notably the National Museum of Contemporary Art, which opened in 2005 in a converted brewery and the proposed new City of Athens Art Gallery, in a converted silk factory in Metaxourgio.

Beautification

As was seen with the examples of Mexico City 1968 (chapter 12) and Atlanta 1996 (chapter 2), beautification of a city is a contentious issue, prioritizing impressing visitors over the interests of the poor, whether through redistribution of resources or displacement of previous residents. These issues arose in the case of Athens, but in the context of the longstanding desire to remake it as a city in keeping with the splendours of its august past. The return of the Games in 2004 witnessed a flurry of activity to beautify the city centre – the focus of the festivities and cultural activities that accompanied the Games, as well as the venue for the cycling road race and the finish of the marathon at the Panathenian Stadium (Sykianaki, 2003, p. 11). Perhaps the most important of the measures taken in relation to the Games was the unification of archaeological sites – a project that dated back to the 1832 plan which suggested that, when cleared and planted, the 'whole would be a museum of ancient building-art second to none in the world' (quoted in Bastéa, 2000, p. 219). The idea of a unified cultural-historic area resurfaced periodically over the next century and a half, but financial and practical problems hindered progress (Papageorgiou-Ventas, 1994, p. 28). In 1993, a formal scheme to link the key classical sites by landscaped pedestrian routes and green open spaces received European Union funding. Its rationale rested in part on romantic nationalism, partly on a wish to marry together the old and the new into a functional whole, and partly on creating a unique tourist amenity that could compete with the great European tourist cities (*Ibid.*, p. 398).

The city's planners considered it imperative to complete a major part of this project in time both to receive Olympic visitors and accommodate the road race which was planned to use the newly-pedestrianized streets around the Acropolis. By the Games, for instance, it was possible to walk from the Panathenian Stadium to the ancient cemetery at Kerameikos, via the Olympieion, the south side of the Acropolis, the Theatre of Dionysus and the ancient agora (see figure 16.1). By contrast, other projects such as the restoration of the Parthenon and the development of the new Acropolis Museum proved impossible to complete before the Games, due particularly to archaeological and conservation issues.

The programme for improving central Athens also encompassed improvements to street lighting, the refurbishment of city squares, restoration of façades, floodlighting monuments and key buildings, planting and landscaping, renewal of street furniture, repaving roads and improving pavements. Work was also carried out to upgrade the waste management systems of the city. The staging of the Paralympic Games had an important impact in improving access for the disabled, with installation of more than 7,000 wheelchair ramps (Bokoyannis, 2006, p. 6), modifications to public transport, and encouragement from ATHOC for businesses to cater for the needs of the disabled (see chapter 5).

Besides the regeneration schemes and other projects that made a permanent contribution to the quality of life of residents and visitors, there were also the

Figure16.1. Pedestrianized street beneath the Acropolis; part of the project unifying the archaeological sites (June 2009).

temporary measures that announced that the city was *en fête*. The notion of giving the city a distinctive 'look' during the Olympic festival, a recurrent theme since Tokyo 1964 (see chapter 2), was again observed at Athens. Like its predecessors, this involved the careful selection of colours, logos, decorations and artwork, with the creation of a Kit of Parts that could be applied city-wide and arranged so that athletes, visitors and television audiences could see the legend 'ATHENS 2004' and the Olympic Rings at all venues and along significant routes. This creation of 'visual identity' (ATHOC, 2005, I, p. 331) involved specification of a twenty-colour palette, centring on blue (sky and sea), yellow and oranges (summertime), red and fuchsia (flowers), green (landscape) and grey (stone) (*Ibid.*, p. 319). Construction sites and ugly buildings disappeared behind large building wraps, with images of ancient Olympia and photographs by Greek artists. Conscious of the over-commercialism of Atlanta – about which the Greeks had made considerable reference when bidding for the Games – attempts were made to control advertising displays throughout the city. By the summer of 2004, 5,000 billboards had been removed and official sites given over to sponsors and used for messages promoting the Olympic ideal. In the process, the Organizing Committee effectively enhanced the value of the investment made by sponsors in offering them 'a whole new level of protection against ambush marketing', comprising 'the most tightly controlled' marketplace to date (Payne, 2006, pp. 262–263, 266).

Legacy

Ensuring that Olympic sports facilities have viable alternative uses is a challenge with which many cities have struggled once the Games are over and Athens certainly made much of the idea that it was creating permanent facilities that would have post-Olympic use (Kissoudi, 2008). Over the seven-year preparation period, official statements constantly speculated on the post-Games legacy, with the city clearly looking for a multifaceted outcome (ATHOC, 2005, II, p. 525). Leisure, cultural, sporting and conference uses were typically mentioned, but unless there is state involvement (as in the case of a government ministry using premises for offices) or end-users are directly identified and involved in construction (e.g. the Press Villages were funded by the universities for halls of residence), it is not so easy to dictate use.

In terms of immediate effect, there was the reality of a city which, with little margin for error, completed the facilities in time for the Games despite the scepticism of journalists who, only weeks earlier, described the rubble on building sites and listed the work still outstanding. There was spectacular television footage of the Opening Ceremony and the striking backdrop of the city. All this confirmed that the 'smoggy Aegean backwater' had indeed been 'transformed' (the most common adjective used) into a city of beautiful boulevards, clear and azure skies, a growing number of art centres, a vibrant and cutting edge spirit and the finest metro in Europe (Correspondent, 2004). Sadly for the organizers, the drug scandal involving Greek athletes on the eve of the Opening Ceremony was a public relations disaster both in the context of Athens promising a return to the core values of the Olympics and in diverting attention away from the city.[8] By the end of the Games however, attention had re-focused on the Games, with consensus being that the Games had been run well, with praise for the scheduling, transport and the athletes' facilities.

The longer term impact of the Games remains contentious. The Official Report (ATHOC, 2005, II, p. 525) outlines their legacy in terms of transport improvements, reduced pollution, land reclamation, sports facilities, beautification of the city, a culture of cooperation, civic spirit and job training, concluding:

> The Games were a 17-day advertisement for our competence and sophistication, potential investors discovered that Greece has the talent, attitude and infrastructure – and the EU membership – to compete internationally. Finally we Greeks proved to ourselves that we can do whatever we set ourselves to doing, under extraordinary pressure, with a global audience. After the Olympic Games, we know we can compete with anybody.

The Director for the Organization for the Planning and Environmental Protection of Athens, Catherine Sykianaki and her colleague Sakis Psihogias (2006, p. 11) maintained that the physical legacy of the Games in terms of 'renewal and regeneration' represented a 'catching up process after some decades of inertia had eroded the competitiveness and quality of life of Athens'. The city now had an infrastructure conducive to economic growth. IOC marketing specialist Michael Payne (2006, p. 271) believed that the Games helped 're-brand Greece as a country' and that they had successfully managed to combine the mythological and traditional images with modern, dynamic designs. The Athens communication team even talked of 'just in time delivery' as if 'it was something that had been planned all the time so that the country could showcase its efficiency and ingenuity at the last minute' (*Ibid.*, p. 269) to counteract the press view that it was in fact a 'last minute approach' (Smith, 2003). However, notwithstanding such promotional gloss, there is no doubt that corners were cut, plans cancelled and tasks left incomplete – issues which impacted on post-Games planning.

Popular tourist literature applauds the changes made in connection with the Games that transformed Athens into a more attractive tourist destination:

> Major urban renewal has breathed new life into Athens' historic centre, spectacularly reconciling its ancient and modern faces with charming car-free streets that wind along well-trodden ancient paths, making it feel like you're walking through a giant archaeological park…The city's radical pre-Olympics makeover went well beyond new infrastructure. There's a newfound confidence and creative energy, particularly in emerging arts, dining and entertainment hotspots in newly hip, urban neighbourhoods. (Kyriakopoulos 2009, p. 7)

By contrast, and despite the frequency with which images of the iconic Olympic complex are reproduced as symbols of the new Athens, their peripheral locations are far removed from the normal tourist circuit and, although easily reached by public transport, do not yet provide the animated public spaces that many assumed they would become.

The Games were praised for placing disability on the agenda, although some warn that the city lags behind other capitals and more needs to be done.[9] Vozikis (2009, p. 496), for example, notes that greater vigilance is required if the gains made in creating a more accessible physical environment for those with mobility problems are to remain effective. She notes that too often lifts remain out of order, disabled toilets are used for storage and illegal parking is tolerated in disabled spaces.

Environmentalists, as mentioned previously, were particularly critical that the rules laid down in the tender for the Olympic Village were largely ignored when reducing construction costs became the priority. In more measured tones, commentators from the United Nations Environment Programme noted that while there had been undoubted achievements in the areas of transport, coastal rehabilitation and improvements in public awareness of environmental issues, in the matter of energy consumption and the building of eco-friendly facilities standards had fallen 'below expectations'. They regretted that there had not been more consultation at the preparation stages with 'key stakeholders, particularly environmental NGOs'.[10] For its part, the environmental assessment of the Games by the World Wildlife Fund (WWF) in July 2004 evaluated eighteen environmental performance indicators with a score from 0 (very disappointing) to 4 (very positive). As table 16.1 shows, Athens's average was just 0.77, scoring zero on no less than eleven of the criteria, including protection of natural habitats, protection of open spaces, siting of Olympic venues, use of green technologies, green energy, water saving, integrated waste management and recycling, and respect for environmental legislation. The highest scores were for public awareness (4), improvement of the built environment (3) and public transport (3). The WWF's assessment was that there had been no effort to integrate the environment into the planning of the Games and that opportunities were missed to improve environmental management in areas where Athens is vulnerable, such as water supply, energy provision and waste disposal. Indeed, nothing was done to promote renewable energy or water conservation or to tackle waste management other than to purchase a new fleet of dust carts.

Finding worthwhile uses for Games facilities once the Games are over is another canon of sustainable Olympic development. This question is the one that has come to bedevil the final reputation of the Games with press coverage that has been relentlessly negative. The summer of 2008 saw a further spate of articles as the Beijing Games loomed, looking back to Athens as an example of how not to plan an Olympics and suggesting that future hosts and bidding cities should take note. Picking just three headlines gives the flavour of the coverage: from the *Daily Telegraph* came 'Athens' deserted Games sites a warning to London Olympics' (Moore, 2008); the *Daily Mail* offered 'Abandoned, derelict, covered in graffiti and rubbish: what is left of Athens' £9billion Olympic "glory"' (Malone, 2008); and the *Chicago Tribune* reported 'Testament to progress atrophies after Games – Athens Olympic venues suffer from lack of long-range planning. Chicago should take note' (Hersh, 2008). Accompanied by photographs of dirty, graffiti-covered, seemingly abandoned facilities in a sea of derelict open space, locked away behind high fences or, in the case of the coastal facilities at Faliro, surrounded by gypsy encampments, it was suggested that resources had been seriously wasted with the *Daily Mail* claiming that only one of twenty-two facilities had found a use (*Ibid.*).[11]

Legacy had already become a political issue in Greece, with the two major national political parties accusing each other as to which bore more blame for the lack of post-Games strategy. The New Democracy Party, in power since March 2004, claimed that PASOK, their Socialist predecessors, had no proper business plans for the Olympic sites. PASOK countered that facilities were being allowed to deteriorate.[12] The New Democracy government established a state-owned holding company, Hellenic Olympic Properties (HOP), to which it transferred twenty-two venues. These included all the Athens sports facilities, the Media Press Centre and the International Broadcasting Centre but not the AOSC complex, the Olympic Village or Press Villages. AOSC is to remain an international sports complex and the Villages had post-Games plans in place. HOP's brief was to

Table 16.1. Olympic Environmental Assessment, Athens 2004.

Issue	Score	Highlighted Examples
Overall Planning		
Environmental planning	0	Principles of the Environmental Policy of ATHOC published 2001 – more a communications tool than an environmental strategy
Environmental assessment	0	Absence of concrete and measurable environmental commitments
Natural Environment		
Protection of natural habitats	0	Schinas Rowing and canoeing centre Fragile environmental areas trapped by the expansion of the urban web
Urban Environment		
Protection of open spaces	0	Use of open space for venues: Galatsi,Maroussi Press facilities, Olympic Village; failure to complete the ecological park at Faliro
Increase of urban green	0	Failure to plant Mediterranean species; planting out of season and requiring irrigation
Improvement of the built environment	3	Façades, removal of billboards, pedestrian network, unification of archaeological sites, street cleaning
Transport		
Public transport	3	Metro, gas powered buses, urban rail and tram network, public awareness campaign to reduce car usage. No cycle facilities
Constructions		
Siting of Olympic venues	0	Lack of public consultation over sites
Use of existing infrastructure	1	Olympic Stadium and Peace and Friendship Stadium used
Use of green technologies	0	Failed to include environmental obligations in the contracts for the Olympic Village: use of solar power, water saving systems, ozone-friendly cooling systems, certified timber. Debris abandoned at constructions sites
Energy		
Green energy	0	Solar and wind energy options not considered for the Olympic sites
Water		
Water saving scheme	0	Tap water used for irrigation of Olympic Village site; 16 km pipeline supplies tap water to Schinais competition reservoirs in dry periods
Waste		
Integrated waste management and recycling	0	No integrated waste management strategy. Recycling bins provided at Olympic venues
Public Participation		
Social consultation	1	No stakeholder consultation. Opposition to the sites for Schinas Rowing Centre, Galatsi, Olympic Village, Press Centre
Transparency	1	Poor information; NGOs with an international base had more success in obtaining information than other groups
Public information	1	Website used as a promotional rather than an information tool. Central role therefore played by the press in highlighting issues
General Issues		
Respect for environmental legislation	0	Existing legislation bypassed, for example in the case of the Press Village Maroussi
Public awareness	4	Good environmental education and awareness to reduce car usage and water consumption
Total Score	0.77	

(4 = very positive; 3 = positive; 2 = fair; 1 = disappointing; 0 = very disappointing)
Source: Compiled from World Wildlife Fund Greece (2004) *Environmental Assessment of the Athens 2004 Olympic Games*, July 2004.

achieve 'sustainable commercial development' in areas of activity compatible with government strategy, with a general framework of permitted uses laid down in legislation passed in 2005–2006 (HOP, 2006). HOP was to manage the remaining sites until lease-holders could be found in the form of foreign or domestic investors or public-private partnerships, thus helping to recoup building costs, avoid the costs of maintaining the venues (estimated at $100 million per annum) and benefit local communities in terms of cultural amenity and jobs.

Understandably, HOP faces the problem that the locations of the venues reflected political, landownership and pragmatic considerations rather than planning for post-Games commercial use. A stated aim for the free-standing venues was to improve the infrastructure of the unplanned suburbs, but the municipalities could not afford to maintain them (MSNBC, 2004). The Faliro and Helleniki complexes were meant to generate critical mass since they contain a number of attractions but it is estimated, for example, that the cost of running Faliro is €5–7 million as against an income from the Marina and Indoor Hall of €2–4 million (Romanos et al., 2005, p. 6).

Therefore, progress towards realizing a new life for the venues has been patchy (see Kissoudi, 2008). Tenders were invited for the Badminton Hall at Goudi, the International Broadcasting Centre, the canoe-kayak slalom course at Helleniki, the sailing centre at Agio Kosmas, and the Galatsi Olympic Indoor Hall in 2005. In March 2006, further tenders were invited for the beach volleyball centre at Faliro. At the time of writing, only two of these projects are operational. In May 2006, a consortium signed a 25-year lease on the Badminton Hall for €12.5 million.[13] The Badminton Theatre opened in 2007 as a 2,500-seater auditorium – the largest in Greece – and capable of staging large-scale productions of opera, ballet, theatre and popular concerts from 'Evita' to Matthew Bourne's 'Swan Lake'.

At the International Broadcasting Centre (IBC) site, the Golden Hall, a luxury shopping mall, opened in November 2008. With 131 shops and 1,400 parking spaces, it was expected to attract between 7 and 9 million visits in its first full year of operation (Michaelidou, 2009, p. 58). Two museums are also planned for the remaining part of the IBC building which abuts the Olympic Stadium. One is a national project, the Museum of the Greek Olympic Games, and the other an International Museum of Athletics and an associated Hall of Fame. An agreement relating to the latter was signed with the International Association of Athletics Federations in 2005 (IAAF, 2005). Neither museum has yet materialized.

The table tennis and rhythmic gymnastics venue at Galatsi was to have been the second Olympic site to host a shopping mall. This demand from the retail sector reflects the fact that Greece reportedly had the lowest ratio of shopping centre space per 1,000 inhabitants in the EU in 2007 at 50 m^2 per 1000 inhabitants compared to the EU average of 150, with Athens not getting its first mall until 2005 (Bouras, 2007). The Galatsi project, unveiled in 2006 was to provide 35,000 m^2 of retail space while retaining the table tennis and rhythmic gymnastics venue for sport. It was originally due for completion in 2008, but was rescheduled for

2009. Subsequent delays in obtaining permits meant the project was then hit by the economic downturn and construction still had not begun by March 2010 (Boston, 2010).

Three further projects have stalled. The canoe-kayak slalom centre is still intended to become a water park, but has not been completed. The Aghios Kosmas Sailing Centre similarly awaits licences for work to be undertaken. The Beach Volleyball on the coast at Faliro has still to receive the relevant permits, despite original assurances that it would open in 2008. A private-public partnership was approved for the work required to adapt the Faliro Pavilion for use as an International Conference Centre and for facility management and maintenance for a 25-year period, but to date nothing has materialized save for hosting the occasional trade fair or concert. It was announced in March 2010 that it had been decided to renegotiate the agreement over the Taekwondo Arena (Correspondent, 2010).

Against this, it should be noted that plans for the site next to the Taekwondo Stadium are moving on apace (see figure 16.2). The Stavros Niarchios Foundation Cultural Centre is planned on the site of the old Athens racecourse, cleared for parking during the Olympics. This development takes advantage of the public works along on the coast, particularly the promenade across the motorway which links the site with the coast and adjacent Olympic venues. The project will

Figure 16.2. Pedestrian promenade over the coastal motorway built for Athens 2004, linking the Taekwando Arena with the site for the Stavros Niarchios Foundation Centre, which will house the National Library and National Opera in a landscaped park (June 2009).

provide new homes for two national institutions – the National Library of Greece, and Greek National Opera surrounded by 42 acres (17 hectares) of landscaped parkland. The $630 million project is being funded by the Foundation, with construction starting in 2010 with a view to completion in 2015 (SNF, 2009).[14] On completion, it will be transferred to the state with the hope of creating a coastal cultural quarter capable of serving the local community, other Athenians, Greek nationals and tourists.

Most of the other sites in the HOP portfolio have acquired public uses. Three have been handed over to Sports Federations: the Faliro Marina to the National Sailing Federation to become a National Sailing Centre; the Markopolou Equestrian Centre to the Hellenic Equestrian Federation; and Schinias Rowing Centre to the Greek Rowing Association for a national and international rowing centre, which in 2008 hosted the European Rowing Championships. The Main Press Centre is to house the Ministry of Health and Social Solidarity; the Markopolou Shooting Centre has become a police shooting academy and headquarters of Police Special Forces; the Nikea weightlifting arena has been given to the University of Piraeus as its second campus; and the Ano Liosia arena used in the wrestling and judo is to be an arts academy.

The old International Airport site has proved a challenge with its concentration of arenas for sports not popular in Greece. The baseball ground has been leased to Ethnikos Football SA, and occasional trade shows have been held in the old fencing hall. The old arrivals, departure and charter buildings have become the Hellenikon Exhibition Centre, but the envisaged Hellenikon Metropolitan Park has not materialized. Nevertheless, it was announced in March 2010 that the site should be opened up to the public by the following summer (Correspondent, 2010).

AOSC raises a familiar problem for Olympic cities, namely, the future of a very large stadium that is scarcely used on any regular basis. The aim is to retain the facilities for sporting use. As elsewhere, there has been usage for football, with the ground now shared by Panathinaikos and AEK Athens, but stadia essentially built for athletics rarely provide ideal conditions for football. Panathinaikos has the long-term aim of developing its own stadium complex, a plan backed by the Athens Municipality which sees this development as spearheading the regeneration of the Votanikos/Alexandros Avenue area to provide open space, cultural, sporting and commercial facilities in a part of Athens lacking good infrastructure (Bokoyannis, 2006, p. 18). AEK Athens, which moved to the Olympic stadium in 2003 when their Nikos Goumas Stadium was demolished, has average gates of only 27,500. The stadium is used for rock concerts (about 15 to 20 a year), but between fixtures the site is bleak (figure 16.3). It is a large site that absorbs the trickle of visitors that come to see the iconic architecture. There are no visitor facilities or stadium tours, but reports of the site being locked are untrue.

Aside from the Olympic venues, the Games were also seen as a means of achieving place promotion goals and the 'soft legacy' of support services, training,

Figure 16.3. The Athens Olympic Sports complex, Maroussi, Athens (June 2009).

employment, attitudinal changes, and organizational knowledge that comes from the successful planning and management of a hallmark event (METREX, 2006, p. 6). In the case of Athens, this included the 'positive climate of opinion within which continued progress could be made' (*Ibid.*, p. 7). Greek politicians quickly latched on to these ideas. Prime Minister Costas Karamanlis, for example, stated at the start of the Games that 'Greece will be a more experienced, a more optimistic and self-confident country' (Beard, 2004). In attempting to learn what such assertions meant in practice, Sykianaki and Psihogias (2006, p. 13) identified four important areas in which Athens 2004 created new working practices that might profoundly affect the city's future development. The first was in pioneering private-public partnerships as a new way of generating development funds. The government introduced legislation in 2005 to provide a framework for such partnerships, then new to Greek practice. This was seen as central to economic policy, something that would support entrepreneurship and make the Greek economy internationally oriented and competitive.[15] Secondly, it was argued that the Games had highlighted the problems of bureaucracy and encouraged a more flexible approach to problem solving. Thirdly, the Games were seen as a vehicle that showed how the city could use major events to lever investment, modernize the built environment and expand Athens's international role. Finally, the Olympics were felt to have mobilized citizens in the affairs of the city.

Conclusion

Calculating the costs and benefits of an Olympic Games is a daunting task given the powerful indirect as well as direct effects of staging the Games for the domestic economy and society. They also depend on political viewpoint. Radical critics on the Left argued that, quite apart from the impact on civil liberties, the long-term consequences of staging the Games included reinforcement of trends towards the militarization of urban space, environmental damage and destruction of heritage. Each could have costs for society beyond those that can be imputed in economic terms. Moreover, assessments of costs also depend on the accounting procedures adopted, particularly judgments as to whether or not investment was purely related to the Games or would have happened anyway (e.g. transport improvements and urban beautification). At the end of 2004, for example, the Economy and Finance Minister George Alogoskoufis assessed the cost of the Games as €8.954 million but consciously omitted costs of the airport and metro, even though their development was expedited for the Games, and the continuing costs of maintaining venues until occupiers can be found.[16]

When looked at in narrow economic terms, ATHOC balanced its books and is eventually expected to declare a profit thanks to a larger-than-expected contribution from IOC broadcast and sponsorship revenues. Games spending helped the sluggish Greek economy to record a 4 per cent annual increase (Payne, 2006, p. 271), but most of the revenue benefited the Athens region. Regional politicians argue that Athens sucked in investment at the expense of other regions, reinforcing the city's primacy and undoing 'past tendencies for decentralisation' (Coccossis et al., 2003, p. 3). There is, however, consensus that the Games were expensive and over-budget, with infrastructural projects costing 37 per cent more than in the original plan. Greece was the smallest nation to host the Games since Finland in 1952, and there is no doubt that the scale of expenditure expected by the start of the twenty-first century was a strain for a small economy. In Greece's case European Union membership and access to its funds were of central importance – in particular the Cohesion Fund (for which Greece was one of the major beneficiaries) and the access to loans from the European Investment Bank. European ties, however, also impose costs. The conditions attached to membership of the European Economic and Monetary Union (EEMU) meant that steps were needed to lower Greece's deficit, which, at 6.1 per cent of Gross Domestic Product in 2004, was more than double the limit set by the terms of the EEMU. This resulted in Greece needing to increase taxes, cut public spending and impose wage restraint measures to realign its economy.[17]

The economic crisis that engulfed Greece by 2008 has further added to the cost of the Games by making the legacy goals of the government more difficult to attain. Yet notwithstanding the cost calculations, Athens 2004 is popularly remembered within Greece as a success that confounded journalist critics and came as a relief to those with any measure of responsibility for staging the Games. After the negative publicity surrounding the delays and descriptions of building sites that were relayed to television viewers and newspaper readers in the weeks leading up to the Olympics, the hurried completion of the sites (even if the landscaping and planting were incomplete), the new public transport and the spectacular Opening Ceremony created the aura of success. The city gained a tangible legacy of infrastructure that can provide the basis for the hoped for cultural, convention and business tourism trade. The centre of Athens is pedestrian friendly and guidebooks wax lyrical on the transformation of the city, although few short break visitors will see the Olympic venues themselves. The cultural sector has benefited from new performance spaces, exhibition spaces and renovated museums. The Games undoubtedly accelerated urban renewal and brought investment in transport and telecommunications. In turn, as Sykianaki and Psihogias (2006, p. 11) argued, these developments produced a more 'conducive environment for economic growth', which would be consolidated in a new Structural Plan for the Athens Metropolitan Area. Whatever costs have been incurred, it is scarcely plausible that the range of changes experienced would have occurred without being driven by the approach of an Olympic Opening Ceremony. Certainly most Greek politicians would have settled for this outcome if they had been offered it before the event.

Notes

1.   The first Zappas Games of 1859 were held in Loudovikou Square (Plateia Eleftheris).

2.   Yannis Pyrgiotis, Executive Director of the Organizing Committee for the Olympic Games (Pyrgiotis, 2003, p. 414).

3.   It was built on the site of the velodrome constructed for the 1896 Games.

4.   Information from a poster entitled 'Athens 96: Return to the Future', produced by the Executive Committee for the Candidacy of Athens for the 1996 Olympic Games.

5.   In the bid document this airport was to be replaced by the new Elefthenos Venizelos International Airport near Sparta, and Helliniki was to continue in operation until the Games were over. Under the new plan it was closed in 2001.

6.   Even so the site manager Xenia Arapogianni was quoted as saying 'We still have misgivings about the sanctuary being used in this way. Ancient Olympia isn't a film or television set', but the local mayor hoped that the television coverage would spur tourist development (Special Correspondent, 2004). Olympia also benefited from renovation and three new museums.

7.   These were the World Wildlife Fund Hellas; Greek Society for the Protection of the Environment and Cultural Heritage; Hellenic Society for the Protection of Nature; and the Hellenic Ornithological Society.

8.   Two of Greece's athletic stars, Kostas Kenteris and Ekaterini Thanou, failed to report for a drugs test on the eve of the Opening Ceremony and ended up in an Athens hospital under somewhat confused circumstances.

9.   Information compiled from Dubin et al. (2004), Facaros and Theodorou (2005) and Sales (2005).

10.   UNEP Press Release 2004/37, August, http://www.unep.org, accessed 26 September 2006.

11.   Alexandridis (2007, p. 13), in his study of the housing impact of the 2004 Games, estimates that 2,700 Roma were affected by the Games either through evictions or the abandonment of relocation projects.

12.   Hellenic Republic Embassy of Greece, press releases, 12 October and 13 November 2004.

13.   Three companies were involved: Adam Productions (event organizers); Half Note Jazz Club (club owners and event organizers); and Allou Fun Park (Greece's largest Amusement park). Information from Hellenic Republic Embassy of Greece, press release, 16 May 2006.

14. The site plan, unveiled in October 2009, is by the Italian architect Renzo Piano.

15. Information from Ministry of Economics, press release, 4 August 2006.

16. Information from Hellenic Republic Embassy of Greece, press release, 14 November 2004.

17. The aim was to get it down to 3 per cent by the end of 2006 (Church, 2005).

Chapter 17

Beijing 2008

Ian G. Cook and *Steven Miles*

It would be difficult not to be impressed with the scale and majesty of the Beijing Olympics in 2008. From the spectacular Opening Ceremony to the almost as impressive Closing Ceremony, the Games were run effectively and efficiently. There were some hitches and glitches, but as a modern mega-event the Beijing Olympics will prove to be difficult for London to live up to, not least because of the global economic recession that commenced in late 2008. As Sebastian Coe, Chair of the London Organising Committee of the Olympic and Paralympic Games (LOCOG), stated to the delight of Xinhua, the Chinese State-Run News Agency, in July 2009 at an African Olympic meeting in Abuja, Nigeria:

> Beijing was fantastic, the venues were superb, the planning was superb, the athletes were well looked after, and they performed well because they were well looked after.[1]

Although Coe suggested that he was excited rather than 'challenged' by the success of Beijing, this was exactly what the Chinese authorities wanted to hear. After all the concerns expressed beforehand concerning human rights, social costs, atmospheric pollution and other issues, the People's Republic of China (PRC) had achieved their objectives to impress as respected an Olympian as Lord Coe and to develop a model for future Olympics. As social scientists, however, it behoves the authors to take a more critical perspective, to note the successes that did occur, but also the problems that arose, and to consider both the pluses and minuses of Beijing's legacy and the longer term implications of the Olympics for the reinvention of China as a participant in the global economy.

Beijing itself is a city that has undergone significant transformation in recent decades, and anyone who has travelled there since the early 1990s will have witnessed enormous changes, with the city rapidly metamorphosing into an 'internationalized metropolis' (Cook, 2006). This period has seen Beijing make not one, but two, bids to host the Summer Olympics. The first bid was submitted in 1992–1993 and was eventually rejected, with Sydney winning the race to host the 2000 Olympics. 'Human rights' were cited as a major reason for the rejection of this bid, unsurprising given that Tiananmen was fresh in the memory, with the tanks being sent in to clear the square on 4 June 1989. Environmental issues, however, were also a major factor. Beijing had hosted the Asian Games by that date, and so the city had already spent a considerable sum on stadia, a Games Village, and on transport infrastructure. Foreign observers noted how most schoolchildren in Beijing in 1992 seemed to sport the bright yellow baseball cap bearing the Asian Games logo. There was an air of expectancy that China would be awarded the 2000 Summer Olympic Games. The disappointment at rejection was palpable.

In contrast, the announcement in June 2001 that Beijing would host the Olympics in 2008 was greeted by mass rejoicing. Even Shanghai, often cast as a rival of Beijing, witnessed warm celebrations when the result was announced, not least because Shanghai was due to co-host the soccer tournament (figure 17.1). The announcement provided a sense of vindication of China's improved standing in the world. When the PRC was founded on 1 October 1949, Mao Zedong said in his address to the new nation that China had stood up and would never be humiliated again. After many years of effort, of marked successes and notable failures, the opportunity to host the 2008 Olympics was proof that China had not only stood up, but also that it was no longer a pariah state and ready to take its rightful place as one of the leading countries on earth. To analyse the Beijing Olympics, therefore, is not only to analyse the specific urban dimension of this Olympic City, but also to contextualize Beijing's successful bid within the rise of the New China, a China that is proud of its past and increasingly proud of its present.

This wider contextualization highlights negatives as well as positives concerning the Beijing Olympics. This chapter, therefore, first examines China's uneven

Figure 17.1. Shanghai joins in the celebrations: Sofitel Hotel, central Shanghai, after the announcement of the successful bid.

transformation, before considering Beijing's development path. The ensuing sections consider the bidding process, the relationship between the Olympics and urban regeneration and the controversies that beset the pre-Olympic period, including the environment, resettlement, human rights, corruption, and obesity. The Games themselves are then examined in terms of their impact and how they were organized, before the legacy is considered in terms of international prestige, environmental impact within Beijing, the social and cultural dimension within the city and beyond, and how the massive Olympic site is to be funded in future.

China's Uneven Transformation

The dramatic changes in China that took place in the second half of the twentieth century are well known (Cannon, 2000; Cook and Murray, 2001). The establishment of the PRC as a communist state led by the Chinese Communist Party (CCP) yielded three alternative models of development: first the Soviet model in which centralization and heavy industry were key features; then the Maoist model in which the decentralized commune was a major element; and finally the Dengist model of market socialism, or 'socialism with Chinese characteristics'. The Dengist model took China, probably irrevocably, down the capitalist road – albeit under strong direction from the Chinese state. It was based on an Open Door for foreign direct investment (FDI), with the objective of modernizing China's agriculture, industry, defence, science and technology. Under the market reforms unleashed by Deng and his successors, China's 'Gold Coast' has been opened up to global connections and China is now in rapid transition from being a closed, poverty-stricken rural society towards being open, wealthy and, for many, urban. In brief, the Chinese state sets the preconditions for investment to enter, the local state (at province, city or town level) provides the infrastructure, and foreign companies provide the necessary investment through which China's resources of land and labour can be fully exploited. The scale and pace of change are phenomenal, especially in China's emerging cities, where the processes of globalization and urbanization interlock so dramatically (Wu, 2006, 2007). The emergence of China as an economic superpower has been built on the apparently limitless potential of cheap labour and an aspirational population that in the aftermath of Tiananmen were happy to accept a social contract in which they were given the freedoms associated with a consumer society in exchange for the maintenance of the political and human rights *status quo*.

China has twenty-nine Provinces, plus four cities run directly via central government (Beijing, Shanghai, Tianjin and Chongqing). Initially, most FDI flowed via Hong Kong into the neighbouring Guangdong Province. In 1997, Guangdong experienced $12.6 billion of actually utilized FDI. Although the annual total dropped slightly in 1998–1999 due to the combined effects of the Asian financial crisis plus a degree of investment saturation in the Pearl River delta, by 2003 FDI in Guangdong was still high at $7.8 billion (National Bureau of Statistics, 1999, 2006). Shanghai and neighbouring provinces in the 'arrowhead' of the Yangtze River delta are fast developing as an alternative attraction for FDI, with the corresponding figures for actually utilized FDI in Shanghai in 1997 and 2003 being \$4.2 billion and \$5.5 billion respectively. As for Beijing itself, the corresponding data show that by 1997 \$1.6 billion FDI was utilized, rising to \$2.2 billion in 2003. Part of the 'China miracle', this type of investment is ploughed into export-oriented manufacturing, the property market, the retail sector and other activities, fuelling the dramatic transformation noted above. Multinational and transnational companies such as Volkswagen, Renault, McDonalds, KFC, Motorola, Nokia, Microsoft, BP, B & Q and many more are engaged in this continuing struggle to enter the lucrative China market.

This investment, however, is spatially uneven. It is clear that the cycle of circular and cumulative causation, to use the old terminology associated with Gunnar Myrdal (e.g. 1968), is very much oriented towards the coast. Chai (1996, p. 57), for instance, in his analysis of East–West income differentials from 1978 to 1991, found that regional income disparity had increased significantly. The trend of concentration of investment resources along the eastern seaboard was reinforced by the export-led growth and FDI policies adopted during this period. The eastern seaboard had ports facilitating the import of raw materials and export of manufacturing. Consequently, most of the export processing facilities tended to concentrate in the coastal areas. Furthermore its proximity to potential foreign investors as well as the special investment incentives created by the central government had attracted most of China's foreign investments into these areas.

Many other studies have similarly indicated the deeply embedded nature of these spatial contrasts (see Cook and Murray, 2001). They are also found with regards to urban–rural differentials and can also vary, as would be expected, at the local scale within provinces, perhaps reflecting upland–lowland contrasts. The new Chinese leadership under Hu Jintao seems particularly concerned to tackle such disparities, emphasizing the importance of investment in the western provinces, and of tackling rural deprivation. The huge stimulus package of 4 trillion yuan (\$586) announced early in 2009 has a significant rural dimension, designed not only to support rural growth *in situ*, but also to slow down the exodus to China's cities and thus reduce spatial imbalances. However, whether the government can effectively redress these imbalances in the light of the massive attraction of development in the eastern seaboard remains to be seen. Investment in the Beijing Olympics, of course, adds still further to this attraction, and thus to the imbalance of development at the national scale.

Beijing's Development Path

Despite a long and distinguished history, under Communism Beijing became an austere, drab producer city, full of steel mills and petrochemical works (Cook, 2006). It was heavily influenced by the Soviet style of planning with wide thoroughfares, mid-rise flats on a large scale, occasional grand buildings, and the expansion of Tiananmen Square to become the new heart of the city. The population of 1.2 million in 1949 within the old boundaries by the early 1980s was probably 4.14 million within its expanded boundaries, including 1.76 million specifically classified as 'urban' (Dong, 1985). In the western outskirts, the Shihjingshan Iron and Steel Works (also known as Shougang, or the Capital Iron and Steel Works) became one of China's largest. The city was worthy but dull, and by the 1970s an increasing proportion of its population were beginning to complain of the endless diet of revolutionary dramas and operas. The average family would aspire to own a radio, watch and bicycle and there was little in the way of luxury available to the mass of the population. As for externalities, Zhou (1992, p. 30) observed that:

> over a rather long period, Beijing put undue emphasis on heavy industry at the expense of light industry, which was underdeveloped. The excessive heavy industry created a shortage of water, electricity and transport capacity, and worsened environmental pollution. Little attention was paid to housing and public facilities... The urban population expanded while the commercial service network decreased.

Today, Beijing is worlds apart from this brief sketch. The reform period has ushered in a period of massive urban change, with new hotels, banks, high-rise residences, ring roads, new subway lines, the largest shopping mall in Asia (Oriental Plaza) and the whole paraphernalia of a city that is seeking to internationalize (Cook, 2006). The total population was officially estimated at 14.93 million in 2004, which include the *liudong renkou*, or 'floating population', who do not have resident status. These are the migrants who are usually tolerated by the authorities, if not by the long-term residents themselves who see the newcomers as 'new urban outcasts' (Solinger, 1995), and supply, for instance, the cheap labour on which the rapid pace of construction is based; work which is '3D' – difficult, demanding and dangerous (Shen, 2002). Urban migrants or 'floaters' are often either exploited by their employers or self-exploited insofar as they work exceptionally long hours, more so given the intensity of the building programme and the tight deadlines associated with the Olympics, often below the minimum wage and often not receiving pay until weeks after it was due. As Friedmann (2005) put it, the urban migrants are the cannon fodder of China's industrial revolution.

Contemporary Beijing often seems to resemble a giant building site. All around, huge new buildings are in various stages of construction, often cloaked in huge nets to prevent tools falling on passers-by. The streets are hazardous due to the trenches which have been dug for pipes and cables, the pavements which are being laid, the trees that have been knocked down or are being replanted, and the trucks and workers' buses which cut across the flows of pedestrians and bicycles into the corrugated iron fortresses which surround the sites. By early 1999, with the advent of the fiftieth anniversary of the PRC, there were an estimated 5,000 building sites in the city (Cook, 2000).

Adoption of the trappings of modern consumer society accompanied this transformation of the built environment. Supermarkets carry Western-style red wines and beer, bread and cakes. The streets have American fast food chains (e.g. McDonalds, Kentucky Fried Chicken and Dunkin' Donut). Chinese tastes now extend to Western motor vehicles (Cherokee Jeep, Audi, Volkswagen, and even Ferrari), clothing (Benetton, Adidas or Wranglers), perfumes (Estée Lauder or Nina Ricci), electrical goods (Sony, Phillips and Panasonic), and housing, with executive-style estates of detached houses complete with nearby golf courses and private schools, perhaps within the complex itself. For the growing middle class, material goods are in full supply. For the working class, too, the department stores are rapidly expanding their size and product range. A night out is increasingly to a Hard Rock Cafe, pub or disco, usually featuring Western music. It is in the light of such changes that Beijing made its bids for the Olympics.

The Bidding Process

As in other Communist societies, sport became an important element in promoting the nation and patriotism. The annual *China Statistical Yearbook* on 'Culture, Sports and Public Health' routinely tabulates such outputs as 'Visits between Chinese and Foreign Sports Delegations', 'Activities of Mass Sports', 'World Records Chalked up by Chinese Athletes' and 'World Championships won by Chinese Athletes'. Dong (2005, p. 533) shows that:

> Chinese political and sports officials openly acknowledged that they viewed sport as an instrument for the promotion of national pride and identity... Contemporary competitive sport in China is motivated by nationalism and in turn contributes to the enhancement of patriotism.

From the mid-1980s, a strategy was developed to maximize gold medals, with an interesting feature being the success of female athletes, and the high proportion of females relative to males in the Chinese team. This has not always been unproblematic. There have been well publicized defections of top athletes plus question marks over the training methods and unprecedented success of 'Ma's Barmy Army' (after their trainer) of female marathon runners as well as the Chinese swimming team, with questions raised as to whether such athletes were 'chemically enhanced'. Dong shows that the first time that the question as to when China could actually host the Olympics was raised as far back as 1908 in the *Tianjin Youth Magazine*, but it was at the end of the successful Asian Games in 1990 that a huge banner was unfurled, stating 'With the success of the Asiad, we look forward to hosting the Olympic Games' (cited by Dong, 2005, p. 538).

As noted above, Beijing failed on this occasion, losing to Sydney by only two votes for the right to host the Millennial Olympics in 2000. There were suggestions (e.g. GamesBids.com, 2006) that there was a vote scandal at this time, but there was also strong opposition from Human Rights groups and the 'Free Tibet' movement, who were vehemently against a successful bid from China. Although the Asian Games had been successful, the shadow of Tiananmen still loomed large as far as many Western governments were concerned (see Broudehoux, 2004), but Beijing was still a severely polluted city at that time, with relatively poor infrastructure. It was certainly no surprise to most observers that the 1990s bid was unsuccessful.

By 2001, however, much had changed. China had decided to bid once again, primarily as part of the drive to modernize and internationalize Beijing. The city, one of five short listed, prepared for the final visit of the bidding panel in February 2001 with great care. *Inter alia*, the short- and longer-term measures taken included investment into awareness of the 2008 bid, for example, illuminations in Olympic colours, billboards, magazines in taxis, the Millennium Museum showing Olympic films and displays, street signs in English, investment in infrastructure (notably the fourth and fifth ring roads), development of new hotels, painting of older buildings to improve appearances, spraying the grass green, establishment of parks, green and silver bins to increase awareness of environment (i.e. waste recycling), removal of older cars from the city to reduce air pollution, banning people burning coal in the city, and the closure of the Shougang factory (steel plant).

The bid adopted the overarching slogan of 'New Beijing: Great Olympics', with subsidiary themes of delivering a 'high-tech Olympics', a 'green Olympics' and a 'people's Olympics'. It featured a plan to construct an Olympic Park and strategies to address the serious environmental issues faced by the Chinese capital. The commitments included:

• An Olympic Park covering an area of 1,215 hectares. It would include an 80,000 seat stadium, fourteen gymnasia, an Athletes' Village and an international exhibition centre, surrounded by a 760 hectare forest and greenbelt.

• During the tenth Five-Year Plan period (2001–2005) Beijing would build three green ecological belts, aiming to raise its green coverage to 48 per cent. By 2005, 'the city will realize the complete and safe disposal of treated waste and 96 per cent waste waster will also be treated'.[2]

• If Beijing gained the nomination 'there will be 5,750 sports venues by 2008 with twenty-three major stadia to hold events. And last year a new airport was opened that can move three million passengers a month. Beijing will have 72,000 rooms in 241 quality hotels and there are plans to build a $500 million national theatre on the edge of Tiananmen Square, to hold cultural events during the Games'.[3]

• 'The government plans to spend the equivalent of $15 billion on anti-pollution efforts through 2008, roughly nine times what China's Olympic Committee organizers estimate the Games would cost'.[4]

Beijing's long-term plan for environmental protection to 2010 had its time-scale reduced to ensure readiness for the 2008 Games. From 1998 to 2007, the plan envisaged such features as:

- total expenditure of $12.2 billion on protection and enhancement of the ecological environment;

- fourteen new wastewater treatment plants to be built to improve the sewage treatment rates to 90 per cent from 42 per cent;

- 240 square kilometres of trees and grass to be planted around Beijing to create a 'green coverage' area of more than 50 per cent;

- 200 industrial enterprises to change production or be shifted out of the downtown area altogether to reduce pollution levels;

- completion of the fourth and fifth ring roads, five new subway lines, 90 per cent of buses and 70 per cent of taxis to use natural gas.[5]

In all, it was forecast at the time that 280 billion yuan ($33.8 billion) of investment would be made in the period to 2008, mainly in stadia and gymnasia, increasing China's annual GNP growth by 0.3–0.4 per cent and Beijing's by 2.5 per cent (Xin, 2001). With these and other activities, the potential impact of the Olympics would be enormous, adding further to China's growing power and prestige on the international stage, and contributing significantly to Beijing's urban development *per se*. The city would move away from being a producer city towards being a city of consumption, of knowledge-based activities, and a city with an enhanced international profile.

For their part, the visiting panel was impressed by these and other evidence not just of the commitment of Beijing's residents to the Olympic ideal, but also that of the nation as a whole. By May 2001 the Olympic Evaluation Commission Report was summarized[6] as:

> This is a government-driven bid with considerable assistance of the NOC (National Olympic Committee). The combination of a good sports concept with complete Government support results in a high quality bid.

> The Commission notes the process and pace of change taking place in China and Beijing and the possible challenges caused by population and economic growth in the period leading up to 2008 but is confident that these challenges can be met.

> There is an environmental challenge but the strong government actions and investment in this area should resolve this and improve the city.

> It is the Commission's belief that a Beijing Games would leave a unique legacy to China and to sport and the Commission is confident that Beijing could organize an excellent Games.

Beijing's success soon afterwards (13 July 2001) was the climax of a series of celebrations, beginning with the return of Hong Kong in 1997, Macao in 1999, the fiftieth anniversary of the PRC in 1999 and the eightieth anniversary of the founding of the CCP in July 2001. Later, China unsuccessfully bid for the 2010 FIFA World Cup and successfully for a World Exposition in Shanghai in 2010. It is difficult to underestimate the symbolic nature of these successes for China's people, the CCP and the leadership of the nation. It is indeed fair to say that the Olympics in particular and the city marketing that they imply serve a strong ideological purpose, not least insofar as it uses the city as and its consumption as a focal point for the naturalization of power (Broudehoux, 2004).

Urban Regeneration

In the years following the bid's success, Beijing saw considerable work and investment towards realizing the Olympic dream. In many respects, the Olympics are a national rather than just a city-based event. Key elements of the Olympics were staged away from Beijing, notably, sailing (Qingdao, Shandong Province), equestrian (Hong Kong), and football (Tianjin, Shanghai, Shenyang and Qinhuangdao). In the case of Qingdao, Shanghai and Hong Kong these cities are located hundreds, one thousand and two thousand miles respectively from Beijing itself.[7] Most of the effort and investment, however, was expended in Beijing. In

Figure 17.2. The Bird's Nest – the National Stadium, August 2008.

2003, work began on four Olympic venues, with a further eleven begun in 2004. By mid-2006, forty-four major projects were under way. The Olympic Village and the National Stadium, with its now-famous 'bird's nest' lattice-work structure (figure 17.2), lie to the north of the central city. Beijing International Airport was considerably modernized and expanded through the building of an enormous Terminal 3. Many new subway lines were built for the Olympics (figure 17.3), while a new loop line was opened to the north of the city in 2002.

The Beijing Organizing Committee for the Games of the Twenty-Ninth Olympiad (BOCOG) held its first plenary session in January 2004 at which it was announced that the first phase of development was complete (Cook, 2006). The second phase would run from 2004 to 2006, leaving the time from 2007 until the Games' Opening Ceremony for test events and fine-tuning. Construction of new hotels, road infrastructure and other essential facilities continued apace, including parks and water recycling centres. The new Opera House (Beijing National Theatre) behind the Great Hall of the People was also completed, notwithstanding the controversies over its huge cost and 'jelly-fish' or 'blob' architectural design (see Broudehoux, 2004). On the symbolic side, the new Beijing Olympic logo – 'Chinese Seal, Dancing Beijing' – was unveiled in August 2003, combining 'elements of engraving, calligraphy, painting and poetry' and bringing together elements of the ancient and the modern.[8]

BOCOG 'is requiring all proprietors … to follow "green" environmental

Figure 17.3. New underground station, Beijing 2008.

guidelines in the construction of Olympic venues' (Lei, 2004). Sustainable development was a key element with the main tasks identified by the executive vice-president of BOCOG as 'controlling air pollution, especially reducing the coal and industrial pollution and vehicle discharges, effective disposal of municipal sewage and municipal refuse, raising the green land acreage to 50 per cent' (*Ibid.*). As an indication of success in these endeavours, in March 2006 Chaoyang District became the first urban area in Beijing to be named a 'model ecological zone', following three suburban districts of Yanqing, Pinggu and Miyun (Li, 2006). Over 60 square kilometres of green zones were created 2004–2008, and according to the municipal authorities: 'Greenbelts cover 43.5 percent of the district, and green public space has reached an average of 15 square meters per person. Meanwhile, air and water quality has improved' (*Ibid.*). The Capital Iron and Steel Works were gradually relocated to a coastal location some distance from the capital in Shandong Province. The regular visitor can vouch for the fact that Beijing's environmental quality is often better than it was, with more blue sky days (one of the set targets), more tree planting, more green spaces, increased use of LPG in buses, and greater restrictions on pollution via industry or vehicles. Nevertheless, there were still many concerns before the Games as to the pollution impact upon Olympic athletes, while a number of other concerns also raised disquiet in some quarters.

Pre-Games Controversies

Despite the environmental focus of the Olympic plans and the improvements noted above, data from the European Satellite Agency in October 2005 stressed that Beijing remained the most polluted city in the world, while it and neighbouring provinces had the world's worst levels of nitrogen dioxide (Watts, 2005). Despite an enormous volume of tree planting in recent years, China's plans were disrupted by a huge sandstorm that hit the city on 16 April 2006. Around 330,000 tons of dust were estimated to have fallen on Beijing that day, while the next saw most of north and north-west China enveloped in sandstorms. This was chastening for the authorities, given that it coincided with the Sixth National Conference on Environmental Protection. Addressing the conference, Premier Wen Jiabao commented: 'Repeated sandstorms should send a warning to us all, we should feel heavy loads on our shoulders while meeting here to discuss environmental problems'.[9] Yet while the government claims to take environmental issues seriously, the pace of social and economic change often outstrips the ability to regulate and control environmental pollution. For example, in 2003 the level of car ownership in Beijing reached the level anticipated for 2010. Much higher taxation rates were announced for large vehicles with rates on small engined cars being reduced, but in a society with such a fast rate of wealth creation and where social status is increasingly a product of conspicuous consumption, it is probable that most people will not be deterred from buying larger vehicles unless punitive measures are taken. The authorities responded by severely restricting vehicle use while the Olympics took place; a decision which caused considerable impact in a city that, for example, is of similar size to Los Angeles.

Another controversial aspect of the Olympics schedule was demolition to make way for the new structures associated with the Olympics. The set target was 9 million square metres of 'dilapidated housing', replaced by new houses that would supply a living area of 18 square metres per capita (Xin, 2001). This is part of an ongoing process of demolition across the whole city, which particularly threatens the old *hutong* and *siheyuan* areas (Cook, 2000, 2006; Cook and Murray, 2001). In brief, these old, often dilapidated, single-storey houses arranged along narrow lanes, originally with access to the 'Hong Tong' or water well, are in areas that ill befit the dreams of planners and developers concerned with creating the grand structures of an internationalized Olympic metropolis. From 1991 to 2003, 1.5 million people were relocated from such areas out to the high-rise residential blocks in the suburbs. The previous Mayor admitted that the difficult problem of resettlement of families affected by this demolition process 'remains to be solved' while the new Mayor, Wang Qishan, although admitting that some of these relocation projects violated the law, stated that older parts of the city would continue to be demolished to make way for the Olympics projects (cited in Cook, 2006). Some estimates suggest that approximately 300,000 people were evicted specifically because of the Olympics, although the government of the PRC denies this (Acharya, 2005).

The last point is a reminder that the issue of human rights refuses to disappear. Organizations such as Amnesty International or Human Rights Watch Asia continue to deplore human rights violations by the Chinese authorities. These crystallize around a number of broad themes, such as the overall lack of democracy, use of the death penalty, the occupation of Tibet, Uighur (Muslim) insurgency in Xinjiang Province and the treatment of the Falun Gong (a Buddhist sect). Security in China, including internet security is tight, so the likelihood of violence marring the Olympics in 2008 was low, but there remained the possibility of public protests concerning these and other issues. Indeed, as in other countries previously, the upheaval created by the Games could actually *contribute* to protest and dissent. For their part, the Chinese authorities retaliate by defending their human rights record by pointing to the lack of basic rights in countries such as the United States and maintain that the war on terrorism and the involvement of the United States and the United Kingdom in Iraq, complete with examples of human rights abuse by American and British soldiers, shows the operation of double standards. The Olympic Torch relay was beset by protests from Free Tibet activists in many countries and cities, particularly Paris, London, San Francisco and Athens. This in turn led to counter-protests from PRC supporters in Hong Kong and China itself. Meanwhile, the Chinese government continues to condemn Western critiques of China's human rights record on the basis that they amount to an imposition of Western cultural values and constitute a fundamental misunderstanding of

Chinese culture and not least the fact that cultural change occurs in China not overnight but over the course of development of a civilization.

Corruption constituted another thorny issue for the Chinese authorities. As shown above, vast sums of foreign investment have entered the country in recent years. Perhaps inevitably, corruption has become a problem for the Chinese government, and some would point to the lack of democratic controls as rendering it very difficult to root out corruption among officials and CCP members. Reports of the first Beijing Olympic official to be sacked over corruption surfaced two years before the Games (Watts, 2006*b*). According to these reports, Liu Zhihua, a Vice Mayor of Beijing responsible for overseeing construction of sporting venues for the Olympics, was removed by the Standing Committee of the Beijing Municipal People's Congress for 'corruption and dissoluteness'. He was liable to face the death penalty for financial crimes if found guilty of taking an alleged 10 million yuan (nearly $1.5 million) as a bribe from developers. The huge amount of money that had been budgeted for the various events and venues means that this may well not be the last such case to come to light. Reporting on the case was suppressed before the Olympics to avoid tarnishing China's image but after the Games in October 2008 Liu did in fact receive a death sentence, suspended for two years to allow his potential 'good behaviour' to commute the sentence to imprisonment.[10]

A final pre-Games concern was the contradictions that apply to the Beijing Olympics in particular (Dickson and Schofield, 2005). The main sponsors for the event include 'calorie-dense beverages (Coca-Cola) and food (McDonalds) as well as motorized transportation (Volkswagen)' (*Ibid.*, p. 170). Such sponsorship runs the risk of exacerbating China's growing obesity problem. Other sponsors such as Samsung or Panasonic produce goods that further contribute to a sedentary lifestyle. They argue that 'the world's most populous nation is at the beginning of an explosion in lifestyle-related disease' (*Ibid.*, p. 177), a point supported by Cook and Dummer (2004) who observed that 'the first "fat camp" was opened in Beijing in 1994'. This, they argued, reflected 'a growing problem of obesity as Western "junk food" becomes increasingly popular in the cities … obesity in young children increasing by over 50% from 1989 to 1997' (*Ibid.*, p. 338). Although the Olympics would help to encourage a proportion of China's population to take more exercise, as has happened in previous Olympic cities, Dickson and Schofield (2005, p. 177) maintained that this would be insufficient to offset 'the opportunities for massive multinational globalization and ultimately, globesity'. This would surely be the ultimate irony that the Beijing Olympics might contribute to the couch potato syndrome in China and the rest of the globe.

The Games Themselves

There are perhaps two abiding images of the 2008 Beijing Olympics: the sheer awe-inspiring scale and richness of the Games' Opening Ceremony and the vision of Usain Bolt smashing the world record whilst de-accelerating long before the finish of the men's 100 metres. The opening ceremony offered a spectacular vision of a city steeped in its own history and yet one that was ready for the challenges facing a nation ready to declare itself a major player in the global economy. Directed by the high profile film director Zhang Yimou, the ceremony featured over 15,000 performers and cost around $100 million to produce. Perhaps most memorable were the mass participation set pieces that offered a timely symbolic reminder of the sheer power of the Communist ideal. The sense of co-operation and united endeavour was undoubtedly reflective of broader social norms in China and also represented a statement of global intent on the part of the Chinese Communist Party. The ceremony was in part a physical manifestation of the Games' slogan 'One World, One Dream', of a world united by the Olympic ideal of peace and harmony. Equally, however, such a notion reaffirmed China's membership of a world united by the possibilities of consumer capitalism, and by the promise that China is now a fully paid up member of the global economy.

In many respects then the Opening Ceremony was more than just a ceremony in constituting a carefully choreographed (in more ways than one) statement of intent and of an arrival on the world stage that mixed Communist images of the obedient masses with the technological wizardry of advanced capitalism. This ceremony and indeed the Games as a whole served to present the Chinese way to the rest of the world and indeed the inherent belief amongst the Chinese people that the Chinese way is the best. This was queried subsequently, however, when it was revealed that a young girl singer was replaced by another who lip-synched on behalf of her plainer colleague behind the scenes. Similarly, the ubiquitously youthful Olympic volunteers fed into the vision of a newly emerging country and one that was blessed by the riches of hundreds of years of unsurpassed civilization, providing 'an almost picture-perfect blend of idealized chinoiserie and ultra-modern convenience'.[11] Even here, however, 'real progress in terms of language fluency and cross-cultural understanding was slight due to the controlled and directed nature of foreigner to volunteer interaction'.[12]

Although for the rest of the world the efforts of Usain Bolt will perhaps stay longest in the memory, the Chinese people were no doubt most affected by Lou Xiang's Olympic experience. Lou Xiang was and is the icon and poster boy of the Chinese people. Reported to have made £12 million in one year alone from endorsements by Nike and other sponsors, the city of Beijing was awash with images of the only male Chinese competitor who had a serious chance of gold on the athletics track. In his hands lay the hopes of a nation. But there was no happy ending. Although Lou Xiang made it on to his starting blocks he did not make it over the hurdles in front of him and as such the dreams of a billion Chinese people were left in tatters. Lou Xiang was literally the face of the Olympics and the fact he was forced to pull out through injury was a devastating blow not only for the people of China but for the CPP itself who were no doubt more than happy to promote Lou Xiang as a symbol of an internationally competitive China and less than happy at his demise. As it happened China topped the Olympic Games medal table achieving fifty-one gold medals in its total medal haul of 100; this justified the massive investment on the part of the Communist party to ensure that China was seen to succeed not only as a host, but, for now at least, as the greatest sporting nation on earth.

The Environmental Impact

At the time of writing it would seem that the Beijing Olympics have, despite the negative environmental impact of the construction process itself, left a positive environmental legacy in a number of ways, although there are also some controversies concerning the exact nature of this legacy. On the positive side, new green areas have been created, including 'Olympic Green' as a resource for Beijing's citizens, while Watts (2009) reported that restrictions on car use have proved to be so successful in reducing air pollution that these restrictions were extended by a further 12 months. This means that, according to the Beijing Traffic Management Bureau one-fifth of the city's 3.6 million private vehicles and a third of official cars will continue to be barred from the roads every weekday, thus reducing emissions by 10 per cent, while plans to widen a ban on high-polluting cars and trucks from the centre to cover the whole city will save a similar amount. Such claims were supported by a report by the United Nations Environment Programme (UNEP), published in February 2009.[13] The report stated that Beijing had 'raised the environmental bar and the Games left a lasting legacy for the city'. Positive elements included increased awareness of environmental issues among residents and businesses alike across China but especially in Beijing, introduction of Euro IV emission standards for cars instead of the Euro II planned, creation of '8,800 hectares of green space … using more than 30 million trees and rose bushes', and a rise in blue sky days from 'less than 180 in 2000 to 274 days in 2008'. Lesser improvements were also recorded in waste disposal and recycling.

This positive 'big tick'[14] for the Olympic environmental improvements was not, however, supported by an analysis of particulate matter in an 8 week period around the Games. The analysis, involving US and Chinese environmental scientists, caused some controversy in China, and led to the Chinese author backtracking on the article's conclusions.[15] The study, by scientists from Oregon State University and Peking University, funded by the National Science Foundations of the United States and China, found that the level of particulate pollution in Beijing was twice as bad as in Athens, Greece; three times as bad as in Atlanta, Georgia; and 3.5 times as bad as in Sydney, Australia. The authors suggested that some pollution was due to the movement of regional air mass from polluted regions beyond the city, but also that good weather on other occasions was responsible for reduction in air pollution to a greater extent than anti-pollution policies. An ongoing analysis by the University of Oxford may in due course help to find a more definitive conclusion between the UNEP findings and those of this transnational study.

The Bird's Nest as a White Elephant

As for the longer term legacy of Beijing 2008, the physical impact of the Games is clear in terms of the massive programme of building work and infrastructural improvements and most notably perhaps the new Olympic subway line reflecting what Li *et al.* (2007, p. 261) describe as the emergence of a 'hybrid global megacity'. Yet the smog soon returned to the city and the key sporting venues have largely stood unused. A major area of concern regarding the legacy of the Beijing Olympics is one that is also found elsewhere with other Olympics, namely who will pay for and use the new Olympic facilities, in particular the spectacular Bird's Nest? During fieldwork in Beijing in March 2009, Cook first became aware that, at least for some, there were concerns that the Bird's Nest might transmogrify into a very expensive White Elephant. The construction cost of this magnificent stadium has been reported as 3.5 billion yuan (approximately $427 million dollars) and the maintenance cost 170 million yuan. There are also loan costs to pay, as well as maintenance. One suggested solution was that the biggest football (soccer) team in Beijing, Beijing Guo An, would take over the stadium, but although football is increasingly popular in China it is highly unlikely that support for this team would be sufficient to maintain such a huge stadium, particularly given that there are also high costs involved in preparing the pitch for each match. Sponsorship for the stadium by the likes of Adidas was also considered, but rejected due to the national importance of the venue. Instead, it would seem at the time of writing that a combination of visitor numbers (thousands pay 50 yuan to enter the stadium) and cultural events including a 'Charm of China' summer concert series involving such celebrities as Placido Domingo and Jackie Chan will be used to raise the funds required to keep this enormous stadium going.[16] Another possibility is that the stadium is reinvented as a shopping and entertainment complex.

The Bird's Nest does not, of course, exist in glorious iconic isolation. It sits beside the Beijing National Aquatic Centre 'The Water Cube', which is equally architecturally striking. The up-keep of such buildings is excessively expensive while the long-term use of facilities is questionable. For example, there appears to be limited need for a public swimming facility of this kind and it is more likely to be used in the long term as a venue for elite aquatic sports. Some of the other facilities available on Olympic Park will no doubt in time inevitably be demolished. What remains is most likely to offer some kind of a private haven: a space of elite consumption founded upon the memories of three weeks in the summer of 2008. This reflects a broader concern that the primary long-term impact of the Olympic Games is to redefine Beijing as a space for consumption so that the Olympic Green area in particular becomes a glitzy space for privatized public pleasures. As Marvin (2008, p. 249) puts it:

> The official version of post-Olympic commercial, exhibition, sports, and entertainment spaces on the Green and elsewhere paints a civic picture of obedient consumers attuned

more to immediate gratification than politics. In Lefebvrian terms the Green is a wholly new conceived space, a cagey gamble by a new generation of rulers who are betting that stripping national space of overt political content will diffuse its potential for 'lived' protest. They are likely to be encouraged by nearly two decades of public response to commercial malls and nighttime strips.

The concern here is that the Olympics have transformed the city of Beijing but they have done so at considerable cost by adopting a model that is all about developing leisure enclaves for the rich that have simply served to impoverish the public life of the city. Of course, the primary role of the Olympics, as we suggested above, is a symbolic one that is concerned with portraying confident harmonious China but the problem is that China is more harmonious for some than it is for others. Indeed, the costs of the Olympics will inevitably fall on those who least benefit from them. In quoting the pertinent figures, the Beijing municipal government spent over $10 billion on transport and infrastructure, for example. Broudehoux (2004) argues that such investment blindly disregards local needs, there being no hard evidence that the local population actually benefits from the anticipated economic boom that would result (which in turn have been cut off at the legs by the effects of a world economic downturn). For Broudehoux (2004) the winners in such a scenario are always the multinational businesses involved in sport through sports, tourism and property while the locals are left to deal with increased taxation, soaring rents and restricted civil liberties.

Branding

In part, this discussion concerns the different levels of branding to which different institutions and actors at different levels are exposed. At the national level, the People's Republic of China has to a great extent overcome many negative external perceptions of China as a severe, autocratic, dictatorial society in which dissent is not tolerated, giving an impression of 'a peaceful China, a civilized China, and a progressive China' according to Te (2009, p. 84). The IOC agrees with this view, insisting that 'lasting legacies' were produced for Beijing and its people, and that as regards criticisms of human rights, 'the games have elevated international dialogue on such issues' as the leader of the IOC's Evaluation Commission put it.[17] Others may be less sanguine, including those who welcomed the alternative Tibetan Freedom Torch that was carried through more than fifty cities before completing its journey near the Tibet border in Ladakh, India,[18] or the 149 people who applied for permission to protest at the officially designated three protest zones – all seventy-seven applications were withdrawn or rejected,[19] 'and in one case two elderly women who had applied to protest were initially sentenced to re-education by labour, though this sentence was later cancelled' (Fahey, 2009. p. 384). The Chinese citizens, none the less, 'displayed new standards of national quality development', of 'civilization', 'passion' and 'smile' (Te, 2009, pp. 88–89).

Such contrasting perspectives are also shown in the survey conducted by Zhang and Zhao (2009) in different locations in Beijing, Tiananmen, Sanlitun and Houhai, with 100 respondents. There were high ratings of Beijing's position and power in international affairs and of the cultural significance of the city. 'In ranking, the respondents considered the tangible, eye-catching indigenous liberal arts and ancient architectures as the foremost representative cultural symbols of Beijing' (*Ibid*, p. 250). In contrast were the low scores on 'liveability', with low ratings for 'ecological conditions, the provision of public amenities, the standard of public services, and urban governance' (*Ibid*.). The sustainability of environmental improvements via the Games was questioned, while there were also concerns about rising property prices, notwithstanding the global recession. Despite successes during the Games:

> the respondents were sceptical about the introduction of a new quality of life and the common good by the Beijing Olympics. While official branding tried to sell the friendly, smiling and comfortable city, people generally thought that a one-time event could not help to satisfy material needs of the economically and socially marginalized groups (including the city's laid-off workers and rural low-skilled migrants working in the city). (*Ibid*., pp. 251–252)

Conclusion

There is no doubt that in many ways the Beijing Olympics were an enormous success and that they succeeded in portraying a new confident China to the global audience. The human rights issue never went away, images of protestors interrupting the Olympic torch procession were undoubtedly damaging to the CPP, but ultimately the image of a revitalized China appears to have generally won through, not least as a result of the awe-inspiring opening ceremony. Certainly in comparison, London's contribution to the closing ceremony was modest to say the least; a modesty that has become an economic necessity given the global recession.

For Brownell (2008) the greatest bequest of the Beijing Games will be its human and cultural legacy and in particular the way in which the Games provided an opportunity to train Chinese people for a globalizing world. As far as the future of China is concerned the Games have of course played an important role in ensuring China's role as a key player on the world stage: its unrelenting enthusiasm and commitment to the Games reflecting its commitment not only to being a full member of the global community but a leading player in the drive towards the construction of a global society (Close *et al.*, 2007). A key concern in this respect is the degree to which the China that emerges from the 2008 Olympics reflects and reinforces a particular set of values broadly described as those associated with global consumer capitalism; a set of values that are more attainable in theory than they are in practice for many social groups including the migrant population discussed above. The concern here is the 'one World, one Dream' to which the Games so vocally referred turns out to be a world in which only some components of Chinese society can actually partake.

Notes

1.   www.chinaview.cn/index.htm/7-7-2009. Accessed 10 July 2009.

2.   www.china.org.cn/english/11125.htm. Accessed 17 April 2001.

3.   *Ibid.*

4.   www.GamesBids.com/archives/2008/Beijing.htm. Accessed 12 June 2006.

5.   www.beijing-olympic.org.cn/xbxa/ztzt/gree/gree-index.shtm, 2001. Accessed 5 May 2001.

6.   www.GamesBids.com/archives/2008/Beijing.htm. Accessed 12 June 2006.

7.   http://en.beijing2008.com/21/65/column212006521.shtml. Accessed 9th June 2006.

8.   *Ibid.*

9.   *Ibid.*

10.   http://www.telegraph.co.uk/news/worldnews/asia/china/3227533/Corrupt-Beijing-vice-mayor-gets-death-sentence.html. Accessed 24 July 2009.

11.   An Olympic Evaluation, E. Setzekorn, http://thechinabeat.blogspot.com/2008/09/olympic-evaluation.html. Accessed 25 November 2009.

12.   *Ibid.*

13.   http://china.org.cn/environment/report_review/2009-02/19/content_17300306.htm. Accessed 10 July 2009.

14.   Beijing Olympics Get Big Green Tick, http://www.unep.org/Documents.Multilingual/Default. asp?DocumentID=562&ArticleID=6086&l=en. Accessed 10 July 2009.

15.   http://www.usnews.com/articles/science/2009/06/21/study-beijings-air-worse-than-at-past-olympics.html. Accessed 10 July 2009.

16.   http://english.peopledaily.com.cn/90001/90782/90873/6690945.html. Accessed 10 July 2009.

17.   IOC Congratulates Itself for Beijing Olympics, http://www.wtop.com/?nid=393&sid=1780288. Accessed 25 November 2009.

18.   The Tibetan Freedom Torch, http://www.tibetnetwork.org/camapigns-Olympics. Accessed 25 November 2009.

19.   Beijing: a Protest-free zone? http://news.sky.com/skynews/Home/World-News/Beijing-Olympics-Protest-Free-Des... Accessed 25 November 2009.

Chapter 18

London 2012

Graeme Evans

On Wednesday, 6 July 2005, the International Olympic Committee's meeting in Singapore voted to award the 2012 Summer Olympics to London. The decision represented a combination of Eurovision-style partisanship, tactical voting,[1] global schmoozing and last minute surprises. London's *coup de grâce*, another steal from the French, was a multicultural-faced group of excited East End children, in contrast to the sombre suited Parisian messieurs. Celebrations began in Stratford, the nondescript town centre of the London borough of Newham, and the heart of the prospective Olympic Village. The next day, four suicide bombers killed fifty-six people, including themselves, in attacks on underground trains and a bus in central London. The 2012 celebration party was cut short and thinking inevitably started to focus on the size of the task ahead, with all its attendant problems. These started with the security considerations in the face of the renewed terror threat and the woefully underestimated capital budget used in the successful bid, which not only excluded the extra security costs, but VAT and other taxes on construction that together added £1.5 billion on to the original £4 billion bid estimate. By March 2007 the publicly-funded Olympic infrastructure budget stood at £9.375 billion, excluding the costs of staging the event, land acquisition and wider regeneration and transport investment.

This chapter provides a critique of the London 2012 Olympic project five years into its post-award, development phase. The first of its four sections provides an analysis of the urban regeneration and renewal context of the London Olympics. The second discusses the cost of the Games and how they are to be financed, with the third focusing on the designation of the Olympic sites in the Lower Lea Valley and their implications for regeneration. The conclusion adds final thoughts about the potential legacy of London 2012.

Regeneration Games

The rationale for hosting hallmark events, as it developed from the early 1960s, is that of 'the city of renewal' (Hall, 1992, p. 29). Nearly fifty years on, it is surprising to note that a recent review of literature on the Olympics (Veal and Toohey, 2005) found only two out of over 1,500 entries specifically on 'regeneration' or 'renewal'. Articles, reports, and a growing number of edited collections are dominated by 'impacts' – embracing the economic, physical, political-economic, and tourism and the cultural – as well as themes of marketing, image and place-making. By contrast, analyses of long-term regeneration effects are notable by their absence. Olympic effects are subsumed into wider redevelopment and competitive city narratives. This makes it problematic to measure the true impact of the Games and similar large-scale, event-based regeneration projects, which become a symbolic but highly temporal event in a city's evolution and another chapter in the Olympic history book.

Notwithstanding the extensive development of facilities undertaken to host even the least ambitious Olympic Games, it is important to distinguish between the now ubiquitous urban renewal (and the US 'revitalization') attached to Olympic plans, and genuine regeneration (see also chapter 9). The latter is associated more with extremes of social decline, multiple deprivation and disadvantage and, in economic terms, below-average performance (for European Union Regional Structural Fund eligibility, below 75 per cent of the EU-average). Unlike industrial and inward investment, regeneration is both a process and an outcome. By definition, it is a response to sustained decline (or *de*-generation) and regeneration therefore seeks to transform a community or place that has displayed the symptoms of environmental (physical), social or economic decline – symptoms that commonly coexist. This instrumental approach to regeneration which now underlies public urban policy initiatives, presumes that such decline can be reversed from the outside, by:

> breathing new life and vitality into an ailing community, industry and area [bringing] sustainable, long-term improvements to local quality of life, including economic, social and environmental needs. (LGA, 2000)

The view of the UK government is that regeneration should now be a 'holistic process of reversing economic, social and physical decay in areas where it has reached a stage when market forces alone will not suffice' (ODPM, 2003*b*). This market failure analysis presents an interesting case for the rationale of being the Olympic host. Neither market nor state can afford (politically and financially) to take the full risk and burden of the Games, and both city and national governments must front and act as guarantor to the bid, and demonstrate a degree of public and cross-party political support. Regeneration and renewal objectives may be wide ranging but will seek to deliver improved work and business opportunities, improved residential attractiveness and improved public services. The distinguishing characteristics are that they have a strong spatial focus and often, as a result, distributional impacts, both positive and negative. They tend to aim at, or contribute to, the overall goals for sustainable development of target areas and groups, and have the specific objective of improving outcomes in social, economic and environmental terms. Spatial and distributive effects are therefore vital in any assessment of the regenerative benefits and impacts arising from the Games. If the ultimate aim of regeneration interventions is to achieve thriving, inclusive and sustainable communities in all regions by raising levels of social inclusion, promoting neighbourhood renewal and fostering regional prosperity, these aims demand a suitably integrated assessment, but such a holistic and balanced approach is still a utopian prospect rather than utilitarian practice (Evans, 2005a). This is evident where redistributive and gentrification effects on host communities are not reflected (or valued) in the official measures of impact and outcomes arising from regeneration – particularly where this is accelerated by the Olympic imperative.

In London's bid, the greatest emphasis is placed on the legacy and after-effects of the Olympic leverage opportunity, rather than the event, its content and purpose. As Allen (2006, p. 3) indicated: 'Talk of the "Olympic Legacy" is so common that it has started to sound like a tautology; shorthand for the perceived wisdom that the Olympics has everything to do with urban regeneration and only a passing concern with patriotism, athletics or public spectacle'. This presents a fundamental problem to the national Olympic and city regeneration delivery agencies. The financial, land ownership and usage, constructional, and related infrastructural and promotional efforts are of necessity dominated by the event delivery objectives and cost pressures and targets. National performance in the competition itself, (i.e. in the final medal league table), is the test of sporting success.[2] It is here that compromises in community benefits (social, local economy and procurement), design quality and after-use, are most likely to be made. As Deyan Sudjic (2006) suggested: 'it's now becoming clear that the idea is something of a smokescreen. In practice, it's becoming apparent that this legacy involves putting the narrowly technical demands of the 17 days of the games above everything else, and then trying to adapt the site for long-term use afterwards'. The visionary masterplans, artists' impressions and promises at the bidding and consultation stage are just that – promises. Barcelona's Olympic Village housing, for example, was privately sold but not 'affordably' as promised (Nel-lo, 1997). The final form and function will therefore be dictated by budget and contractual realities, political stamina and consensus, just as it has been in other regenerating Olympic cities.

No regeneration programme for London's major Olympic sites at Stratford in London's East End, of course, could ignore the lessons of two major regeneration schemes that lie on the periphery of the Olympic zone and influence both the political culture and economy surrounding London 2012. The first is the Docklands regeneration for which the symbolic and economic heart is Canary Wharf and the cluster of newer office towers that have grown up alongside (figure 18.1). This was carried out under the aegis of the London Docklands Development Corporation (LDDC), which was formed by the Conservative government in 1980 and which, until it was wound up in 1998, served to fast track physical regeneration of the declining areas of the inner and outer docklands (see Evans and Taylor, 1997; Brownill, 1990; Colenutt, 1988; and DCC, 1990). The LDDC took control of land-use development by assuming the powers to grant planning permission that would previously have been the prerogative of the incumbent local authorities in the London Docklands. Shortly afterwards, London had no city-wide authority with the winding up of the Greater London Council (GLC) in 1984. As a result, there was neither strategic nor local area planning in this regeneration zone at the time of its peak development. Coupled with property boom and bust cycles (Canary Wharf's Canadian developers, Olympia and York, went into receivership) – and delays to the Jubilee Line Underground Extension (JLE) which links Canary Wharf, Greenwich peninsula and Stratford (Olympic Zone) to central London – regeneration of the wider Docklands area, including the Olympic zone, had been limited.

The viability of the inner ('Enterprise Zone') Docklands office zone relied on public investment and generous investment incentives, and only when the costly (£3.5 billion) JLE reached Canary Wharf in 1999 just in time for the Millennium celebrations in Greenwich, did the so-called private-led development become financially secure. What is of importance here is that this model of urban development is intrinsic to preparing for London 2012. Urban Regeneration and equivalent companies are being used to accelerate development, over and above local planning authorities in the London Thames Gateway and wider region.[3] Following the host city award in 2005 the Olympic Delivery Authority (ODA) and the London Development Agency (LDA) hastily took over compulsory land purchase and strategic planning powers in place of the locally elected authorities. The LDA's initial responsibility for land acquisition and preparation was only a transitory role however, since another unelected body, the Olympic Park Legacy Company (OPLC) was formed in 2009 by the Mayor with Communities (DCLG) and Olympics (DCMS) Ministers, to further develop and dispose of land and facilities post-event.

This fragmented governance structure is in contrast to inner city regeneration organizations in other countries where a long-term agency is established to see through phased redevelopment, such as in La Défence (EPAD), Paris, EuroMéditerranée, Marseilles, and Bilbao's waterfront. This international experience and the lessons from London Docklands in terms of governance, distributive effects and gentrification (Butler, 2007) do not appear to feature in London 2012 Olympic planning, organizational structures and evaluation efforts. Or rather, the current approach can be seen to mirror this earlier regeneration trajectory to which London 2012 is in many senses an extension both spatially and chronologically. London 2012 can therefore be viewed as the 'unfinished business' of the wider docklands and East London regeneration, with the Olympic opportunity the new *force majeure* required to remove the barriers to the exceptional levels of public sector investment and top-down land-use development. Historically this also represents the goal of readdressing the imbalance between west and east London through successive (if not 'sustained') regeneration and

Figure 18.1. The distant skyline of Canary Wharf looking south across from the Olympic Park.

creating a new 'destination', with echoes of earlier London Olympics and World Fairs centred on White City in west London and the promotion of electrified railway and underground routes giving access to and from the newly developed outer London suburbs. The reassertion of London via Olympic branding and massive public regeneration investment – inevitably diverting funding from the regions and regional cities – is enabled, again, by a sporting mega-event (see Evans, 2006a).

The second, more recent public project with sub-regional regeneration goals, was the Millennium Dome across the river from Canary Wharf on the Greenwich peninsula (figure 18.2). The Greenwich site had been selected as the location for the national Millennium celebration (first conceived in 1995) from a shortlist of four including other British Gas-owned derelict sites in Newham and in Derby, and the Birmingham International Exhibition Centre. Like the Olympic Park the site required toxic waste and poisoned soil to be removed prior to construction[4] and formed part of a £4 billion regeneration of the wider Greenwich peninsula. Built as the centre of the nation's celebration of the new Millennium in 2000, its vague purpose and escalating capital cost cast a cloud over such public *grand projets* in Britain. The four criteria for the Millennium Exhibition award, 'the best event of its kind in the world', were also echoed in Olympic visions and delivery programmes promoted by both the national (Labour) and London city (Conservative) governments as well as host (Labour) boroughs (table 18.1).

The main criticisms of the project were the escalating cost and unclear purpose and content, as well the problem of promoting the event as a national celebration in

Table 18.1. Millennium Festival 2000 and London2012 Olympic and Legacy visions.

Millennium Festival 2000	London2012 Olympic Objectives (2005) and Legacy (DCMS, 2007)	London Mayor Olympic Legacy Commitments	London2012 Olympic Legacy Programmes (LDA, 2004)	London2012 Host Borough Legacy Framework
The environment	'Green', sustainable games, Lower Lea Valley regeneration *Making the Olympic Park a blueprint for sustainable living*	Delivering a sustainable Games and developing sustainable communities	Olympic Park & Land delivery	Nexus with physical regeneration
Art, culture	Cultural Legacy, Olympic festivals, Creative Hub *Demonstrating that the UK is a creative, inclusive and welcoming place to live in, visit and for business*	Showcasing London as a diverse, inclusive, creative and welcoming city	Culture; Tourism & Business	Visitor economy
Community activity	Participation in Sport and Culture *Making the UK a world leading sporting nation; inspiring a generation of young people to take part in volunteering, cultural and physical activity*	Increasing opportunities for Londoners to become involved in sport	Sports participation (including Healthy & Active Workplace)	Sporting legacy; Culture
Improved access to the natural and technological world	Park, environmental and transport improvements, Olympic Institute and Media Centre *Transforming the heart of East London*	Ensuring Londoners benefit from new jobs, business and volunteering opportunities *Transforming the heart of East London*	Tourism & Business; London Employment & Skills Taskforce (LEST)	Nexus with physical regeneration

a non-central London location (Evans, 1996*b*, 1999*a*). The final cost of the Dome was £790 million, of which £600 million was funded by the National Lottery (see below) and the balance from ticket sales. The latter, however, were only 50 per cent of the original budget estimate, due to a shortfall in visitor numbers – around 6.5 million people came, compared with 12–18 million ('mid-high' range) in the original business plan (Price Waterhouse, 1994; Evans, 1996*a*).

This experience was exacerbated by the failure to secure its after-use and disposal. By 2005 the costs of annual insurance and security for the vacant facility were put at £1 million. The site had been sold following the year-long 'Millennium Experience' exhibition in December 2001 to Meridian Delta Ltd, a subsidiary of Quintain Estates & Development and Lend Lease[5] (backed by Philip

Anschutz, American billionaire oil, rail, sport and telecoms entrepreneur) with plans for a 20,000 seat sports and entertainment venue, and a housing and office development on the surrounding land of 150 acres. In May 2005 Anschutz sold the rights to the Dome to O_2, a mobile phone company. The refurbished Dome, rebranded 'The O_2', was reopened to the public on 24 June 2007 with a concert by Bon Jovi. A bid for The O_2 to host the UK's first 'super casino' failed in 2007 when the government awarded this licence to Manchester. Although one-third of the ground floor remains undeveloped, the official renaming of the Dome on 31 May 2008 promoted its transition into an entertainment district. For the 2012 Olympics, the Dome and adjoining temporary arenas are designated for use as a venue for the artistic gymnastics, trampolining and basketball finals. Due to IOC sponsorship regulations however, it will officially be known as 'North Greenwich Arena' during the Games.

Figure 18.2. The Millennium Dome, north Greenwich (December 2000).

Financing London 2012

The design and development of the London 2012 Olympic project have taken place during an extreme cycle of economic boom and bust. The bid and cost estimation was produced in an unprecedented period of consumption and construction growth globally, and particularly in residential development in the United Kingdom. This boom had been fuelled and accelerated by further liberalization and availability of credit following the dot.com crash (2000–2001), with low borrowing rates leading to speculation and what became known in the

United States as 'sub-prime' lending, which would later contribute to the downfall of major financial institutions in the United States (e.g. Lehman Brothers), the United Kingdom (e.g. Northern Rock) and elsewhere. London's construction bid estimates were quickly exposed once the award made the project a reality. Construction costs rose rapidly as decisions over venue design looked to existing developers and star architects to produce the required Olympic effect – at a price. History confirms that architects of ambitious schemes seldom come in anywhere near their original budget, whilst global demand for materials and consultants made this a suppliers' market. By the time the global credit crunch and ensuing economic crisis took effect in the United Kingdom during 2007–2008, the Olympic budget overruns were established and not recoverable. To make things worse, the recession and the drying up of credit limited commercial sponsorship interest and the financing by commercial developers of the Olympic Village, necessitating further public funding and increases in the core budget (see below). Proceeds from land ('bought high, sold low') and facility disposals are also likely to be depressed, as Olympic agencies seek to recover capital costs – again increasing the public investment long after the games have been held in 2012.

The Olympic event itself is, of course, a known quantity, and ticket sales will doubtless be enthusiastically promoted and taken up (82 per cent ticket yield is forecast). Britain is a keen 'sporting spectator' nation. British spectators were highly visible at team events at Athens 2004 and at international sporting events such as the World Cup (South Africa 2010). Association football (soccer) and major sporting events regularly draw large crowds, albeit with ticket prices for premier events outside of the reach of lower income groups. The IOC-designated Cultural Olympiad,[6] a national cultural programme is also underway with a Festival of Carnivals, World Shakespeare Festival, Stories of the World and artist-led regional projects (in the case of London, 'Bus Tops' – video screens on the top of bus shelters on which artists and the public can create messages and images to be viewed by passengers on the top of double-decker buses. Over 250,000 Volunteers are also to be recruited, particularly from the London Student Pledge, Olympic Language and Young Ambassadors programmes. However, the proposal for an 'Olympic Friend-Ship' that was to be launched at the Beijing Games in 2008 and sail around the world before arriving in London in 2012 was cancelled. This 'journey of discovery' project was queried by the ODA due to the cost and associated risks, including negative public relations. This was an early example of the Olympic bid promises and visions being downgraded as budget and operational realities took over.

The issues of capital and running cost overruns are the main concern in this development phase, as well as planning for exceptional security and terrorism risks. Like the Millennium Dome, the Olympics are also reliant on National Lottery ticket sales – £2.175 billion, up from £1.5 billion in the original budget, via a special Olympic lottery, and £300 million in ticket revenue (9.6 million tickets will be available), with 75 per cent of all Olympic Game tickets costing £48, but 25 per cent priced above this level (Evans, 1995). The diversion of National Lottery funds to the Olympics remains controversial in terms of the negative impact on existing 'good causes' that were the established beneficiaries of the United Kingdom's state lottery (i.e. the arts, heritage, sports, the community and charity sectors, and education, science and technology), but was also predictable as a 'soft' source of off-balance sheet funding for the government since, technically, it was not 'public' funding or spending.

To elaborate, the Lottery had been established by the previous Conservative government in 1995 to provide funding for good causes, which were 'additional' to government's own spending on public services and provision (Evans, 1999a). It was not designed to meet either a shortfall in public sector spending projects or programmes, or be directed by government, but to respond to applicants based on need. Lottery funded projects are also required to meet a public accessibility test. It is doubtful, however, if either additionality or public benefit tests will be adhered to in the Lottery contributions to the Olympic development costs, or whether any of the contribution will be repaid from subsequent post-event asset sales, given the Millennium 'experience' and recession. The British public, of course, can choose whether or not to buy lottery tickets or to attend the Olympics. By contrast, London council taxpayers have no choice. A £20 per annum or 38p per household per week extra tax will be levied to raise a further £625 million towards the Games. The then London Mayor, Ken Livingstone, pledged that Londoners will pay no more than £240 each towards the Games, despite the rising costs. Overspend by the Mayor's Development Agency (LDA) on land acquisition and other as yet unfunded commitments will inevitably need to be recovered via Londoners – whether through direct tax precepts, or reductions in London services (e.g. transport and regeneration). So it came as no surprise, therefore, that in a 2006 BBC London poll of the public's attitude towards the London Olympics, nearly 80 per cent believed that the Games would end up costing Londoners more than this levy.

The history of cost overruns and unrealistic and unrealized budget and visitor forecasts present the modern Olympics with a major credibility problem. Nevertheless, learning from the past is not high on the agenda. Previous Olympic experiences are seen as 'atypical', although there are, say, comparisons with the much heralded example of Barcelona (Experian, 2006; see also chapter 14). The proportion of the total budget, for example, is comparable between Barcelona and London, with 45–50 per cent on sports facilities, Athletes' Village and infrastructure, and roughly 40 per cent on transport, although London's operations and security costs represent a much higher element. The firm of consultants used to prepare the visitor forecasts and impact assessment for the Millennium 'Dome' ten years earlier (Price Waterhouse, 1994) has again been used for London 2012 in both impact (PriceWaterhouseCoopers, 2005) and evaluation exercises (PriceWaterhouseCoopers, 2009). Distancing and distinguishing the project from its precursors also allows the promoters to ignore warnings and claim immunity when history repeats itself.

The *post hoc* reviews that governments tend to commission are more about attributing blame and non-compliance (e.g. National Audit Office), than implementing a real change in organizational behaviour and assessment regimes. Experience with the Dome, major public facilities such as the Scottish Parliament building (Sudjic, 2005), Jubilee Line Extension and recent sporting stadia – for example, the new Wembley Stadium[7] – suggests that publicly procured mega-event facilities are very hard to cost control and almost guaranteed to degenerate into contractual disputes and political controversy (see the discussion of mega-projects in chapter 9). Ironically the UK has been undergoing a massive public facility building programme – notably in transport, public health care (the largest hospital rebuilding programme in the world), and education ('Building Schools for the Future'). This investment has been substantially funded outside the public spending balance sheet, under the government's Private Finance Initiative (PFI). Nevertheless, the PFI has not been used to finance Olympic capital projects. This is an indication of the poor viability of such facilities, since PFI contractors earn their considerable returns on facility management and leaseback to the public sector, in return for risk capital investment in the development phase.

Only one bidder emerged for the main London 2012 stadium development (figure 18.3; see further discussion below) and the ODA has had difficulty in generating competitive bids for the other venues, with a lack of free market competition driving up price and placing contractors in an unhealthily strong position. The French *grand projects* experienced similar cost spirals, with similar criticisms, but were ultimately driven through by political will or, perhaps, arrogance, in the case of Pompidou and Mitterand: 'The French system is said to be a "cultural monarchy", where he pleases, the minister in office defines his options and takes his decisions in the fashion of a sovereign, according to the principles of "enlightened despotism"' (Wangermée, 1991, p. 35). However, private sector-led major infrastructure projects offer no guarantee of cost restraint either. The joint

Figure 18.3. Olympic Stadium under construction (December 2009).

UK-French EuroTunnel capital cost was two-thirds higher than budgeted and the company has operated under technical insolvency for more than a decade. When combined with major transport and regeneration projects, the capital risk therefore multiplies. In the case of the Olympics, this risk is ultimately underwritten by the state and municipal authorities, with the most direct and acute impacts falling on local communities and businesses.

Attempting to apply a cost-benefit analysis to an Olympic Games impact assessment initially requires estimating capital and revenue costs, but, like the bidding and national campaigning processes, this aspect is also confused and fluid. Short (2008, p. 332) also noted that: 'objective cost-benefit analysis of hosting the Games remains at a rudimentary stage, with few accurate or comprehensive studies and few comparative data'. In the first place, the income and costs of the event from bidding to staging, are distributed between international, national and city-regional organizations and sponsors, and budgeting is not transparent.[8] Whether state-led or heavily private sponsor oriented, much investment and expenditure is 'off-balance sheet', understating the true resource cost and impacts. Secondly, there is the challenge of attributing expenditure to the Olympic event itself. Strictly, commitments made prior to the decision to bid for the Games for, say, transport and other environmental improvements, as well as in sporting, hospitality and media facilities should be discounted. Governments, however, often anticipate bidding for future mega-events as part of place-making and regeneration strategies and investment is also planned, but not necessarily implemented, as part of the competitive bidding process, as putative hosts 'talk up' their capacity to host future Games.

In practice, winning cities use the Games to accelerate, 'divert' and expand infrastructural investment: 'the hosting of mega-events is often deliberately exploited in an attempt to "rejuvenate" or develop urban areas through the construction and development of new infrastructure, road and rail networks, airports, sewage and housing (Hall, 1992, p. 69). This often entails pulling proposals 'off the shelf' as the heightened Olympic prospect offers sources of finance and political opportunities for fast-tracking projects not feasible under 'normal' conditions. Schemes that would otherwise encounter resistance from politicians, the public and local communities may be attached to the Olympic project, with the hope of finding added value (e.g. the 'feel good' factor or 'legacy').

Losing cities also provide 'negative' examples of the additionality test – investment still made in the absence of the Olympic effect, e.g. New York (2008). Regional capital cities such as Birmingham (1992), Manchester (1996, 2000) and Toronto (1996, 2008) have staked the regeneration of major sites on such failed bids, often despite popular resistance, whilst others have been burdened by the financing and failure associated with undeveloped post-event sites, in some cases long after they occurred (e.g. Montreal for Expo 67 and the 1976 Summer Games). Evidence of incentives and their effect on investment decisions indicates that when not granted or withdrawn (e.g. expiry or cessation of public funding), some projects are cancelled or deferred, but many go ahead with alternative finance and at a smaller scale (PACEC, 1990b; Evans, 1999b). Comparing and attributing Olympic Games and related regeneration expenditure, therefore, is as much of an art as a science (Preuss, 2004). When major transport improvements, site clearance and security considerations are taken into account, total investment rises substantially. In the case of Beijing, the estimated costs were $40 billion to get the Chinese capital's infrastructure ready for 2008, with $23 billion for the Games themselves (BBC Sport, 2006). London 2012 is no exception to this conflation, with a credibility gap between bid estimates, promises and naïve assumptions, on the one hand, and the realities of the land acquisition, construction and delivery package, on the other. The line between Olympics and regeneration and renewal becomes impossible to detect.

Table 18.2 summarizes the capital and operating costs and financing included in the candidature file submitted to the IOC in 2005 (LOCOG, 2004) and in the latest official budget estimates. A £4 billion capital budget and £1.5 billion operating budget was supplemented by the additional financing of transport and site infrastructure, the Athletes' Village and investment in sport at community and elite levels. Post-award, the messy process of procurement and the vagaries of construction and materials costs (e.g. steel) driven up by a global building boom, not least in China (including Beijing Olympics) have been fuelled by 'oversights' in costing, which included omitting Value Added Tax on construction and not adequately allowing for inflation. London is also spending £7 billion on rail infrastructure (Channel Tunnel Rail Link – CTRL and East London line) and £1.5 billion on regeneration programmes in the Lower Lea Valley, largely over and above the Olympic budget: '75 percent of every pound we spend is for long-term regeneration' according to an ODA spokesman (BBC Sport, 2008).

The Olympic budget quickly increased from the bid stage. The £1.5 billion operating budget was re-estimated at £2 billion; land compulsory purchases and compensation rose from £478 million to over £1 billion. With construction inflation running at 7 per cent (as against 3 per cent in the original budget), the £2.375 billion capital cost of the sports venues alone was forecast by late-2006 to have risen by £900 million to £3.3 billion. In March 2007, the government announced its revised budget of £9.235 billion for the construction and security costs – £5.3 billion higher than at the bid stage – which excludes the event staging costs (for which LOCOG is responsible), land acquisition (LDA), other government Olympic-related programmes (sports and culture programmes) and wider transport and infrastructure investment in and around the Olympic catchment area. Individual facility budgets such as the main stadium have increased by 20 per cent. The Aquatics Centre originally budgeted at £75 million was forecast to cost £242 million in July 2005, even after design changes (e.g. roof span) imposed early on to reduce costs. The Athlete's Village increased in cost by over 60 per cent and, with private sector financing unable to be delivered by Lend Lease as the credit crunch hit, government also had to put in an additional £324 million of public funding. This may also present an opportunity for greater control over the post-

Table 18.2. London 2012 Olympic capital and revenue budget estimates (£ million).

Capital and Operating Budget	London2012 Bid Nov 2004	Estimates March 2009	Source of Funding
New facilities and upgrades			
Olympic Stadium	280	538	5,975 Central Government
Aquatic Centre		244	
Velodrome, arenas and temporary upgrades	280	118	
International Broadcasting and Press Centre		120	2,175 National Lottery
Transport improvements (Olympic Park)	130	355	925 Greater London Authority
Bridges, tunnels	380	380	
Site security, elite sport, contingencies	350	350	
Athletes' Village	650	1,100	250 London Development Agency (LDA)
Security	200	600	
Other infrastructure and regeneration	1,766	4,120	
Contingency (balance as at December 2009)	–	1,400	
Agreed Funding Package	*4,036*	*9,325*	
Lower Lea Valley Regeneration – site acquisition, preparation, infrastructure	800	1,300	LDA 800 Land sales 500
Running costs [LOCOG]	1,500	2,000	Self-financing – including 560 IOC TV/marketing; 450 sponsorship/official suppliers; 300 tickets from venues; 60 Licensing
Athlete preparations [BOA, UK Sport]	300	600	550 Central Government; 50 sponsorship
Transport – Channel Tunnel Rail Link (CTRL), East London Line Extension	6,620	6,620	Central Government and Transport for London. Of which 380 from the Olympic budget, above
Legacy Trust fund 2007–2012	40	40	34 National Lottery; 6 Central Government
Legacy projects	–	253	253 LDA
Total Olympics & Regeneration	*13,926*	*20,138*	

Sources: London Candidacy File (LOCOG, 2004; HoC 2008).

event use of the converted housing, but government will also be under pressure to maximize the sale disposal value in order to recoup its unforeseen investment and fulfil promises made to return funding, for example, to the Lottery.

The twenty-first century, capital city Olympic Games have proved to be the most expensive to date. Ironically this was the reason why, in the previous century (after Tokyo 1964), these cities became wary of hosting the event, but their interest has returned despite this trend. This has been in part due to their intrinsic high costs, such as land and construction, associated investment in infrastructure and regeneration, but also as a result of poor planning, cost control and governance. London is no exception to this scenario. The spectre of the Athens 2004 Games also hovers over London. This eventually produced expenditure of $12 billion, more than double the budget, with security costs (post-9/11) and poor ticket sales adding to the deficit. This was in addition to $16 billion in transport and other infrastructure development. Before that, Sydney 2000 cost over $2.8 billion against an initial budget of $1 billion (Cashman, 2006), while Beijing's total bill for building the Games and associated transport and clearance is put at $40 billion (Broudehoux, 2007). Rio's bid budget for the 2016 Summer Games was $14 billion, with major investment also scheduled for its 2014 World Cup – these mega-events together representing a national regeneration and profile-raising programme akin to Seoul 1988 and Beijing 2008. Beijing expected a small profit on the 2008 Games and London still aims to make a surplus of £100 million to be reinvested in sport (LOCOG, 2004). Given the post-event attribution problems, however, these small surpluses represent, at best, creative accounting and at worst a public relations sop that is dwarfed by the massive public spending underlying the accelerated regeneration project that the Games opportunity presents to politicians (national and local) and to private developers. Most worryingly, line by line comparison between the cost estimates is difficult to undertake, as the United Kingdom government's Public Accounts Committee observed: 'despite the £5.9 billion increase in the public funding for the Games, the Department has not specified what will be delivered in return for this expenditure and the current budget cannot be reconciled to the commitments in the original bid' (HCCPA, 2008, p. 5).

Winning Ways

London and more so, the outside world, never expected to win the 2012 bid. Land acquisition and relocations had, not surprisingly, been taken less than seriously. The planning, IOC review visit and press support, built up a momentum in the last few months, as credibility and confidence grew – but second place was still regarded as the 'best' outcome. The regeneration legacy was not reliant upon the Olympics; this would be the icing on the cake and provide the international cachet, even to an established world city and cultural capital. London's bid therefore rested pragmatically on both broader regeneration and legacy plans, including explicit 'with' and 'without' Games scenarios.

This formed the consultation roadshow that rolled out to the East London communities who would be most affected by the Regeneration Games. The master-planning team, led by the US firm of AECOM (formerly EDAW), with stadium architects Populous (formerly HOK) and urban designers Allies and Morrison, also employed a firm of community architects, Fluid, to undertake the community consultation on the Olympic and Legacy plans. The Community Engagement included over thirty public events, the distribution of 400,000 public information leaflets to incumbent households and the requisite (if temporary) website. An estimated 5,000 people participated in the event programme held in various community venues in the five Olympic boroughs. Local businesses (around 300 firms) and 'hard to reach' groups were also targeted to ensure their voice was at least heard. The firm undertaking the consultation also worked with the Lea Valley Matrix Group, but this group had been established and led by the LDA itself, comprising businesses, boroughs and local regeneration partnerships. It was neither a representative nor independent community organization (Harskamp, 2006).

Organized opposition to the Olympics was evident locally. Based on experience from other Olympic cities and mega-events, residents, environmentalists, businesses, cultural groups and others were anxious about the negative impacts, spiralling costs and displacement arising from the development. Ideological resistance was also apparent, but the Olympic good news story and the outsider status of the London bid lessened the negative press. Most observers did not expect the city to win and so opposition was not coordinated. Following the award in July 2005, organized resistance has focused on monitoring the development process and legacy promises[9] and on campaigning against land and premises relocation as the pace of issuing compulsory purchase orders (CPOs) intensified. Three years after the 2004 bid feasibility plan, the Olympic Park masterplan was approved by central and local government. With construction commencing, an infamous and impervious blue wall was erected around the Olympic site (figure 18.4) cutting off access to and through the area for local people, with the prospect of over two miles of the wall remaining for a decade or more as residual sites await redevelopment.

Not all sports venues will be concentrated in East London's Olympic Park complex. World-class facilities for specialist events are already available elsewhere, such as Wimbledon for tennis and Lord's cricket ground for archery. Football matches will be staged at Wembley and other United Kingdom football stadia (Cardiff, Glasgow, Birmingham, Newcastle and Manchester), with sailing at Weymouth on the south coast of England. Temporary facilities will be made available for beach volleyball in Horseguards Parade, triathlon in Hyde Park and horse riding events in Greenwich Park, as well as in local exhibition venues. However, the permanent legacy in terms of sports venues, cityscape and landscape resides primarily in the Olympic zone where the local impacts and physical change are most radically felt.

Local Impacts

The broader regeneration growth strategy within which the Olympic site represents a key node, relates to the Thames Gateway, of which the Olympic zone

Figure 18.4. Two views of the blue wall erected around the Olympic construction site (October 2008).

forms a north-western segment. The Thames Gateway stretches from east and south-east London, further south and east to the counties of Essex and Kent, and out to the Medway estuary. It is the subject of large-scale house building plans (240,000 new homes per annum, 3 million by 2020) and forms a key plank of the government's Sustainable Communities strategy (ODPM, 2003*b*, 2003*c*). The annual housing targets required to meet this growth have repeatedly not been met even during the prolonged housing boom period, and the pace of development has been slow (and near-moribund since the credit crunch recession hit in 2008).

The Olympics therefore provide an investment leverage opportunity to accelerate development, with 25 per cent of London's entire housing growth predicated on developments within the Olympic zone.

The heart of the Olympic developments and associated regeneration will therefore be at Stratford. The initial Olympic site plans revealed a park and associated zone of development situated in a linear strip measuring roughly two kilometres from north to south, in the valley of the River Lea – a small river that flows south from the Chiltern Hills to meet the River Thames at Bow Creek. By 2011, when trial events begin, this will contain the main Olympic stadium and Aquatics Centre (figure 18.5) and Village, together with the Paralympic tennis and archery facilities, hockey centre, velopark, fencing hall, handball arena, aquatic centre, basketball arena, media centres and warm-up facilities. These are to be served by a major transport interchange, located one kilometre to the east of the stadium at Stratford and served by underground, national rail, Eurostar and bus services. The Olympic zone and 250 hectare Park are designed to be as compact as possible, covering an area one-third the size of the Beijing Olympics site.

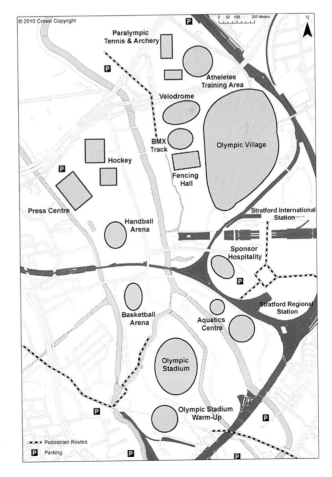

Figure 18.5. Schematic depiction of Olympic Park and Venues.

When designated, however, the area presented a wholly different picture to the observer. Criss-crossed by a maze of river channels and canals, the area contained a mosaic of undeveloped flood plain (figure 18.6) and industrial land. Some of the latter was long derelict, but other sites involved manufacturing facilities and other employment activity which needed to be relocated. In some cases, active regeneration had already started before designation. For instance the Clays Lane residents were approached by the LDA in 2003 to discuss relocation. This area of London has been undergoing piecemeal and selective regeneration for over ten years and reflects successive urban programmes under Conservative and Labour governments (e.g. City Challenge, Single Regeneration Budget, New Deal for Communities and European Regional Development Fund) which have collectively produced a 'patchwork' of regeneration funding schemes. It is perhaps ironic that the new demands made by the 2012 Games have had the result of seeing previously proposed areas of regeneration themselves subsequently subject to compulsory purchase orders.

Figure 18.6. The Pudding Mill River, tributary of the River Lea, bisecting the southern part of the future Olympic Park. The 80,000-seater Olympic stadium will be located to the left and the warm-up tracks to the right (May 2007).

Within months of the award to London, CPOs were sent to nearly 300 businesses within the Olympic Park zone, including those in the Marshgate Lane industrial area where over 5,000 workers were employed. Compensation offered to firms who benefited from cheap and scarce industrial premises in proximity to central London and national transport access was reported to be 20 per cent to 30 per cent less than the original prices paid by owners: 'the Marshgate Lane Business Group argued that the LDA had allocated £450 million to relocate all the businesses when professional advisers to the businesses estimated that the real cost will be more than £1.5 billion' (COHRE, 2007b, p. 14). The LDA has spent £1.3 billion on this exercise, leaving an excess debt of £500 million after intermediate land sales, and this sum is as yet 'unfunded'. Over the course of the land acquisition and clearance of the Lower Lea Valley area, businesses employing nearly 15,000 workers were reportedly forced to move with some firms offered alternative locations over 50 miles (80 km) away. Reluctantly most firms settled or had their appeals turned down at Enquiry. There has surprisingly been little follow up or monitoring of the impact of the enforced relocation of businesses by the LDA or other local authorities, and the direct and indirect loss of employment arising is again not reflected in the headline employment figures predicted for the new leisure-retail economy.

The loss of firms through relocation or cessation obviously has an impact on local employment and multiplier effects on the local economy, but the nature of production also suffers. This included artists and designer-makers, who were located in ACME Studios' Carpenters Road premises. These housed 140 studios that have now been demolished. New studios have been incorporated by Newham borough in mixed-use developments in Stratford, but these have replaced only a fraction of this provision and this studio community will never be replaced at this scale and concentration. It is estimated that over 25 per cent of the United Kingdom's total artist studio provision (6,000 artists in 135 buildings) were located in the Olympic host boroughs, occupying affordable and supportive studio premises. This cultural asset must be at threat (as it was in Beijing's 798 cultural district):

> The irony is that, while London's vibrant, diverse and influential culture has been promoted as a significant aspect of London 2012, the very studio complexes that have contributed to that vitality, along with other supporting businesses such as materials suppliers are under threat and some have disappeared altogether. (Millington, 2009)

There were two main reasons for locating the Olympic Park in this area of East London. The first, which needs little emphasis, was the availability of brownfield land and existing transport extensions to rail and underground systems, including Eurostar and JLE (Evans and Shaw, 2001). The second was the disadvantaged profile of incumbent communities in Newham and the adjoining 'Olympic boroughs'. Relative 'deprivation' is measured in England by a number of economic, environmental and social (including education) factors, weighted by government towards employment and economic participation (ODPM, 2003a, 2004), as opposed to factors such as crime and safety and housing. These include individual domains such as income, education and skills, health, and housing and environment together producing a composite standard by which local areas are ranked nationally, with the score of 1 representing the most deprived area in a national 'Index of Multiple Deprivation' (IMD) (figure 18.7). This therefore

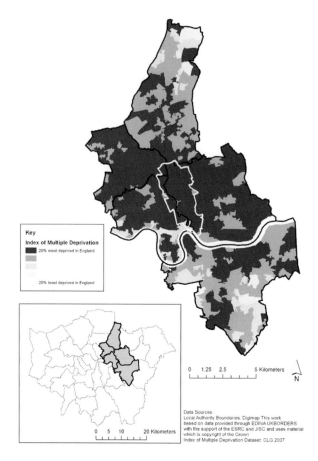

Figure 18.7. Index of Multiple Deprivation in the five Olympic Boroughs showing the Olympic Zone in the centre.

provides a national league table which is used as the prime criteria for regional and other regeneration assistance programmes (i.e. public funding).

Table 18.3 shows the ranking of the income factor in the IMD, comparing the Olympic zone neighbourhoods with Olympic sub-region boroughs, and with London and England as a whole. This shows that 83 per cent of the Olympic zone neighbourhoods (and 39 per cent of the five boroughs) are ranked in the top ten most income-deprived areas in England, and 47 per cent in the worst five. This income ranking had worsened for the Olympic area since the bid was submitted (IMD, 2007) and represents the baseline against which progress and improvement will be measured. The Olympic zone (as opposed to boroughs and Park area) is also not an administratively defined area, but incorporates the Park and permanent venues, including Stratford Village. The changes in deprivation may well start to reflect displacement, as well as the failure of regeneration, at least in the short term, to reach those on lower incomes, but as higher income residents move in, this ranking may well fall.

A key national and regional legacy from the Games is increased sports participation (two million 'more physically active' by 2012) and improved health of residents. Poorer parts of the Olympic boroughs exhibit some of the lowest physical activity rates and highest obesity rates in London. The Olympic borough

Table 18.3. Ranking of lower Super Output Areas (SOAs) on Income Deprivation. Domain of Index of Multiple Deprivation (per cent of SOAs, IMD 2007 with 2004 in parentheses).

Ranking on IMD (% of all SOAs)	Olympic zone (%)	Five Olympic boroughs (%)	London (%)	England (%)
> 10–15	7 (13)	12 (17)	9 (8)	5 (5)
> 5– 10	21 (20)	20 (19)	9 (9)	5 (5)
> 1–5	48 (38)	22 (18)	7 (6)	4 (4)
Up to 1	14 (4)	5 (2)	1 (1)	1 (1)

Source: IMD 2007 (IMD 2007, per PriceWaterhouseCoopers, 2005).

of Newham had the lowest participation rate in regular physical exercise at 14.5 per cent – less than half the rate in the most active borough of Richmond with 29.8 per cent (Sport England, 2006), and reception age (4–5 year old) children had the highest prevalence of obesity in Hackney (16 per cent). As Curtis (2006, p. 9) suggests: 'the journey of the Olympic torch in 2012 will end among some of the laziest and least sporting communities in the UK ... the least likely to leave their couches to take some form of recreational exercise'. Life expectancy is 2.5 years lower than in England as a whole, with higher adult mortality and infant mortality. Another key indicator of quality of life and a target of regeneration intervention is crime and community safety. Violent crime in Newham increased by 5 per cent in 2006–2007 and overall crime rates remain over 20 per cent higher than in London generally (British Crime Survey, 2008–2009). If the inevitable gentrification and 'destination Stratford' strategies accelerate social change and divisions in the post-Olympic zone, crime opportunities and rates are likely to increase and require much greater controls and privatization of public spaces in order to protect new investment, residents and image.

Improved sports facilities and other supply-led interventions to remove barriers to higher levels of participation have targeted local people through Olympic-supported programmes. However, how far the main venues will be accessible to these groups is questionable, again given past experience. The Olympic effect on participation has proved to be weak: 'existing evidence suggests that the presumed trickle down effects of general increase in sports participation and a general improvement in health and fitness are unlikely direct outcomes of a successful Olympic Games' (Coalter, 2004, p. 12). During and after the Sydney Olympics seven sports saw activity levels increase slightly then fall back, but nine others actually declined (Veal, 2003) and sports participation did not improve after Manchester's Commonwealth Games. Participation amongst some minority ethnic groups and women in particular reveal much lower levels, but these represent some of the key groups and supposed beneficiaries of the Olympic 'effect' and sports development programmes. The spectre of a new and improved Olympic Park and recreation area servicing Londoners, visitors and the occasional spectator, rather than the resident community, contrasts markedly with the multicultural young faces presented in London's winning bid.

Legacy Use

The legacy plan shows the key after-use facilities, excluding the temporary facilities which will be removed after the Games (figure 18.8). This includes downsizing the main sports stadium from approximately 80,000 seats to 25,000 and converting the Olympic Village to promised mixed-income housing. The legacy use of the main stadium – originally scheduled to provide a much needed athletics venue – is still undetermined however, with the possibility of a 30,000 or 50,000 seat stadium. Alternative proposals include Premier League football (West Ham United Football Club have shown intermittent interest), or rugby. Post-event stadia use for major league football has taken place in Munich, where

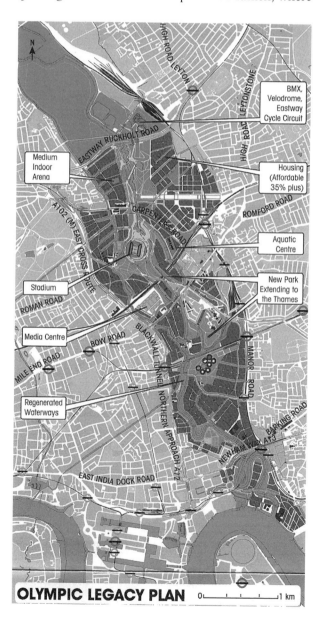

Figure 18.8. Map of Olympic Park in Legacy mode, as presented in public consultation masterplan (Fluid, 2004).

Bayern Munich used the Olympic stadium until 2005. In the case of Manchester, the 2002 Commonwealth Games stadium, originally designed for their failed Olympic 2000 bid, is now occupied after conversion by Manchester City Football Club, who signed a 250 year lease. Elsewhere, Sydney's stadium has been used for a variety of sports including rugby, whereas the Olympic Stadium in Barcelona has housed sports, cultural and celebratory events (including Nit Blanc late night festival and late night swimming). By the same token, the Athens stadium lies largely unused. The London 2012 Aquatics centre will also be downsized from 17,500 to 2,500 seats for community, club and school use with the handball arena and velopark also remaining. Most other venues and facilities will be dismantled or returned to their former use.[10]

Environmental improvements (including transport access) will be the main physical features of the Olympic legacy. However, as outlined in table 18.3, it is the economic regeneration and consequent social benefits – given the association of poor housing, health, education and crime with poverty and lack of work – that have been used to justify the sustainability of London 2012, and ultimately the longer term benefits to offset the explicitly stated and indeterminate direct and indirect costs. Event and post-event economic impacts also rely in part on maintaining increased tourism flows, with 15,000 additional hotel rooms available within 50 kilometres of the Olympic zone.[11] In addition, there will be employment from growth sectors of the economy such as the creative industries, with a 'creative hub' centred on Stratford and post-event usage of the Media Centre and International Press Centre (Evans, 2006c). Attempts at developing a knowledge and creative economy centred on the Olympic legacy have been stunted. Despite a 'shop window' presence by higher education institutions in Stratford, proposals for the legacy use of the Media Centre and International Press Centre, handball arena and other 'permanent' sites for various education, arts and design academy use, and related creative industry development (viz Barcelona's @Media development in the Olympic Poblenou zone) have so far been rejected. The borough of Hackney in which the Olympic Media centre is located still looks to create a retail distribution centre there, despite the public investment in high-tech communications facilities.

Housing

It is claimed that new housing will also attract residents to 2,800 apartments and other dwellings in the Olympic Village and 9,000 to 10,000 in the Olympic Park area as a whole. Like a number of the headline figures used by the Olympic delivery agencies these deliberately exaggerate and conflate existing development activity, since the 'new' homes partly replace demolished housing, for example the former 450 resident/150 dwelling Clays Lane Estate, and include modified housing in Stratford City which was already designated for development even without the Olympics. The net increase may only achieve half the predicted new homes (Cheyne, 2008, p. 14). The masterplan for the swathe of East London along the Lea Valley also allows new housing and amenities to be designed with facilities that are less than the accepted national standards (new housing in London during the 2000s has been built at the lowest space standards per dwelling in Western Europe, closer to East European levels). By contrast, the aspirations of local people[12] are to escape overcrowding and to own houses with gardens (Ryser, 2010). Present policy, therefore, runs the risk of reinforcing a lower quality of life on this historically poorly served community and environment, which has seen its docklands, manufacturing and smoke-stack industrial base (with concomitant pollution and land contamination), irrevocably decline. This also reflects the pace of new development that was already taking place in the Olympic boroughs, and the drive, supported by the then London Mayor Ken Livingstone and central government, for higher density in the shape of so-called 'compact' living and working (Evans *et al.*, 2009; ODPM, 2003*a*).

Sustainable compact living requires quality and levels of amenity, urban design and local employment to counter outward commuting and car use (Evans, 2005*b*). In practice this has resulted in building on previously developed or 'brownfield' land; land that may have amenity value in the form of open space and parkland, which includes backland, infill developments and gardens. London has the lowest amount of brownfield land in all English regions. Most of this is in current use, but has planning permission for higher-value use. The claims for the 'new' Olympic Park likewise do not reflect the loss of pre-existing open space, natural environments and recreation areas (including the Eastway Cycle circuit and other facilities run by the Lea Valley Regional Park). The area was also host to established, but now evicted and rehoused, traveller communities; the two groups were re-housed, much to the chagrin of residents, in newly-built bungalows. Allotment holders in the Manor Gardens allotment site were also evicted and transferred to temporary, less satisfactory sites in 2007, leading to loss of active members. There were promises that the allotments will return to a site within the Park seven years later, although local authority mayors are adamant that they do not want the allotments to return there.

The attraction of the Olympic zone served by new transport links to central London, Canary Wharf and the suburbs had already seen the borough of Newham produce the highest increases in average house prices in the UK between 1999 and 2009 – an increase of 190 per cent over this decade (compared with the national average of 117 per cent), with above-average rises in neighbouring Olympic host boroughs of Hackney (143 per cent) and Tower Hamlets (146 per cent). 'Improved sports venues' were seen as the long-term benefit with most potential by those surveyed nationally. By contrast, regeneration of the area scored highest amongst Londoners, particularly amongst higher (AB) socio-economic groups, who were twice as likely to mention this factor as C2DEs. Similar results were obtained for improved transport (DCMS, 2008, p. 31). The image presented of metropolitan, post-Olympics Newham plays on this aspirational cosmopolitan community as

Burgeoning Bohemian – according to one masterplan proposal for Stratford town centre – using 'vibrant', youthful images of busy street markets from other up-market parts of London.

A key test of legacy benefits and regeneration impacts will, of course, be the housing and employment provision for local people – incumbent, Londoners and migrants – once the infrastructure is in place and life returns to normality. Disposal of the Athletes' Village housing in previous Olympics has failed to meet promised social housing need or affordability. Affordability in housing is another public policy myth, retold in Olympic plans – with 50 per cent of London 2012 Olympic Village housing targeted to be affordable homes once decommissioned and adapted for everyday occupation (via a government housing grant awarded to Triathlon Homes). Yet, 'affordable' is a misnomer in London's property market. With average house prices between £250,000 and £300,000, a first time buyer requires £55,000 per annum income to secure a mortgage (the average household income in Newham is £28,000). Only socially-rented property would meet the housing needs of many local people and families on lower incomes, but this is not a realistic prospect in any legacy scenario or regime.

Employment

Post-event employment and economic development is rather less apparent in the Olympic-related regeneration plans (Experian, 2006; Kornblatt, 2006). Estimates of the contribution of the Games to the *national* economy prior to the Olympic city award was put at only 0.34 per cent over seven years (Patrick, 2005), with a net gain of £82 million (Crookson, 2004).[13] It is the wider *distributive* effects that are attributed to the Olympic regeneration impact, particularly in employment. However, in the government's own initial impact appraisal (PriceWaterhouseCoopers, 2005), projected employment is highly concentrated in pre-event construction activity and benefits the London region more than the local economy (see table 18.4). Olympic boroughs have some of the highest unemployment rates in the United Kingdom, with rates that are 50 to 150 percent higher amongst some ethnic minority groups, such as young Asian and Afro-Caribbeans, than their white counterparts. Economic activity rates in these communities are some 10 per cent lower than the London average.

The Olympic boroughs' policy, and yet another 'vision', has been to address longstanding deprivation through 'stopping the cycle of residents who prosper and for whom conditions improve, moving out of the area, as less well off people move in' (London Borough of Newham, 2009, p. 8). The prospect of new apartment dwellers, professional and shopworkers reversing this process of course risks displacing both established and new lower income settlers, as housing and accessible jobs are priced out of their reach. 'Buy to let' and other property investors will likely take up new apartment housing, as they have in other city development areas (Evans *et al.*, 2009), limiting any prospect for a 'sustainable community', with

Table 18.4. Summary of expected impacts on employment.

Area	Pre-event (2005–2011)	During event (2012)	Legacy/post-event (2013–2016)	Overall (2005–2016)
UK	2,955	3,261	1,948	8,164
London	25,824	3,724	9,327	38,875
North-east London	7,344	311	311	7,966

Source: PriceWaterhouseCoopers (2005).

properties left empty or let to transient occupiers such as students, weekday-only users and 'offshore' owners.

The employment 'saviour' in the Olympic zone is retail, based on a new Westfield shopping complex located just north of the Park and linked to Stratford town with its own shopping centre and street markets (both likely to be hit by the new competition). Westfield will be the largest urban (as opposed to 'out of town') mall in Europe with 1.9 million square feet of floorspace housing over 300 shops (the size of seventy-four Wembley football pitches) and where an estimated 8,500 new jobs are to be created in addition to employment in Olympic Village amenities such as schools, health and new (177,000 square metres) office space. This is resonant of the Liverpool One retail centre which opened during the Capital of Culture 2008 (Evans, 2010), and somewhat similar to Barcelona's Diagonal Mar development of a major retail, hotel and office complex, connected by coast road and extension to the city's metro system. Like Stratford, this 'extension' sought to expand Barcelona's overheated accommodation and consumption cluster from the old city centre and rebalance the post-industrial part of the city, with a major digital media complex ('@22') centred on relocated University Pobra Fabra (Art and Design) campuses and commercial (MediaPro) hi-tech facilities in this former textiles and working-class district on the edge of the Olympic zone (Evans, 2006a).

Delivering the vision for Metropolitan Stratford (London Borough of Newham, 2009) is therefore a litmus test of London 2012's Olympic regeneration and very much its centre. As well as transport connectivity (from 2012 Stratford will be the second most 'connected' transport interchange in the UK after King's Cross-St Pancras, to which it will be linked via Eurostar trains), a prospective Metropolitan Stratford inevitably will see its population profile shift through gentrification, with inflow and outflow of residents and workers. How far its social and multicultural mix will be maintained remains to be seen (at present less than 40 per cent of the population is 'white'). Previous large-scale redevelopment programmes strongly suggest that lower income and more vulnerable residents will be crowded out, move further east or remain in ghetto-like isolation as the doughnut effect takes shape around them, creating greater social and economic divide than already exists. As Fabien Vaujany (2006) suggested: 'The bid said the Olympics would be a one-in-a-lifetime opportunity for the local community. This might prove true: it just depends on what the local community looks like.'

As the Olympic site development commenced, major sports facilities such as the new national football stadium at Wembley (public) and Arsenal Football Club's Emirates Stadium (commercial) were completed in London, involving some of the same Olympic contractors. This boom in facility provision must be seen in the context of an industry which has an endemic lack of capacity and skills, as highlighted in the Egan Review (Egan, 2004; Bailey, 2005), the Urban Task Force's identification of a 'design skills deficit' (CABE, 2001), and regional assessments of regeneration skills (Bagwell *et al.*, 2005). Nationally, an extra 348,000 workers were forecast to be needed by 2010, with the highest demand from east and south-east London regions (CITB, 2006). It is no surprise therefore that foreign contractors and workers have migrated to fill this gap, although since the global recession, particularly impacting on construction activity since late-2008, Polish and other migrant workers have returned home to less severely affected economies. This has reduced an estimated 1.5 million 'new East European' workers to around 750,000. This pattern of inward migration is however long established, particularly in this area of London where Hugenot, Jewish, Irish and Bangladeshi immigrants, among others, have gone before. Today, East European economic migrants underpin the construction and other service activities. What these groups share historically is resistance from incumbent communities as a result of competition for jobs, housing and amenities, and some of the worst discrimination and stigma attaching to their unglamorous and unromantic contribution to London's infrastructure (Evans and Foord, 2005). Ironically, it is members of these residual communities in the East End that now represent some of the highest groups of economic inactivity, and are targets of the Olympic trickle down effect. As Vigor (2006, p. 14) noted:

> If the Lower Lea Valley is to be transformed – socially as well as physically – then these are the people who need to access new employment opportunities. Sustainable regeneration will require a genuine increase in the local employment rate – not just the result of highly skilled population moving in and displacing the indigenous lower skilled one.

A sobering fact is that nearly 20 per cent of the adult population in the Thames Gateway have no formal qualifications and half of the children live in workless households. As the incoming chief executive of the Thames Gateway Partnership, Judith Armitt said: 'educational attainment in the region [is] very depressing, and [is] often overlooked because of a focus on more tangible regeneration such as transport and infrastructure' (*Building Design*, 2006, p. 5).

As Vigor (2006, p. 14) also pointed out: 'past Olympics have focused too closely on hard infrastructure concerns. Organizers have automatically assumed that the people and places most in need of any lasting benefits will receive them. There is little evidence of this'. This scenario is thus worrying. The response from the then Mayor of London was the creation of a London 2012 Employment and Skills Task Force (LEST), with the aim of training low skilled residents so they can compete for any new jobs that arise, and to work with employers to change their recruitment procedures, 'which have sometimes discriminated against such individuals' (LEST, 2006). The government's pre-Olympics target has been to reduce worklessness by 70,000 and achieve an employment rate of 80 per cent by 2020, with host boroughs equal to the London average in 10 to15 years. However, this is a tall order as Olympic boroughs have economic activity rates of 62 per cent in the case of Newham and Tower Hamlets and 65 per cent in Hackney. Olympic LEST programmes costing over £70 million have 'adopted' these same targets, so again any Olympic-derived impacts would not be 'additional', but the new public investment is being used to meet existing government policy targets.

The notion that the least 'skilled', or more accurately those whose skills are now redundant in a post-industrial city will be transformed into the construction and service workers required to deliver the Olympics 'on time, on budget' was perhaps unrealistic (Kornblatt, 2006). Public procurement legislation requires contracts for supplies and services of £90,000 and over to be advertised throughout the European Union and combined with the labour market challenge: 'at present there's no reason why London 2012 should not provide more of a skills legacy for Gdansk (Poland) than Newham' (LCC, 2005). While it is claimed by the ODA (Higgins, 2009) that over 20 per cent of construction jobs are held by residents of the five Olympic boroughs, this will have included migrant workers based there. In addition, local suppliers and food outlets (including many minority ethnic entrepreneurs) will also be excluded from sales during the Games, as global sponsors (Coca Cola, McDonalds, Cadbury/Kraft) receive monopoly status. Plans to regenerate East London formed a key part of the capital's successful bid to host the Games, but as the Chamber of Commerce observed: 'That objective can only be met if the Games itself benefits local businesses' (LCC, 2005).

Conclusion

Writing about an Olympic host city over four years after designation and still two years before the big event, makes any assessment of London 2012 contingent and speculative. Related global and national factors also intervene. The global recession, extreme levels of public debt and consequent spending reductions arising from this, the future shape and timing of the 'recovery', and the changed political landscape arising from the national and local elections of 2010 will have a major impact in the run up to, delivery and aftermath of the 2012 Games. Notwithstanding these factors, the accumulating mega-event and regeneration experience (Evans, 2005a, b) suggests a predictable path and outcome. The history, as Baudrillard once said of the impending entry to the new Millennium, has already been written (Evans, 1999a). The alternative to the Olympic development machine rolling inexorably on would require a leap of imagination and the act of squarely confronting the 'political consequences of creating a blueprint for a less costly, less cumbersome Olympics, without the endless decision-making that permanent buildings demand' (Allen, 2006, p. 3).[14] As Allen (ibid.) went on to ask – pertinently for Rio 2014 and 2016 and other prospective host cities – 'which would be the most meaningful Olympic legacy? A blueprint that makes hosting the Olympic Games a viable aspiration for developing countries? Or a host of mega-structures that have outlived their primary use?'

How the Olympics will be assessed will itself form part of the narratives and history surrounding this latest episode in mega-event regeneration, with impacts that will unfold a generation or more after the event itself. In narrower evaluation and appraisal terms – as required by public bodies dispersing taxpayers' money – official impact studies are seeking to measure change and 'cause and effect' as they can be attributed to Olympic and other programme investment. The Olympic Games Global Impact Study (OGGI) is now a requirement for all hosts, with London undertaking this exercise based on a collection of 120 indicators (Vancouver 2010 being the first Games to do so, following an unsuccessful pilot in Beijing in 2008). A disaggregated set of impact studies is also being commissioned by government departments, including a meta-evaluation study by the DCMS seeking to synthesize all studies (DCMS, 2009). These are driven by government evaluation frameworks and imperatives and are unlikely to reflect the full experience of, or impact on communities, stakeholders, or longer term distributive effects.

The counterfactual – What would have happened without the Olympics in terms of regeneration? What were the opportunity costs from the public investment? – may never be answered, but these are the most important questions underlying the Olympic-regeneration rationale and case, on which the London bid rested. As Hall (1992, p. 83) commented:

> it should be recognised that social impact evaluation will ask the difficult question of who benefits: a question which goes to the very heart of why cities host hallmark events in order to improve or rejuvenate their image and attract tourism and investment.

For his part, Getz (2009, p. 76) optimistically suggests: 'the effect would be to ensure that the usual claims of economic benefits are not accepted at face value, and that social, cultural and environmental measures of value would be equal to the economic'. In reality the political inability to embrace the full impacts and decision-making rationales honestly and transparently, is partly a reflection of the fragmented governance and delivery structure and the stop-go regeneration regimes imposed over a fifty year period. In addition, agencies are affected by the limitations of political and budget horizons and are unable to commit to programmes beyond their likely corporate lives. In some respects this is likely to let the Olympic machine 'off the hook' in terms of full blown evaluation and attribution, but this is not a reason for failing to try and capture as full an analysis and assessment of 'impact' and 'legacy' as is possible – particularly with the benefit of renewed academic and public interest in the phenomenon, and a wider range of data and tools to analyse this than has previously been available.

The day after the 1992 Olympic Games closed, a Commission for the Olympic Legacy convened in Barcelona, although they had not anticipated the extent of the Olympic effect that has become associated with the city. It might be suggested that an independent Commission for the Olympic Legacy would need to convene permanently in London to ensure that the promises and regeneration aspirations are also delivered. Poetry and dance might have been integral to the Olympics of classical Greece, but without this legacy guarantee, it will be hard to avoid Kunzmann's (2004, p. 2) gloomy prediction that: 'Each story of regeneration begins with poetry and ends with real estate'.

Notes

1. A misplaced vote might have helped London win the 2012 Olympics. An International Olympic Committee member (President of the Greek Olympic Committee) had mistakenly voted for Paris rather than Madrid. Paris received 33 votes to Madrid's 31 in the third round, eliminating the Spanish capital. Moscow and New York were eliminated in the first two rounds. Had Madrid received the vote rather than Paris, the cities would have tied with 32 each, seven fewer than London, and entered a tiebreaker. London beat Paris 54–50 in the final round. In the run up to the IOC vote in Singapore, London was still ranked third after Paris, the clear favourite, and Madrid. No city had hosted the Games more than twice (London and Paris) and London had never won by competition, only hosting by default in 1908 and 1948. New York was originally the obvious choice for the 2012 Olympics due to sympathy over 9/11, but much of this support had ebbed away, leaving New York as an unlikely choice. Moreover, public opposition to the city's first location of the Olympic stadium complicated its bid, compounded by protracted disputes over the design and rebuilding of the World Trade Centre and post-9/11 site, and the deferral of schemes such as the proposed Gehry-designed Guggenheim museum over the Hudson River. Madrid and Moscow planned city centre sites. By contrast, Paris had most facilities in place, having hosted the FIFA World Cup in 1998.

2. According to the Chief Executive of the British Olympic Association, Simon Clegg: 'The sole measurement of the Games won't be on how efficient the organizing committee is, or how beautifully architectured the design of the stadiums are – it'll be decided on how many British athletes stand on the podium and collect medals' (http://ukolympics.org.uk. Accessed 1 December 2006). The official target is to improve the place in the Olympic medal table from tenth in 2004 to fourth in 2012.

3. This includes the London Thames Gateway Development Corporation (LTGDC), which includes the five Olympic boroughs (excluding Hackney), plus Lewisham and Bexley in the south-east and Barking & Dagenham and Havering in the north-east, the Thames Gateway London Partnership (TGLP), and over thirty government and area based partnerships responsible for delivering the Thames Gateway Delivery Plan (DCLG, 2007).

4. The Olympic site located in this part of East London had traditionally been the dumping ground for toxic waste, including mustard gas stored during World War I, as well as of engineering and manufacturing that produced pollutants resulting in poisoned soil and water.

5. Lend Lease, an Australian property development company is also the developer of the Olympic Village, housing athletes and providing a mix of social and private housing after the 2012 games. The Chief Executive (CEO) of the Olympic Delivery Authority (ODA) David Higgins was also CEO of the Lend Lease Group from 1995.

6. The Cultural Olympiad is an IOC 'branded' event, encompassing the opening, medal and closing ceremonies, torch relay and a national event programme delivered for London 2012 regionally by the Arts Council, the BBC and Royal Philharmonic Orchestra with local events promoted by the Greater London Authority, local and regional authorities. The Olympic Park

Legacy Company is also responsible for public art, installations and related events as well as other cultural aspects of the Park design and heritage.

7. Massively over-budget and failing to complete to agreed timetables, Wembley left the Australian Multiplex developer near-bankrupt.

8. Government claims for 'transparency' in decision-making and financing of the Olympics are able to be side-stepped under the mask of 'commercial confidentiality' in the procurement process and in special adviser contracts.

9. Games Monitor: debunking the Olympic myths (see www.gamesmonitor.org/uk).

10. Decommissioning and retrofitting costs continue post-event, representing ongoing expenditure in addition to the Olympic budget, as will maintenance and insurance costs until the assets are sold or transferred to new owners.

11. IOC members and their partners are however already booked into West End hotels with fast track road access resulting in road closures and delays for residents and commuters.

12. London Citizens (www.londoncitizens.org.ukaffordablehomes/index.html).

13. In the case of another iconic regeneration project, Guggenheim Bilbao, the contribution to the Basque regional GNP was estimated at 0.47 per cent in 1997, similar to London 2012, with substantial prior public investment in transport infrastructure (Evans and Foord, 2003). As Cerro (2006) concluded 'Bilbao's economic performance since 1994 was not fundamentally due to Gehry's Guggenheim building'. However remarkably the €126m public investment in this project will have been returned to the city via tax and other income on visitor activity in only ten years (Plaza, 2006). The net economic impact of Barcelona 1992 was $30m (Brunet, 1995).

14. Allen (2006, p. 3) suggests that 'the business of temporary public spectacle would be better left to the professional event designers; to those who know how to do it best'. In an effort to produce spectacular buildings, the Olympic commissioning agencies have selected star architects such as Zaha Hadid, whose costly Aquatic Centre design has been substantially scaled back. ODA Chief Executive David Higgins claimed that 'Design is at the Heart of what we are doing here' (*Building Design*, 1 December 2006) and then Culture Minister Tessa Jowell said that the ODA must: 'ensure design is as much of a pre-occupation as cost control' – the ODA had no architect on its board, but in late-2006 appointed design advisers Ricky Burdett (ex-London School of Economics, Greater London Authority Architecture and Urbanism Unit); Peter Cook (University College London and the 1960s group Archigram); and the Tate Gallery director, Nicholas Serota. None has a significant track record of design practice, or of major sports buildings (primarily academic or curatorial careers). Andrew Altman, US-born CEO of the Olympic Park Legacy Company (OPLC) is also on the Board of LSE's Urban Age, which is directed by Burdett who no longer advises the ODA but has a new role as design adviser to the OPLC.

Chapter 19

Rio de Janeiro 2016

John R. Gold

It was a moment of pure theatre, staged for television and based on a model which originated at the Oscar ceremony in 1941 when the Academy of Motion Picture Arts and Sciences first introduced the format of an announcer opening sealed envelopes to reveal the winners (Levy, 2003, p. 53). The voting for the city that would stage the 2016 Summer Olympic and Paralympic Games had been completed over an hour earlier. The President of the International Olympic Committee (IOC), Jacques Rogge, and the other IOC members all knew the result, but were sworn to silence. The audience in Copenhagen's Bella Convention Centre had been cleared to allow in two substantial phalanxes of supporters of the bids for Madrid and Rio de Janeiro – the two cities that had survived until the final round of voting. A suitably svelte blonde Danish athlete brought in an oversized envelope which she presented to Rogge. As he began to open the envelope, he intoned the words: 'I have the honour to announce that the Games of the Thirty-First Olympiad are awarded to the city of…'. After the obligatory dramatic pause, which in this instance lasted fully thirteen seconds, he had clumsily withdrawn the card from the envelope, turned it to the cameras of the world's television networks, and completed his sentence with the words 'Rio de Janeiro'.

The watching television audiences were then confronted with a blur of jump cut images as production teams tried to capture the contrasting emotions of the moment. Inside the hall, the exuberant celebrations of the Brazilian delegates were juxtaposed with the stunned bewilderment of their Spanish counterparts. The explosion of noise from an estimated 30,000 people on Copacabana beach contrasted with the shocked silence of the crowd of around 6,000 in front of the giant screens in Madrid's Plaza de Oriente. 'Expert' commentators were called in to supply instant analyses of what had just occurred. Why did Rio win? What were the features that made its bid strong? Could the Brazilians *really* deliver the Games? How could Chicago, the bookmakers' longstanding favourite, have been eliminated in the *first* round of voting? Had President Obama's brief trip to Copenhagen constituted more of an own goal than proving a decisive act of support for his home city's bid? What did this all mean for the future of the Obama

Presidency and the standing of the United States in the world, the Olympic movement, Latin America, Brazil and the city of Rio de Janeiro?

This chapter traces the path to that decisive moment of realized candidacy at the IOC's meeting on 2 October 2009 – a journey that, for Rio as well as the other candidate cities, had begun at least a decade earlier. In the first section of this chapter, therefore, we trace the previous occasions on which the municipal regime in Brazil's leading port-city had expressed serious interest in staging the Games, followed by analysis of steps that Rio took to improve its credentials as potential host city. The second section deals with the bidding process for 2016, with discussion of the initial long-list of seven applicant cities, followed by analysis of the short-listing process, the eventual submission of the files for the four candidate cities and the campaigns waged in advance of the Copenhagen meeting. The final section briefly takes stock of the situation as the OCOG looks ahead to the process of converting the initial plans, as laid out by the bid documents, into concrete reality.

First Attempts

As with any modern Olympic city, it is difficult to identify with any precision the exact moment when enthusiastic expressions of interest by leading local citizens or significant civic bodies become consolidated into serious initiatives to host the Games. However, if one judges matters on the basis of bids formally submitted and voted on by the IOC, it is apparent that Latin American interest in staging the Games can be traced back to Havana's bid in 1914 for the 1920 Games, with Buenos Aires notably having made four attempts over the years (for the Games of 1936, 1956, 1968 and 2004). None was successful other than when Mexico City received the nomination to stage the 1968 Games at the IOC's Baden-Baden meeting in October 1963. Since that time, no further Latin American city has successfully bid for the Olympics and, indeed, no South American nation had ever done so before Rio de Janeiro in 2009.

At the outset, it should be recognized that while Rio annually stages the world's largest street carnival, the nation's experience of staging sporting mega-events during the twentieth century was limited to just two festivals. The first was the 1950 FIFA World Cup Finals. These were shared between six cities, with the deciding match[1] being played in front of almost 200,000 spectators in the vast concrete bowl of Rio's Maracanã Stadium (Estádio do Maracanã). The second was the Fourth Pan-American Games, held in São Paulo in 1963 with twenty-two competing nations. There was no attempt to assemble a formal bid to host the Summer Olympics[2] from any Brazilian city until a proposal was initiated by Brasília as candidate city for the Millennium Games. Although short-listed, its candidacy was withdrawn before the final voting process took place in April 1993 following an unfavourable report on its facilities by the IOC's inspection team. Rio itself entered the arena with candidacy for the 2004 Games, with a plan commissioned by the Mayor that proposed constructing an Olympic Park and Village in the south-western suburb of Barra da Tijuca (Anon, 2000) – a feature that persisted through into the plans for 2016.

This proposal, however, failed to advance to the short-listing stage. Looking back on it, Carlos Roberto Osorio, the Secretary-General of the Brazilian Olympic Committee, recognized that the bid was deeply flawed (see Monteiro and Shropshire, 2010). He noted that:

> When we first tried to get the Olympic Games for the year 2004, we had a very basic project, and not a very deep understanding of the Olympic world and the requirements to host the Olympic Games.

Nevertheless, he argued that it was a vital initial step in two respects. First, it had inculcated an understanding of the broader context in that the sports sector could not organize such events without the support of the public sector , especially given the associated demands for additional public services and additional infrastructure. Secondly, it had underlined the need to gain experience in running large-scale sports festivals if the city was to gain the chance to stage the 'most complex and the largest event that exists on our planet during times of peace' (*Ibid.*).

That process received a significant stimulus in August 2002 when Rio was nominated to stage the 2007 Pan American Games and Paralympic Pan American Games. While described as a 'second order' sporting mega-event (e.g. Black, 2008), the Fifteenth Pan American Games in Rio de Janeiro would ramp up the festival through new levels of investment – the Games had a budget of $1.9 billion. Its organizers also recognized the importance of media coverage. They provided improved broadcasting facilities and arranged newsworthy devices, such as a large-scale torch relay, with an eye to attracting national interest (BBC News, 2007).[3] They also recognized the lasting importance of commemorative film. The documentary made by Scott Givens of its spectacular Opening Ceremony won the award for best film in the Sports and Society category at the 26th Milan International FICTS (Federation Internationale Cinema Television Sportifs) Festival in November 2007. Givens and his California-based production company FiveCurrents would later be rehired to undertake presentations, videos and creative support for Rio's campaign for the 2016 nomination.

This link between earlier and successor events was symptomatic of the broader chain of connection between the Pan-American Games and the Olympics; a relationship that would have three distinct elements. First, the Pan American Games showed organizational and logistic competence in running a major Games and gave the international community a measure of reassurance that the Brazilians could deliver a larger event. The necessary funding was mobilized, with full support from local, regional and central government. The new and rehabilitated stadia were completed on time and the sporting programme ran smoothly. Fears over crime and security – recurrent concerns in a city that is a major transit point for the Latin American drug trade (Brennan-Galvin, 2002) – were allayed, albeit with a concentrated approach that saturated venues and the surrounding areas with police for the duration of the Games. That approach led to the cancellation of associated festivities that might have provided possible flashpoints. For example, the Brazilian leg of the Live Earth concerts, due to take place on the Copacabana beach on the eve of the Games, was cancelled at short notice (Phillips, 2007). The judge who reviewed the matter referred to recent clashes between drug traffickers and security forces in giving her ruling, stating (*Ibid.*): 'It is far too risky putting on a concert for 700,000 people on the eve of the Pan-American Games and when the police are also involved in the frequent conflicts in the [Complexo do] Alemao [shantytown network]'.

Secondly, preparations for the Pan American Games supplied the legacy of sporting infrastructure suitable for staging such events, which was especially important given that the continental Pan American Games mirrors the Olympics in terms of its multi-sports basis and in having an Athletes' Village. The new facilities included the 45,000-seater João Havelange Stadium (the Engenhão), which was used in 2007 for soccer, track and field; the Maria Lenk Aquatic Park, used for swimming and diving events; and the Barra Velodrome. The revamped Maracanã Stadium, now reduced to around 90,000 seats, staged the Opening and Closing Ceremonies, with the associated Maracanãzinho Gymnasium housing volleyball events. The Athletes' Village, custom-built for the Games at Barra da Tijuca, covered an area of 91 acres (37 hectares) and comprised seventeen ten-storey buildings that supplied a total of 1,480 apartments (Goulartt, 2007, p.18). Noticeably, the venues were situated at four nodes that were all located within a span of 15 miles (25 kilometres) and have good connections to the city's motorway system. They provided an integrated core of facilities that might be used for any subsequent multi-sports festival.

Thirdly, and related, the successful staging of the Pan American Games, with its powerful boost to the state and municipal revenues, reinforced the city's ambition to seek other more prestigious mega-events. Thoughts quickly returned to Rio de Janeiro's aspirations to stage the Olympics even before the Pan American Games were held, when the city put forward a bid for the 2012 Olympics. In gaining the national nomination over Sao Paulo in July 2003, the Rio delegation argued that their city could undercut their rivals given the extent of investment already committed for the Pan American Games. Understandably, the bid offered a Games based on a scaled-up version of the 2007 Pan American project, with deliberate emphasis on the IOC's preference for a nucleated Games. The bidding team's overall message stressed the known sporting passion of the Cariocas and the Brazilian nation, with the message: 'In 2012, we will bring our passion to the world... [because the city] loves everything to do with the Games' (quoted in Tomlinson, 2005, p.186). At this stage, Rio's candidacy did not convince the IOC's Candidature Acceptance Working Group, who concluded on the basis of the eleven key evaluation criteria[4] of the first phase questionnaire that Rio de

Janeiro along with Leipzig, Istanbul and Havana did not have the requisite level of capability at this time to host the 2012 Olympic Games (IOC, 2004a, p. 90). It, thus, again failed to make the shortlist.

Like most recent applicants, the bidding team from Rio saw their failure to secure the nomination not as a permanent rebuff but as a temporary setback that would serve as useful experience from which to hone a subsequent Olympic bid. It was fully recognized that such a bid would benefit from the city consolidating its *curriculum vitae* by hosting other large sporting events. In May 2007, the International Military Sports Council nominated Rio de Janeiro as host city for the Fifth Military World Games. This four-yearly ambulatory sporting festival, closely based on the Olympic template, began in 1995 and now includes twenty-four sports. Further reinforcement of Rio's position came in October 2007 from the success of the national football association (Confederação Brasileira de Futebol) in attracting the FIFA World Cup in 2014, with Rio's position confirmed in May 2009 as one of twelve Brazilian host cities and the probable location for the final match. The likely impact of this event was increased by the linked award to Brazil of FIFA's Confederations Cup in 2013, which will be used as a test event for the following year's finals.[5]

Securing the right to stage the FIFA World Cup Finals, widely regarded as second only to the Olympics in terms of sporting festivals, led the Brazilian government to announce an extensive associated programme of stadia upgrading and infrastructural improvement focused especially on the tourism and communications sectors. Although some elements of the plans either embraced pre-existing projects (e.g. extensions to the metro) or, as in the case of improvements to interior road networks, were likely to have occurred anyway, some significant projects were prompted by the award for 2014. Prominent among them, were the plans for the creation of the Trem de Alta Velocidade Rio-São Paulo (TAV), the first high-speed railway line in Latin America. Costing $9 billion, the 322 mile (518 kilometres) TAV line will move passengers at speeds of up to 220 miles (354 kilometres) an hour, allowing trips between São Paulo and Rio to be completed in under 90 minutes (Zoltan, 2010). Yet despite repeated political assurances, delays in awarding tenders to contractors for construction and for the supply of motive power suggest that the line will not open until 2015 and will miss the staging of the World Cup (Doherty, 2009).

Bidding for 2012

Any renewed candidacy from Rio de Janeiro for the Summer Olympics, whether for 2016 or later, therefore was set against a socio-economic and political landscape that was qualitatively different from that which applied in the mid-1990s when the city had planned a possible bid for the 2004 Games. Nationally, the booming Brazilian economy – with its positive balance of external trade, stable currency and real GDP growth averaging 4.7 per cent between 2003 and 2008 (Jaeger,

2009) – provided an impression of stability to the outside world that was far removed from the usual negative stereotypes of Latin American economies. More locally, Rio could now draw on the legacy of having hosted a major event without serious problems of logistics and security, with the steady accumulation of new infrastructure and world-class facilities. It could also point to having the endorsement of other internationally-constituted bodies by virtue of having received the nomination to stage their sporting festivals. Importantly, Rio gained unanimous national support to be applicant city when the Brazilian Olympic Committee met on 1 September 2006. Nevertheless, the city was never the favourite to receive the nomination for the 2016 Games. Although its campaign had noticeably established a powerful momentum and closed the gap in the last months before the Copenhagen meeting, it seemed, almost until the last stages of voting, that Rio's best result might be to receive a respectable share of the IOC members' votes.

Applicant Cities

The initial timetable saw the IOC send invitations on 16 May 2007 to the 203 National Olympic Committees to nominate applicant cities. When the list closed on 13 September 2007, the seven cities on the long-list of applicant cities had varying pedigrees. Three others besides Rio had previous experience of bidding for the Olympics, with the remainder bidding for the first time. Of the previous applicants, none had histories that extended further back than Chicago. Originally awarded the 1904 Games, the city had relinquished its rights to act as host in the face of the spoiling tactics deployed by the organizers of the 1904 International Exposition at St Louis (see chapter 2). Subsequently Chicago had itself hosted notable World's Fairs (Gold and Gold, 2005), but had failed in three subsequent bids in 1921, 1947 and 1949. Opinions were divided as to whether Chicago's chances might suffer from the recency of other successful US candidacies for the Games (Los Angeles 1984 and Atlanta 1996) or whether the twenty years since the Games had last visited the Americas would be a positive factor in its favour.

Madrid, too, had a significant history of interest in the Games. It had bid for the 1972 Summer Olympics in 1966 and, more recently, came third in the voting for the 2012 Games. Although always likely to face an uphill battle for the 2016 Olympics on grounds of the implicit principle of continental equity – given that the 2012 Games were in London and the 2014 Winter Games were in Sochi (Russia) – its renewed candidacy might have been seen as a determined effort to establish the city as Europe's contender-in-waiting. That impression was reinforced by the fact that its 2016 bid was not hugely different from the failed bid for 2012.

Tokyo was the only city previously to have successfully bid for the Olympics, being the original hosts for the aborted 1940 Olympics before gaining the Games of the Eighteenth Olympiad in 1964. In seeking a further nomination, the bidding team sought to reprise the success of the 1964 Summer Olympics – an event that had played an important part in the ensuing history of both Tokyo and Japan. As with the previous event, the Games would be linked to a major urban planning exercise. The Olympic areas would deploy brownfield land along the waterfront along with land reclaimed from Tokyo Bay that would afterwards leave a legacy of parkland, new housing, retailing, and entertainment venues. The event would also fit in with transportation and open space strategies to allow the creation of a green corridor to reconnect the city centre to the waterfront.

By contrast, Rio's other three rivals on the long-list were all first-time bidders. Although there had been previous bids from Alexandria and Cairo in Egypt for the Summer Games,[6] the bid from Doha (Qatar) still constituted one of the first bids from the Arab world. It might be expected to draw in powerful regional support, especially as it had successfully hosted the 2006 Asian Games. Its Achilles' heel, however, was always likely to be the ferocity of its summer heat if it abided by the normal calendar. Oil-rich Baku, the capital of a country (Azerbaijan) that had only gained its independence in 1991, was understandably a new entrant to the competition for the Olympic nomination. Although possessing the necessary resources, its lack of experience of staging such events and a perception of political instability in the surrounding region were probable drawbacks. Finally, Prague's sixty-six member local assembly voted on 23 March 2007 – somewhat late in the day – to submit a bid for the 2016 Games. This was, at best, a half-hearted effort, clearly lacking real depth of public support. Certainly, initial pronouncements from Prague's leaders gave no sense of any real expectation of winning the bid in view of the fact that the city was a first-time applicant and that, like Madrid, it was a European contender. Rather, the city's leadership regarded candidacy for 2016 primarily as an investment, providing much needed experience for staging succeeding bids to hold the Olympics in either 2020 or 2024 (PDM, 2007).

Candidate Cities

The applicant cities provided their responses to the eleven criteria first phase questionnaire by 14 January 2008. These were then evaluated by the IOC's Candidature Acceptance Working Group and deliberated by the IOC Executive Board at the SportAccord International Convention in Athens on 4 June 2008. The final weighted scores for each bid were Tokyo 8.3, Madrid 8.1, Chicago 7.0, Doha 6.9, Rio de Janeiro 6.4, Prague 5.3, and Baku 4.3, with 6.0 regarded as the minimum required benchmark score to run a satisfactory Games (Anon, 2009). The two lowest performing cities were eliminated by virtue of not achieving the benchmark, but the IOC courted controversy by then selecting Rio de Janeiro rather than Doha. The latter had outperformed Rio on most criteria but wanted to hold the Games in October – outside the normal time-frame – in order to avoid the mid-Summer temperatures. Rejection on that premise rested as much with IOC tradition as with the given reason of 'not wanting to interfere with the international sporting calendar' (Kelso, 2008), although there was also underlying unease about the small size of the potential host city (just 415,051 in 2007) and its existing infrastructure. Its omission from the short-list in favour of Rio, however, brought inevitable claims of political bias. Despite denials from the IOC, the head of the Doha 2016 campaign Hassan Ali Bin Ali, for example, angrily contended: 'it is a great pity that they [the IOC] have closed the door on a bid from the Middle East. If the Games are only going to be held in Europe, Asia and America then I do not know why the IOC want us in the Olympic movement' (GB Staff, 2008).

This narrow escape from consecutive eliminations at the short-listing stage had two linked consequences. First, it left the impression of a bid that was comfortably trailing its competitors at the short-listing phase. Secondly, and in response, it led the Rio team to redouble efforts to improve the technical quality of the city's candidature before the submission of the Candidature Files ('Bid Books') on 12 February 2009 and the visit of the ten members of the IOC's Evaluation Commission between 29 April and 2 May 2009. The effectiveness of the campaign team's subsequent actions can be discerned from the fact that Rio had moved to the top of the list by the time that the Evaluation Commission's report was published on 2 September 2009.

Arguably, the Candidature Files displayed a greater uniformity than seen in any previous bidding for Olympic and Paralympic Games. The likely reason is an increasing professionalization of the process as campaign teams pay close attention to the known predilections of the IOC and seek out developments explicitly held up as examples of best practice. Hence, all bids made a point of offering highly nucleated Games venues, whereby almost all sports would take place within the city boundaries. All reports recognizably responded to the prevailing rhetoric of social, environmental and economic sustainability. With the exception of Tokyo, each proposal had a specific environmental slogan, with Rio proposing a 'Green Games for a Blue Planet', Chicago the 'Blue-Green Games' and Madrid 'Happy Green Games' (GCE, 2009). The key selling themes and slogans used by the campaign teams, as shown in table 19.1, also collectively addressed a somewhat similar set of issues and values thought to be of paramount concern. They include support for the Olympic movement and strengthening national and international sporting culture, along with elements that had come through strongly in the bidding for 2012 and other recent Games: notably multiculturalism and urban regeneration.

The variations in budget figures for the Games largely reflect the varying amounts earmarked for spending on urban regeneration and infrastructural improvement, given that the strict cost of the Games, as reflected by the OCOG budget, only ranges from Madrid's $2.67 billion to Chicago's $3.8 billion. Rio's plans included $5.5 billion for transport infrastructure (airport, road and railways), $1.2 billion for environmental management systems, $770 million for power and electricity infrastructure and $813 million for security equipment. In locational terms, the foci for regeneration were the brownfield areas of the port. Madrid sought to achieve a legacy of urban and social regeneration through the Olympic

Table 19.1. Selling the candidate cities.

City	Budget US $	Key Selling Points
Chicago	4.83 billion (Comprising 3.8 billion OCOG and 1.03 billion non-OCOG)	• The Games would symbolize the nation's desire to reach out and renew bonds of friendship with the world • A cityscape uniquely designed to host global celebrations • 25 million visitors p.a. already come to celebrate festivals in the lakefront parklands where the Games would be staged • A diverse, multicultural population who are passionate about sport • The prospect of strengthening America's commitment to the Olympic movement for generations to come Slogan: *Let Friendship Shine*
Madrid	6.11 billion (Comprising 2.67 billion OCOG and 3.44 billion non-OCOG)	• Promoting social and physical regeneration • Repositioning Madrid on the international stage • Providing a role model of best practice to other cities • Making a significant contribution to the development of the Olympic movement • Reinforcing the value and importance of the Games to athletes worldwide Slogan: *Hola Everyone*
Rio de Janeiro	13.92 billion (Comprising 2.82 billion OCOG and 11.1 billion non-OCOG)	• Uniting the power of sport with the spirit of Brazil • Games of celebration and transformation • Engaging and inspiring the youth of the world • Games delivery aligned with legacy plans • Promoting the Olympic and Paralympic values globally Slogan: *Live Your Passion*
Tokyo	5.95 billion (Comprising 2.86 billion OCOG and 3.09 billion non-OCOG)	• Inspire and reinvigorate a city and its people • Uniting our worlds • A 100-year legacy for the Olympic movement • Promoting sports and pursuing peace: Tokyo after the Games • National economic ripple effect Slogan: *Uniting Our Worlds*

Sources: Compiled from Candidature Files (2009).

project to the two areas that contained the Olympic venues – the 'Core' zone in the east of the city and an elongated 'River' zone, along the course of the Manzanares. The goal was to 'transform a current landscape of 780 desolate hectares into green spaces for sport and recreation' (Madrid2016, 2009, I, p. 17). Tokyo looked back fifty years to the regenerative impact of the 1964 Games and looked forward to ensuring another half-century of urban development on the back of hosting the 2016 Games. Chicago similarly sought to embed the Games in its own urban history, with specific allusion to Daniel Burnham's unrealized 1909 plan for the city and his famous injunction to: 'Make no little plans... Make big plans; aim high in hope and work' (CHICOG, 2009, p. 29). As such the potential legacy of the Olympics, especially in terms of development of the lakeshore areas, would be shaped to fit in with the Chicago Central Area Action Plan. This ambitious $15.5 billion programme, which was approved by the city in August 2009, sought to consolidate the mixed-use expansion of Chicago's downtown by 2020 (CPC, 2009, p. 23).

With specific reference to Rio, the broad locational plan laid out by the Candidature File (ROCOG, 2009) outlined the proposals that, in the fullness of time, will supply the template for the 2016 Games. This will see all sports housed within the city apart from soccer, which in addition to the Maracanã will also use stadia in Brasília, Belo Horizonte, São Paulo and Salvador. Four main zones ('clusters') are designated within Rio: Barra da Tijuca, Copacabana, Deodoro and Maracanã. The Olympic Park itself will be at Barra, which will host nineteen Olympic and thirteen Paralympic sports. These will partly be housed in facilities that were introduced for the Pan American Games such as the Maria Lenk Aquatic Park and the Velodrome, but there will be construction of a new Olympic Village, Olympic Training Centre, and the International Broadcast Centre and the Main Press Centre. Copacabana, roughly 10 miles (16 kilometres) to the east will house some aquatic disciplines, triathlon and beach volleyball. Deodoro, situated around five miles (8 kilometres) north of the Olympic Park, will stage BMX and mountain bikes, white-water canoeing, equestrianism, shooting and pentathlon. Finally, the Maracanã cluster will provide the Olympic Stadium (the Maracanã), to be used for soccer and the main ceremonies, with the João Havelange stadium staging track and field.

Before leaving the subject of the Bid Books, it is worth noting that making the case for the Games involved striking a balance between natural advantages and potential sources of weakness. The former particularly involved touting the city's natural scenic splendours and cultural heritage. The report writers extensive use of superlatives – e.g. 'spectacular' (19 times), 'iconic' (15) and 'stunning' (12) – in connection with the carnival, the Copacabana and Ipanema beaches, the Sugar Loaf and the Maracanã stadium was perhaps simply acknowledgment that Rio contains more features that are readily recognizable to the outside world than any other Latin American city. The nation's passionate sporting culture was also strongly featured. The potential sources of weakness included problems of crime and concerns about the temperatures to be experienced even during a tropical winter. With regard to crime, for example, the organizers were able to point to the success of management plans introduced for the Pan American Games and could also point out that, in a post-9/11 age, Brazil per se was not a major target for international terrorism. Any concerns about climate were lightly brushed aside. Rio's climate was 'strongly influenced by the landscape and ocean', with the 'mild southern hemisphere [providing] the optimal environment for athlete performance' (ROCOG, 2009, I, p 107). Throughout, too, the writers delicately addressed lingering doubts about Brazil's ability to deliver the Olympic festivals by reference to recent experience of running large-scale events – the Pan American Games receive no less than ninety-one mentions in the Candidature File – and the importance of trust in a young and dynamic nation.

Copenhagen

Preparing final presentations for IOC Meetings, like compiling Olympic candidacy files, has become something of a black art. Copenhagen, itself having won the right to stage this IOC meeting against competition from eight other cities,[7] saw the unfolding and expensive ritual of Candidate Cities carrying out last minute attempts to influence the final outcome. In the weeks before the 2 October 2009 meeting, they prepared promotional videos, choreographed speakers, and brought in distinguished celebrities to make their case. Heads of state and noted members of the sports community lobbied the IOC members, who were widely thought to contain more waiverers than usual. On the day of the meeting, the four cities each received an hour in which to make a 45-minute presentation followed by 15 minutes answering questions. The order was decided by drawing of lots, with Chicago going first and then Tokyo, Rio de Janeiro and Madrid.

The Rio presentation featured a passionate speech by the Brazilian President Lula Da Silva, who made a direct appeal to the unwritten law of continental equity, when he argued that:

> I honestly think it is Brazil's turn... It is South America's bid. This is a continent that has never held the Games. It is time to address this imbalance. It is time to light the Olympic cauldron in a tropical country. (Gardner, 2010)

He was followed by Carlos Arthur Nuzman, the President of the Olympic Games Organizing Committee (ROCOG), who reprised a theme that the bid team had constantly used when making presentations to IOC members; namely, showing a map with the location of Olympic cities spread throughout the world – apart from Africa and South America.[8] This was followed by Fernando Meirelles's short film 'Passion unites Us' (see also chapter 7). Made by a director whose credits include 'The City of God' (2002) and 'The Constant Gardener' (2005), 'Passion unites Us' offered a glowing portrait of life in the city, celebrated the Brazilian love of sport and provided the ubiquitous shots of the 2007 Pan American Games. A succession of other municipal leaders and prominent figures completed the presentation. Sergio Cabral, Governor of the State of Rio de Janiero took the stage and informed IOC members that *Forbes Magazine* had voted Rio the 'happiest city in the world' (GB Editor, 2009). The President of the Central Bank of Brazil provided an upbeat account of national finances and support for the bid's budget proposals. The city's mayor reminded delegates that the FIFA World Cup was effectively providing a test event for the Olympics.

By late afternoon, the meeting reached the voting phase. At the start of the day, the bookmakers William Hill had made Chicago odds-on favourite at 8/11, followed by Rio de Janeiro (11/4), Tokyo (5/1) and Madrid (8/1). Understandably, audible gasps of amazement resounded round the Convention Centre when Rogge announced that Chicago was the first city to be eliminated. The voting figures, as subsequently released, revealed that there was little between the four cities on the first round: Madrid 28, Rio 26, Tokyo 22, Chicago 18. Had Chicago survived a round where regional preferences often shape the pattern, it can be speculated that it might have done rather better than the lacklustre Tokyo bid or the hard-to-approve European candidacy of Madrid. In Chicago's absence, Rio simply gathered the votes of the eliminated cities, as the unfolding of the subsequent voting shows. Round two had Rio on 46 votes, Madrid 29 and Tokyo 20. The final round finished with Rio on 66 votes and Madrid 32. In other words, Madrid had picked up just four more votes after the first round, relative to the 44 that accrued to Rio. However interpreted, it was an enormous vote of confidence in a city that, had the IOC adhered to its own conventions, would have been eliminated in the previous year at the short-listing stage.

Conclusion

With the IOC's decision in Copenhagen and the signing of the Host City Contract by the Brazilian Olympic Committee and the IOC that evening, Rio de Janeiro embarked on a path that replicates in reverse the feat of Mexico City in 1968–1970 by hosting the world's two major sporting mega-events in just two years. Capturing them represents an extraordinary coup for the city and for Brazil at a time when competition for such events has never been fiercer. Understandably, it is a programme that will bring problems for a city and state where social issues linked to the extreme poverty of the *favelas* and to law and order remain serious problems. On the day before the start of *Carnaval* in February 2010, for example, heavily armed members of Rio de Janeiro's police force fought a pitched battle with suspected drug traffickers in the slums of Jacarezinho, leaving seven suspects and one policeman dead. This form of violence, as one observer noted 'has become a tedious certainty in Brazil's slums' (McAdams, 2010).

In addition, as with most recent Olympics apart from Beijing 2008, disputes over finance will inevitably arise. One such crisis emerged in March 2010, when the lower house of the Brazilian Congress (Chamber of Deputies) voted to share the proportion of national oil revenue that accrues to state budgets equally between the states rather than in proportion to output. If that policy became law, officials claimed that the state of Rio de Janeiro, the leading oil producer, would see its royalty revenues share fall to about $134 million from about $4.3 billion and, *inter alia*, put the Olympic projects at risk (Barrionuevo, 2010). Carlos Arthur Nuzman weighed into the debate on behalf of ROCOG with a suitably doom-laden forecast:

During the process of candidature, the Brazilian government presented a number of guarantees that were included as part of the contract signed with the International Olympic Committee and became one of the Brazilian State's obligations, represented by the federal, state and municipal government, according to their specific constitutional competences.

The reduction of income for the exploration of petroleum will leave the state of Rio de Janeiro without the resources to do the necessary construction work for the Rio 2016 Games. Any decision that affects the capacity of the State of Rio de Janeiro to fulfil their many obligations has a negative impact on the organization of the games and, if it is not remedied, it will represent a breach in the contract. (Nuzman, 2010)

Clearly, the scale of this reduction in resources would seem to pose a threat to revenues if implemented and, *prima facie*, would threaten the financing of the Games. The federal government, however, was quick to give assurances that the commitments to the Olympics would be met and, if the lessons of recent history are any guide, trimming routinely occurs at the margins leaving the core commitments unimpaired. In the modern era, it is highly unlikely that we will again see a repetition of Rome 1908 or Denver 1976 – the only two occasions when nominated cities have subsequently withdrawn from staging the Games. Quite simply, these are the Olympics; the pinnacle of events for which cities compete internationally. Battles over finance are *de rigueur* and invariably resolved. In an uncertain world, few things can be predicted with greater accuracy than that the Opening Ceremony of the Thirty-First Summer Olympic Games will take place in the Maracanã Stadium on 5 August 2016.

Notes

1.   The 1950 tournament was the only soccer World Cup in which the final result was reached by winning a four-nation league rather than a knock-out match.

2.   This is despite a Wikipedia-inspired source of misinformation, endlessly repeated by the World's press, that the city had bid for the 1936 Games (a confusion with Buenos Aires). See Anon (2010).

3.   This saw the flame lit at the Teotihuacán Pyramids and conveyed to the stadium by a route that took in most state capitals in Brazil.

4.   The criteria were political and social support, general infrastructure, sports venues, Olympic Village, environment, accommodation, transport, security, past experience, finance, and legacy. The result is based on an aggregated average score to each city.

5.   This is a tournament involving the host country, the world champion and the champions of each of the six regional football associations.

6.   For the 1916 (aborted) and 2008 Games respectively.

7.   Strictly speaking, the vote was for the staging of the 13th Olympic Congress, with which this meeting (the 121st Session of the IOC) was associated. The other candidates were Athens, Busan (South Korea), Cairo, Lausanne, Mexico City, Riga, Taipei and Singapore.

8.   Admittedly this was not the first time this tactic had been used, since the bid team had frequently used this map in making presentations to IOC members.

Chapter 20

Afterword

John R. Gold and *Margaret M. Gold*

Branding, n. *Marketing*. The application of a trade mark or brand to a product; the promotion of consumer awareness of a particular brand of goods or services.[1]

In 2007, Dennis Spurr, owner of the Fantastic Sausage Factory in Weymouth – the resort that is venue for the 2012 sailing events – devised a vinyl sign featuring the five Olympic rings rendered by Cumberland sausages. He quickly found himself threatened with legal action for infringement of copyright by LOCOG on the grounds that he was not an official sponsor of the Games. The problem blew over when he replaced the circles with squares (Slot, 2009). By application of the same principle, retailers in Vancouver who were seeking to resell tickets for the 2010 Olympics – which is permissible under British Columbian law – were threatened with legal action if they did so, because the tickets contained the copyrighted term 'Vancouver 2010'. The same city sought to remove a mural from outside the Crying Room art gallery, which comprised a set of black Olympic rings, four of which had sad faces and one outcast sporting a smile. In this instance, the city denied that its removal was due to the artwork being critical of the Games but was justified under anti-graffiti by-laws (Maguire, 2009).

These draconian uses of legal measures to protect the Olympic symbol and other features associated with the Games are not new, but there is little doubt that their prevalence has intensified since formal structures of sponsorship were introduced through TOP and other programmes (see chapter 6; also MacRury, 2009). Sponsors want value for money and expect to see action taken to prevent competitors from having a free ride. Each OCOG takes steps to ensure its share of the lucrative returns from marketing by registration of its own symbols and trademarks. Their actions seem counter to arguments about the regional multiplier effects of staging the Games, in that they seem to target small local retailers and producers that cannot afford expensive sponsorship deals in favour of protecting the interests of large multinational corporations. They also seem directed against those that seek to register public disapproval; actions which might otherwise be seen as preventing citizens from exercising their democratic rights.

At the heart of these issues, of course, lie the wider issues connected with the financing of the Games that have been touched on at various points in this book. The near-death experience of the Olympics in the 1970s, when few bidding cities could be found, led to the need to look again at ways to finance the colossal expense involved in hosting the Games (see chapter 6). This has led to frequent compromises between the internationalism and humanism intrinsic to the IOC's own philosophy and forces of commercialism. Capitalizing on the Olympic Games' potential to be powerful tools for product advertising and promotion of consumer brand identity has dramatically increased available funding, both directly through sponsorship and indirectly through selling media rights to television networks who can sell peak audience advertising slots. At the same time, the message of the Games can become embedded 'in a broader process of commerce whereby the media/marketing/advertising/corporate nexus is concerned less with the values underpinning Olympism per se and more with how such values can help build markets, construct and enhance brand awareness' (Maguire *et al.*, 2008, p. 63). Certainly for many observers, the Games look more like a celebration of the marketing muscle of large commercial companies 'than a display of human prowess and courage' (Drozdiak, 1999; quoted in Rivenburgh, 2002, p. 40).

To some extent, this also represents the consolidation of the process of branding the Olympics themselves. Certainly, the actions of the IOC are analagous to those of a commercial company in the way that it has striven to build and maintain the strength of its brand. The words 'Olympic', 'Olympiad', 'Paralympic', 'Paralympiad' and close derivatives are legally registered as trademarks.[2] The motto '*Citius, Altius, Fortius*' is similarly protected. The five-ring logogram, arguably one of the world's most readily identifiable symbols, is fiercely protected, even to the point where some associated events, such as those within the Cultural Olympiad, are restricted in whether or not they can use it. This protective cocoon was strengthened considerably after the experience of ambush advertising at Atlanta 1996 whereby businesses attempted to attach themselves to the Games without paying sponsors' fees. Although this legal framework can be represented as a safeguard for the integrity of the Olympics, looked at another way it constitutes a rigorous commitment to maintaining brand identity and to extracting the maximum value from it (MacRury, 2009, p. 53).

Yet, as so often with the Olympics, contradictions abound and not everything need be represented as an inexorable drift towards narrow corporate branding and commercialism. From 2010 onwards, two new series of ambulatory Olympic events are to be added to the sporting calendar and, with them, further additions to the lists of Olympic cities. Conscious of its Charter obligations to seek 'to create a way of life based on the joy of effort, the educational value of good example and respect for universal fundamental ethical principles' (IOC, 2004b, p. 9; see also chapter 4), the IOC sought to reignite interest in Olympic sports by introducing two new youth festivals – the Youth Summer Olympic Games and the Youth Winter Olympic Games. These festivals, which were approved by the IOC General Assembly in Guatemala City on 6 July 2007, were seen as sporting events for 14–18 year-olds that would balance sport, education and culture. Specifically, the IOC's statement stressed that 'alongside the sports element of the event' would run 'educational programmes on the Olympic values, the benefits of sport for a healthy lifestyle, the social values sport can deliver and the dangers of doping and of training to excess and/or of inactivity' (*Daily News*, 2008).

The Games would follow the standard four year pattern with Summer Games commencing in 2010 and Winter Games in 2012. These will commence with the First Summer Youth Olympic Games, to be held in Singapore from 14 to 16 August 2010. Its selection followed the same pattern as the adult version with invited bidding competitions. Nine cities initially showed interest, with five shortlisted: Athens, Bangkok, Moscow, Singapore, and Turin. After a report of the IOC Evaluation Commission in January 2008, the list was reduced to two finalists (Singapore and Moscow), from which Singapore was chosen by postal ballot. Following a similar process, it was decided to hold the First Youth Winter Olympics in Innsbruck from 13 to 22 January 2012. Innsbruck itself defeated Kuopio (Finland) in a postal ballot, with Harbin (China) and Lillehammer (Norway) previously eliminated by the Evaluation Commission.

In many respects this expansion of the IOC's festival calendar could be seen as another step in consolidating and enhancing the already-premier Olympic brand. New events have been initiated on the old four year ambulatory model. Athletes will be introduced to the Olympic ethos and encouraged to aspire to the festival. There will be new rounds of choosing host cities which, as has already been indicated above, will witness something of the lengthy and costly operation of Olympic selection procedures. The new host cities may be supplying scaled down versions of the existing Games, but will still require a set of facilities to accommodate a multi-sports festival, replete with Athletes' Villages. Some will use existing sporting infrastructure, perhaps from earlier Olympics; others will be new choices and will need to supply new facilities – Singapore, for example, is constructing an equestrian centre. There will be concern for legacy and talk of sustainable urbanism.

Yet, it may be convincingly argued that this interpretation is too narrowly ideological. Although the Youth Olympic festivals have generated controversy (e.g. Judge *et al.*, 2009), there is reason to suggest that they are an important step in helping to return the Olympics to something of their roots. In the early years at least, these will be amateur sportspeople for whom the experience of attending and of belonging to a wider individual collectivity is as important as the competitions (see also Roche, 2002). The reduced size of the festival will allow smaller cities like Singapore to enter the Olympic arena and counter the trend towards only larger metropolitan cities being suitable candidates. It might also help to counter the associated tendency towards gigantism that has long afflicted the Olympics, especially the 'bloated beast' that is now the Summer Games (Tomlinson, 2004, p. 158). If so, it can only work to the good of the Olympic movement and ensure that the human scale remains part of the brand.

Notes

1. *Oxford English Dictionary*, vol. 1, 1971, p. 264.

2. For example, under British Law, this is protected by the Olympic Symbol etc. (Protection) Act 1995 (c. 32), augmented by the London Olympic Games and Paralympic Games Act 2006 (c. 12). Under US law, it is covered by 36 U.S.C. § 220506.

References

The references listed in this bibliography include both the primary and secondary sources used in writing this book. Full publication details are not always given for the small number of sources listed here that were published before 1900, since some were privately published and bear only the names of their printers.

2010 Legacies Now (2008) *Collaborate, Participate, Celebrate: Annual Review 2007–08*. Vancouver: 2010 Legacies Now.

2010 Legacies Now (2009) *About us website*. http://www.2010legaciesnow.com/about_us/, accessed 12 August 2009.

Acharya, S.K. (2005) Urban development in post-reform China: insights from Beijing. *Norsk Geografisk Tidsskrift*, **59**, pp. 229–236.

ACLU (2001) Q and A On Face-Recognition. http://www.aclu.org/privacy/spying/14875res2003 0902.html, accessed 1 October 2009.

ACOG (Atlanta Committee for the Olympic Games) (1990) *Welcome to a Brave and Beautiful City*. Atlanta, GA: Atlanta Committee for the Olympic Games.

Agamben, G. (2005) *State of Exception*. Chicago, IL: University of Chicago Press.

Alberts, H.C. (2009) Berlin's failed bid to host the 2000 Summer Olympic Games: Urban development and the improvement of sports facilities. *International Journal of Urban and Regional Research*, **33**(2), pp. 502–516.

Alexandridis, T. (2007) *The housing impact of the 2004 Olympic Games in Athens. Background paper*. Geneva: Centre on Housing Rights and Evictions

Alibés, J.M.R., Campo, M.J., Giral, E., Huertas Claveria, J.M., Pradas, R. and Tarragó, S. (1975) *La Barcelona de Porcioles*, 2nd ed. Barcelona: Editorial Laia.

Allen, I. (2006) Should regeneration be based on a fleeting and extraordinary event? *Architects' Journal*, **224**, 30 November, p. 3.

Alpha Bank (2004) *The Impact of the Olympic Games on the Greek Economy*. Athens: Alpha Bank.

AMSUBC (Alma Mater Society of University of British Colombia) (2009) *The 2010 Winter Olympics: Community, Student and Campus Impacts*. Vancouver: AMSUBC.

Andranovich, G., Burbank, M.J. and Heying, C.H. (2001) Olympic Cities: lessons learned from mega-event politics. *Journal of Urban Affairs*, **23**, pp. 113–131.

Anon (1904) *Universal Exposition, Saint Louis 1904: Preliminary Programme of Physical Culture, Olympic Games and World's Championship Contests*. St. Louis, MO: Organizing Committee.

Anon (1907) The Olympic Games. *The Times*, 30 March, p. 10.

Anon (1910) Dover, Robert. *Encyclopaedia Britannica*, 11th ed., vol. 8. Cambridge: Cambridge University Press, p. 453.

Anon (1963) Two cities battle to host the Olympics. *Business Week*, 23 February, p. 36.

Anon (1987) The future of Athens: a city in transition. *Financial Times*, 6 May.

Anon (2000) Olympics: Brazil president pushes for Rio 2012 bid. *Reuters News*, 24 May. http://global.factiva.com/ha/default.aspx, accessed 29 March 2010.

Anon (2003) Athens prays for Zorba to rescue its 'shambolic' Olympic Games. *Observer*, 13 July.

Anon (2004) Securing the Olympic Games. *Wall Street Journal*, 22 August.

Anon (2005) How the bid financing breaks down. *Daily Telegraph*, 4 July.

Anon (2006) Don't make grassroots pay for Olympics. *The Observer*, March 26.

Anon (2007) Olympic FriendShip may run aground. *thelondonpaper*, 4 January, p. 5.

Anon (2008) Think what the Olympic budget could have bought us. *Country Life*, 10 December, p. 23.

Anon (2009) Rio Olympic Games 2016. http://www.olympicsgames2016.com/, accessed 28 March 2010.

Anon (2010) Rio de Janeiro bid for the 2016 Summer Olympics. http://en.wikipedia.org/wiki/Rio_de_Janeiro_bid_for_the_2016_Summer_Olympics, accessed 28 March 2010.

AOBC (Athens 2004 Olympic Bid Committee) (1997) *Athens Candidate City*. Athens: AOBC.

Arbena, J.L. (1991) Sport, development, and Mexican nationalism, 1920–1970. *Journal of Sport History*, **18**, pp. 350–364.

Arbena, J.L. (1996) Mexico City 1968: The Games of the XIXth Olympiad, in Findling, J.E. and Pelle, K.D. (eds.) *Historical Dictionary of the Modern Olympic Movement*. Westport, CT: Greenwood Press, pp. 139–147.

Arnold, B. (1992) The past as propaganda. *Archaeology*, **45**(July/August), pp. 30–37.

Askew, K. (2006) Debt sinks Stadium Australia: ANZ to take control for $10m. *Sydney Morning Herald*, 16 November.

Aso, N. (2002) Sumptuous repast: the 1964 Tokyo Olympic Arts Festival. *Positions*, **10**, pp. 7–38.

ATC (Australian Tourist Commission) (1998) *1996 Olympic Games Atlanta Report*. September. Sydney: ATC.

ATC (2000) *The Sydney Olympic Games*. ATC research update. April. Sydney: ATC.

ATC (2001) *Australia's Olympics*. Special Post Games Tourism Report. Sydney: ATC.

Athens Indymedia (2005) CCTV cameras all around us (but some destroyed). http://athens.indymedia.org/features.php3?id=394, accessed 1 April 2008.

ATHOC (Athens Organizing Committee for the Olympic Games) (2004) Archery in the shadow of the Acropolis (advertisement), in Konstandaras, K. *Greece: The Ideal Destination*. Athens: Hellenic Sun Editions.

ATHOC (Athens Organizing Committee for the Olympic Games) (2005) *Official Report of the XXVIII Olympiad*, 2 vols. Athens: Liberis Publications Group.

Auf der Maur, N. (1976) *The Billion-Dollar Game*. Toronto: James Lorimer.

Augustin, J.-P. and Gillon, P. (2004) *L'Olympisme: Bilan et enjeux géopolitiques*. Paris: Armand Colin.

Australian Democrats (2001) *An Australian Cultural Plan*. http://www.democrats.org.au/policies/#, accessed 21 January 2007.

Baade, R.A., Baumann, R. and Matheson, V.A. (2008) Slippery Slope? Assessing the Economic Impact of the 2002 Winter Olympic Games in Salt Lake City, Utah. Department of Economics Faculty Research Series, Paper 08-15, College of the Holy Cross Worcester, MA.

Baade, R.A. and Matheson, V. (2002) Bidding for the Olympics: fool's gold, in Baros, C.P., Ibrahimo, M. and Szymanski, S. (eds.) *Transatlantic Sport: The Comparative Economics of North America and European Sports*. Cheltenham: Edward Elgar, pp. 127–151.

BAB (British Assessment Bureau) (2010) ISO 14001:2004 (ISO 14000) Certification. http://www.british-assessment.co.uk/ISO-14001-certification-services.htm, accessed 6 April 2010.

Bagwell, S., Foord, J. and Lewis, J. (2005) *Regeneration Skills and Training Needs Survey*. London: Cities Institute for the Higher Education Innovation Fund (HEIF2), London Metropolitan University.

Bailey, N. (2005) The great skills debate: defining and delivering the skills required for community regeneration in England. *Planning Practice and Research*, **20**(3), pp. 341–352.

Bailey S. (2008) *Athlete First: A History of the Paralympic Movement*. Oxford: Wiley-Blackwell.

BALASA (British Amputee and Les Autres Sports Association) (2007) Les Autres Athletes. http://www.patient.co.uk/showdoc/26739787/, accessed 12 March 2007.

Bandy, S.J. (1988) The Olympic celebration of the arts, in Seagrave, J.O. and Chu, D. (eds.) *The Olympic Games in Transition*. Champaign, IL: Human Kinetics, pp. 163–169.

Barcelona City Council (1971) *Barcelona 2000*. Barcelona: Ayuntamiento de Barcelona.

Barcelona City Council (1983) *Plans i projectes per a Barcelona, 1981–1982*. Barcelona: Ajuntament de Barcelona.

Barcelona City Council (1987a) *Arees de nova centralitat*, Barcelona: Ajuntament de Barcelona.

Barcelona City Council (1987b) *Plans cap al 92*. Barcelona: Ajuntament de Barcelona.

Barcelona City Council (1996) *Barcelona: La segona renovació*. Barcelona: Ajuntament de Barcelona.

Barcelona City Council (1999*a*) *Barcelona 1979–2004: del desenvolupament a la ciutat de qualitat*. Barcelona: Ajuntament de Barcelona.

Barcelona City Council (1999*b*) *Urbanisme a Barcelona*. Barcelona: Ajuntament de Barcelona.

Barcelona Regional (1999) *Barcelona New Projects*. Barcelona: Ajuntament de Barcelona.

Barkham, P. (2005*a*) Chirac's reheated food jokes bring Blair to the boil. *The Guardian*, 5 July.

Barkham, P. (2005*b*) Spielberg (ET, Jaws) and Besson (Nikita, Léon). The winner: Goodrich (Travelex ads). *The Guardian,* 7 July.

Barker, P. (2006) London 1948. *Journal of Olympic History*, **14**(2), pp. 65–69.

Barkin, D. and King, T. (1970) *Regional Economic Development: The River Basin Approach in Mexico*. Cambridge: Cambridge University Press.

Barnett, C.R. (1996) St. Louis 1904: the Games of the 3rd Olympiad, in Findling, J.E. and Pelle, K.D. (eds.) *Historical Dictionary of the Modern Olympic Movement*. Westport, CT: Greenwood Press, pp. 18–25.

Barney, R.K., Wenn, S.R. and Martyn, S.G. (2004) *Selling the Five Rings: The International Olympic Committee and the Rise of Olympic Commercialism*, revised ed. Salt Lake City, UT: University of Utah Press.

Barrionuevo, A. (2010) Rio de Janeiro is in fight over Brazil's oil riches. http://www.nytimes.com/2010/03/18/world/americas/18brazil.html, accessed 28 March 2010.

Bastéa, E. (2000) *The Creation of Modern Athens: Planning the Myth*. Cambridge: Cambridge University Press.

Bataillon, C. and Rivière d'Arc, H. (1979) *La Ciudad de México*. Mexico City: Sep Diana.

Bauman, Z. (2000) *Liquid Modernity*. Cambridge: Polity Press.

BBC (British Broadcasting Corporation) (2007) Brazil hopes for Rio Games boost. http://news.bbc.co.uk/1/hi/world/americas/6921814.stm, accessed 28 March 2010.

BBC (2008) Sochi's mixed feelings over Olympics. http://bbc.co.uk/mpapps/print/news.bbc.co.uk/1/hi/world/europe/7746114.stm, accessed 12 August 2009.

BBC News 24 (2006) London's Olympic victory. Broadcast 1 January.

BBC News (2007) Pan American Games Open in Brazil. http://news.bbc.co.uk/1/hi/world/americas/6898137.stm, accessed 7 July 2010.

BBC Sport (2006) Beijing eyes Games profit in 2008. www.news.bbc.co.uk/go/pr/fr/-/sport1/hi/other_sports/4559728stm, accessed 26 December 2006.

BBC Sport (2008) Olympic stadium 'hits £525m mark'. BBC News, 18 June. http:/news.bbc.co.uk/1/hi/England/London/7460188.stm, accessed 7 July 2010.

BC Arts News (2010) www://www.bcartnews.ca/category/cultural-olympiad, accessed 30 March 2010.

Beard, M. (2004) The Greek heroes, a missed drugs test and a 'motorbike accident' that upset the Games. *The Independent*, 14 August.

Beckett, A. (2007) Cordon Blue. http://www.guardian.co.uk/society/2007/sep/21/communities, accessed 21 September, 2007.

Beriatos, E. and Gospodini, A. (2004) 'Glocalising' urban landscapes: Athens and the 2004 Olympics. *Cities*, **21**(3), pp. 187–202.

Berkaak, O.A. (1999) In the heart of the volcano: the Olympic Games as mega drama, in Klausen, A.M. (ed.) *Olympic Games as Performance and Public Event: The Case of the XVII Winter Olympic Games in Norway*. New York: Bergham Books, pp. 49–75.

Berlin, P. (2003) What did the Olympics bring to Sydney? *New York Times*, 24 December. http://www.nytimes.com/2003/12/24/news/24iht-t1_2.html?pagewanted=1, accessed 24 April 2010.

Best, S. (2000) Public art in the Olympic city. *Architecture Australia*, **89**(5), pp. 80–85.

Bianchini, F. and Parkinson, M. (eds.) (1993) *Cultural Policy and Urban Regeneration: The West European Experience*. Manchester: Manchester University Press.

Bijkerk, A.T. (2006) Amsterdam 1928. *Journal of Olympic History*, **14**, pp. 29–31.

Binyon, M. (1980) The way the Games were won. *The Times*, 4 August.

Black, D. (2008) Dreaming big: The pursuit of 'second order' games as a strategic response to globalization. *Sport in Society*, **11**, pp. 467–480.

Blair, T. (2004) A message, in Anon, *A Vision for the Olympic Games and Paralympic Games*. London: LOCOG, p. 1.

Blitz, R. (2008) Olympic sponsors unite to increase influence. *Financial Times*, 14 November, p. 4.

BOBICO (Beijing 2008 Olympic Bid Committee) (2001) *Beijing Candidature File*, vol. 1. http://en.beijing2008.com, accessed 13 February 2006.

BOCOG (Beijing Organizing Committee for the Games of the XXXIX Olympiad) (2003) *Beijing Olympic Action Plan*. Beijing: BOCOG.

BOCOG (2008) *Culture Guide Beijing 2008*. Beijing: BOCOG

BOGVWCG (Beijing Olympic Games Volunteer Work Coordination Group) 2008 *Manual for Being Olympic Volunteers*. Beijing: China Renmin University Press.

Bohigas, O. (1985) *Reconstrucció de Barcelona*. Barcelona: Edicions 62.

Bohigas, O. (1999) Valorización de las periferias y recuperación del centro: recuperación del frente marítimo, in Maragall, P. (ed.) *Europa próxima: Europa, regiones y ciudades*. Barcelona: Edicions de la Universitat Politècnica de Catalunya, pp. 199–214.

Bokoyannis, D. (2006) Athens: The Making of a Contemporary and Friendlier City. Speech, 9 February, Athens Concert Hall. http://www.cityofathens.gr/files/pdf/highlights/apologismos_omilia_en.pdf, accessed 1 September 2006.

Bondonio, P. and Campaniello, N. (2006) Torino 2006: An Organisational and Economic Overview. Working Paper 1/2006, Mega-Events Observatory, University of Turin.

Booth, D. (1999) Gifts of corruption? Ambiguities of obligation in the Olympic movement. *Olympika*, **8**, pp. 43–68.

Booth, D. and Tatz, C. (1999) *One-Eyed: A View of Australian Sport*. Sydney: George Allen and Unwin.

Borges, W., Lennartz, K., Quanz, D.R. and Teutenberg, W. (1995) *Deutsche Olympiade Kalender. Daten zur Olympischen Bewegung in Deutschland, Teil 1: I. bis XIII. Olympiade (1896–1945) mit Interludium (393–1889) und Praeludium (1889–1996)*. Kassel: Agon-Sportverlag.

Borja, F. (1992) *The Winter Olympic Games. Albertville 1992: A Case Study*. Paris: American University of Paris.

Borja, J. (ed.) (1995) *Barcelona: A Model of Urban Transformation 1980–1995*. Quito: Urban Management Series (PGU-LAC).

Borja, J. and Castells, M. (1997) *Local y Global: La gestión de las ciudades en la era de la informació*. Madrid: Taurus.

Boston, W (2010) Global recession and nation's financial crisis force property companies to rethink projects and look abroad. http://online.wsj.com/articles/SB10001424052748703798904575069423368502324.html, accessed 3 April 2010.

Bottomley, G. (1994) Post-multiculturalism? The theory and practice of heterogeneity. *Culture and Policy*, **6**, pp. 139–152.

Bouras, S. (2007) Greek mall boom challenges tradition. http://www.nytimes.com/2007/06/11/business/worldbusiness/11iht-regreece.1.6096546.html, accessed 2 April 2010.

Bourne, C. (2006) *A Future for Presentism*. Oxford: Oxford University Press.

Boyle, P. and Haggerty, K. (2009) Spectacular security: mega-events and the security complex. *International Political Sociology*, **3**, pp. 257–274

BPA (British Paralympic Association) (2007) Sydney 2000. http://www.paralympics.org.uk/paralympic_games.asp?section=000100010003&games_code=00010003000300010003, accessed 11 February 2007.

Bradby, D. and McCormick, J. (1978) *People's Theatre*. London: Croom Helm.

Bradsher, K. (2007) China finds American allies for security. http://www.nytimes.com/2007/12/28/business/worldbusiness/28security.html, accessed 15 March 2010.

Brennan-Galvin, E. (2002) Crime and violence in an urbanizing world. *Journal of International Affairs*, **56**, pp. 123–145.

Brent Ritchie, J.R. and Smith, B.H. (1991) The impact of a mega-event on host region awareness: a longitudinal study. *Journal of Travel Research*, **30**(1), pp. 3–10.

Brewster, K. (2005) Patriotic pastimes: the role of sport in post-revolutionary Mexico. *International Journal of the History of Sport*, **22**, pp. 139–157.

Brewster, K. and Brewster, C. (eds.) (2009) The Mexico City Olympics, *International Journal of the History of Sport*, **26**(6), pp. 711–880.

Brichford, M. (1996) Munich 1972: the Games of the 20th Olympiad, in Findling, J.E. and Pelle,

K.D. (eds.) *Historical Dictionary of the Modern Olympic Movement*. Westport, CT: Greenwood Press, pp. 148–152.

Bristow, M. (2008) Empty Olympic seats causes concern. http://news.bbc.co.uk/1/hi/world/asia-pacific/7555509.stm, accessed 12 August 2008.

British Crime Survey (2008–2009) *Crime in England and Wales 2008/09*. Volume 1. *Findings from the British Crime Survey and Police Recorded Crime*. London: Home Office. http://www.homeoffice.gov.uk/rds/pdfs09/hosb1109vol1.pdf, accessed 12 January 2010.

Brittain, I. (2008) The evolution of the Paralympic Games, in Cashman R. and Darcy S. (eds.) *Benchmark Games: The Sydney 2000 Paralympic Games*. Sydney: Walla Walla Press, pp. 19–34.

Brittain, I. (2010) *The Paralympic Games Explained*. London: Routledge.

Broudehoux, A.-M. (2004) *The Making and Selling of Post-Mao Beijing*. London: Routledge.

Broudehoux, A.-M. (2007) Spectacular Beijing: the conspicuous construction of an Olympic Metropolis. *Journal of Urban Affairs*, **29**(4), pp. 383–399.

Brown, D. (1996a) Pierre de Coubertin's Olympic exploration of modernism, 1894–1914: aesthetics, ideology and the spectacle. *Research Quarterly for Exercise and Sport*, **67**, pp. 121–135.

Brown, D. (1996b) Revisiting the discourses of art, beauty, and sport from the 1906 Consultative Conference for the Arts, Literature and Sport. *Olympika*, **5**, pp. 1–24.

Brown, D. (2001) Modern sport, modernism and the cultural manifesto: de Coubertin's *Revue Olympique*. *International Journal of the History of Sport*, **18**, pp. 78–109.

Brown, G. (2001) Sydney 2000: an invitation to the world. *Olympic Review*, **37**, pp. 15–20.

Brown, M. (2010) 2012 Olympic festival to be at centre of cultural celebration around Games. http://www.guardian.co.uk/uk/2010/mar/17/olympics-cuoture-festival=showcase-arts, accessed 30 March 2010.

Brownell, S. (2008) *Beijing's Games: What the Olympics Mean to China*. Lanham. MD: Rowman and Littlefield.

Brownill, S. (1990) *Developing London's Docklands*. London: Paul Chapman.

Browning, M. (2000) Olympics under the gun. *The Guardian*, 8 March. http://www.cpa.org.au/gachive2/991games.html, accessed 1 April 2000.

Brundage, A. (1951) Report of Commission appointed by the IOC at its meeting in Copenhagen in 1950 to study conditions in Latin America. *Bulletin of the International Olympic Committee*, 27 June, pp. 37–39.

Brunet, F. (1995) An economic analysis of the Barcelona '92 Olympic Games: resources, financing and impact, in Moragas, M. de and Botella, M. (eds.) *The Keys of Success: The Social, Sporting, Economic and Communications Impact of Barcelona '92*. Barcelona: Bellaterra, pp. 203–237.

Brunet, F. (2009) The economy of the Barcelona Olympic Games, in Poynter, G. and MacRury, I. (eds.) *Olympic Cities: 2012 and the Remaking of London*. Farnham: Ashgate, pp. 97–119.

Brunet, F. and Xinwen, Z. (2009) The economy of the Beijing Olympic Games: an analysis of prospects and first impacts, in Poynter, G. and MacRury, I. (eds.) *Olympic Cities: 2012 and the Remaking of London*. Farnham: Ashgate, pp. 163–180.

Bryson, J.M. (2004). What to do when stakeholders matter: stakeholder identification and analysis techniques. *Public Management Review*, **6**(1), pp. 21–53.

Buchanan, I. and Mallon, B. (2001) *Historical Dictionary of the Olympic Movement*. Lanham, MD: Scarecrow Press.

Buchanan, P. (1984) Regenerating Barcelona: projects versus planning – nine parks and plazas. *Architectural Review*, **175**(6), pp. 32–46.

Buchanan, P. (1992) Barcelona: a city regenerated. *Architectural Review*, **191**(August), pp. 11–14.

Building Design (2006) Gateway skills crisis highlighted. *Building Design*, 15 December, p. 5.

Burbank, M.J., Andranovich, G.D., and Heying, C.H. (2001) *Olympic Dreams: The Impact of Mega-Events on Local Politics*. Boulder, CO: Lynne Rienner.

Burbank, M.J., Andranovich, G.D. and Heying, C.H. (2002) Mega-events, urban development, and public policy. *Review of Policy Research*, **19**, pp. 179–202.

Burns, J. (2005) Written Statement to the US Senate Subcommittee on Trade, Tourism and Economic Development. *Field Hearing on The Economic Impact of the 2010 Vancouver, Canada, Winter Olympics on Oregon and the Pacific Northwest*. Washington DC: US Government Printing Office.

Burroughs, A. (1999) Winning the bid, in Cashman, R. and Hughes, A. (eds.) *Staging the Olympics: The Event and Its Impact*. Sydney: University of New South Wales Press, pp. 35–45.

Business File. (2004) *Going for Gold? A survey on the economics of the 2004 Olympic Games*. Athens: Greek Special Survey Series.

Busquets, J. (1992) *Barcelona: evolución urbanística de una capital compacta*. Madrid: Mapfre.

Butler, T. (2007) Re-urbanizing London's Docklands: gentrification, suburbanization or new urbanism? *International Journal of Urban and Regional Research*, **31**(4), pp. 759–781.

CABE (Commission for Architecture and the Built Environment) (2001) *Urban Design Skills Working Group: Report to the Minister for Housing, Planning and Regeneration*. London: DTLR.

Calavita, N. and Ferrer, A. (2000) Behind Barcelona's success story: citizens' movements and planners' power. *Journal of Urban History*, **26**, pp. 793–807.

California Olympic Commission (1960) *VIII Olympic Winter Games Squaw Valley, California, Final Report*. Squaw Valley, CA: Organizing Committee.

Calvert, P. (1973) *Mexico: Nation of the Modern World*. London: Ernest Benn.

Campbell, D. (2005) The day Coe won gold. *The Observer*, 10 July.

Campbell, T. and Wilk, D. (1986) Plans and plan-making in the valley of Mexico. *Third World Planning Review*, **8**, pp. 287–313.

Cannon, T. (2000) *China's Economic Growth: The Impact on Regions, Migration and the Environment*. London: Macmillan.

Capel, H. (2005) *El modelo Barcelona: un examen crítico*. Barcelona: Edicions del Serbal.

Carisbroke, Lord, Porritt, A., Webb-Johnson, Lord, Heyworth, Lord, Templer, E.M., Londin, H., Summers, S., Bannister, R., Faure, J.C.A. and Guttmann, L. (1956) Games for the paralysed. *The Times*, 20 March, p. 11.

Cashman, R. (1999) The greatest peacetime event, in Cashman, R. and Hughes, A. (eds.) *Staging the Olympics: The Event and Its Impact*. Sydney: University of New South Wales Press, pp. 3–17.

Cashman, R. (2006) *The Bitter-Sweet Awakening: The Legacy of the Sydney 2000 Olympic Games*. Sydney: Walla Walla Press.

Cashman, R. (2009) Regenerating Sydney's West: framing and adapting an Olympic vision, in Poynter, G. and MacRury, I. (eds.) *Olympic Cities: 2012 and the Remaking of London*, Farnham: Ashgate, pp.133–143.

Cashman R. and Darcy S. (2008) (eds.) *Benchmark Games. The Sydney 2000 Paralympic Games*, Sydney: Walla Walla Press, pp. 19–34.

Caust, J. (2003) How has the discourse about cultural policy been captured by the economists and the marketers and what should be done about it? *International Journal of Cultural Policy*, **9**, pp. 51–63.

CEC (Commission of the European Communities) (1992) *Urbanisation and the Function of Cities in the European Community. Regional Development Studies*. Brussels: CEC.

Cerro, G. del (2006) *Bilbao: Basque Pathways to Globalization*. Oxford: Elsevier.

Chai, J.C.H. (1996) Divergent development and regional income gap in China. *Journal of Contemporary Asia*, **26**, pp. 46–58.

Chalip, L. (2004). Beyond impact: a general model for sport event leverage, in Ritchie, B.W. and Adair, D. (eds.), *Sport Tourism: Interrelationships, Impacts and Issues*. Clevedon: Channel View Publications, pp. 226–252.

Chalip, L. and Leyns, A. (2002) Local business leveraging of a sport event: managing an event for economic benefit. *Journal of Sport Management*, **16**(2), pp. 132–158.

Chalkley, B. and Essex, S. (1999) Urban development through hosting international events: a history of the Olympic Games. *Planning Perspectives*, **14**, pp. 369–394.

Chandler, R. (1776) *Travels in Greece; or, an Account of a Tour made at the Expense of the Society of Dilettanti*. Dublin.

Chappelet, J.-L. (1997) From Chamonix to Salt Lake City: evolution of the Olympic Village Concept at the Winter Games, in Moragas, M. de, Llines M. and Kidd, B. (eds.) *Olympic Villages: A Hundred Years of Urban Planning and Shared Experiences*. International Symposium on Olympic Villages. Lausanne: Documents of the IOC Museum, pp. 81–88.

Chappelet, J-L. (2002a) *A Short Overview of the Olympic Winter Games*. Barcelona: Centre d'Estudis Olimpics I de l'Esport, Universitat Autònoma de Barcelona.

Chappelet, J-L. (2002*b*) From Lake Placid to Salt Lake City: the challenging growth of the Olympic Winter Games since 1980. *European Journal of Sport Science*, **2**(3), pp. 1–21.

Chappelet, J-L. (2008) Olympic environmental concerns as a legacy of the Winter Games. *International Journal of the History of Sport*, **25**(14), pp. 1884–1902.

Charmetant, R. (1997) Albertville: Olympism and architecture, in Moragas, M. de, Llines M. and Kidd, B. (eds.) *Olympic Villages: A Hundred Years of Urban Planning and Shared Experiences*. International Symposium on Olympic Villages. Lausanne: Documents of the IOC Museum, pp. 109–115.

Chernushenko, D. (2004) Sustainable Urban Development in the Beijing Olympic Bid. Speech given during a private presentation to the Beijing Deputy Mayor and the Beijing Olympic Organizing Committee. http://www.ottawagreens.ca/ottawa-centre2/about/trackrecord/speech-sud_e.php, accessed 13 December 2006.

Cheyne, J. (2008) London2012 Olympic evictions: Jowell's 'Parliamentary' answer and an evictee's response. http://gamesmonitor.org.uk/node/558, accessed 11 January 2010.

CHICOG (Chicago Organising Committee for the 2016 Olympic and Paralympic Games) (2009) *Candidature File Highlights*. Chicago, IL: CHICOG.

Chinyo, E.A. and Akintoyee, A. (2008) Practical approaches for engaging stakeholders: findings from the UK. *Construction Management and Economics*, **26**, pp. 591–599.

Church, B. (2005) Forgotten games. *Houston Chronicle*, 13 August.

CIIC (China Internet Information Centre) (2004) Beijing subways improve access for handicapped. *China Daily* (English language edition), 17 August. http://www.china.org.cn/english/2004/Aug/104219.htm, accessed 11 February 2007.

CITB (Construction Industry Training Board) (2006) *Construction Skills Network Report*. London: CITB.

Clancy, M.J. (1999) Tourism and development: evidence from Mexico. *Annals of Tourism Research*, **26**, pp. 1–20.

Close, P. Askew, D. and Xu Xin (2007) *The Beijing Olympiad: The Political Economy of a Sporting Mega-Event*. London: Routledge.

Clusa, J. (1999) La experiencia urbanística de Barcelona 1986–1992 y las expectativas del Forum 2004. *Ciudades*, **5**, pp. 85–102.

Clusa, J. (2000) The Barcelona Olympic Experience (1986–1992) and the 2004 Forum Expectations. Paper given to the World Direct Investment Forum, Lisbon, 5–6 June.

Coaffee, J. (2009) *Terrorism, Risk and the Global City: Towards Urban Resilience*. Farnham: Ashgate.

Coaffee, J. and Shaw, T. (2005) The liveability agenda: new regionalism, liveability and the untapped potential of sport and recreation. *Town Planning Review*, **76**(2), pp. i–v.

Coaffee, J. and Murakami Wood, D. (2006) Security is coming home: rethinking scale and constructing resilience in the global urban response to terrorist risk. *International Relations*, **20**, pp. 503–517.

Coalter, F. (2004) Future sports or future challenges to sports? in *Sport England, Driving up Participation: The Challenge for Sport*. London: Sport England, pp. 78–86. http://www.sportni.net/Publications/documents/Driving_up_participation_the_challenge_for_sport.pdf, accessed 12 January 2010.

Coccossis, H., Deffner, A. and Economou, D. (2003) Urban/regional Co-operation in Greece: Athens, a Capital City under the Shadow of the State. Paper presented to 43rd European Congress of the Regional Science Association (ERSA), University of Jyväskylä, 27–30 August. http://www.jyu.fi/ersa2003/cdrom/papers/358.pdf, accessed 1 March 2007.

Cochrane, A., Peck, J. and Tickell, A. (1996) Manchester plays games: exploring the local politics of globalisation. *Urban Studies*, **33**(8), pp. 1319–1336.

COCO (Commission d'Enquête sur le Coût de la 21e Olympiade) (1980) *Rapport*, 3 vols. Quebec: Éditeur Officiel.

COHRE (Centre on Housing Rights and Evictions) (2007*a*) *Fair Play for Housing Rights: Mega-Events, Olympic Games and Housing Rights*. Geneva: COHRE.

COHRE (2007*b*) *Hosting the 2012 Olympic Games: London's Olympic Preparations and Housing Rights Concerns*. Geneva: COHRE. http://www.cohre.org/store/attachments/London_background_paper.pdf, accessed 12 January 2010.

COHRE (2007*c*) *One World, Whose Dream? Housing Rights Violations and the Beijing Olympic Games*. Geneva: COHRE. Available at http://www.cohre.org/beijingreport, accessed 12 January 2010.

COJO (Comité d'Organisation des Xemes Jeux Olympiques d'Hiver) (1968) *Official Report Xth Winter Olympic Games*. Grenoble: Organizing Committee.

Colenutt, B. (1988) Local democracy and inner city regeneration. *Local Economy*, **3**, pp. 119–125.

Colvin, S. (1878) Greek Athletics, Greek Religion and Greek Art at Olympia: An Account of Ancient Usages and Modern Discoveries. Paper given to the Liverpool Art Club, 4 February.

Comitato Olimpico Nazionale Italiano (1956) *VII Giochi Olimpici Invernali, Cortina D'Ampezzo, Rapporto ufficiale*, Rome: Comitato Olimpico Nazionale Italiano.

CONI (Comitato Olimpico Nazionale Italiano) (1956) *VII Giochi Olimpico Inversnali: Cortina d'Ampezzo. Rapporto Ufficiale*. Rome: CONI.

COOB (Barcelona Olympic Organizing Committee) (1992) *Official Report of the Games of the XXV Olympiad*, 3 vols. Barcelona: COOB.

Cook, I.G. (2000) Pressures of development on China's cities and regions, in Cannon, T. (ed.) *China's Economic Growth: The Impact on Regions, Migration and the Environment*. London: Macmillan, pp. 33–55.

Cook, I.G. (2006) Beijing as an 'internationalized metropolis', in Wu, F. (ed.) *Globalisation and China's Cities*. London: Routledge.

Cook, I.G. and Dummer, T.J.B. (2004) Changing health in China: re-evaluating the epidemiological transition model. *Health Policy*, **67**, pp. 329–343.

Cook, I.G. and Murray, G. (2001) *China's Third Revolution: Tensions in the Transition to Post-Communism*. London: Curzon.

Cook, T.A. (1909) *International Sport: A Short History of the Olympic Movement from 1896 to the Present Day, containing the Account of a Visit to Athens in 1906 and of the Olympic Games of 1908 in London together with the Code of Rules for 20 Different Forms of Sport and Numerous Illustrations*. London: Archibald and Constable.

Correspondent (2004) Going for gold: the Olympics can pay off, but only if you have a city to sell. *Financial Times*, 14/15 August.

Correspondent (2010) Olympic sites to get new life. http://www.ekathimerini.com/4dcgi/_w_articles_politics_2_19/03/2010_115743, accessed 4 April 2010.

COWGOC (Calgary Olympic Winter Games Organizing Committee/Calgary Olympic Development Association) (1988) *XV Olympic Winter Games: Official Report*. Calgary: Organizing Committee.

CPC (Chicago Planning Commission) (2009) *Central Area Action Plan adopted by the Chicago Plan Commission, August 20, 2009: Executive Summary*. Chicago, IL: Chicago Planning Commission.

Crookson, M. (2004) Making the Games work: a sustainable employment legacy, in Vigor, A., Mean, M. and Tims, C. (eds.) *After the Gold Rush: A Sustainable Olympics for London*. London: IPPR, pp. 51–68.

Crowther, N.B. (2003) Elis and Olympia: city, sanctuary and politics, in Phillips, D.J. and Pritchard, D. (eds.) *Sport and Festival in the Ancient Greek World*. Swansea: Classical Press of Wales, pp. 75–100.

Crowther-Dowey, C. and Fussey, P. (2010) *Researching Crime: Approaches, Method and Application*. Basingstoke: Palgrave.

CTV (2006) Vancouver homeless population may triple by 2010. www.ctv.ca/servlet/ArticleNews/story/CTVNews/20060921/vancouver_homeless, accessed 14 August 2009.

Culf, A. (2006) Five-ringed circus comes under unfriendly financial fire. *The Guardian*, 19 May.

Curtis, P. (2006) A question of sport: half of Britons do no exercise at all. *The Guardian*, 8 December.

Daily News (2008) IOC Press Release: Announcement Ceremony of 2010 Youth Olympic Games. http://www.designtaxi.com/news.php?id=15957, accessed 3 April 2010.

Daley, R. (1963) Lyons makes a lavish pitch to be site for 1968 Olympics. *New York Times*, 17 October, p. 47.

Dansero, E., Segre, A. and Mela, A. (2003) Spatial and environmental transformations towards Torino 2006: Planning the legacy of the Future, in de Moragas, M., Kennett, C. and Puig, N. (eds.) *The Legacy of the Olympic Games 1984–2000*, Documents of the Museum. Lausanne: IOC, pp. 83–93.

Davenport, J. (1996) Athens 1896: the Games of the 1st Olympiad, in Findling, J.E. and Pelle, K.D. (eds.) *Historical Dictionary of the Modern Olympic Movement*. Westport, CT: Greenwood Press, pp. 3–11.

Dayan, D. and Katz, E. (1994) *Media Events: The Live Broadcasting of History*. Cambridge, MA: Harvard University Press.

DCC (Docklands Consultative Committee) (1990) *The Docklands Experiment: A Critical Review of Eight Years of the London Docklands Development Corporation*. London: DCC.

DCITA (Department of Communications Information Technology and the Arts) (1994) *Creative Nation: Commonwealth Cultural Policy*. Canberra: DCITA.

DCLG (Department for Communities and Local Government/Office for National Statistics) (2006) *Land Use Change in England: Residential Development to 2005* (LUCS21). London: DCLG.

DCLG (2007) *Thames Gateway Delivery Plan*. London: DCLG

DCMS (Department of Culture, Media and Sport) (2007a) *Our promise for 2012: how the UK will benefit from the Olympic Games and Paralympics Games*. http://www.culture.gov.uk/reference_library/publications/3660.aspx/, accessed 3 April 2010.

DCMS (2007b) *Before, during and after: making the most of the London 2012 Games*. http://www.culture.gov.uk/images/publications/2012LegacyActionPlan.pdf, accessed 3 April 2010.

DCMS (2008) *London 2012: Lessons from Beijing*. http://www.publications.parliament.uk/pa/cm200809/cmselect/cmcumeds/25/8100703.htm, accessed 15 March 2010.

DCMS (2009) *London: Meta-Evaluation of the Impacts and Legacy of the London 2012 Olympic and Paralympic Games*, www.podium.ac.uk/opportunities/download/109/1/dcms-meta-evaluation.pdf, accessed 11 January 2010.

DCMS (2010) *London 2012: A Legacy for Disabled People*. London: DCMS, Office for Disability Issues.

Delgado, M. (2005) *Elogi del vianant: del 'model Barcelona' a la Barcelona real*. Barcelona: Edicions de 1984.

de Pauw, K.P. and Gavron, S.J. (2005) *Disability Sport*, 2nd ed. Champaign, IL: Human Kinetics.

DETR (Department of Environment, Transport and the Regions) (1999) *Towards an Urban Renaissance: The Report of the Urban Task Force chaired by Lord Rogers of Riverside*. London: Office of the Deputy Prime Minister.

Dickson, G. and Schofield, G. (2005) Globalisation and globesity: the impact of the 2008 Beijing Olympics on China. *International Journal of Sport Management and Marketing*, **1**, pp. 169–179.

Diem, C. (1912) *Die Olympischen Spiele 1912*. Berlin: Ausgabe.

Diem, C. (1942) *Olympische Flamme: Das Buch vom Sport*. Berlin: Deutscher Archiv.

Doherty, B. (2009) *UKTI Railway Sector: Fact Finding Mission to Argentina and Brazil. Part II – Brazil*. London: UK Trade and Investment.

Dong, J. (2005) Women, nationalism and the Beijing Olympics: preparing for glory. *International Journal of the History of Sport*, **22**, pp. 530–544.

Dong, L. (1985) Beijing: the development of a socialist capital, in Sit, V.F.S. (ed.) *Chinese Cities*. Oxford: Oxford University Press, pp. 67–93.

Drees, L. (1968) *Olympia: Gods, Artists, Athletes* (trans. G. Onn). London: Pall Mall Press.

Drozdiak, W. (1999) Torching the Olympic myth. *Washington Post*, 14 February, B01.

Dubin, M.S., Ellingham, M., Fisher, J. and Jansz, N. (2004) *The Rough Guide to Greece*. London: Rough Guides.

Dunn, K.M. and McGuirk, P. (1999) Hallmark events, in Cashman, R. and Hughes, A. (eds.) *Staging the Olympics: The Event and Its Impact*. Sydney: University of New South Wales Press, pp. 18–34.

Duran, P. (2005) The impact of the Olympic Games on tourism. Barcelona: the legacy of the Games 1992–2002, in Urdangarin, I. and Torres, D. (eds.) *New Views on Sport Tourism*. Mallorca: Calliope Publishing, pp. 77–91.

Eccles, J. (1997) Smart individuals are no match for the clever people. *The Australian Financial Review*, 4 October, p. 14.

Eckert, R. and Schäche, W. (1992) *Zu Geschichte und Bestand des ehemaligen Reichssportfeldes in Berlin-Charlottenburg: Expertise im Auftrag der Senatsverwaltung für Stadtentwicklung und Umweltschutz*. Berlin.

Egan, J. (2004) *The Egan Review: Skills for Sustainable Communities*. London: Office for the Deputy Prime Minister.

Emery, P.R. (2002) Bidding to host a major sports event: the local organising committee perspective. *International Journal of Public Sector Management*, **1**, pp. 316–335.

Espy, R. (1979) *The Politics of the Olympic Games*. Berkeley, CA: University of California Press.

Essex, S. and Chalkley, B. (1998) Olympic Games: catalyst of urban change. *Leisure Studies*, **17**, pp. 187–206.

Essex, S. and Chalkley, B. (2002) Il ruolo dei Giochi Olimpici nella trasformazione urbana, in Bobbio, L. and Guala, C. (eds.) *Olimpiadi e Grandi Eventi*. Rome: Carocci, pp. 57–76.

Essex, S. and Chalkley, B. (2004) Mega-sporting events in urban and regional policy: a history of the winter Olympics. *Planning Perspectives*, **19**, pp. 201–232.

Esteban, J. (1999) *El Projecte Urbanístic: valorar la perifèria i recuperar el centre*. Barcelona: Aula Barcelona.

Evans, G.L. (1995) The National Lottery: Planning for Leisure or Pay Up and Play the Game? *Leisure Studies*, **14**(4), pp. 225–244.

Evans, G.L. (1996a) Planning for the British Millennium Festival: establishing the visitor baseline and a framework for forecasting. *Journal of Festival Management and Event Tourism*, **3**, pp. 183–196.

Evans, G.L (1996b) The Millennium Festival and urban regeneration: planning, politics and the party, in Robinson, M. and Evans, N. (eds.) *Managing Cultural Resources*. Newcastle: Business Education Publishers, pp. 79–98.

Evans, G.L. (1999a) Last chance lottery and the Millennium City, in Whannel, G. and Foley, M. (eds.) *Leisure, Culture and Commerce: Consumption and Participation*, Publication 64. Eastbourne: Leisure Studies Association, pp. 3–22.

Evans, G.L. (1999b) Leisure investment incentives in the European Community: changing rationales, in McPherson, G. and Foley, M. (eds.) *Sustainability and Environmental Policies*, vol. 1, Publication 50. Eastbourne: Leisure Studies Association, pp. 1–27.

Evans, G.L. (2005a) Measure for measure: evaluating the evidence of culture's contribution to regeneration. *Urban Studies*, **42**, pp. 959–984.

Evans, G.L. (2005b) Mixed-use and urban sustainability. *Planning in London*, **52**(1), pp. 43–46.

Evans, G.L. (2006a) Branding the city of culture: the death of city planning? in Monclus, J. and Guardia, M. (eds.) *Culture, Urbanism and Planning*. Aldershot, Ashgate: pp. 197–214.

Evans, G.L. (2006b) *Creative Spaces: Case Study Barcelona*. www.creativelondon.org.uk/upload/pdf/SFCS_Barcelona_Case_Study_Nov_2006.pdf, accessed 20 April 2007.

Evans, G.L. (2006c) *Creative Spaces: Case Study London*. London: London Development Agency. www.creativelondon.org.uk/upload/pdf/SFCS_London_Case_Study_Nov_2006.pdf, accessed 20 April 2007.

Evans, G.L. (2010) Cities of culture and the regeneration game. *Journal of Policy Research in Tourism, Leisure and Events* (in press).

Evans, G.L. and Foord, J. (2000) European funding of culture: promoting common culture or regional growth? *Cultural Trends*, **36**, pp. 53–87.

Evans, G.L. and Foord, J. (2003) Cultural planning in East London, in Kirkham, N. and Miles, M. (eds.) *Cultures and Settlement: Advances in Art and Urban Futures*, vol. 3. Bristol: Intellect Books, pp. 15–30.

Evans, G.L. and Foord, J. (2005) Rich mix cities: from multicultural experience to cosmopolitan engagement. *Journal of European Ethnology*, **34**(2), pp. 71–84.

Evans, G.L., Foord, J. and Aiesha, R. (2009) Urban sustainability: mixed use or mixed messages? in Cooper, R., Boyko, C. and Evans, G. (eds.) *Designing Sustainable Cities*. Oxford: Wiley-Blackwell, pp. 190–217.

Evans, G.L. and Shaw, S. (2001) Urban leisure and transport: regeneration effects. *Journal of Leisure Property*, **1**(4), pp. 350–372.

Evans, G.L. and Taylor, M. (1997) *Destination Marketing East London*. London: Taylormade Solutions for London Docklands Development Corporation.

Experian (2006) *Hosting the 2012 Olympics: Skills and Employment Challenges*, Draft Final report, version 2. Prepared for Learning and Skills Council and London Development Agency, April.

Facaros, D. and Theodorou, L. (2005) *Athens and Southern Greece*, Cadogan Guides 84. Guildford: Globe Pequot Press.

Fahey, M.R. (2009) China, World Affairs China, *Britannica Book of the Year: Events of 2008*, Chicago, IL: Encyclopaedia Britannica, pp. 383–386.

Falk, N. (2003) Urban renaissance: lessons from Turin. *Town and Country Planning*, **72**(7), pp. 213–215.

Farrell, F. (1999) Australian Identity, in Cashman, R. and Hughes, A. (eds.) *Staging the Olympics: The Event and Its Impact*. Sydney: University of New South Wales Press, pp. 59–69.

Fellmann, B. (1973) The history of excavations at Olympia. *Olympic Review*, Nos. 64/65, pp. 109–118, 162.

Finn, P. (2008) Putin directs organisers of 2014 Winter Olympics to protect wilderness. *The Washington Post*, 3 July.

Fischer, D.H. (1971) *Historians' Fallacies: Toward a Logic of Historical Thought*. London: Routledge and Kegan Paul.

Fluid (2004) *London's Bid for the 2012 Olympic Games. Have Your Say*. London: Fluid/Lower.

Flyvbjerg, B., Bruzelius, N. and Rothengatter, W. (2003) *Megaprojects and Risk: An Anatomy of Ambition*. Cambridge: Cambridge University Press.

Frankland, R. (2000) Media Briefing, 26 November. Sydney: Indigenous Unit, Australian Film Commission.

Freeman, R.E. (2006) The Wal-Mart effect and business, ethics and society. *Academy of Management Perspectives*, August, pp. 37–41.

French, S.P. and Disher, M.E. (1997) Atlanta and the Olympics. *American Planning Association Journal*, **63**, pp. 379–392.

Friedmann, J. (2005) *China's Urban Transition*. Minneapolis, MN: University of Minnesota Press.

Frooman, J. (1999) Stakeholder influence strategies. *Academy of Management Review*, **24**(2), pp. 191–205.

Fussey, P. (2007) Observing potentiality in the global city: surveillance and counterterrorism in London. *International Criminal Justice Review*, **17**(3), pp. 171–192.

GameBids.com (2006) Review of Olympic bid news and information. http://www.gamesbids.com/english/index.shtml, accessed 30 January 2007.

GameBids.com (2009) Supreme Court rejects environmentalists appeal of Sochi 2014, 21 March, 2007. www.gamesbid.com/eng/other_news/1174503225.html, accessed 14 August 2009.

García, B. (2001) Enhancing sports marketing through cultural and arts programmes: lessons from the Sydney 2000 Olympic Arts Festivals. *Sport Management Review*, **4**, pp. 193–220.

García, B. (2002a) The Concept of Olympic Cultural Programmes: Origins, Evolution and Projections, Paper. Centre d'Estudiis Olimpics I de l'Esport, Universitat Autònoma de Barcelona.

García, B. (2002b) *Towards a Cultural Policy for Great Events: Local and Global Issues in the Definition of the Olympic Games Cultural Programme. Lessons from the Sydney Olympic Arts Festivals 1997–2000*. Barcelona: Universitat Autònoma de Barcelona.

García, B. (2003) Securing sustainable legacies through cultural programming in sporting events, in Moragas, M. de, Kennet, C. and Puig, N. (eds.) *The Legacy of the Olympic Games 1984–2000: International Symposium (14–16 Nov 2002)*. Lausanne: Olympic Museum, pp. 314–320.

García, B. (2004) Urban regeneration, arts programming and major events: Glasgow 1990, Sydney 2000 and Barcelona 2004. *International Journal of Cultural Policy*, **10**, pp. 103–118.

García, B. (2008) Beijing 2008 Cultural festivals: bigger, but not always better. *Culture @ the Olympics*, **10**(4), pp. 25–29.

García, B. and Miah, A. (2000) Olympic ideals and Disney dreams: cultural representation during Sydney's Opening Ceremony. *Culture @ the Olympics*, **2**(4), pp. 15–20. www.culturalolympics.org.uk, accessed 21 January 2007.

García, B. and Miah, A. (2004) Non-accredited media, the Olympic Games and the host city: The British Academy 2004 project. *Culture @ the Olympics*, **6**(1), pp. 1–7, www.culturalolympics.org.uk, accessed 21 January 2007.

García-Espuche, A., Guárdia, M., Monclús, F.J. and Oyon, J.L. (1991) Modernization and urban beautification: the 1888 Barcelona World's Fair. *Planning Perspectives*, **6**, pp. 125–138.

Gardner, D. (2010) Slap in the face for Obama as his personal plea to back Chicago backfires for the U.S. and the 2016 Olympics goes to Rio, *Mail Online*. http://www.dailymail.co.uk/news/worldnews/article-1217595/Rio-Janeiro-awarded-2016-Olympics.html#ixzz0k25O56t6, accessed 3 April 2010.

Garrido, M. (2003) The Olympic Ideal. *Property People*, 19 June, pp. 8–9.

Gartner, W.C. and Shen, J. (1992) The impact of Tiananmen Square on China's tourism image. *Journal of Travel Research*, **30**(4), pp. 47–52.

GB Editor (2009) President Lula's impassioned remarks highlight Rio 2016 Olympic bid presentation. http://www.gamesbids.com/eng/olympic_bids/rio_2016/1216134728.html, accessed 2 April 2010.

GB Staff (2008) Doha accuses IOC of 'closing the door'. http://www.gamesbids.com/eng/olympic_bids/2016_bid_news/1212681800.html, accessed 2 April 2010.

GCE (Green Cross Espana) (2009) *Environmental Comparative Analysis of Bid Cities to Host the 2016 Summer Olympic Games*. http://www.deportesostenible.es/doc/Environmental_Comparative_UK.pdf, accessed 1 April 2010.

Gehl, J. and Gemzoe, L. (2001) *New City Spaces*. Copenhagen: Danish Architectural Press.

Gehl, J. and Gemzoe, L. (2004) *Public Spaces, Public Life: Copenhagen 1996*. Copenhagen: Danish Architectural Press and Royal Academy of Fine Arts.

Georgiadis, K. (1996) Olympic ceremonies in the Athens Games of 1896 and 1906, in Moragas, M. de, MacAloon, J.J. and Llinés, M. (eds.) *Olympic Ceremonies: Historical Continuity and Cultural Exchange*. Lausanne: IOC, pp. 81–91.

Getz, D. (1997) *Event Management and Event Tourism*. New York: Cognizant Corporation.

Getz, D. (2009) Policy for sustainable and responsible festivals and events: institutionalization of a new paradigm. *Journal of Policy Research in Tourism, Leisure and Events*, **1**(1), pp. 61–78.

Gibson, O. (2009*a*) Tearful Pele and weeping Lula greet historic win for Rio. *The Guardian*, 3 October, pp. 2–3.

Gibson, O. (2009*b*) London's tenacious campaigner Lee makes it back-to-back triumphs in the complexities of bidding. *The Guardian*, Sport section, 3 October, pp. 8–9.

Gilbert, K. and Schantz, O.J. (eds.) (2009) *The Paralympic Games: Empowerment or Side Show?* Aachen: Meyer and Meyer.

Giniger, H. (1968*a*) Mexicans rushing Olympics' complex. *New York Times*, 21 July, V, p. 5.

Giniger, H. (1968*b*) Olympic building is behind schedule. *New York Times*, 8 September, V, p. 10.

Girginov, V. and Hills, L. (2008) A sustainable sports legacy: creating a link between the London Olympics and sports participation. *International Journal of the History of Sport*, **25**(14), pp. 2091–2116.

GLA (Greater London Authority) (2006) *Lower Lea Valley Opportunity Area Planning Framework*, Consultation Draft for Mayor of London. London: Greater London Authority.

Glancey, J. (2004) Comment and analysis: the games have already started: don't let the Olympic bid serve as an excuse for another gimcrack redevelopment scheme. *The Guardian*, 23 January, p. 28.

Gleeson, B. (2001) Disability and the open city. *Urban Studies*, **38**, pp. 251–265.

Glendinning, M. (2006) Finance: NSW still paying for Olympics. *Sport Business International*, No. 112, April, p. 51.

Goeritz, M. (1970) 'The Route of Friendship': sculpture. *Leonardo*, **3**(4), pp. 397–407.

Gold, J.R. and Gold, M.M. (2005) *Cities of Culture: Staging International Festivals and the Urban Agenda, 1851–2000*. Aldershot: Ashgate.

Gold, J.R. and Gold, M.M. (2007) Access for all: the rise of the Paralympics within the Olympic movement. *Journal of the Royal Society for the Promotion of Health*, **127**(3), pp. 133–141.

Gold, J.R. and Gold, M.M. (2008) Olympic cities: regeneration, city rebranding and changing urban agendas. *Geography Compass*, **2**, pp. 300–318.

Gold, J.R. and Gold, M.M. (2009) 'Future indefinite? London 2012, the spectre of retrenchment and the challenge of Olympic sports legacy. *London Journal*, **34**, pp.180–197.

Gold, J.R. and Revill, G. (2003) Exploring landscapes of fear: marginality, spectacle and surveillance. *Capital and Class*, **80**, pp. 27–50.

Gold, J.R. and Revill, G.E. (2006) Gathering the voices of the people? Cecil Sharp, cultural hybridity and the folk music of Appalachia. *GeoJournal*, **63**, pp. 55–66.

Golden, M. (1998) *Sport and Society in Ancient Greece*. Cambridge: Cambridge University Press.

Goldstein, E.S. (1996) Amsterdam: the Games of the 9th Olympiad, in Findling, J.E and Pelle, K.D. (eds.) *Historical Dictionary of the Modern Olympic Movement*. Westport, CT: Greenwood Press, pp. 68–83.

Good, D. (1999) The Cultural Olympiad, Cashman, R. and Hughes, A. (eds.) *Staging the Olympics: The Event and Its Impact*. Sydney: University of New South Wales Press, pp. 159–169.

Goodman, S. (1986) *Spirit of Stoke Mandeville: The Story of Sir Ludwig Guttmann*. London: Collins.

Gordon, B.F. (1983) *Olympic Architecture: Building for the Summer Games*. New York: John Wiley.

Goulartt, A. (2007) *XV Pan American Games Sailing Competition: Final Report*. Rio: Organising Committee for the XV Pan American Games.

Gratton, C., Shibli, S. and Coleman, R. (2005) Sport and economic regeneration in cities. *Urban Studies*, **42**, pp. 985–999.

Gratton, C. and Taylor, P. (2000) *Economics of Sport and Recreation*, 2nd ed. London: E. and F.N. Spon.

Green, D.A. (2003) *Olympic Impacts: Should We Expect An Employment Boom?* Vancouver, BC: Canadian Centre for Policy Alternatives.

Green, M. (1986) *Mountain of Truth: The Counter Culture begins, Ascona, 1900–1920*. Hanover, NH: Tufts University/University Press of New England.

Greer, G. (2005) Two tribes go to war. *The Guardian*, G2, 15 December, pp. 12–13.

Grey-Thompson, T. (2006) The Olympic Generation: How the 2012 Olympics and Paralympics can Create the Difference. Inaugural Lecture, Staffordshire University, 26 October. http://www.staffs.ac.uk/news/article/dame_tanni.php, accessed 2 February 2007.

Grose, T. (2001) White City Stadium. *UK Running Track Directory 2001*. http://www.runtrackdir.com/uk/london(wc).htm, accessed 30 November 2006.

Guárdia, M., Monclus, F.J. and Oyon, J.L. (eds.) (1994) *Atlas Histórico de Ciudades Europeas*, vol.1: *Península Ibérica*. Barcelona: CCCB-Salvat.

Guillain, J.-Y. (2005) The end of the Olympic Arts contests: when art and sport became strangers to each other. *Journal of Olympic History*, **13**(3), pp. 24–30.

Guillain, J.-Y. (2006) Paris 1924. *Journal of Olympic History*, **14**, special edition, pp. 22–43.

Guoqi, X. (2008) *Olympic Dreams: China and Sports, 1895–2008*. Cambridge, MA: Harvard University Press.

Guttmann, A. (1984) *The Games Must Go On*. New York: Columbia University Press.

Guttmann, A. (2002) *The Olympics: A History of the Modern Games*, 2nd ed. Urbana, IL: University of Illinois Press.

Guttmann, L. (1976) *Textbook of Sport for the Disabled*. Aylesbury: H.M. & M. Publishers.

Halifax plc (2004) Houses go for Gold in Olympic Host Cities. Press Release, 18 October.

Hall, C.M. (1992) *Hallmark Tourist Events: Impacts, Management and Planning*. London: Belhaven.

Hall, P. (1980) *Great Planning Disasters*. London: Weidenfeld and Nicolson.

Hall, P. (1988) *Cities of Tomorrow: An Intellectual History of Urban Planning and Design in the Twentieth Century*. Oxford: Basil Blackwell.

Hall, T. and Hubbard, P. (eds.) (1998) *The Entrepreneurial City: Geographies of Politics, Regime and Representation*. Chichester: John Wiley.

Hampton, J. (2008) *The Austerity Olympics*. London: Aurum Press.

Hanna, M. (1999) *Reconciliation in Olympism: The Sydney 2000 Olympic Games and Australia's Indigenous People*. Sydney: Walla Walla Press.

Harlan, H.V. (1931) *History of Olympic Games: Ancient and Modern*. Topanga, CA: Athletic Research Bureau.

Harding, L. (2009) Russia's Winter Olympic vision for Sochi earns IOC praise. *Guardian*, 14 May.

Hargreaves, J. (2000) *Freedom for Catalonia? Catalan Nationalism, Spanish Identity and the Barcelona Olympic Games*. Cambridge: Cambridge University Press.

Harskamp, M. van (2006) Lost in translation. *Rising East*, No. 3, January. www.uel.ac.uk/risingeast/currentissue/essays/vanharkskamp.htm, accessed 20 September 2006.

Hart, S. (2008) London is fortunate to be hosting Olympics, says Mayor Boris Johnson. *Daily Telegraph*, 14 November, p. 13.

Hart Davis, D. (1986) *Hitler's Games: The 1936 Olympics*. London: Century.

Hawthorne, F.H. and Price, R. (2001) *The Soulless Stadium: A Memoir of London's White City*. Upminster: 3-2 Books.

Haynes, J. (2001) *Socio-Economic Impact of the Sydney 2000 Olympic Games*. Lucerne: Olympic Studies Centre/Universitat Autònoma de Barcelona.

Haynes, R. (1999) There's many a slip 'twixt the eye and lip': an exploratory history of football and running commentaries on BBC Radio, 1927–1939. *International Review for the Sociology of Sport*, **34**, pp. 143–156.

HCCPA (House of Commons Committee of Public Accounts) (2008) *The Budget for the London 2012 Olympic and Paralympic Games*. London: HMSO.

He, G. (ed.) (2008) *Olympic Architecture: Beijing 2008*. Basle: Birkhäuser.

Hebbert, M. (2000) El Grupo de Trabajo – *Task Force* – y el nuevo enfoque del urbanismo británico. *Urban*, **4**, pp. 82–90.

Hersh, P. (2008) Testament to progress atrophies after Games: Athens Olympic venues suffer from lack of long-range planning. Chicago should take note. http://archives.chicagotribune.com/2008/aug/05/sports/chi-05-athens-olympicsaug05, accessed 12 May 2009.

Higgins, D. (2009) What the Victorians Did for Us – Invention, Industrialisation and the Here and Now on the Olympic Park. Paper presented to the New London Architecture Conference 'London 2012: Raising the Bar for London's Future Development', 11 December.

Hill, C.R. (1996) *Olympics Politics: Athens to Atlanta, 1896–1996*, 2nd ed. Manchester: Manchester University Press.

Hiller, H.H. (1990) The urban transformation of a landmark event: the 1988 Calgary Winter Olympics. *Urban Affairs Quarterly*, **26**, pp. 118–137.

Hiller, H.H. (2000) Mega-events, urban boosterism and growth strategies: an analysis of the objectives and legitimations of the Cape Town 2004 Olympic bid. *International Journal of Urban and Regional Research*, **24**, pp. 439–458.

Hiller, H. and Moylan, D. (1999) Mega-events and community obsolescence: redevelopment versus rehabilitation in Victoria Park East. *Canadian Journal of Urban Research*, **8**, pp. 47–81.

Hinkson, M. (2003) Encounters with aboriginal sites in Metropolitan Sydney: a broadening horizon for cultural tourism? *Journal of Sustainable Tourism*, **11**, pp. 295–306.

HoC (House of Commons Committee of Public Accounts) (2008) *The Budget for the London 2012 Olympic and Paralympic Games*. London: The Stationery Office.

Hoffmann, H. (1993) *Mythos Olympia: Autonomie und Unterwerfung von Sport und Kultur*. Berlin: Aufbau-Verlag.

Hofstadter, D. (ed.) (1974) *Mexico 1946–73*. New York: Facts on File.

Holden, M., MacKenzie, J. and VanWynsberghe, R. (2008) Vancouver's promise of the world's first sustainable Olympic Games. *Environment and Planning C: Government and Policy*, **26**(5), pp. 882–905.

Holt, R. and Mason, T. (2000) *Sport in Britain, 1945–2000*. Oxford: Blackwell.

Home Office (2009) *London 2012 Olympic and Paralympic Safety and Security Strategy*. London: HMSO.

HOOWI (Herausgegeben vom Organisationskomitee der IX Olympischen Winterspiele in Innsbruck) (1967) *Offizieller Bericht der IX Olympischen Winterspiele Innsbruck 1964*. Vienna: Österreichischer Bundesverlag für Unterricht, Wissenschaft und Kunst.

HOP (Hellenic Olympic Properties SA) (2006) Hellenic Olympic Properties: public real estate & sustainable commercial development. http://www.olympicproperties.gr/, accessed 7 August.

Hope, K. (1990) A chance to save Athens. *Financial Times*, 27 February.

Hornbuckle, A.R. (1996) Helsinki 1952: the Games of the 15th Olympiad, in Findling, J.E. and Pelle, K.D. (eds.) *Historical Dictionary of the Modern Olympic Movement*. Westport, CT: Greenwood Press, pp. 109–118.

Horne, J. and Manzenreiter, W. (eds.) (2006) *Sports Mega-Events: Social Scientific Analyses of a Global Phenomenon*. Oxford: Blackwell.

Howe, P.D. (2008) *The Cultural Politics of the Paralympic Movement through an Anthropological Lens*. London: Routledge.

Howell, R.A. and Howell, M.L. (1996) Paris 1900: the Games of the 2nd Olympiad, in Findling, J.E. and Pelle, K.D. (eds.) *Historical Dictionary of the Modern Olympic Movement*. Westport, CT: Greenwood Press, pp. 12–17.

Hughes, H.L. (1993) Olympic tourism and urban regeneration. *Journal of Festival Management and Event Tourism*, **1**, pp. 157–162.

Hughes, R. (1996) *Barcelona*. New York: Alfred A. Knopf.

IAAF (International Association of Athletics Federations) (2005) The International Museum of Athletics is born, Press Release, 23 June. http://www.iaaf.org/news/kind=101/newsid=29896.html, accessed 2 April 2010.

IMD (2007) *The English Indices of Deprivation 2004* (revised). http://www.communities.gov.uk/publications/communities/englishindices, accessed 7 July 2010.

Imrie, R. (1996) *Disability and the City: International Perspectives*. London: Sage.

IOC (International Olympic Committee) (1997) *Marketing Matters*, No. 11, special issue, August.

IOC (1999*a*) Final Recommendations for IOC Reform Published. Press release, 24 November. Lausanne: IOC.

IOC (1999*b*) *IOC Crisis and Reform Chronology*. Lausanne: IOC.

IOC (2000*a*) IOC and IPC Sign Cooperation Agreement. Press release, 20 October. Lausanne: IOC.

IOC (2000*b*) *The Environment: The Third Dimension of Olympism*. http://www.olympic.org/uk/ organisation/missions/environment_uk.asp, accessed 21 January 2007.

IOC (2001) IOC and IPC Sign Agreement on the Organisation of the Paralympic Games. Press release, 10 June. Lausanne: IOC.

IOC (2002) *Sydney 2000 Sponsorship*. Sydney 2000 Marketing Report. http://multimedia.olympic.org/ pdf/en_report_253.pdf, accessed 21 January 2007.

IOC (2003*a*) IOC and IPC sign Amendment to 2001 Agreement. Press release, 25 August. Lausanne: IOC.

IOC (2003*b*) *The Legacy of the Olympic Games 1984–2000: Conclusions and Recommendations*. http: //multimedia.olympic.org/pdf/en_report_635pdf, accessed 16 March 2007.

IOC (2004*a*) *2012 Candidature Procedure and Questionnaire: Games of the XXX Olympiad in 2012*. Lausanne: Lausanne: IOC.

IOC (2004*b*) *The Olympic Charter*. Lausanne: IOC.

IOC (2005*a*) *A Report of the IOC Evaluation Commission for the Games of the XXX Olympiad in 2012*. Lausanne: IOC.

IOC (2005*b*) *Olympic Broadcasting*. http://www.olympic.org/uk/orgnaistion/facts/broadcasting/index_ uk.asp, accessed 2 January 2005.

IOC (2006*a*) IOC and IPC sign Agreement Extension for 2014 and 2016. Press release, 22 June. Lausanne: IOC.

IOC (2006*b*) *Marketing Fact File*. Lausanne: IOC Press.

IOC (2006*c*) Olympic Movement's Agenda 21: Sport for Sustainable Development. Lausanne: IOC. http://www.turin2006.com/Documents/Reports/EN/en_report_300.pdf, accessed 12 March 2010.

IOC (2007*a*) *Olympic Winter Games*. http://www.olympic.org/uk/games/index_uk.asp, accessed 15 March 2007.

IOC (2007*b*) *IOC 2014 Evaluation Committee Report for XXII Olympic Winter Games in 2014*. Lausanne: IOC.

IOC (2008) *The Olympic Marketing Factfile* (2008 edition). http://multimedia.olympic.org/pdf/en_ report_344.pdf, accessed 21 August 2009.

IOC (2009*a*) *Marketing Report: Beijing*. http://multimedia.olympic.org/pdf/en_report_1428.pdf, accessed 27 September 2009.

IOC (2009*b*) *Olympic Winter Games*. http://www.olympic.org/uk/games/index_uk.asp, accessed 9 June 2009.

IOC (2009*c*) Pandemonium in Beijing. *Olympic News*. http://www.olympic.org/uk/news/olympic_ news/full_story_uk.asp?id=2752, accessed 29 September 2009.

IOC (2010) *The Olympic Charter*. Lausanne: IOC.

IOC Olympic Studies Centre (various) *Archives: Documentation Files*. Lausanne: IOC OSC.

IPC (International Paralympic Committee) (2005) *Annual Report 2004*. Bonn: IPC.

IPC (2006*a*) *About the IPC*. Bonn: IPC. http://www.paralympic.org/release/Main_Sections_Menu/ IPC/About_the_IPC, accessed 29 October 2006.

IPC (2006*b*) *Annual Report 2005*. Bonn: IPC.

IPC (2006*c*) *IPC Strategic Plan 2006–2009*. Bonn: IPC.

IPC (2008) New Russian law upholds Paralympic standards. http://www.paralympic.org/Media_ Centre/News/General_News/2008_11_07_a.html, accessed 14 March 2010.

IPC (2009) *Annual Report 2008*. Bonn: IPC. http://www.paralympic.org/export/sites/default/IPC/ Reference_Documents/2009_05_Annual_Report_2008_web.pdf, accessed 31 March 2010.

IPC (2010) *Organization*. http://www.paralympic.org/IPC/Organization/, accessed 31 March 2010.

Iton, J. (1977) *The Economic Impact of the 1976 Olympic Games: A Study Undertaken for the Organizing Committee of the 1976 Olympic Games*. Montreal: McGill University Industrial Research Centre.

IVC (Intervistas Consulting) (2002) *The Economic Impact of the 2010 Winter Olympic and Paralympic Games: An Update*. Vancouver: Intervistas Consulting.

Jaeger, M. (2009) *Brazil 2020: Economic & Political Scenarios – Update*. Frankfurt: Deutsche Bank Research. https://www.dws-investments.com/EN/docs/insight/brazil_2020.pdf, accessed 29 March 2010.

Jakubowicz, A. (1981) State and ethnicity: multiculturalism as ideology. *Australian and New Zealand Journal of Sociology*, **17**, pp. 4–13.

Jakubowicz, A. (1994) Australian (dis)contents: film, mass media and multiculturalism, in Rizvi, F. and Gunew, S. (eds.) *Arts for a Multicultural Australia: Issues and Strategies*. Sydney: George Allen and Unwin, pp. 86–107.

Jefferies, M. (2006) Critical success factors of public private sector partnerships: a case study of the Sydney SuperDome. *Engineering, Construction and Architectural Management*, **13**(5), pp. 451–462.

Jenkins, R. (2008) *The First London Olympics 1908*. London: Aurum Books.

Jenkins, S. (2006) Let's have commonsense games, not an extravagant festival of chauvinism. *The Guardian*, 24 November, p. 37.

Jennings, A. and Sambrook, C. (2000) *The Great Olympic Swindle: When the World Wanted Its Games Back*. London: Simon and Schuster.

Johnston, C. (2005) Olympic ad director speaks of delight. *The Guardian*, 7 July.

Judge, L. W., Petersen, J. and Lydum, M. (2009) The best kept secret in sports: the 2010 Youth Olympic Games. *International Review for the Sociology of Sport*, **44**(2–3), pp. 173–191.

Kasimati, E. (2003) Economic aspects and the Summer Olympics: a review of related research. *International Journal of Tourism Research*, **5**, pp. 433–444.

Kasparov, G. (2008) Editorial: Russia's Pre-Olympic nightmare. *Wall Street Journal*, 26 April, p. A9.

Kelso, P. (2008) Doha hits out after ejection from 2016 bidding race. *The Guardian*, 5 June, Sport section, p. 9.

Keogh, L. (2009) *London 2012 Olympic Legacies: Conceptualising Legacy, the Role of Communities and Local Government and the Regeneration of East London*. London: Department of Communities and Local Government.

Kettle, M. (1999) Corruption probe spares Samaranch. *Guardian*, 2 March.

Kidd, B. (1992*a*) The culture wars of the Montreal Olympics. *International Review for the Sociology of Sport*, **27**, pp. 151–161.

Kidd, B. (1992*b*) The Toronto Olympic commitment: towards a social contract for the Olympic Games, in Barney, R.K. and Meier, K.V. (eds.) *Proceedings of the Second International Symposium for Olympic Research*. London, Ontario: Centre for Olympic Studies, University of Western Ontario, pp. 67–77.

Kidd, B. (1996) Montreal 1976: the Games of the 21st Olympiad, in Findling, J.E. and Pelle, K.D. (eds.) *Historical Dictionary of the Modern Olympic Movement*. Westport, CT: Greenwood Press, pp. 153–160.

Killanin, Lord (1983) *My Olympic Years*. London: Secker and Warburg.

Kim, J. and Choe, S.-C. (1997) *Seoul: The Making of a Metropolis*. Chichester: John Wiley.

Kissoudi, P. (2008) The Athens Olympics: optimistic legacies: post-Olympic assets and the struggle for their realization. *International Journal of the History of Sport*, **25**(14), pp. 1972–1990.

Koolhaas, R. (1995) What ever happened to urbanism? in Sigler, J. (ed.) *Small, Medium, Large, Extra-Large*. Rotterdam: 010, pp. 958–971.

Kornblatt, T. (2006) Setting the Bar: Preparing for London's Olympic Legacy. IPPR Discussion Paper 8. London: IPPR.

Krauze, E. (1997) *Biography of Power: A History of Modern Mexico 1810–1996*. New York: Harper Collins.

Kunzmann, K. (2004) Keynote Speech, Intereg III Mid-Term Conference, London, 19 November.

Kyrieleis, H. (2003) The German excavations at Olympia: an introduction, in Phillips, D.J. and Pritchard, D. (eds.) *Sport and Festival in the Ancient Greek World*. Swansea: Classical Press of Wales, pp. 41–60.

Kyriakopoulos, V. (2009) *Athens Encounter*. London: Lonely Planet.

Lane, P. (2006) The Paralympics 2012. Unpublished lecture, symposium on 'Profiling London', London Metropolitan University, 26 April.

Lappo, G., Chikishev, A. and Bekker, A. (1976) *Moscow, Capital of the Soviet Union: A Short Geographical Survey*. Moscow: Progress Publishers.

LAOOC (Los Angeles Olympic Organizing Committee) (1985) *Official Report of the Games of the XXIInd Olympiad Los Angeles, 1984*. Los Angeles: LAOOC.

Larson, R. and Staley, T. (1998) Atlanta Olympics: the big story, in Thompson, P., Tolloczko, J.J.A. and Clarke, J.N. (eds.) *Stadia, Arenas and Grandstands: Design, Construction and Operation*. London: Spon, pp. 276–283.

Law, C.M. (1994) Manchester's bid for the Millennium Olympic Games. *Geography*, **79**, pp. 222–231.

LCC (London Chamber of Commerce) (2005) *Meeting the Olympic Skills Challenge*. London: LCC.

LDA (London Development Agency) (2004) *Statement of Participation: Introduction – Context Document for the Lower Lea Valley Olympic and Legacy Planning Application*. London: LDA.

Leake, W.M. (1830) *Travels in the Morea*, 3 vols. London: John Murray.

Lee, J.K. (2005) Marketing and promotion of the Olympic Games. *The Sport Journal*, **8**(3), pp. 25–27. www.thesportjournal.org/2005Journal/Vol 8-No3/lee-aug1.asp, accessed 28 January 2007.

Lei, L. (2004) Beijing evolves into Olympic 'Green'. *China Daily*, 1 March. www.chinadaily.com.cn, accessed 17 April 2006.

Lennartz, K. (2006*a*) Stockholm 1912. *Journal of Olympic History*, **14**, pp. 10–11.

Lennartz, K. (2006*b*) Antwerp 1920. *Journal of Olympic History*, **14**, p. 18.

Lenskyj, H.J. (1992) More than Games: community involvement in Toronto's bid for the 1996 Summer Olympics, in Barney, R.K. and Meier, K.V. (eds.) *Proceedings of the Second International Symposium for Olympic Research*. London, Ontario: Centre for Olympic Studies, University of Western Ontario, pp. 78–87.

Lenskyj, H.J. (2000) *Inside the Olympic Industry: Power, Politics and Activism*. Albany, NY: State University of New York Press.

Lenskyj, H.J. (2002) *The Best Olympics Ever? The Social Impacts of Sydney 2000*. Albany, NY: State University of New York Press.

Lenskyj, H. (2004) Making the world safe for global capital: the Sydney 2000 Olympics and beyond, in Bale, J. and Christensen, M. (eds.) *Post-Olympism? Questioning Sport in the 21st Century*. Oxford: Berg, pp. 231–242.

Leontidou, L. (1990) *The Mediterranean City in Transition: Social Change and Urban Development*. Cambridge: Cambridge University Press.

LEST (London Employment and Skills Taskforce for 2012) (2006) *Action Plan*. http://www.lda.gov.uk/server.php?show=nav.00100i003001, accessed 11 January 2006.

Levin, M. (2001) *London 1908*. http://www.lib.umd.edu/ARCH/honr219f/1908lond.html, accessed 10 February 2004.

Levy, E. (2003) *All About Oscar: The History and Politics of the Academy Awards*. New York: Continuum.

LGA (Local Government Association) (2000) *A Change of Scene: The Challenge of Tourism in Regeneration*. London: DCMS/Local Government Association.

Li, Y. (2006) Green Chaoyang part of Olympic preparations. *Beijing Today*, 24 March.

Li, L.M., Dray-Novey, A.J. and Kong, H. (2007) *Beijing: From Imperial City to Olympic City*. Basingstoke: Palgrave Macmillan.

Littlewood, A.R. (2000) Olympic Games, in Speake, G. (ed.) *Encyclopaedia of Greece and the Hellenic Tradition*, vol. 2. Chicago. IL: Fitzroy Dearborn, pp. 1176–1179.

LOCOG (London Organizing Committee for the Olympic Games) (2004) *London 2012: Candidate File*. London: LOCOG. http://www.london2012.com/en/news/publications/Candidatefile/Candidatefile.htm, accessed 14 April 2006.

LOCOG (2008) *London 2012: Inspire Mark Guidelines*. http://www.london2012.com/documents/brand-guidelines/inspire-mark-guidelines.pdf, accessed 31 March 2010.

Loland, S. (1995) Coubertin's ideology of Olympism from the perspective of the history of ideas. *Olympika*, **4**, pp. 49–78.

London Borough of Newham (2009) *Masterplan for Metropolitan Stratford: Consultants Brief*. London: London Borough of Newham.

Lorey, D.E. (1997) The Revolutionary Festival in Mexico: November 20 celebrations in the 1920s and 1930s. *The Americas*, **54**, pp. 39–82.

Lovett, C. (1997) *Olympic Marathon: A Centennial History of the Games Most Storied Race*. Westport, CT: Praeger.

LPOOC (Lake Placid Olympic Organizing Committee) (1932) *Official Report III Olympic Winter Games, Lake Placid*. New York: III Olympic Winter Games Committee.

LPOOC (Lake Placid Olympic Organizing Committee) (1980) *XIII Olympic Winter Games, Lake Placid New York, Final Report*. Lake Placid: LPOOC.

Lyons, J. (2008) Credit crunch hits 2012 Olympics: MPs call for 'Austerity' Games. *Daily Mirror*, 14 November.

MacAloon, J.J. (1981) *This Great Symbol: Pierre de Coubertin and the Origins of the Modern Olympic Games*. Chicago, IL: University of Chicago Press.

MacAloon, J.J. (1984) Olympic Games and the theory of spectacle in modern societies, in MacAloon, J.J. (ed.) *Rite, Drama, Festival, Spectacle: Rehearsals Towards a Theory of Cultural Performance*. Philadelphia, PA: Institute for the Study of Human Issues, pp. 241–280.

MacAloon, J.J. (1989) Festival, Ritual and TV (Los Angeles 1984), in Jackson, R. and McPhail, T. (eds.) *The Olympic Movement and the Mass Media*, part 6. Calgary: Hunford Enterprises, pp. 21–40.

Macko, S. (1996) Security at the Summer Olympic Games is ready. *EmergencyNet NEWS Service*, **2**, p. 191.

MacMasters, M. (2008) Retrieve the artwork from Mexico 68. *La Jornada*, 24 July.

MacRury, I. (2009) Branding the Games: commercialism and the Olympic city, in Poynter, G. and MacRury, I. (eds.) *Olympic Cities: 2012 and the Remaking of London*. Farnham: Ashgate, pp. 43–71.

Madrid2016 (2009) *Candidature file: Madrid 2016*, 3 vols. Madrid: Madrid2016.

Magdalinski, T, and Nauright, J. (2004) Commercialisation and the modern Olympics, in Slack, T. (ed.) *The Commercialisation of Sport*. London: Taylor and Francis, pp. 185–204.

Magnier, M. (2007) Beijing Olympics visitors to come under widespread surveillance. *Los Angeles Times*, 7 August. http://articles.latimes.com/2008/aug/07/world/fg-snoop7, accessed 15 March 2010.

Maguire, J., Barnard, S., Butler, K. and Golding, P. (2008) 'Celebrate humanity' or 'consumers?' A critical evaluation of a brand in motion. *Social Identities*, **14**, pp. 63–76.

Maguire, R. (2009) Vancouver forces gallery to remove Anti-Olympic mural. http://artthreat.net/2009/12/olympic-mural-banned/, accessed 3 April 2010.

Mahne, C. (2004) Did the Sydney Olympics pay off? *BBC Online*. http://newbbc.co.uk/1/hi/business/3549580.stm, accessed 10 August 2004.

Mallon, B. (1998) *The 1900 Olympic Games: Results for All Competitors in All Events with Commentary. Results from the Early Olympics 2*. Jefferson, NC: McFarland and Company Inc.

Mallon, B. (1999a) *The 1904 Olympic Games: Results for All Competitors in All Events with Commentary. Results from the Early Olympics 3*. Jefferson, NC: McFarland and Company Inc.

Mallon, B. (1999b) *The 1906 Olympic Games: Results for All Competitors in All Events with Commentary. Results from the Early Olympics 4*. Jefferson, NC: McFarland and Company Inc.

Mallon, B. and Buchanan, I. (2009) *The 1908 Olympic Games: Results for All Competitors in All Events with Commentary. Results from the Early Olympics 5*. Jefferson, NC: McFarland and Company Inc.

Mallon, B. and Widland, T. (1998) *The 1896 Olympic Games: Results for All Competitors in All Events with Commentary. Results from the Early Olympics 1*. Jefferson, NC: McFarland and Company Inc.

Mallon, B. and Widland, T. (2002) *The 1912 Olympic Games: Results for All Competitors in All Events with Commentary*. Jefferson, NC: McFarland and Company Inc.

Malone, A. (2008) Abandoned, derelict, covered in graffiti and rubbish: what is left of Athens' £9 billion Olympic 'glory'. http://www.dailymail.co.uk/news/worldnews/article-1036373/, accessed 5 April 2009.

Maloney, L. (1996) Barcelona 1992: the Games of the 25th Olympiad, in Findling, J.E. and Pelle, K.D. (eds.) *Historical Dictionary of the Modern Olympic Movement*. Westport, CT: Greenwood Press, pp. 185–193.

Mandell, R.D. (1976) *The First Modern Olympics*. London: Souvenir Press.

Mangan, J.A. (2008) Prologue: guarantees of global goodwill: post-Olympic legacies – too many limping white elephants, *International Journal of the History of Sport*, **25**(14), pp. 1869–1883.

Maragall, P. (ed.) (1999a) *Europa Próxima: Europa, regiones y ciudades*. Barcelona: Edicions de la Universitat de Barcelona and Edicions de la Universitat Politècnica de Catalunya.

Maragall, P. (1999b) Foreword, in Department of Environment, Transport and the Regions, *Towards an Urban Renaissance*, London: E. and F.N. Spon, pp. 5–6.

Marrs, C. (2003) The benefits of believing. *Regeneration and Renewal*, 13 June, p. 23.

Marsan, J.-C. (1994) *Montréal en Évolution*, 3rd ed. Montreal: Éditons Le Méridien.

Marshall, T. (1996) City entrepreneurialism in Barcelona in the 1980s and 1990s. *European Planning Studies*, **4**, pp. 147–165.

Marshall, T. (ed.) (2004) *Transforming Barcelona*. London: Routledge.

Martins, L. (2004) *Bidding for the Olympics; A Local Affair? Lessons Learned from the Paris and Madrid 2012 Olympic Bids*. Marne-La-Vallée: Laboratoire Techniques, Territoires et Sociétés, École Nationale des Ponts et Chaussées.

Marvin, C. (2008) 'All under heaven': megaspace in Beijing, in Price, M.E. and Dayan, D. (eds.) *Owning the Olympics: Narratives of the New China*. Ann Arbor, MI: University of Michigan Press, pp. 229–259.

Masterson, D.W. (1986) The modern Olympic Games and the arts, in International Olympic Committee. *Report of the 26th International Academy 3–18 July 1986*. Lausanne: IOC, pp. 104–115.

Matthews, G.R. (1980) The controversial Olympic Games of 1908 as viewed by the *New York Times* and *The Times* of London. *Journal of Sports History*, **7**, pp. 40–53.

Matzerath, H. (1984) Berlin, 1890–1940, in Sutcliffe, A. (ed.) *Metropolis, 1890–1940*. London: Mansell, pp. 289–318.

May, V. (1995) Environmental implications of the 1992 Winter Olympic Games. *Tourism Management*, **16**, pp. 269–275.

McAdams, M. (2010) Can Brazil get Olympic Medal for fighting crime, child sex and police brutality? http://www.brazzil.com/component/content/article/217-march-2010/10372-can-brazil-get-olympic-medal-for-fighting-crime-child-sex-and-police-brutality.html, accessed 28 March 2010.

McCann, B. (2005) Complete the street! *Planning*, **71**(5), pp. 18–23.

McCarthy, S. (2008) Beijing's green Games? *Building*, 26 August. http://www.building.co.uk/story.asp?storycode=3120949#, accessed 10 February 2004.

McDonald, D. (1994) Interview. *Arts Today*, December.

McGehee, R.V. (1993) The origins of Olympianism in Mexico: the Central American games of 1926. *International Journal of the History of Sport*, **10**, pp. 319–323.

McGeoch, R. and Korporaal, G. (1994) *The Bid: How Australia Won the 2000 Games*. Melbourne: William Heinemann Australia.

McGuirk, P.M. (2003) Producing the capacity to govern a global Sydney: a multiscaled account. *Journal of Urban Affairs*, **25**, pp. 201–223.

McIntosh, M.J. (2003) The Olympic bid process as a starting point of the legacy development, in Moragas, M. de, Kennett, C. and Puig, N. (eds.) *The Legacy of the Olympic Games 1984–2000*. Lausanne: IOC, pp. 450–456.

McKay, D. (2000) *La Recuperació del Front Maritim*. Barcelona: Quaderns de Gestió.

McManus, P. (2004) Writing the palimpsest, again: Rozelle Bay and the Sydney 2000 Olympic Games. *Urban Policy and Research*, **22**, pp. 157–167.

McMill, E. (1999) NSW Ethnic Communities, Advocacy and Lobbying: Past, Present and Future, in Multicultural Arts Alliance. Conference on 'The Future of Multicultural Arts', 7 November, Australian Museum, Sydney.

McNeill, D. (1999) *Urban Change and the European Left: Tales from the New Barcelona*. London: Routledge.

Mendelow, A.L. (1991) Environmental scanning: the impact of the stakeholder concept, in *Proceedings from the Second International Conference on Information Systems*. Cambridge, MA, pp. 407–418.

Metera, D., Pezold, T. and Piwowarski, W. (2005) *Implementation of Natura 2000 in New EU Member States of Central Europe: An Assessment Report*. Warsaw: The World Conservation Union.

METREX (The Network of European Metropolitan Regions and Areas) (2006) The Legacies from Major Events: Findings and Conclusions. Symposium on 'Planning for Major Events', Turin, 25–26 March. Glasgow: METREX. http://www.eurometrex.org/Docs/Expert_Groups/Major_Events/Torino_Report_2003.pdf, accessed 1 March 2007.

Metropolitan Police Authority (2007) Metropolitan Police Service Olympic Programme Update. http://www.mpa.gov.uk/committees/x-cop/2007/070201/06/, accessed 1 October 2009.

Meyer-Künzel, M. (2002) *Der planbare Nutzen: Stadtentwicklung durch Weltausstellungen und Olympische Spiele*. Hamburg: Dölling and Galitz.

MIC (Melbourne Invitation Committee) (1948) *The Melbourne Invitation Committee extends a most cordial Invitation to the Esteemed International Olympic Committee to celebrate the XVI Olympiad in Melbourne, Australia in 1956*. Melbourne: G.W. Grant and Sons.

Michaelidou, T. (2009) Main stream. *Athens 4U*, Spring, pp. 7–60.

Miller, D. (1994) *Olympic Revolution: The Olympic Biography of Juan Antonio Samaranch*. London: Papillion Books Limited.

Miller, D. (2003) *Athens to Athens: The Official History of the Olympic Games*. Edinburgh: Mainstream.

Miller, S.G. (2003) The organization and functioning of the Olympic Games, in Phillips, D.J. and Pritchard, D. (eds.) *Sport and Festival in the Ancient Greek World*. Swansea: Classical Press of Wales, pp. 1–40.

Millington, Val (2009) London 2012: what legacy for artist's studios? *Axis webzine*, Autumn. http://www.axisweb.org/dlForum.aspx?ESSAYID=18066, accessed 12 January 2010.

Minnaar, A. (2007) The implementation and impact of crime prevention/crime control open street closed-circuit television surveillance in South African Central Business Districts. *Surveillance and Society*, **4**(3), pp. 174–207.

Mitchell, R.K., Agle, B.R. and Wood, D.J. (1997) Toward a theory of stakeholder identification and salience: defining the principle of who and what really counts. *Academy of Management Review*, **22**(4), pp. 853–886.

MLA (Museums, Libraries and Archives Council) (2009) *Stories of the World*. London: MLA. Available at www.mla.gov.uk/what/~/media/Files/pdf/2009/Stories_Prospectus_web.ashx, accessed 6 July 2010.

Museums Libraries Archives Council (2009) Stories of the world launch. http://www.mla.gov.uk/news_and_views/press/releases/2009/Stories_of_the_World, accessed 31 March 2010.

Monclús, F.J. (ed.) (1998) *La Ciudad Dispersa: Suburbanización y nuevas periferias*. Barcelona: Centre de Cultura Contemporània de Barcelona.

Monclús, F.J. (2000) Barcelona's planning strategies: from 'Paris of the South' to the 'Capital of West Mediterranean'. *GeoJournal*, **51**, pp. 57–63.

Monclús, F.J. (2003) The Barcelona Model: an original formula? From 'reconstruction' to strategic urban projects (1979–2004). *Planning Perspectives*, **18**, pp. 399–421.

Monclús, F. J. (2004) International Expos and Planning Culture: Innovation and Tradition in Strategic Urban Projects. Paper presented to 11th International Planning History Conference, Barcelona, 14–17 July.

Monclús, F.J. (2006) International exhibitions and planning: hosting large-scale events as place promotion and as catalysts of urban regeneration, in Monclús, F.J. and Guardia, M. (eds.) *Culture, Urbanism and Planning*. Aldershot: Ashgate, pp. 215–239.

Montaner, J.M. (1990) El modelo Barcelona. *Geometría*, **10**, pp. 2–19.

Montaner, J.M. and Muxí, Z. (2002) Los modelos Barcelona: de la acupuntura a la prótesis. *Arquitectura Viva*, **84**, pp. 28–32.

Monteiro, F. and Shropshire, K. (2010) How Rio Won its Olympic Bid. http://www.latinbusinesschronicle.com/app/article.aspx?id=4059, accessed 4 April 2010.

Moore, M. (2008) Athens' deserted Games sites a warning to London Olympics. http://www.telegraph.co.uk/news/worldnews/europe/greece/2062541/Athens-deserted-Games-sites-a-warning-to-London-Olympics.html, accessed 13 May 2009.

Moragas, M. de (1992) *Cultura, Símbols i Jocs Olímpics*. Barcelona: Centre d'Investigació en Comunicació, Generalitat de Catalunya.

Moragas, M. de, Rivenburgh, N.K. and Larson, J.F. (1995) *Television in the Olympics*. London: John Libbey.

Moreno, E. and Vazquez-Montalbán, M. (1991) *Barcelona, cap a on vas?* Barcelona: Libres de l'índex.

Morgan, J. (1999) Opera to ask its audiences for top notes at Games. *Sydney Morning Herald*, 30 July, p. 15.

Morin, G.R. (1997) *La Cathédrale Inachevée: l'histoire rocambolesque des installations Olympiques de Montréal … et des idées pour en finir*. Montreal: Éditions XYZ.

Morse, J. (2001) The Sydney 2000 Olympic Games: how the Australian Tourist Commission leveraged the games for tourism. *Journal of Vacation Marketing*, 7, pp. 101–107.

Moss, M.L. (1985) Telecommunications and the Future of Cities. Paper presented to 'Landtronics' Conference, London, June.

MSNBC (Microsoft/National Broadcasting Corporation) (2004) No concrete plans for Greek athletics venues. http://www.msnbc.msn.com/, accessed 26 September 2006.

Müller, N. (1994) *One Hundred Years of Olympic Congresses, 1894–1994*. Lausanne: IOC.

Müller, N. (ed.) (2000) *Pierre de Coubertin, 1893–1937: Olympism, Selected Writings*. Lausanne: IOC.

Muñoz, F. (1997) Historic evolution and urban planning typology of the Olympic Village, in Moragas Spà, M. de, Llinés, M. and Kidd, B. (eds.) *Olympic Villages: A Hundred Years of Urban Planning and Shared Experiences*. Lausanne: IOC, pp. 27–51.

Myrdal, G. (1968) *Asian Drama: An Inquiry into the Poverty of Nations*. New York: Pantheon Books.

National Bureau of Statistics (1999) *China Statistical Yearbook 1998*. Beijing: China Statistical Publishing House.

National Bureau of Statistics (2006) *China Statistical Yearbook 2005*. Beijing: China Statistical Publishing House.

National Library of Australia (2000) ausarts2000, in *Pandora. Australia's Web Archive*. http://pandora.nla.gov.au/nph-arch/2000/Z2000-Sep12/http://www.ausarts2000.com/index.html, accessed 21 January 2007.

Nel-lo, O. (1997) *The Olympic Games as a Tool for Urban Renewal: The Experience of Barcelona'92 Olympic Village*. Barcelona: Centre d'Estudis Olimpics, Universitat Autònoma de Barcelona. http://olympicstudies.uab.es/pdf/wp090_eng.pdf, accessed 16 May 2006.

Ness, A. (2002) Blue skies for the Beijing Olympics. *China Business Review*, March.

Nguyen, L. (2009) When the Olympic Flame Burns Out. *BC Business Online*. http://www.bcbusinessonline.ca/bcb/top-stories/2009/03/01/when-flame-burns-out?page=0%2C1, accessed 29 September 2009.

Nikolaou, L.W. (1986) Olympism and art, in International Olympic Committee, *Report of the 26th International Academy, 3–18 July 1986*. Lausanne: IOC, pp. 77–82.

No 2010 (2009) Natives and 2010: Background. www.no2010.com/node/205, accessed 14 August 2009.

Nolan, M.L. and Nolan, S. (1988) The evolution of tourism in twentieth-century Mexico. *Journal of the West*, **27**(4), pp. 14–25.

NSW Ministry for the Arts (1997) *The Arts and Cultural Diversity*. Sydney: New South Wales Ministry for the Arts.

Nuzman, C.A. (2010) *Rio 2016: Official Notice*. http://www.rio2016.com/en/Noticias/Noticia.aspx?idConteudo=1145, accessed 29 March 2010.

O'Bonsawin, C.M. (2010) 'No Olympics on stolen native land': contesting Olympic narratives and asserting indigenous rights within the discourse of the 2010 Vancouver Games. *Sport in Society*, **13**, pp.143–156.

O'Connor, A. (2008) Disabled groups outraged by Beijing snub. http://www.timesonline.co.uk/tol/sport/olympics/article4009610.ece, accessed 29 March 2010.

O'Connor, A. (2009) Vancouver struggling to cover cost of Winter Olympics. *The Times*, 12 February 2009.

ODA (Olympic Delivery Authority) (2007) Security Industry Day: call for security tenders. http://www.london2012.com/documents/oda-industry-days/oda-security-industry-day-presentation.pdf, accessed 3 December 2008.

ODPM (Office of the Deputy Prime Minister) (2003a) *Assessing the Impacts of Spatial Interventions: Regeneration, Renewal and Regional Development. Main Guidance*. London: ODPM.

ODPM (2003b) *Sustainable Communities: An Urban Development Corporation for the London Thames Gateway*, Consultation Paper. London: ODPM.

ODPM (2003c) *Sustainable Communities: Building for the Future*. London: ODPM.

ODPM (2004) *The English Indices of Deprivation 2004: Summary (revised)*. London: ODPM.

Office for Disability (2009) New legacy promise puts disabled people at the heart of London 2012. Press release. http://www.officefordisability.gov.uk/docs/wor/new/0912-paralympics.pdf, accessed 4 April 2010.

Olds, K. (1998) Urban mega-events, evictions and housing rights: the Canadian case. *Current Issues in Tourism*, **1**, pp. 2–46.

Olson, L.L.K. (1974) Power, Public Policy and the Environment: The Defeat of the 1976 Winter Olympics in Colorado. Unpublished PhD thesis, Department of Political Science, University of Colorado.

Øresundstid (2003) History and Culture during the Past 1000 Years: The 19th Century. http://www.oresundstid.dk/dansk/engelsk/oresundstid/1800/index.htm, accessed 21 December 2006.

Organisasjonskomiteen (1952) VI Olympiske Vinterleker Oslo 1952. Oslo: Organisasjonskomiteen.

Organizing Commitee (1908) The Fourth Olympiad: London 1908 Official Report. London: British Olympic Association.

Organizing Committee (1924) The Eighth Olympiad: Paris 1924 Official Report. Paris: Organizing Committee.

Organizing Committee (1928) The Ninth Olympiad, Amsterdam 1928: Official Report. Amsterdam: R.H. de Bussig.

Organizing Committee (1932) Official Report of the III Olympic Winter Games. Lake Placid, NY: III Olympic Wintre Games Committee.

Organizing Committee (1936) The Eleventh Olympiad, Berlin 1936. Berlin: Amtlicher Bericht.

Organizing Committee (1948) The Official Report of the Organising Committee for the XIV Olympiad: London 1948. London: British Olympic Association.

Organizing Committee (1952) The Official Report of the Games of the XV Olympiad. Helsinki: Organizing Committee.

Organizing Committee (1958) The Official Report of the Olympic Committee for the Games of the XVI Olympiad Melbourne 1956. Melbourne: W.M. Houston, Government Printer.

Organizing Committee (1960) The Official Reports of the Olympic Committee for the Games of the XVII Olympiad. Rome: Olympic Committee.

Organizing Committee (1964) The Official Reports of the Olympic Committee for the Games of the XVIII Olympiad. Tokyo: Olympic Committee.

Organizing Committee (1968) The Official Report, 2 vols. Mexico: Organizing Committee of the Games of the XIX Olympiad, Mexico.

Organizing Committee (1972) The Official Report of the Olympic Committee for the Games of the XX Olympiad, Munich 1972. Munich: Pro-Sport Munchen.

Organizing Committee (1976) Official Report of the Games of the XXI Olympiad. Ottawa: COJO-76.

Organizing Committee (1980) Official Report of the Organizing Committee for the Games of the XXII Olympiad. Moscow: Progress Publishers.

Organizing Committee (1984) Final Report. Sarajevo: Organizing Committee for the XIVth Winter Olympic Games 1984 at Sarajevo.

Organizing Committee (1989) Official Report of the Games of the XXIV Olympiad. Seoul: Seoul Olympic Organizing Committee.

Organizing Committee (1992) Official Report of the XVI Olympic Winter Games of Albertville and Savoie. Albertville: Organizing Committee.

Organizing Committee (1996) Official Report of the Games of the XXVI Olympiad. Atlanta: Atlanta Committee for the Olympic Games.

Ortloff, G.C. and Ortloff, S.C. (1976) Lake Placid: The Olympic Years, 1937–1980. Lake Placid: Macromedia.

Osborne, A. and Kirkup, J. (2008) Tessa Jowell: Britain would not have bid for 2012 Olympics if we knew about recession. Daily Telegraph, 12 November, p. 1.

PACEC (PA Cambridge Economic Consultants) (1990a) An Evaluation of Garden Festivals, Inner Cities Research Programme, Department of the Environment. Cambridge: PACEC.

PACEC (1990b) Additionality in Section 4 Tourism Grants. Cambridge: PACEC.

Painter, J. (1998) Entrepreneurs are made, not born: learning and urban regimes in the production of entrepreneurial cities, in Hall, T. and Hubbard, P. (eds.) The Entrepreneurial City: Geographies of Politics, Regime and Representation. Chichester: John Wiley, pp. 259–273.

Papageorgiou-Ventas, A. (1994) Athens: The Ancient Heritage and Historic Townscape in a Modern Metropolis, Library Report 140. Athens: The Archaeological Society at Athens.

Patrick, A. (2005) Olympics offers little benefit for economy. Daily Telegraph, 21 May.

Payne, M. (2006) *Olympic Turnaround: How the Olympic Games Stepped Back from the Brink of Extinction to Become the World's Best Known Brand*. Westport, CT: Praeger.

PDM (2007) Olympics 2016: Prague says it won't be expensive. *Prague Daily Monitor*. http://www.praguemonitor.com/en/171/prague_news/12173, accessed 14 October 2007.

Peek, L. (2004) How I strolled into the heart of the Games. *The Times*, 14 May, p. 4.

Peng, J. and Yu, Y. (2008) Beijing Olympics Security Plan. Paper presented at 'Security and Surveillance at Mega Sport Events: from Beijing 2008 to London 2012' conference, 25 April.

Perrottet, T. (2004) *The Naked Olympics: The True Story of the Olympic Games*. New York: Random House.

Petrakos, G. and Economou, D. (1999) Internationalisation and structural changes in the European urban system, in Economou, D. and Petrakos, G. (eds.) *The Development of Greek Cities*. Athens: Gutenberg and University of Thessaly Publications.

Phillips, T. (2007) Rio's Live Earth concert cancelled over security concerns. http://www.guardian.co.uk/environment/2007/jul/05/brazil.musicnews, accessed 28 March 2010.

Phillips, T. (2009) Twelve dead and helicopter downed as Rio de Janeiro drug gangs go to war. www.guardian.co.uk/world/2009/oct/17/rio-favela-violence-helicopter, accessed 24 October 2009.

Pierce, A. (2008) Foreign workers on their marks for Olympics jobs. *The Daily Telegraph*, 14 November, p. 8.

Pinson, G. (2002) Political government and governance: strategic planning and the reshaping of political capacity in Turin. *International Journal of Urban and Regional Research*, **26**(3), pp. 477–493.

Pitts, A. and Liao, H. (2009) *Sustainable Olympic Design and Urban Development*. London: Routledge.

Plaza, B. (2006) The return on investment of the Guggenheim Museum Bilbao. *International Journal of Urban and Regional Research*, **30**(32), pp. 452–467.

PMSU (Prime Minister's Strategy Unit) (2005) *Improving the Life Chances of Disabled People*. Final Report Joint report with Department of work and Pensions; Department of Health; Department for Education and Skills; Office of the Deputy Prime Minister. London: PMSU.

Poast, P.D. (2007) Winning the bid: analyzing the International Olympic Committee's host city selections. *International Interactions*, **33**, pp. 75–95.

Portas, N. (1998) L'emergenza del progetto urbano. *Urbanistica*, No. 110.

Poulios, P.C. (2006) The 2004 Athens Olympics: a cost-benefit analysis. *Entertainment and Sports Lawyer*, **24**(1), pp. 1, 18–31.

Pound, R. (2006) *Inside the Olympics*. Toronto: John Wiley and Sons Canada.

Poynter, G. and Roberts, F. (2009) Atlanta 1996: the Centennial Games, in Poynter, G. and MacRury, I. (eds.) *Olympic Cities: 2012 and the Remaking of London*, Farnham: Ashgate, pp.121–131.

Prasad, D. (1999) Environment, in Cashman, R. and Hughes, A. (eds.) *Staging the Olympics: The Event and Its Impact*. Sydney: University of New South Wales Press, pp. 83–92.

Preston, J. and Dillon, S. (2004) *Opening Mexico: The Making of a Democracy*. New York: Farrar, Straus and Giroux.

Preuss, H. (2000) *Economics of the Olympic Games: Hosting the Games 1972–2000*. Sydney: Walla Walla Press.

Preuss, H. (2002) Economic Dimension of the Olympic Games. Lecture, Centre d'Estudis Olimpics i de l'Esport, Universitat Autònoma de Barcelona.

Preuss, H. (2004) *The Economics of Staging the Olympics: A Comparison of the Games, 1972–2008*. Cheltenham: Edward Elgar.

Price Waterhouse (1994) *Britain's Millennium Festival Project at Greenwich*. London: Price Waterhouse.

PriceWaterhouseCoopers (2002) *Business and Economic Benefits of the Sydney 2000 Olympics: A Collation of Evidence*. Sydney: NSW Department of State and Regional Development.

PriceWaterhouseCoopers (2004) *European Economic Outlook*. London: PriceWaterhouseCoopers.

PriceWaterhouseCoopers (2009) *London Development Agency 2012 Games Legacy Impact Evaluation Study: Feasibility Study Report*. London: PriceWaterhouseCoopers.

PriceWaterhouseCoopers (2005) *Olympic Games Impact Study: Final Report*. London: Department for Culture Media and Sport.

Promyslov, V. (1980) *Moscow: Past and Present*. Moscow: Progress Publishers.

Purcell, S. and McKenna, B. (1980) *Drapeau*. Toronto: Clarke, Irwin and Co.

Pyrgiotis, Y. (2003) Athens 2004: planning and organising Olympic legacy, in Moragas, M. de, Kennett, C. and Puig, N. (eds.) *The Legacy of the Olympic Games, 1984–2000*. Lausanne: IOC, pp. 414–418.

Radbourne, J. and Fraser, M. (1996) *Arts Management: A Practical Guide*. Sydney: Allen and Unwin.

Readman, P. (2005) The place of the past in English culture, c. 1890–1914. *Past and Present*, **186**, pp. 147–199.

Redmond, G. (1988) Toward modern revival of the Olympic Games: the various pseudo-Olympics of the nineteenth century, in Seagrave, J.O. and Chu, D. (eds.) *The Olympic Games in Transition*. Champaign, IL: Human Kinetics, pp. 7–21.

Reeve, S. (2001) *One Day in September: The Full Story of the 1972 Munich Olympic Massacre and Israeli Revenge Operation 'Wrath of God'*. New York: Arcade.

Renson, R. (1996) Antwerp 1920: the Games of the 7th Olympiad, in Findling, J.E. and Pelle, K.D. (eds.) *Historical Dictionary of the Modern Olympic Movement*. Westport, CT: Greenwood Press, pp. 54–60.

Renson, R. and Hollander, M. den (1997) Sport and business in the city: the Antwerp Olympic Games of 1920 and the urban elite. *Olympika*, **6**, pp. 73–84.

Reyes, R. (2009) Personal communication with M. Barke, 5 October.

RIA Novosti (2009) Olympic Sochi approves master plan despite environmental doubts. http://en.rian.ru/russia/20090714/155521578-print.html, accessed 14 July 2009.

Richards, G. and Wilson, J. (2004) The impact of cultural events on city image: Rotterdam, cultural capital of Europe 2001. *Urban Studies*, **41**, pp. 1931–1951.

Richie, J.R.B. (2000) Turning 16 days into 16 years through Olympic legacies. *Event Management*, **6**, pp. 155–165.

RICS (Royal Institution of Chartered Surveyors) (2004) Beijing Revolution Underway. News Release, 10 September.

Riding, A. (1987) *Mexico: Inside the Volcano*. London: Hodder and Stoughton.

Riley, D. (2005) Written Statement to the US Senate Subcommittee on Trade, Tourism and Economic Development. *Field Hearing on The Economic Impact of the 2010 Vancouver, Canada, Winter Olympics on Oregon and the Pacific Northwest*. Washington: US Government Printing Office.

Ritchard, K. (2004) The hotel industry is pinning its hope on gold at Beijing in 2008: but is it a sure winner? *Hotel Asia Pacific*, December.

Rivas, C. and Sarhandi, D. (2005) This is 1968…This is Mexico. *Eye*, No 56.

Rivenburgh, N.K. (2002) The Olympic Games: twenty-first century challenges as a global media event. *Culture, Sport, Society*, **5**(3), pp. 32–50.

Roberts, K. (2003) Ebersol finds profit in Olympic passion. *SportBusiness International*. October, pp. 32–33.

Roberts, P. and Sykes, H. (eds.) (2000) *Urban Regeneration: A Handbook*. London: Sage.

Roche, M. (2000) *Mega-Events and Modernity: Olympics and Expos in the Growth of Global Culture*. London: Routledge.

Roche, M. (2002) The Olympics and 'global citizenship'. *Citizenship Studies*, **6**(2), pp. 165–181.

ROCOG (Rio di Janeiro Organising Committee for the Olympic Games) (2009) *Candidature File for Rio de Janeiro to host the 2016 Olympic and Paralympic Games*, 3 vols. Rio di Janeiro: ROCOG.

Rodríguez Kuri, A. (2003) Hacia México 68: Pedro Ramírez Vázquez y el proyecto olímpico. *Secuencia*, **56**, pp. 37–73.

Rognoni, G. (1996) The ideas and creativity of the Barcelona '92 Paralympic Ceremonies, in Moragas, M. de, MacAloon, J.J. and Llinos, M. (eds.) *Olympic Ceremonies: Historical Continuity and Cultural Exchange*. Lausanne: IOC.

Romanos, A., Vellissaraton, J. and Liveris, K. (2005) Re-shaping Urban Environment through Major Events: The Athens Olympic Games. Paper presented to the 41st ISOCARP Congress 2005. http://www.isocarp.net/Data/case_studies/665.pdf, accessed 6 March 2007.

Rosso, E. (2004) Torino: Policies and Actions at a Metropolitan Level. Paper presented at the La Gouvernance Metropolitaine Conference, Montreal, 7–8 October.

Rowe, C. and Koetter, F. (1978) *Collage City*. Cambridge, MA: MIT Press.

Rowe, P.G. (1991) *The Urban Public Spaces of Barcelona 1981–87*. Cambridge, MA: Graduate School of Design, Harvard University.

Rowe, P.G. (1997) *Civic Realism*. Cambridge, MA: MIT Press.

Rürup, R. (ed.) (1996) *1936: Die Olympischen Spiele und der Nationalsozialismus: eine Dokumentation*. Berlin: Argon.

Rustin, M. (2009) Sport, spectacle and society: understanding the Olympics, in Poynter, G. and MacRury, I. (eds.) *Olympic Cities: 2012 and the Remaking of London*. Farnham: Ashgate, pp. 3–21.

RUVR (Voice of Russia) (2008) Fair exchange for Sochi residents. http://www.ruvr.ru/Sochi-2014, accessed 12 August 2009.

Ryser, J. (2010) Olympics: a legacy for the locals? *Planning in London*, No. 72, pp. 18–19.

Sajo, J. (2006) *Turin: A Local's Guide to the Olympic City*. Livermore, CA: WingSpan Publishing.

Salázar, R. (1968) Wonderland of colour welcomes Olympics. *Los Angeles Times*, 13 October, p. 8.

Sales, E. (ed.) (2005) *Time Out: Athens*, 2nd ed. London: Ebury.

Samatas, M. (2004) *Surveillance in Greece: From Anticommunist to Consumer Surveillance*. New York: Pella Publishing.

Samuel, H. (2008) Gallic glee at London's Olympic headache. *The Daily Telegraph*, 15 November, p. 24.

Sanahuja, R. (2002) Olympic City – The City Strategy 10 Years after the Olympic Games in 1992. Paper to the International Conference on Sports Events and Economic Impact, Copenhagen, Denmark, April.

Sanan, G. (1996) Olympic Security Operations 1972–94, in Thompson, A. (ed.) *Terrorism and the 2000 Olympics*. Sydney: Australian Defence Force Academy, pp. 33–42.

Sandomir, R. (1999) Olympics: Inquiry cites Olympic 'culture' of impropriety. *The New York Times*, 2 March.

Santacana, F. (2000) *El Planejament Estratègic*. Barcelona: Aula Barcelona.

Sassen, S. (1994) *Cities in a World Economy*. Thousand Oaks, CA: Pine Forge Press.

SCCOC (Southern California Committee for the Olympic Games) (2010) Los Angeles' bid for the 2012 Olympic Games. www.the84games.com/webapp/2012-olympic-bid, accessed 28 March 2010.

Schäche, W. (1991) *Architektur und Städtebau in Berlin zwischen 1933 und 1945: Planen und Bauen unter der Ägide der Stadtverwaltung*. Berlin: Mann-Verlag.

Schäche, W. (2001) *Das Reichssportfeld: Architektur im Spannungsfeld von Sport und Macht*. Berlin: Bebra.

Schmidt, T. (1992) *Werner March: Architekt des Olympiastadions, 1894–1976*. Basel: Birkhauser Verlag.

Schmitt, H.F. (1971) The Olympic Villages. *Olympic Review*, **44**, pp. 258–261.

Scott, C. (2004) The Olympics in Australia: museums meet mega and hallmark events. *International Journal of Arts Management*, **7**, pp. 34–44.

Scruton, J. (1998) *Stoke Mandeville: Road to the Paralympics: Fifty Years of History*. Aylesbury: Peterhouse.

Searle, G. (2002) Uncertain legacy: Sydney's Olympic stadiums. *European Planning Studies*, **10**, pp. 845–860.

Segrave, J.O. (2005) Pietro Metastasio's L'Olimpiade and the survival of the Olympic idea in eighteenth century Europe. *Olimpika*, **14**, pp. 1–28.

Séguillon D (2002) The origins and consequences of the first World Games for the Deaf: Paris, 1924. *International Journal of the History of Sport*, **19**, pp. 119–136.

Senn, A.E. (1999) *Power, Politics and the Olympic Games*. Champaign, IL: Human Kinetics.

Shank, M. (2005) *Sports Marketing*, 3rd ed. Harlow: Prentice Hall.

Sheil, P. (1998) *Olympic Babylon*. Sydney: Pan Macmillan.

Shen, J. (2002) A study of the temporary population in Chinese cities. *Habitat International*, **26**, pp. 363–377.

Shilbury, David and Deane, John (2001) *Sport Management in Australia: An Organisational Overview*. East Bentleigh, Vic: Strategic Sport Management.

Shipway, R. (2007) Sustainable legacies for the 2012 Olympic Games. *Journal of the Royal Society for the Promotion of Health*, **127**, pp. 119–124.

Short, J.R. (2008) 'Globalization, cities and the Summer Olympics', *City*, **12**(3), pp. 321–340.

Simson, V. and Jennings, A. (1992) *The Lord of the Rings: Power, Money and Drugs in the Modern Olympics*. Toronto: Stoddart.

SLOC (Salt Lake Organising Committee) (2002) *Salt Lake 2002: Official Report of the XIX Olympic Winter Games*, Salt Lake City, UT: SLOC.

Slot, O. (2009) World in motion: making a song and dance about the haka. *The Times Online*. http://www.timesonline.co.uk/tol/sport/rugby_union/article5730001.ece, accessed 3 April 2010.

Smith, A. (n.d.) The Impact of Sports Events on City Images. London: University of Westminster, unpublished paper (*c*. 2003).

Smith, H. (2003) Athens prays to Zorba to rescue its 'shambolic' Olympic Games. *The Observer*, 13 July.

Smith, H. (2004) Athens shows doubters it will hit games deadline. *The Guardian Online*. http://sport.guardian.co.uk/olympics/story/0,1278221,00.html, accessed 7 August 2004.

SNF (Stavros Niarchos Foundation) (2009) Recent News: The Stavros Niarchos Foundation Cultural Centre. http://www.snf.org/snfcc/EN.index.php?ID=the_park_EN, accessed 3 April 2010.

SOBL (Sydney Olympic Bid Ltd) (1992) *Sydney Bid Books*. Sydney: SOBL.

SOC (Stockholm Organizing Committee) (1913) *The Fifth Olympiad; The Official Report of the Olympic Games of Stockholm, 1912: Issued by the Swedish Olympic Committee* (ed. E. Bergvall and trans. E. Adams-Ray). Stockholm: Wahlstrom and Widstrand.

Sochi2014 (2010) *Culture*. http://sochi2014.com/en/games/culture, accessed 30 March 2010.

SOCOG (Sydney Organizing Committee for the Olympic Games) (1997–2000) *Olympic Arts Festivals: Fact Sheets*. Sydney: SOCOG.

SOCOG (1998) *Olympic Marketing. Marketing Communications Manual*. Sydney: SOCOG.

SOCOG (1999*a*) Sydney 2000: A 'Total Olympic Experience'. Press release. Sydney: SOCOG.

SOCOG (1999*b*) *Games Time Structure*. Sydney: SOCOG.

SOCOG (1999*c*) *Summary Budget: Olympic Arts Festivals*. Sydney: SOCOG.

SOCOG (1999*d*) SOCOG Revised Games Budget. News release, 22 July. Sydney: SOCOG.

SOCOG (1999*e*) *Turning Green into Gold: Making an Environmental Vision a Reality*. Sydney: SOCOG.

SOCOG (1999*f*) *The Harbour of Life: Complete Guide to the Festival*. Sydney: SOCOG.

SOCOG (2000*a*) *Media Guide*. Sydney: SOCOG.

SOCOG (2000*b*) *Official Report of the XXVII Olympiad*. http://www.gamesinfo.com.au/postgames, accessed 19 August 2003.

Sokoloff, B. (1999*) Barcelone, ou comment refaire une ville*. Montreal: Les Presses Universitaires de Montréal.

Sola-Morales, I. (1992) Uso y abuso de la ciudad histórica: la Villa Olímpica de Barcelona. *A&V Monografías*, **37**, pp. 28–32.

Solinger, D. J. (1995) The floating population in the cities: chances for assimilation? in Davis, D.S. Kraus, R. Naughton, B. and Perry, E.J. (eds.) *Urban Spaces in Contemporary China: The Potential for Autonomy and Community in Post-Mao China*. Cambridge: Cambridge University Press, pp. 113–139.

Sonne, W. (2003) *Representing the State: Capital City Planning in the Early Twentieth Century*. Munich: Prestel.

SOOC (Sochi Olympic Organising Committee) (2009) Games 2014 will double Sochi power supply. http://sochi2014.com/87868, accessed 10 August 2009.

Special Correspondent (1948) Games for paralysed archery tournament at Ministry Hospital. *The Times*, 30 July, p. 7.

Special Correspondent (2004) Olympia shot put aims to revive stadium of ancient Games. *Financial Times*, 18 August.

Speer, A. (1969) *Erinnerungen*. Berlin: Propylaen Verlag.

Spencer, R. (2008) Beijing Olympic 2008 opening ceremony giant firework footprints 'faked'. http://www.telegraph.co.uk/sport/othersports/olympics/2534499/Beijing-Olympic-2008-opening-ceremony-giant-firework-footprints-faked.html, accessed 13 March 2010.

Spilling, O. (1998) Beyond intermezzo? On the long-term industrial impacts of mega-events: the case of Lillehammer 1994. *Festival Management and Event Tourism*, **5**, pp. 101–122.

Spivey, N. (2004) *The Ancient Olympics*. Oxford: Oxford University Press.

Sport England (2006) *Active People Survey*, 1. London: Sport England.

Stanhope, J.S. (1824) *Olympia: Or Topography Illustrative of the Actual State of the Plain of Olympia, and of the Ruins of the City of Elis*. London.

Stanton, R. (2000) *The Forgotten Olympic Art Competitions: The Story of the Olympic Art Competitions of the Twentieth Century*. Victoria, BC: Trafford.

Stevenson, D. (2003) *Cities and Urban Cultures*. Maidenhead: Open University Press.

Stone, C.M. (1989) *Regime Politics: Governing Atlanta 1946–1988*. Lawrence, KS: University of Kansas Press.

Stone, C.M. (1993) Urban regimes and the capacity to govern: a political economy approach. *Journal of Urban Affairs*, **15**, pp. 1–28.

Stump, A.J. (1988) The Games that almost weren't, in Seagrove, J.O. and Chu, D. (eds.) *The Olympic Games in Transition*. Champaign, IL: Human Kinetics, pp. 191–199.

Sudjic, D. (2005) *The Edifice Complex*. London: Allen Lane.

Sudjic, D. (2006) Where are the Olympic building plans heading? *The Observer*, May 28.

Swart, K. and Bob, U. (2004) The seductive discourse of development: the Cape Town 2004 Olympic bid. *Third World Quarterly*, **25**, pp.1311–1324.

Sykianaki, C. (2003) Case Study: Athens and Olympic Games 2004. Paper given to symposium on 'The Legacies from Major Events', Turin, 25–26 March. http://www.eurometrex.org/Docs/Expert_Groups/Major_Events/Torino_Report_2003.pdf, accessed 1 March 2007.

Sykianaki, C. and Psihogias, S. (2006) Athens Case Study. Paper given to symposium on 'Planning for Major Events', Turin, 24–25 March. Glasgow: METREX. http://www.eurometrex.org, accessed 2 March 2007.

Taillibert, R. (1977) *Construire l'Avenir*. Paris: Presses de la Cité.

Tatz, C. (1999) Aboriginal Representation in the Olympics. Olympic lecture series, University of Technology, Sydney.

Te, B. (2009) Beijing Olympics: a new brand of China. *Asian Social Science*, **5**(3), pp. 84–90.

Teigland, J. (1999) Mega-events and impacts on tourism; the predictions and realities of the Lillehammer Olympics. *Journal of Impact Assessment and Project Appraisal*, **17**, pp. 305–317.

Tello, R. (1993) Barcelona post-olímpica: de ciudad industrial a escenario de consume. *Estudios Geográficos*, **212**, pp. 507–519.

Tenorio-Trillo, M. (1996) *Mexico at the World's Fairs: Crafting a Modern Nation*. Berkeley, CA: University of California Press.

Thamnopoulos, Y. and Gargalianos, D. (2002) Ticketing of large-scale events: the case of Sydney 2000 Olympic Games. *Facilities*, **20**, pp. 22–33.

Thompson, A. (1999) Security, in Cashman, R. and Hughes, A. (eds.) *Staging the Olympics: The Event and Its Impact*. Sydney: University of New South Wales Press, pp. 106–120.

Thompson, J. (2000) Aboriginal Tent Embassy set to stay. *Green Left Weekly*, No. 418, 30 August.

TOC (Tenth Olympic Committee of the Games of Los Angeles) (1933) *Tenth Olympiad: Los Angeles 1932 Official Report*. Los Angeles, CA: TOC.

Tomlinson, A. (1996) Olympic spectacle: opening ceremonies and some paradoxes of globalization. *Media, Culture and Society*, **18**, pp. 583–602.

Tomlinson, A. (1999) *The Game's Up: Essays in the Cultural Analysis of Sport, Leisure and Popular Culture*. Aldershot: Ashgate.

Tomlinson, A. (2004) The Disneyfication of the Olympics? Theme parks and freak-shows of the body, in Bale, J. and Christensen, M.K. (eds.) *Post-Olympism? Questioning Sport in the Twenty-First Century*. Oxford: Berg Publishers, pp. 147–163.

Tomlimson, A. (2005) The commercialization of the Olympics: cities, corporations and the Olympic commodity, in Young, K. and Wamsley, K.B. (eds.) *Global Olympics: Historical and Sociological Studies of the Modern Games*. Oxford: Elsevier, pp. 179–200.

Toohey, K. and Veal, A.J. (2007) *The Olympic Games: A Social Science Perspective*, 2nd ed. Wallingford: CAB International.

TOROC (Organizing Committee of the XX Turin 2006 Olympic Winter Games) (2005) *Italyart Cultural Olympiad Turin*. Turin: TOROC.

Townsend, M. and Campbell, D. (2005) London 2012 to be the greenest Games. *The Observer*, 13 February.

Travel Utah (2002) *Beyond the Games: Assessing the Impact of the 2002 Olympic Winter Games and the Future of Utah Tourism*. Salt Lake City, UT: Utah Division of Travel Development.

Travlos, J. (1981) Athens after the Liberation: planning the new city and exploring the old. *Hesperia*, **50**, pp. 391–407.

Tufts, S. (2001) Building the 'competitive city': labour and Toronto's bid to host the Olympic Games. *Geoforum*, **35**, pp. 47–58.

Tuppen, J. (2000) The restructuring of winter sports resorts in the French Alps: problems, processes and policies. *International Journal of Tourism Research*, **2**, pp. 327–344.

Turismo Torino (2004) *Olympic Games and Tourism: Turin's Tourist Strategy for the 2006 Winter Olympics*. Turin: Turismo Torino.

Turismo Torino (2006) *Torino 2006: One Year On*. Turin: Turismo Torino

Tzonis, A. (2005) *Santiago Calatrava: The Athens Olympics*. New York: Rizzoli.

Ueberroth, P. (1986) *Made in America: His Own Story*. New York: Morrow.

USA Today (2006) Host city hopes Games recast its image: Torino officials think new look will boost business, tourism. *USA Today*, 17 February.

Vancouver2010 (2010) *CODE*. http://www.vancouver2010.com/more-2010-information/cultural-festivals-and-events/code-connect-create-collaborate/, accessed 31 March 2010.

Vanlerberghe, C. (2008) 'Des Jeux Olympiques déjà trop chers pour Londres', *Le Figaro*, 14 November. http://www.lefigaro.fr/economie/2008/11/13/04001-20081113ARTFIG00643-des-jeux-olympiques-deja-trop-chers-pour-londres-.php, accessed 27 November 2008.

Varley, A. (1992) Barcelona's Olympic facelift. *Geographical Magazine*, **64**(7), pp. 20–24.

Vaubel, R. (2005) The role of competition in the rise of Baroque and Renaissance music. *Journal of Cultural Economics*, **29**, pp. 277–297.

Vaujany, F. (2006) Hardly heroic: Olympics housing plans. *Rising East*, 3. January. http://www.uel.ac.uk/risingeast/archive03/essays/vaujany.htm, accessed 11 January 2010.

Veal, A.J. (2003) Tracking change: leisure participation and policy in Australia, 1985–2002. *Annals of Leisure Research*, **6**(3), pp. 245–277.

Veal, A. J. and Toohey, K. (2005) *The Olympic Games: A Bibliography*. Sydney: School of Leisure, Sport and Tourism, University of Technology. www.business.uts.edu.au/lst/research.index, accessed 4 February 2007.

Videl, J. (2004) Village damned: Olympic hosts fail green test. *The Guardian*, 25 August.

Vigor, A. (2006) Olympic's legacy must focus on jobs. *Regeneration and Renewal*, No. 24, p. 14.

Vigor, A., Mean, M. and Tims, C. (eds.) (2004) *After the Gold Rush: A Sustainable Olympics for London*. London: IPPR/DEMOS.

Voeltz, R.A. (1996) London 1948: the Games of the 14th Olympiad, in Findling, J.E. and Pelle, K.D. (eds.) *Historical Dictionary of the Modern Olympic Movement*. Westport, CT: Greenwood Press, pp. 103–108.

Vozikis, K. (2009) Are there accessible environments in Athens, Greece today? *WSEAS Transactions on Environment and Development*, **5**(7), pp. 488–497.

Waitt, G. (2003) Social impacts of the Sydney Olympics. *Annals of Tourism Research*, **30**, pp. 194–215.

Waitt, G. (2004) A critical examination of Sydney's 2000 Olympic Games, in Yeoman, I., Robertson, M., Ali-Knight, J., Drummond, S. and McMahon-Beattie, U. (eds.) *Festival and Events Management*. Oxford: Elsevier Butterworth Heinemann, pp. 391–407.

Wangermée, R. (1991) *Cultural Policy in France, European Programme for the Appraisal of Cultural Policies*. Strasbourg: Council for Cultural Cooperation, Council of Europe.

Ward, P.M. (1990) *Mexico City: The Production and Reproduction of an Urban Environment*. London: Belhaven Press.

Ward, P.M. (1998) Future livelihoods in Mexico City: a glimpse into the new millennium. *Cities*, **15**, pp. 63–74.

Ward, S.V. (1998) *Selling Places*. London: E. and F.N. Spon.

Ward, S.V. (2002) *Planning the Twentieth-Century City: The Advanced Capitalist World*. Chichester: John Wiley.

Ward, S.V. (2006) 'Cities are fun!' Inventing and spreading the Baltimore model of cultural urbanism, in Monclús, F.J. and Guardia, M. (eds.) *Culture, Urbanism and Planning*. Aldershot: Ashgate, pp. 271–285.

Wark, M. (1994) *Virtual Geography: Living with Global Media Events*. Bloomington, IN: Indiana University Press.

Warren, R. (2002) Situating the city and September 11th: military urban doctrine, 'pop-up' armies and spatial chess. *International Journal of Urban and Regional Research*, **26**(3), pp. 614–619.

Waterfield, R. (2004) *Athens: A History from Ancient Ideal to Modern City*. London: Macmillan.

Watts, J. (2005) Satellite data reveals Beijing as air pollution capital of world. *The Guardian*, 31 October.

Watts, J. (2006*a*) Beijing to ban drivers for blue sky Olympics. *The Guardian*, 7 April.

Watts, J. (2006*b*) Beijing Olympic official sacked over corruption. *The Guardian*, 13 June.

Watts, J. (2009) Beijing keeps Olympic restrictions on cars after air quality improves, *The Guardian*, 6 April.

Weaver, M. (2005) Livingstone promises green Olympics. *Guardian Unlimited*, 8 September. society.guardian.co.uk/communities/news/0,,1565373,00.html, accessed 4 April 2007.

Weed, M. (2008) *Olympic Tourism*. Oxford: Elsevier.

Weed, M. and Bull, C. (2009) *Sports Tourism: Participants, Policy and Providers*, 2nd ed. Oxford: Elsevier.

Wei, Y.H.D. and Yu, D.L. (2006) State policy and the globalisation of Beijing: emerging themes. *Habitat International*, **30**, pp. 377–395.

Weirick, J. (1999) Urban design, in Cashman, R. and Hughes, A. (eds.) *Staging the Olympics: The Event and Its Impact*. Sydney: University of New South Wales Press, pp. 70–82.

Welch, P.D. (1996) Paris 1924: the Games of the 8th Olympiad, in Findling, J.E. and Pelle, K.D. (eds.) *Historical Dictionary of the Modern Olympic Movement*. Westport, CT: Greenwood Press, pp. 61–67.

Wendl, K. (1998) The route of friendship: a cultural/artistic event of the Games of the XIX Olympiad in Mexico City, 1968. *Olympika*, **7**, pp. 113–134.

Wenn, S.R. (1993) Lights! Camera! Little action: television, Avery Brundage, and the Melbourne Olympics. *Sporting Traditions*, **1**, pp. 38–53.

Wenn, S.R. (1995) Growing pains: the Olympic movement and television, 1966–1972. *Olympika*, **4**, pp. 1–22.

Whitelegg, D. (2000) Going for gold: Atlanta's bid for fame. *International Journal of Urban and Regional Research*, **24**, pp. 801–817.

Wilson, H. (1996) What is an Olympic city? *Media, Culture and Society*, **18**, pp. 603–618.

Wimmer, M. (1976) *Olympic Buildings*. Leipzig: Edition Leipzig.

Winkler, A. (2007) *Torino: City Report*. London: Centre for Analysis of Social Exclusion, London School of Economics.

Witherspoon, K.B. (2003) Protest at the Pyramid: The 1968 Mexico City Olympics and the Politicization of the Olympic Games. Unpublished PhD thesis, Florida State University.

Woodman, E. (2004) Stratford's glamour gameplan. *Building Design*, 30 January, p. 8.

WOS (Wenlock Olympian Society) (2006) Wenlock Olympian Society. http://www.wenlock-olympian-society.org.uk/, accessed 22 December 2006.

Wrynn, A. (2004) The human factor: science, medicine and the International Olympic Committee, 1900–70. *Sport in Society*, **7**, pp. 211–231.

Wu, F. (ed.) (2006) *Globalisation and China's Cities*. London: Routledge.

Wu, F. (ed.) (2007) *China's Emerging Cities*. London: Routledge.

WWF (World Wildlife Fund) (2004) *Environmental Assessment of the Athens 2004 Olympic Games*. Athens: WWF Greece.

Wynn, M. (ed.) (1984) *Planning and Urban Growth in Southern Europe*. London: Mansell.

Xin, Y. (2001) Olympic economy: a huge temptation. www.bjreview.com.cn/bjreview/EN/2001/200134/Nationalissues-200134(A).htm, accessed 7 February 2002.

Yannopoulos, D. (2003) Entrepreneurs Set Eyes on Post-Olympic Windfall. *Athens News*, 26 August.

Yarborough, C.R. (2000) *And They Call Them Games: An Inside View of the 1996 Olympics*. Macon, GA: Mercer University Press.

Yew, W. (1996) *The Olympic Image: The First 100 Years*. Edmonton, Alberta: Quon Editions.

Yiftachel, O. (1994) The dark side of modernism: planning as a control of an ethnic minority, in Watson, S. and Gibson, K. (eds.) *Postmodern Cities and Spaces*. Oxford: Blackwell, pp. 216–242.

Yoon, H. (2009) The legacy of the 1988 Seoul Olympic Games, in Poynter, G. and MacRury, I. (eds.) *Olympic Cities: 2012 and the Remaking of London*. Farnham: Ashgate, pp. 121–131.

Young, D.C. (1987) The origins of the modern Olympics: a new version. *International Journal of the History of Sport*, **4**, pp. 271–300.

Young, D.C. (1996) *The Modern Olympics: A Struggle for Revival*. Baltimore, MD: Johns Hopkins University Press.

Young, D.C. (1998) Further thoughts on some issues of early Olympic history. *Journal of Olympic History*, **6**(3), pp. 29–41.

Young, D.C. (2004) *A Brief History of the Olympic Games*. Oxford: Blackwell.

Zhang, L. and Zhao, S.X. (2009) City branding and the Olympic effect: a case study of Beijing. *Cities*, **26**, pp. 245–254.

Zhou, S. (1992) *China: Provincial Geography*. Beijing: Foreign Languages Press.

Zimmerman, P. (1963) Financial nightmare ruins Detroit's Olympic Dream. *Los Angeles Times*, 10 March, D, p. 2.

Zoltan, M. (2010) Brazilian football, FIFA, infrastructure and planning. http://brazil.suite101.com/article.cfm/world_cup_2014_soccer_in_brazil, accessed 29 March 2010.

Zolov, E. (1999) *Refried Elvis: The Rise of the Mexican Counterculture*. Berkeley, CA: University of California Press.

Zolov, E. (2004) Showcasing the 'land of tomorrow': Mexico and the 1968 Olympics. *The Americas*, **61**, pp. 159–188.

Index

Aboriginal peoples, *see* First Nations
accessibility for disabled 113, 118–
    122, 124, 125, 330
aesthetics 32, 38, 39, 43, 82, 245, 271,
    291
airport improvements 37, 41, 42, 46,
    64, 73, 74, 183, 184, 188, 251, 257,
    319, 320, 324, 326, 347, 397
Amateur Athletic Club 21–22
ambush advertising 328, 404
amateur status 3, 35, 91, 140
Angelopoulos-Daskalaki, Gianna 321,
    322
anti-Olympic protest 74, 217, 243–
    245, 351, 356, 373
archaeology 18–19, 25, 44, 51, 98,
    316, 321, 322, 325, 326, 327
architecture 5, 36, 46, 52, 80, 85,
    86–87, 88, 186, 192, 256, 265, 309,
    316, 323–324
arts competitions 29, 80, 86–92
arts festivals 36, 80, 92–106, 253, 287,
    294, 296, 297, 306, 308–310, 311
Asian Games 44, 341
Austerity 3, 21, 34–36, 182

ballet 84, 88, 92, 100, 333
Barcelona model 46, 185–188, 205,
    207, 208, 268–269, 270, 284–285
Basque separatists 47, 170
beautification, urban 47, 185, 298,
    313–317, 322, 327–328, 337
Beckham, David 161, 165

bidding for Olympic Games 2, 30,
    31, 34, 41, 45, 49, 52, 67, 113, 118,
    123–124, 147, 148, 150, 151–153,
    154, 156, 164, 201, 215, 236,
    248–251, 275, 288–289, 318–320,
    340–341, 345–348, 360, 369, 391–
    401, 405
Bourgault-Ducoudray, Louis 86
boycotts, political 9, 38, 41, 44, 170,
    217, 245, 288
branding 38, 104, 136–137, 149, 153,
    166, 179, 204, 284, 291, 356–357,
    363, 403–406
British Empire Games 29
broadcasting revenue 37, 39, 46, 57,
    63, 65, 76, 188, 120–121, 131, 134,
    137, 139, 140, 149, 234, 320
Brookes, William Penny 21, 23
brownfield land 26, 39, 48, 69, 273,
    278–279, 322, 376, 377, 382
Brundage, Avery 78, 92, 235, 237,
    238, 241
Burnham, Daniel 398–399

Calatrava, Santiago 323
candidature files 153–154, 173, 177,
    277–278, 318–320, 397
Central American Games 237, 238
ceremonies 24, 26, 48, 53, 83–84, 89,
    98–99, 103, 105, 116–117, 121,
    143, 172, 224–225, 234, 253, 287,
    292, 296, 310, 311, 329, 340, 352–
    353, 392, 393

Chandler, Richard 17–18

Chirac, Jacques 148, 159, 169, 265

city marketing 5, 11, 148–166, 248–253, 264, 282, 296, 328

city rivalries 31, 32, 148, 150, 152–153, 185

civil liberties 52, 172, 179; see also human rights

closed circuit television (CCTV) 169, 171, 172, 174, 175, 178

coastal regeneration 271, 277, 278, 324, 334–335

Coe, Sebastian 156, 165, 340

Cold War politics 9, 21, 41–43, 236

commemorative coins 144–145

commercialism 42–3, 46–48, 54, 131, 153, 161, 162, 318, 328, 404

commodification 165

Commonwealth Games 155

congestion 39, 47, 190, 317, 319, 325

conservation 42, 44, 65, 191, 192, 327, 331

convention centres 324, 390

copyright protection 117, 403–404

corruption 67, 68, 352

cosmopolitanism 235, 257, 382–383

cost-benefit analysis 5, 147, 254–255, 367–271

Coubertin, Baron Pierre de 22–23, 29, 54, 56, 80, 82–83, 85, 97, 255, 260, 317

crime rates 177, 181, 379, 392–393, 401

cultural diversity, see multiculturalism

Cultural Olympics 6, 11, 46, 80–107, 240, 242, 287–314, 320, 366

cultural industries 47–48, 96, 149, 377, 381, 384

curatorship 104

dance 82, 84, 89, 102, 242, 309

De Gaulle, Charles 251, 252

decentralization 42, 277, 279, 321–322, 399

deindustrialization 68, 269

densification, urban 382

deprivation 185, 245, 360, 377–378, 385

Diem, Carl 84, 89–90, 216, 218, 222, 224, 225, 230

diplomacy, sport as 8, 11, 35, 108–127

disability sport 8, 11, 35, 108–127

Docklands, London 361–362, 382

Dover, Robert 21

Drapeau, Jean 40, 151, 153, 249–251, 256, 257, 259, 260, 261, 263, 265, 266

education 5, 8, 23, 33, 187, 218, 292, 385, 404–405

employment 46, 181, 185, 317, 383–386

environmental audit 191, 325, 331–332

environmental improvement 43–5, 181, 185, 189–190, 381

environmental sustainability 3–4, 48–51, 66, 70, 73, 165, 181, 189–193, 304–305, 331, 381, 397

environmentalism 3–4, 5, 7, 48–51, 66, 70, 73, 165, 181, 189–93, 304–305, 331, 381, 397

ethics 67, 404

ethnographic displays 26–27

eurhythmy 82, 83

European Athletics Championships 50, 318, 323

European Cities of Culture 55

evictions, see resettlement

FIFA (Fédération Internationale de Football Association) World Cup 149, 196, 215, 226, 239, 240, 366, 372, 391, 394

film and video 32, 100, 159–160, 353, 392, 400

finance 1–2, 11, 32–33, 37, 42, 50, 61,

96, 118, 131–3147, 149, 154, 190,
197, 236, 247, 250, 259, 294, 311,
312, 320, 365–372, 377, 397, 404
fireworks 25, 29
First Nations 27, 49, 73, 74, 84, 93,
94, 97–98, 102, 241, 253, 287,
288–290, 294, 296, 297, 311–3312

galleries 100, 106, 149, 310, 326
games, classical 17–19, 315, 321
gated communities 47, 246
gigantism 4, 32, 94, 405
globalization 149–150, 181, 269, 270,
282, 285, 317, 342
governance, urban 77–78, 259–264,
357
graphic design 36, 38, 39, 234, 245,
246
Grey-Thompson, Tanni 108, 122
Guttmann, Ludwig 108–109, 111,
114–115

health, public 7, 37, 181, 185, 381
heritage 44, 80, 96, 102, 186, 241, 318,
324, 337
historiography 9, 234
Holmenkollen Week 56, 78
hospitality, corporate 49, 143
hotels 35, 37, 39, 42, 57, 61, 74, 77,
125, 162, 184, 236, 237, 324, 349,
381
housing 2, 35, 37, 44, 45, 49, 61, 74,
181, 182, 192, 258–259, 285, 325,
374, 380, 381–383
human rights 52, 76, 164, 210, 289,
340, 346, 351
humanism 24, 209, 404

identity 24, 81, 102, 149, 186, 291,
315, 328, 404
ideology 21, 22–23, 33, 35, 41–43,
89–90, 93, 104, 121, 151, 234, 238,
239, 246, 404

illuminations 25, 29, 84, 309
indigenous cultures, see First Nations
infrastructure 2, 5, 6, 7, 10, 21, 33,
34, 37, 39–40, 42, 43–53, 57, 60,
62, 63, 65, 67–368, 69, 77, 94, 109,
119, 125, 146, 153, 179, 180, 182,
184, 185, 190, 210, 239, 245, 257–
3258, 271, 272, 283, 288, 291, 317,
319, 321, 322, 325–326, 341, 342,
359–389, 392, 393, 394, 397, 405
intellectual property 117, 143–144
international expositions 8, 25–326,
27–28, 45, 58, 172, 181–182, 235,
248, 249–250, 256, 257, 260, 270–
271, 284, 288, 348, 363, 395
International Federations 131–147,
321
International Olympic Committee
(IOC)
established 22–324
ethical problems, 67, 68, 352
Evaluation Commissions 118,
124–125, 154, 319, 347, 356,
391, 397
International Paralympic Committee
(IPC) 117–118, 123
internationalism 23, 33, 151, 161, 162,
241, 404
investment, inward 69, 148, 149, 180,
198, 311, 317, 342
Isthmian Games 81

Johnson, Boris 2, 7, 145, 178, 362
Jowell, Tessa 1–2, 6, 125, 389

land acquisition 370, 372, 376–377,
382
legacy 2–37, 9, 35, 66, 73–74, 77, 123,
125–126, 147, 173, 179, 181, 182,
185, 191–193, 208–209, 255, 256,
287, 311–312, 315, 322, 329–336,
338, 347, 361, 380–386, 387–388,
393

leverage 132, 196–204, 205–211, 247, 269, 284, 296, 336, 361, 375
licensing 143–144, 320
literature 36, 80, 85, 87, 88, 102
Livingstone, Ken 193, 367, 382
lobbying 156–159
logos 73, 117, 166, 241, 296, 306, 349
'look', *see* visual unity
lotteries 37, 144, 254, 320, 364, 366–367, 371
Lula da Silva, Luiz Inácio 159, 400

Maragall, Pasqual 151, 164, 188, 274–275
March, Otto 213
March, Werner 33, 218–3219, 220–221, 222–223, 229
mascots 143, 250
Mateos, Adolfo López 235, 237
media 1–2, 32, 33, 42, 47, 57, 62, 69, 102, 120–121, 124, 125, 148, 150, 154, 161, 184, 196, 203, 210, 234, 288, 292, 298, 302–303, 318, 322, 369, 375, 381, 384, 392, 399
Media Centres 42, 52, 57, 105, 296, 298, 305, 364, 375, 381
mega-events 1, 3, 6, 77, 105, 149, 172, 177, 181, 306, 317, 340, 363, 368, 373, 391
megaprojects 6
metros, *see* railways
Millennium Dome, see O$_2$ Arena
modernization 37, 43–46, 52–53, 63, 65, 69, 172, 190, 238, 271, 263, 336, 349
monorails 37, 183
monumentality 37, 40, 44, 183, 229
Much Wenlock Games 21, 23
multiculturalism 5, 27, 49, 74, 97–98, 104, 162, 253, 266, 287, 288, 290–291, 292, 294, 296, 308, 311, 359, 379, 384
museums 36, 38, 87, 88, 90, 97, 100, 105–3106, 149, 284, 305–306, 310, 324, 326, 333, 338, 346
music 8, 25, 27, 29, 38, 80, 88, 90, 100, 102, 300, 309

narratives 10–11, 287
National Olympic Association 21–22
National Olympic Committees 62, 90–91, 131–147, 150, 242, 249, 250, 262, 265, 346, 395
National Parks 65, 75–76, 325
nationhood, sense of 3, 316–317
Nemean Games 81
Nordic Games 56, 78

O$_2$ Arena 59, 363–365, 366
obesity 352, 379
Olympia (Greece) 8, 17–19, 81–82, 224, 321, 328
Olympic anthem 83, 224–225
Olympic Charter 24, 56, 66, 81, 82, 91, 92, 134, 135, 140, 170, 319, 404
Olympic flame 83–84
Olympic Games (Summer)
    Amsterdam (1928) 31–32, 84, 88, 182, 216
    Antwerp (1920) 30, 56, 88, 182, 216, 255
    Athens (1896) 9, 11, 19, 24–25, 50–51, 96, 181, 317; (1906) 19, 27, 317; (2004) 4, 5, 12, 21, 64, 98, 118–119, 121, 142, 146, 150, 167, 170, 171–172, 179, 190–191, 207–209, 265, 292, 311, 315–339, 366, 372, 381
    Atlanta (1996) 4, 46–48, 78, 96–97, 106, 146, 153–154, 156, 162, 164, 171, 188, 261, 263, 265, 293, 311, 319, 327, 395, 404
    Barcelona (1992) 3, 12, 21, 44–46, 73, 96, 157, 162, 164, 185–188, 193, 200, 205, 207, 208, 257, 268–286, 290, 292, 293, 367, 388

Beijing (2008) 5, 9, 11, 12, 21, 52–53, 78, 84, 98–100, 103, 121, 126, 162, 164, 172–173, 191–192, 209–211, 340–358, 375

Berlin (1916, not held) 30, 32, 216; (1936) 3, 8, 12, 19–20, 33–34, 84, 89–90, 151, 182, 215–232

Helsinki (1940, not held) 35; (1952) 35, 91–92

London (1908) 27–29, 56, 86–87, 182; (1948) 34–35, 90, 110, 182; (2012) 1–2, 5, 11, 12, 35, 103–104, 123–126, 141–142, 144, 152, 156, 162–163, 165, 173–177, 192–193, 212, 359–389, 395

Los Angeles (1932) 32–33, 88–89, 152, 182; (1984) 9, 21, 42–43, 93, 113, 137, 140, 142, 145, 146, 152, 170, 184, 189, 197, 257, 262, 263, 317, 395

Melbourne (1956) 4, 35–36, 94

Mexico City (1968) 12, 38, 84, 93, 94, 113, 134, 183–184, 233–246, 257, 327

Montreal (1976) 4, 12, 35, 39–41, 46, 84, 94, 140, 144–145, 169, 184, 247–267

Moscow (1980) 9, 41–42, 113–114, 144, 155, 169, 247–248, 257

Munich (1972) 9, 38–39, 67, 84, 94, 114, 134, 163, 168–169, 184, 247–248, 259

Paris (1900) 24, 25–26; (1924) 31, 88, 182

Rio de Janeiro (2016) 9, 12, 13, 152, 154, 156, 159, 162, 372, 390–402

Rome (1960) 3, 4, 36, 94, 112–113, 121, 134, 156, 177

St. Louis (1904) 26–27, 181, 385

Seoul (1988) 43–44, 94, 116, 144, 151, 170, 179, 185, 372

Stockholm (1912) 29–30, 87, 182

Sydney (2000) 4, 12, 21, 94, 97–98, 105–106, 118–119, 143–146, 155, 157, 162, 171, 179, 189–190, 193, 205–207, 257, 262, 265, 287–314, 372

Tokyo (1964) 8, 37–38, 48–50, 84, 93, 112–113, 134, 179, 183, 328, 371, 395, 398

Olympic Games (Winter)

Albertville (1992) 65–66, 78, 116

Calgary (1988) 4, 65, 76–77, 94, 100–102, 116, 197–198, 261

Chamonix (1924) 56, 57, 59, 216

Cortina d'Ampezzo (1956) 62, 100

Denver (1976, withdrew) 64–65, 77

Garmish-Partenkirchen (1936) 58

Grenoble (1968) 63–64, 78, 94, 100

Innsbruck (1964) 63; (1976) 64, 100, 114

Lake Placid (1932) 58, 60–61; (1980) 62, 65, 100, 114, 169

Lillehammer (1994) 65–66, 76, 78, 168, 198

Nagano (1998) 65

Oslo (1952) 62

St. Moritz (1928) 58, 60, 61; (1948) 78

Salt Lake City (2002) 4, 61, 66–68, 77, 118, 121, 150, 158, 198–200, 202, 262–263

Sapporo (1972) 63, 65

Sarajevo (1984) 100

Sochi (2014) 73–76, 77, 104–105, 395

Squaw Valley (1960) 62

Turin (2006) 5, 68–72, 77–78, 102, 119, 142, 200–202

Vancouver (2010) 5, 73, 94, 102–103, 126, 202–204

Olympic Games Global Impact (OGGI) project 5, 307

Olympic hymn 83

Olympic motto 83, 404

Olympic oaths 83

Olympic pins 143–144, 306

Olympic Programme, The (TOP) 54, 136–137, 140, 294–296, 300, 403

Olympic torch relay 83–84, 105, 224, 233, 252, 292, 296, 309, 310, 357, 379

Olympic Villages 31, 32, 37, 41, 42, 44, 49, 57, 61, 63–64, 65, 66, 69, 74, 77, 113, 116, 119, 145, 169, 182, 190, 191, 223–224, 228, 229, 238, 240, 242, 245–246, 255, 258–259, 277, 278–279, 280, 319, 320, 322, 325, 346, 349, 366, 367, 375, 383, 393, 405

Olympics, revival of 21–24, 81–84

Olympism 4, 24, 32, 52, 74, 82, 304, 404

open space 44, 45, 69, 190, 227, 272, 274, 304–306, 319, 324, 382

opera 29, 93, 289, 296, 308, 309, 324, 349

opportunity cost 66

oratory 8, 81

Ordaz, Gustavo Díaz 235, 241

Organizing Committees (OCOGs) 3, 5, 19–20, 24, 27, 31, 41, 50, 117–118, 119, 124, 131–147, 150–151, 168, 169, 170, 184, 185, 189, 219, 223, 225, 233, 258–259, 260–261, 265, 291–293, 294–296, 298, 303, 328, 340, 346, 403

painting 36, 80, 85, 86, 87, 90, 349

Pan-American Games 237, 238, 391–393, 400

panegyris 8, 17, 60–62

Paralympics 8, 10, 11, 35, 80, 103, 108–127, 308, 327, 397

paraplegia 109, 110

parklands 2, 44, 47, 49, 179, 192, 272

participation, sports 4, 7, 126, 317, 378–379, 404–405

partnerships, public-private 67, 69, 297, 334, 336

patriotism 83

pedestrianization 39, 47, 51, 104

philately 24, 144

philosophy 4, 10, 24, 82, 237

place promotion 6, 11, 21, 148–166, 201–202, 235, 248–253, 317

poetry 8

policing 167, 168, 169, 178

pollution, environmental 26, 44, 48, 189, 317, 319, 323, 325–326, 340, 346, 350, 354

pregacy 5

presentism 10–11

press, see media

processions 25, 33, 81

propaganda 3, 33, 42–43, 89–90, 217, 229

property values 47, 149

pseudo-Olympics 23

Pythian Games 81

Quebec separatists 251, 261, 264, 265

racecourses 48, 219, 323, 324

racial supremicism 8, 26–27, 215, 217

railways 28, 33, 39, 44, 46, 64, 68, 69, 70, 74, 125, 183, 191, 257, 258, 279, 283, 319, 320, 323, 325–326, 349, 375, 377, 384, 394, 397

rationing 35

receptions 25, 29, 32, 81, 87

recession 1, 32, 33, 74, 142, 181, 334, 357, 365–366, 374

regime politics 151, 262

resettlement 44, 47, 52, 172, 179, 258, 351, 377, 381, 382

road improvements 39, 42, 44, 64,
67, 69, 73, 103, 183, 188, 191, 239,
240, 271, 273, 283, 319, 320, 323,
326, 349, 397
Rogers, Lord Richard 187, 274
Romanticism 82, 327
rugby union 9, 13, 196

Samaranch, Juan Antonio 49–50, 164,
189, 271, 322
Schartau, Gustav Johan 21
sculpture 80, 85, 86, 87, 88, 240–241,
245, 312
security 11, 39, 41, 66, 76, 77, 141,
145–146, 167–179, 251, 359, 372,
392–393, 397
Serra, Narcis 151, 275
skills 5, 77, 383–386
spectacle 25, 33, 34, 52–53, 80, 82, 84,
89–90, 149, 171, 179, 215, 269, 304
sponsorship 5, 24, 42, 46, 57, 131,
137, 139, 140, 149, 288, 292, 294,
300–302, 320, 366, 403
stadia 5, 19, 22, 24–53, 61, 65–66, 67,
69, 89, 115–116, 174, 182, 183,
190, 192, 215–30, 240, 247, 251,
253, 256, 318, 320, 321, 323–323,
327, 335–336, 341, 346, 349, 355–
356, 375, 381–382, 385, 393, 399
stakeholder analysis 131, 132–140,
291, 297–303
Stoke Mandeville 35, 108, 109–112,
114–115, 119, 124
street art and decorations 25, 29, 32,
252, 297
street entertainments 94, 98, 206,
298–300, 304–305
superpower rivalries 41–43
surveillance 168, 169, 171, 174, 176,
177–179
symbolism 25, 28, 51, 74, 149, 165, 328

Taillibert, Roger 40, 251, 260

telecommunications 37, 46, 74, 184,
252, 338
terrorism 39, 43, 67, 141, 167, 168–
169, 170–177, 359
Thames Gateway 373–375, 385
theatre 25, 39, 69, 82, 84, 85, 87, 89,
93, 100, 102, 222, 299, 304, 323–
324, 326, 327, 333, 346, 349
ticketing 38, 46, 142–143, 172, 209,
238, 241, 302, 305, 310, 320, 321,
364, 366, 372
Thatelolco massacre 243–245, 246
tourism 5, 6, 11, 35, 50, 74, 77, 81,
87, 102, 140, 149, 150, 172, 185,
194–212, 239, 284, 292, 311, 312,
327–328, 330, 338, 356
tree planting 44, 47, 68, 323, 344, 345,
347, 350, 354

uneven development 234, 342–343
urban design 186, 253, 268, 274
urban entrepreneurialism 57, 77, 149,
262, 281, 282
urban regeneration 3, 4, 10, 11,
36–39, 44–45, 69, 77, 81, 94, 102,
109, 140, 147, 148, 153, 180–193,
253–259, 264, 287, 348–350, 359–
389, 397
urban renewal 11, 44–46, 180–193,
258, 269, 281–284, 338, 360
urban space, militarization of 167,
170, 337

visual unity ('look') 32, 38, 39, 43,
252, 292, 293, 306, 322, 328
volunteers 5, 73, 122, 170, 171, 184,
250, 261, 303, 322, 366

water supply and sewage 37, 44, 183,
188, 192, 279, 283, 327, 350
waterfronts 277, 278, 362
wetlands 324–325
'white elephants' 28–29, 47, 50, 51,

311, 331–333, 335–336, 355–356, 381

Youth Olympic Games 12, 404–405

Zappas Games 22–23